Constitutional L
Text, Cases and Ma

Constitutional Law:
Text, Cases and Materials

By
Oran Doyle

Trinity College, Dublin

Published by
Clarus Press Ltd,
Griffith Campus,
South Circular Road,
Dublin 8.

Typeset by
Datapage International Limited,
18 Docklands Innovation Park,
East Wall Road,
Dublin 3.

Printed by
Printed in Ireland by SPRINT-print Ltd.

ISBN
978-1-905536-16-0

Reprinted in 2009, 2010, 2011, 2012 and 2013

All rights reserved. No part of this publication may be reproduced, or transmitted in any form or by any means, including recording and photocopying, without the written permission of the copyright holder, application for which should be addressed to the publisher. Written permission should also be obtained before any part of the publication is stored in a retrieval system of any nature.

All extracted materials reproduced in this publication have been done so with the kind permission of the copyright holder, author and/or publisher.

Disclaimer
Whilst every effort has been made to ensure that the contents of this book are accurate, neither the publisher nor author can accept responsibility for any errors or omissions or loss occasioned to any person acting or refraining from acting as result of any material in this publication.

© Oran Doyle 2008

To Kevin

FOREWORD

Although the literature on Irish constitutional law is voluminous—not to say formidable—a challenging text and materials book suitable for the needs of the contemporary undergraduate has been awaited for at least a generation. The highly acclaimed O'Reilly and Redmond, *Cases and Materials on the Irish Constitution* was published in 1980 and (unfortunately) a second edition was never published. Dr Doyle's present book more than fills a gap in this market: it combines an overview of the present law, with appropriate extracts from the case-law, together with a stimulating and strikingly original commentary. It would be hard to think of a better introduction to constitutional law for the undergraduate (and, indeed, post-graduate) student.

It is the very originality of the commentary which has set me thinking. I suspect that Dr Doyle is correct to suggest (at [4-56]) that (leaving the possible issue of socio-economic rights aside) "the unenumerated rights doctrine ... has done its job and can now gracefully be abandoned.... With those rights now secured as part of the *acquis constitutionel*, there is no longer a need to enumerate wholly new rights." As he points out, whatever qualms one might have had about the methodology, the "results were generally unexceptionable." In reality, the courts used the unenumerated rights doctrine to fill in the gaps of standard civil and political rights which had been omitted—probably through oversight—from express collection of such rights in the fundamental rights provisions of the Constitution itself. In any event, many of the rights could just as easily have been said to derive by necessary implication from express provisions of the Constitution itself. Obvious examples here are the right to marry, which is clearly (at least) implicit in Art 41 (see the discussion of this in *O'Shea v Ireland*, 17 October 2006 (HC)) and the right to bodily integrity. It is hard to see how the latter right is any way different from the right to the protection of the person, which is, of course, expressly protected by Art 40.3.2° (see the discussion of this in *Fitzpatrick v K (No 2)*) [2008] IEHC 104). Even in the case of rights with less obvious connections to the actual wording of the Constitution itself, a textual basis of some faint kind can often be found. Thus, the dignity of the individual (to use the words of the Preamble) would scarcely be assured if the courts were not prepared to protect the right to privacy.

A further consequence of the unenumerated rights doctrine and (just as importantly) the subsequent development of the *acquis constitutionel* has been to mitigate the potential importance of the European Convention of Human Rights Act 2003. None of this is to downplay the role or huge importance of the Convention (not least in terms of the torrent of precedent generated by Strasbourg), but it is rather to make a different point. If the right to privacy is already constitutionally protected, does it really make a difference that Art 8 ECHR guarantees the right to a private life in express terms? Certainly, it would not seem that any of the recent important privacy cases—such as *Caldwell v Mahon* [2006] IEHC 86, *Herrity v Associated Newspapers, Irish Times*, 18 July 2008 or *Sinnott v Carlow Nationalist, Irish Times*, 31 July 2008—would have been decided any differently if Art 8 had been in play as opposed to the constitutional right to privacy.

Dr Doyle's treatment of Art 41 is also most interesting. No one nowadays doubts but that the best interests of the child must be (at least) a prominent consideration in any case where its welfare is at stake. Many children's rights campaigners seek to go further and endeavour to have Art 41 amended to ensure that the "best interests" tests is the primary consideration. They cite cases such as *N v HSE* [2006] IESC 60 as examples of this unfortunate "parent centred" approach. The difficulty, however, is this: who exactly is to decide what is in the "best interests" of the child and, in the case of a legal dispute, how is this to be decided? If, for example, there is a custody dispute between a young, uneducated mother who is dependent on State assistance on the one hand and adoptive parents who are affluent professionals on the other, is it to be said that (all other things being equal) the courts should opt to give custody to the latter couple *simply* because many people consider that the child would be better off in comfortable surroundings with adoptive parents possessing an enhanced level of life and social skills? Or should the courts be prepared on "best interests" grounds to intervene (effectively) to compel a mother to accept routine medical treatment which she considers to be contrary to her religious beliefs, simply because she will otherwise die and leave her new born child abandoned in the State (see *Fitzpatrick v K (No 2)*). The best interests of the child test is certainly an appealing slogan and, at the level of abstract generalisation, it might be thought to have much to commend it, but those who argue for such a test do not always appear to have considered how such a principle might have to be applied by the courts to cases which come before them. How many of these protagonists have ever read judgments such as *HW, McK* or *N*?

This is not to deny that the wording of Art 41 currently presents many difficulties. Many of the potential problems stem from the fact that, as things stand, Art 41 applies only to the family based on marriage, yet with over one third of first time births being born to parents who are not married, the Supreme Court's much criticised judgment in *Nicolaou* will be have to be re-visited. Can one realistically say that the result in either *North Western Health Board v HW* or *McK v Information Commissioner* ought to have been different if the parents had not been married? If one, for example, changes the facts in *HW* and assumes that the parents had never married and, furthermore, that the natural mother had died: is it to be said that in that situation the natural father looking after the child could invoke no constitutional rights whatever to object to the administration of the PKU test to his infant son?

HW was, of course, a very difficult case and the majority and the minority judgments are both compellingly argued. If forced to choose, I would incline to the views expressed by the majority and then only with considerable hesitation. As Murphy J pointed out for the majority, any other conclusion could bring about a situation where "numerous applications would be made to the courts to overrule decisions made by caring but misguided parents." Yet the *HW* test is not without its difficulties. If the State can only intervene where there is something exceptional "arising from a failure of [parental] duty"–the test posited by Murray J in that case, then how should one approach a case such as *In re Baby B, The Irish Times*, 27 December 2007? Here the Jehovah Witness parents of a new born baby objected on religious grounds to the administration of a blood transfusion which the clinicians treating the baby considered might well become necessary. It seems hard to characterise the parents' decision as a "failure of duty" in this sense, given that the parents are, after all, simply exercising religious freedoms which enjoy constitutional protection under Art 44. Yet in the High Court Bermingham J

Foreword

(correctly) intervened to protect the child's right to life, thereby overruling the parents' conscientious religious objections. Is there any difference in principle here between *Baby B* and *HW* other than judicial perceptions as to the degree of risk to the child?

The consequences of a finding of unconstitutionality is another perpetually vexed question, but Dr Doyle's illuminating analysis cannot, I think, be improved upon as an introduction to this topic. The problem here is that there is really no completely satisfactory solution to this question and it is an illusion to think that there is. The judicial task, however, is to find a solution which best addresses a number of potentially competing considerations, including the language of the Constitution itself (especially Art 15.4, Art 34.3.2° and Art 50); the judicial duty to provide redress for infringements of constitutional rights; the need to avoid legal chaos and the duty to safeguard the rights of third parties, while at the same time ensuring that an injustice is not done to litigants by arbitrary line-drawing. No solution will be logically perfect or totally coherent, but it may be thought that, on the whole, the Supreme Court has provided as good solutions to this problem as it is reasonably possible to find. The ground work was laid by the judgments of Henchy J in *Corrigan v Irish Land Commission* [1977] IR 317, *The State (Byrne) v Frawley* [1978] IR 326 and *Murphy v Attorney General* [1982] IR 241.

A v Governor of Arbour Hill Prison [2006] IESC 45 was, of course, another hard case and, just as with *HW*, it is not easy to choose as between the judgment of Laffoy J on the one hand and those of the Supreme Court reversing her on the other. Laffoy J's willingness to uphold the primacy of the Constitution and her steadfast commitment to the rule of law even though the legal and political heavens were about to fall is strikingly admirable. Yet there is also much to be said for what Geoghegan J's observation to the effect that the courts cannot permit a declaration of unconstitutionality to have catastrophic effects for third parties and, indeed, society at large.

One of the chief merits of this book is that it demonstrates clearly the extent to which the Constitution has penetrated almost every element of Irish life and society. Even though Constitution remains unfashionable in some quarters–certainly conference organisers consider a conference on the influence of the ECHR to be a far more glamorous and attractive option–for good or for ill, it remains stubbornly a part of what we are. No one who takes a serious interest in contemporary Irish law and society can fail to be fascinated by the development of Irish constitutional law over the last 70 years and no finer introduction to these developments will be found outside of the pages of this outstanding work.

Gerard Hogan
Distillery Building,
Church St.,
Dublin 7
1 September 2008

PREFACE

This book was conceived as a response to the difficulties of teaching constitutional law. It aims to provide students with a thorough introduction to constitutional law in a way that does not simplify the subject but rather presents the difficult issues and opposing viewpoints in a coherent and manageable way. It is not intended as a substitute for reading important cases and articles in full, but should hopefully provide the core of any undergraduate constitutional law curriculum. The book takes the format of Text, Cases and Materials. I have integrated extracts from the leading cases and the seminal articles into my own account of the development of constitutional law. In this regard, I am hugely grateful to those authors and publishers who have given permission for their work to be reproduced in this book. Without their generosity, it quite simply would not have been possible. In particular, I wish to express my gratitude to the Incorporated Council of Law Reporting in Ireland for its permission to reproduce the Irish Reports and to Round Hall Thomson and Westlaw.ie for their permission to reproduce the Irish Law Reports Monthly and a large number of extracts from journal articles and books.

The book begins by introducing the reader to a number of key concepts concerning the Irish people, their language, their State and its powers. Chapters 2-10 then deal with the fundamental rights provisions of the Constitution. Chapters 11-13 deal with the separation of powers, addressing the legislative power, the executive power and the judicial power, with a focus on the difficult interaction between them. It may prove controversial to have dealt with the fundamental rights before the separation of powers. They are ordered in this way because, in my experience, students cannot assess and independently analyse the issues raised by the separation of powers without first having been exposed to a wider range of constitutional issues. Chapter 14 addresses the changes made to Irish constitutional law to ensure Ireland's effective membership of the European Communities and the European Union. Chapter 15 analyses the political and referendum process, a discrete area of Irish law that has attracted much constitutional litigation. Chapter 16 addresses the procedural issues that arise in relation to all constitutional litigation: standing, presumption of constitutionality, declarations of unconstitutionality, *etc.* Chapter 17 provides an introduction to the debate over constitutional interpretation, dealt with as a last chapter again on the basis that students cannot independently assess the fundamental problems raised by interpretation without being exposed to a wide range of doctrinal issues first.

A difficult issue that arises in relation to a book on constitutional law is the extent to which the law of the European Convention on Human Rights ought to be addressed. In most cases, the Convention is now pleaded alongside the Constitution. Moreover, the Convention has become much more influential in the development of Irish constitutional law than it used to be. Nevertheless, I have generally avoided discussion of the Convention except where absolutely necessary to explain a radical change in the Irish courts' interpretation of the Constitution. The increasing overlap between the Convention and the Constitution should not lead us to overlook their differences nor to rule out the possibility of students learning about the Constitution on its own terms. Just because issues of contract law, torts law, equity, restitution and land law often intersect in litigation does not require that there be a composite book on that subject. Nevertheless, as the Convention exerts greater influence and as the teaching of the Convention in the undergraduate curriculum is changed to reflect its significance, this academic division of labour may need to be reassessed.

Several chapters of the book were tested on members of the constitutional law class in Trinity College. This considerably helped to refine the style of the book. I am grateful to them. I am also grateful to many people who have commented on various chapters and who have had discussions with me that greatly assisted in the writing of this book: Patricia Brazil, Donal Coffey, Neville Cox, Estelle Feldman, Gerard Hogan, David Langwallner, Brian Murray, Paul O'Connell, Macdara Ó Drisceoil, David Prendergast, Des Ryan and Gerry Whyte. Dr Hogan initiated me into constitutional law as a First Year law student in Trinity College and has encouraged me in my efforts to understand the subject since then. I am honoured that he agreed to write the Foreword.

Two people in particular have made an enormous contribution to this book. Fergus Ó Domhnaill was my research assistant throughout. I cannot overstate his assistance in sourcing and compiling the extracts that have been reproduced in this book. David McCartney of Clarus Press approached me in July 2006 and asked me what book I would like to publish. He has been exceptionally helpful (and occasionally forgiving) in all aspects of the design and production process. I am also grateful to those at Clarus Press involved in the proofing, indexing, tabling and design of this book.

Above all, I thank Kevin. I could not have written this book without his love, support and encouragement.

Oran Doyle
Law School
Trinity College, Dublin
1 September 2008

CONTENTS

Foreword vii
Preface xi
Table of Constitutional Provisions xix
Table of Legislation xxiii
Treaties and Conventions xxxi
Table of Cases xxxiii

Chapter 1: Nation, State, People and Language 1
I.   The Nation and its People 3
II.   The Rights of the People 5
III.   The State and its Powers 6
IV.   Language 11

Chapter 2: The Constitution and the Criminal Law 15
I.   Introduction 17
II.   The Concept of Trial in Due Course of Law 17
III.   What is a Criminal Charge? 19
IV.   Unconstitutionally Obtained Evidence 20
V.   The Right to be Provided with a Lawyer 28
VI.   The Right to Silence 33
VII.   Unfair Pre-Trial Publicity 37
VIII. The Duty to Seek Out and Preserve Evidence 39
IX.   The Right to an Early Trial 41
X.   The Presumption of Innocence 45
XI.   No Right to Confrontational Cross-Examination 48
XII.   The Right to Jury Trial 48
XIII. No Retroactive Penal Sanctions 55
XIV. Vague Criminal Offences 55
XV.   Blameworthiness 56

Chapter 3: Equality 59
I.   Introduction 61
II.   Formal Equality 61
III.   Aristotelian Equality 63
          Legitimate Recognition of Difference 63
          Other Legitimate Reasons for Legislative Discrimination 70
          No Obligation to Treat Unequals Unequally 71
IV.   Standards of Review 71
V.   Levelling Up or Down 72
VI.   Indirect Discrimination 73
VII.   The Human Personality Doctrine 74

Chapter 4: The Unenumerated Rights Doctrine 83
I.   Textual Basis and Early Days 85
II. Methods for the Identification of Unenumerated Rights 87
     Christian and Democratic Nature of the State 87
     The Human Personality 88
     The Natural Law 92
     Rights Implied From Other Constitutional Provisions 96
III. The Difficulties with the Unenumerated Rights Doctrine 97
IV. The Apotheosis of the Natural Law in Irish Constitutional
     Law 100
V.   Current Status of Unenumerated Rights Doctrine 104

Chapter 5: Personal Rights 109
I.   Introduction 111
II.   The Right to Life 111
III. The Right to Life of the Unborn 114
IV.   The Right to a Good Name 123
V.   The Right to Bodily Integrity 124
VI.   The Right to Work and Earn a Livelihood 125
VII. The Right to (Marital) Privacy and Autonomy 127
VIII. The Right of Access to the Courts and the Right to Litigate 128

Chapter 6: Property Rights 133
I.   Introduction 135
II. Early Case Law and the Interaction Between Art 40.3.2°
     and Art 43 136
III. What is Property? 140
     Constitutionally Protected Property 140
     Economic Value Created by Law 141
IV. Standing to Invoke Property Rights 147
V.   Testing the Legitimacy of Restrictions of Property Rights 149
     Introduction 149
     The Proportionality Test 149
     Regulation of Ownership Rights 152
     Regulation of Land Use 155
     Taxation 156
     Retrospective Restrictions of Property Rights 158
     Imposing the Cost of Achieving a Public Good on One
     Section of the Community 158
     Anomalous Legislation as Distinct from Clearly
     Focused Legislation 160
VI. Compensation 162
VII. Postscript 165

Chapter 7: Liberty and the Dwelling Place 167
I.   Introduction 169
II. Procedural or Substantive Guarantee 169
III. Illegalities Leading to Unconstitutional Detention 172
IV. Rights of Prisoners 175
V.   Liberty and the Legality of Detention Powers 179

VI.	Preventive Detention	186
VII.	Inviolability of the Dwelling	188

Chapter 8: Freedoms of Expression, Assembly and Association 191

I.	Introduction	193
II.	Public Order and Morality	193
III.	Freedom of Expression	194
	Rationale	194
	The Freedom to Express What?	195
	The Freedom of Whom?	197
	Restrictions on Freedom of Expression	199
	Blasphemy	205
IV.	Freedom of Assembly	207
V.	Freedom of Association	207
	Trade Unions	208
	Political Parties	211
	Sports Clubs	212
	Restrictions on Freedom of Association	213
	The Extent of the Freedom	215

Chapter 9: Family and Education 219

I.	Introduction	221
II.	Marital Families and Recognition for Other Types of Family Unit	223
	Definition of "Marriage" and "Family"	223
	Legislative Recognition of Non-Marital Families	226
III.	The Right to Marry	232
IV.	The Rights of Married Couples and Families	234
	Family Rights	234
	Rights of Married Couples	235
V.	The Position of Non-Marital Families	235
	The limits of Art 41	235
	Alternative Means of Constitutional Protection	236
VI.	Standing of Non-Nationals to Invoke Arts 41 and 42	240
VII.	Derivative Rights to Reside in Ireland	241
	The Right of a Child Citizen to Reside in the State	244
	The Child Citizen's Right to the Care and Companionship of her Parents in the State	245
	Species of Common Good that can Override the Right	246
VIII.	Woman's Life Within the Home	249
	Legitimising Discrimination by Reference to Art 41.2	249
	Attempts to Expand Art 41.2	250
	Proposals for Change	252
IX.	The Autonomy of Married Couples	253
X.	Children's Rights and Family Autonomy	255
	Children's Rights	255
	Parental Autonomy in the Custody Context	256
	Parental Autonomy in the Health Context	260
	Parental Autonomy in the Education Context	267

XI.	Primary Education	274
	The Meaning of (Primary) Education	274
	Parental Choice in Primary Education	283
XII.	At Risk Children	285

Chapter 10: Religion 287
I.	Introduction	289
II.	Freedom of Conscience and Free Practice and Profession of Religion	289
III.	Non-discrimination	292
IV.	Non-endowment	298
V.	Overview of Case Law on Art 44	303

Chapter 11: The Legislative Power and the Oireachtas 307
I.	Introduction	309
II.	Delegated Legislation	312
III.	Henry VIII Clauses: the Interaction of the Non-delegation Doctrine and the *Ultra Vires* Doctrine	321
IV.	Primary Legislation as a Deliberative Process	327
V.	Investigative Powers of the Oireachtas	330

Chapter 12: The Executive Power and the Government 333
I.	Introduction	335
II.	Implicit Executive Powers	335
III.	Explicit Executive Power Over External Relations	341
IV.	Composition of the Government	348
V.	Cabinet Confidentiality	349

Chapter 13: The Judicial Power and the Courts 351
I.	Introduction	353
II.	The Character of the Judicial Power	353
III.	The Reservation of the Judicial Power to the Courts	357
IV.	Oversight of Other Governmental Powers as an Aspect of the Judicial Power	362
	The Majority's View of the Separation of Powers: A High Constitutional Value	363
	The Majority's View on when the Courts may make a Mandatory Order	365
	The Minority's View of the Separation of Powers: A Framework for Government	367
	The Minority's View on when the Courts may make a Mandatory Order?	368
	Difficulties in Both the Majority and Minority Positions	369
	The Distinction between Commutative and Distributive Justice	372
V.	The Separation of Powers and Competing Visions of Democracy	376
VI.	Judicial Impeachment	378
	The Constitutionality of the Impeachment Process	378

  The Constitutionality of the Power to Compel Judges 380
  The Direction to Produce the Computer 381

Chapter 14: The European Union 383
I. Introduction 385
II. The Principal Constitutional Amendments 385
III. Amendment of the Treaties 387
IV. Methods of Incorporating Community Law 392

Chapter 15: Referendums and the Political Process 403
I. Introduction 405
II. Referendums: the Constitutional Provisions and Early Cases 405
III. The Referendum Cases: a More Interventionist Role 409
IV. The Substance of Referendum Proposals 416
V. The Electoral Process 419
  Drawing of Constituency Boundaries 419
  Secret Ballot 425
  Rules Governing Candidates at Elections 426

Chapter 16: Principles Governing Constitutional Litigation 429
I. Introduction 431
II. Standing 431
III. The Presumption of Constitutionality 437
IV. Judicial Restraint 439
V. The Double Construction Rule 441
VI. Severance 443
VII. Effects of a Finding of a Declaration of Unconstitutionality 445
  Introduction 445
  When Do Declarations of Unconstitutionality Date To? 446
  What is the Effect of a Declaration of Unconstitutionality? 447
  The Continuing Effect of Official Decisions Taken Before the
  Declaration of Unconstitutionality 452

Chapter 17: Constitutional Interpretation 455
I. Introduction 457
II. The Constitution: Interpreting Words 458
III. The Constitution: Interpreting Values 461
IV. Conclusions 468

Index 469

TABLE OF CONSTITUTIONAL PROVISIONS

Constitution

Constitution of the Irish Free State 1922
Art 2 .... 1–15, 1–17, 1–19
Art 2A 4–36-4–37, 7–03-7–04
Art 6 .... 7–01-7–06, 7–09
Art 10 9–116
Art 11 1–20
Art 51 .... 1–14, 1–17
Art 71 17–22
Art 73 1–15

Bunreacht na hÉireann 1937
Preamble 4–1-4–14, 4–18, 7–08, 8–25, 12–23
Art 1 1–03
Art 2 .... 1–03-1–06, 4–44, 12–19, 12–23, 15–25
Art 3 .... 1–03-1–04, 12–19, 12–23, 15–25
Art 5 .... 1–19-1–20, 4–13, 12–25, 15–34
Art 6 .... 1–07, 4–18, 11–01, 11–50, 12–20, 13–01, 13–11, 15–08
Art 6.1 .... 12–25, 13–02, 15–02
Art 6.2 .... 12–25, 13–02
Art 8 .... 1–22-1–23, 9–125
Art 9 .... 1–05, 9–57
Art 9.2 1–05-1–06
Art 9.2.1 1–06
Art 10 1–12
Art 10.1 1–20
Art 10.3 1–20
Art 12.9 12–31
Art 13.6 .... 13–15, 13–16
Art 15 .... 8–26, 12–25, 16–29
Art 15.1 14–24
Art 15.2 .... 11–07, 11–16, 11–20, 11–23, 11–31-11–32, 11–34, 11–40, 11–45, 12–15, 14–23
Art 15.2.1 .... 11–01, 11–03, 11–18, 11–24, 11–36-11–37, 11–48, 13–16, 14–23, 16–24
Art 15.2.2 .... 11–02, 16–29
Art 15.4 .... 6–08, 16–23, 16–29, 16–37, 16–45
Art 15.4.1 11–03
Art 15.4.2 .... 11–04, 16–24, 16–29
Art 15.5 11–03
Art 15.5.1 2–83
Art 15.5.2 .... 2–85, 5–02
Art 15.10 13–65
Art 15.11.1 13–61

Art 16	7–20, 15–38, 15–47
Art 16.1.1	15–49
Art 16.1.2	3–25, 4–38, 7–21
Art 16.1.4	4–13, 15–34, 15–41
Art 16.2	9–73, 15–31, 15–34
Art 16.2.3	15–32, 15–34-15–35
Art 16.2.4	15–36, 15–39
Art 16.3	15–36
Art 17	6–52
Art 24	12–31
Art 25	11–45, 11–47
Art 25.4.1	16–37
Art 25.4.3	11–44
Art 25.4.5	11–44
Art 26	11–44, 11–47-11–48, 13–02, 15–06
Art 26.1.1	11–44, 11–47-11–48
Art 27	1–07
Art 28	6–52, 7–15, 12–01, 12–25-12–26, 12–29
Art 28A	15–48
Art 28.1	12–30
Art 28.2	12–03, 13–40
Art 28.3	12–27
Art 28.3.2	12–01
Art 28.3.3	5–02, 7–15, 12–28
Art 28.4.1	12–25, 12–32
Art 28.4.2	12–03, 12–31-12–32
Art 28.4.3	12–33
Art 28.4.4	12–01
Art 28.5	12–30
Art 28.6.2	12–30
Art 28.6.3	12–30-12–31
Art 28.12	12–03
Art 29	12–01, 12–24-12–25, 15–25
Art 29.1	12–23, 12–25
Art 29.2	12–23, 12–25
Art 29.3	12–25, 12–25
Art 29.4	12–20, 14–03, 14–13
Art 29.4.1	12–01
Art 29.4.3	12–20, 14–03, 14–10-14–12, 14–20, 14–23-14–24
Art 29.4.4	14–03, 14–20
Art 29.4.5	14–03, 14–20, 14–24
Art 29.4.10	14–03, 14–07, 14–10, 14–18
Art 29.5.1	12–25
Art 29.6	12–25, 14–06
Art 29.7	15–25
Art 29.7.3	15–25
Art 30	2–59
Art 34	2–90, 13–06, 13–11
Art 34.1	8–14-8–15, 13–01, 13–02

Table of Constitutional Provisions

Art 34.2.3	13–52
Art 34.3.2	6–08, 11–04, 13–01, 13–18, 13–40
Art 34.4.3	17–10, 17–12
Art 34.4.4	6–08
Art 34.4.5	14–09
Art 35	13–11
Art 35.4	13–59
Art 35.4.1	13–60-13–62, 13–64-13–67
Art 35.5	11–03
Art 36	13–11
Art 36.1	11–03
Art 37	13–02-13–03, 13–11
Art 38	2–01, 2–05, 2–41, 2–55, 2–65, 17–22
Art 38.1	2–01-2–04, 2–07-2–08, 2–33-2–34, 2–63-2–64, 2–69, 2–86-2–87, 16–25
Art 38.2	2–71
Art 38.5	2–71, 2–78-2–82, 3–09
Art 40	2–90, 3–08, 3–10-3–11, 3–19, 4–02, 4–18, 4–46, 5– 15, 6–12, 7–31, 7–35, 8–05, 9–35, 9–118, 11–50, 15–43, 17–07
Art 40.1	2–01, 2–20, 2–78, 2–86-2–87, 3–01-3–04, 3–07-3–11, 3–16, 3–19, 3–21, 3–23-3–26, 3–33-3–40, 3–46, 3–50, 3–53-3–54, 4–38, 5–39-5–40, 6–33-6–34, 7–32, 8–25, 8–44, 9–29, 9–73, 9–118, 10–07, 10–09, 15–34, 15–47, 17–03, 17–07, 17–14
Art 40.3	2–01, 2–86, 4–01, 4–17-4–18, 4–24, 5–01, 5–16, 5–20, 6–18, 6–33, 6–35, 6–54, 6–72, 8–07, 9–05, 9–35-9–36, 9–74, 9–90, 13–19, 17–16, 17–21
Art 40.3.1	4–02-4–03, 4–07, 4–11-4–13, 4–15-4–17, 4–24-4–27, 4–30, 4–46-4–47, 4–50, 4–54-4–56, 5–01, 5–34, 5–43, 6–17, 6–66, 7–19, 7–35, 8–04, 8–06-8–07, 8–35, 9–25, 13–21, 13–40
Art 40.3.2	4–02-4–03, 4–07, 4–11,5–02, 5–15, 5–37, 6–01, 6–06, 6–08-6–14, 6–17, 6–33-6–34, 6–37, 6–44, 6–48, 6–54, 6–66, 6–72, 8–30, 13–40, 17–07
Art 40.3.3	5–11, 5–14-5–16, 5–18, 5–20, 5–23-5–26, 8–26, 15–04, 15–07, 16–07
Art 40.4	2–09, 2–20, 7–10, 7–27, 7–32, 7–36
Art 40.4.1	2–20, 2–86, 7–01-7–02, 7–07, 7–09-7–11, 7–39
Art 40.4.2	7–01, 7–13, 7–34, 13–08-13–09, 16–27, 16–44
Art 40.4.6	7–37
Art 40.5	2–09, 7–39-7–42
Art 40.6	8–01, 8–24, 8–42, 8–48
Art 40.6.1	2–34, 8–02, 8–11, 8–20, 8–28, 8–46, 8–50, 8–53
Art 40.6.1(i)	8–02, 8–04-8–12, 8–14, 8–23, 8–26, 8–30, 8–50
Art 40.6.1(iii)	8–35, 8–38, 8–40, 8–42, 8–45, 8–49, 8–51-8–52, 15–42
Art 40.6.2	11–03
Art 41	4–11, 4–18, 4–18, 4–22, 5–15, 6–52, 9–01-9–04-9–08, 9–11, 9–13-9–14, 9–17, 9–22-9–23, 9–27-9–28, 9–30-9–33, 9–35-9–36, 9–40, 9–42-9–47, 9–70, 9–80, 9–85, 9–90, 9–93, 9–118, 16–34, 17–19
Art 41.1	9–02
Art 41.1.1	4–38, 9–23, 9–70
Art 41.1.2	9–23
Art 41.2	3–10-3–11, 4–34, 9–31, 9–62-9–69
Art 41.2.1	3–19
Art 41.3	9–05, 9–09, 17–19

Art 41.3.1	9–18, 9–23
Art 41.3.2	9–32, 11–03
Art 42	4–18, 4–22, 4–34, 9–01-9–04-9–05, 9–35, 9–42-9–46, 9–70, 9–80, 9–85, 9–87, 9–102, 9–106, 9–113-9–119, 9–124, 9–126, 10–15
Art 42.1	9–80, 9–102, 9–106, 9–116, 9–118
Art 42.1.1	4–38
Art 42.2	9–102, 10–15, 10–18
Art 42.2.1	10–18
Art 42.2.4	10–18
Art 42.3	9–113
Art 42.3.1	9–102
Art 42.3.2	9–102-9–105, 9–107-9–109, 9–111, 9–113, 9–121, 9–124, 9–126
Art 42.4	9–115-9–121, 9–124, 9–127, 10–19, 17–23
Art 42.5	4–24, 9–44, 9–74, 9–80, 9–98-1–101, 9–113, 9–118, 9–127, 9–129, 13–19
Art 43	4–18, 4–22, 4–34, 6–02, 6–05-6–06, 6–09, 6–17, 6–30, 6–33, 6–35, 6–66, 6–72, 17–21
Art 43.1.1	6–72
Art 43.1.2	6–08, 11–03
Art 43.2	6–52
Art 44	4–18, 8–25, 9–03, 10–02-10–04, 10–10, 10–15, 10–22-10–27
Art 44.1	10–07, 10–08, 10–23
Art 44.1.1	10–07
Art 44.1.2	10–03
Art 44.1.3	10–03
Art 44.2	10–01, 10–23, 17–08
Art 44.2.1	10–01-10–02, 10–07, 10–11, 10–13, 17–08
Art 44.2.2	10–01, 10–15-10–16, 10–19
Art 44.2.3	10–01, 10–07, 10–09-10–11, 10–13-10–14, 17–08-17–09
Art 44.2.4	10–01, 10–15, 10–20-10–21
Art 44.2.5	10–10
Art 45	5–34, 6–08
Art 45.2(i)	9–62
Art 45.3.1	5–34
Art 45.4	9–62
Art 46	1–07-1–08, 4–42, 15–02, 15–11, 15–12, 15–24-15–25, 15–28
Art 46.1	4–38, 15–02, 15–28
Art 46.3	15–29
Art 46.4	15–04, 15–29
Art 47	1–07-1–08, 15–12
Art 47.1	15–02
Art 49	1–13, 1–17
Art 50	3–16
Art 50.1	16–30, 16–43, 16–45

TABLE OF LEGISLATION

Adoption Act 1952 .... 3–17, 4–47, 9–35, 16–16
    s 10 4–09
    s 12 10–14
    s 14 .... 4–21, 9–36, 9–76
    s 14(1) 3–17, 9–05
    s 16(1) 3–17, 9–05
    s 24(b) 9–35
    s 5(1) 9–63
    s 15 9–76
Adoption Act 1974
    s 3 .... 4–21, 9–36
    s 5 3–19
    s 5(1) 3–19
Adoption Acts 1952–1988 9–44
Aliens Act 1935 .... 11–15-11–16, 11–43, 11–48, 12–09
    s 5 11–42
    s 5(1)(e) 11–14-11–16, 11–18, 11–22, 12–15, 12–18
    s 5(1)(h) 11–20-11–22, 11–42
An Blascaod Mór National Historic Park Act 1989 3–48
    s 4(2)a 3–48
    s 4(4) 3–48
Broadcasting Authority Act 1960
    s 18 15–21
    s 31 8–02
Broadcasting, Wireless and Telegraphy Act 1988
    s 3 8–21
    s 4 8–21
Building Societies Act 1989
    s 4 11–37
Canals Act 1986
    s 13 11–37
Censorship of Films Act 1923
    s 7(2) 8–25
Child Care Act 1991
    s 2(1) 9–121
Children Act 1987
    s 12 9–39
Civil Legal Aid Act 1995 5–45
Civil Liability Act 1961
    s 9 6–17
    s 12 6–36
    s 14 6–36
Civil Registration Act 2004
    s 2(2)(e) 9–27

Civil Service (Employment of Married Women) Act 1973 3–20
Civil Service Regulation Act 1956.. 3–20
Committee of Public Accounts (Privilege and Procedures) Act 1970
   s 3(4)... 5–29
Committees of the Houses of the Oireachtas (Compellability, Privileges
and Immunity of Witnesses) Act 1997
   s 3 13–59-13–60
   s 3A 13–68-13–69
Common Law Procedure (Ireland) Act 1853 5–43
Companies Act 1990
   s 10(5)... 16–25
   s 10(6)... 16–25
   s 18 2–41-2–42
   s 19(6)... 2–43
   s 24 11–37
Courts Act 1991
   s 16(1)... 11–37
Courts of Justice Act 1924 17–22
   s 39 13–62
Criminal (Evidence) Act 1992
   s 13 2–70
Criminal Justice (Evidence) Act 1924 9–31
Criminal Justice (Legal Aid) Act 1962... 2–25, 2–27
   s 2 2–27
Criminal Justice Act 1951 17–22
   s 23 13–16
Criminal Justice Act 1984
   s 18 .... 2–37, 2–43
   s 19 .... 2–37, 2–43
Criminal Law (Amendment) Act 1935
   s 1(1).. 2–89-2–91, 16–27, 16–43-16–45,
                                                                               17–29-17–30
   s 6 3–53
Criminal Law Act 1935
   s 17 4–11
   s 17(1)... 4–11, 5–07
Criminal Law Amendment Act 1885
   s 11 .... 4–13, 16–05
Customs (Temporary Provisions) Act 1945
   s 5(1).. 6–11
Customs Consolidation Act 1876
   s 186 .... 2–71, 13–13
Dairy Produce (Price Stabilisation) Act 1935
   s 24 2–71
Deceased Brother's Widow's Marriage Act 1921
   s 1(2)(b) 9–25
Deceased Wife's Sisters Marriage Act 1907
   s 3(2).. 9–25

Table of Legislation

Defamation Act 1961
  s 8 8–24
Defamation Act 1961
  s 13(1) 8–25
Disease of Animals Act 1966 2–27
Education (Welfare) Act, 2000
  s.2(1) 9–121
Electoral (Amendment) Act 1959 15–34
Electoral (Amendment) Act 2002 15–47
Electoral (Amendment) Act 2005 15–37-15–38
Electoral Act 1923 15–41
Fifth Schedule 15–41
Electoral Act 1963 15–41
  s 13(2) 8–38, 15–42
  s 16 15–43
  s 16(2) 15–41
  s 17 15–41
Electoral Act 1997 15–40
  s 2(a) 15–40
  s 2(c) 15–40
  s 31 16–22
Electricity (Supply) Act 1927
  s 53 6–66-6–67
Employment Equality Acts 1998–2004 3–03
Equal Status Act 2000 8–40
  s 8 .... 8–39- 8–40, 8–47
Equal Status Acts 2000–2004 3–03
European Communities (Amendment) Act 1986 14–09
European Communities (Amendment) Act 2007
  s 2 14–28
  s 4 14–28
  s 5 14–28
European Communities Act 1972 14–06-14–07
  s 1 14–06
  s 2 .... 14–06, 14–18, 14–24, 14–28
  s 3 .... 14–06, 14–19-14–20,
                                                                14–23-14–24, 14–28
  s 3(2) 14–18-14–19,14–23
  s 3(3) 14–26-14–27
  s 4 14–24
Extradition Act 1965 7–30
Family Law Act 1981 9–22
  s 2(1) 9–22
Finance Act 1976
  s 46 11–13
Finance Act 1980
  s 18-21 9–12
Finance Act 1980
  s 21 .... 9–12-9–13, 16–35

Finance Act 1987
  s 18 6–40
  Part III 6–40
Finance Act 1990
  s 26(1) 6–40
Garda Síochána Act 1977
  s 1 8–46
Greyhound Industry Act 1958 16–20
  s 43 16–20
  s 44 16–20
  s 47 13–02-13–03
Ground Rents (No 2) Act 1978
  s 8 6–46-6–47
Guardianship of Infants Act 1964
  s 2 9–80
  s 3 9–79-9–80
  s 6(4) 4–24
  s 6A 9–39
  s 10 4–21
  s 10(2)(a) 4–24, 9–39
Health Act 1970 11–34
  s 46 11–34
  s 46(3) 11–34
  s 52 11–34
  s 56 11–34
  s 71 11–34
  s 72 11–34-11–35
  s 72(1) 11–34
  s 72(2) 11–34
Health Insurance Act 1994
  s 12 6–62
Housing Act 1966
  s 120 6–44
  Third Schedule 12–03
Housing of the Working Classes Acts 1890–1958 6–44
Immigration Act 1999
  s 2 .... 11–41-11–45, 11–48
  s 2(1) 11–43-11–44
  s 3 9–61
Imposition of Duties Act 1957
  s 1(d) 11–12-11–13
Income Tax Act 1967 9–12
Industrial and Provident Societies Act 1978
  s 5 8–45
Industrial Training Act 1967 11–09-11–10
  s 21 11–09
  s 23 11–09
Irish Nationality and Citizenship Act 1956 3–29
  s 6(1) 1–05

Table of Legislation

s 8 3–29
Judicial Separation Act 1989..9–32
s 3 9–32
Juries Act 1927 .... 2–78, 2–80, 3–10, 16–33
s 3 2–80
s 3(1)...3–08
s 5 .... 3–08, 9–63
s 16 .... 3–11, 9–63
Labourers Acts 1883–1958 6–44
Land Clauses Consolidation Act 1845
s 63 6–48
Landlord and Tenant (Amendment) Act 1984
s 7(4)...6–46
Larceny Act 1916
s 42 7–42
Local Government (No 2) Act 2003
s 2 15–48
Local Government (Planning and Development) Act 1963
s 26(2)...6–21
s 82(3B)(a) 6–18
Part VI...6–65
Local Government Act 1946
s 11 6–54
Local Government Act 2001
s 13A 15–48
Married Women's Property Acts 1882 to 1907 3–20
Married Women's Status Act, 1957..3–20
Mental Treatment Act 1945 7–35
s 162 .... 7–33, 13–07
s 163 7–35
s 165(1) 7–10, 7–32
s 171 ....7–33-7–35, 13–07-13–08
s 172 .... 7–35, 13–09
s 172(2)...7–35
Ministers and Secretaries Act 1924...12–31
National Monument Act 1931
s 8 6–69
Nineteenth Amendment of the Constitution Act 1998.........................15–25
Offences against the Person Act 1861 3–53
s 58 .... 5–11, 5–25
s 59 .... 5–11, 5–25
s 61 16–05
s 61 .... 3–32, 4–13
s 62 3–53
Offences against the State (Amendment) Act 1972
s 3(2)...2–63
Offences against the State Act 1939..2–71
s 21 2–63
s 24 2–63

xxvii

s 30 .... 2–28, 3–03, 7–30-7–31
s 34 16–37
s 35 2–35
s 52 .... 2–34-2–37, 2–39
s 52(1) 2–34
s 52(2) 2–34
s 55 7–08
Official Languages Act 2003 1–25
Petty Sessions (Ireland) Act 1851 14–22
s 10(3) 14–23
s 29 5–41
Pigs and Bacon Act 1935 16–12
Pigs and Bacon Act 1937 16–12
Planning and Development Act 2000 10–07
Radio and Television Act 1988 10–04
s 10 8–23
s 10(3) 8–08, 8–22, 10–04
Referendum Act 1994 .... 15–12, 15–14, 15–17
s 26 15–22
s 42 15–17
s 43 15–17
s 43(1) 15–17
Rent Restrictions Act 1960 6–44
s 7 6–44
s 9 6–44
Part II 6–44
Road Traffic Act 1961 .... 7–28, 17–22
s 26 2–73
s 49 2–73
s 109 7–28
Road Traffic Act 1968
s 44(2)(a) 13–12, 16–24
School Attendance Act 1926 .... 9–105-9–107, 9–117
s 17 9–105
Shops (Hours of Trading) Act 1938
s 25 .... 3–34, 10–07
Sinn Féin Funds Act 1947 .... 6–08, 13–10
s 10 .... 6–08, 13–10
Statute of Limitations 1957
s 11 5–43
s 11(2)(b) 16–02
Part III 5–43
Succession Act 1965 .... 3–22, 9–33-9–34
s 67 3–22
s 67(3) 9–33
s 69 3–22
Teachers' Superannuation Act 1928
s 3 .... 6–19, 11–39
Third Amendment of the Constitution Act, 1972 14–06

Table of Legislation

Trade Disputes Act 1906 8–31
   s 2 8–30
   s 3 8–30
Trade Union Act 1941
   s 26 8–43
Trustee Act 1893 .... 6–08, 13–10
Vagrancy Act 1824
   s 4 2–86
Valuation Act 1988
   s 4 11–37
Valuation Acts 1852–1918 6–54
Wireless and Telegraphy Act 1926
   s 3 8–21
   s 4 8–21
   s 6 8–21

TREATIES AND CONVENTIONS

African Charter on Human and Peoples' Rights Art 7 2–64
American Convention on Human Rights 1969 Art 8 (2) 2–64
European Convention on Human Rights and Fundamental
    Freedoms 1950 .... 2–32, 8–05, 8–09, 8–19-8–20, 9–59, 9–116, 12–13
        Art 6(1) 2–02, 2–39
        Art 6 (2) 2–64
        Art 8 9–67
        Art 10 .... 5–12, 8–20
Single European Act 12–20, 14–08, 14–10-14–12, 14–16
        Art 30 .... 12–21, 14–15
        Art 6(ii) 14–13
        Title II 14–13
        Title III 12–20-12–21, 14–13, 14–14, 14–16
Treaty establishing the European Community 1957 14–20
        Art 189 14–23
        Art 234 5–12
Treaty of Amsterdam 14–03, 14–17
Treaty of Lisbon 14–17
Treaty of Maastricht 14–03, 15–09
Treaty of Nice 14–03, 14–17
Treaty of Rome 12–20, 14–06, 14–08, 14–10, 14–12, 14–24
        Art 2 14–12
        Art 3 14–12
Treaty on European Union 15–07
UN International Covenant on Civil and Political Rights Art 14(8)(3)(g) 2–02
United Nations Convention and Resolution of the General Assembly 9–116

TABLE OF CASES

A
A and B v Eastern Health Board [1998] 1 IR 464 5–21-5–22
A v Governor of Arbour Hill Prison [2006] IESC 45...................... 11–04, 16–27-16–45
Aherne v RTÉ [2005] IEHC 180..8–17
An Blascaod Mór Teoranta v Commissioners of Public Works
    [2000] 1 IR 6.. 3–48-3–49, 3–51-3–52
Attorney General (Society for the Protection of Unborn Children
    (Ireland) Ltd) v Open Door Counselling Ltd [1988] IR 593 .... 5–12, 5–25
Attorney General for England and Wales v Brandon Books [1986] IR 597 8–18
Attorney General v Hamilton (No 1) [1993] 2 IR 250 12–32
Attorney General v Paperlink [1984] ILRM 373............................... 5–34, 8–04, 17–06
Attorney General v Southern Industrial Trust (1961) 109 ILTR 161 .... 6–11, 6–15
Attorney General v X [1992] 1 IR 1.. 2–46, 5–13-5–20, 5–25
Aughey v Ireland [1989] ILRM 87.. 8–46, 8–53

B
Baby O v Minister for Justice [2002] 2 IR 169..5–25
Barry v Medical Council [1998] 3 IR 387..5–37
Blake v Attorney General [1982] IR 117......................... 6–12, 6–44-6–45, 6–63, 11–16
Bode v Minister for Justice, Equality and Law Reform
    [2006] IEHC 341.. 9–58-9–60
Bode v Minister for Justice, Equality and Law Reform
    [2007] IESC 62... 9–58, 12–13
Boland v An Taoiseach [1974] IR 338.................................. 12–19, 13–18, 13–29, 13–42
Botta v Italy (1998) 26 EHRR 241 9–67
Bowes and McGrath v DPP [2003] 2 IR 25...2–54
Braddish v Director of Public Prosecutions [2001] 3 IR 127 2–51-2–52
Breathnach v Ireland [2001] 3 IR 230 ....7–21-7–23, 7–26
Brennan v Attorney General [1983] ILRM 449 (HC);
    [1984] ILRM 355 (SC) 3–23, 3–27, 3–39- 3–41,
                                                                                                    6–52, 6–54, 6–63
Browne v Attorney General [2003] 3 IR 205 ....14–26, 14–28
Buckley v Attorney General [1950] IR 67 ....6–08-6–10, 6–15,
                                                                                13–10-13–11, 13–18, 13–21, 16–13
BUPA Ireland Ltd v Health Insurance Authority, 23 November 2006 (HC) 6–62
Byrne v Government of Ireland, 11 March 1999 (SC) 3–06
Byrne v Ireland [1972] IR 241 .... 1–08-1–09, 1–14-1–15, 1–17, 4–40

C
C v Ireland (No 1) [2005] IESC 48..2–89
C v Ireland (No 2) [2006] IESC 33..2–89-2–91, 17–29
Cahill v Sutton [1980] IR 269 .... 16–02-16–04, 16–10
Campaign to Separate Church and State v Minister for Education
    [1998] 3 IR 321 10–15-10–20

xxxiii

Constitutional Law: Text, Cases & Materials

Carrigaline Community Television Broadcasting Co Ltd v Minister
  for Transport, Energy and Communications *(No 2)* [1997] 1 8–21
Cassidy v Minister for Industry and Commerce [1978] 1 IR 297 11–05
Central Dublin Development Association v Attorney General (1975)
  109 ILTR 69 .... 6–15, 6–49-6–50, 6–62, 6–64-6–65
Chen v Secretary of State for the Home Department [2004] ECR I-9925 9–53
Chestvale Properties Ltd v Glackin [1992] ILRM 221 6–16
Cityview Press v An Comhairle Oiliúna [1980] IR 381 .... 11–09, 11–23,
                              11–25, 11–27-11–30, 11–34, 11–39, 14–26
Clinton v An Bord Pleanála [2005] IEHC 84 6–51
Colgan v Independent Radio and Television Commission [2000] 2 IR 490 8–23
Comerford v Minister for Education [1997] 2 ILRM 134 .... 9–117, 9–127
Commission of the European Communities v United Kingdom of Great Britain
  and Northern Ireland *(Case 804/79)* [1981] 2 ECR 1045 14–26
Conroy v Attorney General [1965] IR 411 .... 2–73, 17–22
Cooke v Walshe [1984] IR 710 11–34
Corway v Independent Newspapers (Ireland) Ltd [1999] 4 IR 484 8–24-8–26
Coughlan v Broadcasting Complaints Commission [2000] 3 IR 1 15–21
Cox v Ireland [1992] 2 IR 53 16–37
Croke v Smith *(No 2)* [1998] 1 IR 101 .... 7–33-7–35, 13–07-13–09
Crotty v An Taoiseach [1987] IR 713 .... 12–20-12–25, 14–03,
                              14–06-14–17, 15–12, 16–08, 16–10
Crowley v Ireland [1980] I.R. 102 .... 9–107, 9–115, 9–121, 9–125
CT v DT [2003] 1 ILRM 321 9–09
Curtin v Clerk of Dáil Éireann [2006] IESC 14 13–59-13–69

D

D v DPP [1994] 1 IR 374 2–55
D v DPP [1994] 2 IR 564 2–45
D v HSE 9 May 2007 *(HC)* 5–22
Daly v Revenue Commissioners [1995] 3 IR 1 .... 6-40-6–41, 6–54
DB v Minister for Justice [1999] 1 IR 29 13–26
de Búrca v Attorney General [1976] IR 38 ..... 1–23, 2–78-2–81, 3–08-3–12, 9–63, 16–33
Deaton v Attorney General [1963] IR 170 13–13-13–15
Dennehy v Minister for Social Welfare, 24 July 1984 *(HC)* 9–64
Desmond v Glackin *(No 2)* [1993] 3 IR 67 15–25
Dillane v Attorney General [1980] ILRM 167 17–07
Dimbo v Minister for Justice [2008] IESC 26 .... 9–61 de
Director of Public Prosecutions v Best [2000] 2 I.R. 17 9–121
Director of Public Prosecutions v Dunne [1994] 2 IR 537 2–17
Director of Public Prosecutions v Healy [1990] ILRM 313 7–31
Donnelly v DPP [1998] 1 IR 321 2–70
Doyle v An Taoiseach [1986] ILRM 693 2–84
Doyle v Croke (1988) 7 JISLL 170 .... 8–36, 8–49
(DPP) v Balfe [1998] 4 IR 50 2–17
(DPP) v Buck [2002] 2 IR 268 2–29
DPP (Stratford) v Fagan [1994] 3 IR 265 7–28-7–29
DPP *(Walsh)* v Cash [2007] IEHC 108 2–23
DPP v Best [2000] 2 IR 17 9–105-9–113

Table of Cases

DPP v Corrigan [1986] IR 290 7–40
DPP v Haugh (No 2) [2001] 1 IR 162 2–49
DPP v McCreesh [1992] 2 IR 239 7–40
DPP v McMahon [1986] IR 393 7–40
Draper v Attorney General [1984] IR 277 3–25
Dreher v Irish Land Commission [1984] ILRM 94 .... 6–13, 6–66
DT v CT [2003] 1 ILRM 321 9–68
Dublin College ASA v City of Dublin VEC, 31 July 1981 (HC) 8–37
Dubsky v Government of Ireland [2005] IEHC 442 12–26-12–29
Dunne v DPP [2002] 2 IR 305 2–52-2–53
Dunnes Stores Ireland Co Ltd v Ryan [2002] 2 IR 60 .... 2.43

E
East Donegal Co-operative Livestock Market Ltd v Attorney General
 [1970] IR 317 .... 11–32, 16–21
Eastern Health Board v An Bord Uchtála [1994] 3 IR 207 9–44
ED v Health Services Executive, 28 April 2005 (SC) 9–129
Educational Company of Ireland v Fitzpatrick [1961] IR 345 .... 8–30-8–33, 8–41
Electricity Supply Board v Gormley [1985] 1 IR 129 6–66
Ennis v Butterly [1996] 1 IR 426 9–22-9–24
Equality Authority v Portmarnock Golf Club [2005] IEHC 235 8–39
ER v JR [1981] ILRM 125 9–32

F
Fajujonu v Minister for Justice [1990] 2 IR 151;[1990] 1 ILRM 234 9–47-9–50
Finn v Minister for the Environment [1983] IR 154 15–04-15–06
FN v Minister for Education [1995] 1 IR 409 .... 4–53, 9–127-9–128
Foley v Sunday Independent Ltd [2005] IEHC 14 8–17
FP v Minister for Justice [2002] 1 IR 164 .... 1–12, 12–10
Funke v France (1993) 16 EHRR 297 2–02

G
G v An Bord Uchtála [1980] IR 32 4–21-4–25,
 4–29, 4–47, 4–48, 4–53, 5–10, 9–08, 9–107, 9–36-9–37, 9–74, 15–04
Gilligan v Revenue Commissioners [2006] IEHC 404 .... 3–53, 17–25
Goodman International v Hamilton (No 1) [1992] 2 IR 542 13–04-13–06
Greene v Minister for Agriculture [1990] 2 IR 17 9–14
Gregory v Windle [1994] 3 IR 613 7–38

H
H v EHB [1988] IR 747 9–14
Hanafin v Minister for the Environment [1996] 2 IR 321 15–17-15–21
Hanley v Minister for Defence [1999] 4 IR 392 3–06
Hardy v Ireland [1994] 2 IR 550 2–68
Harvey v Minister for SocialWelfare [1990] 2 IR 232 11–35-11–37
Haughey v Moriarty [1999] 3 IR 1 .... 4–10, 12–05
Heaney v Ireland [1994] 3 IR 593 .... 2–02, 2–34-2–37, 6–24, 6–37
Heaney v Ireland [1996] 1 IR 580 .... 2–34, 2–35
Hegarty v O'Loughran [1990] 1 IR 148 5–43

XXXV

Hempenstall v Minister for the Environment [1994] 2 IR 20......................................6–32
Holland v Governor of Portlaoise Prison [2004] 2 IR 573......................7–24-7–26, 8-07
Horgan v Ireland [2003] 2 IR 468 12–26
Howard v Commissioners of Public Works [1994] 1 IR 101...................................1–18
Hunter v Duckworth [2003] IEHC 81 8–20
Hyland v Minister for Social Welfare [1989] IR 629 9–14
Hynes-O'Sullivan v O'Driscoll [1988] IR 436 8–20

I
Iarnród Éireann v Ireland [1996] 3 IR 321 ....6–18, 6-33-6–34, 6–36-6–39
In re C (A Child) (H.I.V. Testing) (Fam. D.) [2000] Fam. 48.............................9–90
In re T (A Minor) (C.A.) [1997] 1 WLR 242... 9–90-9–91
Independent Newspapers of Ireland Ltd v Judge Anderson [2006] IEHC 62 8–15
Institute of Patent Agents v Lockwood [1894] AC 347..17–27
Irish Times Ltd v Ireland [1998] 1 IR 359 .... 8–51, 8–05, 8–10, 8–14

K
K v W [1990] 2 IR 437 9–39
Kavanagh v the Governor of Mountjoy Prison [2002] 3 IR 97 12–25
Kelly v Minister for the Environment [2002] 4 IR 191 .... 15–44-14–45, 16–22
Kennedy v Ireland [1987] IR 587 .... 4–10, 5–36
Kennedy v Law Society of Ireland (No 3) [2002] 2 IR 458......................11–05, 11–31
Kerry Co-Operative Creameries Ltd v An Bord Bainne [1990] ILRM 664 6–18
King v Attorney General [1981] IR 233 ....2–86, 7–12, 16–10
King v Minister for Environment [2006] IESC 61 15–47

L
L v L [1989] ILRM 528 (HC); [1992] 2 IR 77 (SC); [1992] ILRM
  115 (SC)...9–65, 9–70, 9–31
Landers v Attorney General (1975) 109 ILTR 1 .... 5–34, 9–73
Laurentiu v Minister for Justice [1999] 4 IR 26...11–14-11–18,
                                                        11–21, 12–12, 12–15-12–18
Lavery v Member in Charge, Carrickmacross Garda Station [1999] 2 IR 390 2–29
Leontjava v DPP and Chang v DPP [2004] 1 IR 591.................................11–19-11–23,
                                                        11–41-11–48, 14–28, 17–27
Lobe and Osayande v Minister for Justice [2003] 1 IR 1 .... 1–05, 9–50-9–57, 9–96-9–97
Loftus v Attorney General [1979] IR 221 ....3–21, 8–38, 15–42
Lovett v Minister for Education [1997] 1 ILRM 89.............................. 6–19, 11–39
Lowth v Minister for Social Welfare [1998] 4 IR 321 ....3–20, 3–47, 9–64

M
M v An Bord Uchtála [1977] IR 287 ....9–76 -9–78, 16–16
M v Drury [1994] 2 IR 8 8–16
Macauley v Minister for Posts and Telegraphs [1966] IR 345..............3–33, 4–26, 5–42
MacCárthaigh v Éire [1999] 1 IR 186 1–23
MacFarlane v DPP [2007] 1 IR 134 ....2–59-2–60, 2–62
Madigan v Attorney General [1986] ILRM 136..6–52,16–10
Magee v Culligan [1992] 1 IR 233 2–84
Magee v O'Dea [1994] 1 IR 500 2–48

Table of Cases

Maguire v Ardagh [2002] 1 IR 385 11–49-11–51
Maher v Attorney General [1973] IR 140 .... 13–12, 16–24
Maher v Minister for Agriculture, Food and Rural Development
  [2001] 2 IR 139 .... 6–26-6–31, 14-24-14–26
Mahon v Post Publications Ltd [2007] IESC 15 .... 8–06, 8–19
Massachusetts Board of Retirement v Murgia 427 US 307 (1976) 3–45
McDaid v Sheehy [1991] 1 IR 1 .... 11–12-11–13, 11–16
McDonald v Bord na gCon [1965] IR 217 .... 13–02-13–03, 16–20
McDonnell v Ireland [1998] 1 IR 134 .... 16–37-16–42, 16–44
McEneaney v Minister for Education [1941] IR 430 17–23
McGee v Attorney General [1974] IR 284 .... 4–11-4–12, 4–14,
    4–18-4–19, 4–22, 4–34-4–36, 4–42 -4–43, 4–48, 4–51, 5–07,
    5–09, 5–14, 5–35, 9–42, 10–02, 16–05, 17–16, 17–25, 17–29
McGimpsey v Ireland [1990] 1 IR 110 .... 1–04, 12–23-12–24
McGrath v Trustees of Maynooth College [1979] ILRM 166 10–10-10–11
McKenna v An Taoiseach (No 1) [1995] 2 IR 1 .... 15–09-15–10, 15–44
McKenna v An Taoiseach (No 2) [1995] 2 IR 10 .... 13–18, 13–30,
    13–40, 13–43, 15–12-1, 16–09, 16–10
McKinley v Minister for Defence [1992] 2 IR 333 3–20
McLoughlin v Tuite [1989] IR 82 2–07
McMahon v Attorney General [1972] IR 69 15–41
McMahon v Leahy [1984] IR 525 3–05
McPhillips and McShane (1986) 3 Frewen 36 7–31
Meagher v Minister for Agriculture [1994] 1 IR 329 14–20-14–26
Melling v Ó Mathghamhna [1962] IR 1 .... 2–05-2–07, 2–71-2–73
Meskell v CIE [1973] IR 121 8–34
MhicMhathúna v Attorney General [1989] IR 505 .... 13–21, 16–10
MhicMhathúna v Ireland [1989] IR 504 (HC);
  [1995] 1 IR 484 .... 6–53, 9–15-9–19
Mitchell v Ireland [2007] IEHC 280 3–53-3–54
Morris v Minister for the Environment [2002] 1 IR 326 15–27-15–29
Moynihan v Greensmith [1977] IR 55 6–17
Muckley v Ireland [1985] IR 472 .... 9–12-9–14, 9–18-9–19,16–35-16–40
Mulloy v Minister for Education [1975] IR 88 .... 10–12-10–13, 10–23
Murphy v Attorney General [1982] IR 241 .... 9–09, 9–12,
    9–15, 9–18-9–19, 9–32, 11–04, 16–29-16–31, 16–34-16–45
Murphy v DPP [1989] ILRM 71 2–50
Murphy v Dublin Corporation [1972] IR 215 .... 12–03, 12–06
Murphy v GM [2001] 4 IR 113 2–07
Murphy v Independent Radio and Television Commission [1999] 1 IR 12 8–06,
    8–08-8–09, 8–13, 8–22-8–23, 10–04-10–05
Murphy v Minister for Environment [2007] IEHC 185 15–37-15–40
Murphy v Roche [1987] IR 106 16–17-16–18
Murphy v Stewart [1973] IR 97 .... 8–29, 8–35
Murray v Ireland [1985] IR 532 .... 7–19-7–20, 9–08, 9–32
Murray v United Kingdom (1996) 22 EHRR 29 2–40
Murtagh Properties v AG [1972] IR 335 5–34
Murtagh Properties v Cleary [1972] IR 330 5–34-3–35

N

N v HSE [2006] IEHC 278 9–82-9–85
N v K [1985] IR 733 9–09
National Irish Bank v RTÉ [1998] 2 IR 465 8–18
National Union of Railwaymen and Others v Sullivan and Others
  [1947] IR 77 8–30
NC v DPP [2001] IESC 54 2–61
Norris v Attorney General [1984] IR 36 .... 3–31, 4–13-4–16,
  5–34, 5–35-5–36, 15–04, 16–05-16–06
Northants County Council v ABF [1982] ILRM 64 9–42-9–43
Northwestern Health Board v HW [2001] 3 IR 622 .... 9–02-9–03, 9–87-9–97
NUR v Sullivan [1947] IR 77 8–43-8–48

O

Ó Beoláin v Fahey [2001] 2 IR 279 1–24
Ó Domhnaill v Merrick [1984] IR 151 5–43
O'Brien v Keogh [1972] IR 144 6–17
O'Brien v Manufacturing Engineering Co Ltd [1973] IR 334 6–17
O'Brien v Stoutt [1984] IR 316 .... 3–22, 9–06, 9–33, 9–41
O'Brien v Wicklow UDC, 10 June 1994 *(HC)* 13–50
O'Callaghan v Attorney General [1993] 2 IR 17 2–81
O'Callaghan v Commissioners of Public Works [1985] ILRM 364 6–69
O'Carolan v Minister for Education [2005] IEHC 296 9–123
O'Donoghue v Legal Aid Board [2004] IEHC 413 5–45
O'Donoghue v Minister for Health [1996] 2 I.R. 20 .... 9–107, 9–116, 9–121
O'Donohoe v Ó Baróid 23 April 1999 *(HC)* 8–39
O'Donovan v Attorney General [1961] IR 114 .... 15–32-15–34, 16–10
O'G v Attorney General [1985] ILRM 61 .... 3–19, 9–63
O'Leary v Attorney General [1993] 1 IR 102 2–63-2–67
O'Malley v An Taoiseach [1990] ILRM 461 .... 15–36, 15–38
O'Neill v Ryan [1993] ILRM 557 6–18
O'Reilly v Limerick Corporation [1989] ILRM 181 .... 13–48, 13–55, 13–57
O'Reilly v Minister for the Environment [1986] IR 143 15–43
O'Shea v Ireland, 17 October 2006 *(HC)* 9–25-9–26
O'Sheil v Minister for Education [1999] 2 IR 321 .... 9–124-9–127, 10–25
O'T v B [1998] 2 IR 321 .... 4–46-4–52, 4–54-4–55
Oblique Financial Services Ltd v The Promise Production Company Co Ltd
  [1994] 1 ILRM 74 .... 8–04, 8–18
Ojo v Minister for Justice, 8 May 2003 *(HC)* 9–55
Open Door Counselling Ltd v Ireland (1992) 14 EHRR 131 .... 5–12.
Osheku v Ireland [1986] IR 733 .... 1–12, 9–47, 11–16, 12–09

P

People (Attorney General) v O'Brien [1965] IR 142 2–11-2–18
People (Attorney General) v O'Callaghan [1966] IR 501 .... 7–11, 7–36-7–37
People (DPP) v Draper, 24 March 1988, *The Irish Times* 10–06
People (DPP) v Eccles 7–31
People (DPP) v Finn [2001] 2 ILRM 211 13–16
People (DPP) v Finnerty [1999] 4 IR 364 2–43

Table of Cases

People (DPP) v Healy [1990] 2 IR 73 2–28
People (DPP) v Kenny [1990] 2 IR 110 .... 2–15-2–18, 2–20, 2–23, 7–28
People (DPP) v Lawless 3, Frewen 30 7–40
People (DPP) v O'Brien [2005] 2 IR 206 2–29
People (DPP) v O'Shea [1982] IR 384 .... 2–76-2–77, 17–10-17–13
People (DPP) v Quilligan (No 3) [1992] 2 IR 305 .... 2–61, 3–03, 7–31
People (DPP) v Shaw [1982] IR 1 .... 2–14-2–15, 2–19-2–21
People (DPP) v T (1988) 3 Frewen 141 9–31
People (DPP) v Walsh [1980] IR 294 7–31
PH v J Murphy & Sons Ltd [1987] IR 621; [1988] ILRM 542 9–30
Phonographic Performance (Ireland) Ltd v Cody [1998] 4 IR 504 6–16
Pigs Marketing Board v Donnelly [1939] IR 413 16–12-16–13
Pine Valley Developments v Minister for the Environment [1987] IR 23 6–22-6–23
PMPS v Attorney General [1983] IR 339 .... 8–45, 8–53
Pok Sun Shun v Ireland [1986] ILRM 593 9–47
Portmarnock Golf Club v Ireland [2005] IEHC 235 .... 8–39-8–41, 8–47, 8–53-8–54
Private Motorists Provident Society v Attorney General
  [1983] IR 339 .... 6–18, 6–33
Purcell v Attorney General [1995] 3 IR 287; [1996] 2 ILRM 153 3–05

Q
Quinn v Ireland (2001) 33 EHRR 334 2–39
Quinn's Supermarket v Attorney General [1972] IR 1 3–34-3–38,
                                                                                3–42, 10–07-10–08, 10–23, 17–08

R
R v Central Independent Television PLC [1994] Fam. 192;
  [1994] 3 WLR 20 8–19
R v R [2006] IEHC 359 2–23-2–28
R(S) v Chief Constable of South Yorkshire [2002] 1 WLR 3223 16–14
Re a Ward of Court (withholding medical treatment) (No 2)
  [1996] 2 IR 79 .... 5–03-5–06, 5–38-5–40
Re Article 26 and Part V of the Planning and Development Bill 1999
  [2000] 2 IR 321 .... 6–24-6–25, 6–42-6–43, 6–51, 6–62, 6–68
Re Article 26 and sections 5 and 10 of the Illegal Immigrants (Trafficking)
  Bill 1999 [2000] 2 IR 360 5–44
Re Article 26 and the Adoption (No 2) Bill 1987 [1989] IR 656 9–30
Re Article 26 and the Electoral (Amendment) Bill 1961 [1961]
  IR 169 15–35-15–37
Re Article 26 and the Emergency Powers Bill 1976 [1977] IR 159 .... 7–12, 7–15-7–16
Re Article 26 and the Employment Equality Bill 1996 [1996] 2
  IR 321 .... 2–88, 3–44-3–45, 3–51, 6–16, 6–57-6–59, 10–09, 10–15, 11–48
Re Article 26 and the Health (Amendment) (No 2) Bill 2004
  [2005] IESC 7 .... 6–03-6–05, 6–14, 6–17, 6–55-6–56, 6–60-6–61,
                                                                                6–67, 11–07-11–08, 11–24-11–27, 17–18
Re Article 26 and the Illegal Immigrants (Trafficking) Bill 1999
  [2000] 2 IR 360 .... 3–27, 12–10
Re Article 26 and the Matrimonial Home Bill 1993 .... 9–70-9–72, 9–89
Re Article 26 and the Offences Against the State (Amendment) Bill 1940 7–10

Re Article 26 and the Regulation of Information (Services Outside the State for Termination of Pregnancies) Bill 1995 [1995]
1 IR 1 .... 1–10, 4–401-4–45, 15–11, 15–23
Re Article 26 and the School Attendance Bill 1942 [1943]
IR 334.. 9–103-9–104, 9–107, 9–108
Re Haughey [1971] IR 217 .... 2–70, 2–73, 5–29-5–30
Re JH [1985] IR 375 .... 9–79-9–81, 9–85
Re National Irish Bank [1999] 3 IR 145................................2–34, 2–41-2–42
Re Philip Clarke [1950] IR 235 .... 7–10, 7–32, 7–34-7–35
Re The Emergency Powers Bill, 1976 [1977] IR 159..............................7–31
Re Tilson [1951] IR 1 3–17
Redmond v Minister for the Environment [2001] 4 IR 61............................15–46-15–47
Representatives of Chadwick and Goff v Fingal County Council
[2007] IESC 49..6–48
Reynolds v Malocco [1999] 2 IR 203 8–17
Rice v Connolly [1966] 2 QB 414..7–28
Ring v Minister for the Environment [2004] 1 IR 185.................15–48-15–49
Riordan v An Taoiseach (No 1) [1999] 4 IR 321................................... 15–24
Riordan v An Taoiseach (No 2) [1999] 4 IR 343............... 15–25-15–26, 15–28
Riordan v An Taoiseach [1997] 3 IR 502 12–31
Riordan v Government of Ireland, 14 February 2002 *(HC)* 15–29
Roche v Ireland 17 June 1983 *(HC)*... 15–03
Rock v Ireland [1997] 3 IR 484.. 2–37-2–38
Rodgers v ITGWU [1978] ILRM 51...8–35
Rogers v ITGWU [1978] ILRM 51...5–34
Russell v Fanning [1988] IR 505 12–23
Ryan v Attorney General [1965] IR 294................................4–02-4–07, 4–26,
4–46, 4-49, 5–31, 9–25, 9–30, 9–86, 9–108,
9–115-9–116, 17–26
Ryan v DPP [1989] IR 399...7–37
Ryan v O'Callaghan, 22 July 1987 *(HC)* 7–39, 7–42

S

S v S [1983] IR 68..3–17
Saunders v Midwestern Health Board, 23 June 1987 *(SC)* 9–43
Saunders v United Kingdom (1997) 23 EHRR 313................................2–39
SH v DPP [2006] 3 IR 575 ....2–57-2–58, 2–62
Sherwin v Minister for Environment [2004] 4 IR 279 (1997)................ 15–22
Shirley v AO Gorman & Company Ltd [2006] IEHC 27......................6–46-6–47, 6–63
Sinnott v Minister for Education [2001] 2 IR 545........................ 9–66-9–67,
9–118-9–122, 13–19, 13–40, 17–04, 17–23-17–24
Slattery v An Taoiseach [1993] 1 IR 286 15–07-15–08
Society for the Protection of Unborn Children (Ireland) Ltd v Grogan [1989]
IR 753..5–12
Society for the Protection of Unborn Children v Coogan
[1989] IR 734 .... 5–17, 16–07
Somjee v Minister for Justice [1981] ILRM 324.......................... 1–06, 3–29
State (Burke) v Lennon [1940] IR 36.. 7–08-7–09
State (Byrne) v Frawley [1978] IR 326................. 1–23, 16–33- 16–34, 16–43

Table of Cases

State (C) v Frawley [1976] IR 365.. 5–31, 7–17
State (Comerford) v Governor of Portlaoise Prison [1981] ILRM 86 7–18
State (DPP) v Walsh [1981] IR 412 .... 2–82, 3–16
State (FPH Properties SA) v An Bord Pleanála [1987] IR 698 6–21
State (Healy) v Donoghue [1976] IR 325 2–25-2–27
State (Healy) v Donoghue [1976] IR 325 2–90
State (Lynch) v Cooney [1982] IR 337 8–02
State (M) v Attorney General [1979] IR 73 4–08-4–09
State (McDonagh) v Frawley [1978] IR 131 .... 7–14, 7–16
State (McKeever) v Governor of Mountjoy Prison, 19 December 1966 *(SC)* 7–14
State (Nicolaou) v An Bord Uchtála [1966] IR 567 .... 3–17, 4–17,
                            4–22, 9–05-9–06, 9–23, 9–33, 9–35, 9–38, 9–74, 17–19-17-20
State (O'Connell) v Fawsitt [1986] IR 362 2–55-2–56
State (Quinn) v Ryan [1965] IR 70 5–41
State (Richardson) v Governor of Mountjoy Prison [1978] IR 131 5–33
State (Ryan) v Lennon [1935] IR 170 .... 4–36, 7–02-7–07
State (Trimbole) v Governor of Mountjoy Prison [1985] IR 550 7–30
State (Walshe) v Murphy [1981] IR 275 11–03

T
TD v Minister for Education [2001] 4 IR 259 4–53-4–54,
                                                5–08, 5–33, 9–129, 13–19-13–51, 16–10
TF v Ireland [1995] 1 IR 321 9–32
The Adoption (No. 2) Bill, 1987 [1989] I.R. 656 9–88
Toal v Duignan and others [1991] ILRM 135 5–43
Tuohy v Courtney [1994] 3 IR 1 .... 5–43, 6–17

W
W v W [1993] 2 IR 476 3–17
Walsh v O Buachalla [1991] 1 IR 56 2–22
Webb v Ireland [1988] IR 353 .... 1–16-1–17, 1–19-1–20
White v Dublin City Council [2004] 1 IR 545 .... 5–44, 16–18-16–19

X
X v Flynn, 19 May 1994 *(HC)* 5–37

Z
Z v DPP [1994] 2 IR 476 2–46-2–47
Zappone v Revenue Commissioners [2006] IEHC 404 9–27-9–29
Zoe Developments v DPP, 3 March 1999 *(HC)* 2–49

CONTENTS – CHAPTER 1

Nation, State, People and Language

The Nation and its People. . . . .[1–01]
The Rights of the People. . . . . [1–07]
The State and its Powers. . . . . [1–11]
Language. . . . . [1–22]

Overview

The Constitution distinguishes between the Irish nation and the Irish State. The Irish nation consists of the Irish people – the people are those who are citizens, either by virtue of Article 9 of the Constitution (as amended in 2004) or by statutory law. The people are sovereign and have the right both to designate the rulers of the State and, in final appeal, to decide all questions of national policy. The Constitution further provides that the powers of government that the State holds derive, under God, from the people. The State has certain powers granted to it by the Constitution but also has other implicit powers. The courts have held that the State does not retain the royal prerogatives that inhered in the Crown in the United Kingdom. However, the courts have recognised that sovereign, democratic states must have certain powers in order to be states. These powers include a power to control immigration and a power akin to treasure trove. Irish is the national language of the State and the first official language. The courts have recognised a right of citizens to conduct their own side of official business with the State through Irish.

CHAPTER 1

Nation, State, People and Language

The Nation and its People

Desmond Clarke has analysed what constitutes a nation: [1–01]

> The term "nation", like so many terms in ordinary English, has no precise definition but the lack of precision or sharp boundaries is an obstacle only for those who fail to appreciate how terms acquire and continue to have a definite meaning without having a precise one.... A nation is usually understood as a group of people who share a common history, a common culture and/or language, and who think of themselves as forming a distinctive community among other peoples. David Miller summarizes his analysis of the concept of nationality as follows: "These five elements together—a community (1) constituted by shared belief and mutual commitment, (2) extended in history, (3) active in character, (4) connected to a particular territory, and (5) marked off from other communities by its distinct public culture—serve to distinguish nationality from other collective sources of personal identity." These identifying features are not offered as necessary and sufficient conditions for what constitutes a nation; all nations may not satisfy the same criteria, and it may remain undecided in some cases whether or not a given community qualifies as a nation.
>
> One of the most important features of this concept of nationality—but one which is widely acknowledged—is that whether a community of people constitutes a nation cannot be decided simply by reference to objective facts about them which are independent of their beliefs. Their shared history, ethnicity, or geographical location are not enough to constitute them as a nation; "what holds nations together are beliefs." That means that they must think of themselves as a nation, assume the obligations of national identity and collectively present themselves, both to the world outside and to each other, as members of the same nation. Their shared beliefs may be supported by shared myths, a shared understanding of their common history, participation in a common public culture and an on-going willingness to assume the ethical and civic duties which flow from nationhood. All these elements are widely discussed and contested in the literature; the lack of agreement about them serves only to emphasize that the concept of a nation (or nationality) should be used with due caution in constitutional discussions. Desmond Clarke, "Nation, State and Nationality in the Irish Constitution" [1998] 16 *Irish Law Times* 252, at 252.

Clarke has argued that the Irish Constitution is not fully consistent in how it uses the term "nation". At times, it is used in a broad way to refer to the Irish people; at other times, it seems to refer to a narrower group of people who have a specific legal connection to the Irish State. Nevertheless, despite these inconsistencies, the Constitution seems to strive for a concept of "nation" that distinguishes it from the more legalistic entity that is the "State". [1–02]

Article 1 of the Constitution identifies the Irish nation, affirming its inalienable, indefeasible and sovereign right to choose its own form of government. Articles 2 and 3 were amended pursuant to a referendum in 1998 as part of the Belfast Agreement. Article 2 now provides: [1–03]

> It is the entitlement and birthright of every person born in the island of Ireland, which includes its islands and seas, to be part of the Irish Nation. That is also the entitlement of all persons otherwise qualified in accordance with law to be citizens of Ireland. Furthermore, the Irish nation cherishes its special affinity with people of Irish ancestry living abroad who share its cultural identity and heritage.

[1–04] Article 3 now notes an aspiration for Irish unity but recognises that such unity can only be brought about by peaceful means with the consent of a majority of the people, democratically expressed, in both jurisdictions in the island. This replaced the territorial claim that existed in the old Art 3. In *McGimpsey v Ireland* [1990] 1 IR 110, the Supreme Court had held that the old Arts 2 and 3 amounted to a claim as of right by Ireland to the territory of the whole island of Ireland. The new Articles clearly take a more consensual approach.

[1–05] The language of the new Art 2 appears to write a *ius soli* entitlement to citizenship into the Constitution. Under this conception of citizenship, a person becomes a citizen if she is born in the particular territory—citizenship is tied to the soil. This contrasts with a *ius sanguinis* entitlement to citizenship, whereby citizenship depends on one's blood relationship to an existing citizen. Common law countries traditionally adopted a *ius soli* approach to citizenship. Indeed, s 6(1) of the Irish Nationality and Citizenship Act 1956 explicitly followed previous legislation in providing for a *ius soli* entitlement to citizenship. In *Lobe v Minister for Justice* [2003] 1 IR 1, certain members of the Supreme Court commented that the revised Art 2 had raised this *ius soli* entitlement from a statutory to a constitutional basis. Prompted by a concern that this might encourage migrants to come to Ireland in order to have children who would be Irish citizens, the Government proposed certain amendments to Art 9 of the Constitution in 2004. These amendments were overwhelmingly approved by the People in a referendum. Article 9(2) now provides:

> 1° Notwithstanding any other provision of this Constitution, a person born in the island of Ireland, which includes its islands and seas, who does not have, at the time of the birth of that person, at least one parent who is an Irish citizen or entitled to be an Irish citizen is not entitled to Irish citizenship or nationality, unless provided for by law.
> 2° This section shall not apply to persons born before the date of the enactment of this section.

[1–06] The effect of this provision is to preclude persons born in Ireland from gaining Irish citizenship, unless they have one parent who is an Irish citizen or entitled to be an Irish citizen. The phrase "notwithstanding any other provision of this Constitution" means that this more specific provision takes precedence over the terms of Art 2. The phrase "unless provided for by law" allows the Oireachtas to extend citizenship on a statutory basis more widely. This has been done. The Irish Nationality and Citizenship Act 2004 provides that where a person is born in Ireland to a non-citizen parent, but that parent has been living in Ireland for more than three of the past four years, then the child is entitled to Irish citizenship. However, Estelle Feldman and I have argued that the phrase "notwithstanding any other provision of this Constitution" has potentially wider effects:

> This phrase effectively elevates Article 9.2.1° over Article 2 and immunises the legislative regime envisaged by Article 9.2.1° from constitutional challenge by reference to Article 2. However, it also immunises that legislative regime from constitutional challenge by reference to any other provision of the Constitution. Thus it is no longer open to a

person, as it was in *Somjee v Minister for Justice* [1981] ILRM 324, to challenge citizenship laws by reference to other provisions of the Constitution, such as Article 40.1. Assuming that "provision" does not mean "Article", it also appears that citizenship laws can no longer be invalidated by reference to Article 9.1.3°, which provides that no person may be excluded from Irish nationality and citizenship by reason of the sex of such person. In short, citizenship legislation cannot be constitutionally challenged, save by reference to Article 9.2.1°. Raymond Byrne and William Binchy eds, *Annual Review of Irish Law 2004* (Thomson Round Hall, 2005), at 163–164.

The Rights of the People

Article 6 of the Constitution provides that the people have the right to designate the rulers of the State and, in final appeal, to decide all questions of national policy. This appears to be primarily a reference to Arts 46 and 47 which provide that the Constitution can only be amended by way of referendum. It may also refer to Art 27 of the Constitution which allows Bills to be referred to the people. This procedure has never been utilised. [1–07]

The courts have also derived the doctrine of popular sovereignty from the Constitution. In *Byrne v Ireland* [1972] IR 241, the plaintiff sued the State for personal injuries. She had tripped over a subsidence in a footpath, caused by a trench that had been dug and refilled (albeit not very effectively) by employees of the State. The plaintiff was unsuccessful in the High Court, as Murnaghan J ruled that the sovereignty of the State—referred to in Art 5 of the Constitution—precluded the State from being sued in its own courts. The Supreme Court overturned this decision on appeal. Walsh J reasoned as follows: [1–08]

> By the Constitution which was adopted and enacted by the People and came into force on the 29th December, 1937, the People created a State which is described in Article 5 of the Constitution as "a sovereign, independent, democratic state" and under Article 4 the name of the State in the English language is "Ireland". If the State can be sued, then in my opinion it can be sued by its official name which is "Ireland" in the English language.
> Article 6 of the Constitution provides that all powers of government—legislative, executive and judicial—"derive, under God, from the people, whose right it is to designate the rulers of the State and, in final appeal, to decide all questions of national policy, according to the requirements of the common good." Article 46 of the Constitution provides that every proposal for an amendment of the Constitution shall, upon having been passed or deemed to have been passed by both Houses of the Oireachtas, be submitted by referendum to the decision of the People, and Article 47 provides that every such proposal for an amendment shall be held to have been approved by the People if, upon having been so submitted, a majority of the votes cast at such referendum shall have been cast in favour of its enactment into law. The preamble to the Constitution is a preamble by the People formally adopting, enacting and giving themselves a Constitution.
> It appears to me abundantly clear from those provisions that the State is the creation of the People and is to be governed in accordance with the provisions of the Constitution which was enacted by the People and which can be amended by the People only, and that in the last analysis the sovereign authority is the People [1972] IR 241, at 261–262.

Accordingly, Walsh J held that the State could be sued in its own courts: the State was subject to the Constitution which in turn was subject to the People. As the courts were responsible for the enforcement of the Constitution, it followed that a person was entitled to assert her rights against the State in court. This did not affect the external [1–09] sovereignty of the State. Externally, the State was fully competent to deal with other nations. Internally, however, the State was the creature of the People.

[1–10] A number of practical propositions have followed from this sovereignty of the People. Most notably, the courts have held that the People have an unfettered power to amend the Constitution: *Re Article 26 and the Regulation of Information (Services outside the State for Termination of Pregnancies) Bill 1995* [1995] 1 IR 1. This case is discussed in detail in chapter 4. The demise of royal prerogatives (see below) may also be attributable to the doctrine of popular sovereignty.

The State and its Powers

[1–11] As noted above, the Constitution provides separate recognition for the Nation and for the State. Desmond Clarke has helpfully described the State as "a legal entity or a cluster of political and legal structures which have been established by the people." [1998] 16 *Irish Law Times* 252, at 256.

[1–12] The Constitution explicitly recognises certain powers on the part of the State. For instance, Art 10 provides that all natural resources, including the air and all forms of potential energy, within the jurisdiction of the State belong to the State. Article 29 recognises the State's power in external relations. In addition to this, certain powers may be recognised as belonging to the State by reason of its character as a state. Most notably, the courts have held that the State has the power to control immigration. In *Osheku v Minister for Justice* [1986] IR 733, the High Court considered the State's role in relation to immigration. Gannon J observed:

> The control of aliens which is the purpose of the Aliens Act 1935, is an aspect of the common good related to the definition, recognition, and the protection of the boundaries of the State. That it is in the interests of the common good of a State that it should have control of the entry of aliens, their departure, and their activities and duration of stay within the State is and has been recognised universally and from earliest times. There are fundamental rights of the State itself as well as fundamental rights of the individual citizens, and the protection of the former may involve restrictions in circumstances of necessity on the latter. The integrity of the State constituted as it is of the collective body of its citizens within the national territory must be defended and vindicated by the organs of the State and by the citizens so that there may be true social order within the territory and concord maintained with other nations in accordance with the objectives declared in the preamble to the Constitution. [1986] IR 733, at 746.

These sentiments have been approved by the Supreme Court in *Re Article 26 and the Illegal Immigrants (Trafficking) Bill 1999* [2000] 2 IR 360 and more recently by Hardiman J in *FP v Minister for Justice* [2002] 1 IR 164, at 168–169.

[1–13] Article 49 of the Constitution identifies a category of "powers, functions, rights and prerogatives" which existed in the Irish Free State, declaring them to belong to the People but to be exercisable by or on the authority of the Government. This appears to refer back to certain royal prerogatives that were recognised by British constitutional theory. In British constitutional theory, the King (or the Crown) was regarded as the personification of the State; he was also the supreme authority within the State. Certain powers were deemed to inhere in the Crown. Over time, these powers came to be exercisable by or on the authority of the executive. Some of these powers were very regal in character, relating to the personality of the Crown as supreme authority. Others, however, could reasonably be seen as necessary powers for any State to have. For instance, the power to control immigration was generally seen as an aspect of the royal prerogative. See Hallsbury (1917), Book 1, 705. It had been generally assumed that the royal prerogatives that attached to the British Crown had been carried over by Art 49 of the Constitution so that they belonged to the Irish people and could be exercised by the Government. This, however, turned out not to be the case.

In *Byrne v Ireland* [1972] IR 241, the State attempted to rely on the former royal prerogative of the Crown's immunity from suit. The Supreme Court held that the royal prerogatives had not carried over into the Irish Free State and therefore could not have been carried over from the Irish Free State into the new Ireland in 1937. Article 51 of the Irish Free State Constitution provided: [1–14]

> The Executive Authority of the Irish Free State (Saorstát Éireann) is hereby declared to be vested in the King, and shall be exercisable, in accordance with the law, practice and constitutional usage governing the exercise of the Executive Authority in the case of the Dominion of Canada, by the Representative of the Crown.

However, in *Byrne* the Supreme Court did not accept that this reference to the Crown in the 1922 Constitution carried over any of the Crown prerogatives. [1–15]

Walsh J reasoned as follows:

> The position and power granted to the King in that Constitution owed everything to the express provisions to that effect in that Constitution. In Saorstát Éireann he was not the personification of the State and, therefore, the common-law immunities or prerogatives of the King which were personal to him did not exist in Saorstát Éireann because any such claim postulated, of necessity, the acceptance in the Constitution of Saorstát Éireann of the King as the personification of the State. All royal prerogatives to be found in the common law of England and in the common law of Ireland prior to the enactment of the Constitution of Saorstát Éireann, 1922, ceased to be part of the law of Saorstát Éireann because they were based on concepts expressly repudiated by Article 2 of that Constitution and, therefore, were inconsistent with the provisions of that Constitution and were not carried over by Article 73 thereof. [1972] IR 241, at 274–275.

The Crown prerogative of immunity from suit was generally objectionable. Few lamented its passing. However, 16 years later the Supreme Court came to the same conclusion with regard to a more acceptable aspect of the Crown prerogative. In *Webb v Ireland* [1988] IR 353, the plaintiffs had been searching for buried treasure with a metal detector. They discovered the Derrynaflan Chalice, described as "one of the most significant discoveries of early Christian art ever made." The plaintiffs brought the hoard to the National Museum and gave it to the Director, with a letter stating that this was "for its care and pending the determination of the legal ownership or status thereof". The plaintiffs subsequently sought the return of the hoard, but the State pleaded treasure trove, by way of defence. Treasure trove was an aspect of the royal prerogative that allowed the Crown to claim buried gold and silver. [1–16]

The Supreme Court followed *Byrne v Ireland* in holding that all royal prerogatives had ceased to exist in relation to the Irish Free State in 1922 and therefore could not have [1–17] been carried over by Art 49 in 1937. Finlay CJ reviewed the history of this royal prerogative, reasoning:

> Treasure trove as we know it, is a creature of the common law. It is part of the more general right of *bona vacantia* which in the common law of England belonged to the Crown. The general purpose of the vesting of the property in *bona vacantia* in the Crown is usually stated to have been to prevent the strife and contention to which title by occupancy might otherwise give rise in relation to goods, land or rights to which no one can make a lawful claim.
>
> With regard to the prerogative of treasure trove, however, it would seem clear that, historically, it also had the major purpose of being a source of revenue for the Royal Mint.
>
> It applied only to valuable chattels which it could be established were concealed for the purpose of protecting them and with the intention of subsequently recovering them on the part of the person who hid them and which were made of the precious metals of silver or gold, a combination of them or an alloy containing a substantial ingredient of either or both of them. The right of the Crown to the possession and ownership of such treasure trove was subject always to the obligation to restore it or its value to the "true owner" if he could be found.
>
> It would appear obvious that the confining according to the common law of the right of treasure trove to gold and silver objects or objects substantially made of either or both of those metals was directly associated with the purpose of enriching the Royal Mint, and it is stated in most of the textbooks concerning this topic that in early days treasure trove when recovered by the Crown was frequently melted down into coin.
>
> It would appear that since the accession of George III the right to treasure trove vested in the Crown has been part of the surrendered revenue of the Crown, surrendered by each succeeding monarch to the Treasury for his lifetime in return for the provision of the Civil List.
>
> It would appear that from the earliest times the right to treasure trove was enforced on the one hand by penalties imposed on the finders of such treasure trove who failed to reveal to the appropriate authorities the find and failed to yield them to the Crown, and on the other hand by the giving of rewards to those who did reveal their finds and yielded them to the Crown.
>
> By the nineteenth century it is quite clear that the prerogative of treasure trove in England and in Ireland continued to be exercised on behalf of the Crown by the Government of Great Britain and Ireland but for a purpose wholly different from that which had been its historical origin. Its purpose now clearly was the retention by the State, for the common good, of antiquarian objects of interest and value, which formed part of the heritage of the People.
>
> Thus, during this period it would appear, for example, that internal arrangements were made by the Treasury of the British Government, dealing with the scale and measure of rewards for the finding of treasure trove which were quite inconsistent with the possibility of the acquisition by the State of the objects of treasure trove for the purpose of profit. Furthermore, the right or franchise of treasure trove in Ireland was apparently *de facto* exercised on behalf of the State by the Royal Irish Academy who received a grant from the Treasury for the purpose of providing rewards and who do not appear to have had any obligation to account in any way to the State for the value of what they might have acquired under this right.
>
> In general terms, it would appear that at common law the payment of a reward to the finder of treasure trove was an act of grace and the finding and giving up of treasure trove to the State or its agent was not considered to confer on the finder any right enforceable at law to the payment of any particular reward or of a reward at all.
>
> Having regard to this very brief summary of the apparent history and characteristics of the prerogative of treasure trove, I have, with regard to the submissions made on

behalf of the defendants, under two separate headings, come to the following conclusions.

I agree with the view reached by the learned trial judge in this case that on the authority of *Byrne v Ireland* [1972] IR 241 no royal prerogative in existence prior to the enactment of the Constitution of 1922 was by virtue of the provisions of that Constitution vested in the Irish Free State. I agree with the judgment of Walsh J in *Byrne v Ireland* which was expressly concurred in by a majority of the Court that the provisions of article 2 of the Constitution of 1922 declaring the Irish Free State to be a sovereign State and the provisions of article 51 of the same Constitution expressly vesting in the King certain executive functions, being the executive functions of the Irish Free State, are inconsistent with the transference to that State of any royal prerogative. As is also set out in the decision in *Byrne v Ireland*, it must follow from this conclusion that the royal prerogatives were not prerogatives exercisable in Saorstát Éireann immediately before the 11th December, 1936, and were therefore not captured by Article 49, section 1 of the Constitution.

It was contended on this appeal that it was possible to distinguish between a prerogative of immunity from suit, which was the subject matter of the decision in *Byrne v Ireland* [1972] IR 241 and which could be traced to the royal dignity of the King and a prerogative of treasure trove which it was stated could be traced or related not to the dignity of his person but to his position as sovereign or ruler. Such a distinction does not alter the view which I have expressed with regard to the effect of the provisions of the Constitution of 1922, and appears to me to ignore the essential point which is that by virtue of the provisions of the Constitution of 1922 what was being created was a brand new sovereign State and that the function, power or position of the King in that sovereign State was such only as was vested in him by that Constitution and by the State created by it. [1988] IR 353, at 381–382.

This strong attitude against royal prerogatives was again confirmed in *Howard v Commissioners of Public Works* [1994] 1 IR 101. Here the applicants sought to halt the building of an interpretative centre on the basis that the Commissioners had not applied for planning permission. Finlay CJ held that there was no principle of common law to the effect that the State was presumed not to be subject to statutes of general application that could be freed from the particular position of the Crown in English constitutional theory, or which has by any means been divested of its association with the entire doctrine and history of the Crown prerogative. [1–18]

The decision in *Webb* has been heavily criticised, most notably by Kelly: [1–19]

> If the major premise leading to this conclusion is, that the Irish Free State, as established in 1922, was a sovereign state, it seems to me extremely dubious. It is all very well now, with hindsight of the 1920s and 1930s during which the British did not hinder, and even encouraged, the gradual evolution of Dominion independence, to say that in 1922 "a brand-new sovereign state" was being created. This proposition, *then*, was not asserted even by the Provisional Government which had to put the best face on the Treaty and to steer the draft Constitution through the Dáil; and it would have been derided by the very substantial minority which fought a civil war precisely because they did not think a sovereign state had been achieved. The Constitution itself did not, in fact, describe the Irish Free State as "sovereign", either in Article 2 – to which the Supreme Court majority pointed in *Webb's* case – or anywhere else; and I believe the use of the word "sovereign" in our present Article 5 had the deliberate purpose of emphasising in 1937 what no one thought could be claimed in 1922 ...
>
> The apparently general legislative, governmental, and judicial powers conferred by Article 2 were to be exercised within the terms of the Constitution; and there was no power

in the country—neither in the people nor in the Oireachtas—to amend the Constitution itself in such a way that it no longer conformed with a Treaty negotiated with, or more correctly imposed by a foreign state. The Irish doctrine certainly was that the Dáil and not the British Parliament had imposed this limitation; but a sovereign power cannot conclude itself, and the doctrine was therefore a very odd one for a sovereign state to have to accept. It was also a highly individual form of sovereignty which could accommodate appeals from its own Supreme Court to a tribunal sitting in a foreign capital, the legislation of its parliament becoming law only on the signature of the representative of a foreign monarch, and the members of that parliament, before taking their seats, being required to swear that they would be faithful to the king of a foreign country.

The Irish Free State, then, was not "sovereign" in the normal sense of the word; and if I am right in saying this, the main plank on which the Supreme Court rested its rejection of the idea of a qualified survival of the royal prerogative beyond 6 December 1922 disappears. But apart from this I feel the Court may not have paid enough attention to the general policy of the old Constitution, once the substance of the legislative independence had been established—in other words, did not apply to its construction the very sensible doctrine of harmonious interpretation which in recent years it has elaborated for our present Constitution. That policy appears to me to have been—very understandably after the years of instability which preceded it—to effect the transition of regime with as little friction and disruption of familiar patterns as possible. Thus while the old Constitution did not mention prerogative rights specifically, it did provide, in terms which clearly encompassed the common law—and the prerogative was part of the common law—for the substantial continuance in force of the pre-existing body of law. ...

The present Supreme Court is therefore now in the position of asserting a sovereignty for the Irish Free State which its own Constitution and its own judges did not assert; and of using that as the basis for denying the continuance of the royal prerogative beyond 1922, which judges who were in the best position to know the old Constitution's intent, explicitly acknowledged. John Kelly, "Hidden Treasure and the Irish Constitution" (1988) 10 *DULJ* 5, at 8-10.

[1–20] The practical problems posed by the elimination of the royal prerogative of treasure trove were avoided by the Supreme Court's discovery of a constitutional doctrine remarkably akin to treasure trove:

With regard to the second submission made by the defendants concerning the question of the prerogative of treasure trove, I have come to the following conclusions.

Article 5 of the Constitution declares that "Ireland is a sovereign, independent, democratic state." Article 10.1 of the Constitution provides as follows:—

"All natural resources, including the air and all forms of potential energy, within the jurisdiction of the Parliament and Government established by this Constitution and all royalties and franchises within that jurisdiction belong to the State subject to all estates and interests therein for the time being lawfully vested in any person or body."

Article 10.3 provides as follows:—

"Provision may be made by law for the management of the property which belongs to the State by virtue of this Article and for the control of the alienation, whether temporary or permanent, of that property."

I am satisfied that the phrase "all royalties" contained in Article 10.1 of the Constitution, construed in the light of Article 5, must be widely construed and must include one of the definitions of royalty to be found in the Shorter Oxford English Dictionary, namely, the sovereignty or sovereign rule of a State.

It would, I think, now be universally accepted, certainly by the People of Ireland, and by the people of most modern states, that one of the most important national assets belonging to the people is their heritage and knowledge of its true origins and the buildings and objects which constitute keys to their ancient history. If this be so, then it would appear to me to follow that a necessary ingredient of sovereignty in a modern state and certainly in this State, having regard to the terms of the Constitution, with an emphasis on its historical origins and a constant concern for the common good is and should be an ownership by the State of objects which constitute antiquities of importance which are discovered and which have no known owner. It would appear to me to be inconsistent with the framework of the society sought to be created and sought to be protected by the Constitution that such objects should become the exclusive property of those who by chance may find them.

The existence of such a general ingredient of the sovereignty of the State, does, however, seem to me to lead to the conclusion that the much more limited right of the prerogative of treasure trove known to the common law should be upheld not as a right derived from the Crown but rather as an inherent attribute of the sovereignty of the State which was recognised and declared by Article 11 of the 1922 Constitution.

For the purpose of determining the issues in this case, therefore, I would conclude that there does exist in the State a right or prerogative of treasure trove, the characteristics of which are the characteristics of the prerogative of treasure trove at common law which I have already outlined in this judgment as they stood in 1922.

As I have already indicated, it would appear that the characteristics of the right or prerogative of treasure trove at common law included the practice of rewarding a diligent and honest finder who revealed his find and yielded the object of it to the Crown. This practice is, however, apparently established as one of grace only and not as conferring a legal right enforceable by the courts. [1988] IR 353, at 383–384.

Thus it appears that in much the same way as the control of immigration—once considered an aspect of the royal prerogative—has been held to be an inherent state power, so treasure trove—or something like it—is an inherent state power. If the courts adopt this approach more generally, it may be that all the non-objectionable aspects of the royal prerogative (*ie* those that are appropriate to a republican democracy) may be resurrected by the courts as inherent state powers. If this transpires to be the case, one wonders whether it might not have been simpler just to declare unconstitutional those prerogatives that were inconsistent with the character of the State, leaving the others in place. [1–21]

Language

Article 8 of the Constitution provides: [1–22]

1. The Irish language as the national language is the first official language.
2. The English language is recognised as a second official language.
3. Provision may, however, be made by law for the exclusive use of either of the said languages for any one or more official purposes, either throughout the State or in any part thereof.

Given that English is spoken by 98 percent of the population as their vernacular, Art 8 is perhaps best seen as an aspirational statement in support of the Irish language. It has been successfully relied on by a number of litigants who wanted to transact their official business with the State through Irish. A number of court cases have established the right of persons to conduct their own side of a court case in Irish but have rejected the contention that a person is entitled to a process conducted entirely through Irish. This [1–23] position is illustrated by the judgment of the Supreme Court in *MacCárthaigh v Éire* [1999] 1 IR 186. Hamilton CJ accepted that the accused was entitled to conduct his defence in Irish but rejected the suggestion that the accused was entitled to be tried by a jury all of whom had a good spoken knowledge of Irish. Such an approach would be inconsistent with Art 38.5, as interpreted in *de Búrca v Attorney General* [1976] IR 38:

> Tá sé sin fíor go leor, ach caithfear a rá, in Éireann faoi láthair, nach bhfuil réiteach níos fearr ann. Dá mbeadh ar gach ball den ghiúiré bheith in ann cúrsaí dlí a thuiscint as Gaeilge gan cabhair ateangaire, chuirfí formhór de mhuintir na hÉireann ar leataobh. Dhéanadh sé sin sarú ar Airteagal 38.5 den Bhunreacht, mar a mhínigh an Chúirt Uachtarach é i gcás *de Búrca v Attorney General* [1976] IR 38 agus *State (Byrne) v Frawley* [1978] IR 326.

[1–24] There is also a general entitlement to conduct one's own side of official business with the State in Irish. Article 25.4.4° provides that where the President signs the text of a Bill in one only of the official languages, a translation shall be issued in the other official language. In *Ó Beoláin v Fahey* [2001] 2 IR 279, an issue arose as to whether this obligation had to be complied with within a particular time, the State not having provided an Irish translation of most Acts enacted since 1980. The applicant faced prosecution in the District Court and sought an official translation of the Road Traffic Acts 1994 and 1995, as well as a translation of the Rules of the District Court. McGuinness J reasoned as follows in relation to the statutes:

> Article 25.4.4, as was pointed out by counsel on both sides, does not provide any time frame within which an official translation of each bill/act is to be provided. However, the Article as a whole seems to envisage a fairly rapid procedure—where time limits are provided they are short, and the former pre-1980 system of providing a translation virtually simultaneously with the enactment of the statute seems considerably more in accordance with the general tenor of the article than the present system which, as far as the court can ascertain, provides a translation only when a special or urgent demand is made for it. The respondents' argument for a reasonable time to be allowed for translation would ring more sincerely were it not for the fact that virtually *no* official translations of statutes have been provided for the past 20 years. This could not be described as a "reasonable time". Indeed it seems probable that the statutes in question in this case—statutes which are used daily in the District Court—would never have been translated were it not for the efforts of the applicant and his legal advisers....
>
> In the present situation it is clear that the State is simply unwilling to provide the resources to fulfil its clear constitutional duty. Counsel for the respondents submits that the duty to provide translations of the statutes falls, not on his clients, but on the Clerk of the Dáil. He grounds this claim not on the Constitution or on any statutory authority, but on the Standing Orders of the Dáil. It does not appear that this argument was made in the High Court. [2001] 2 IR 279, at 307–308.

[1–25] A majority of the court also ruled that the applicant was entitled to an official translation of the District Court Rules, Hardiman J deriving this obligation on the State from Art 8 of the Constitution:

> It appears to me that ... a person, whether an official or not, [has] a right to choose which of the official languages he will use for any particular official transaction. This choice relates to his side of the transaction: no-one can dictate another's choice of language.... Similarly a defendant may conduct his defence in Irish, although proceedings might have been commenced against him in English. In view of the terms of Art 8, and the official policy of bilingualism to which the State is committed, the State must facilitate the use of

either language without discrimination. The production of laws in one language only is totally inconsistent with bilingualism, and is not paralleled to my knowledge in any other bilingual country.

On the specific topic of the rules [of the District Court], I have no doubt that an Irish version of the rules of every court is an absolute essential for the conduct of litigation as effectively in Irish as in English. It would be the grossest negligence for any practitioner to approach a court without a competent knowledge of the rules. If the equal right to litigate, whether as plaintiff or defendant, in Irish as in English is to be more than a shibboleth, this material must be provided....

These rules, as noted above, are extremely important for the conduct of litigation in that court. In relation to the trial of summary offences, they contain provisions for such vital matters as service, powers of adjournment, powers of amendment, and the effect of variations between the offence alleged in the summons and the evidence actually given in court. Furthermore, the rules provide the appropriate forms to be used for such basic purposes as the summoning of a witness and the giving of notice of appeal. In the absence of an official version of these forms in Irish an unwilling witness served with a summons in Irish might omit to attend and, if it were sought to compel him, object that the summons was not in the prescribed form. A party served with notice of appeal might take a similar point. Again, the document containing the result of the analysis conducted by the medical bureau of road safety must, if it is to be admissible in evidence, be in the statutorily prescribed form and a non-statutory translation might be the subject of objection. I express no opinion on the validity of any such objection as envisaged above: they are mentioned to illustrate the additional difficulties which may beset either party seeking, in the absence of official translations of acts and orders, to conduct his or its legal business in the national language.

It is noteworthy that an Irish translation was provided for the former Rules of the District Court, made in 1948. It would appear that in this regard, as with the statutes, there has been a grave shortfall in the provision of legal materials in Irish since about the year 1980. This can only be described as a failure to observe the constitutional imperative contained in Art 8, and a failure for which apparent lack of staff in the office of the Chief Translator in the Houses of the Oireachtas is no sort of excuse. [2001] 2 IR 279, at 343–344.

The Official Languages Act 2003 now imposes a wide range of obligations on public bodies in relation to their use of both official languages.

CONTENTS – CHAPTER 2

The Constitution and the Criminal Law

Introduction	[2–01]
The Concept of Trial in Due Course of Law	[2–02]
What is a Criminal Charge?	[2–05]
Unconstitutionally Obtained Evidence	[2–09]
The Right to be Provided with a Lawyer	[2–25]
The Right to Silence	[2–33]
Unfair Pre-Trial Publicity	[2–45]
The Duty to Seek Out and Preserve Evidence	[2–50]
The Right to an Early Trial	[2–55]
The Presumption of Innocence	[2–63]
No Right to Confrontational Cross-Examination	[2–70]
The Right to Jury Trial	[2–71]
No Retroactive Penal Sanctions	[2–83]
Vague Criminal Offences	[2–86]
Blameworthiness	[2–88]

Overview

The courts have used various Articles of the Constitution to write several procedural and substantive requirements into the criminal law. The Article most commonly relied on has been Art 38.1, which provides that no person shall be tried on any criminal charge save in due course of law. This ensures that where a person is being investigated or prosecuted for a criminal offence, she has certain procedural and substantive protections. The courts have held that evidence obtained as a result of an unconstitutional act (typically an unauthorised search of a dwelling or an unauthorised deprivation of liberty) cannot be admitted against an accused person, unless there are extraordinary excusing circumstances. The courts have identified a right to a lawyer but, in the pre-trial stages, an accused person only has a right of reasonable access to a lawyer. The courts have held that the right to silence is protected by Art 38.1. In particular, answers that a person is legally compelled to provide cannot be used against that person in a criminal trial. However, it is permissible for adverse inferences to be drawn at trial from silence during pre-trial questioning, subject to certain procedural safeguards. The courts have held that criminal trials can be prohibited where there is a real risk of an unfair trial arising from pre-trial publicity, delay or any failure of the gardaí to seek out and preserve relevant evidence.

The presumption of innocence is constitutionally protected by Art 38.1. For non-minor offences (other than offences which are tried before the Special Criminal Court or Military Tribunals), an accused person is constitutionally entitled to a jury trial. The main criterion for determining whether an offence is minor or non-minor is the severity of the possible punishment. The jury must be drawn from a representative cross-sample of the population. The courts have held that it was unconstitutional to exclude non-ratepayers and presumptively to exclude women. The Constitution explicitly prohibits retroactive penal sanctions.

Certain other substantive requirements of criminal law have also been derived from the Constitution: criminal offences cannot be vague; there must be some *mens rea* requirement, at least for serious and "traditional" criminal offences.

CHAPTER 2

The Constitution and the Criminal Law

Introduction

One of the areas in which the Constitution has had the most influence is the criminal law. This has been most acute in the area of criminal procedure: the Constitution has been invoked to introduce norms of fairness that protect the position of suspects both at trial and during pre-trial investigation. However, the Constitution has also had a limited influence on the content of criminal law, principally in relation to the sort of conduct that it is legitimate to criminalise. Many of these norms of fairness—both procedural and substantive—are not easily traceable to a specific constitutional provision. For the most part, they have been introduced under the rubric of "due course of law", protected by Art 38.1. However, other provisions such as Art 40.1 (equality) and Art 40.3 (unenumerated rights) have also been invoked. The more specific protections in Art 38 have also been the subject of judicial interpretation. This chapter consists of a thematic exploration of the most significant ways in which the Constitution has influenced the substance and process of criminal law. [2–01]

The Concept of Trial in Due Course of Law

Article 38.1 provides: [2–02]

> No citizen shall be tried on any criminal charge save in due course of law.

It is not immediately clear what "due course of law" means. At its narrowest, it could simply mean that trials of criminal charges must be held in accordance with the law. Such an interpretation would provide no additional legal protections, simply making it a constitutional requirement that legal rules be followed. The courts have taken a far wider approach to the phrase than this. In *Heaney v Ireland* [1994] 3 IR 593, at 605–606, Costello J characterised the scope of Art 38.1 in the following terms:

> This Article provides that "No person shall be tried on any criminal charge save in due course of law", an Article which, as the courts have shown, implies a great deal more than a simple assertion that trials are to be held in accordance with laws enacted by parliament. It is an Article couched in peremptory language and has been construed as a constitutional guarantee that criminal trials will be conducted in accordance with basic concepts of justice. Those basic principles may be of ancient origin and part of the long established principles of the common law, or they may be of more recent origin and widely accepted in other jurisdictions and recognised in international conventions as a basic requirement of a fair trial. Thus, the principle that an accused is entitled to the presumption of innocence, that an accused cannot be tried for an offence unknown to the law, or charged a second time with the same offence, the principle that an accused must

know the case he has to meet and that evidence illegally obtained will generally speaking be inadmissible at his trial, are all principles which are so basic to the concept of a fair trial that they obtain constitutional protection from this Article. Furthermore, the Irish courts have developed a concept that there are basic rules of procedure which must be followed in order to ensure that an accused is accorded a fair trial and these basic rules must be followed if constitutional invalidity is to be avoided.

The first immunity I will consider is that of an accused at his trial, as a result of which he is not obliged to give evidence or be required to adduce evidence on his own behalf, and cannot be questioned against his will. This is an immunity long established in the common law world and has been a basic concept of criminal trials in this country for many years. It was enacted as the 5th Amendment to the American Constitution. It was declared in article 14(8)(3)(g) of the UN International Covenant on Civil and Political Rights that in the determination of any criminal charge against him everyone shall be entitled not to be compelled to testify against himself or to confess guilt. It was provided in article 6(1) of the European Convention on Human Rights that in the determination of a criminal charge against him everyone has the right to a fair hearing and the European Court of Human Rights has construed that article as conferring on an accused person the right to remain silent and not to incriminate himself (see *Funke v France* (1993) 16 EHRR 297). I am of the opinion that the concept is such a long-standing one and so widely accepted as basic to the rules under which criminal trials are conducted that it should properly be regarded as one of those which comes within the terms of the guarantee of a fair trial contained in Article 38.1.

But this case is of course concerned with the immunity conferred by law on a *suspect in custody* not with an *accused on trial* and it was submitted on behalf of the Attorney General that as this Article clearly relates to trials of persons on criminal charges and makes no mention of suspects in custody, the right to silence of a suspect cannot obtain protection from this Article. I think that is too restrictive a view of the Article. The fairness of a trial may be compromised by what has happened prior to it and this is why, for example, evidence which has been obtained prior to the trial by improper means may vitiate the trial itself. It would follow, in my opinion, that if the right to silence of a suspect can properly be regarded as a basic requirement for our system of criminal justice then it would be protected by this Article.

[2–03] Thus Art 38.1 has been used by the courts as a means of giving constitutional protection to principles of fairness pertaining to the criminal trial. These principles of fairness may have their origins in the common law or in generally accepted international conventions. Despite this traditionalist and largely conservative content of Art 38.1, the courts' approach has led to considerable tension with other organs of government. For popular culture is ever more characterised by a fear of and reaction to crime. In particular, changes to the substance and process of criminal law are—rightly or wrongly—seen as an appropriate response to increasing crime rates. In these circumstances, a desire on the part of elected representatives to change the criminal law rules can be thwarted by the constitutionalisation and rigid enforcement of previously evolutionary principles. This dynamic leads to conflict.

[2–04] This dynamic has a further interesting facet. Despite the overtly counter-majoritarian stance of the courts and the lack of any clear basis in the Constitution for most of the rights that have come to be protected under the rubric of Art 38.1, there is little debate (at least within the legal world) of the legitimacy of the courts' actions. Certainly as compared with the unenumerated rights debate (see chapter 4) or the concern over the enforcement of socio-economic rights (see chapter 12), there is little agonising over judicial deference or the rights of elected representatives to make democratic decisions over how to control crime. The sanguine attitude to judicial power in this domain appears to rest on a deeply conservative notion that the criminal process lies at the core of the judicial power and is therefore uniquely subject to judicial regulation under the fig leaf of Art 38.1. This conservative position allows the courts simultaneously to take a less interventionist approach in more constitutionally innovative areas, such as the right to free primary education.

What is a Criminal Charge?

The various guarantees of Art 38 clearly only apply to persons who are being tried on a criminal charge. This raises the question, uncontroversial in most cases, of what constitutes a criminal charge. In *Melling v Ó Mathghamhna* [1962] IR 1, the Supreme Court considered whether a statutory provision that allowed a person, who smuggled certain goods into the country, to be fined three times the duty paid value of the goods was a "criminal charge". Lavery J adopted a functional approach to this issue: [2–05]

> [A] proceeding, the course of which permits the detention of the person concerned, the bringing of him in custody to a Garda Station, the entry of a charge in all respects in the terms appropriate to the charge of a criminal offence, the searching of the person detained and the examination of papers and other things found upon him, the bringing of him before a District Justice in custody, the admission to bail to stand his trial and the detention in custody if bail be not granted or is not forthcoming, the imposition of a pecuniary penalty with the liability to imprisonment if the penalty is not paid has all the *indicia* of a criminal charge. The penalty is clearly punitive in character, being £100 or treble the duty-paid value of the goods. [1962] IR 1, at 9.

In contrast, Kingsmill Moore J adopted a more conceptual approach, focusing on the fact that the offences in question were committed against the community at large (not an individual), the penalty was punitive in character (not reparatory), and there was a requirement of *mens rea*. In addition, Ó Dálaigh J noted that the following features were not generally considered aspects of a civil wrong: punishment rather than redress as the primary sanction, imprisonment for failure to make redress, preliminary detention in jail unless bail be found, search and seizure of goods in a defendant's house and premises. These various criteria have been applied by the courts in a number of cases to determine whether tax penalties were civil or criminal in character. [2–06]

This issue was re-examined more recently in *Murphy v GM* [2001] 4 IR 113, in which the Supreme Court considered the constitutionality of the Proceeds of Crime Act 1996. The Act provided for the forfeiture of property which was established, on the balance of probabilities, to be the proceeds of crime. Keane CJ, delivering the judgment of the Court, accepted that—if the provisions were deemed to be a criminal trial—they would unquestionably fall foul of Art 38.1 due to the virtual absence of the presumption of innocence, the provision that proof would be on the balance of probabilities and the admissibility of hearsay evidence. However, the Court concluded that the provisions did not amount to the trial of a person on a criminal charge: [2–07]

> It is clear from the judgments of Lavery J (with whom Maguire CJ and Maguire J concurred) and from the judgment of Ó Dálaigh J [in *Melling*], that the *ratio* of that decision was that the presence of a number of *indicia*, which are conspicuously absent in the present case, rendered the proceedings criminal in character, *viz* the provision for the detention of the person concerned, the bringing of him in custody to a garda station,

the searching of the person detained, his admission to bail, the imposition of a pecuniary penalty with liability to imprisonment in default, the reference in the statute to a party having been "convicted of an offence" and the provision for the withdrawal of proceedings by the entry of a *nolle prosequi*. The court is satisfied that the emphasis placed by the appellants on the three elements indicated by Kingsmill Moore J as essential ingredients of a criminal offence is misplaced: in another passage in his judgment, cited by Finlay CJ in *McLoughlin v Tuite* [1989] IR 82, he refers expressly to some of these *indicia* as pointing clearly to the criminal nature of the proceedings. In contrast, in proceedings under sections 3 and 4 of the Act of 1996, there is no provision for the arrest or detention of any person, for the admission of persons to bail, for the imprisonment of a person in default of payment of a penalty, for a form of criminal trial initiated by summons or indictment, for the recording of a conviction in any form or for the entering of a *nolle prosequi* at any stage. [2001] 4 IR 113, at 147.

[2–08] In the vast majority of cases, it will be uncontentious whether a legal provision creates a criminal offence or not. In the contentious cases, it appears that the courts assess whether a provision creates an offence by ascertaining whether the provision (and provisions related to it) contains a number of features that are generally shared by provisions which are uncontroversially accepted to be criminal in character. Once a provision is deemed to be criminal in character, the protections afforded to the accused person dramatically increase as Art 38.1 comes into play.

Unconstitutionally Obtained Evidence

[2–09] The Gardaí are provided with extensive powers to facilitate the investigation of crime. They can detain people for questioning in anticipation of a charge. They can search premises for evidence. Ordinarily the evidence obtained through the use of these powers will be admissible at trial—that was the very purpose for which it was gathered. However, issues arise where the evidence was gathered illegally, for instance where a person is questioned for longer than is permitted or where evidence is seized without a warrant. Given Arts 40.4 and 40.5 of the Constitution (see chapter 7), evidence that was obtained illegally will often also have been acquired unconstitutionally. Article 40.4 provides that a person's liberty can be deprived only in accordance with law; Art 40.5 provides that dwellings can only be forcibly entered in accordance with law. It follows, therefore, that an illegal deprivation of liberty or entry of a dwelling is also unconstitutional. The question for the courts has been how to deal with evidence that has been obtained in an illegal or unconstitutional manner.

[2–10] The answer to this question is hotly contested. On the one hand, it can be argued that there is no particular reason why the process by which evidence was obtained should affect the use which can now be made of that evidence. The ordinary touchstones for admissibility of evidence are relevance and reliability. There is no reason why relevant evidence that has been obtained unconstitutionally should be considered unreliable. Of course, if evidence were obtained by means of torture (in breach of the right to bodily integrity), there would be serious doubts as to its reliability and it should—on that basis alone—be excluded. However, there is no general reason why unconstitutionally obtained evidence should be any more or less reliable than evidence that has been constitutionally obtained. On the other hand, it can be argued that a person should not suffer by reason of a breach of her constitutional rights. If agents of the State unconstitutionally deprive a person of her liberty or unconstitutionally enter her dwelling, she is entitled to a remedy that puts her in the same situation as if her rights had not been violated. Such a remedy requires that the evidence that was obtained unconstitutionally not be used against her. Moreover, the State should not be rewarded for breaching the rights of a citizen by gaining the benefit of the unconstitutional act.

These issues were first considered in *People (Attorney General) v O'Brien* [1965] IR 142. [2–11] The accused had been convicted of housebreaking and receiving stolen goods. The items in question had been found during a police search of Number 118 Captain's Road, Crumlin, where the two accused lived. However, the search warrant authorised the search of Number 118 Cashel Road, Crumlin—an adjacent street. Because of the error in the search warrant, the search was arguably illegal and, if so, unconstitutional. The Supreme Court unanimously held that the evidence was properly admitted at the trial, although different members of the Court differed substantially in their approach to the issue. Kingsmill Moore J (with whom Lavery and Budd JJ agreed) held that a trial judge should have a discretion whether to admit such evidence:

> It is desirable in the public interest that crime should be detected and punished. It is desirable that individuals should not be subjected to illegal or inquisitorial methods of investigation and that the State should not attempt to advance its ends by utilising the fruits of such methods. It appears to me that in every case a determination has to be made by the trial judge as to whether the public interest is best served by the admission or by the exclusion of evidence of facts ascertained as a result of, and by means of, illegal actions, and that the answer to the question depends on a consideration of all the circumstances. On the one hand, the nature and extent of the illegality have to be taken into account. Was the illegal action intentional or unintentional, and, if intentional, was it the result of an *ad hoc* decision or does it represent a settled or deliberate policy? Was the illegality one of a trivial and technical nature or was it a serious invasion of important rights the recurrence of which would involve a real danger to necessary freedoms? Were there circumstances of urgency or emergency which provide some excuse for the action?...
>
> I turn to the facts of the case now before us. It appears that the circumstances were such that on the information sworn by Sergeant Healy a warrant to search 118 Captain's Road would have been signed almost as a matter of course. The issue of a warrant to search for goods suspected to have been stolen was authorised even by the common law. No reason has been suggested why a warrant should not have as readily been issued for a search of 118 Captain's Road as for 118 Cashel Road. The mistake was a pure oversight and it has not been shown that the oversight was noticed by anyone before the premises were searched. I can find no evidence of deliberate treachery, imposition, deceit or illegality; no policy to disregard the provisions of the Constitution or to conduct searches without a warrant; nothing except the existence of an unintentional and accidental illegality to set against the public interest of having crime detected and punished. Assuming that the Judge had a discretion to exclude or receive evidence of what was discovered in the course of the search because the search was illegal, I am of opinion that such discretion was rightly exercised in receiving the evidence. [1965] IR 142, at 160–161.

Walsh J, with whom Ó Dálaigh CJ agreed, came to the same conclusion but for very [2–12] different reasons. Walsh J reasoned that the courts should take a far stricter view of unconstitutionally obtained evidence than of illegally obtained evidence, but that even the former might be admissible in some circumstances:

> In my judgment the law in this country has been that the evidence in this particular case is not rendered inadmissible and that there is no discretion to rule it out by reason only of the fact that it was obtained by means of an illegal as distinct from an unconstitutional seizure....

I come now to deal with the ground which was based upon the Constitutional issue. Article 40.5, of the Constitution provides as follows:—"The dwelling of every citizen is inviolable and shall not be forcibly entered save in accordance with law." That does not mean that the guarantee is against forcible entry only. In my view, the reference to forcible entry is an intimation that forcible entry may be permitted by law but that in any event the dwelling of every citizen is inviolable save where entry is permitted by law and that, if necessary, such law may permit forcible entry. In a case where members of a family live together in the family house, the house as a whole is for the purpose of the Constitution the dwelling of each member of the family. If a member of a family occupies a clearly defined portion of the house apart from the other members of the family, then it may well be that the part not so occupied is no longer his dwelling and that the part he separately occupies is his dwelling as would be the case where a person not a member of the family occupied or was in possession of a clearly defined portion of the house. In this case the appellants are members of a family living in the family dwelling-house and also appear to have their own respective separate bedrooms. Each of the appellants would therefore have a constitutional right to the inviolability of No. 118 Captain's Road. I have already referred, in the earlier part of this judgment, to what are sometimes, regrettably, the competing interests of the trial and conviction of criminals and the frustration of police illegalities. When the illegality amounts to infringement of a constitutional right the matter assumes a far greater importance than is the case where the illegality does not amount to such infringement. The vindication and the protection of constitutional rights is a fundamental matter for all Courts established under the Constitution. That duty cannot yield place to any other competing interest. In Article 40 of the Constitution, the State has undertaken to defend and vindicate the inviolability of the dwelling of every citizen. The defence and vindication of the constitutional rights of the citizen is a duty superior to that of trying such citizen for a criminal offence. The Courts in exercising the judicial powers of government of the State must recognise the paramount position of constitutional rights and must uphold the objection of an accused person to the admissibility at his trial of evidence obtained or procured by the State or its servants or agents as a result of a deliberate and conscious violation of the constitutional rights of the accused person where no extraordinary excusing circumstances exist, such as the imminent destruction of vital evidence or the need to rescue a victim in peril. A suspect has no constitutional right to destroy or dispose of evidence or to imperil the victim. I would also place in the excusable category evidence obtained by a search incidental to and contemporaneous with a lawful arrest although made without a valid search warrant.

In my view evidence obtained in deliberate conscious breach of the constitutional rights of an accused person should, save in the excusable circumstances outlined above, be absolutely inadmissible. It follows therefore that evidence obtained without a deliberate and conscious violation of the accused's constitutional rights is not excludable by reason only of the violation of his constitutional right.

In the present case it is abundantly clear from the evidence that it was through an error that the wrong address appeared on the search warrant and that the searching officers were unaware of the error. There was no deliberate or conscious violation of the right of the appellants against arbitrary intrusion by the Garda officers. The evidence obtained by reason of this search is not inadmissible upon the constitutional ground. [1965] IR 142, at 168–170.

[2–13] In Walsh J's view, therefore, evidence that was obtained in deliberate and conscious violation of a citizen's constitutional rights would be automatically inadmissible, unless there were "extraordinary excusing circumstances". The concept of "deliberate and conscious violation" of rights introduces a number of difficulties. If the courts' role is to protect constitutional rights, it is not particularly relevant whether those rights are being breached deliberately or otherwise. The court is excluding evidence not to punish those who breached the rights but rather to protect those whose rights were breached. Also, Walsh J's conclusion that the evidence in this case was not obtained in conscious and deliberate violation of rights suggests that this requirement relates not to the act but to the legal character of the act. That is, the search of the dwelling was clearly conscious and deliberate. However, as the Gardaí were unaware of the error in the search warrant, the illegality and unconstitutionality were not conscious and deliberate.

Notwithstanding these difficulties, the courts moved to adopt the majority position of Walsh J in preference to the majority position of Kingsmill Moore J. Thereafter there was much debate on whether the "conscious and deliberate" requirement related only to the doing of the act (making the search, for example) or whether it also related to the question of whether the act was unconstitutional. Walsh J himself came to the view (apparently at odds with his decision in *O'Brien*) that evidence was *prima facie* inadmissible if it had been obtained both unconstitutionally and consciously and deliberately. It did not matter whether those obtaining the evidence were conscious of the fact that it was obtained unconstitutionally. In *People (DPP) v Shaw* [1982] IR 1, at 31, he put it as follows: [2–14]

> When the act complained of was undertaken or carried out consciously and deliberately, it is immaterial whether the person carrying out the act may or may not have been conscious that what he was doing was illegal or, even if he knew it was illegal, that it amounted to a breach of the constitutional rights of the accused. It is the doing of the act which is the essential matter, not the actor's appreciation of the legal consequences or incidents of it.

This position has now been definitively adopted by the courts. In *People (DPP) v Kenny* [1990] 2 IR 110, it was held that a search warrant had been illegally obtained from a peace commissioner because the commissioner had not inquired into the basis for the Garda's suspicion that a controlled drug was present on a premises. This was a novel finding. A majority of the Supreme Court held that this evidence ought to be excluded, Finlay CJ reasoning: [2–15]

> The constitutional rights with which all these cases are concerned are personal rights, being either the right to liberty: *Walsh's* case; *Madden's* case; *Shaw's* case, or the inviolability of the dwelling: *O'Brien's* case and the instant case.
> The duty of the Court pursuant to Article 40.3.1 of the Constitution is as far as practicable to defend and vindicate such rights.
> As between two alternative rules or principles governing the exclusion of evidence obtained as a result of the invasion of the personal rights of a citizen, the Court has, it seems to me, an obligation to choose the principle which is likely to provide a stronger and more effective defence and vindication of the right concerned.
> To exclude only evidence obtained by a person who knows or ought reasonably to know that he is invading a constitutional right is to impose a negative deterrent. It is clearly effective to dissuade a policeman from acting in a manner which he knows is unconstitutional or from acting in a manner reckless as to whether his conduct is or is not unconstitutional.
> To apply, on the other hand, the absolute protection rule of exclusion whilst providing also that negative deterrent, incorporates as well a positive encouragement to those in authority over the crime prevention and detection services of the State to consider in

detail the personal rights of the citizens as set out in the Constitution, and the effect of their powers of arrest, detention, search and questioning in relation to such rights.

It seems to me to be an inescapable conclusion that a principle of exclusion which contains both negative and positive force is likely to protect constitutional rights in more instances than is a principle with negative consequences only. The exclusion of evidence on the basis that it results from unconstitutional conduct, like every other exclusionary rule, suffers from the marked disadvantage that it constitutes a potential limitation of the capacity of the courts to arrive at the truth and so most effectively to administer justice.

I appreciate the anomalies which may occur by reason of the application of the absolute protection rule to criminal cases.

The detection of crime and the conviction of guilty persons, no matter how important they may be in relation to the ordering of society, cannot, however, in my view, outweigh the unambiguously expressed constitutional obligation "as far as practicable to defend and vindicate the personal rights of the citizen."

After very careful consideration I conclude that I must differ from the view of the majority of this Court expressed in the judgment of Griffin J in *The People v Shaw* [1982] IR 1. I am satisfied that the correct principle is that evidence obtained by invasion of the constitutional personal rights of a citizen must be excluded unless a court is satisfied that either the act constituting the breach of constitutional rights was committed unintentionally or accidentally, or is satisfied that there are extraordinary excusing circumstances which justify the admission of the evidence in its (the court's) discretion.

In the instant case there cannot be any question but that the acts of the gardaí which obtained the warrant by the submission to the peace commissioner of the sworn written information in the form in which I have recited it, and which then forcibly entered the dwellinghouse were neither unintentional nor accidental, and counsel for the respondent agrees that there are no extraordinary excusing circumstances in this case. Even though, then, I would accept that neither of the two gardaí concerned had any knowledge that they were invading the constitutional rights of the accused and would also accept that they were carrying out the process of obtaining and executing a search warrant in a manner which has been customary over a long period with the gardaí, I am satisfied that the evidence obtained as a result of the forcible entry into the house should not have been admitted at the trial of the accused and that, accordingly, the conviction of the accused should not have occurred. [1990] 2 IR 110, at 133–134.

[2–16] Although the rationale for the rule of absolute protection is easy to understand, it is somewhat difficult to square it with the phrase "conscious and deliberate violation". One is left wondering what unconscious and non-deliberate act could be a violation of a citizen's rights: a garda accidentally falling into a building and searching it, perhaps?

[2–17] There is still some reluctance on the part of the courts to follow through on *Kenny* to the conclusion that all deliberate searches of dwellings, if not precisely authorised, are unlawful and unconstitutional leading to the exclusion of evidence. Thus in *People (DPP) v Balfe* [1998] 4 IR 50, the Court of Criminal Appeal ruled admissible evidence obtained pursuant to a search, notwithstanding that there were several defects in the search warrant and in the manner in which it was obtained. The address on the information was incorrect; the date given for the larceny was incorrect and the name Eddie Balfe, not that of the applicant, appeared on the information. In addition, the search warrant was addressed to a person other than the applicant and the search warrant contained an amendment which was considered "unsuitable, inappropriate, unclear, ambiguous and unlawful." Murphy J delivered the judgment of the Court, distinguishing *Kenny* on the following basis:

> The present case can be distinguished on its facts in that there was no forcible entry involved. Furthermore there was no evidence of deliberate treachery, imposition or deceit, no policy to disregard the provisions of the Constitution or to conduct searches without a warrant. No point was raised at the trial when the search warrant was under scrutiny that there was any defect in respect of an omission to specify the nature of the property, the subject of the search. The Circuit Court Judge made inquiry as to the circumstances of the issue of the search warrant and properly exercised his discretion not to exclude the evidence obtained on foot of the search warrant....
>
> Whilst it must be recognised that the jurisprudence relating to "the deliberate and conscious violation of constitutional rights" is still evolving, it is clear that a search warrant which innocently but vitally misdescribes premises which may be searched on foot thereof is not without operative effect. Property seized in innocent reliance thereon may be admissible in evidence on a subsequent criminal charge. On the other hand, it would seem clear that the occupiers of 118 Captains Road would have been perfectly entitled to refuse admission to the gardaí in pursuance of a warrant expressly entitling them to search 118 Cashel Road. Nevertheless, for the reasons stated by the Supreme Court in *The People (Attorney General) v O'Brien* [1965] IR 142, there was sufficient validity in the warrant or order to justify the admission in evidence of the goods which were in fact seized pursuant to the warrant despite its defects. *The People (Director of Public Prosecutions) v Kenny* [1990] 2 IR 110, is different; the warrant on its face gave no indication of the inherent flaw. Only the Peace Commissioner and the garda concerned were aware or could have been aware of the fact that no inquiry was made by the Peace Commissioner of the garda as to the basis for his suspicions and indeed it was accepted that neither appreciated the legal significance of that omission. The terms of the warrant in *The People (Director of Public Prosecutions) v Kenny* might indeed have given it an apparent validity. However, the subsequent examination of the circumstances in which the search warrant was issued revealed the flaw which deprived it of legal effect. This is the basis on which the majority decision in *Kenny* (and indeed the decision in *Director of Public Prosecutions v Dunne* [1994] 2 IR 537) can be reconciled with the majority decision in *The People (Attorney General) v. O'Brien*; that is to say, where a judge of the District Court acting within his jurisdiction agrees to issue a search warrant, a mistake, however gross, in the recording of his order will not necessarily render the warrant invalid for all purposes though it might justify persons to whom it was addressed, or intended to be addressed, declining to cooperate with it. Where, however, the search warrant is made without authority, then it has no value in law, however innocent the mistake in granting the same or however apparently plausible the document issued. [1998] 4 IR 50, at 58–60.

The court thus drew distinctions between a lack of authority for a search warrant and a defect in the drawing up of the warrant; and between an obvious defect to which the occupier of a dwelling could object and a latent defect of which the occupier would have no knowledge. Taking these together, it seems the Court was prepared to conclude that the search, although not quite lawful, was not so unlawful as to merit the exclusion of the evidence. Lawfulness is not usually considered to be a matter of degree. [2–18]

In *People (DPP) v Shaw* [1982] IR 1, the Supreme Court considered the meaning of the phrase "extraordinary excusing circumstances." In this case, the accused had been arrested in Galway for being in possession of a stolen motor car. However, the gardaí suspected that he was involved with the disappearance of two young women, one in Wicklow a month previously and one in Mayo four days previously. Fearing for the safety of the two women, the gardaí continued to hold the accused in custody rather than bring him before the District Court at the first reasonable opportunity as required by law. While in custody, the accused made a statement incriminating himself. He [2–19] subsequently, at his own suggestion, went on a car journey with the gardaí during which he pointed out various places, including where the second young woman had been killed and her clothes burned. He was then charged and convicted of the rape, murder and false imprisonment of the young woman.

[2–20] A majority of the Supreme Court agreed with a judgment delivered by Griffin J which held that the breach of the accused's constitutional rights had not been conscious and deliberate. This ratio did not survive the subsequent ruling in *People (DPP) v Kenny* [1990] 2 IR 110 (above). However, Walsh J held that the detention was unlawful, the breach of constitutional rights conscious and deliberate; nevertheless extraordinary excusing circumstances rendered the evidence admissible:

> The net question is whether an arrest or imprisonment which is not in accordance with law can be rendered lawful by a belief that such arrest or imprisonment may vindicate one or more of those rights of another citizen which the Constitution in Article 40.3, guarantees to defend, protect and vindicate. In the instant case there arises the question of a belief that another person's life, already imperilled, may be saved by effecting or maintaining an unlawful arrest or detention. In my opinion the answer must be that the unlawful character of the act remains unchanged however well intentioned it may be.
>
> The Constitution expressly provides that no person may be deprived of his personal liberty save in accordance with law: Article 40.4.1. There is nothing in the Constitution which authorises the commission of an unlawful act. If an act is unlawful and the law or the laws which render it unlawful is or are not inconsistent with, or invalid having regard to the provisions of the Constitution, it is quite clear that the Constitution cannot and does not purport to render lawful an act which is unlawful and that no court is competent or permitted to do so. To suggest that an effort in vindicating the life of another person, *eg*, to enable that person to gain the benefit of the constitutional provision for the protection or vindication of his life, is sufficient in itself to render lawful any act however unlawful, provided it is motivated by an honest desire to save or vindicate a life, is simply to state that the end may justify the means, unlawful though they may be. The specific question raised in the certificate of the Court of Criminal Appeal, namely, whether the arrest and imprisonment of the appellant after 10.30 a.m. on Monday, the 27th September, 1976, was lawful by reason of the obligation of the Gardaí to attempt to vindicate the right to life appears to me to beg the question. The Constitution, by reason of its express provision that no person shall be deprived of his personal liberty save in accordance with law, means what it says. It entrenches the law and raises it to the level of a constitutionally guaranteed right. To take the example which was considered by the trial judge, if an application for the release of the appellant at the time in question had been made to the High Court under Article 40 of the Constitution and the only justification which could be offered by the custodians, namely, the Garda Síochána, was their belief, albeit a reasonable one, that holding the appellant under continued arrest might lead to the saving of the life of Mary, the High Court would have had no alternative but to order the release of the appellant forthwith on the grounds that he was not being detained in accordance with the law. The custodians would not have been able to point to any law which justified the appellant's continued detention. If it were sought simply to justify it by showing a good motive, such as an effort or a hope to save a life in so doing, the court would have had to hold, in accordance with Article 40.4.2, of the Constitution, that such detention, however well intentioned, was not in accordance with the law — whether it be the law stated in the Constitution or the law in force by virtue of statute or common law. To do otherwise would be to disobey the mandatory express injunction of Article 40. Therefore, I am of opinion that the statements would not have been admissible because such arrest and imprisonment were contrary to law and, therefore, amounted to a breach of the

constitutional rights of the appellant. For the reasons I have already given, the answer to that question does not govern this case....

[T]he answer must be that the provisions of the Constitution did not permit the Garda Síochána to deprive the appellant of his personal liberty for the period in question in the belief that such deprivation might vindicate the constitutional right or rights of another citizen. For the reasons already given, that arrest and imprisonment were unlawful. But, for the reasons already given, in the circumstances of this case such unlawful arrest did not render inadmissible the incriminating evidence furnished by the appellant during the period of the unlawful arrest. The circumstances prevailing at the time the appellant made his Galway confession were capable of amounting in law to extraordinary excusatory circumstances. [1982] IR 1, at 40–42.

Although there was a significant doctrinal disagreement over the issue of "conscious and deliberate violation" between Walsh J and the other members of the court, it was accepted that the possibility of saving the life of the woman was an extraordinary excusing circumstance that would render the unconstitutionally obtained evidence admissible. [2–21]

The courts have emphasised a requirement that there be a causative connection between the breach of constitutional rights complained of and the evidence obtained. In *Walsh v Ó Buachalla* [1991] 1 IR 56, the applicant had been arrested on a charge of drunk driving but was refused permission to have his solicitor present while a doctor was taking a blood sample. Blayney J refused to rule the evidence inadmissible, even if there had been a breach of the applicant's constitutional rights: [2–22]

> It was submitted on behalf of the applicant that if he had had access to a solicitor he could have been advised by him. But what advice could a solicitor have given him? He would certainly not have advised him to commit an offence by refusing to give one or other of the specimens. All he could have done was to confirm that the applicant was required by law to provide a specimen of blood or urine. No advice could have prevented the specimen being obtained and, accordingly, the applicant's not having had access to a solicitor in no way affected its being obtained.
>
> I am satisfied accordingly that even if the applicant's constitutional rights were violated there was no causal connection between such violation and the applicant giving a specimen of his blood and accordingly the first respondent was correct in admitting the certificate in evidence. [1991] 1 IR 56, at 60.

In the recent case of *DPP (Walsh) v Cash* [2007] IEHC 108, Charleton J was strikingly critical of the rationale and decision in *Kenny*, concluding: [2–23]

> I have difficulty in accepting that the separation of powers doctrine allows the courts to invent rules whereby juries, or judges as triers of fact in criminal cases, are deprived, on a non-discretionary basis, of considering evidence which is inherently reliable. I am bound by the decision in *The People (DPP) v. Kenny* [1990] 2 IR 110. A rule which remorselessly excludes evidence obtained through an illegality occurring by a mistake does not commend itself to the proper ordering of society which is the purpose of the criminal law.
>
> Any system of the exclusion of improperly obtained evidence must be implemented on the basis of a balancing of interests. The two most fundamental competing interests, in that regard, are those of society and the accused. I would also place the rights of the victim in the balance. I note, in writing this judgment, that the third anniversary of the March, 2004 train bombings in Madrid is being marked. That atrocity led to the death of

191 commuters making their way to work and was inspired, apparently, because of the involvement of Spain in a foreign policy with which an international terrorist organisation did not agree. It is entirely conceivable, were the same thing to occur in Ireland, that vital evidence that might lead to the conviction of the perpetrators might have been uncovered through the infringement of someone's privacy as they spoke on a telephone or as a result of a comparison of DNA samples which the prosecution could not strictly prove were obtained by consent or through the proper exercise of statutory powers. The original test, as propounded by the Supreme Court in *O'Brien's* case would have allowed for a balancing of the rights of parties. In particular, the gravity of the offence and the nature of the infringement by the State authorities would have been taken into account. The current rule, as set forth by the Supreme Court in *Kenny's* case, automatically requires the exclusion of any evidence obtained through a mistake which had the accidental, and therefore unintended, result of infringing any constitutional right of one individual, namely the accused. The entire rational of the original Supreme Court decision in *O'Brien's* case is undermined by *Kenny's* case. The principle that extraordinary excusing circumstances can allow for the admission of evidence obtained in breach of a constitutional right can no longer be applied. It is an impossibility to make a mistake while, at the same time, acting to rescue a victim in peril or prevent the destruction of vital evidence. The whole rationale for a balanced rule with exceptions, set out in *O'Brien's* case, has been replaced.

I would also note that in every other respect, where constitutional rights conflict, a balance is sought to be struck; *In Re Article 26 of the Constitution and the Regulation of Informa*tion (*Services Outside the State for the Termination of Pregnancy*) *Bill, 1995* [1995] 1 IR 1. I should further note privileges in the law of evidence, whether State or diplomatic, are all now decided on a balancing test. Medical privilege can be argued for on analogous basis of resolving conflicting rights; see *Simon P O'Leary*, March 2007 in the Bar Review (2007) 12(1) *BR* 33. There can be no doubt that exclusion is sometimes the only correct response to egregious police misconduct. The admission of evidence obtained in flagrant violation of fundamental rights without excusing circumstances can amount to an attack on the very administration of justice. The problem identified, however, is the isolation of the rule of exclusion formulated in *Kenny's* case from any principle of balance as it otherwise operates within the constitutional scheme. [2007] IEHC 108, at [65]–[67].

[2–24] Whether this presages a change of view on the part of the Supreme Court as to the exclusionary rule remains to be seen.

The Right to be Provided with a Lawyer

[2–25] In *State (Healy) v Donoghue* [1976] IR 325, the Supreme Court elevated to constitutional status the right of an accused person to be provided with a lawyer. The Criminal Justice (Legal Aid) Act 1962 provided an entitlement to criminal legal aid in certain circumstances. The entitlement arose where the means of a person charged with an offence and the gravity of the charge or exceptional circumstances made it essential in the interests of justice that legal aid be granted. Mr Healy, an 18-year old whose formal education ceased when he was 13, had been convicted of two offences. In relation to the first, he had not been told of his right to legal aid and was unrepresented. In relation to the second, he had been granted a legal aid certificate but had not been able to secure legal representation and advice before he was convicted. He sought judicial review of both convictions. The Supreme Court quashed both convictions, O'Higgins CJ reasoning:

> [C]riminal charges vary in seriousness. There are thousands of trivial charges prosecuted in the District Courts throughout the State every day. In respect of all these there must be

fairness and fair procedures, but there may be other cases in which more is required and where justice may be a more exacting task-master. The requirements of fairness and of justice must be considered in relation to the seriousness of the charge brought against the person and the consequences involved for him. Where a man's liberty is at stake, or where he faces a very severe penalty which may affect his welfare or his livelihood, justice may require more than the application of normal and fair procedures in relation to his trial. Facing, as he does, the power of the State which is his accuser, the person charged may be unable to defend himself adequately because of ignorance, lack of education, youth or other incapacity. In such circumstances his plight may require, if justice is to be done, that he should have legal assistance. In such circumstances, if he cannot provide such assistance by reason of lack of means, does justice under the Constitution also require that he be aided in his defence? In my view it does.

The general view of what is fair and proper in relation to criminal trials has always been the subject of change and development. Rules of evidence and rules of procedure gradually evolved as notions of fairness developed. The right to speak and to give evidence, and the right to be represented by a lawyer of one's choice were recognised gradually. To-day many people would be horrified to learn how far it was necessary to travel in order to create a balance between the accuser and the accused.

If the right to be represented is now an acknowledged right of an accused person, justice requires something more when, because of a lack of means, a person facing a serious criminal charge cannot provide a lawyer for his own defence. In my view the concept of justice under the Constitution ... requires that in such circumstances the person charged must be afforded the opportunity of being represented.

This opportunity must be provided by the State. Only in this way can justice be done, and only by recognising and discharging this duty can the State be said to vindicate the personal rights of the person charged. To hold otherwise would be to tolerate a situation in which the nature and extent of a man's ability to defend himself, when accused, could depend on the nature and extent of his means; that would be to tolerate injustice....

[T]he Act of 1962 lays down as a condition for the grant of legal aid both in the District Court and on return for trial, that the person seeking it must apply for it. No one can be compelled to accept legal aid, and a person charged is entitled to waive his right in this respect and to defend himself. No objection can be raised if these provisions of the Act operate to cover such cases where a person, knowing of his right, does not choose to exercise it and, therefore, decides not to apply. However, if a person who is ignorant of his right fails to apply and on that account is not given legal aid then, in my view, his constitutional right is violated. For this reason it seems to me that when a person faces a possible prison sentence and has no lawyer, and cannot provide for one, he ought to be informed of his right to legal aid. If the person charged does not know of his right, he cannot exercise it; if he cannot exercise it, his right is violated.

The Act of 1962 provides for a choice of both solicitors and counsel from amongst those in both branches of the legal profession who have agreed to operate the Act. This Act has been in effective operation for a number of years. It has provided for accused persons, who are held to be entitled to avail of it, the means whereby they can have the solicitor and counsel of their choice. The only limitation on this choice has been that the practitioner concerned must have declared himself willing to provide legal aid by going on the panel. While I regard the Act as a recognition by the State of what is the constitutional right of a poor person facing a serious criminal charge, I do not say that the provisions of the Act match exactly what the Constitution requires. In particular I would be slow to hold that the Constitution requires the choice which the statute gives. I can imagine circumstances in which, for one reason or another, the State cannot provide a choice of lawyer; in such circumstances the provision of a designated lawyer or lawyers, trained and experienced for the task, is an adequate discharge of the State's duty to provide legal assistance for the person without means. [1976] IR 325, at 350–352.

[2–26] Henchy J neatly captured the rationale in the following terms:

> A person who has been convicted and deprived of his liberty as a result of a prosecution which, because of his poverty, he has had to bear without legal aid has reason to complain that he has been meted out less than his constitutional due. This is particularly true if the absence of legal aid is compounded by factors such as a grave or complex charge; or ignorance, illiteracy, immaturity or other conditions rendering the accused incompetent to cope properly with the prosecution; or an inability, because of detentional restraint, to find and produce witnesses; or simply the fumbling incompetence that may occur when an accused is precipitated into the public glare and alien complexity of courtroom procedures, and is confronted with the might of a prosecution backed by the State. [1976] IR 325, at 354.

[2–27] Although recognising a constitutional right to legal aid, the Court was careful not to over-specify the level of legal aid or the manner in which it required to be provided. In a sense, the defect corrected in *Healy* was not a wholesale failure on the part of the State but rather an inadequate operation of the 1962 Act. More recently, in *Carmody v Minister for Justice, Equality and Law Reform* [2005] IEHC 10, an argument was advanced that an accused person should be entitled to be represented by a barrister where the prosecutor would be represented by a barrister. Mr Carmody was charged with certain offences under the Disease of Animals Act 1966, as amended, and was being prosecuted by the Minister for Agriculture in the District Court. It was established in evidence that the Minister nearly always retained a barrister for the purposes of prosecutions under the 1966 Act. However, under s 2 of the Criminal Justice (Legal Aid) Act 1962, an accused person can only be granted a legal aid certificate in respect of a solicitor. Laffoy J rejected the contention that this created an inequality of arms such as to breach the right to a fair trial as recognised in *Healy*. She concluded:

> The fact that there may, in terms of lawyers, be a numerical imbalance or a divergence of legal qualification between the prosecution team and the defence team does not disadvantage the accused person to the extent that his guarantee to a fair trial is imperilled unless the lawyer defending him cannot do so effectively. In my view it has not been shown that such is the case.

This case is under appeal.

[2–28] The right to legal representation does not extend, however, to a comprehensive right of access to legal advisors in the pre-trial stages. Instead, the courts have held that a person detained in police custody has a right of reasonable access to a solicitor. After some uncertainty in the case law, this right was raised to constitutional status in *People (DPP) v Healy* [1990] 2 IR 73. The accused had been arrested under s 30 of the Offences against the State Act 1939; after several hours, he began to make a statement. While he was making the statement, a solicitor organised by his family arrived at the garda station. However, the solicitor was refused admission to see the accused on the basis that it would be rude to interrupt the interview. The Supreme Court unanimously held that the accused's evidence was inadmissible on the basis that the right of reasonable access to a solicitor had been infringed:

> The undoubted right of reasonable access to a solicitor enjoyed by a person who is in detention must be interpreted as being directed towards the vital function of ensuring that such person is aware of his rights and has the independent advice which would be

appropriate in order to permit him to reach a truly free decision as to his attitude to interrogation or to the making of any statement, be it exculpatory or inculpatory. The availability of advice from a lawyer must, in my view, be seen as a contribution, at least, towards some measure of equality in the position of the detained person and his interrogators.

Viewed in that light, I am driven to the conclusion that such an important and fundamental standard of fairness in the administration of justice as the right of access to a lawyer must be deemed to be constitutional in its origin, and that to classify it as merely legal would be to undermine its importance and the completeness of the protection of it which the courts are obliged to give.

The vital issue which arises, therefore, if a breach of the right of access to a solicitor has occurred as a result of a conscious and deliberate act of a member of the Garda Síochána, is whether there is a causative link between that breach and the obtaining of an admission.

A right of reasonable access to a solicitor by a detained person, I am satisfied, means, in the event of the arrival of a solicitor at the garda station in which a person is detained, an immediate right of that person to be told of the arrival and, if he requests it, immediate access. The only thing that could justify the postponement of informing the detained person of the arrival of the solicitor or of immediately complying with a request made by the detained person when so informed, for access to him, would be reasons which objectively viewed from the point of view of the interest or welfare of the detained person, would be viewed by a court as being valid. I reject completely the submission made on behalf of the Director of Public Prosecutions that the test to be applied to the question of reasonable access is a subjective test in the mind of the jailer of the detained person. The test is whether the superintendent's refusal of access was a conscious and deliberate act, as it clearly was. The fact that he may not have appreciated that his refusal was a breach of the defendant's constitutional right is immaterial. Furthermore, I would also reject the submission made on behalf of the Director that the fact that a detained person was in the course of making a statement, whether it was exculpatory of incriminatory, at the time of the arrival of the solicitor could possibly be an objectively valid reason for postponing informing him of that arrival, and asking him whether he wished to suspend the making of the statement in order to have access to the solicitor.

Having regard to these conclusions, it is clear on the evidence in this case that the defendant should have been informed at 4.00 p.m. of the arrival of the solicitor, and if he had asked to see him at that time, should have been permitted to see him. The failure to follow that course and the postponement both of the access to the solicitor and of the informing of the defendant of the presence of the solicitor until after the completion of the statement was, in my view, both a deliberate and conscious violation of the defendant's constitutional right and also a complete failure to observe reasonable standards of fairness in the procedure of his interrogation. [1990] 2 IR 73, at 81–82.

[2–29] It has not proven easy, however, to identify the precise parameters of the right of reasonable access to a solicitor. In *Lavery v Member in Charge, Carrickmacross Garda Station* [1999] 2 IR 390, the Supreme Court rejected the contention that an accused person had a right to have his solicitor present while being questioned. In *People (DPP) v Buck* [2002] 2 IR 268, the accused requested access to a solicitor but it proved impossible to obtain the services of the solicitor for five hours. Although the accused did not actually make any statements prior to the arrival of the solicitor, Keane CJ suggested *obiter* that any such statement would have been admissible. This issue was further considered in *People (DPP) v O'Brien* [2005] 2 IR 206. The accused was arrested and brought to Pearse Street Garda station in the centre of Dublin. He requested a solicitor but was unable to name one. On his behalf, the gardaí requested a particular solicitor, Mr Gaffney, who practised in Tallaght, on the outskirts of Dublin, and was unable to be present for several hours. The accused made certain inculpatory statements before the arrival of his solicitor; he then consulted with his solicitor for approximately half an hour. After his solicitor left, the accused was again interviewed and again made certain inculpatory statements. The Circuit Court trial judge ruled that the selection of Mr Gaffney was a breach of the accused's right of reasonable access to a solicitor as the gardaí must have known that a considerable delay would occur before Mr Gaffney could be present. Accordingly, the statements admitted prior to the arrival of the solicitor were inadmissible. However, once Mr Gaffney arrived, the breach was cured and the subsequent statements could be admitted. The accused appealed his conviction on the ground that the subsequent statement should not have been admitted in evidence. The Supreme Court rejected this appeal on the basis that there was no causative link between the breach of the accused's rights and the evidence subsequently obtained. McCracken J reasoned:

> If the inculpatory statement or admission ultimately made by the accused was elicited from him by the use of information disclosed by him while he was in unlawful detention, there would clearly have been a causative link between the breach of his constitutional rights and the making of the statements or admissions. In those circumstances, material which had been wrongfully obtained in breach of the accused's constitutional rights would have been used to obtain an inculpatory statement or admission. However, the corollary to this also appears to me to be valid, namely that if the statements were not made as the result of any material obtained in breach of the accused's rights, then they are not tainted by unconstitutionality and, provided the accused's detention was lawful at the time they were obtained, they are admissible. [2005] 2 IR 206, at 211–212.

[2–30] McCracken J also rejected the contention that the breach of the right of reasonable access to a solicitor rendered the accused's detention unlawful; at the very least, if the detention were unlawful, it became lawful again once the solicitor attended.

[2–31] Daly has criticised this judgment, arguing that far greater weight should have been attached to the fact that the gardaí consciously and deliberately breached the accused's rights and that the Court should have examined more closely the possibility of a causative link between the earlier breach and the subsequent evidence:

> [I]t seems somewhat unusual that neither the Court of Criminal Appeal nor the Supreme Court embarked on any exploration of the possibility that the eventual consultation with the solicitor did not fully remedy the original breach of the accused's right to legal advice or fully sever the causative link between such breach and the statements later made. The exact content of the two sets of statements made by O'Brien is unclear from the judgments of the Court of Criminal Appeal and the Supreme Court. It is also unclear whether it was argued by the defence either at trial or on appeal that, despite the eventual consultation with a solicitor, there was an ongoing causative link between the breach of his right to legal advice and the statements made even after consultation with Mr Gaffney. Nonetheless, it is submitted that, by contrast to the situation in Buck, it seems plausible that there may have been a causative link in existence between the breach of O'Brien's right to legal advice, the statements obtained by the gardaí at that time, and the later statements obtained after he had in fact consulted with his solicitor. Yvonne Daly, "Does the Buck Stop Here: An Examination of the Right to Pre-Trial Legal Advice in the Light of *O'Brien v DPP*" (2006) 28 *DULJ* 345, at 352.

[2–32] The decisions in cases such as *Lavery*, *Buck* and *O'Brien* may raise issues under the European Convention of Human Rights—particularly where the right to silence is at issue by reason of the fact that an adverse inference may be drawn from the accused's remaining silent in police custody. This is discussed further in the next section.

The Right to Silence

At common law, there existed a privilege against self-incrimination. This ensured that an accused person could not—at trial or otherwise—be required to give answers or provide information that could incriminate herself. In the context of increased police powers, several questions have arisen for the consideration of the courts. Is the right to silence constitutionally protected, under Art 38.1 or elsewhere? In what circumstances and in what manner can the right be restricted? Is it permissible to allow inferences to be drawn at trial from the fact that an accused remained silent during police interviewing? Each of these issues will now be addressed. [2–33]

In *Heaney v Ireland* [1996] 1 IR 580, the Supreme Court considered the constitutionality of s 52 of the Offences Against the State Act 1939. Section 52(1) empowered a garda to demand of a person arrested under Part IV of the Act "a full account of his movements and actions during any specified period and all information in his possession in relation to the commission or intended commission by another person of any offence under any section or sub-section of this Act or any scheduled offence." Section 52(2) provided that it was an offence not to comply with such a request, carrying a sentence not exceeding six months. O'Flaherty J, with whom the other members of the Court agreed, held that the right to silence was constitutionally protected not by Art 38.1 (as held in the High Court) but by Art 40.6.1, the corollary of the freedom of expression being a freedom not to express oneself. However, in the subsequent case of *Re National Irish Bank Ltd* [1999] 3 IR 145, the Supreme Court also appeared to find some support for the right to silence in Art 38.1. [2–34]

In *Heaney* itself, the Supreme Court held that s 52 was a justified limit on the right to silence. O'Flaherty J explained the Court's conclusion: [2–35]

> [T]he matter calling for resolution on this appeal is whether the power given to the Garda Síochána in the circumstances by the section is proportionate to the objects to be achieved by the legislation. As previously pointed out, the case falls to be resolved under a Constitution which guarantees liberty for the exercise of certain rights including the right of citizens to express freely their convictions and opinions. The right to freedom of expression necessarily implies the right to remain silent.... However, it is clear that the right to freedom of expression is not absolute. It is expressly stated in the Constitution to be subject to public order and morality. The same must hold true of its correlative right-the right to silence.
> The Offences against the State Act, 1939, is described in its long title to be *inter alia*:—
> > "An Act to make provision in relation to actions and conduct calculated to undermine public order and the authority of the State..."
> Section 52, the section complained of, appears in Part V of the Act. Part V is in the nature of an exceptional provision. It comes into operation only when the Government is satisfied that the ordinary courts are inadequate to secure the effective administration of justice and the preservation of public peace and order and makes and publishes a proclamation to that effect pursuant to the provisions of section 35 of the Act. The Government made such a proclamation on the 26th May, 1972, and it is still in force. Dáil Éireann has power at any time, under the provisions of section 35, to pass a resolution annulling the Government proclamation, but it has not done so.

It is in this context that the problem which arises in the present case falls to be resolved. On the one hand, constitutional rights must be construed in such a way as to give life and reality to what is being guaranteed. On the other hand, the interest of the State in maintaining public order must be respected and protected. We must, therefore, ask ourselves whether the restriction which section 52 places on the right to silence is any greater than is necessary having regard to the disorder against which the State is attempting to protect the public....

[T]he State is entitled to encroach on the right of the citizen to remain silent in pursuit of its entitlement to maintain public peace and order. Of course, in this pursuit the constitutional rights of the citizen must be affected as little as possible. As already stated, the innocent person has nothing to fear from giving an account of his or her movements, even though on grounds of principle, or in the assertion of constitutional rights, such a person may wish to take a stand. However, the Court holds that the *prima facie* entitlement of citizens to take such a stand must yield to the right of the State to protect itself. *A fortiori*, the entitlement of those with something relevant to disclose concerning the commission of a crime to remain mute must be regarded as of a lesser order.

The Court concludes that there is a proper proportionality in the provision between any infringement of the citizen's rights with the entitlement of the State to protect itself. [1996] 1 IR 580, at 589–590.

[2–36] This is deeply unsatisfactory reasoning. The Court was very quick to conclude that a criminal penalty for maintaining silence did not breach the constitutionally protected right to silence. O'Flaherty J implied that it was only the guilty who would seek to invoke their right to remain silent, making it very easy for the State's interest in crime control to override the accused person's right. However, it is questionable whether arguments of this type carry any weight once one has already accepted that the right to silence is constitutionally protected. That is, the only basis on which one can afford constitutional protection to the right to silence is that one accepts that there is an important value served in allowing persons to remain silent notwithstanding that (in strict theory) this will be of most assistance to those who have something incriminating to say. O'Flaherty J was thus overriding the right on a basis that was flatly inconsistent with the recognition of the right in the first instance. What the Court gave with one hand, it took away with the other. Of particular significance, the Court did not examine whether the evidence obtained under s 52 could then be used against that person at trial. If this were the case, an accused person would be faced with the sort of choice that one would expect the right to silence to protect against: provide the police with self-incriminating evidence (possibly leading to one's own conviction) or be convicted for failing to provide such evidence.

[2–37] The Supreme Court continued with this weak protection of the right to silence in *Rock v Ireland* [1997] 3 IR 484. In this case, the Court considered the constitutionality of ss 18 and 19 of the Criminal Justice Act 1984. Section 18 allows the trial court to draw an inference from the fact that an accused person failed, when requested on arrest by a garda, to provide an explanation for an object, substance or mark in her possession at the time of her arrest. Section 19 similarly allows inferences to be drawn from an accused person's failure to explain her presence in a certain place at the time of her arrest. Hamilton CJ, delivering the judgment of the Court, noted that the effect of ss 18 and 19 of the 1984 Act was far more significant than the effect of s 52 of the Offences Against the State Act 1939, considered in *Heaney*. The consequence of a failure to answer in relation to s 52 was, at worst, a six-month prison sentence. In contrast, under ss 18 and 19 of the 1984 Act, adverse inferences could be drawn at trial. Moreover, the

Criminal Justice Act 1984 covered a far broader range of offences than did the Offences Against the State Act 1939. Nevertheless, the Court concluded that ss 18 and 19 were constitutional:

> It is clear from [section 18 of the 1984 Act] that, while a court may draw such inferences from an accused's failure or refusal to account for the presence of an object, substance or mark in the circumstances provided for in the section, it is not obliged to draw any inference from such failure or refusal.
>
> It is, however, entitled to draw such inferences as appear proper. It is purely a matter for the court, or subject to the judge's directions, the jury, to decide whether any inferences should be drawn or what inferences may be properly drawn from the failure or refusal of the accused person to account for the presence of such substances.
>
> In deciding what inferences may properly be drawn from the accused person's failure or refusal, the court is obliged to act in accordance with the principles of constitutional justice and having regard to an accused person's entitlement to a fair trial must be regarded as being under a constitutional obligation to ensure that no improper or unfair inferences are drawn or permitted to be drawn from such failure or refusal....
>
> If inferences are properly drawn, such inferences amount to evidence only; they are not to be taken as proof. A person may not be convicted of an offence solely on the basis of inferences that may properly be drawn from his failure to account; such inferences may only be used as corroboration of any other evidence in relation to which the failure or refusal is material. The inferences drawn may be shaken in many ways, by cross-examination, by submission, by evidence or by the circumstances of the case....
>
> It is the opinion of this Court that, in enacting sections 18 and 19 of the Act of 1984, the legislature was seeking to balance the individual's right to avoid self-incrimination with the right and duty of the State to defend and protect the life, person and property of all its citizens. In this situation, the function of the Court is not to decide whether a perfect balance has been achieved, but merely to decide whether, in restricting individual constitutional rights, the legislature have acted within the range of what is permissible. In this instance, this Court finds they have done so, and must accordingly uphold the constitutional validity of the impugned statutory provisions. While it is true that sections 18 and 19 could lead to an accused being convicted of a serious offence in circumstances where he or she might otherwise have been acquitted, there are two important, limiting factors at work. Firstly, an inference cannot form the basis for a conviction in the absence of other evidence.... Secondly, only such inferences "as appear proper" can be drawn: that is to say, an inference adverse to the accused can only be drawn where the court deems it proper to do so. If it does not, then neither judge nor jury will be permitted to draw such inference. Thus, for example, a court could refuse to allow an inference in circumstances where its prejudicial effect would wholly outweigh its probative value as evidence.
>
> The Court is not satisfied that the provisions of the impugned sections are so contrary to reason and fairness as to constitute an unjust attack on the applicant's constitutional rights and the appeal herein must be dismissed. [1997] 3 IR 484, at 497–501.

Again, the Court's conclusion did not accord much force to the right to silence. Although invoking the proportionality test, there is little assessment of the manner in which the Oireachtas has sought to facilitate the investigation of crime. Rather the individual's right to avoid self-incrimination is simply stated to be in balance with the State's right and duty to protect and defend the life, person and property—of citizens. Characterised in that way—without an examination of the power wielded by the police and the pressures experienced while in police custody, it would be difficult to support a stronger protection for the right to silence.

[2–38]

[2–39] Around about this time, however, the European Court of Human Rights was developing its own jurisprudence on the right to silence. In *Saunders v United Kingdom* (1997) 23 EHRR 313, the European Court of Human Rights held that the right to silence and the right not to incriminate oneself were generally recognised international standards which lay at the heart of the notion of a fair criminal procedure protected by Art 6(1) of the Convention. Specifically, it held that the powers of government-appointed inspectors to require answers to certain questions did not breach Art 6, but that the subsequent use of the answers to those questions in criminal proceedings violated the accused's right to silence. This was the issue avoided by the Supreme Court in *Heaney*. Indeed, Mr Heaney subsequently successfully challenged Ireland in the European Court of Human Rights—*Quinn v Ireland* (2001) 33 EHRR 334. The Court concluded that the operation of s 52 of the Offences Against the State Act 1939 breached Art 6 in circumstances in which it was legally unclear whether the answers obtained could be used in evidence at the trial of the person questioned.

[2–40] In *Murray v United Kingdom* (1996) 22 EHRR 29, the Court held that the right to silence did not absolutely prohibit the drawing of adverse inferences from silence. In the circumstances of that case, the Court concluded that adverse inferences had been permissibly drawn for several reasons: the accused had been warned of the possible consequences of remaining silent; there was no evidence that the accused had misunderstood the warnings; the inferences could only be drawn where a *prima facie* case had already been established. However, the Court held that, given the potential for adverse inferences to be drawn from silence, it was imperative that an accused person have access to a lawyer at the early stages of police interrogation. The Irish constitutional right of reasonable access to a solicitor (considered above) may not be stringent enough to achieve this end where an accused person—under threat of an adverse inference provision or a penalty for remaining silent—makes an incriminating statement before her solicitor has arrived.

[2–41] These developments in the jurisprudence of the European Court of Human Rights appear to have been a factor in the Irish courts significantly strengthening the level of protection provided by the Irish Constitution. In *Re National Irish Bank* [1999] 3 IR 145, the Supreme Court reconsidered these issues. Section 18 of the Companies Act 1990 provided that statements made by an officer or agent of a company to a court-appointed inspector could be used in evidence against her. There were certain powers under the Act effectively to compel officers and agents of companies to answer the questions of inspectors. Having cited a number of decisions of the European Court of Human Rights, Barrington J (with whom the other members of the Court agreed), reasoned as follows:

> It appears to me that the better opinion is that a trial in due course of law requires that any confession admitted against an accused person in a criminal trial should be a voluntary confession and that any trial at which an alleged confession other than a voluntary confession were admitted in evidence against the accused person would not be a trial in due course of law within the meaning of Article 38 of the Constitution and that it is immaterial whether the compulsion or inducement used to extract the confession came from the executive or from the legislature. [1999] 3 IR 145, at 186–187.

[2–42] Barrington J then upheld the constitutionality of s 18, but only on the basis that it did not authorise the introduction into evidence in a criminal trial of a non-voluntary confession on the part of the accused. The difficult question of whether any particular statement was voluntary (made yet more difficult by the fact that any such statement would be made against the background of a possible statutory compulsion to answer questions) was left over for trial judges in particular cases.

This more robust approach on the part of the courts is evidenced by *Dunnes Stores Ireland Co Ltd v Ryan* [2002] 2 IR 60, in which Kearns J struck down s 19(6) of the Companies Act 1990 on the basis that answers provided to a statutory demand under that section would be admissible in Court. Also, in *People (DPP) v Finnerty* [1999] 4 IR 364, the Supreme Court quashed a rape conviction on the basis that the prosecution had been permitted to cross-examine the accused as to why he had not answered questions while in garda custody. The accused's counsel had maintained in his cross-examination of the complainant that the sexual relations had been consensual but the accused had provided no detail on this when questioned by the police. The Supreme Court considered that it was impermissible to cross-examine the accused on why this was the case, Keane J reasoning: [2–43]

> [I]t is a usual practice for solicitors to advise their clients while they are in custody, not to answer any questions put to them by the gardaí, if they consider that it would not be in their interests to do so. However, if the jury could be invited to draw inferences from the failure to reply to such questions, the result would be that persons in custody would have to be advised by solicitors that, notwithstanding the terms of the caution, it might be inimical to their client's interests not to make a full statement to the gardaí, thereby eroding further the right of silence recognised at common law.
>
> Had the Oireachtas intended to abridge the right of silence in this manner, it would have expressly so legislated. Sections 18 and 19 of the Act of 1984, enable the court of trial to draw inferences from the failure or refusal of a person arrested by the gardaí, to account for the presence of certain objects in his possession, or his having been found at a particular place. Such inferences may afford corroboration of any evidence, but the person may not be convicted, of an offence solely on the basis of such inferences. This leads to the inevitable conclusion that no such general abridgement of the right of silence was intended to be effected where a person declined to answer questions put to him by the gardaí during the course of such a detention.
>
> It follows that the right of suspects in custody to remain silent, recognised by the common law, is also a constitutional right and the provisions of the Act of 1984, must be construed accordingly. Absent any express statutory provisions entitling a court or jury to draw inferences from such silence, the conclusion follows inevitably that the right is left unaffected by the Act of 1984, save in cases coming within sections 18 and 19, and must be upheld by the courts.

As well as protecting the right to silence, the courts have also developed an elaborate jurisprudence designed to ensure that only voluntary statements are admissible in evidence. Drawing the line between permissible and impermissible psychological pressure in interrogations has not proven easy; the case law on this complex issue lies beyond the scope of this book. [2–44]

Unfair Pre-Trial Publicity

On a number of occasions, the courts have been called on to consider whether they should prohibit a trial on the basis that prejudicial pre-trial publicity rendered it impossible for the accused to receive a fair trial. In *D v DPP* [1994] 2 IR 564, the accused sought to prohibit his rape trial on this ground. He had been tried on two [2–45] previous occasions, but on each occasion a mistrial occurred. After the second mistrial, a Sunday newspaper prominently carried a lengthy interview with the complainant. Although neither the complainant nor the accused was named, it would have been possible to identify the story as relating to the trial that had just been halted. Six months elapsed between the collapse and the scheduled third trial. The High Court held that the trial should be prohibited, but a majority of the Supreme Court allowed the appeal and directed that the trial should proceed. The Court agreed that the trial should be prohibited if there was a real and serious risk that the trial would be unfair should it proceed. The majority focused on the fact that there was only one newspaper article, that it had been published six months previously, that the parties had not been named, and that jurors were bound by oath to disregard such matters. In contrast, the minority's concerns were not assuaged by these factors. In their view, the article was seriously prejudicial to the accused and there was a serious risk that any juror who had read it would not be able to put it out of her mind.

[2–46] Shortly after *D*, the Supreme Court had to consider a far greater level of pre-trial publicity in *Z v DPP* [1994] 2 IR 476. Z was accused of raping X, the young girl at the centre of the *X Case* (see chapter 5). Z's principal arguments were (a) that considerable publicity had been given to a genetic testing of X's foetus which allegedly identified Z as being guilty of raping X and (b) that the ambient publicity surrounding the *X Case* would have made a fair trial impossible. The Supreme Court unanimously held that the trial should not be prohibited. Finlay CJ (with whom the other members of the Court agreed) repeated the test from *D*, namely that an accused bore the onus of proving that a fair trial would not be possible by reason of the pre-trial publicity. He clarified that this meant a risk which could not be avoided by appropriate direction on the part of the trial judge to the jury. Finlay CJ was satisfied that the pre-trial publicity could be addressed by appropriate direction:

> Not only am I satisfied, as I have already indicated, that it is agreed in these proceedings that the charges against the accused are in respect of the girl who was the respondent in *The Attorney General v X* [1992] 1 IR 1 and that the facts surrounding those charges must inevitably be some of the facts which were adumbrated in that case, but I am also satisfied that as a matter of practical probability it will not be possible to empanel a jury in this case who will not, either as to the great majority of them or more likely as to all of them, be aware of this identity of the case.
>
> It is against that fact that the effect upon the jury and upon the deliberations of the jury and therefore upon the fairness of the trial of this saturation publicity of an ambient or general kind must be viewed.
>
> In many instances, pre-trial publicity may be particularly damaging in regard to the question of a fair and unprejudiced trial; where a trial judge is faced with a dilemma that, to remind the members of the jury at the commencement and during the course of the case of that publicity, and to point out that they must in its entirety ignore it in carrying out their deliberations which must be completely confined to the evidence sworn before them, he may be reminding jurors of a publicity or of a link between the publicity and the case they were trying of which they were unaware. No such danger exists in this case and I take the view that a trial judge will be able in a specific way, and with considerable specific detail, to point out to a jury at the very commencement of the trial accepting the admitted fact that the trial must be associated with *The Attorney General v X* [1992] 1 IR 1 that the controversy, media publicity, newspaper and magazine commentary arising from that case and from other issues of national policy which were in a sense raised by it are wholly irrelevant to the trial and must be completely put out of their minds. I am satisfied that a

jury so fully and amply instructed will be able to bring to the trial of the case an impartial mind and will be particularly scrupulous about preventing themselves or indeed, in a sense preventing each other, from deciding the case based on any view arising from this type of general publicity or controversy.

I would therefore be satisfied that this submission on the hearing of this appeal must be rejected. [1994] 2 IR 476, at 508–509.

Finlay CJ also rejected the more specific argument about the DNA testing on the basis that it would be open to the trial judge to give very specific directions in relation to such evidence (or the need to disregard any evidence not adduced at the trial) if necessary. [2–47]

Following on from *Z*, it might have been thought that there could never be such a level of unfair pre-trial publicity that would preclude a trial. However, in *Magee v O'Dea* [1994] 1 IR 500, Flood J prohibited the extradition of Mr Magee to the United Kingdom. There had been extensive newspaper coverage which included photographs of Mr Magee who was effectively identified as the murderer. Despite the fact that the newspaper coverage had occurred two years previously and that the English trial judge could be assumed to issue all appropriate directions to the jury, Flood J concluded that there was a real risk of an unfair trial. [2–48]

More recently, the courts have adopted the approach of postponing trials to allow for the fade factor to operate. In *DPP v Haugh* (*No 2*) [2001] 1 IR 162, the DPP challenged the decision of Judge Haugh to stay the prosecution of former Taoiseach Charles Haughey on grounds of obstructing the Moriarty Tribunal. The stay was granted on the grounds of pre-trial publicity, consisting of a planned public rally and prejudicial comments by the Tánaiste, Ms Mary Harney. In the High Court, Carroll J refused to overturn the trial judge's decision that the prosecution should be stayed. Similarly, in *Zoe Developments v DPP*, 3 March 1999 (HC), Geoghegan J did not think there was a serious risk of an unfair trial but directed that the trial should be postponed for a further six months to allow for the fade factor to come into effect. [2–49]

The Duty to Seek Out and Preserve Evidence

In *Murphy v DPP* [1989] ILRM 71, the High Court prohibited a trial in circumstances in which the accused had sought to examine forensically the car which he was charged with stealing. The gardaí allowed the car to leave their possession without either acceding to this request or examining the car forensically themselves. The High Court held that this was a breach of fair procedures. This basic principle has been developed considerably by the Supreme Court in recent years. [2–50]

In *Braddish v DPP* [2001] 3 IR 127, the applicant sought to prohibit his trial for robbery on the basis that a video surveillance tape had not been retained by the gardaí. A garda viewed the tape and came to the conclusion that Mr Braddish was the person who had committed the robbery. While in police custody, Mr Braddish confessed to the crime. Nine months later, he was charged with the robbery. On his first appearance in the District Court, his solicitor sought the video tape but it transpired that the gardaí had returned it to the shop in which the robbery had occurred. The Supreme Court granted an order prohibiting the trial, Hardiman J reasoning: [2–51]

It is well established that evidence relevant to guilt or innocence must, so far as necessary and practicable, be kept until the conclusion of a trial. This principle also applies to the preservation of articles which may give rise to the reasonable possibility of securing relevant evidence....

The first respondent, however, states that in the present case the video tape is not of evidential use. Firstly (and the learned High Court Judge was obviously impressed by this point) the case is not being put forward on the basis of identification either of the applicant or of a video of the perpetrator. It is being advanced solely on the basis of the alleged inculpatory statement.

If anyone is at a loss because the video tape is missing, it was submitted, it is the prosecution. The video has no actual or potential use to the defendant and its absence is not a ground for affording him any relief.

In the criminal trial for this robbery, the applicant is pleading not guilty despite the alleged existence of an inculpatory statement signed by him. This statement was allegedly made while he was in garda custody after an arrest allegedly based wholly on the video tape evidence. If the applicant wished to object to the statement on the basis of the illegality of his detention it is difficult to see how he could do so unless he could show that the ground put forward for his arrest did not in fact support it and could not reasonably be supposed to do so. This seems impossible to do without the video tape. The stills, certainly in the form of which they were presented to this court are quite useless for identification purposes.

More fundamentally, this is a video tape which purports actually to show the robbery in progress. It is not acceptable, in my view, to excuse the absence of so vital and direct a piece of evidence simply by saying that the prosecution are not relying on it, but prefer to rely on an alleged confession. Firstly, the confession is hotly disputed. Secondly, a confession should if possible be corroborated and relatively recent history both here and in the neighbouring jurisdiction has unfortunate examples of the risks of excessive reliance on confession evidence. Thirdly, the video tape has a clear potential to exculpate as well as to inculpate.

This video tape was real evidence and the gardaí were not entitled to dispose of it before the trial. It is now admitted that they should not have done so. Lest, however, the sentence already quoted from the State Solicitor's letter, (and which can only have been based on his instructions from the gardaí), can be read to suggest that because the prosecution was based wholly on an alleged confession, other items of evidence can be destroyed or rendered unavailable, I wish to state emphatically that this is not so. It is the duty of the gardaí, arising from their unique investigative role, to seek out and preserve all evidence having a bearing or potential bearing on the issue of guilt or innocence. This is so whether the prosecution proposes to rely on the evidence or not, and regardless of whether it assists the case the prosecution is advancing or not. [2001] 3 IR 127, at 131–133.

[2–52] In the subsequent case of *Dunne v DPP* [2002] 2 IR 305, the Supreme Court emphasized that the duty on the gardaí extended not only to preserving evidence, but to seeking it out. The case concerned similar facts: the accused was charged with the robbery of a petrol station. Although there had been previous robberies from the same petrol station in respect of which the gardaí had sought and obtained video evidence, it was unclear whether a video tape had been obtained in this instance. If a video tape had been obtained and then lost, then it would follow that the *Braddish* principle had been infringed. However, if the video had not been sought in the first place, that would raise equivalent problems, Hardiman J reasoning:

> The matter is not concluded even if one accepts the uncontradicted statement in the respondent's affidavit that the video was never given to or obtained by any member of An Garda Síochána. Why was that? It is clear that it would have been reasonable for any guard attending the scene to have inquired about the video. It is not averred that this took place.

If it did take place, no explanation has been offered as to why they did not obtain a tape. Since the duty of the gardaí extends to "seeking out" as well as "preserving" evidence, the distinction of the facts here from those of *Braddish v Director of Public Prosecutions* [2001] 3 IR 127 does not appear to me to address the central issue. [2002] 2 IR 305, at 316.

McGuinness J agreed with Hardiman J, but Fennelly J dissented on the basis that the Court should only interfere where the missing evidence had at some stage been in the hands of the prosecution. [2–53]

In *Bowes and McGrath v DPP* [2003] 2 IR 25, the Supreme Court reconsidered the *Braddish* principles in two separate appeals. In *Bowes*, the applicant was charged with possession of heroin for the purposes of sale and supply. The case against him was based on the discovery of drugs in a car of which he was the alleged driver. 20 months after the proceedings were initiated and just a few days before his trial commenced, he sought details of any technical examination carried out on the car by the gardaí. In *McGrath*, the applicant was accused of dangerous driving causing death. The gardaí had carried out a technical examination of the motorcycle which she had hit. Shortly after proceedings were commenced, the applicant sought to make a technical examination of the motorcycle but the gardaí had parted with it several months previously. Addressing the general principles to be applied, Hardiman J (with whom the other members of the Court agreed) adopted the "real risk of an unfair trial" test used by Finlay CJ in the publicity cases *D* and *Z*. He emphasised that the aim of the courts was to ensure a fair trial not to sit as a form of disciplinary body on police procedures. He held that the motorcycle in *McGrath* was a crucial piece of evidence which should have been preserved. However, in *Bowes*, there was only a negligible possibility that an examination of the car would have offered the applicant a way of rebutting the case against him. Accordingly, the trial of Ms McGrath was prohibited while the trial of Mr Bowes was allowed to proceed. [2–54]

The Right to an Early Trial

In *State (O'Connell) v Fawsitt* [1986] IR 362, the Supreme Court held that Art 38.1 guaranteed a right to a trial with reasonable expedition. Many cases arose from the 1990s onwards as Irish society began to address a long history of child abuse. Frequently, prosecutions in this context would arise many years after the alleged offences, creating obvious issues of delay. The courts accorded considerable importance to the question of whether the complainant could justify the delay in making her complaint. It was generally possible to justify the delay as it is a feature of sexual abuse cases that the abuser often holds a position of dominance over the victim which could explain the victim not making a complaint. The need to treat sexual abuse differently was recognised by the Supreme Court in *D v DPP* [1994] 1 IR 374, at 380, Finlay CJ commenting: [2–55]

> The court asked to prohibit the trial of a person on such offences, even after a very long time, might well be satisfied and justified in reaching a conclusion that the extent to which the applicant had contributed to the delay in the revealing of the offences and their subsequent reporting to the prosecution authorities meant that as a matter of justice he should not be entitled to the order.

However, the need to explore this issue caused considerable complication as psychological examination and cross-examination of complaints could be necessary to ascertain the situation in any particular case. The Supreme Court recently [2–56] undertook an exhaustive survey of the case law in the area and, in the light of experience, opted for a simpler approach.

[2–57] In *SH v DPP* [2006] 3 IR 575, Murray CJ restated the Court's view in the following terms:

> [T]he court's experience extends to a broader set of issues and it has found that there is a range of circumstances extending beyond dominion or psychological consequences flowing directly from the abuse which militate or inhibit victims from bringing complaints of sexual abuse to the notice of other persons, in particular those outside their family and even more particularly the gardaí with a view to a possible trial.
>
> Over the last decade the courts have had extensive experience of cases where complaints are made of alleged sexual abuse which is stated to have taken place many, many years ago. It is an unfortunate truth that such cases are routinely part of the list in criminal courts today.
>
> At issue in each case is the constitutional right to a fair trial. The court has found that in reality the core inquiry is not so much the reason for a delay in making a complaint by a complainant but rather whether the accused will receive a fair trial or whether there is a real or serious risk of an unfair trial. In practice this has invariably been the essential and ultimate question for the court. In other words it is the consequences of delay rather than delay itself which has concerned the court.
>
> The court approaches such cases with knowledge incrementally assimilated over the last decade in some of which different views were expressed as to how these issues should be approached. In such cases when information was presented concerning the reasons for the delay it was invariably a preliminary point to the ultimate and critical issue as to whether the accused could obtain a fair trial. In all events, having regard to the court's knowledge and insight into these cases it considers that there is no longer a necessity to inquire into the reason for a delay in making a complaint. In all the circumstances now prevailing such a preliminary issue is no longer necessary.
>
> This particular case illustrates the extensive affidavits and oral evidence along with psychological and medical reports which have come before the court for the purpose of explaining the reason for a lapse of time between the alleged offence and the making of a complaint. Yet, in the end, what concerns the court is whether an accused will receive a fair trial or whether there is a real or serious risk of an unfair trial....
>
> These cases have come before the court after a decision to prosecute has been made by the respondent. The respondent is independent in the performance of his functions. The decision to prosecute may be a complex decision involving the balancing of many factors.
>
> Article 30 of the Constitution of Ireland 1937 specifies that prosecutions for serious crimes "shall be prosecuted in the name of the People". This provision reflects the fact that the prosecution of serious crimes is vital to the public interest. The State can only initiate a prosecution when it is aware that a crime has been committed and there is sufficient evidence available to charge somebody with it. Once that happens the State has, in principle, a duty to prosecute. Although the bringing of a prosecution may undoubtedly be central to vindicating the rights or interests of a victim of a crime, the interests of the People in bringing a prosecution is, in the interest of society as a whole, of wider importance. The fact that a person who was the victim of a serious crime had delayed in bringing the commission of that crime to the notice of the State authorities is not of itself a ground upon which the State should refuse to bring a prosecution or the courts to entertain one. In particular circumstances delay in reporting such a crime, because of its extent or in combination with other factual matters, may be considered to affect the credibility of a complainant. That could not in general be a ground for prohibiting a trial proceeding. It is a matter in the first instance for the prosecuting authorities in deciding whether there is evidence of sufficient weight to warrant a charge

being preferred. It is also the duty of the respondent, in exercising his independent functions with regard to the bringing of a prosecution, to consider whether, in all the circumstances, a fair trial can be afforded to an accused. This is an onerous and strict duty since, as some of the decisions of this court demonstrate, there are circumstances in which the bringing of a prosecution in respect of offences that are alleged to have happened very many years ago would be to visit a serious injustice on the person accused of them. Where a prosecution is in fact brought following a complaint made after a long lapse of time since the alleged offence, any issue concerning the credibility of a complainant by reason of a lengthy delay is a matter to be considered at the trial should the defence raise such an issue. There is no reason why the prosecution of serious offences involving sexual abuse of minors should be treated differently from other serious offences in this regard.

Test

... I am satisfied that it is no longer necessary to establish such reasons for the delay. The issue for the court is whether the delay has resulted in prejudice to an accused so as to give rise to a real or serious risk of an unfair trial. The court would thus restate the test as:-

"The test is whether there is a real or serious risk that the applicant, by reason of the delay, would not obtain a fair trial, or that a trial would be unfair as a consequence of the delay. The test is to be applied in light of the circumstances of the case."

Thus, the first inquiry as to the reasons for the delay in making a complaint need no longer be made. As a consequence any question of an assumption, which arose solely for the purpose of applications of this nature, of the truth of the complainants' complaints against an applicant no longer arises. The inquiry which should be made is whether the degree of prejudice is such as to give rise to a real or serious risk of an unfair trial. The factors of prejudice, if any, will depend upon the circumstances of the case.

There is no doubt that difficulties arise in defending a case many years after an event. However, the courts may not legislate, the courts may not take a policy decision that after a stated number of years an offence may not be prosecuted. Also, as the legislature has not itself established a statute of limitations that itself may be viewed as a policy of the representatives of the People. Thus each case falls to be considered on its own circumstances. [2006] 3 IR 575, at [36]–[49]

The effect of *SH* is to preclude an accused person—in a sexual abuse case—from relying on the length of delay *per se* as a reason for prohibiting a trial. The courts are prepared to assume that there are good reasons justifying the delay. Instead, the accused must be able to point to some prejudice, linked to the delay, that results in a real or serious risk that the accused could not obtain a fair trial. As with the courts' jurisprudence on unfair pre-trial publicity, the ability of the trial judge to mitigate unfairness by means of appropriate direction to the jury must be taken into account. [2–58]

In *MacFarlane v DPP* [2007] 1 IR 134, the Supreme Court considered the issue of a delay in a context other than sexual abuse. Here the applicant was charged with the false imprisonment of a businessman some 15 years after the alleged commission of the offence. For much of that time, the applicant had been in prison in Northern Ireland; however, the DPP contended that there was not sufficient evidence to charge the applicant with the offence prior to his arrest in 1998. The Court held that the applicant could not simply point to delay prior to charge *per se* as a reason for prohibiting the applicant's trial. Instead, it was necessary for the applicant to identify some specific prejudice associated with that delay. In this regard, the applicant pointed to the fact that items allegedly bearing his fingerprints had been lost by the gardaí. This essentially raised the *Braddish* ground that the gardaí have a duty to preserve the [2–59] evidence. Although expressing his concern at the loss of the items, Hardiman J emphasised that the purpose of the Court's jurisdiction was not to seek for fault on the part of the gardaí but rather to assess whether there was a real risk of an unfair trial. In this regard, the risk of unfairness was significantly mitigated by the fact that photographs had been taken of the fingerprints:

> [T]here was in fact a forensic examination of the missing items prior to their disappearance and that the *results* of the forensic analysis have been preserved. It appears from the book of evidence, exhibited by the applicant, that there is a chain of evidence covering the identification of the fingerprints on the items, the photographing of the fingerprints on the items and the preservation of the photographs. These photographs are available for comparison purposes: they have in fact been compared with the applicant's fingerprints and are available, if desired, for further comparison on behalf of the applicant. A significantly different situation would arise if this independent comparison were not possible. No attempt has been made in the present case to suggest that meaningful comparison is not possible, using the photographs, or that any additional advantage might have accrued to the applicant on the basis of a comparison with the actual marks made on the items as opposed to photographs of them. [2007] 1 IR 134, at [22].

[2–60] This distinguished the case from cases such as *Braddish*, *Dunne* and *Bowes*. As a result, Hardiman J held that there was no real or serious risk of an unfair trial such as would warrant prohibiting the trial. A majority of the Court agreed with this conclusion. Kearns J dissented.

[2–61] The courts have identified other factors which might, in the context of a delay, give rise to the sort of specific prejudice which could warrant the prohibition of a trial. In *People (DPP) v Quilligan (No 3)* [1992] 2 IR 305, Finlay CJ considered that the death of an alibi witness towards the end of the delay was sufficient prejudice to cause a serious risk of an unfair trial. In *NC v DPP* [2001] IESC 54, the Supreme Court prohibited a sexual abuse trial in which the applicant was accused of abusing two of his sisters. In the intervening period, their mother had died. Hardiman J considered that this was a significant prejudice to the applicant:

> The role of the deceased mother of the Applicant and the two complainants is a conspicuous one in this case. Allegations about her actions are found in the statements of the complainants: they are generally contradicted or disparaged by the Applicant.
>
> In many cases of a very long lapse of time it is found that witnesses or potential witnesses had died. On occasions it is open to the Prosecution to submit that no prejudice has been shown because it is not clear that the deceased person would have had any evidence to give. In this case it is apparent from the statements of the complainants themselves that she would have, on their account, highly relevant evidence to give. Moreover her attitude to the allegations was quite clearly one favourable to the Applicant, so much so that Counsel for the Director conceded in this Court that:-
>
> "Everyone knows the mother would say these things didn't happen"....
>
> It appears to me that the centrality of the mother as a witness emerges clearly from the statements of each of the complainants, as well as from other sources.... In summary it appears to me that the following can be said about the mother's evidence, as presented by the prosecution. The particular arrangements in the household of which she was the effective head, and in particular sleeping arrangements for her large family in a small house, are central to the allegations in relation to K in the form in which they now stand. Similarly, her alleged, continuing and sometimes violent demeanour towards M, in particular by way of insisting that she present herself for baby sitting in the Applicant's

house at a much later date are central to the account given of those alleged assaults. Thirdly, her disbelief and total lack of receptivity to these two ladies' complaints, both an early age and more recently are relied on by them and in the psychological evidence as explaining and excusing the delay in complaining. Fourthly, by reason of the mother's death the only realistic prospect of finding the hypnotist whose role is so central is gone. Fifthly, by reason of her absence it is now impossible to contradict the prosecution's speculation that the person to whom she brought the child may not have a hypnotist at all but that she simply decided to use that word. Sixthly, allegations about much more recent years such as the extraordinary allegations that she locked one of these complainants in a cupboard and subsequently threatened to commit suicide are both significant in the complainant's accounts and quite beyond the reach of contradiction or investigation in the absence of the mother. [2001] IESC 54, at 13–20.

In light of the attitude adopted by the Supreme Court in *SH* and *MacFarlane*, it appears that the courts must adopt a fact-specific approach to the question of prejudice in each case. It is thus difficult to extrapolate general rules as to what may or may not constitute sufficient prejudice. [2–62]

The Presumption of Innocence

Unsurprisingly, the courts have held that the presumption of innocence is constitutionally protected by Art 38.1. Although this presumption may underpin the protections afforded to the accused person in the pre-trial process, it comes most sharply into focus in the context of the burden of proof at trial. In *O'Leary v Attorney General* [1993] 1 IR 102, the plaintiff challenged the constitutionality of s 24 of the Offences Against the State Act 1939 and s 3(2) of the Offences Against the State (Amendment) Act 1972, both of which relate to the offence of being a member of an unlawful organisation contrary to s 21 of the 1939 Act. Section 24 of the 1939 Act provided that proof that the accused was in possession of an incriminating document relating to the organisation would count as evidence, until the contrary was proven, that the accused was a member of the organisation. Section 3(2) of the 1972 Act provided that where a member of the Garda Síochána, not below the rank of Chief Superintendent, gives evidence of her belief that the accused was a member of the unlawful organisation, that would count as evidence that the accused was a member of the organisation. Mr O'Leary was found guilty of being a member of an unlawful organisation and of being in possession of an incriminating document (37 posters bearing the legend, "The IRA Calls the Shots"). He subsequently sought to challenge the constitutionality of s 24 of the 1939 Act and s 3(2) of the 1972 Act on the basis that they required him to prove his innocence. [2–63]

Costello J first accepted that the presumption of innocence was protected by Art 38.1: [2–64]

> I have little difficulty in accepting the basic contention on which these arguments are posited and in construing the Constitution as conferring on every accused in every criminal trial a constitutionally protected right to the presumption of innocence. This right is now widespread and indeed enjoys universal recognition. Article 11 of the United Nations Universal Declaration of Human Rights, 1948, provides that "Everyone charged with a penal offence has the right to be presumed innocent until proved guilty according to law …"; Article 6 (2) of the European Convention on Human Rights and Fundamental Freedoms, 1950, provides that "Everyone charged with a criminal offence shall be presumed innocent until proved guilty according to law"; Article 8 (2) of the American Convention on Human Rights, 1969, prepared within the Organisation of

American States provides that "Every person accused of a criminal offence has the right to be presumed innocent so long as his guilt has not been proven according to law."; Article 7 of the African Charter on Human and Peoples' Rights provides that every individual has the right to have his cause heard and declares that this, *inter alia*, comprises "the right to be presumed innocent until proven guilty by a competent Court or tribunal."

By construing the Constitution in the light of contemporary concepts of fundamental rights (as I am entitled to do; see *The State (Healy) v Donoghue* [1976] IR 325) the plaintiff's claim obtains powerful support. But in addition, although the Constitution was enacted before these international instruments were adopted in 1937, the presumption of innocence had long been an integral part of the common law tradition which constituted an important part of the legal order which this State then adopted (as pointed out by McCarthy J in *Ryan v Director of Public Prosecutions* [1989] IR 399). The Constitution of course contains no express reference to the presumption but it does provide in Article 38 that "no person shall be tried on any criminal charge save in due course of law." It seems to me that it has been for so long a fundamental postulate of every criminal trial in this country that the accused was presumed to be innocent of the offence with which he was charged that a criminal trial held otherwise than in accordance with this presumption would, *prima facie*, be one which was not held in due course of law. It would follow that *prima facie* any statute which permitted such a trial so to be held would be unconstitutional. The contentious issue in the case, therefore, is not whether the plaintiff had a constitutionally protected right to the presumption of innocence but whether the impugned provisions of the Acts of 1939 and 1972 infringed that right. [1993] 1 IR 102, at 107–108.

[2–65] However, Costello J did not accept that the presumption of innocence was infringed by the impugned provisions. He reasoned that the provisions merely reversed the evidential burden of proof by allowing in evidence which the accused could challenge, rather than reversing the legal burden of proof:

It is obvious that the difference in the manner in which the statute shifts the onus of proof may produce different legal consequences and so any statute which does so must be carefully considered to appreciate exactly the effect it may have on an accused's constitutional rights.... By providing that once a fact is established...the court is then required to draw an inference which is specified in the section. It is the nature and effect of the inference or conclusion that requires careful analysis.

Secondly, it is important to bear in mind that the phrase "the burden of proof" is used in two entirely different senses and that when it is said that a statute "shifts" the burden of proof onto the accused this may mean two entirely different things. The phrase is used firstly to describe as a matter of substantive law the burden which is imposed on the prosecution in a criminal trial to establish the case against the accused beyond a reasonable doubt. This burden is fixed by law and remains on the prosecution from the beginning to the end of the trial. It is this burden which arises from the presumption of the accused's innocence and it is the removal of this burden by statute that may involve a breach of the accused's constitutional rights. It is now usual to refer to this burden as the legal or persuasive burden of proof. But the phrase is also used to describe the burden which is cast on the prosecution in a criminal trial of adducing evidence to establish a case against an accused, a burden which is now usually referred to as the evidential burden of proof. In criminal cases the prosecution discharges this evidential burden by adducing sufficient evidence to raise a "prima facie" case against an accused. It can then be said that an evidential burden has been cast on to the accused. But the shifting of the evidential burden does not discharge the legal burden of proof which at all times rests on the prosecution. The accused may elect not to call any evidence and will be entitled to an acquittal if the evidence adduced does not establish his or her guilt beyond a reasonable doubt. Therefore if a statute is to be construed as merely shifting the evidential burden no constitutional infringement occurs. (For a discussion on the two meanings see: Glanville Williams, *Criminal Law* (1961), at [287]–[288] and *Phipson on Evidence* (1982), at chapter 4.)

Whilst it may not be desirable or indeed possible to lay down any hard and fast rule for the construction of statutes involving the shifting of a burden of proof, it is clear that if the effect of the statute is that the court *must* convict an accused should he or she fail to adduce exculpatory evidence then its effect is to shift the legal burden of proof (thus involving a possible breach of the accused's constitutional rights) whereas if its effect is that notwithstanding its terms the accused *may* be acquitted even though he calls no evidence because the statute has not discharged the prosecution from establishing the accused's guilt beyond a reasonable doubt then no constitutional invalidity could arise.

Thirdly, it does not necessarily follow that a statute is unconstitutional merely because its effect is that the failure of an accused to adduce exculpatory evidence must result in a conviction. The statute may merely give legal effect to an inference which it is reasonable to draw from facts which the prosecution establish. The presumption of the accused's innocence is therefore rebutted not by the statute but by the inference.…

Fourthly, the Constitution should not be construed as absolutely prohibiting the Oireachtas from restricting the exercise of the right to the presumption of innocence. The right is to be implied from Article 38, which provides that trials are to be held "in accordance with law", and it seems to me that the Oireachtas is permitted in certain circumstances to restrict the exercise of the right because it is not to be regarded as an absolute right whose enjoyment can never be abridged.… [1993] 1 IR, 102, at 108–110.

Although Costello J held that the presumption of innocence could be infringed by the Oireachtas in certain circumstances, he held that no infringement had occurred here. Both sections merely accorded evidential weight to evidence that might otherwise be inadmissible. There was nothing to prevent the accused from challenging and seeking to undermine the relevance of the evidence (*eg* by explaining how the document was not really incriminating) nor to prevent the court from evaluating and weighing the evidence. Neither section made it necessary for the accused to introduce exculpatory evidence in order to prove his guilt. Accordingly, the legal burden of proof had not shifted and the presumption of innocence had not been infringed. [2–66]

The Supreme Court approved this conclusion on appeal, employing the presumption of constitutionality to emphasise that the sections merely gave evidential weight to the opinion of the Chief Superintendent and to the possession of the incriminating document, rather than shifting the burden of proof. [2–67]

In *Hardy v Ireland* [1994] 2 IR 550, the Supreme Court similarly upheld the constitutionality of s 4(1) of the Explosive Substances Act 1883. This provided that any person who knowingly had in her possession or under her control any explosive substance, under such circumstances as to give rise to a reasonable suspicion that she did not have it in her possession or under her control for a lawful object would be guilty of an offence unless she could show that she it in her possession or control for a lawful object. Mr Hardy argued that this unconstitutionally transferred the legal burden of proof on to him to establish that the explosive was in his control for a lawful object. The Supreme Court rejected this claim, reasoning that the prosecution had to prove all elements of the offence beyond a reasonable doubt (possession of an explosive substance giving rise to a reasonable suspicion that it was not for a lawful purpose). The final clause merely provided a statutory defence in relation to which it was permissible to place the legal burden of proof on the accused. [2–68]

[2–69]   In summary, it is clear that the presumption of innocence is protected by Art 38.1, although there may be some slight scope for the Oireachtas to restrict this right. However, it is permissible for the Oireachtas to shift the evidential burden of proof. Moreover, statutes which might appear at first glance to shift the legal burden of proof will, if possible, be read as shifting only the evidential burden of proof, thereby making them constitutionally sound.

No Right to Confrontational Cross-Examination

[2–70]   In *Re Haughey* [1971] IR 217, the Supreme Court had held that an accused person has a right cross-examine every person giving evidence against him. However, in *Donnelly v DPP* [1998] 1 IR 321, the Supreme Court rejected a challenge to s 13 of the Criminal (Evidence) Act 1992 which allowed for persons under the age of 17 to give evidence by way of video link. Hamilton CJ delivered the judgment of the Court:

> [T]he central concern of the requirements of due process and fair procedures is ... to ensure the fairness of the trial of an accused person. This undoubtedly involves the rigorous testing by cross-examination of the evidence against him or her.
>
> The Court recognises, as did the learned trial judge, that it is an undeniable fact that children may be manipulated by malevolent adults, or in some cases, by over-zealous social workers into making false accusations of sexual abuse and that fair procedures require that there are proper means to assess the credibility of all the testimony in the prosecution case, including the testimony of child witnesses.
>
> The Court is satisfied, however, that the assessment of such credibility does not require that the witness should be required to give evidence in the physical presence of the accused person and that the requirements of fair procedures are adequately fulfilled by requiring that the witness give evidence on oath and be subjected to cross-examination and that the judge and jury have ample opportunity to observe the demeanour of the witness while giving evidence and being subjected to cross-examination. In this way, an accused person's right to a fair trial is adequately protected and vindicated. Such right does not include the right in all circumstances to require that the evidence be given in his physical presence and consequently there is no such constitutional right. [1998] 1 IR 321, at 356–358.

The Right to Jury Trial

[2–71]   Article 38.5 of the Constitution provides a general right to jury trial, save for three exceptions: non-minor offences, special courts where it is determined by law that the ordinary courts are inadequate to secure the effective administration of justice, and military tribunals. The Special Criminal Court was established to try, *inter alia*, offences under the Offences Against the State Act 1939. It is Art 38.2 that provides that non-minor offences can be tried summarily, *ie* without a jury. The courts have developed an elaborate jurisprudence on what constitutes a non-minor offence. In *Melling v Ó Mathghamhna* [1962] IR 1, the Supreme Court laid down four criteria to establish if an offence was non-minor. Mr Melling was charged in the District Court on 15 charges relating to the smuggling of butter into the State. The offences alleged constituted a contravention of s 24 of the Dairy Produce (Price Stabilisation) Act 1935 and s 186 of the Customs Consolidation Act 1876. The Revenue Commissioners elected under s 186 to proceed for a penalty of £100 in each of the fifteen charges, *ie* treble the duty paid value of the goods.

[2–72]   Having reviewed US authority on a similar point, Lavery J held that four criteria were relevant to the issue of whether an offence was non-minor:

It appears to me that these principles may be stated thus:
First: in the construction of a statute and, at least equally in construing a provision in a constitution as a fundamental law, it is necessary to consider how the law stood when the statute was passed. Second: the severity of the penalty involved. Third: the moral quality of the act. Fourth: its relation to common law crimes. [1962] IR 1.

Applying these principles to the offence in question, a majority of the Court concluded that it was a non-minor offence. Lavery J emphasised that the severity of the penalty was the most important of the criteria involved, a point reiterated in several later cases. The case law also establishes that the severity of the penalty should be assessed from the perspective of the ordinary citizen (Ó Dálaigh J dissenting on the conclusion in *Melling*) and that the severity of the penalty should be assessed by reference to the penalty authorised by statute and not the penalty actually imposed (*Re Haughey* [1971] IR 217). More controversially, the courts have introduced a distinction between primary and secondary punishment, the latter not being relevant to the calculation of whether an offence is non-minor. In *Conroy v Attorney General* [1965] IR 411, the Supreme Court considered whether s 49 of the Road Traffic Act 1961, making it an offence to drive while under the influence of alcohol, constituted a non-minor offence. A person convicted, after a summary trial, under s 49 was liable to a fine of £100 and/or a six-month prison sentence. However, under s 26 of the Act, a person convicted of such an offence would also be disqualified from holding a driving licence for not less than one year in the case of a first offence and not less than three years in the case of a second any subsequent offence. Walsh J delivered the judgment of the Court: [2–73]

> A disqualification whether imposed by a Court or otherwise may result in considerable hardship for some people and in little more than a recreational inconvenience for others. It may well be ... that to some people a driver's licence may be just as valuable as a licence to engage in an occupation or profession. That, however, does not determine the matter. In the opinion of this Court, so far as punishment is concerned, the punishment which must be examined for the purpose of gauging the seriousness of an offence is what may be referred to as "primary punishment." That is the type of punishment which is regarded as punishment in the ordinary sense and, where crime is concerned, is either the loss of liberty or the intentional penal deprivation of property whether by means of fine or other direct method of deprivation. Any conviction may result in many other unpleasant and even punitive consequences for the convicted person. By the rules of his professional association or organisation or trade association or any other body of which he is a member he may become liable to expulsion or suspension by reason of his conviction on some particular offence or perhaps on any offence. His very livelihood may depend upon the absence of a conviction in his record. These unfortunate consequences are too remote in character to be taken into account in weighing the seriousness of an offence by the punishment it may attract.
>
> The disqualification from holding a driving licence is in the same category because it amounts to the withdrawal of a right granted by the Act in a manner prescribed by the Act. The fact that the Act grants the holder of a licence or the person entitled to a licence the benefit of a judicial hearing on the question of disqualification itself and the fact that the judicial hearing is conducted by the person who imposes the conviction which in some eases is a necessary condition precedent to disqualification does not alter the nature of it. In so far as it may be classed as a punishment at all it is not a primary or direct punishment but rather an order which may, according to the circumstances of the particular individual concerned, assume, though remotely, a punitive character.
>
> One must not lose sight, however, of the real nature of the disqualification order which is that it is essentially a finding of unfitness of the person concerned to hold a driving

licence. Apart from the statutory minimum which is imposed in certain cases, this is a matter which must be determined by the Court in the light of evidence which it hears on this aspect of the case and in the light of that evidence it may determine what period of disqualification will be appropriate. A motor car, if not driven properly, is a potential danger not merely to the driver himself but to all other persons using the highway. It is obvious that the protection of the common good requires that the right to drive a motor car cannot be unrestricted. The right may therefore be lost if a Court, on a consideration of the relevant facts and materials, determines that the person concerned, by reason of his general recklessness or thoughtlessness or of his propensity to drink, or by reason of disease or other disability or his abuse of the right by exercising it in the furtherance of criminal activities, is unfit to exercise the right to drive a motor car. Such disqualification is not a punishment notwithstanding that the consequence of such finding of unfitness might be both socially and economically serious for the person concerned.... Undoubtedly disqualification may have a deterrent quality but that does not make it a punishment. It is a regulation of the exercise of a statutory right in the interest of public order and safety....

Though it may have punitive consequences disqualification cannot be regarded as a punishment in the sense in which that term is used in considering the gravity of an offence by reference to the punishment it may attract upon conviction such as imprisonment or a fine, but rather is a finding of unfitness. [1965] IR 411, at 440–442.

[2–74] This approach has been endorsed in a number of other cases, but criticised by Kelly:

Apart from the instinct which must protest against admitting – at any rate in the context of identifying a minor offence – any distinction between "primary" and "secondary" punishment, it seems wrong to present a forfeiture, revocation or disqualification as a "regulation" or "withdrawal" of a statutory right. The truth, historically, in this State or any other, must be that once upon a time everyone was free to sell drink, lay bets or travel in a vehicle; only when the State perceived a potential public injury in this uncontrolled liberty (in the case of the mechanically propelled vehicle, no doubt almost immediately after its emergence) was it proposed to avert this injury, or reduce the risk of it, by a regime of licensing. This was, if from the best of motives, a general though conditional curtailment of freedom, though not a punishment. To make, however, in the case of an individual infringing one of the terms on which limited freedom was still allowed him, a conditional liberty into an absolute deprivation of liberty in the sphere concerned, is a real punishment. This is how the Legislature which creates such disqualifying rules regards them, and how it marks as serious the infraction for which they are invoked. Measured against this fact, the superficial distinction between the modalities of punishment which underlies the words "primary" and "secondary" does not seem significant in the context of appraising the gravity of the offence. Gerard Hogan and Gerry Whyte eds, *Kelly: The Irish Constitution* (4th ed, Butterworths LexisNexis, 2003), at [6.5.305].

[2–75] In recent years, there have been very few cases on the question of what constitutes a non-minor offence. The heavy emphasis on the severity of punishment and the clarification on the issue of secondary punishment (notwithstanding Kelly's views) may have provided the certainty necessary for the Oireachtas to legislate without opening up the possibilities for too many constitutional challenges. It seems to be generally accepted that it is permissible to assign cases for summary (*ie*, to treat them as minor) trial if the term of imprisonment is 12 months or less and if (on the latest estimation) the monetary penalty is €5,000 or less.

[2–76] Once an offence is non-minor—and does not fall within the exception for special courts or military tribunals—the accused is entitled to a jury trial. The courts have consistently emphasised the value of jury trials. In *People (DPP) v O'Shea* [1982] IR 384, Henchy J put it in the following terms:

> I am satisfied that the indissoluble attachment to trial by jury of the right after acquittal to raise the plea of *autrefois acquit* was one of the prime reasons why the Constitution of 1937 (like that of 1922) mandated trial with a jury as the normal mode of trying major offences. The bitter Irish race-memory of politically appointed and Executive-oriented judges, of the suspension of jury trial in times of popular revolt, of the substitution therefor of summary trial or detention without trial, of cat-and-mouse releases from such detention, of packed juries and sometimes corrupt judges and prosecutors, had long implanted in the consciousness of the people and, therefore, in the minds of their political representatives, the conviction that the best way of preventing an individual from suffering a wrong conviction for an offence was to allow him to "put himself upon his country", that is to say, to allow him to be tried for that offence by a fair, impartial and representative jury, sitting in a court presided over by an impartial and independent judge appointed under the Constitution, who would see that all the requirements for a fair and proper jury trial would be observed, so that, amongst other things, if the jury's verdict were one of not guilty, the accused could leave court with the absolute assurance that he would never again "be vexed" for the same charge. [1982] IR 384, at 432–433.

[2–77] Although this statement formed part of a dissenting judgment as to whether the prosecution could appeal a jury acquittal to the Supreme Court (see chapter 17 for some discussion of this issue), it seems likely that there was considerable judicial agreement on the importance of the jury's role.

[2–78] In *de Búrca v Attorney General* [1976] IR 38, the Supreme Court held that sections of the Juries Act 1927 which limited jury service to ratepayers and exempted women from jury service (subject to a right to opt in) were unconstitutional. O'Higgins CJ and Walsh J approached the case on the basis of Art 40.1 (equality), agreeing that the exclusion of non-ratepayers was unconstitutional but disagreeing over whether the *prima facie* exemption of women was permissible (see chapter 3). The other members of the Court approached the case on the basis of Art 38.5. Henchy J identified the primary purpose of Art 38.5 and the method for assessing compliance with its provisions in the following terms:

> There is no doubt that the primary aim of section 5 of Article 38 in mandating trial by jury for criminal offences other than minor ones (and offences triable in special courts established under section 3, or in military tribunals established under section 4 of that Article) is to ensure that every person charged with such an offence will be assured of a trial in due course of law by a group of laymen who, chosen at random from a reasonably diverse panel of jurors drawn from the community, will produce a verdict of guilty or not guilty free from the risks inherent in a trial conducted by a judge or judges only, and which will therefore carry with it the assurance of both correctness and public acceptability that may be expected from the group verdict of such a representative cross-section of the community. Obviously, in order to carry out its constitutional function, a jury must have certain indispensable attributes in both its composition and its operation. However, neither the issues raised by the pleadings nor the scope of the argument would justify an attempt in this case to identify those attributes. In only one respect do the plaintiffs question the constitutionality of the jury that will try them; they question the representative character of the jury. They say it will be unrepresentative because of the requirements of a minimum rating qualification for eligibility to serve as a juror, and because of the right given to women to elect not to serve as jurors. In

determining whether a particular method of jury selection will produce a jury that fairly represents a cross-section of the community, it is not enough to show that a particular class or particular classes are not represented or are under-represented. Competence to fulfil the duties of a juror is an individual rather than a class attribute. No group or class can lay claim to have any special qualification to produce representative jurors. Ideally, as many identifiable groups and classes as possible should be included by the standard of eligibility employed, so that a jury drawn from the panel will be seen to be a random sample of the whole community of the relevant district. But, because jurors are drawn by lot, a particular jury may turn out to be quite unrepresentative of the community. The Constitution cannot be read as postulating a system of jury selection that will avoid that risk. Therefore, the Courts will not test the constitutionality of an impugned system of jury selection by seeing whether it provides the most comprehensive choice possible. Of course, the jury must be drawn from a pool broadly representative of the community so that its verdict will be stamped with the fairness and acceptability of a genuinely diffused community decision. The particular breadth of choice necessary to satisfy this requirement cannot be laid down in advance. It is left to the discretion of the legislature to formulate a system for the compilation of jury lists and panels from which will be recruited juries which will be competent, impartial and representative. We are not required in the present case to rule on the standards or procedures necessary to satisfy the requirements of competency and impartiality, for those are matters not raised by the issues in this litigation. What is called for—and this goes to the essence of this aspect of the case—is a judicial determination as to whether jury panels drawn exclusively from persons rated in respect of property of the prescribed rateable valuation can be said to be representative of the citizenry of the relevant jury district.

When a system of jury recruitment is assailed for being exclusionary to the point of unconstitutionality, the test is whether, by intent or operation, there is an exclusion of any class or group of citizens (other than those excluded for reasons based on capacity or social function) who, if included, might be expected to carry out their duties as jurors according to beliefs, standards, or attitudes not represented by those included. If such a class or group is excluded, it cannot be said that a resulting jury will be representative of the community. The exclusion will leave untapped a reservoir of potential jurors without whom the jurors' lists will lack constitutional completeness. [1976] IR 38, at 74–76.

[2–79] Applying this test for whether a method of jury selection ensured that juries were sufficiently representative, Henchy J held that the minimum rating qualification was unconstitutional:

The minimum rating qualification, in my opinion, produces that result. The line it draws between the eligible and the ineligible produces what some people would call a socio-economic classification. A rating qualification shuts the door on all citizens who are not liable to pay rates. This embargo is constitutionally objectionable not simply because it renders ineligible a substantial section of the citizenry but because it ensures that a jury will not include non-ratepayers. A jury so circumscribed in composition is no less wanting in the representativeness demanded by the guarantee in section 5 of Article 38 than would be a jury drawn from a panel confined to taxpayers. It excludes a range of mental attitudes which, because they will be absent from the jury-box and the jury-room, will leave an accused with no hope of the contribution they might make in the determination of guilt or innocence. This is particularly so in the trial of offences involving damage to property and, more particularly, in the trial of offences involving damage for which ratepayers are liable to make compensation. A jury which is so selective and exclusionary is not stamped with the genuine community representativeness necessary to classify it as the jury guaranteed by section 5 of Article 38. It is, therefore, unconstitutional. [1976] IR 38, at 76.

Henchy J came to a similar conclusion in relation to the exclusion of women: [2–80]

> In regard to the exemption of women, section 3 of the Act of 1927, in laying down the qualifications for jury service, excludes those who are disqualified or exempt. Section 5 of the Act, by reference to the first schedule, places women in the category of those who are exempt but who are entitled to serve if they make application. It is the exemption of *all* women, save those who opt for jury service, that the plaintiffs say is constitutionally objectionable. They concede that an exemption of certain women (such as mothers of young children) on the ground of capacity or social function would be constitutionally permissible. But it is their case that the total exemption of women (unless they opt for jury service) is neither necessary nor desirable—that in practice it produces juries which are exclusively male and that, as a result, an accused who has to stand trial before such a jury does not get the jury trial to which he or she is constitutionally entitled.
>
> There is no doubt that a consequence of the exemption of women, unless they claim eligibility, is that women hardly ever serve on juries. Official records show that out of the hundreds of jury trials of criminal offences that took place in this State in the ten years prior to 1973, and out of the thousands of jurors who served in that period, only two women did jury service. For practical purposes, therefore, jury service is a male preserve and the plaintiffs are correct in saying that the operation of the statutory exemption of women virtually ensures that the jury before whom they will stand trial will be entirely male. True, the Act of 1927 does not compel this result but, in erecting a rating qualification which in this society rules out most women and in requiring further that those women not thus excluded should elect for inclusion, the Act of 1927 is the foundation on which the all-male jury rests. If the all-male jury is constitutionally unacceptable, the statutory exemption of women cannot stand.
>
> In my judgment, a system of jury selection which operates so that there is a total absence of women from juries amounts to a denial of the right to trial by jury assured by Article 38.5. It is the result of the operation of the Act of 1927 that must be considered in determining whether an accused person's constitutional rights have been infringed. The absence of women from juries is due, in part, to the permissiveness of the Act in allowing women to remain exempt unless they claim eligibility and, in part, to the almost universal way in which women themselves have used that permissiveness to avoid what they apparently consider to be the unwelcome task of serving on juries. For the purposes of an accused person who impugns the jury system on the ground of unrepresentativeness, the Act of 1927 stands condemned in that the unrepresentativeness would not exist without the statutory provisions as to the eligibility of women.
>
> The absence of women from juries means an unconstitutional system of selection for two reasons. First, it fails the test of representativeness because it means that some 50% of the adult population will never be included in the jury lists. Granted that many of the women who make up that 50% would be entitled to exemption on personal grounds such as pregnancy; nevertheless, the fact remains that a whole swathe of the citizenry (including some 200,000 single women) will be outside the range of choice open to an accused person facing a trial by jury. Secondly, and of even greater importance, that narrowed choice means that a woman's experience, understanding, and general attitude will form no part in the jury processes leading to a verdict. Whatever may have been the position at common law or under statute up to recent times, it is incompatible with the necessary diffusion of rights and duties in a modern democratic society that important public decisions such as voting, or jury verdicts involving life or liberty, should be made by male citizens only. What is missing in decisions so made is not easy to define; but reason and experience show that such decisions are not calculated to lead to a sense of general acceptability, or to carry an acceptable degree of representativeness, or to have the necessary stamp of responsibility and involvement on the part of the community as a

whole. Juries recruited in that way fall short of minimum constitutional standards no less than would juries recruited entirely from female citizens.

While the plaintiffs have not shown that their chances of a fair trial will be diminished because the jury will be all-male, and while it is not possible to ensure a mixed jury, nevertheless the statutory provisions which operate to make an all-male jury virtually certain, thus depriving the plaintiffs of any real chance of having a mixed jury, cannot be reconciled with the choice of jurors necessarily comprehended by Article 38.5. Those statutory provisions must therefore be held unconstitutional.

The result is that the system of jury selection laid down by the Juries Act, 1927, because it is based on a minimum rating qualification and results in the invariable absence of women from juries, is to that extent constitutionally defective as it does not produce the jury guaranteed by Article 38.5 of the Constitution. [1976] IR 38, at 76–78.

[2–81] Although *de Búrca* established that juries had to be representative, it is not clear what other requirements flow from the guarantee of jury trial in Art 38.5. In his judgment, Walsh J made clear that it was not necessarily the case that all the historical incidents of jury trial (12 members, unanimous verdicts, *etc*) were constitutionally mandated. The Oireachtas was entitled to adapt the jury system. This was borne out by the subsequent case of *O'Callaghan v Attorney General* [1993] 2 IR 17, in which the Supreme Court upheld the constitutionality of s 25 of the Criminal Justice Act 1984 which allowed jury verdicts to be by majority provided there are at least 11 jurors and 10 of them agree. This covers the situation where a juror might withdraw from a trial due to ill health or some other reason. The Supreme Court rejected the claim that the lack of a requirement for unanimity was unconstitutional, Finlay CJ delivering the judgment of the Court:

> The purpose of trial by jury is to provide that a person shall get a fair trial, in due course of law, and be tried by a reasonable cross-section of people acting under the guidance of the judge, bound by his directions on law, but free to make their findings as to the facts. The essential feature of a jury trial is to interpose, between the accused and the prosecution, people who will bring their experience and commonsense to bear on resolving the issue of the guilt or innocence of the accused. A requirement of unanimity is not essential to this purpose.
>
> *Advantages of majority verdicts*
> Majority verdicts such as are permitted in the impugned legislation may rebound to the advantage of the accused as well as to the prosecution on occasion; the chances of a disagreement are reduced and the aim of the zealot who glories in dissent and who may make his or her way onto a jury from time to time is defeated. Sufficient protection is provided in the legislation to give enough time to a minority to win others over to their point of view. The delicate balance required to give effect to the constitutional mandate of jury trials in criminal cases involving non-minor offences is preserved in the legislation. The Court approves what the learned High Court Judge said, that "a decision might lose its character of being a decision of the jury if the majority required was substantially lowered". The Court agrees with his view that where the majority has to be at least a majority of ten it cannot be objected that a decision by such a majority is not the decision of the jury. [1993] 2 IR 17, at 25–26.

[2–82] The courts have had some difficulty in deciding the precise role of the jury in relation to trials for criminal contempt of court. In *State (DPP) v Walsh* [1981] IR 412, the Supreme Court held that the offence of criminal contempt of court was peculiarly within the control and summary jurisdiction of the courts, distinct from the substantive criminal law to which Art 38.5 pertained. However, an accused contemptor would have a right to jury trial on a disputed issue of fact that might arise in a trial for criminal contempt. This introduces an unusual distinction into the jury's role. Moreover, it is difficult to see why (at least from the perspective of the accused person or based on a reading of the constitutional text) the non-minor offence of contempt of court should be treated differently from other non-minor offences.

No Retroactive Penal Sanctions

The most obvious constitutional limit on the content of the criminal law is provided by Art 15.5.1° of the Constitution: [2–83]

> The Oireachtas shall not declare acts to be infringements of the law which were not so at the date of their commission.

This principle is one of the cornerstones of the Rule of Law and it is appropriate for it to receive explicit constitutional protection. Perhaps because of this explicit protection, it has not been judicially considered in many cases. However, in *Doyle v An Taoiseach* [1986] ILRM 693, the Supreme Court confirmed—applying the double construction rule—that legislation declaring acts to be infringements of the law should be read as having only prospective effect if possible. In *Magee v Culligan* [1992] 1 IR 233, the Supreme Court confirmed that Art 15.5.1° applied to the civil law as much as the criminal law. [2–84]

In 2001, the people enacted Art 15.5.2° of the Constitution, prohibiting the Oireachtas from enacting any law providing for the imposition of the death penalty. [2–85]

Vague Criminal Offences

The courts have also inferred from the Constitution certain norms governing the substance of the criminal law. In *King v Attorney General* [1981] IR 233, the Supreme Court struck down parts of s 4 of the Vagrancy Act 1824 which created the offence of "loitering with intent" which applied to "every suspected person or reputed thief" who was proved to have been frequenting or loitering in various public places "with intent to commit a felony". To prove the intent it was not necessary to prove any overt act; the intent could be inferred from the circumstances and from the accused's previous convictions. Henchy J identified the following constitutional defects in this criminal offence: [2–86]

> In my opinion, the ingredients of the offence and the mode by which its commission may be proved are so arbitrary, so vague, so difficult to rebut, so related to rumour or ill-repute or past conduct, so ambiguous in failing to distinguish between apparent and real behaviour of a criminal nature, so prone to make a man's lawful occasions become unlawful and criminal by the breadth and arbitrariness of the discretion that is vested in both the prosecutor and the judge, so indiscriminately contrived to mark as criminal conduct committed by one person in certain circumstances when the same conduct, when engaged in by another person in similar circumstances, would be free of the taint of criminality, so out of keeping with the basic concept inherent in our legal system that a man may walk abroad in the secure knowledge that he will not be singled out from his fellow-citizens and branded and punished as a criminal unless it has been established beyond reasonable doubt that he has deviated from a clearly prescribed standard of conduct, and generally so singularly at variance with both the explicit and implicit characteristics and limitations of the criminal law as to the onus of proof and mode of proof, that it is not so much a question of ruling unconstitutional the type of offence we are now considering as identifying the particular constitutional provisions with which such an offence is at variance.

> I shall confine myself to saying, without going into unnecessary detail, that the offence, both in its essential ingredients and in the mode of proof of its commission, violates the requirement in Article 38.1, that no person shall be tried on any criminal charge save in due course of law; that it violates the guarantee in Article 40.4.1, that no citizen shall be deprived of personal liberty save in accordance with law—which means without stooping to methods which ignore the fundamental norms of the legal order postulated by the Constitution; that, in its arbitrariness and its unjustifiable discrimination, it fails to hold (as is required by Article 40.1) all citizens to be equal before the law: and that it ignores the guarantees in Article 40.3, that the personal rights of citizens shall be respected and, as far as practicable, defended and vindicated, and that the State shall by its laws protect as best it may from unjust attack and, in the case of injustice done, vindicate the life, person, good name, and property rights of every citizen.

[2–87] It is apparent from this reasoning that substantive provisions of the criminal law must be certain. What is less clear is the precise textual basis for this conclusion. The constitutional rule against vague criminal offences was almost assumed to be self-evident.

Blameworthiness

[2–88] More recently, the courts have identified some level of constitutional protection for *mens rea* requirements. In *Re Article 26 and the Employment Equality Bill 1996* [1996] 2 IR 321, the Supreme Court considered the constitutionality of, *inter alia*, ss 15 and 16 of the Bill. In effect, s 15 imposed vicarious criminal liability on an employer for acts of an employee that infringed s 14 (unlawful discrimination and victimisation), subject to the defence that the employer took such steps as were reasonably practicable to prevent the employee from infringing s 14. The Court held that this breached both Art 38.1 and Art 40.1 of the Constitution:

> [T]he Court is of the opinion that the conditions by which [the offences] may be held to pass muster under our present constitutional system is that...they should essentially be regulatory in character; apply where a person has a particular privilege (such as a licence) or a duty to make sure that public standards as regards health or safety or the environment or the protection of the consumer, and such like, are upheld, and where it might be difficult, invidious or redundant to seek to make the employee liable.
>
> However, what is sought to be done by this provision is that an employer, devoid of any guilty intent, is liable to be found guilty on indictment of an offence carrying a fine of £15,000 or a prison sentence of two years, or both such fine and imprisonment, and to be tainted with guilt for offences which are far from being regulatory in character but are likely to attract a substantial measure of opprobrium. The social policy of making the Act more effective does not, in the opinion of this Court, justify the introduction of so radical a change to our criminal law. The change appears to the Court to be quite disproportionate to the mischief with which the section seeks to deal.
>
> The Court concludes that to render an employer liable to potentially severe criminal sanctions in circumstances which are so unjust, irrational and inappropriate would make any purported trial of such a person not one held in due course of law and, therefore, contrary to Article 38.1 of the Constitution and also repugnant to the provisions of Article 40.1 of the Constitution. [1996] 2 IR 321, at 374–375.

[2–89] This case appeared to suggest a general principle that, outside the domain of regulatory offences, it was constitutionally impermissible to provide for criminal offences that had no *mens rea* element. In *C v Ireland (No 2)* [2006] IESC 33, the Supreme Court—in effect—stated this general principle. This judgment followed on from that in *C v Ireland (No 1)* [2005] IESC 48, in which the Supreme Court held that s

1(1) of the Criminal Law (Amendment) Act 1935 did not allow an accused person to plead a reasonable mistake as to age as a defence to a charge of unlawful carnal knowledge of a girl under the age of 15 years. Mr C, who was charged with having on several occasions had unlawful carnal knowledge of a female under the age of 15, then challenged the constitutionality of s 1(1) on the grounds that he was unable to plead in his defence that he had a reasonable belief that the complainant was over the age of 15.

Hardiman J, with whom all other members of the Court agreed, noted the absolute character of the offence: once the *actus reus* was established, no defence was open to the accused person. He reasoned that it was proper to assess the seriousness of the offence by reference to the maximum punishment that could be ordered. The maximum sentence of penal servitude for life, the social stigma attached to the offence and the consequences of enrolment on the Sexual Offenders Register combined to render the offence created by s 1(1) very serious. Hardiman J reasoned: [2–90]

> It appears to us that to criminalise in a serious way a person who is mentally innocent is indeed "to inflict a grave injury on that person's dignity and sense of worth" and to treat him as "little more than a means to an end", in the words of Wilson J quoted earlier in this judgment. It appears to us that this, in turn, constitutes a failure by the State in its laws to respect, defend and vindicate the rights to liberty and to good name of the person so treated, contrary to the State's obligations under Article 40 of the Constitution. These rights seem fundamental in the sense of that word as used in *Jedowski*; cited above....
>
> The English decisions, of course, were addressing matters of construction and not of compatibility with a Constitution. But they, like this Court in the Employment Equality Bill case, and like the Canadian Supreme Court in the cases cited, speak powerfully to the central importance of a requirement for mental guilt before conviction of a serious criminal offence, and the central position of that value in a civilised system of justice. Speaking of such a system in a constitutional context, O'Higgins CJ in *The State (Healy) v Donoghue* [1976] IR 325 said:
>
>> "In the first place the concept of justice, which is specifically referred to in the preamble in relation to the freedom and dignity of the individual appears again in the provisions of Article 34 which deals with the Courts. It is justice which is to be administered in the Courts and this concept of justice must import not only fairness and fair procedures, but also regard to the dignity of the individual. No court under the Constitution has jurisdiction to act contrary to justice."
>
> I cannot regard a provision which criminalises and exposes to a maximum sentence of life imprisonment a person without mental guilt as respecting the liberty or the dignity of the individual or as meeting the obligation imposed on the State by Article 40.3.1 of the Constitution....

Hardiman J rejected any utilitarian justification (*eg*, the protection of young girls) for the abrogation of the right of an accused person not to be convicted of a true criminal offence in the absence of *mens rea*. It is this heavy emphasis on dignity that appears to provide the philosophical underpinning for this development in constitutional law. On this argument, the state must respect each individual as an independent, autonomous agent. Individuals must not be treated as means to an end. Accordingly, as a matter of constitutional law (as well as criminal law theory), it is impermissible for the state to punish people for crimes of which they are mentally innocent. Although s 1(1) of the Criminal Law Act 1935 was unquestionably a serious offence (or a "true crime", if one prefers that terminology), it is possible that Hardiman J's comments may have some application to less serious (or "regulatory") offences. [2–91]

CONTENTS – CHAPTER 3

Equality

Introduction.	[3–01]
Formal Equality.	[3–03]
Aristotelian Equality.	[3–07]
Legitimate Recognition of Difference.	[3–07]
Other Legitimate Reasons for Legislative Discrimination	[3–21]
No Obligation to Treat Unequals Unequally	[3–24]
Standards of Review.	[3–26]
Levelling Up or Down	[3–29]
Indirect Discrimination.	[3–31]
The Human Personality Doctrine.	[3–33]

Overview

The courts have generally interpreted Art 40.1 in a less than robust fashion. Although Art 40.1 protects formal equality (the equal application of rules to those covered by the rules), it has also been held to protect Aristotelian equality, requiring that legislative differentiation should reflect real differences. The courts have been generally sceptical of discriminations based on sex. However, the courts have been far quicker to strike down outdated common law rules that are based on the view that women were subservient to men than they have been to strike down modern legislation that discriminates against men in the general context of parenting. The courts have held that discriminations are justified where they reflect a real difference, where they are relevant to a legitimate legislative purpose or where they advance another constitutional value, such as respect for the marital family. In applying such tests, the courts have been deferential to the legislature's assessment of the issues.

The courts relied on the phrase "as human persons" to restrict the ambit of the equality guarantee, particularly in the 1960s, 1970s and 1980s. The courts gave two interpretations to this phrase. One held that only discriminations that arose in the context of a person's essential human attributes could be held unconstitutional. Applying this interpretation, the courts never identified any such discrimination. The other interpretation held that discriminations based on an assumption that some humans are intrinsically inferior by reason of their human attributes could be unconstitutional. More recently the courts appear to have adapted this latter interpretation to suggest that discriminations based on essential human attributes, such as race and sex, require a greater level of justification from the State.

Chapter 3

Equality

Introduction

Article 40.1 of the Constitution provides: [3–01]

> All citizens shall, as human persons, be held equal before the law.
> This shall not be held to mean that the State shall not in its enactments have due regard to individual differences of capacity, physical and moral, and of social function.

This is the first of the fundamental rights guaranteed by the Constitution. It has generally been interpreted in a restrictive way by the courts. Different aspects of the guarantee—"as human persons", "equal before the law" and "due regard to differences"—have all been relied on by the courts to produce a constitutional equality doctrine that is less robust than it might have been. Furthermore, the guarantee has traditionally been subordinated to constitutional guarantees of apparently more substantive rights, such as respect for the marital family. That said, in the past decade Art 40.1 has become a more useful constitutional guarantee for litigants. It may be that the current generation of judges—accustomed to applying the non-discrimination guarantees of European Community law, as well as domestic legislation such as the Employment Equality Acts 1998–2004 and the Equal Status Acts 2000–2004—may be more prepared to develop some of the potential of this constitutional provision. [3–02]

Formal Equality

Foundational documents, such as constitutions, tend to guarantee equality (in some form), whereas legislation tends to prohibit particular types of discrimination. Different formulae are used to guarantee equality, the most common being "equal protection of the laws" and "equality before the law". On a purely textual analysis, "equality before the law" might appear to protect purely formal equality. This is a requirement merely that a rule or law be applied equally to all to whom it is stated to apply. Such a requirement allows for no scrutiny of whether the law or rule itself respects equality, *ie* whether the distinctions drawn by the rule or law are permissible. On occasion, the courts have interpreted Article 40.1 in this way. In *People (DPP) v Quilligan (No 3)* [1993] 2 IR 305, the Supreme Court considered a challenge to the constitutionality of s 30 of the Offences Against the State Act 1939, which allowed persons suspected of committing certain subversive-type offences to be detained for up to 48 hours prior to being charged. Among the grounds on which the legislation was challenged was Art 40.1. The Supreme Court rejected this, Finlay CJ reasoning: [3–03]

> Every person who is suspected of the commission of an offence under the Act of 1939 or an offence scheduled for the purposes of that Act is subject in law to the same rights and obligations and to the possibility of detention for the same period or periods.... The mere fact that a law discriminates as between one group or category of persons and another

does not, of itself, render it constitutionally invalid. What is necessary to establish such invalidity is the existence of invidious discrimination, and the court is satisfied that that has not been established with regard to section 30 of the Act of 1939 in this case. [1993] 2 IR 305, at 320–321.

[3–04] In this passage, Finlay CJ seemed to imply that the fact that the impugned law applied only to those to whom it was stated to apply rescued it from any inconsistency with Art 40.1. But what if the distinctions drawn by the law itself were objectionable? Should a law making it an offence for black people to use a particular beach satisfy Art 40.1 on the grounds that it applies to all black people? In general, the courts have not interpreted Art 40.1 in this narrow fashion. Perhaps implicit textual authorisation for the broader approach can be found in the second sentence of Art 40.1. This authorises the State to draw certain types of distinctions in its legislation. If the first sentence of Art 40.1 did not preclude the State from drawing distinctions in general, such an explicit authorisation would not be necessary.

[3–05] Just because Art 40.1 is not limited to a protection of formal equality, however, does not mean that formal equality is not protected by the guarantee. In *Purcell v Attorney General* [1995] 3 IR 287; [1996] 2 ILRM 153, the Supreme Court held that, where an Act of the Oireachtas evidenced no intention to discriminate between persons to whom the Act applied, it would be unconstitutional for such discriminations to be introduced into the administration of the Act. Indeed, the courts have relied on Art 40.1 to develop a general obligation of consistency for state officials. In *McMahon v Leahy* [1984] IR 525, the plaintiff challenged an extradition order made against him. The plaintiff was accused of escaping from lawful custody in Northern Ireland a few years previously. A number of others had escaped with him but had been arrested shortly after their escape. However, their release had been ordered on the basis that their offence was "a political offence or an offence connected with a political offence", an exception under the legislation. The State had not contested the release of two of these persons and had not appealed against the orders for the release of the other two. In the intervening years, however, the courts had changed their interpretation of the political offence exception with the result that the plaintiff would no longer fall within the exception. O'Higgins CJ rejected the State's submission that each application for the political offence exception had to be considered separately:

> If the State were successful in this submission, it would mean that contradictory declarations in relation to the same incident would have issued from our Courts. If such occurred, respect for the administration of justice in our Courts would surely suffer, and the Courts' process would certainly have been abused.... In such circumstances, could it be said that all these five citizens had been held equal before the law? This obligation to provide equal treatment for citizens of the State is ordained by Article 40 of the Constitution. It is the clear duty of the Courts to see this duty discharged. [1984] IR 525, at 537–538.

[3–06] This obligation of consistency still has some force in Irish law, being cited in cases such as *Hanley v Minister for Defence* [1999] 4 IR 392, by Denham J, in support of a method for ensuring consistency in compensation awards for army deafness. However, it is doubtful if it still applies in relation to decisions taken by prosecutorial authorities. In *Byrne v Government of Ireland*, 11 March 1999 (SC), the Supreme Court refused to invalidate a decision of the Director of Public Prosecutions (DPP) to return certain persons for trial in the Special Criminal Court when other persons, charged in relation to the same incident, were returned for trial to the Circuit Criminal Court. Hamilton CJ held that the DPP's decision could only be quashed if there were evidence of mala fides on his part. Absent such bad faith, the DPP was under no enforceable obligation to act consistently.

Aristotelian Equality

Legitimate Recognition of Difference

Notwithstanding the dicta of Finlay CJ in *Quilligan*, the courts have generally interpreted Art 40.1 in a non-formal manner. The approach generally adopted by the courts has often been referred to as the Aristotelian understanding of equality. This is because it reflects Aristotle's understanding of equality: [3–07]

> For equals share alike in the honourable and the just, as is just and equal. But that the unequal should be given to equals, and the unlike to those who are alike, is contrary to nature, and nothing which is contrary to nature is good. Aristotle, *Politics* VII.3, at 5, *et seq*. Translated by Benjamin Jowett (Oxford, 1885).

This captures the idea that all persons are different and that affording sameness of treatment to those who are differently situated would be unjust. In short, equals should be treated equally and unequals should be treated unequally. This approach was most explicitly stated by Walsh J in *de Búrca v Attorney General* [1976] IR 38, in which the plaintiffs challenged certain provisions of the Juries Act 1927. Section 3(1) of that Act provided that a person would be qualified and liable for jury service if the rateable valuation of his or her land equalled or exceeded the minimum rating qualifications prescribed for that jury district by the Minister for Justice. Section 5 provided that certain classes of persons would be exempted from jury service but could opt in to such service. Although 10 of these classifications were based on the occupation of the persons concerned, the first was based on sex: women were exempted from jury service unless they specifically applied to be on the jury register. Although there were over 700,000 women in the age bracket of 20–64, in 1975 only nine had been inserted on the list of jurors. The plaintiffs challenged both of these discriminations. Walsh J summarised the requirements of Art 40.1 as follows: [3–08]

> Article 40 does not require identical treatment of all persons without recognition of differences in relevant circumstances but it forbids invidious or arbitrary discrimination. It imports the Aristotelian concept that justice demands that we treat equals equally and unequals unequally. [1976] IR 38, at 68.

This approach requires an identification of relevant differences. If a difference naturally existing between two classes of persons is relevant to the matter being regulated by the legislation, it is permissible for the legislation to reflect that distinction and discriminate accordingly. If the difference is irrelevant, however, the legislation cannot reflect that distinction. In *de Búrca*, O'Higgins CJ and Walsh J addressed the case on the basis of Art 40.1, the other judges relying on the right to a jury trial protected by Art 38.5. It is instructive to consider how each addressed the question of whether the distinctions drawn by the Juries Act were relevant to the matter being regulated. Walsh J addressed the property qualification in the following way: [3–09]

> The property qualification undoubtedly discriminates between those citizens who have the qualification and those who have not and does so solely upon the basis of the amount of the poor-law valuation of property in a particular district. This property qualification could not conceivably be said to refer to the physical or moral capacity of a prospective juror. Can it seriously be suggested that a person who is not the rated occupier of any property, or who is not the rated occupier of property of a certain value, is less intelligent or less honest or less impartial than one who is so rated? The answer can only be in the negative. Can such a discrimination be based on social function? Just as a man's intelligence and honesty is not directly or at all proportionate to the poor-law valuation of his house or lands, which seems to be the underlying assumption of the property qualification, so it cannot be said that such a qualification marks him out as having a social function which makes him more fitted for jury service than another—if, indeed, it does in any way constitute a social function within the meaning of Article 40.1, of the Constitution.
>
> If a case could be made for having a property qualification, it could not reasonably be confined to one particular type of property. It would be just as rational to suggest that jury service should be confined to the owners of motor cars exceeding a certain horse-power, or motor cars of more than a certain value. This particular type of property qualification totally ignores the realities of wealth. A man may be a most highly-qualified person for jury service and may be a very wealthy man and yet he may not be the rated occupier of any property. On the other hand, the rated occupier of property may be illiterate and poverty stricken; he may even be a person of unsound mind. For the reasons I have stated, I am of opinion that such discrimination as is created by the distinction between the rated occupier of property of a certain value and everybody else is one that is inconsistent with and violates Article 40.1, of the Constitution and, therefore, is a distinction which could not be validly the subject of legislation by the Oireachtas. [1976] IR 38, at 68–69.

[3–10] Although Walsh J and O'Higgins CJ agreed that the property qualification was relevant, they disagreed over the relevance of the sex discrimination. O'Higgins CJ reasoned as follows:

> In this respect it is submitted that the provisions of the Act of 1927, in so far as they exempt women as such, constitute a discrimination which is invidious and contrary to Article 40.1, of the Constitution. It is urged that this discrimination cannot be excused by the second sentence of Article 40.1, which permits the State to have regard in its enactments to differences of capacity, physical and moral, and of social function. In the context of this case it seems to me to be immaterial whether jury service is regarded as an obligation or burden, or as a right. The fact is that under the Act of 1927 men and women are treated differently. The names of qualified male citizens are entered, by force of the statute, on the appropriate jury list for service as jurors, whereas the names of qualified women citizens can only so appear after application for inclusion is made by each woman concerned. That this is discrimination can scarcely be denied. The question is whether this is discrimination of a kind which can fairly be described as being invidious: see Ó Dálaigh CJ in *O'Brien v Keogh*.
>
> Article 40 permits the State to have regard in its laws to differences of capacity, physical and moral, and of social function. It does not seem incongruous or inappropriate for the State, under this Article, to temper or cushion obligations generally imposed in so far as they affect women. In particular, one would expect this to be done under a Constitution which expressly recognises that by her life within the home, woman gives to the State a support without which the common good cannot be achieved: see section 2 of Article 41. Where, therefore, as in the case of jury service, the State imposes on all citizens an obligation to serve, the discharge of which necessarily takes the citizen concerned away

Equality

from his occupation and his home, special provisions must obviously be made in respect of women. In my view. such special provision is permissible under the second sentence of section 1 of Article 40 and is almost mandatory under section 2 of Article 41. Such special provision could be made by putting all women citizens of the prescribed ages on the jury lists, and by providing that each of them must serve on being duly called unless she applies to have her name removed. In the Act of 1927 special provision has been made by providing that no woman citizen shall appear on the jury list unless she applies for inclusion. In either case there is a recognition of the woman's right to serve, but there is also a recognition that for many women jury service could be a severe burden and handicap. The State, therefore, while recognising and safeguarding the right, permits each woman to decide for herself, in accordance with her own circumstances and special responsibilities, whether service on a jury is a right she ought to exercise or a burden she ought to undertake. I cannot see how this can be regarded as an invidious discrimination. In my view, it is not invidious, unjust, or unfair having regard to the Constitution as a whole. The important feature of such special provision is that the decision is left to the woman herself, and the right to serve is preserved for her. [1976] IR 38, at 58–60.

O'Higgins CJ reasoned that it was appropriate for the State to "temper or cushion" obligations that apply to women. Walsh J took a different approach: [3–11]

It is undoubtedly true that the Constitution, in dealing with the family, draws attention to and stresses the importance of woman's life within the home and makes special provision for the economic protection of mothers who have home duties: see section 2 of Article 41. Women fulfil many functions in society in addition to, or instead of, those mentioned in section 2 of Article 41. Women are actively engaged in all of the professions, in most branches of business, in art and literature, and in virtually every human activity; this is scarcely surprising in the light of the fact that women constitute approximately one half of the adult human race. In this State approximately half the adult population consists of women; in urban areas, which are the most likely source of prospective jurors, there are more women than men. According to the 1971 census, there were just over 700,000 women in the age group of 20–64 years; of these, approximately 200,000 were unmarried, 470,000 were married and approximately 38,000 were widows. According to figures provided by the Department of Justice for the ten years immediately preceding the hearing of this action and put in evidence at the hearing, the total number of women whose names were inserted in the jurors' lists under section 16 of the Act of 1927 was the startlingly low figure of 9; the numbers who were called for jury service and who served on juries were 5 and 2 respectively.

Within the terms of Article 40.1, of the Constitution, the reference to social function, as well as the reference to physical and moral capacity, is applicable to both sexes. The evidence in this case indicates that a very small number of those women who are eligible for jury service have volunteered for jury service, or have succeeded in serving when they volunteered. Even assuming that the vast majority of women [do] not wish to serve on juries, in itself that is not a good ground for legislative discrimination in their favour. From one viewpoint, jury service may be regarded as a privilege but from another an exemption from jury service may be regarded as a privilege—just as liberty to avoid any obligation or duty which falls on other people may be regarded as a privilege. The question is whether the "privilege" is of a type which can be validly conferred by statute. There can be little doubt that the Oireachtas could validly enact statutory provisions which could have due regard, within the provisions of Article 40, to differences of capacity both physical and moral and of social function in so far as jury service is concerned. For example, it could provide that all mothers with young children could be exempt from jury service. On virtually the same considerations, it could provide that all widowers, husbands with invalid wives, and husbands deserted by their wives would be entitled to a similar exemption if they were looking after their young children. It might also provide exemptions for the proprietors of one-man businesses who have no assistance, whether the proprietors be men or women. It could provide that certain occupations, such as a general practitioner in the medical profession (whether man or woman), be exempt because of the importance of the social function fulfilled by persons of such occupation.

However, the provision made in the Act of 1927, is undisguisedly discriminatory on the ground of sex only. It would not be competent for the Oireachtas to legislate on the basis that women, by reason only of their sex, are physically or morally incapable of serving and acting as jurors. The statutory provision does not seek to make any distinction between the different functions that women may fulfil and it does not seek to justify the discrimination on the basis of any social function. It simply lumps together half of the members of the adult population, most of whom have only one thing in common, namely, their sex. In my view, it is not open to the State to discriminate in its enactments between the persons who are subject to its laws solely upon the ground of the sex of those persons. If a reference is to be made to the sex of a person, then the purpose of the law that makes such a discrimination should be to deal with some physical or moral capacity or social function that is related exclusively or very largely to that sex only. [1976] IR 38, at 70–71.

[3–12] As with O'Higgins CJ, relevance is the touchstone for Walsh J. However, he assesses the relevance of the distinction in a different way. Although he notes that distinctions between some women (pregnant mothers for example) and others would be relevant to the issue of who should be obliged to sit on juries, he considers that the bald distinction between all men and all women is not relevant to the matter being regulated. In a sense, the difference between the sexes (an easy to state and recognise ground of distinction) cannot be used as a convenient proxy for other relevant grounds of distinction.

[3–13] If relevant difference suffices to justify a discrimination, two potentially troubling consequences arise. First, the more deeply entrenched the difference between two classes of persons is perceived to be, the more likely the courts are to uphold a legislative discrimination that reflects the difference. But perhaps the perception of difference is itself a cause of concern for equality. Viewed from this perspective, it is arguable that the reason for the conflicting approaches of Walsh J and O'Higgins CJ was simply that Walsh J did not perceive any broad and general distinction between the sexes (that was relevant to the issue at hand) whereas O'Higgins CJ did. This raises the danger that objectionable discriminations may be upheld and buttressed simply because they are so persistent and entrenched that they appear to the courts to be reflective of reality.

[3–14] Secondly, and more subtly, if relevant difference is the touchstone of inequality, it is arguable that a person must demonstrate that she is the same as the person who already receives the preferential treatment in order to receive that treatment herself. Writing in the US context, MacKinnon J has been scathingly critical of this approach to equality:

> Unquestioned is how difference is socially created or defined, who sets the point of reference for sameness, or the comparative empirical approach itself. Why should anyone have to be like white men to get what they have, given that white men do not have to be like anyone except each other to have it? Since men have defined women as different to the extent that they are female, can women be entitled to equal treatment only to the extent that they are not women? Why is equality as consistent with systematic advantage as with systematic disadvantage, so long as both correlate with differences? Catherine MacK-

innon, "Reflection on Sex Equality under Law" 100 *Yale Law Journal* 1281, at 1287 (1991).

Some of these difficulties can be seen in a number of other cases in which the courts have addressed discriminations on the basis of sex. These cases can broadly be divided into two types. On the one hand, the courts have rather summarily held unconstitutional a number of archaic common law rules that discriminated against women in their civil status. On the other hand, the courts have been far more circumspect in addressing more recent legislative discriminations against men in the context of their family and social lives. [3–15]

In *State (DPP) v Walsh* [1981] IR 412, the Supreme Court held that the common law defence of coercion, which had been available to a wife in respect of certain offences if the act was done by her in the presence of her husband, had not been carried over by Art 50 of the Constitution. This defence operated as a prima facie presumption which could be rebutted by evidence of initiative on the part of the wife. Henchy J reasoned: [3–16]

> A legal rule that presumes, even on a *prima facie* and rebuttable basis, that a wife has been coerced by the physical presence of her husband into committing an act prohibited by the criminal law, particularly when a similar presumption does not operate in favour of a husband for acts committed in the presence of his wife, is repugnant to the concept of equality before the law guaranteed by the first sentence of [Article 40.1] and could not, under the second sentence of that Article, be justified as a discrimination based on any difference of capacity or of social function between husband and wife. [1981] IR 412, at 450.

Note that, compared with *de Búrca*, there is very little consideration of whether the discrimination could reflect any difference between men and women that is relevant to the matter being regulated. Based on similar reasoning, the courts have struck down common law rules that a father's authority over his children was paramount (*Re Tilson* [1951] IR 1), that the courts could not admit a wife's evidence to prove that a child borne during wedlock was not that of her husband (*S v S* [1983] IR 68) and that a wife was deemed to have the domicile of her husband (*W v W* [1993] 2 IR 476). In all these cases, it was nearly taken as self-evident that the common law rule at issue infringed Art 40.1. A possible side-effect of this has been that the courts have not built up a large body of case law to help identify whether a particular measure (whether legislative or common law in character) infringes the equality guarantee. When addressing legislative measures, however, the courts have generally been slower to conclude that the discrimination was not based on a relevant difference. For example, in *State (Nicolau) v An Bord Uchtála* [1966] IR 567, the Supreme Court rejected an argument that provisions of the Adoption Act 1952 unfairly discriminated against unmarried fathers as compared with unmarried mothers. Sections 14(1) and 16(1) of the Act excluded all persons from the adoption process, except the specified persons. Section 14(1) provided that the consent of the child's mother, guardian or person having charge of or control over the child had to be obtained prior the making of an adoption order, save in specified circumstances. These persons also had a right, under s 16(1) to be heard prior to the making of an adoption order, as did a number of other persons. However, the natural father had no such role. In this case, the natural father claimed that the sections of the Act discriminated against him on the basis of his sex. Walsh J, unlike his [3–17] judgment a decade later in *de Búrca*, considered that the discrimination here was relevant to a real difference:

> When it is considered that an illegitimate child may be begotten by an act of rape, by a callous seduction or by an act of casual commerce by a man with a woman, as well as by the association of a man with a woman in making a common home without marriage in circumstances approximating to those of married life, and that, except in the latter instance, it is rare for a natural father to take any interest in his offspring, it is not difficult to appreciate the differences in moral capacity and social function between the natural father and the several persons described in the sub-sections in question. [1966] IR 567, at 641.

[3–18] In *de Búrca*, Walsh J held that sex could not be used as a legislative ground of discrimination where there was a reason to exclude only some women from jury service. In *Nicolau*, however, he allowed sex to be used as a legislative ground of discrimination where only some men (rapists, callous seducers and those engaged in casual acts of commerce) should be excluded.

[3–19] In *O'G v Attorney General* [1985] ILRM 61, an adopting widower successfully challenged the constitutionality of s 5(1) of the Adoption Act 1974, which precluded adoption orders being made in favour of childless widowers. Childless widows were allowed to adopt. McMahon J did not accept that there was any difference between widowers and widows, or between women and men, which justified this sex discrimination:

> Why then is the plaintiff excluded from consideration on his merits as an adopter of this child? Widowers as a class are not less competent than widows to provide for the material needs of children and their exclusion as a class must be based on a belief that a woman by virtue of her sex has an innate capacity for parenthood which is denied to a man and the lack of which renders a man unsuitable as an adopter. This view is not supported by any medical evidence adduced before me and the fact that section 5 permits a widower who has already custody of a child to adopt another appears to be an admission that a man may acquire skills or capacities necessary to be an adopter.... Counsel for the Attorney General did not claim that there was anything in the Constitution to justify this discrimination apart from the *proviso to Article 40*. He submitted that to be of either sex without more is not in itself to have a social function but the law may have regard to the fact that certain functions are more usually performed by one person and the functions of widow or widower are motherhood or fatherhood and adoption legislation recognises this difference. The culture of our society has assigned distinct roles to father and mother in two parent families in the past just as families on the land recognised a distinction between men's work and women's work but this is a feature of our culture which appears to be changing as the younger generation of married people tend to exchange roles freely. No medical or psychological evidence has been adduced to explain the difference between these roles and its significance for the welfare of the child or to establish that the roles are mutually exclusive or that both are essential for the proper upbringing of children or to establish that there is any difference in capacity for parenthood between a widow and a widower.
>
> Counsel for the Attorney General referred to *Article 41.2.1* in which the State recognises that by her life in the home woman gives to the State a support without which the common good cannot be achieved as conferring on a widow an advantage over a widower as an adopter. The article recognises the social value of a mother's services in the

home but that does not involve a denial of the capacity of widowers as a class to be considered on their merits as suitable adopters.

I am satisfied that in the circumstances envisaged by section 5 of the Act of 1974 that is where a married couple have received an infant for adoption and the wife dies before the final adoption order is made it is unreasonable and unjust to exclude the widower from being considered as a suitable person to adopt the child. It is unreasonable because the widower's relationship with the child and his suitability as an adopter from the point of view of the emotional needs of the child is something which a qualified psychologist can readily assess by observing the inter-action between the widower and the child. Disputation of the bond between the child and the widower will in many cases subject the child to emotional trauma. It is therefore unjust to the child as well as unreasonable. I am satisfied that the *proviso to* section 5 is founded on an idea of difference in capacity between men and women which has no foundation in fact and the proviso is therefore an unwarranted denial of human equality and repugnant to Article 40.1 of the Constitution. *Subparagraph (ii)* is repugnant to the Constitution since it requires as a condition for the validity of the consent to adoption by a widower something which is not required where the adopter is a woman. [1985] ILRM 64–65.

McMahon J placed considerable emphasis on the fact that the State was not able to adduce evidence to support the view that a widower would make a competent adopter. This appears to place the onus on the State to justify the appropriateness of the discrimination. Compare this with the approach adopted by the Supreme Court in *Lowth v Minister for Social Welfare* [1998] 4 IR 321. In this case, the plaintiff challenged provisions of the social welfare code which effectively discriminated against deserted husbands in comparison with deserted wives. Deserted husbands were only entitled to a lone parent's allowance, whereas deserted wives were entitled to a specific deserted wife's allowance which was, in a number of respects, more advantageous than the lone parent's allowance. The Supreme Court upheld this legislative discrimination, Hamilton CJ stating: [3–20]

> The facts proved in evidence before the learned High Court Judge show clearly how women in employment at the material times were at a financial disadvantage in comparison to men. Again the statistics adduced in evidence established the relatively small proportion of married women in the work force. Moreover the provisions of the Constitution dealing with the family recognise a social and domestic order in which married women were unlikely to work outside the family home. Furthermore the Married Women's Property Acts, 1882 to 1907, which significantly limited the rights of a married woman to deal with her own property were not repealed until the Married Women's Status Act, 1957. An even more obvious impediment to the married woman engaging in business was the Civil Service Regulation Act, 1956, which required the retirement on marriage from the civil service of women who were civil servants. It was not until 1973, that that prohibition was repealed by the Civil Service (Employment of Married Women) Act, 1973. At about the same time a comparable restriction on married women working in banks was lifted. These realities confirm and enliven the picture provided by the statistics given in evidence by the defendants. It is no function of this Court to adjudicate upon the merits or otherwise of the impugned legislation. It is only necessary to conclude, as this Court has done, that there were ample grounds for the Oireachtas to conclude that deserted wives were in general likely to have greater needs than deserted husbands so as to justify legislation providing for social welfare whether in the form of benefits or grants or a combination of both to meet such needs. [1998] 4 IR 321, at 341–342.

Other Legitimate Reasons for Legislative Discrimination

[3–21] Although the courts have often referred to the second sentence of Art 40.1 in upholding legislative discrimination, they have consistently held that it is legitimate for the Oireachtas to discriminate for other reasons. First, the courts have held that differences other than those listed in the second sentence can be used to justify discriminations. For instance, in *Loftus v Attorney General* [1979] IR 221, the Supreme Court held that the difference between political parties represented in Dáil Éireann and political parties not so represented justified a requirement that the latter satisfy the Registrar of Political Parties that they were genuine political parties.

[3–22] Secondly, the courts have held that legislative discriminations which serve another constitutional value are permissible. In *O'Brien v Stoutt* [1984] IR 316, the Supreme Court upheld the constitutionality of ss 67 and 69 of the Succession Act 1965. As interpreted by the court, these provisions required that, where property was distributed on intestacy, non-marital children of the deceased did not qualify for any share in the property being distributed. Walsh J put the matter as follows:

> The essential question is whether, in recognising the undoubted social function of the family, the validity of a law designed to protect the family depends upon compliance with the proviso in so far as it distinguishes, in questions of intestate succession, between those born inside marriage and those born outside marriage. Does a law aimed at maintaining the primacy of the family as the fundamental unit group of society require to come within the words of the proviso to be valid? The Court is of opinion that it does not....
>
> Having regard to the constitutional guarantees relating to the family, the Court cannot find that the differences created by the Act of 1965 are necessarily unreasonable, unjust or arbitrary. Undoubtedly, a child born outside marriage may suffer severe disappointment if he does not succeed to some part of his parents' property on intestacy, but he can suffer the same disappointment if the parent or parents die testate and leave that child no property—an event which could occur even if the Act of 1965 did enable intestate succession on the part of such child. However, the decision to change the existing rules of intestate succession and the extent to which they are to be changed are primarily matters for the Oireachtas. Even if the present rules were to be found to be invalid having regard to the provisions of the Constitution, it would avail the defendant nothing as the resultant absence of any rules would leave her without any claimable share. [1984] IR 316, at 335–336.

[3–23] Finally, the courts have also evolved a general principle that it is permissible for the Oireachtas to make discriminations that are relevant to a legitimate, legislative purpose. This test was first stated by Barrington J in *Brennan v Attorney General* [1983] ILRM 449, but is now applied generally by the courts. For instance, in *Re Article 26 and the Illegal Immigrants (Trafficking) Bill 1999* [2000] 2 IR 360, at 403 the Supreme Court rejected an Art 40.1 argument against a provision in the Bill which required legal challenges to certain immigration decisions to be taken in an unusually short two-week period (subject to a discretion on the part of the Court to extend time). The Court observed that the section served "a legitimate public policy objective of seeking to bring about at an early stage legal certainty as regards the administrative decisions in question. It also facilitates the better administration and functioning of the system for dealing with applicants for asylum or refugee status."

No Obligation to Treat Unequals Unequally

Notwithstanding the courts' characterisation of their constitutional equality doctrine as an Aristotelian conception of equality, it only reflects the first half of the Aristotelian injunction. For Aristotle required that equals be treated equally and unequals unequally. Although the courts have required—albeit not in a very strict way—that the State treat equals equally, they have never required that the State treat unequals unequally. Such an approach would arguably be inconsistent with the second sentence of Art 40.1, which allows—but does not require—the State to legislate in recognition of certain differences. As I have pointed out elsewhere, the draft of Art 40.1 was changed in response to concerns expressed by the Department of Finance specifically to ensure that the second sentence did not impose any obligation to treat unequals unequally. See Oran Doyle, *Constitutional Equality Law* (Thomson Round Hall, Dublin, 2004), at 61. [3–24]

The case that most clearly illustrates that the courts only approve of half of the Aristotelian conception is *Draper v Attorney General* [1984] IR 277. The plaintiff claimed that the failure of the State to provide her with a facility for postal voting amounted to a breach of Art 40.1. The Supreme Court rejected this argument, O'Higgins CJ reasoning: [3–25]

> The case made by the plaintiff in this action rests entirely on the failure of the State to provide special facilities for her and for those similarly situated. In the opinion of the Court, such failure does not amount to an interference by the State in the exercise of the right to vote under Article [16.1.2], of the Constitution. Nor is it, in the opinion of the Court, a breach by the State of the provisions of [Article 40.1]. While under this Article the State could, because of the plaintiff's incapacity, have made particular provisions for the exercise by her of her voting rights, the fact that it did not do so does not mean that the provisions actually made are necessarily unreasonable, unjust or arbitrary. For the reasons already stated, the Court could not so find. [1984] IR 277, at 290–291.

Standards of Review

The courts have thus interpreted Art 40.1 in a way that permits the Oireachtas to discriminate in order to reflect differences and/or to achieve legitimate legislative purposes. A crucial feature of constitutional law, however, is that it involves one organ of government (the courts) reviewing the decisions of another organ of government. When one is called on to review the decision of another, one can exhibit a greater or lesser degree of deference. Foley has explained deference in the following terms: [3–26]

> Suppose that a younger brother defers to the views of his oldest brother about how best to play a particular computer game. Insofar as little brothers actually think about these kinds of things, there are two general types of reason for such deference. First are reasons which relate to his brother's *identity* as the eldest. He may defer simply because the fact-of-being-the-eldest warrants some degree of "respect". Alternatively, he may defer because he equates the fact-of-being-the-eldest with assumptions about how good his brother *qua* the eldest actually is at playing the game. The latter deference is not justified simply by reason of the older brother's identity-as-the-eldest, what he *is*, but by reason of assumptions made about how the eldest actually does a particular thing, ie what he *does*. A similar distinction can be drawn in the constitutional sphere. For example, deference in the United Kingdom has been justified, in the words of *R(S) v Chief Constable of South Yorkshire*, on the basis of the "unimpeachable democratic credentials" of Parliament. It is

the fact-of-being-elected which counts here — a fact about the legislature's *democratic identity*. On the other hand, one may defer not simply because of the democratic identity of the legislature — a factor relevant to what the legislature "is" — but because of assumptions made about how a democratic legislature actually conducts constitutional scrutiny — assumptions about what parliament "does". That, for example, seems to be the guiding principle behind one form of the "due deference" approach whereby some British courts have held that deference must be based on a preliminary assessment as to whether the legislature has actually reached an opinion on the matter now before the court. The presumption of constitutionality, it is submitted, appeals *both* to images of what the legislature "is" and what it "does." Brian Foley, "Presuming the Legislature Acts Constitutionally: Legislative Process and Constitutional Decision-Making" (2007) 29 *DULJ* 141, at 147–148.

[3–27] In testing the legitimacy of legislative classifications, the courts have always adopted some level of deference to the legislature's assessment of the issues. That is, the courts do not require that legislation conform to the courts' view of what is a relevant difference, but rather that the Oireachtas have reached an acceptable view as to what is a relevant difference. The clearest statement of a standard of review comes from Barrington J in *Brennan v Attorney General* [1983] ILRM 449. Considering a claim that the Valuation Acts breached the equality guarantee, Barrington J set out the constitutional requirement that, in order to be valid, a classification must be for a legitimate legislative purpose, relevant to that purpose and each class must be treated fairly. There are two significant aspects to this formulation. First, the purpose itself must be legitimate. Secondly, there must be an adequate relationship between the purpose and the means adopted to pursue it. Although Barrington J's conclusions on the equality arguments of the plaintiffs were overturned on appeal, his legitimate legislative purpose test has since become well-established in the case law. See, for instance, *Re Article 26 and the Illegal Immigrants (Trafficking) Bill 1999* [2000] 2 IR 360.

[3–28] One can take the analysis further and identify that there are four aspects to any standard of review. First, who bears the onus of justification: must the plaintiff demonstrate that the legislation is unjustified or must the State demonstrate that the legislation is justified? Secondly, how significant must the purpose for the classification be: must it merely be a "legitimate legislative purpose" (as in *Brennan*) or should it perhaps be a "compelling legislative purpose", or something in between these two extremes? Thirdly, how closely must the means adopted for pursuing the purpose fit that purpose: must the means be merely "relevant" to achieving the purpose or should they perhaps be "closely tailored" or "necessary" for achieving the purpose? Finally, do the courts require actual justification (*ie* that the Court itself be satisfied that the measure was justified according to the above criteria) or is it sufficient that there be hypothetical justification (*ie* that the Court merely be satisfied that the Oireachtas might reasonably have thought that the measure was justified)? In general, the Irish courts have adopted weak standards of review, thereby making it much easier for the State to defend the constitutionality of legislation.

Levelling Up or Down

[3–29] In *Somjee v Minister for Justice* [1981] ILRM 324, Keane J upheld a discrimination effected by s 8 of the Irish Nationality and Citizenship Act 1956. This section provided that a non-national woman who married an Irish citizen could acquire Irish citizenship immediately, provided that she lodged a declaration. No such facility was afforded to a non-national man who married an Irish citizen. Such a person had to satisfy a residency requirement of five years, subject to a power of the Minister to reduce that period. Keane J held that this legislative measure was justified. However, even if it had not been, he identified a crucial flaw in the plaintiffs' case. He noted that the plaintiffs' claim, if successful, would only result in the invalidation of certain sections of the Irish Nationality and Citizenship Act 1956, a result which would confer no benefit on the plaintiffs. As the courts had no power to direct the Oireachtas to enact legislation so as to remedy an inequality, the plaintiffs' claim should fail. It was not the function of the court to "indulge in an academic exercise which will be utterly futile so far as the plaintiffs are concerned". This situation arises where a legislative provision which confers an advantage is under-inclusive.

A different approach was taken in relation to a common law rule in *McKinley v Minister for Defence* [1992] 2 IR 333. Here the plaintiff challenged the common law rule which allowed an action for loss of consortium to a husband but not to a wife. The Court, by a three-two majority, developed the common law rule so as to allow a right of action to the wife as well. [3–30]

Indirect Discrimination

Indirect discrimination occurs where a legislative measure, although not discriminatory on its face as between two groups, nevertheless is considered to be discriminatory either because it is motivated by a discriminatory purpose or because it produces a discriminatory impact. The Irish courts have not accepted that indirect discrimination is constitutionally prohibited. In *Norris v Attorney General*, both the High Court and the Supreme Court rejected the plaintiff's contention that the criminalisation of anal sex constituted a discrimination between homosexuals and heterosexuals. McWilliam J reasoned as follows: [3–31]

> A certain act is declared to be unlawful. It may be performed by either homosexual or heterosexual men with either men or women. Although it is perfectly obvious that such acts will usually be performed between homosexual males, which is probably what the legislature had in mind, that does not constitute an invidious or arbitrary discrimination against homosexual citizens any more than the statutes making theft an offence constitute an invidious or arbitrary discrimination against congenital kleptomaniacs, supposing there were such a group of people. [1984] IR 36, at 44.

Section 61 of the offences against the person Act 1861 was a classic example of indirect discrimination where the legislative measure was highly salient to an unstated ground of classification; although the criminalisation of buggery applies to all persons, it clearly impacts more on those for whom anal sex is a significant form of sexual intimacy. This group consists mostly of gay men. As noted by McWilliam J, this differential impact was probably intended. That said, the discrimination was not categorically related to male homosexuality; some heterosexuals practise anal sex. The Court's rejection of the plaintiff's contention amounted to a rejection of the concept of indirect discrimination where the discrimination was salient to a ground of classification, but not necessarily where the discrimination was categorically related to a ground of classification. [3–32]

The Human Personality Doctrine

[3–33] The interpolated phrase "as human persons" is the most significant textual novelty in the equality guarantee. Its interpretation by the courts has attracted more criticism than almost any area of constitutional doctrine. In *Macauley v Minister for Posts and Telegraphs*, Kenny J rejected an equality argument on the basis that "the guarantee in the Constitution of equality before the law relates to the position of the citizen as a human person". [1966] IR 345, at 355. This comment suggested that the human personality phrase restricted the application of constitutional equality to legislation that bore on the citizen as a human person, but it remained unclear what the courts understood by that restriction. Two different conceptions of the human personality phrase have emerged in the case law. On the one hand, some judges have held that the phrase limits the ambit of Art 40.1 to those discriminations that occur in a *context* that implicates some essential attribute of the human personality. On the other hand, some judges have held that the phrase limits the ambit of Art 40.1 to those discriminations that are *based on* some essential attribute of human personality.

[3–34] Kenny J was the leading judicial exponent of the context of discrimination approach. In *Quinn's Supermarket v Attorney General* [1972] IR 1, the Supreme Court considered a challenge to the provisions of a Ministerial Order which exempted the proprietors of Kosher shops from a ban on evening opening. The plaintiffs challenged the provisions of the Victuallers' Shops (Hours of Trading on Weekdays) (Dublin, Dun Laoghaire and Bray) Order 1948 made by the Minister for Industry and Commerce under s 25 of the Shops (Hours of Trading) Act 1938. Article 2 of the Order effectively exempted Kosher butcher shops from a ban on evening opening. Kenny J offered the following interpretation of the human personality phrase as a justification for his rejection of the plaintiff's claim under Art 40.1:

> This guarantee, however, is one of equality before the law in so far as the characteristics inherent in the idea of human personality are involved: it does not relate to trading activities or to the hours during which persons may carry on business for neither of these is connected with the essentials of the concept of human personality. [1972] IR 1, at 31.

[3–35] Kenny J focused not on the basis of the discrimination (religion) but on the context of the discrimination (trading activities). As that context did not implicate any essential attribute of the human personality, the equality guarantee was not breached. In *Murtagh v Cleary*, Kenny J elaborated on what was meant by "essential attributes of human personality", asserting that the guarantee of equality related only to the plaintiffs' "essential attributes as persons, those features which make them human beings"; it thus had, in his view, no application to trading activities or conditions of employment. [1972] IR 330, at 335. Kenny J thus rendered restrictive the context of discrimination approach by adopting a naturalist interpretation of the human personality. One's human personality was considered a shorthand for the essence of one's existence as a human being. More peripheral and transient aspects of one's personality, such as the ability to work, the liability to pay tax and the entitlement to receive social welfare benefits, were not considered part of one's human personality. As such, a legislative discrimination could only be subjected to judicial equality scrutiny if it were made in a context that implicated the essential attributes of one's human personality. If it were made in a context that merely implicated more peripheral aspects of one's life, judicial equality scrutiny was not appropriate as "human equality" was not at stake.

The "basis of discrimination" interpretation of the human personality phrase also emerged in *Quinn's Supermarket*. In a memorable and oft-cited passage, Walsh J elaborated on the equality guarantee: [3–36]

> [Article 40.1] is not a guarantee of absolute equality for all citizens in all circumstances but it is a guarantee of equality as human persons and (as the Irish text of the Constitution makes quite clear) is a guarantee related to their dignity as human beings and a guarantee against any inequalities grounded upon an assumption, or indeed a belief, that some individual or individuals or classes of individuals, by reason of their human attributes or their ethnic or racial, social or religious background, are to be treated as the inferior or superior of other individuals in the community. [1972] IR 1, at 13–14.

This conception of equality focused not on the context of discrimination (in this case, trading activities), but on the basis of discrimination (in this case, religion). Wherever discrimination was based on an impermissible assumption that some individuals were inferior to others, the guarantee of human equality was breached. Impermissible assumptions were understood to be those that assumed inferiority by reference to the human attributes of the people so distinguished. Once again, there were naturalist overtones to this conception of equality. However, the effect of the naturalist influence was not as restrictive of equality argumentation here as it was in the context of discrimination approach. For although it is difficult to imagine a legislative context that impinges on the essential attributes of the human personality, it is relatively easy to imagine a legislative basis of discrimination that rests on an assumption that some individuals are inferior to others by reason of their human attributes. The following example illustrates this point. As part of a general campaign against Jewish people, it is stipulated that all Jews should wear a yellow star on their clothes for ease of identification. Kenny J's approach would, if pursued to its logical conclusion, hold that this is merely discrimination within the context of clothing and fabric design and, as such, does not prejudice the essential attributes of the human person. In contrast, Walsh J's approach could conceivably hold that the discrimination in question implicitly rests on an assumption that Jewish people are intrinsically inferior to others in the community. If religion were considered to be a human attribute, the constitutionally guaranteed ideal of human equality would be subverted by such an assumption. [3–37]

Unfortunately, the clear distinction between the context of discrimination approach and the basis of discrimination approach was then confused by the actual decision of Walsh J in *Quinn's Supermarket*. Walsh J rejected any application of Art 40.1 to the case, stating simply that no question of human equality or inequality arose. This conclusion perhaps followed from Walsh J's assertion that his list of human attributes was intended to show that the equality guarantee referred to human persons for what they were in themselves rather than to any lawful activities, trades or pursuits which they might engage in or follow. This concluding assertion was redolent of the Kenny J context of discrimination approach and, as such, was wholly incompatible with the basis of discrimination approach cogently outlined by Walsh J. Walsh J's conclusion thus not only dulls the clarity of the distinction between the context of discrimination [3–38] and the basis of discrimination approach but also undermines support for the basis of discrimination approach.

[3–39] In *Brennan v Attorney General*, Barrington J provided the most considered analysis of the difference between the context of discrimination approach and the basis of discrimination approach:

> Article 40.1 is not dealing with human beings in the abstract but with human beings in society. There may be differences and distinctions made between individuals in society in the course of their trading activities or otherwise which are not based upon an assumption that those individuals are superior or inferior to other people. With such distinctions Article 40.1 is not normally concerned. But a law can be based upon an assumption that some individuals are inferior to others as human persons and yet manifest itself, in the social or economic sphere, in some superficially trivial regulation, such as who may or may not sit on a park bench; who may or may not own a horse worth more than five pounds; or who may or who may not serve drink in a public bar. [1983] ILRM 449, at 481.

[3–40] For Barrington J, therefore, the context of the discrimination was irrelevant. The controlling question was whether the basis of the discrimination suggested an assumption that some individuals were superior or inferior to others. Such an assumption could have existed even where the context of the legislation was wholly socio-economic. It is important to emphasise that Barrington J's judgment did not expand from a naturalist conception of the human personality to a social and economic conception. Article 40.1 applied to "human beings in society", but only where there was legislation based on an assumption that some individuals were inferior to others by reason of their human attributes, a requirement that still had naturalistic overtones.

[3–41] Citing the judgment of Walsh J in *de Búrca*, Barrington J implicitly concluded that discrimination on the basis of property ownership prejudiced the constitutionally guaranteed human equality. Nevertheless, it is questionable whether Barrington J's conclusion correctly followed from the basis of discrimination approach. The discrimination at issue was based on differences between parcels of land, not on differences between the human persons who owned the land. All possible owners of a particular piece of property would be treated in the same way. Indeed, given that Barrington J accepted that the discrimination in the legislation was inadvertent—more of a historical accident than anything else—it is difficult to see how it could have been described as resting on an assumption of the inferiority of some humans to other humans. The discrimination at issue was not referable to any distinction drawn between persons by reason of their human attributes; accordingly, human equality, even under the basis of discrimination approach, was not at issue. Although Barrington J's discussion of the human personality doctrine was welcome as a rare elaboration of a coherent equality argument, it is arguable that it did not apply to the facts of the case. (In contrast to Barrington J, the Supreme Court focused on the context of the discrimination (property tax) and held that the equality guarantee was not at issue because human equality was not affected. [1984] ILRM 355, at 365). Nevertheless, the Court upheld the judgment of Barrington J on the basis that the property rights of the plaintiffs had been unjustly attacked.

[3–42] The basis of discrimination interpretation of the human personality phrase focuses judicial scrutiny on the basis of discrimination, the criterion of classification. It demands that legislation not discriminate on the basis of human attributes. In *Quinn's Supermarket*, Walsh J asserted that the following were among the attributes proscribed as a basis of discrimination: ethnic or racial, social or religious background. Curtin describes Walsh J's dicta as "an important, and powerful, statement of the circumstances in which discrimination occurs" which "relates discrimination directly to the effect of impairment of human dignity". Deirdre Curtin, *Irish Employment Equality Law* (Round Hall, Dublin, 1989), at 23. She argues that the core of dignity is that people should be treated for what they are and should not be discriminated against on the basis of insignificant and irrelevant characteristics. It is an approach that emphasises people's common humanity as the justification for equality; equality is breached where the State denies human equality by treating some people as inferior on account of their human attributes. Realised in constitutional law, this approach would give meaning to the equality guarantee by focusing the attention of the courts on certain offensive bases of discrimination. It would require that, in the legislative process, all persons should be treated as equals and particular groups should not be *a priori* targeted for legislative disadvantage on the basis of their alleged inferiority to other groups of individuals in the community. Recent dicta of the Supreme Court, without explicitly reconsidering their interpretation of the human personality phrase, suggest that such a development of constitutional equality doctrine may be taking place in Irish law.

[3–43] Before considering the impact of these recent cases, it is useful to reconsider, in brief, the basic aspects of a standard of review, set out above. First, there is the onus of justification. Does the onus lie on the State to justify the measure or on the plaintiff to show that there is no justification for the measure? Until recently, it was considered that the plaintiff bore the onus of justification at all stages. Secondly, there is the standard of justification. What quality of purpose must the legislature have and how close a relationship must the measure have to that purpose? The test established by Barrington J in *Brennan* tended to be deferential to the legislature's judgment: the purpose need only be *legitimate* and the means need only be *relevant* to that purpose. Thirdly, there is the difference between actual and hypothetical justification. Does the court question whether, in its own judgment, the measure is in fact justified or does it question whether the measure might reasonably be justified? The Irish courts have generally adopted the deferential approach of hypothetical justification.

[3–44] In *Re Article 26 of the Constitution and the Employment Equality Bill 1996* [1997] 2 IR 321 (hereinafter referred to as "the *Employment Equality Bill Case*"), the Supreme Court considered, *inter alia*, a number of statutory provisions which dealt with age discrimination in the context of employment. Section 6 of the Bill provided, *inter alia*, that discrimination would be taken to occur where one person was treated less favourably than another on the basis of age. However, there were two age-based exceptions to the prohibition of age discrimination. Section 6(3) provided that treating a person over the age of 65 or under the age of 18 more or less favourably than another, whatever that person's age, would not be regarded as discrimination on the age ground. In addition, s 33(1) provided that the anti-discrimination measures of the Bill were not to be taken as preventing measures for the integration into employment of persons over the age of 50, among others. Counsel assigned by the Court to argue against the constitutionality of the Bill challenged these three cut-off ages (18, 50 and 65) as themselves being unconstitutional discrimination on the basis of age. Hamilton CJ, for the Court, having cited Walsh J's views that Art 40.1 guaranteed human equality, expressed the view that, having regard to Art 40.1, a number of forms of discrimination were prima facie invalid:

> The forms of discrimination which are, presumptively at least, proscribed by Article 40.1 are not particularised: manifestly, they would extend to classifications based on sex, race, language, religious or political opinions. [1997] 2 IR 321, at 347.

[3–45] This dictum parallels Walsh J's comments in *Quinn's Supermarket* to the effect that human attributes could not be used as a basis of discrimination. However, although Walsh J had suggested that discriminations based on such attributes were wholly prohibited, in this case the Supreme Court more subtly stipulated that such discriminations were presumptively invalid. This shifts the onus of justification onto the State. In addition, the Court expanded somewhat on the list of human attributes to cover sex, language and political opinions. The attribute of age raised greater analytical difficulties. In considering whether age should also be considered a presumptively proscribed ground, the Court referred to the US case of *Massachusetts Board of Retirement v Murgia* 427 US 307 (1976) and in particular to the judgment of Justice Marshall. Although the Irish Supreme Court's analysis was not as rigid or formalised as that currently employed by the United States Supreme Court, it clearly suggested that certain classifications were to be treated as *prima facie* invalid, thus reversing the onus of proof and imposing an onus of justification on the State. Further support for this proposition can be derived from the subsequent reasoning of the Court. In upholding the exclusion from the Bill's provisions of employment in the Defence Forces, the Garda Síochána and the prison service, the Court made the following observation:

> Once, however, it is accepted that discrimination on the grounds of age falls into a different constitutional category from distinction on grounds such as sex or race, the decision of the Oireachtas not to apply the provisions of the Bill to a relatively narrowly defined class of employees in the public service whose duties are of a particular character becomes more understandable. [1997] 2 IR 321, at 349.

[3–46] This further suggests that a differentiated standard of review applies to legislative classifications. Although classifications based on age are subject to Art 40.1, requiring justification under the legitimate purpose test, they are easier, in the view of the Court, to justify than classifications based on race or sex. By implication, classifications based on race or sex are subject to a standard of review more difficult to meet than that contained in the legitimate purpose test. It is not quite clear in what way this new standard of review is more onerous. At the very least, given that these classifications are "presumptively invalid", the onus of proof lies on the State to show that the measure is justified. However, it may be that there is also a move from hypothetical to actual justification and that a closer relationship to a more compelling purpose is also required. In this regard, it is worth noting that the Court considered the standard of review stipulated by Justice Marshall in *Murgia* not to be essentially different from the legitimate purpose test of Irish constitutional law. Justice Marshall's test required the State to show a "reasonably substantial interest" and a scheme "reasonably closely tailored to achieving that interest". Notwithstanding the Court's comments, this is clearly a higher standard than mere relevance to a legitimate legislative purpose. The purpose or interest, for Justice Marshall, must not merely be "legitimate" but "reasonably substantial"; the means must not merely be "relevant" to that purpose but "reasonably closely tailored". The use of the word "reasonably" suggests that this standard of review is still about hypothetical justification but a higher standard of hypothetical of justification. If this is the standard of review that applies to age based classifications under Art 40.1, the standard for race and sex based classifications must be higher still.

The basis of discrimination interpretation of the human personality phrase is the unspoken justification of this doctrinal development in Irish constitutional law. That justification also identifies the limits of the doctrine: proscribed as presumptively invalid are those (and only those) classifications based on an assumption that certain individuals are inferior to other individuals in the community by reason of their human attributes. Even if the only change effected by the *Employment Equality Bill Case* is a reversal of the onus of proof, the significance of this should not be underestimated. In *Lowth v Minister for Social Welfare*, as noted above, the plaintiff's claim failed largely because of his own inability to provide statistics to illustrate that he, as a deserted husband, was similarly situated to a deserted wife, thereby grounding a claim that he should receive the same treatment. Had the onus been on the State to justify the discrimination, it would have been necessary for it to produce the statistics to demonstrate the difference in situation. However, the fact that *Lowth* was decided after the *Employment Equality Bill Case* does cast some doubt on whether any change was effected in constitutional doctrine by the latter case. [3–47]

That said, the more recent case again of *An Blascaod Mór Teoranta v Commissioners of Public Works* [2000] 1 IR 6 ("the *Great Blasket* Case") provided further support for a new constitutional doctrine that some legislative classifications would *a priori* be treated differently by the courts. An Blascaod Mór National Historic Park Act 1989 provided for the delegation to the OPW of the power to acquire land compulsorily on the Great Blasket Island, for the purpose of establishing and maintaining a national park. However, s 4(2)(a) of the Act provided that this power did not apply to land owned or occupied by a person who had owned or occupied it since 17 November 1953 and was ordinarily resident on the island before that date, nor to land owned or occupied by a relative of such a person. Section 4(4) defined relative as a parent, lineal ancestor, spouse, widow, widower, child, lineal descendant, uncle, aunt, brother, sister, nephew or niece. Barrington J (speaking for the Supreme Court) again cited the basis of discrimination human personality dicta of Walsh J in *Quinn's*, as well as his own legitimate purpose test from *Brennan*. He concluded: [3–48]

> In the present case the classification appears to be at once too narrow and too wide. It is hard to see what legitimate legislative purpose it fulfils. It is based on a principle — that of pedigree — which appears to have no place (outside the law of succession) in a democratic society committed to the principle of equality. This fact alone makes the classification suspect. The Court agrees with the learned trial judge that a Constitution should be pedigree blind just as it should be colour blind or gender blind except when those issues are relevant to a legitimate legislative purpose. This Court can see no such legitimate legislative purpose in the present case and has no doubt but that the plaintiffs are being treated unfairly as compared with persons who owned or occupied and resided on lands on the island prior to November 1953 and their descendants. [2000] 1 IR 6, at 19.

[3–49] The reference to suspect classifications and the idea of constitutional blindness to certain irrelevant legislative criteria were clear echoes of US constitutional equality doctrine. Although Barrington J did not use the language of "presumptive invalidity", he was clearly suggesting that some "suspect" legislative criteria should be evaluated more closely than others. Again the basis of discrimination interpretation of the human personality phrase is the unspoken justification and should be used to identify those suspect criteria. The *Great Blasket Case* thus strengthens the contention that the Irish Supreme Court is adopting a doctrine whereby objectionable legislative criteria are identified in the abstract and accorded special treatment. However, the exact parameters of the new doctrine remain unclear.

[3–50] It is perhaps useful to summarise the development in constitutional equality doctrine that has occurred over the last few years. A number of dicta of the courts have suggested a move, analogous to that undergone in the US, whereby some legislative classifications would impose an onus of justification on the State. The doctrinal and rhetorical underpinning for such a development has arguably been the basis of discrimination interpretation of the human personality phrase, extant in Irish law since the early 1970s, identified earlier. The value of human equality, guaranteed by Art 40.1, mandates that the organs of the State treat its citizens with equal respect and esteem. This is not an obligation of mechanical equal treatment, but it does preclude classifications which are based on an assumption that some individuals are inherently inferior or superior to other individuals in the community by reason of their human attributes. The justification for legislation which appears to be based on such assumptions must therefore be evaluated more closely, through the expedient of reversing the onus of justification and, possibly, through raising the standard of justification.

[3–51] Although the *Employment Equality Bill Case* and the *Great Blasket Case* have not signalled any move from hypothetical to actual justification on the part of the courts, they have suggested three possible changes to the standard of review of objectionable legislative classifications. First, the onus of justification is reversed. Secondly, but less likely, the legislative measure may have to be closely tailored to achieving the purpose as opposed to being merely relevant to that purpose. Thirdly, but also less likely, the purpose may have to be compelling as opposed to being merely legitimate. The effect of the dicta in the *Employment Equality Bill Case* and the *Great Blasket Case* is to circumscribe the scope of the courts to imagine legislative purposes.

[3–52] However, one must be careful not to overstate the doctrinal development effected by these decisions. Following the *Great Blasket Case*, the Supreme Court was poised on the brink of an egalitarian development. It remains to be seen whether the current Court, the composition of which has altered substantially since these two cases, determines to fulfil this egalitarian potential. Nevertheless, it is apparent that the possibility of a constitutional equality doctrine based on differentiated tiers of scrutiny analysis is at least being considered by the courts.

[3–53] In *Gilligan v Revenue Commissioners*, for instance, it was argued that the ban on same-sex marriage amounted to a discrimination on the grounds of sexual orientation, which required a greater level of justification. Dunne J avoided this argument, as she reasoned that the sexual orientation discrimination was justified by reference to the importance placed by the Constitution on opposite-sex marriage. In *Mitchell v Ireland* [2007] IEHC 280, the plaintiff successfully challenged the constitutionality of s 62 of the Offences against the Person Act 1861, which provided that a person convicted of committing an indecent assault upon a male could be sentenced to penal servitude for any term not exceeding 10 years. In contrast, the maximum sentence for the same offence committed on a female is two years—under s 6 of the Criminal Law (Amendment) Act 1935. Laffoy J held in favour of the plaintiff on the following grounds:

> Section 62 of the Act of 1861, in mandating a maximum penalty for the offence of indecent assault when committed against a male person which is substantially different from the maximum penalty mandated by law when the same offence is committed against a female, is *prima facie* discriminatory on the ground of gender in contravention of Article 40.1. It is inconsistent with the Constitution unless the differentiation it creates is legitimated by reason of being founded on difference of capacity, whether physical or moral, or difference of social function of men and women in a manner which is not invidious, arbitrary or capricious.
>
> The core question is whether the classification of persons convicted of indecent assault on male persons for different treatment in sentencing is for a legitimate legislative purpose and is relevant to that purpose. In endeavouring to identify the purpose which the classification serves, there is really nothing to go on other than what may be gleaned from the context of the impugned provision within the legislative scheme of the Act of 1861. The impugned provision is an integral part of provisions ... which manifest a societal repugnance to homosexual activity in the terminology used, for instance, the references to "unnatural" offences and the "abominable" crime of buggery. The same degree of societal disapproval is not apparent in the terminology used in the Act of 1861 dealing with sexual offences against women....
>
> What else can be extrapolated from the submissions as supporting a legitimate legislative purpose? There are two possibilities in the defendants' submissions. One is that male and female victims require different degrees of protection against sexual offences necessitating different levels of denunciation as reflected in sentencing. The other is that gravity of the sexual offence against a woman is inherently greater than that against a man because of the risk of an unwanted pregnancy. The imposition of a substantially more severe maximum penalty for indecent assault of a male person most certainly would not address the second possibility, nor would it address the first possibility if, as I think it is reasonable to assume for present purposes, women are more vulnerable to sexual assault than men.
>
> I can find nothing in the Act of 1861 or in an objective consideration of the differences of physical capacity, moral capacity and social function of men and women which points to a legitimate legislative purpose for imposing a more severe maximum penalty for indecent assault on a male person than for the same offence against a female person. Therefore, I have come to the conclusion that the relevant provision is inconsistent with Article 40.1.
>
> I have come to that conclusion on the basis of the case as presented without having to reach any conclusion on whether the burden of establishing justification lies with the defendants or with the plaintiff. It is also unnecessary to express any view on whether gender-based discrimination warrants a strict scrutiny approach. In my view, no rational justification for the different maximum penalties which statute law prescribes where the offence of indecent assault is committed, whether by a man or a woman, against a male and a female can be divined even on the basis of the most deferential form of scrutiny. That discrimination is the legacy of Victorian mores and social attitudes. It is an anomaly which just over a quarter of a century ago the Oireachtas eliminated prospectively.

[3–54] While Laffoy J's judgment is a welcome and robust application of Art 40.1, it does not significantly advance equality doctrine. For Laffoy J found it possible to reach her conclusion—that the legislation was invalid—even applying the most generous of standards to the State. The possibility cannot be discounted, however, that discussion of standards of review and an emphasis on how weakly such standards have been applied in the past may have caused the Court to apply the low standards somewhat more rigorously.

Contents – Chapter 4

The Unenumerated Rights Doctrine

Textual Basis and Early Days .... [4–01]
Methods for the Identification of Unenumerated Rights. .... [4–08]
   Christian and Democratic Nature of the State .... [4–08]
   The Human Personality .... [4–11]
   The Natural Law .... [4–17]
   Rights Implied From Other Constitutional Provisions .... [4–26]
The Difficulties with the Unenumerated Rights Doctrine .... [4–28]
The Apotheosis of the Natural Law in Irish Constitutional Law .... [4–34]
Current Status of Unenumerated Rights Doctrine .... [4–46]

Overview

The courts have held that Art 40.3 of the Constitution protects certain rights that are not explicitly enumerated. Taking this approach, the courts have identified the following rights as among those constitutionally protected, notwithstanding the absence of any clear textual basis: a right to bodily integrity, a right to travel, a right to marital privacy, a right to privacy. The courts have used different approaches to identify these rights. The courts have protected rights that they consider: (a) follow from the Christian and democratic nature of the State; (b) inhere in people by reason of their human personality; (c) are protected by the natural law; or (d) are implicitly protected by other provisions of the Constitution. This development in Irish constitutional law was strongly criticised by academics who pointed to the lack of certainty in these sources of rights and the scope for undemocratic judicial discretion in identifying the rights.

In 1995, the Supreme Court was (in effect) asked to declare a constitutional amendment unconstitutional on the basis that it breached the natural law. The Supreme Court refused to do this, pronouncing that the people were sovereign and that the natural law was not superior to the Constitution. This marked the beginning of a general demise in the unenumerated rights doctrine. The judicial consensus now seems to be that new rights should be identified only where they are clearly implicit either in the text of the Constitution or as corollaries of rights that have already been identified by the courts under the unenumerated rights doctrine.

Chapter 4

The Unenumerated Rights Doctrine

Textual Basis and Early Days

Article 40.3 of the Constitution provides as follows: [4–01]

> 1° The State guarantees in its laws to respect, and, as far as practicable, by its laws to defend and vindicate the personal rights of the citizen.
> 2° The State shall, in particular, by its laws protect as best it may from unjust attack and, in the case of injustice done, vindicate the life, person, good name, and property rights of every citizen.

The fact that Art 40.3.2° enumerates a number of specific rights that are protected, prefaced by the phrase "in particular", implies that there are other, unenumerated rights protected by Article 40.3.1°. This possibility was first seized on in *Ryan v Attorney General* [1965] IR 294. The plaintiff objected to plans to fluoridate the public water supply. This was proposed as a public health measure to reduce the incidence of dental caries in children. Among the arguments relied on by the plaintiff was that the fluoridation would affect the right of herself and her children to bodily integrity. This right was not explicitly protected by any provision of the Constitution. Mrs Ryan's claim was that it was implicitly protected by Art 40.3.1°. Kenny J accepted this proposition: [4–02]

> [T]he personal rights which may be involved to invalidate legislation are not confined to those specified in Article 40 but include all those rights which result from the Christian and democratic nature of the State....
>
> The next matter to be considered ... is whether the general guarantee in Article 40, section 3, relates only to those personal rights which are specified in Article 40 or whether it extends to other unspecified personal rights of the citizen. If it extends to personal rights other than those specified in Article 40, the High Court and the Supreme Court have the difficult and responsible duty of ascertaining and declaring what are the personal rights of the citizen which are guaranteed by the Constitution. In modern times this would seem to be a function of the legislative rather than of the judicial power but it was done by the Courts in the formative period of the Common Law and there is no reason why they should not do it now. A number of factors indicate that the guarantee is not confined to the rights specified in Article 40 but extends to other personal rights of the citizen. Firstly, there is sub-s. 2° of section 3 of Article 40. It reads:—"The State shall, in particular, by its laws protect as best it may from unjust attack and, in the case of injustice done, vindicate the life, person, good name, and property rights of every citizen." The words "in particular" show that sub-s. 2° is a detailed statement of something which is already contained in sub-s. 1° which is the general guarantee. But sub-s. 2° refers to rights in connection with life and good name and there are no rights in connection with these two matters specified in Article 40. It follows, I think, that the general guarantee in sub-s. 1° must extend to rights not specified in Article 40. Secondly, there are many personal rights of the citizen which follow from the Christian and democratic nature of the State

which are not mentioned in Article 40 at all—the right to free movement within the State and the right to marry are examples of this. This also leads to the conclusion that the general guarantee extends to rights not specified in Article 40.

In my opinion, one of the personal rights of the citizen protected by the general guarantee is the right to bodily integrity. I understand the right to bodily integrity to mean that no mutilation of the body or any of its members may be carried out on any citizen under authority of the law except for the good of the whole body and that no process which is or may, as a matter of probability, be dangerous or harmful to the life or health of the citizens or any of them may be imposed (in the sense of being made compulsory) by an Act of the Oireachtas. This conclusion, that there is a right of bodily integrity, gets support from a passage in the Encyclical Letter, "Peace on Earth":— "Beginning our discussion of the rights of man, we see that every man has the right to life, to bodily integrity and to the means which are necessary and suitable for the proper development of life; these are primarily food, clothing, shelter, rest, medical care, and finally the necessary social services." If then the Act of 1960 imposes the consumption of fluoridated water on the citizens and if that is or may, as a matter of probability, be dangerous or harmful to the life or health of any of the citizens, the plaintiff's right to bodily integrity would be infringed and the legislation would be unconstitutional. [1965] IR 245, at 312–314.

[4–03] Thus the unenumerated rights doctrine was born. Kenny J identified three different arguments in support of the assertion that the right to bodily integrity was protected by the Constitution. The first argument turned on the textual implication in Art 40.3.2° that there were unenumerated rights protected by Art 40.3.1°. The second was that there were rights of the citizen that followed from the Christian and democratic nature of the State that, although not explicitly mentioned in the Constitution, must be constitutionally protected. The third was that Catholic social teaching recognised a right to bodily integrity.

[4–04] On closer examination, however, it is apparent that these arguments are very different. If one accepts that there is any distinction between positive (written down) law and general principles of morality and that judges' duties relate (at least primarily) to the positive law, the first argument is the most appealing. For it identifies a basis in positive law for the judicial identification and protection of rights that are not explicitly stated in the positive law. However, it provides no guidance as to what those rights might be. In contrast, the third argument moves from the general moral premise that people have a right to bodily integrity to the conclusion that the Irish Constitution legally protects the right to bodily integrity. If one accepts that there is a distinction between positive law and morality and that judges' duties relate primarily to positive law, this is an untenable argument. For it simply allows judges, without any basis in positive law, to import general moral principles into positive law, thereby collapsing any distinction between positive law and morality. The second argument falls somewhere between the first and the third: assuming that Kenny J inferred the "Christian and democratic" character of the State from the text of the Constitution (although this is not entirely clear), it could be argued that judges are required to give effect to those rights that are required by the character of the State as established by the Constitution. This approach has more textual basis than the third approach but less textual basis than the first approach.

[4–05] Perhaps the best interpretation of Kenny J's reasoning is that the first argument was a necessary precondition for the existence of the judicial power to recognise rights at all, the other two arguments only being relevant to the question of which rights should be judicially recognised. That is, given that the Constitution textually implies the existence of unenumerated rights, it is permissible for the courts to rely on the Christian and democratic nature of the State, as well as papal encyclicals, in determining what those rights are. Nevertheless, this approach still raises difficulties. One reason for recognising a distinction between positive law and morality is to limit the power of judges to make moral choices that should, in a democracy, be made by the people in general. By allowing themselves to appeal to such amorphous concepts as the Christian and democratic character of the State in order to recognise and potentially enforce rights as against the wishes of the Oireachtas, have the courts given to themselves a *carte blanche* to write their own moral preferences into the fundamental law of the State?

These are essentially the arguments that beset the unenumerated rights doctrine over its 30 or so years of existence. In the immediate aftermath of Kenny J's judgment, however, they received little scrutiny. Although Kenny J held that plaintiff had a right to bodily integrity, he concluded that the right had not been illegitimately restricted: [4–06]

> Let me say then that I am satisfied beyond the slightest doubt that the fluoridation of the public water supplies in this country at a concentration of 1 p.p.m. will not cause any damage or injury to the health of anybody, young, old, healthy or sick, who is living in this country and that there is no risk or prospect whatever that it will. [1963] 2 IR 245, at 316.

On appeal, the Supreme Court approved Kenny J's judgment but added little analysis of Art 40.3: [4–07]

> The Court agrees with Mr. Justice Kenny that the "personal rights" mentioned in section 3, 1° are not exhausted by the enumeration of "life, person, good name, and property rights" in section 3, 2° as is shown by the use of the words "in particular"; nor by the more detached treatment of specific rights in the subsequent sections of the Article. To attempt to make a list of all the rights which may properly fall within the category of "personal rights" would be difficult and, fortunately, is unnecessary in this present case. [1965] IR 245, at 344–345.

The identification of Art 40.3.2° rights consumed much judicial time over the next 20 years.

Methods for the Identification of Unenumerated Rights

Christian and Democratic Nature of the State

In *Ryan*, Kenny J had identified the right to travel within the State as one right following from the Christian and democratic nature of the State. In *State (M) v Attorney General* [1979] IR 73, Finlay P expanded on this reasoning to conclude that a *prima facie* right to travel followed from the Christian and democratic nature of the State: [4–08]

> [T]he citizens of the State may have a right (arising from the Christian and democratic nature of the State—though not enumerated in the Constitution) to avail of such facilities [for travel] without arbitrary or unjustified interference by the State. To put the matter more simply and more bluntly, it appears to me that, subject to the obvious conditions

which may be required by public order and the common good of the State, a citizen has the right to a passport permitting him or her to avail of such facilities as international agreements existing at any given time afford to the holder of such a passport.... [O]ne of the hallmarks which is commonly accepted as dividing States which are categorised as authoritarian from those which are categorised as free and democratic is the inability of the citizens of, or residents in, the former to travel outside their country except at what is usually considered to be the whim of the executive power. Therefore, I have no doubt that a right to travel outside the State in the limited form in which I have already defined it (that is to say, a right to avail of such facilities as apply to the holder of an Irish passport at any given time) is a personal right of each citizen which, on the authority of the decisions to which I have referred, must be considered as being subject to the guarantees provided by Article 40 although not enumerated. [1979] IR 73, at 80–81.

[4-09] Finlay P held unconstitutional that portion of s 10 of the Adoption Act 1952 which prohibited a non-marital child under the age of one from being removed from the State. (The child's mother had wanted the child to travel to Nigeria to live with the family of the child's father there). This reasoning perhaps shows the "Christian and democratic nature" test at its most convincing. There are good and relatively uncontroversial grounds for characterizing a state that does not allow its citizens to travel as undemocratic.

[4-10] In *Kennedy v Ireland* [1987] IR 587, at 592, Hamilton P stated—without analysis perhaps because the point was not contested—that the right to privacy flowed from the Christian and democratic nature of the State, a point endorsed by Hamilton CJ in *Haughey v Moriarty* [1999] 3 IR 1, at 58. As will be seen below, however, a different basis for the right to privacy was cited in other cases.

The Human Personality

[4-11] In *McGee v Attorney General* [1974] IR 284, the plaintiff challenged the constitutionality of s 17(1) of the Criminal Law Act 1935 which prohibited the sale of contraceptives in Ireland or the import of contraceptives in Ireland. The plaintiff was a married woman who had four children. She had been informed by her medical advisors that another pregnancy could have serious consequences for her, including possibly putting her life at risk. Henchy J held for the plaintiff on the basis of a personal right to privacy protected by Art 40.3.1°:

> [T]he unspecified personal rights guaranteed by sub-s. 1 of s. 3 of Article 40 are not confined to those specified in sub-s. 2 of that section. It is for the Courts to decide in a particular case whether the right relied on comes within the constitutional guarantee. To do so, it must be shown that it is a right that inheres in the citizen in question by virtue of his human personality. The lack of precision in this test is reduced when sub-s. 1 of s. 3 of Article 40 is read (as it must be) in the light of the Constitution as a whole and, in particular, in the light of what the Constitution, expressly or by necessary implication, deems to be fundamental to the personal standing of the individual in question in the context of the social order envisaged by the Constitution. The infinite variety in the relationships between the citizen and his fellows and between the citizen and the State makes an exhaustive enumeration of the guaranteed rights difficult, if not impossible.
>
> The dominant feature of the plaintiff's dilemma is that she is a young married woman who is living, with a slender income, in the cramped quarters of a mobile home with her husband and four infant children, and that she is faced with a considerable risk of death or crippling paralysis if she becomes pregnant. The net question is whether it is

constitutionally permissible in the circumstances for the law to deny her access to the contraceptive method chosen for her by her doctor and which she and her husband wish to adopt. In other words, is the prohibition effected by s. 17 of the Act of 1935 an interference with the rights which the State guarantees in its laws to respect, as stated in sub-s. 1 of s. 3 of Article 40?

The answer lies primarily in the fact that the plaintiff is a wife and a mother. It is the informed and conscientious wish of the plaintiff and her husband to maintain full marital relations without incurring the risk of a pregnancy that may very well result in her death or in a crippling paralysis. Section 17 of the Act of 1935 frustrates that wish. It goes further; it brings the implementation of the wish within the range of the criminal law. Its effect, therefore, is to condemn the plaintiff and her husband to a way of life which, at best, will be fraught with worry, tension and uncertainty that cannot but adversely affect their lives and, at worst, will result in an unwanted pregnancy causing death or serious illness with the obvious tragic consequences to the lives of her husband and young children. And this in the context of a Constitution which in its preamble proclaims as one of its aims the dignity and freedom of the individual; which in sub-s. 2 of s. 3 of Article 40 casts on the State a duty to protect as best it may from unjust attack and, in the case of injustice done, to vindicate the life and person of every citizen; which in Article 41, after recognising the family as the natural primary and fundamental unit group of society, and as a moral institution possessing inalienable and imprescriptible rights antecedent and superior to all positive law, guarantees to protect it in its constitution and authority as the necessary basis of social order and as indispensable to the welfare of the nation and the State; and which, also in Article 41, pledges the State to guard with special care the institution of marriage, on which the family is founded, and to protect it against attack.

Section 17, in my judgment, so far from respecting the plaintiff's personal rights, violates them. If she observes this prohibition (which in practice she can scarcely avoid doing and which in law she is bound under penalty of fine and imprisonment to do), she will endanger the security and happiness of her marriage, she will imperil her health to the point of hazarding her life, and she will subject her family to the risk of distress and disruption. These are intrusions which she is entitled to say are incompatible with the safety of her life, the preservation of her health, her responsibility to her conscience, and the security and well-being of her marriage and family. If she fails to obey the prohibition in s. 17, the law, by prosecuting her, will reach into the privacy of her marital life in seeking to prove her guilt.

In my opinion, s. 17 of the Act of 1935 violates the guarantee in sub-s. 1 of s. 3 of Article 40 by the State to protect the plaintiff's personal rights by its laws; it does so not only by violating her personal right to privacy in regard to her marital relations but, in a wider way, by frustrating and making criminal any efforts by her to effectuate the decision of her husband and herself, made responsibly, conscientiously and on medical advice, to avail themselves of a particular contraceptive method so as to ensure her life and health as well as the integrity, security and well-being of her marriage and her family. [1974] IR 284, at 325–326, 328.

The concept of rights that inhere in citizens by virtue of their personality is, if anything, even more vague than the concept of rights that flow from the Christian and democratic nature of the State. Henchy J maintained that the vagueness of the test could be reduced by assessing what the Constitution views "as fundamental to the personal standing of the individual in question in the context of the social order envisaged by the Constitution." But it is questionable whether that provides any further guidance. How fundamental is "fundamental"? What does personal standing mean? Does the Constitution clearly envisage one form of social order? In any event, what does it mean for a right to inhere in an individual? The core of Henchy J's decision seems to turn on the way in which the legislation intruded on a particularly [4–12] private part of the plaintiff's life and prevented her from making decisions for herself, along with her husband, in relation to that part of her life. Using more contemporary language, it could be argued that the legislation offended her dignity. Yet Henchy J did not reduce the Art 40.3.1° protection to simply a protection of privacy, autonomy or dignity. Instead he viewed the right to privacy as just one of many rights that could inhere in the citizen by virtue of her human personality and was therefore protected by Art 40.3.1°.

[4–13] Henchy J took a similar approach to the right to privacy in *Norris v Attorney General* [1984] IR 36. In this case, the plaintiff challenged the constitutionality of s 61 of the Offences against the Person Act 1861 (criminalising anal sex) and s 11 of the Criminal Law Amendment Act 1885 (criminalising "gross indecency" between men). A majority of the Supreme Court held against the plaintiff, Henchy and McCarthy JJ dissenting. Henchy J expanded somewhat on his understanding of the privacy that was protected by Art 40.3.1°:

> That a right of privacy inheres in each citizen by virtue of his human personality, and that such right is constitutionally guaranteed as one of the unspecified personal rights comprehended by Article 40, s. 3, are propositions that are well attested by previous decisions of this Court. What requires to be decided—and this seems to me to be the essence of this case—is whether that right of privacy, construed in the context of the Constitution as a whole and given its true evaluation or standing in the hierarchy of constitutional priorities, excludes as constitutionally inconsistent the impugned statutory provisions.
>
> Having regard to the purposive Christian ethos of the Constitution, particularly as set out in the preamble ("to promote the common good, with due observance of Prudence, Justice and Charity, so that the dignity and freedom of the individual may be assured, true social order attained, the unity of our country restored, and concord established with other nations"), to the denomination of the State as "sovereign, independent, democratic" in Article 5, and to the recognition, expressly or by necessary implication, of particular personal rights, such recognition being frequently hedged in by overriding requirements such as "public order and morality" or "the authority of the State" or "the exigencies of the common good", there is necessarily given to the citizen, within the required social, political and moral framework, such a range of personal freedoms or immunities as are necessary to ensure his dignity and freedom as an individual in the type of society envisaged. The essence of those rights is that they inhere in the individual personality of the citizen in his capacity as a vital human component of the social, political and moral order posited by the Constitution.
>
> Amongst those basic personal rights is a complex of rights which vary in nature, purpose and range (each necessarily being a facet of the citizen's core of individuality within the constitutional order) and which may be compendiously referred to as the right of privacy. An express recognition of such a right is the guarantee in Article 16, s. 1, sub-s. 4, that voting in elections for Dáil Éireann shall be by secret ballot. A constitutional right to marital privacy was recognized and implemented by this Court in *McGee v. The Attorney General* [1974] I.R. 284; the right there claimed and recognized being, in effect, the right of a married woman to use contraceptives, which is something which at present is declared to be morally wrong according to the official teaching of the Church to which about 95% of the citizens belong. There are many other aspects of the right of privacy, some yet to be given judicial recognition. It is unnecessary for the purpose of this case to explore them. It is sufficient to say that they would all appear to fall within a secluded area of activity or non-activity which may be claimed as necessary for the expression of an individual personality, for purposes not always necessarily moral or commendable, but

meriting recognition in circumstances which do not engender considerations such as State security, public order or morality, or other essential components of the common good.

Put in specific terms, the central issue in this case is whether the plaintiff's claim to be entitled to engage in homosexual acts in private must give way to the right and duty of the State to uphold considerations of public order and morality. In my opinion the legal test by which that issue should be determined is this: where, as in this case, a pre-Constitution legislature has condemned as criminal all homosexual acts between males (ranging from acts of gross indecency, the commission of which does not require even physical contact, to acts of sodomy) and thereby blights and thwarts in a variety of ways the life of a person who is by nature incapable of giving expression to his sexuality except by homosexual acts, and who wishes to be entitled to do so consensually in private, the onus lies on the Attorney General, representing the State, if he is to defeat the individual's claim, to show that to allow him that degree of privacy would be inconsistent with the maintenance of public order and morality.

In my judgment the Attorney General has signally failed to discharge that onus. [1984] IR 36, at 71–72.

Although Henchy J provided compelling accounts of the way in which the restrictions in *Norris* and *McGee* affected the dignity of the two plaintiffs, the question remains as to whether inherence in human personality is a sufficiently clear basis for judges to afford constitutional recognition and protection to rights. One of the obvious difficulties is the potential for conflict between this test and the "Christian and democratic" test. For the conclusion reached by Henchy J in *McGee* was directly at odds with Catholic teaching while his conclusion in *Norris* was at odds with the vast bulk of Christian teaching. How could this be consistent with the Christian character of the State, not to mention the reliance placed by Kenny J on papal encyclicals? McCarthy J adverted to this problem: [4–14]

> In so far as the judgment of Kenny J. in McGee's Case [1974] I.R. 284, in referring to the Christian and democratic nature of the State, is a relevant identification of source (cited by the President of the High Court in *The State (C.) v. Frawley* [1976] I.R. 365 at p. 373 and in *The State (M.) v. The Attorney General* [1979] I.R. 73 at p. 80), I would respectfully dissent from such a proposition if it were to mean that, apart from the democratic nature of the State, the source of personal rights, unenumerated in the Constitution, is to be related to Christian theology, the subject of many diverse views and practices, rather than Christianity itself, the example of Christ and the great doctrine of charity which He preached. Jesus Christ proclaimed two great commandments—love of God and love of neighbour; St. Paul, the Apostle to the Gentiles, declared that of the great virtues, faith, hope and charity, the greatest of these is charity (1 Cor. 13, 13). I would uphold the view that the unenumerated rights derive from the human personality and that the actions of the State in respect of such rights must be informed by the proud objective of the people as declared in the preamble "seeking to promote the common good, with due observance of prudence, justice and charity, so that the dignity and freedom of the individual may be assured, true social order attained, the unity of our country restored, and concord established with other nations." The dignity and freedom of the individual occupy a prominent place in these objectives and are not declared to be subject to any particular exigencies but as forming part of the promotion of the common good. [1984] IR 36, at 99–100.

Although McCarthy J recognises the problem, his solution is scarcely convincing, at least not if one is concerned about judicial activism. While his view of Christianity, and human dignity, is compelling (perhaps more compelling than the official version of [4–15]

Christianity presented by Roman Catholic teaching), as a matter of constitutional doctrine what it amounts to is the proposition that Art 40.3.1° authorises judges to read their own understanding of Christianity into the Constitution. At the same time, the majority in *Norris* were relying on their understanding of Christianity to hold against the plaintiff:

> From the earliest days, organised religion regarded homosexual conduct, such as sodomy and associated acts, with a deep revulsion as being contrary to the order of nature, a perversion of the biological functions of the sexual organs and an affront both to society and to God. With the advent of Christianity this view found clear expression in the teachings of St. Paul, and has been repeated over the centuries by the doctors and leaders of the Church in every land in which the Gospel of Christ has been preached. To-day, as appears from the evidence given in this case, this strict view is beginning to be questioned by individual Christian theologians but, nevertheless, as the learned trial judge said in his judgment, it remains the teaching of all Christian Churches that homosexual acts are wrong....
>
> The preamble to the Constitution proudly asserts the existence of God in the Most Holy Trinity and recites that the people of Ireland humbly acknowledge their obligation to "our Divine Lord, Jesus Christ." It cannot be doubted that the people, so asserting and acknowledging their obligations to our Divine Lord Jesus Christ, were proclaiming a deep religious conviction and faith and an intention to adopt a Constitution consistent with that conviction and faith and with Christian beliefs. Yet it is suggested that, in the very act of so doing, the people rendered inoperative laws which had existed for hundreds of years prohibiting unnatural sexual conduct which Christian teaching held to be gravely sinful. It would require very clear and express provisions in the Constitution itself to convince me that such took place. When one considers that the conduct in question had been condemned consistently in the name of Christ for almost two thousand years and, at the time of the enactment of the Constitution, was prohibited as criminal by the laws in force in England, Wales, Scotland and Northern Ireland, the suggestion becomes more incomprehensible and difficult of acceptance. [1984] IR 36, at 61, 64.

[4–16] Thus the same Preamble on which McCarthy J relied to identify a right to dignity and privacy that would extend to permitting homosexual conduct in private was relied on by the majority almost to the point of suggesting that it would be unconstitutional to permit homosexual activity. Different understandings of Christianity led the minority and majority to different conclusions. The net effect of Art 40.3.1°, therefore, was to assign to judges a power not just to interpret the rights that *were* constitutionally protected but to decide what rights *ought to be* constitutionally protected.

The Natural Law

[4–17] In *State (Nicolaou) v An Bord Uchtála* [1966] IR 567, at 642, Walsh J observed:

> It is ... abundantly clear that the rights referred to in section 3 of Article 40 are those which may be called the natural personal rights and the very words of sub-section 1, by the reference therein to "laws", exclude such rights as are dependent only upon law.

[4–18] This reliance on the natural law came to the fore in *McGee v Attorney General* [1974] IR 289. Here Walsh J, like Henchy J, held in favour of the plaintiff, but on the basis of a somewhat more specific right to marital privacy derived from Article 41, as distinct from individual privacy. However, he also identified the natural law as a source of constitutional rights:

Articles 40, 41, 42 and 44 of the Constitution all fall within that section of the Constitution which is titled "Fundamental Rights." Articles 41, 42 and 43 emphatically reject the theory that there are no rights without laws, no rights contrary to the law and no rights anterior to the law. They indicate that justice is placed above the law and acknowledge that natural rights, or human rights, are not created by law but that the Constitution confirms their existence and gives them protection. The individual has natural and human rights over which the State has no authority; and the family, as the natural primary and fundamental unit group of society, has rights as such which the State cannot control. However, at the same time it is true, as the Constitution acknowledges and claims, that the State is the guardian of the common good and that the individual, as a member of society, and the family, as a unit of society, have duties and obligations to consider and respect the common good of that society....

Both in its preamble and in Article 6, the Constitution acknowledges God as the ultimate source of all authority. The natural or human rights to which I have referred earlier in this judgment are part of what is generally called the natural law. There are many to argue that natural law may be regarded only as an ethical concept and as such is a re-affirmation of the ethical content of law in its ideal of justice. The natural law as a theological concept is the law of God promulgated by reason and is the ultimate governor of all the laws of men. In view of the acknowledgment of Christianity in the preamble and in view of the reference to God in Article 6 of the Constitution, it must be accepted that the Constitution intended the natural human rights I have mentioned as being in the latter category rather than simply an acknowledgment of the ethical content of law in its ideal of justice. What exactly natural law is and what precisely it imports is a question which has exercised the minds of theologians for many centuries and on which they are not yet fully agreed. While the Constitution speaks of certain rights being imprescriptible or inalienable, or being antecedent and superior to all positive law, it does not specify them. Echoing the words of O'Byrne J. in *Buckley and Others (Sinn Féin) v. The Attorney General*, I do not feel it necessary to enter upon an inquiry as to their extent or, indeed, as to their nature. It is sufficient for the court to examine and to search for the rights which may be discoverable in the particular case before the court in which these rights are invoked....

In this country it falls finally upon the judges to interpret the Constitution and in doing so to determine, where necessary, the rights which are superior or antecedent to positive law or which are imprescriptible or inalienable. In the performance of this difficult duty there are certain guidelines laid down in the Constitution for the judge. The very structure and content of the Articles dealing with fundamental rights clearly indicate that justice is not subordinate to the law. In particular, the terms of s. 3 of Article 40 expressly subordinate the law to justice. Both Aristotle and the Christian philosophers have regarded justice as the highest human virtue. The virtue of prudence was also esteemed by Aristotle as by the philosophers of the Christian world. But the great additional virtue introduced by Christianity was that of charity—not the charity which consists of giving to the deserving, for that is justice, but the charity which is also called mercy. According to the preamble, the people gave themselves the Constitution to promote the common good with due observance of prudence, justice and charity so that the dignity and freedom of the individual might be assured. The judges must, therefore, as best they can from their training and their experience interpret these rights in accordance with their ideas of prudence, justice and charity. It is but natural that from time to time the prevailing ideas of these virtues may be conditioned by the passage of time; no interpretation of the Constitution is intended to be final for all time. It is given in the light of prevailing ideas and concepts. [1974] IR 284, at 310, 317–319.

As Henchy J had done in the same case, Walsh J identified the structure of the Constitution as providing guidance for judges. However, on closer examination it [4–19] transpires that the guidance provided is to the effect that justice (perhaps mitigated by charity) is above the law and therefore protected by the Constitution. Put another way, the natural law is constitutionally protected. The natural law is a set of moral principles which can be applied, by means of a natural law style of reasoning, to particular factual situations with a view to providing normative guidance to individuals, in the sense of providing *reasons* to behave in a particular way. Walsh J was putting it mildly when he stated that theologians were not yet fully agreed on the content of the natural law. There remains considerable disagreement among theologians—not to mention philosophers—about both the proper principles of natural law and the proper method of applying those principles to factual situations. Indeed, many natural lawyers would baulk at Walsh J's apparent conclusion that the natural law should be read into the Constitution. For many natural lawyers, the distinction between positive law and natural law is an important element of the natural law and not one that should be so readily collapsed.

[4–20] Uncertainty and disagreement over the content, mode of application and status of the natural law are not in and of themselves problems. It becomes problematic, however, when the courts decide that the Constitution gives positive law status to the natural law. For then, the courts' political power to re-order society becomes a power fettered not by any clear text, nor by any relatively clear political theory but rather only by each individual judge's own sense of what the natural law requires. And whether that constitutes a fetter at all is open to question.

[4–21] These difficulties came to the fore in *G v An Bord Uchtála* [1980] IR 32. Section 14 of the Adoption Act 1952 states that an adoption order shall not be made without the consent of the non-marital mother of the child, and that the consent may be withdrawn at any time before the adoption order is made. Where the child has been placed with the proposed adoptive parents but the mother, before the adoption order is made, withdraws her consent, she can apply to court, under s 10 of the Guardianship of Infants Act 1964. Where consent has been withdrawn, the proposed adoptive parent can apply to the High Court under s 3 of the Adoption Act 1972 for an order dispensing with the consent of the natural mother; such an order can be made if it is in the best interests of the child to do so. In this case, the plaintiff had given up her child for adoption but withdrew her consent before the adoption order was made. The natural mother sought an order returning the child to her custody; the proposed adoptive parents sought an order dispensing with the natural mother's consent. In order to determine the issue, the High Court and the Supreme Court had to identify the constitutional rights of the natural mother and her child, and then interpret the relevant statutory provisions in that light. Three members of the Supreme Court held that the child should be returned to its mother; two members dissented.

[4–22] Walsh J identified the constitutional rights of mother and child as follows:

> The mother and her illegitimate child are human beings and each has the fundamental rights of every human being and the fundamental rights which spring from their relationship to each other. These are natural rights. It has already been decided by this Court in *Nicolaou's Case* [1966] I.R. 567 that among the mother's natural rights is the right to the custody and care of her child. Rights also have their corresponding obligations or duties. The fact that a child is born out of lawful wedlock is a natural fact. Such a child is just as entitled to be supported and reared by its parent or parents, who

are the ones responsible for its birth, as a child born in lawful wedlock. One of the duties of a parent or parents, be they married or not, is to provide as best the parent or parents can the welfare of the child and to ward off dangers to the health of the child....In my judgment in [*McGee*], I referred (at p. 310) to Articles 41, 42 and 43 of the Constitution and expressed the view, which I still hold, that these Articles "acknowledge that natural rights, or human rights, are not created by law but that the Constitution confirms their existence and gives them protection. The individual has natural and human rights over which the State has no authority..." Later, at p. 317 of the report, I stated:— "The natural or human rights to which I have referred earlier in this judgment are part of what is generally called the natural law."

Not only has the child born out of lawful wedlock the natural right to have its welfare and health guarded no less well than that of a child born in lawful wedlock, but *a fortiori* it has the right to life itself and the right to be guarded against all threats directed to its existence whether before or after birth. The child's natural rights spring primarily from the natural right of every individual to life, to be reared and educated, to liberty, to work, to rest and recreation, to the practice of religion, and to follow his or her conscience. The right to life necessarily implies the right to be born, the right to preserve and defend (and to have preserved and defended) that life, and the right to maintain that life at a proper human standard in matters of food, clothing and habitation. It lies not in the power of the parent who has the primary natural rights and duties in respect of the child to exercise them in such a way as intentionally or by neglect to endanger the health or life of the child or to terminate its existence. The child's natural right to life and all that flows from that right are independent of any right of the parent as such. I wish here to repeat what I said in *McGee's Case* [1974] I.R. 284. at p. 312 of the report:— "... any action on the part of either the husband and wife or of the State to limit family sizes by endangering or destroying human life must necessarily not only be an offence against the common good but also against the guaranteed personal rights of the human life in question." In these respects the child born out of lawful wedlock is in precisely the same position as the child born in lawful wedlock. [1980] IR 32, at 67–69.

Based on this analysis of the constitutional rights, Walsh J held that the consent of the mother, within the meaning of the Act, was only given where the mother acted to surrender or abandon the natural rights that inhered in her. He concluded that the mother had not in a free and fully informed way surrendered her rights to her child. [4–23]

O'Higgins CJ provided a slightly different natural law account of the rights of mother and child: [4–24]

> [T]he plaintiff is a mother and, as such, she has rights which derive from the fact of motherhood and from nature itself. These rights are among her personal rights as a human being and they are rights which, under Article 40, s. 3, sub-s. 1, the State is bound to respect, defend and vindicate. As a mother, she has the right to protect and care for, and to have the custody of, her infant child. The existence of this right was recognised in the judgment of this Court in *The State (Nicolaou) v. An Bord Uchtála* [1966] I.R. 567. This right is clearly based on the natural relationship which exists between a mother and child. In my view, it arises from the infant's total dependency and helplessness and from the mother's natural determination to protect and sustain her child. How far and to what extent it survives as the child grows up is not a matter of concern in the present case. Suffice to say that this plaintiff, as a mother, had a natural right to the custody of her child who was an infant, and that this natural right of hers is recognised and protected by Article 40, s. 3, sub-s. 1, of the Constitution. Section 6, sub-s. 4, and s. 10, sub-s. 2(*a*), of the Guardianship of Infants Act, 1964, constitute a compliance by the State with its obligation, in relation to the mother of an illegitimate child, to defend and vindicate in its

laws this right to custody. These statutory provisions make the mother guardian of her illegitimate child and give the mother statutory rights to sue for custody.

However, these rights of the mother in relation to her child are neither inalienable nor imprescriptible, as are the rights of the family under Article 41. They can be alienated or transferred in whole or in part and either subject to conditions or absolutely, or they can be lost by the mother if her conduct towards the child amounts to an abandonment or an abdication of her rights and duties.

The Child's Rights

The child also has natural rights. Normally, these will be safe under the care and protection of its mother. Having been born, the child has the right to be fed and to live, to be reared and educated, to have the opportunity of working and of realising his or her full personality and dignity as a human being. These rights of the child (and others which I have not enumerated) must equally be protected and vindicated by the State. In exceptional cases the State, under the provisions of Article 42, s. 5, of the Constitution, is given the duty, as guardian of the common good, to provide for a child born into a family where the parents fail in their duty towards that child for physical or moral reasons. In the same way, in special circumstances the State may have an equal obligation in relation to a child born outside the family to protect that child, even against its mother, if her natural rights are used in such a way as to endanger the health or life of the child or to deprive him of his rights. In my view this obligation stems from the provisions of Article 40, s. 3, of the Constitution. [1980] IR 32, at 55–56.

[4–25] O'Higgins CJ then disagreed with Walsh J in coming to the conclusion that, by agreeing to place her child for adoption, the natural mother had dispensed with her constitutional rights over the child. Although it is not unusual for judges to disagree over matters of interpretation, the disagreement between Walsh J and O'Higgins CJ is of a different order. For it is not in any sense a disagreement over text, but is rather a disagreement over which version of natural law theory should, by virtue of Article 40.3.1°, be accorded the status of constitutional law: a natural law theory that accords strong (difficult to waive) rights to the natural mother or a natural law theory that accords less strong rights?

Rights Implied From Other Constitutional Provisions

[4–26] In quite a number of cases, the courts have held that rights implicit in other constitutional provisions fall to be protected by Art 40.3.1°. For instance, in *Macauley v Minister for Posts and Telegraphs* [1966] IR 345, Kenny J held that Art 34.1, providing that justice shall be administered in courts established by law, implied a right of access to the courts, which right fell to be protected by Art 40.3.1°. In other cases, the courts have identified constitutional rights that could fairly be characterised as implicit in other constitutional provisions, even if the judges did not rely on those other provisions in their identification of the right. For instance, in *Ryan* itself, Kenny J spoke of the right to marry as being derived from the Christian and democratic nature of the State. However, the right to marry could also reasonably be said to be implicit in the special status afforded to marriage under Art 41.

[4–27] These methods of enumerating rights under Art 40.3.1° do not pose the same difficulties as those other methods considered above. For here there remains a textual basis for the recognition of rights and the problems that arise are chiefly problems of interpretation. Interpretation may, of course, be problematic. There are better and worse methods of constitutional interpretation. There may even be correct and incorrect methods of interpretation. These issues arise generally with regard to law, albeit possibly in more pressing form with constitutional law, where the courts have the power to overturn the decisions of democratically elected legislators. The issues posed by interpretation shall be considered separately in chapter 17. As significant as these issues are, they are not as acute as those raised by cases such as *McGee*, *G* and *Norris*. For where the courts utilise Art 40.3.1° to read into the Constitution each judge's own understanding of the natural law or each judge's own understanding of what is inherent in the human personality or each judge's own understanding of what a Christian and democratic State requires, this is not interpretation, but enactment.

The Difficulties with the Unenumerated Rights Doctrine

Perhaps more than any other of constitutional law, the unenumerated rights doctrine attracted significant academic criticism that subsequently informed the development of constitutional doctrine. As well as highlighting the scope for manoeuvre afforded to judges by the unenumerated rights doctrine, Desmond Clarke identifies some of the philosophical problems presented by the particular natural law theories to which the courts—on occasion—apparently committed themselves: [4–28]

> The use of the term "nature" or "natural" to designate a moral law or fundamental legal rights often involves a conflation of two distinctions, viz. "nature" meaning law-governed, and "natural" as opposed to artificial. The attractiveness of the former derives from the necessity which is characteristic of physical laws: while the motivation for the latter seems to depend on the idea that human agents should not interfere in God's (natural) causal agency. Both of these ideas require some elaboration to make the rest of the discussion intelligible.
>
> Physical phenomena, in so far as they are though to occur according to laws of nature, *necessarily* occur in the way that they do. That means that, given a certain set of prior conditions, the outcome is inevitable. This does not imply that the scientific laws which we use to describe physical events are necessarily true; evidently, they are merely hypothetical. However, at the time in which the natural law theory was adopted by scholastic philosophy, the distinction was not clearly made between the kind of necessity involved in the way the laws operate, and the non-necessary status of the laws as knowledge-claims. So that one gets the impression that the laws of nature are both necessarily true and that they determine the occurrence of physical events necessarily. Such laws were the ideal principles for a science of nature according to the model of science proposed by Aristotle and endorsed by the scholastic tradition up to the middle of the seventeenth century. This model demanded that any scientific—*ie* reliable or worthwhile—knowledge must be based on first principles which were necessarily true or self-evident, and that these principles should describe the natures of whatever one hoped to scientifically understand.
>
> If this model of an ideal science is applied to ethics and jurisprudence, then we would need to formulate basic principles which function in approximately the same way in which the physical laws of nature were mistakenly thought to function in Aristotelian science. These first principles of ethics and law would have to be necessarily true or self-evident, and they would relate to human behaviour in some way which is analogous to the relationship between the laws of nature (in the scientific sense) and physical events. Therefore they could be called by analogy, "laws of nature" or "natural laws".
>
> This historically explicable but philosophically counterproductive analogy, between physical science and ethics, obscured a number of very important distinctions: [...] between what *is* the case, as in physical science, and what *ought to be* the case, in ethics or law. The attempt to logically derive the latter from the former is so suspect that it has

earned a special title, the naturalistic fallacy. The fallacy involved here is, technically, the attempt to deduce claims about how people ought to behave from descriptions of how either agents or events naturally (in senses II and III) act or occur. No series of merely factual descriptions of anything can logically imply conclusions about how human agents ought to behave. In a less technical sense and perhaps more often in practice, the fallacy is committed by ignoring the difficulties involved in drawing analogies between physical laws and moral or legal laws. In this approach one does not attempt to formally deduce values from facts; however, one does apparently justify evaluative conclusions on the basis of evidence of a factual character which cannot logically support them. This kind of move is sometimes facilitated by analogies between "nature" and an ideal of moral behaviour but such analogies do not save these arguments from the charge of fallacious reasoning. Desmond Clarke, "The Role of Natural Law in Irish Constitutional Law" (1982) 17 *Irish Jurist* 187, at 192–194.

[4–29] A lack of philosophical sophistication on the part of judges, Clarke argues, led the courts either to commit the naturalistic fallacy in their enumeration of rights or to fail to articulate which natural law theory justified the right's existence. Addressing O'Higgins CJ's judgment in *G v An Bord Uchtála* [1980] IR 33, at 55–56, Clarke comments as follows:

> This opinion suggests a query about the natural law basis of the various rights which are said to be constitutionally guaranteed. The Chief Justice claimed that the relevant rights "*derive from* the fact of motherhood and from nature itself", or that the mother's right is "*clearly based* on the natural relationship which exists between a mother and child. It *arises* ... from the infant's total dependency ... and from the mother's natural determination to protect and sustain her child."
>
> One non-contentious interpretation of this paragraph would be to read the word "natural" as a purely descriptive epithet which is applied to constitutional rights which pertain to natural relationships, where "natural" is understood according to sense IV above. In that case, the basis of such rights would not be natural law theory at all but either the explicit text of the Constitution or a theory of rights which are implicitly guaranteed by the Constitution. This interpretation would fail to do justice, however, to the apparent justificatory force of the words italicised in the previous paragraph.
>
> Another interpretation would be to read the text as if it blatantly committed the naturalistic fallacy of attempting to deduce rights from facts, as in the right of a mother *deriving* from the fact of motherhood. Evidently, the fact of motherhood, in itself, could not give rise to either moral or legal rights of any description.
>
> The only other interpretation suggested by the text is to introduce some natural law theory as the appropriate bridge between "the fact of motherhood" and "the natural right to custody". And this, in turn, requires that the natural law theory in question be made explicit in order to test its assumed validity[.] Desmond Clarke, "The Role of Natural Law in Irish Constitutional Law" (1982) *Irish Jurist* 187, at 205.

[4–30] Gerard Hogan summed up the difficulties posed by the unenumerated rights doctrine in the following terms:

> [W]hile the language of Article 40.3.1 would seem to compel the courts to arrive at the analysis approved in *Ryan*, this is not necessarily a result which should meet with out unqualified approval, since the lack of objectivity in the method whereby such unenumerated rights are arrived at, coupled with the attendant uncertainty thereby entailed, all seriously undermine the important legal values of objectivity and certainty. In other words, the gist of the objection is that the rather loose language of Article 40.3.1 has resulted in a vast—and, it must be said, somewhat unprincipled—expansion of the power

of judicial review. While the protection of such various unenumerated rights—such as the right to privacy, the right to earn a livelihood and the right of an unwed mother to custody and care of her child – may well be beneficial and salutary, it is often difficult to take this jurisprudence completely at face value, since there is nothing whatever in the actual text of the Constitution to show that these rights were intended to enjoy constitutional protection. Gerard Hogan, "Unenumerated Personal Rights: *Ryan's* Case Re-evaluated" (1990–1992) 25–27 *Irish Jurist* 95, at 114.

In response to Hogan, Humphreys mounted a spirited defence of judicial reliance on the natural law. His argument essentially makes three points: the Constitution mandates judicial reliance on the natural law; the exclusion of natural law from the Constitution could lead to a disregard for human rights; there is in fact a wide body of material that can guide judges in their elaboration of the natural law: [4–31]

> One can like it or not, but the existence of God and natural law are given constitutional facts. This is not to say of course that these concepts have any reality in themselves. Views differ on this question and there is little point in elaborating my own view here. But what is significant is that the judge who is asked to interpret the Constitution must set his or her scepticism about natural rights aside. Such personal scepticism could scarcely be more irrelevant. For the purpose of any practical exercise in constitutional interpretation, natural rights exist because the Constitution says that they do.
>
> It is not difficult to see why the framers of constitutions and great charters of international rights have chosen to phrase their documents in terms of natural law. Natural rights theory is poetic, overarching, mysterious, immense. It places us in awe of the wonder of the human condition. It asserts that the challenges of our condition have meaning, and that the denial of life, liberty and well-being violates an awesome moral character which pre-exists the insignificant circumstances of mere human governments and laws. Natural law is an affirmation of the significance of the human person and of his or her sacred entitlement to respect. It refutes, with the ultimate argument of the transcendent, the sometimes horrendous suffering inflicted on our fellow men and women. [...]
>
> Perhaps it would be more courageous, existentially, to declare that constitutional rights are simply those posited in a particular document, and have no meaning outside of that. There is not shortage of literature which can be read as a call to such a positivistic rejection. But history suggests that this approach has its dangers. Mr Justice Walsh has pointed to the disasters of legal positivism in South Africa and Nazi Germany as events which proved to be the downfall of the vogue for that particular interpretive methodology. It seems that a case can be made that the natural rights model has better prospects of acting as a successful theoretical underpinning for the factual enforcement of rights than has positivism. In other words, if natural rights are a fiction, they are a necessary fiction. The argument then really comes down to whether this is sufficient to justify a role for natural rights, or whether it is an unhealthy or even dishonest symptom of result-orientated jurisprudence at work. Perhaps it is sufficient to say that the expression of natural rights theories in constitutional law is simply an imperfect articulation of the insight that the human condition has a mystery and wonder about it which cannot be captured by any single written text. [...]
>
> Natural rights theory presupposes that the individual human being has rights which exist prior to law and which inhere in him or her simply by virtue of being a person. By definition, such rights are good for all persons everywhere in the world. This being so, one would expect to find some reflection of them in international human rights instruments and in national constitutions and laws throughout the world. A court in any given jurisdiction which is charged with the task of identifying the existence of a particular personal right thus has a body of external material to assist in this task. It may be

additionally guided, as an Irish court would be, to particular traditions which may be of special value to this task. Richard Humphreys, "Interpreting Natural Rights" (1993–1995) 28–30 *Irish Jurist* 221, at 222; 224–225.

[4–32] Humphreys is surely right that the explicit constitutional references to the natural law are the soundest basis for a natural rights-based jurisprudence. However, this rooting of natural law's authority in the Constitution cuts both ways. For there is no guarantee that the natural law referred to by the Irish Constitution actually is the natural law. Nor is there any particular reason to believe that judicial invocation of the language of natural law is likely to lead to a better protection of human rights.

[4–33] None of this determines the appropriate method for interpreting the Constitution in general. It may well be that those constitutional provisions that are informed by natural law theory (such as property rights and family rights) should be interpreted in a way that is consistent with natural law theory. For present purposes, the point is a narrower one. The judicial enumeration (as distinct from interpretation) of rights by reference to indeterminate external sources, whether natural law, human personality, or Christianity, raises significant problems.

The Apotheosis of the Natural Law in Irish Constitutional Law

[4–34] Of all the methods for the enumeration of rights, Walsh J's natural law theory raised the greatest number of questions about the constitutional order. As was seen above, in *McGee v Attorney General* [1974] IR 245, at 310, Walsh J described the interaction between the Constitution and the natural law in the following terms:

> Articles 41, 42 and 43 emphatically reject the theory that there are no rights without laws, no rights contrary to the law and no rights anterior to the law. They indicate that justice is placed above the law and acknowledge that natural rights, or human rights, are not created by law but that the Constitution confirms their existence and gives them protection. The individual has natural and human rights over which the State has no authority; and the family, as the natural primary and fundamental unit group of society, has rights as such which the State cannot control.

[4–35] Lest there was any doubt, Walsh J later in the judgment clarified that the constitutional references to the natural law were not simply an acknowledgement of the ethical content of law but were rather a statement that the natural law was the ultimate governor of the laws of man.

[4–36] In *McGee*, Walsh J gave effect to the natural law in order to strike down legislation. However, if justice is placed above the law and if the State has no authority over natural and human rights, it follows that the natural law is superior to the Constitution itself. Given that the Constitution requires judges to give effect to the natural law, this raised the intriguing proposition that certain constitutional provisions might be unconstitutional. An argument of this type had been made in relation to the Irish Free State Constitution in *State (Ryan) v Lennon* [1935] IR 170, in which the Supreme Court considered Art 2A of that Constitution. Originally, the 1922 Constitution allowed for amendment by ordinary legislation for a period of eight years. However, prior to that period running out, the Constitution was amended (by ordinary legislation) to allow for amendment by ordinary legislation to continue for a further eight years.

Subsequent to this provision, Art 2A was inserted into the Constitution. This was a [4–37] lengthy provision that effectively came into operation by order of the Executive Council. This order could be made whenever, in the opinion of the Executive Council, circumstances existed which rendered it expedient. The Article established a tribunal, staffed by military personnel, to try certain offences and also granted a number of powers to police officers in relation to the arrest and detention of persons. The Article also provided that, in the event of an inconsistency between its provisions and other provisions contained in the Constitution, its own provisions took precedence. The prosecutors were detained under the provisions of the Article and sought their release. The Court considered a number of arguments in relation to whether Art 2A was a valid amendment of the Constitution, a majority concluding that it was. Kennedy CJ, however, strongly dissented:

> [I]f any legislation of the Oireachtas (including any purported amendment of the Constitution) were to offend against that acknowledged ultimate Source from which the legislative authority has come through the people to the Oireachtas, as, for example, if it were repugnant to the Natural Law, such legislation would be necessarily unconstitutional and invalid, and it would be, therefore, absolutely null and void and inoperative. [1935] IR 170, at 204–205.

This argument came more forcibly back into focus in 1995. In 1983, the Constitution [4–38] had been amended to give explicit protection to the right to life of the unborn child. In 1992, this provision itself was amended to ensure that it did not limit the freedom to obtain or make available, in the State, information relating to abortion services lawfully available in other states. In order to give legislative effect to this amendment of the Constitution, the Oireachtas passed the Regulation of Information (Services Outside the State for Termination of Pregnancies) Bill 1995. The President referred the Bill to the Supreme Court under Art 26 of the Constitution. Arguments against the Bill were presented both by counsel assigned to represent the interests of the unborn and by counsel assigned to represent the interests of the mother. Counsel on behalf of the unborn essentially argued, relying on the dicta of Walsh J in McGee as well as on other provisions of the Constitution and other dicta, that the Bill was unconstitutional because the amendment on which it was based was itself unconstitutional: enactments of the people (constitutional amendments) had to comply with the natural law in order to be valid. Citing both constitutional provisions and case law, Mr Justice O'Hanlon, writing extra-judicially, made the following argument:

> If important aspects of a most fundamental human right can be set aside in this manner, the question must arise as to whether there are *any* limits to the power to make laws which are contrary to basis human rights. Would it be constitutionally licit, for example, for the people to enact a provision allowing the elderly, disabled or infirm to be killed on the advice of a doctor? Is there any limitation on the power in Article 46.1 of the Constitution by which "Any provision of this Constitution may be amended"?
>
> This question goes to the root of the nature of law. It obliges us to consider the relationship between basic human rights and the process of political resolution of issues of public controversy. It is clearly not sufficient that the formal requirements of the legislative process be observed for a law to be considered just and in accordance with human dignity. In fact, the origin of all modern Charters of Human Rights lies in the recognition that there *are* limits, grounded in human nature, to any law-making power.[. . .]

> Fortunately, Bunreacht na hEireann leaves us in little doubt as to where it stands on this question. It acknowledges the authority of a higher law as the source of "inalienable and imprescriptable" rights which are "antecedent and superior to all positive law" (Article 41.1.1). It identifies "man in virtue of his rational being" as the subject of fundamental rights (Article 42.1.1) and human personality as the basis for equality before the law (Article 40.1). These are important indicators of the legal philosophy on which the Constitution is based and they must govern our understanding of Irish law so long as they remain part of the Constitution. [...]
>
> Some tentative conclusions may be reached at this stage.
> 1. The State is founded on a Constitution which acknowledges that all authority comes from the Most Holy Trinity to Whom, as our final end, all actions both of men and States must be referred, and which states that all powers of government derive under God from the people.
> 2. It would appear to follow, as affirmed by Chief Justice Kennedy and Mr Justice Henchy, that no law could be enacted, no amendment of the Constitution could lawfully be adopted, and no judicial decision could lawfully be given, which conflicted with the Natural Law (which we recognise as being of divine origin).
>
> Roderick O'Hanlon, "Natural Rights and the Irish Constitution" (1993) 11 *ILT* 8, at 8, 10.

[4–39] The argument against this proposition is that the people are entitled to amend the Constitution in whatever way they see fit. The amending power in Art 46 is, at least on its own terms, unfettered:

> Any provision of this Constitution may be amended, whether by way of variation, addition or repeal, in the manner provided by this Article.

[4–40] Also, in a number of other cases, the courts had suggested that the people were sovereign. Indeed, in *Byrne v Ireland* [1972] IR 241, at 263, Walsh J himself had commented:

> [T]he State is the creation of the people and is to be governed in accordance with the provisions of the Constitution which was enacted by the people and which can be amended by the people only, and ... the sovereign authority is the people.

[4–41] In effect, in two different lines of cases the courts had come to two different conclusions. On the one hand, the Constitution was subordinate to (and dependent for its authority on) the people. On the other hand, the Constitution was subordinate to (and dependent for its authority on) the natural law. These two conclusions could co-exist provided that the people never acted in a way that could be considered incompatible with the natural law. However, where a constitutional amendment was inconsistent with the natural law (as was arguably, though not necessarily, the case with the abortion information amendment), the conclusions to be drawn from the two lines of case law were mutually inconsistent. In *Re Article 26 and the Regulation of Information (Services Outside the State for Termination of Pregnancies) Bill 1995* [1995] 1 IR 1, the Supreme Court had to decide between these two propositions. The manner in which it did so was deeply unsatisfactory.

[4–42] Having reviewed previous case law, including many of the cases considered in this chapter, the Supreme Court concluded on this issue:

> It is clear from the passages from these judgments set forth herein that the courts in interpreting the Constitution and in ascertaining and declaring what are the personal

rights which are guaranteed by the Constitution and in determining, where necessary, the rights which are superior or antecedent to positive law or which are imprescriptible or inalienable, must act in accordance with the aforesaid guidelines as laid down in the Constitution and must interpret them in accordance with their ideas of prudence, justice and charity.

As stated by Walsh J. in the course of his judgment in *McGee v. The Attorney General* [1974] I.R. 284 at p. 318 of the report:—

> In a pluralist society such as ours, the Courts cannot as a matter of constitutional law be asked to choose between the differing views, where they exist, of experts on the interpretation by the differing religious denominations of either the nature and extent of these natural rights as they are to be found in the natural law.

From a consideration of all the cases which recognised the existence of a personal right which was not specifically enumerated in the Constitution, it is manifest that the Court in each such case had satisfied itself that such personal right was one which could be reasonably implied from and was guaranteed by the provisions of the Constitution, interpreted in accordance with its ideas of prudence, justice and charity.

The courts, as they were and are bound to, recognised the Constitution as the fundamental law of the State to which the organs of the State were subject and at no stage recognised the provisions of the natural law as superior to the Constitution.

The People were entitled to amend the Constitution in accordance with the provisions of Article 46 of the Constitution and the Constitution as so amended by the Fourteenth Amendment is the fundamental and supreme law of the State representing as it does the will of the People. [1995] 1 IR 1, at 42–43.

The Supreme Court's conclusion that the courts "at no stage recognised the provisions of the natural law as superior to the Constitution" flatly contradicts Walsh J's statements in *McGee* to the effect that the State has no authority over natural rights, not to mention with the Court's own description of those rights—a few sentences previously—as being "superior or antecedent to positive law". Nevertheless, the case amounted to a judicial assertion that popular sovereignty trumped the natural law. [4–43]

Although the Supreme Court's reasoning leaves much to be desired, the case itself raises fundamental issues as to the character of the Irish legal system and the source of authority for the Irish Constitution. I have outlined these issues elsewhere as follows: [4–44]

> The paradox of a higher law the content of which is determined by the agents of positive law reflects a deeper paradox. Duncan argues:
>> The difficulty ... is that the theory that the natural law stands above the Constitution is being justified by the terms of a human instrument, the Constitution, which is itself subject to the natural law. The Constitution cannot be both subject to the natural law and the legal justification for that subjection.
>
> This undermines the basic premise of the O'Hanlon thesis: the Constitution (and *a fortiori* judicial decisions) cannot, argues Duncan, be cited as authority for the superiority of natural law to positive law. But the same argument applies to the popular sovereignty thesis: the Constitution (and *a fortiori* judicial decisions) cannot be cited as authority for the superiority of the people to positive law. The natural law argument and the popular sovereignty argument as to the source of legal validity are both contingent on positive law. The former locates the source of validity outside the Constitution in the natural law, while the latter locates the source of validity outside the Constitution in the popular will. In the former image, the Constitution derives its authority from the natural law and is valid only to the extent that it complies with the natural law: it was on this basis that the 14th Amendment was argued to be invalid. In the latter image, the Constitution derives

its authority from the people and is valid to the extent that it represents the popular will. On this basis, the 14th Amendment could not but be valid.

The problem with each argument is that it purports to draw its authority from within the constitutional order itself. This phenomenon can be described in two ways. First, it can be said that both the natural law and the popular sovereignty arguments have dual status as moral and legal claims. Each is a contingent claim of positive law, but purports to identify itself as a proposition of absolute, political morality. Secondly, it can be said that both arguments are circular. In making claims about the validity of the Irish constitutional order, each argument purports to locate legal validity externally; by using material from within the positive legal system as authority for that location, however, each argument allows the chain of validity to loop back into the system. Each argument is circular, telling one nothing of Irish law's actual justification. The story of legal validity, law's explanation of its own existence, *is a* story of self-justification.

This circularity of argumentation manifests itself in a further and related way. The popular sovereignty argument purports to locate the source of validity in the people. It is they who have the authority to amend the Constitution. However, "the people" is a construct of the Constitution, a product of Art.2 and Art.16.1.2. These two provisions constitute "the people" in the sense of the source of validity under the popular sovereignty claim. It is clearly a construct of the Constitution in the first instance and of statutory law in the second instance. If the Constitution is a construct of the people, the people are equally a construct of the Constitution and any search for the source of validity between the two leads one into a circle of analysis. Similarly, it can be argued that the natural law to which the Irish Constitution is supposedly subordinate is itself, depending as it does on judicial enumeration, a creature of the Constitution and did not pre-exist the Constitution for which it is claimed as a source of authority. Oran Doyle, "Legal Validity: Reflections on the Irish Constitution" (2003) 25 *DULJ* 56, at 65–66, citing William Duncan, "Can Natural Law Be Used In Constitutional Interpretation?" (1995) 45 *Doctrine & Life* 125, at 127.

[4–45] Setting aside the broader issues raised by the case and the unsatisfactory reasoning employed by the Court, the decision of *Re Article 26 and the Regulation of Information (Services Outside the State for Termination of Pregnancies) Bill 1995* is clear: the power of the people to amend the Constitution trumps any natural law rights. The message of the judgment also seems clear. Prior to the case, the rate of enumeration of rights under Art 40.3.1° had drastically slowed. The case indicated a general wariness about the natural law, at least suggesting that the heyday of the unenumerated rights doctrine was over. Shortly after the Supreme Court's decision, Twomey predicted that the decision might herald the death of natural law within Irish constitutional jurisprudence:

> One of the great tragedies of the bitter debate on abortion and related matters which has raged in this country over the last number of years is that it has caused other issues to become clouded and confused. Now it would seem that the abortion debate has claimed as its latest victim a *corpus* of law which has a centuries-old tradition and an immense value. If the Supreme Court decision has proved anything, it is that "hard cases" do not only make bad law, but that they also destroy good law. For the foreseeable future at least then it would seem that positivists and black-letter lawyers will hold sway in the Supreme Court. It is to be hoped that history will not remember them as the architects of the death of natural law. Adrian Twomey, "The Death of Natural Law" (1995) *ILT* 270, at 272.

Current Status of Unenumerated Rights Doctrine

[4–46] Following the Supreme Court's decision in the *Abortion Information Case*, there continued to be some, albeit diminishing, vitality for the unenumerated rights doctrine.

In *O'T v B* [1998] 2 IR 321, an issue arose as to whether a person was entitled to know the identity of her mother. The judgments in these cases considered two conjoined cases in which two people, both of whom had been informally adopted prior to the introduction of the adoption code in 1952, sought to establish the identity of their mother. The legislation invoked and the procedures employed in the two sets of proceedings were slightly different, but the constitutional issue that arose was the same. The Supreme Court unanimously agreed that the lower courts (*ie* courts other than the High Court and the Supreme Court) had no role in declaring constitutional rights. Although such courts should defend and vindicate rights that were explicit in the Constitution or had been clearly declared by the higher courts, they could not enumerate rights themselves. The Court disagreed, however, over whether rights should be enumerated by the higher courts under Art 40.3.1°. Hamilton CJ, Denham, Barrington and Barron JJ confirmed that the High Court and the Supreme Court had the role of enumerating such rights. Hamilton CJ, delivering a judgment with which the three other majority judges (at least on these points) agreed, reasoned:

> It is clear from the foregoing passage that Kenny J. considered that the responsible duty of ascertaining and declaring what are the personal rights of the citizen, other than those specified in Article 40, rests on the High Court and the Supreme Court.
>
> In many cases, too numerous to mention, since the decision in *Ryan v. The Attorney General* [1965] I.R. 294, the High Court and the Supreme Court have fulfilled the responsible duty referred to by Kenny J. In no case, has either the District Court or the Circuit Court sought to exercise such jurisdiction.
>
> I am satisfied that it was the intention of the framers of the Constitution that all matters pertaining to the interpretation of the provisions of the Constitution should be decided by the courts whose jurisdiction derives from the Constitution itself and not by courts of limited and local jurisdiction, whose jurisdiction is derived from Acts of the Oireachtas. [1998] 2 IR 321, at 342.

Hamilton CJ then held that the right of a natural child to know the identity of her natural parents had not been declared in *G v An Bord Uchtála*. If it were to be relied on, therefore, it would have to be declared first by the High Court or the Supreme Court. He then considered whether it was a right protected by Art 40.3.1°: [4–47]

> The existence of such right is not dependent on the obligation to protect the child's right to bodily integrity or such rights as the child might enjoy in relation to the property of his or her natural mother but stems directly from the aforesaid relationship.
>
> It is not, however, an absolute or unqualified right: its exercise may be restricted by the constitutional rights of others, and by the requirement of the common good.
>
> Its exercise is restricted in the case of children who have been lawfully adopted in accordance with the provisions of the Adoption Act, 1952 as the effect of an adoption order is that all parental rights and duties of the natural parents are ended, while the child becomes a member of the family of the adoptive parents as if he or she had been their natural child.
>
> The applicant and the plaintiff are not in the same position as children who have been adopted in accordance with the provisions of the Adoption Act, 1952. They remain the children of their natural mother and are entitled to the benefit of such rights as arise from such relationship. While they enjoy the constitutional right to know the identity of their respective natural mothers, the exercise of such right may be restricted by the constitutional right to privacy and confidentiality of the natural mothers in respect of their dealings with the Society. Whether they are so restricted depends on the

circumstances of the case and whether they, or either of them wish to exercise this right to privacy. [1998] 2 IR 321, at 348–349.

[4–48] This judgment could be characterised as a return to the very strong enumeration of rights seen in cases such as *G* and *McGee*. Hamilton CJ derived the right to know one's parent's identity from the very fact of the parent-child relationship. However, it was not such a naked exercise of political power as were the earlier judgments in *G* and *McGee*. For the right recognised here, although not easily inferable from the text of other constitutional provisions, was inferable from the rights of natural parents and children that had been accorded constitutional recognition in *G*. That is, the right was derived as much from the existing *corpus* of constitutional law as it was from the precepts of the natural law.

[4–49] Keane J delivered a judgment that was markedly sceptical of the unenumerated rights doctrine, and was considerably more reserved in its approach to the enumeration of rights. Having reviewed Kenny J's decision in *Ryan*, he noted:

> There was no discussion in [the judgment of the Supreme Court delivered by Ó Dálaigh CJ] of the question as to whether, given that the unenumerated rights clearly existed in the contemplation of the framers of the Constitution, it was intended by them that the duty of declaring what those rights were should be the function of the judiciary rather than the Oireachtas, although that fundamental issue is referred to in the judgment of Kenny J. Nor was there any explicit endorsement of Kenny J.'s proposed criterion that they might flow from the Christian and democratic nature of the State. This may have been because the right under discussion was conceded, on behalf of the Attorney General, to be such an unenumerated right, although not in the precise form of a right to bodily integrity. [1998] 2 IR 321, at 369–370.

[4–50] Notwithstanding the concerns over the courts' use of Art 40.3.1°, it is difficult to see how—in our constitutional scheme—it would be possible for the Oireachtas to have the role in identifying constitutional rights. Although a general interpretative power is not assigned by the Constitution to the courts, it is the only organ of government with any constitutional power to interpret the Constitution. It alone has the power to determine whether a law is consistent with the Constitution. In short, the Constitution does not appear to envisage a role for the Oireachtas in the interpretation of constitutional rights.

[4–51] Keane J then noted the difficulties with the unenumerated rights doctrine, called for restraint in the identification of new rights and well-illustrated how that restraint might operate in practice:

> It would unduly prolong this judgment to consider in detail the problems that have subsequently been encountered in developing a coherent, principled jurisprudence in this area. It is sufficient to say that, save where such an unenumerated right has been unequivocally established by precedent, as, for example, in the case of the right to travel and the right of privacy, some degree of judicial restraint is called for in identifying new rights of this nature....
>
> In the present case, it is argued that the right to know who one's natural parents are is so essential to realising one's personality and dignity as a human being that it should be recognised as such an unenumerated right. However, it is also possible to take another view....
>
> In the overwhelming majority of families, where children happily know the identity of their parents, the question which is under consideration in this case does not arise. Nor

will it arise where, through an intermediary such as An Bord Uchtála, or an adoption society, communication is established between a natural mother and her child and a reunion is voluntarily effected between the two. It can only arise, where, as here, the possibility exists that the mother may not be willing to effect a reunion with the child.

It is in that context, and that context alone, that, in my view, the issue can be addressed as to whether the child enjoys a unenumerated right to know the identity of the mother. There may be cases, of which the right to travel is an obvious example, where the right derives so conspicuously from the democratic nature of the State that its recognition affords little difficulty. Similarly, freedom of expression is so universally acknowledged and central a value in all democratic societies that, if the view is taken that it does not derive complete and express recognition from Article 40.6.1(i), it would seem to demand acceptance as an unenumerated personal right of the citizen.

Such considerations are, however, of little assistance in resolving the issue in this case. Once it is accepted, as I think emerges inevitably from the remarks of Walsh J. in *McGee v. Attorney General* [1974] I.R. 284 and the judgment of this Court in *Information (Termination of Pregnancies) Bill, 1995* [1995] 1 I.R. 1, that there exists no identifiable and superior *corpus* of law to which judges may have recourse in a case such as the present, it follows that the existence of the right will depend on the opinions of individual judges as to whether, in the circumstances with which they are confronted, it would be just or unjust to deny the existence of the right. The relevance of that approach in the present case is, of course, that it immediately brings into the equation the right to privacy of the natural mothers.

Purists may object to that approach, because, it could be said, the right either exists as a right superior to positive law or it does not. That may be a philosophically irreproachable position. But it leaves judges still without any guidance as to how they are to determine whether the right exists. Ultimately, there is no escape from the conclusion that while the right, as a matter of philosophical theory, may exist, the legal question, which it is the function of the court to resolve, is whether, assuming its existence, it is outweighed by the right of privacy of the mothers....

[T]he claim on behalf of the applicants in the present case not merely necessitates a finding by this Court that a constitutional right of the nature asserted exists, however uncertain its jurisprudential origins: it must also of its nature be superior to that extent to the established right of privacy, recognised in the decisions of the High Court and this Court which no one in the present case has sought to challenge. I am satisfied that that claim is not well founded.

Clearly, most people in the position of the applicants, perhaps the overwhelming majority, would have a deep-seated wish to know the identity of their mother. But what is at issue is whether they have a discrete, unenumerated personal right to such knowledge which is one of the personal rights acknowledged by the Constitution and which imposes a corresponding duty on the mothers to reveal their identity to them. I am satisfied that they have not. It remains to be considered whether they have such a right deriving from their expressly guaranteed rights under the Constitution or from an unenumerated right identified by the courts. [1998] 2 IR, at 370–375.

Whereas the majority were prepared to enumerate a right to know one's identity, which right could then be subjected to exceptions to respect the parent's right to privacy, Keane J was not prepared to enumerate a new right in circumstances where it would inevitably lead to conflict with the right to privacy. Although Keane J was a sole dissenting voice, his attitude to unenumerated rights appears now to represent the prevailing consensus on the Supreme Court. [4–52]

Keane CJ repeated his call for restraint in *TD v Minister for Education* [2001] 4 IR 259. In this case, the applicants sought a mandatory injunction requiring the Minister to implement the policy that he had formulated to deal with the general problem of [4–53] children with special needs. In the earlier case of *FN v Minister for Education* [1995] 1 IR 509, Geoghegan J, relying on the judgment of O'Higgins CJ in *G v An Bord Uchtála*, had concluded that a child had a right—under Art 40.3—as against its parents to be fed and to live, to be reared and educated, and to have the opportunity of working and realising his or her full personality and dignity as a human being. Where the parents failed in their duty towards the child, the State was required to step in and meet those rights. In *FN*, Geoghegan J thus concluded that the State had a constitutional obligation to establish as soon as reasonably practicable suitable arrangements of containment with treatment for the applicant, a troubled youngster. Although *TD* concerned the power of the courts to make mandatory orders against other branches of government, some members of the Court considered whether the applicants had the sorts of right that had been recognised in *FN*.

[4–54] Having reiterated his concerns from *O'T v B*, Keane CJ commented that he had the gravest doubts as to whether the courts should assume the function of declaring socio-economic rights to be unenumerated rights protected by Art 40.3.1°. Although the point had not been argued before the Court, Murphy J (expressing sentiments endorsed by Keane CJ) considered the issue:

> There are, as I would see it, serious arguments against inferring the existence of positive socio-economic rights (apart from the anomalous rights relating to education) but there are impressive authorities to the contrary. [Having quoted from *G* and *FN*, Murphy J continued:] It is, of course, entirely understandable, and desirable politically and morally, that a society should, through its laws, devise appropriate schemes and by means of taxation raise the necessary finance to fund such schemes as will enable the sick, the poor and the underprivileged in our society to make the best use of the limited resources nature may have bestowed on them. It is my belief that this entirely desirable goal must be achieved and can only be achieved by legislation and not by any unrealistic extension of the provisions originally incorporated in Bunreacht na hÉireann. [2001] 2 IR 259, at 318, 321–322.

[4–55] Despite the absence of any definitive judgment resiling from the unenumerated rights doctrine, that doctrine seems to have withered. The restraint advocated by Keane CJ in *O'T v B* has become almost the defining characteristic of the courts, particularly the Supreme Court. Following cases such as *Sinnott* and *TD*, it is almost inconceivable that the courts will enumerate any socio-economic right under Art 40.3.1°. Indeed it seems unlikely that Art 40.3.1° will in the future play any role other than a location for rights that could reasonably be said to be implicit in other constitutional provisions.

[4–56] Perhaps the unenumerated rights doctrine was a necessary constitutional device that has done its job and can now be gracefully abandoned. The courts used the doctrine to enhance the protection of individual rights. While one might have qualms over the process, the results were generally unexceptionable. With those rights now secured as part of the *acquis constitutionel*, there is no longer a need to enumerate wholly new rights. Rights can be inferred from the provisions of the Constitution and indeed from the rights previously enumerated by the courts under Art 40.3.1°. There is—perhaps—no need for the courts to identify any radically new ones. Of course, if one strongly supports socio-economic rights and believes, for instance, that a right to shelter is more important than a right to bodily integrity, one could not agree with this conclusion.

Contents – Chapter 5

Personal Rights

Introduction.	[5–01]
The Right to Life.	[5–02]
The Right to Life of the Unborn.	[5–11]
The Right to a Good Name.	[5–29]
The Right to Bodily Integrity.	[5–31]
The Right to Work and Earn a Livelihood.	[5–34]
The Right to (Marital) Privacy and Autonomy.	[5–35]
The Right of Access to the Courts and the Right to Litigate.	[5–41]

Overview

The courts have extensively interpreted the various rights that are protected in the Constitution. The right to life has been held to encompass a right to die a natural death. The courts suggested that the right to life of the unborn was implicitly protected by the Constitution. Nevertheless, an amendment was passed in 1983 to copper-fasten this right, protecting the right to life of the unborn with due regard to the equal right to life of the mother. In the *X case*, the Supreme Court held that a suicidal teenager, pregnant as a result of rape, was entitled to an abortion in Ireland as her own life was in danger. The Constitution has since been amended to allow people to travel outside Ireland for the purposes of procuring an abortion and to allow the distribution of information about abortion services available in other jurisdictions. However, the position on the substantive issue of abortion remains the same. More recently, the courts have held that embryos fertilised *in vitro* do not constitute unborn life for the purposes of the Constitution and have no right to life prior to implantation. The courts have identified a right to bodily integrity as a protection from invasive medical procedures but have been slow to develop it into a positive right to demand medical treatment from the State. The courts have protected a right to (marital) privacy and autonomy in a way that protects certain types of personal decision from State intervention. The courts have protected a right of access to the courts and a right to litigate, including a limited right to civil legal aid.

Chapter 5

Personal Rights

Introduction

The purpose of this chapter is to examine the personal rights protected by the Constitution, whether those rights are explicit in the text of Art 40.3 or enumerated pursuant to Art 40.3.1°. Property rights are dealt with in their own chapter. Enumerated rights that are thematically related to rights explicitly protected elsewhere in the Constitution are considered in conjunction with those rights. For instance, the right to communicate is addressed during the discussion of freedom of expression and the rights of non-marital family members are addressed during the discussion of family rights. This chapter will address the other personal rights protected by Art 40.3, including the right to life of the unborn. [5–01]

The Right to Life

Article 40.3.2° requires the State to protect as best it may from unjust attack and, in the case of injustice done, to vindicate the life of every citizen. This right has rarely been pleaded before the courts, perhaps because interference with the right to life is so seldom. Interestingly, the constitutionality of the death penalty was never challenged. This may be explained, however, by the fact that no one has been executed since 1954. The Constitution now explicitly prohibits the death penalty. Article 15.5.2° provides that the Oireachtas shall not enact any law providing for the imposition of the death penalty. Article 28.3.3° has also been amended to ensure that even laws enacted during a time of war for the purposes of securing public safety (which, loosely speaking, in general have a constitutional immunity) cannot provide for the death penalty. [5–02]

Although the right to life, as such, has had little direct consideration in the case law, the courts have inferred from it a right to die a natural death. *Re a Ward of Court (withholding medical treatment) (No 2)* [1996] 2 IR 79 concerned a woman who had been in a near persistent vegetative state since 1972. The ward of court was initially fed through a nasogastric tube which she seemed to find somewhat distressing and after 20 years or so this was replaced by a gastrostomy tube in April 1992. The ward required full nursing care. She was spastic and both arms and hands were contracted. Both her legs and feet were extended. Her jaws were clenched and she had a tendency to bite the insides of her cheeks and her tongue, her back teeth were capped to prevent the front teeth from closing. She could not swallow or speak. She was incontinent and bedridden. She had no capacity for speech or for communicating. A speech therapist failed to elicit any means of communication. She had a minimal capacity to recognise: she could only follow or track people with her eyes and react to [5–03] noise. The ward's heart and lungs functioned normally. If she continued to be nourished by tube, the ward might have lived for many years but could have died if she developed some infection unless it was treated aggressively with antibiotics. In the High Court, Lynch J held that it was in the best interests of the Ward that the feeding be discontinued and that, in effect, she be allowed to die. On appeal, four judges of the Supreme Court upheld this conclusion. Hamilton CJ explicitly relied on the right to life:

> The right to life is one of the fundamental rights which under the Constitution the State guarantees in its laws to respect and, as far as practicable, to defend, vindicate and protect as best it may from unjust attack.
>
> The sanctity of human life is recognised in all civilised jurisdictions and is based on the nature of man.
>
> The Constitution recognises this right and grants to it the protection set forth in the Constitution. The courts have recognised that the right to life springs from the right of every individual to life.
>
> There are many other fundamental rights, express or implied, which are acknowledged by the Constitution and which are afforded similar protection.
>
> It has been well established by many decisions of this Court that where there exists an interaction of constitutional rights, the first objective of the courts in interpreting the Constitution and resolving any problems thus arising should be to seek to harmonise such interacting rights....
>
> I am satisfied that in this case, if there was an interaction of constitutional rights which I was not capable of harmonising, the right to life would take precedence over any other rights.
>
> The nature of the right to life and its importance imposes a strong presumption in favour of taking all steps capable of preserving it, save in exceptional circumstances. The problem is to define such circumstances.
>
> The definition of such circumstances must, of necessity, involve a determination of the nature of the right to life acknowledged by the Constitution....
>
> As the process of dying is part, and an ultimate, inevitable consequence, of life, the right to life necessarily implies the right to have nature take its course and to die a natural death and, unless the individual concerned so wishes, not to have life artificially maintained by the provision of nourishment by abnormal artificial means, which have no curative effect and which is intended merely to prolong life.
>
> This right, as so defined, does not include the right to have life terminated or death accelerated and is confined to the natural process of dying. No person has the right to terminate or to have terminated his or her life, or to accelerate or have accelerated his or her death.
>
> In this case, the ward is in the condition described in the judgment of the learned trial judge, to portions of which I have referred in the course of this judgment.
>
> Her life is being artificially maintained by the provision of life sustaining nourishment through a gastrostomy tube inserted in her body. Such treatment is in no way, nor intended to be, curative and she will continue to be in the condition in which she now is, and has been for over twenty years, if she continues to be provided with nourishment in this manner. [1996] 2 IR 79, at 122–124.

[5–04] It is noteworthy that Hamilton CJ applied the naturalistic fallacy to come to his conclusion that the ward ought to be allowed to die: because people *do* die natural deaths, people *ought* to die natural deaths. As was seen in chapter 4, this is a very dubious form of natural law reasoning.

Part of Hamilton CJ's judgment appeared to turn on the quality of life (or lack thereof) available to the Ward. O'Flaherty J was more explicit in his focus on this issue: [5–05]

> The ward may be alive but she has no life at all. Lynch J. found as a fact that although the ward is not fully PVS, she is very nearly so and such cognitive capacity as she possesses is extremely minimal....
>
> Thus, the circumstances of the current case are clearly distinguishable from the position as regards, for example, a seriously mentally handicapped person. A mentally handicapped person is conscious of his or her situation and is capable of obtaining pleasure and enjoyment from life. It is fanciful to attempt to equate the position of the ward in this case with that of a person whose life has been impaired by handicap. The analogy is both false and misleading; the quality of the ward's life was never in issue; she is not living a life in any meaningful sense. We are concerned here only with allowing nature to take its course and for the ward to die with dignity. We are not thereby going down any slippery slope or stepping into any abyss.
>
> It is the fact that indubitably the ward is alive. All life is sacred.... I move to the concept of death. For those of religious belief, death is not an end but a beginning. In the submissions at bar on behalf of the committee of the ward death was said to be part of life—indeed the only certainty in life.... [I]n everyone's subconscious there is a hope of a peaceful and dignified death. We console the bereaved when a death occurs unexpectedly if the deceased was spared suffering.
>
> In my judgment, this case is not about terminating a life but only to allow nature to take its course which would have happened even a short number of years ago and still does in places where medical technology has not advanced as far as it has in this country, for example. But now the advance of medical science may result in rendering a patient a prisoner in a ward from which there may be no release for many years without any enjoyment or quality of life: indeed without life in any acceptable meaning of that concept except in the sense that by means of various mechanisms life is kept in the body. [1996] 2 IR 79, at 130–131.

O'Flaherty J's focus on the ward's quality of life was somewhat disturbing. How bad does one's life have to become before the courts decide that one is "not living in any meaningful sense"? O'Flaherty J's test seems to be that a person be: (a) conscious of her situation and (b) capable of obtaining pleasure and enjoyment from life. Is either of these sufficient to lead the courts to a decision that a person, whose own wishes are unknown, should now die a natural death? [5–06]

Some of the other issues in this case are brought more sharply into focus by its discussion of privacy and autonomy rights, which are considered below.

In *McGee v Attorney General* [1974] IR 284, the plaintiff challenged the constitutionality of s 17(1) of the Criminal Law Act 1935 which prohibited the sale of contraceptives in Ireland or the import of contraceptives in Ireland. The plaintiff was a married woman who had four children. She had been informed by her medical advisors that another pregnancy could have serious consequences for her, including possibly putting her life at risk. Walsh J partly relied on the right to life in holding that the legislation was unconstitutional: [5–07]

> [O]ne of the personal rights of a woman in the plaintiff's state of health would be a right to be assisted in her efforts to avoid putting her life in jeopardy. I am of opinion also that not only has the State the right to do so but, by virtue of the terms of the proviso to s. 1

and the terms of s. 3 of Article 40, the State has the positive obligation to ensure by its laws as far as is possible (and in the use of the word "possible" I am relying on the Irish text of the Constitution) that there would be made available to a married woman in the condition of health of the plaintiff the means whereby a conception which was likely to put her life in jeopardy might be avoided when it is a risk over and above the ordinary risks inherent in pregnancy. It would, in the nature of things, be much more difficult to justify a refusal to do this on the grounds of the common good than in the case of married couples generally. [1974] IR 284, at 315–316.

[5–08] Although this dictum appears to give positive force to the right to life, perhaps creating a socio-economic entitlement to life, it should probably be limited to the specific context of the case, *ie* that of the State precluding a woman from taking reasonable measures to protect her own life. This is particularly the case given the dicta in *TD v Minister for Education* [2001] 4 IR 257, considered in chapter 4, to the effect that the courts should not enumerate socio-economic rights.

[5–09] In the same case, Walsh J made a more significant statement about the right to life of the unborn, sharply distinguishing the constitutional treatment of abortion from that of contraception:

> [A]ny action on the part of either the husband and wife or of the State to limit family sizes by endangering or destroying human life must necessarily not only be an offence against the common good but also against the guaranteed personal rights of the human life in question. [1974] IR 284, at 315–316.

[5–10] He made this point even more explicitly in *G v An Bord Uchtála* [1980] IR 32, at 69:

> Not only has the child born out of lawful wedlock the natural right to have its welfare and health guarded no less well than that of a child born in lawful wedlock, but *a fortiori* it has the right to life itself and the right to be guarded against all threats directed to its existence whether before or after birth. The child's natural rights spring primarily from the natural right of every individual to life, to be reared and educated, to liberty, to work, to rest and recreation, to the practice of religion, and to follow his or her conscience. The right to life necessarily implies the right to be born, the right to preserve and defend (and to have preserved and defended) that life, and the right to maintain that life at a proper human standard in matters of food, clothing and habitation. It lies not in the power of the parent who has the primary natural rights and duties in respect of the child to exercise them in such a way as intentionally or by neglect to endanger the health or life of the child or to terminate its existence.

It thus appeared that the right to life of the unborn was implicitly protected by the Constitution. This copper-fastened the statutory protection provided by ss 58 and 59 of the Offences against the Person Act 1861.

The Right to Life of the Unborn

[5–11] Notwithstanding this implicit protection for the right to life of the unborn, a substantial political movement culminated in 1983 with the insertion into the Constitution of explicit protection. Article 40.3.3° provides:

> The State acknowledges the right to life of the unborn and, with due regard to the equal right to life of the mother, guarantees in its laws to respect, and, as far as practicable, by its laws to defend and vindicate that right.

In *Attorney General (Society for the Protection of Unborn Children (Ireland) Ltd) v Open Door Counselling Ltd* [1988] IR 593, the Supreme Court granted an injunction restraining the defendants from assisting pregnant women "to travel abroad to obtain abortions by referral to a clinic, by the making of their travel arrangements or by informing them of the identity and location and method of communication". However, this decision was later found to be in breach of Art 10 the European Convention on Human Rights in *Open Door Counselling Ltd v Ireland* (1992) 14 EHRR 131. In *Society for the Protection of Unborn Children (Ireland) Ltd v Grogan* [1989] IR 753, SPUC obtained an interlocutory injunction restraining the defendants from distributing abortion information pending the decision of the European Court of Justice on a reference under Art 234 of the Treaty. This success was undermined, however, by the judgment of the Court to the effect that abortion was a service within the meaning of the Treaty and that a commercial agent of an abortion clinic, lawful in another Member State, could distribute information about that abortion service in Ireland. [5–12]

The underlying issue of the permissibility of abortion came more starkly into focus in *Attorney General v X* [1992] 1 IR 1. Ms X was a 14-year-old girl, pregnant as a result of a then alleged (later proved) rape. She and her parents decided that the best course of action was for Ms X to travel to the United Kingdom to obtain an abortion there. They informed the gardaí of this, raising the possibility of carrying out scientific tests on the foetus to identify the father. A legal opinion was sought on the admissibility of this evidence. The DPP informed the Attorney General of the matter. The Attorney obtained interim injunctions the following day, restraining Ms X from travelling to the United Kingdom. Ms X and her family were already in the United Kingdom at this stage, but they returned to Ireland to contest the injunctions. A senior psychologist gave evidence that, in view of the girl's threatened intentions, there was a risk that she might commit suicide. This raised a possible conflict between the right to life of the unborn child and the right to life of her mother. The High Court granted permanent injunctions restraining Ms X from travelling to the United Kingdom for the purposes of obtaining an abortion. She successfully appealed to the Supreme Court. [5–13]

Finlay CJ first held that the Court was competent to enforce the right to life of the unborn, notwithstanding the absence of any statutory law giving effect to Art 40.3.3°. He then addressed the manner in which the Court should reconcile the right to life of the unborn and the right to life of the mother: [5–14]

> I accept the submission made on behalf of the Attorney General, that the doctrine of the harmonious interpretation of the Constitution involves in this case a consideration of the constitutional rights and obligations of the mother of the unborn child and the interrelation of those rights and obligations with the rights and obligations of other people and, of course, with the right to life of the unborn child as well.
>
> Such a harmonious interpretation of the Constitution carried out in accordance with concepts of prudence, justice and charity, as they have been explained in the judgment of Walsh J in *McGee v Attorney General* [1974] IR 284 leads me to the conclusion that in vindicating and defending as far as practicable the right of the unborn to life but at the same time giving due regard to the right of the mother to life, the Court must, amongst the matters to be so regarded, concern itself with the position of the mother within a family group, with persons on whom she is dependent, with, in other instances, persons who are dependent upon her and her interaction with other citizens and members of society in the areas in which her activities occur. Having regard to that conclusion, I am

satisfied that the test proposed on behalf of the Attorney General that the life of the unborn could only be terminated if it were established that an inevitable or immediate risk to the life of the mother existed, for the avoidance of which a termination of the pregnancy was necessary, insufficiently vindicates the mother's right to life.

I, therefore, conclude that the proper test to be applied is that if it is established as a matter of probability that there is a real and substantial risk to the life, as distinct from the health, of the mother, which can only be avoided by the termination of her pregnancy, such termination is permissible, having regard to the true interpretation of Article 40.3.3° of the Constitution. [1992] 1 IR 1, at 53–54.

[5–15] Finlay CJ then applied this test in the following way:

I am satisfied that the only risk put forward in this case to the life of the mother is the risk of self-destruction. I agree with the conclusion reached by the learned trial judge in the High Court that that was a risk which, as would be appropriate in any other form of risk to the life of the mother, must be taken into account in reconciling the right of the unborn to life and the rights of the mother to life. Such a risk to the life of a young mother, in particular, has it seems to me, a particular characteristic which is relevant to the question of whether the evidence in this case justifies a conclusion that it constitutes a real and substantial risk to life.

If a physical condition emanating from a pregnancy occurs in a mother, it may be that a decision to terminate the pregnancy in order to save her life can be postponed for a significant period in order to monitor the progress of the physical condition, and that there are diagnostic warning signs which can readily be relied upon during such postponement.

In my view, it is common sense that a threat of self-destruction such as is outlined in the evidence in this case, which the psychologist clearly believes to be a very real threat, cannot be monitored in that sense and that it is almost impossible to prevent self-destruction in a young girl in the situation in which this defendant is if she were to decide to carry out her threat of suicide.

I am, therefore, satisfied that on the evidence before the learned trial judge, which was in no way contested, and on the findings which he has made, that the defendants have satisfied the test which I have laid down as being appropriate and have established, as a matter of probability, that there is a real and substantial risk to the life of the mother by self-destruction which can only be avoided by termination of her pregnancy. [1992] 1 IR 1, at 52.

McCarthy J came to the same conclusion but for slightly different reasons:

The right of the girl here is a right to a life in being; the right of the unborn is to a life contingent; contingent on survival in the womb until successful delivery. It is not a question of setting one above the other but rather of vindicating, as far as practicable, the right to life of the girl/mother (Article 40.3.2°), whilst with due regard to the equal light to life of the girl/mother, vindicating, as far as practicable, the right to life of the unborn. (Article 40.3.3°). If the right to life of the mother is threatened by the pregnancy, and it is practicable to vindicate that right, then because of the due regard which must be paid to the equal right to life of the mother, it may not be practicable to vindicate the right to life of the unborn. What then does "threatened" mean? The learned trial judge identified the question in these words:—

"What the court, therefore, is required to do is to assess by reference to the evidence the danger to the life of the child and the danger that exists to the life of the mother. I am quite satisfied that there is a real and imminent danger to the life of the unborn and that if the court does not step in to protect it by means of the injunction sought its life would be terminated. The evidence also establishes that if the court grants the injunction sought there is a risk that the defendant may take her own life. But the risk that the defendant may take her own life if an order is made is much less and is of a different order of magnitude than the certainty that the life of the unborn will be terminated if the order is not made. I am strengthened in this view by the knowledge that the young girl has the benefit of the love and care and support of devoted parents who will help her through the difficult months ahead. It seems to me, therefore, that having had regard to the rights of the mother in this case, the court's duty to protect the life of the unborn requires it to make the order sought."

In my judgment, this was an incorrect approach to the problem raised by the terms of the Eighth Amendment. It is not a question of balancing the life of the unborn against the life of the mother; if it were, the life of the unborn would virtually always have to be preserved, since the termination of pregnancy means the death of the unborn; there is no certainty, however high the probability, that the mother will die if there is not a termination of pregnancy. In my view, the true construction of the Amendment, bearing in mind the other provisions of Article 40 and the fundamental rights of the family guaranteed by Article 41, is that, paying due regard to the equal right to life of the mother, when there is a real and substantial risk attached to her survival not merely at the time of application but in contemplation at least throughout the pregnancy, then it may not be practicable to vindicate the right to life of the unborn. It is not a question of a risk of a different order of magnitude; it can never be otherwise than a risk of a different order of magnitude.

On the facts of the case, which are not in contest, I am wholly satisfied that a real and substantial risk that the girl might take her own life was established; it follows that she should not be prevented from having a medical termination of pregnancy. [1992] 1 IR 1, at 79-80.

O'Flaherty and Egan JJ also agreed that Ms X should be allowed to travel, but Hederman J strongly dissented: [5–16]

[Article 40.3.3°] expressly spelled out a guarantee of protection of the life of the mother of the unborn life, by guaranteeing her life equality — equality of protection, to dispel any confusion there might have been thought to exist to the effect that the life of the infant in the womb must be saved even if it meant certain death for the mother. The death of a foetus may be the indirect but foreseeable result of an operation undertaken for other reasons. Indeed it is difficult to see how any operation, the sole purpose of which is to save the life of the mother, could be regarded as a direct killing of the foetus, if the unavoidable and inevitable consequences of the efforts to save the mother's life leads to the death of the foetus. But like all examples of self-defence, of which this would be one, the means employed to achieve the self-protection must not go beyond what is strictly necessary. The most significant aspect of the provisions of Article 40, s. 3 and of the Eighth Amendment is the objective of protecting human life which is the essential value of every legal order and central to the enjoyment of all other rights guaranteed by the Constitution. The constitutional provisions amount to a dedication to the fundamental value of human life. The Eighth Amendment establishes beyond any dispute that the constitutional guarantee of the vindication and protection of life is not qualified by the condition that the life must be one which has achieved an independent existence after birth. The right of life is guaranteed to every life born or unborn. One cannot make distinctions between individual phases of the unborn life before birth, or between unborn and born life. Clearly the State's duty of protection is far reaching. Direct State interference in the developing unborn life is outlawed and furthermore the State must protect and promote that life and above all defend it from unlawful interference by other persons. The State's duty to protect life also extends to the mother. The natural connection between the unborn child and the mother's life constitutes a special relationship. But one cannot consider the unborn life only as part of the maternal organism. The extinction of unborn life is not confined to the sphere of private life of the mother or family because the unborn life is an autonomous human being protected by the Constitution. Therefore the termination of pregnancy other than a natural one has a legal and social dimension and requires a special responsibility on the part of the State. There cannot be a freedom to extinguish life side by side with a guarantee of protection of that life because the termination of pregnancy always means the destruction of an unborn life. Therefore no recognition of a mother's right of self-determination can be given priority over the protection of the unborn life. The creation of a new life, involving as it does pregnancy, birth and raising the child, necessarily involves some restriction of a mother's freedom but the alternative is the destruction of the unborn life. The termination of pregnancy is not like a visit to the doctor to cure an illness. The State must, in principle, act in accordance with the mother's duty to carry out the pregnancy and, in principle must also outlaw termination of pregnancy.

The State's obligation is to do all that is reasonably possible having regard to the importance of preserving life. [1992] 1 IR 1, at 71–72.

[5–17] In Hederman J's view, the evidence tendered in the case did not come close to establishing that there was such a threat to the life of the mother that an abortion could be carried out:

The Eighth Amendment does contemplate a situation arising where the protection of the mother's right to live has to be taken into the balance between the competing rights of both lives, namely the mother's and the unborn child's. Abortion as a medical procedure is unique in that it involves three parties. It involves the person carrying out the procedure, the mother and the child. It is inevitable that if the procedure is adopted the child's life is extinguished. Therefore before that decision is taken it is obvious that the evidence required to justify the choice being made must be of such a weight and cogency as to leave open no other conclusion but that the consequences of the continuance of the pregnancy will, to an extremely high degree of probability cost the mother her life and that any such opinion must be based on the most competent medical opinion available. In the present case neither this Court nor the High Court has either heard or seen the mother of the unborn child. There has been no evidence whatever of an obstetrical or indeed of any other medical nature. There has been no evidence upon which the courts could conclude that there are any obstetrical problems, much less serious threats to the life of the mother of a medical nature. What has been offered is the evidence of a psychologist based on his own encounter with the first defendant and on what he heard about her attitude and behaviour from other persons, namely the Garda Síochána, and her parents. This led him to the opinion that there is a serious threat to the life of the first defendant by an act of self-destruction by reason of the fact of being pregnant. This is a very extreme reaction to pregnancy, even to an unwanted pregnancy. But as was pointed out in this Court in *SPUC v Coogan* [1989] IR 734, the fact that a pregnancy is unwanted was no justification for terminating it or attempting to terminate it. If there is a suicidal tendency then this is something which has to be guarded against. If this young person without being pregnant had suicidal tendencies due to some other cause then nobody would doubt that the proper course would be to put her in such care and under such supervision as would counteract such tendency and do everything possible to prevent suicide. I do not think the terms of the Eighth Amendment or indeed the terms of the Constitution before amendment would absolve the State from its obligation to vindicate, and protect the life of a person who had expressed the intention of self-destruction. This young girl clearly requires loving and sympathetic care and professional counselling and all the protection which the State agencies can provide or furnish.

> There could be no question whatsoever of permitting another life to be taken to deal with the situation even if the intent to self-destruct could be traced directly to the activities or the existence of another person. [1992] 1 IR 1, at 75–76.

Cox has advanced four serious criticisms of the manner in which the majority of the Supreme Court reached its conclusion in *X*: [5–18]

> First, despite the fact that a Thomistic view of Natural law had been informing the process of constitutional interpretation in Ireland for most of the previous thirty years its significance received no mention from the majority judges in this case.
> Secondly, it seems quite clear that Article 40.3.3° was seen by those who voted for it as an "anti-abortion" amendment. Although the originalist reliance on the intentions of those who voted the Constitution into place has not held much sway in Irish constitutional jurisprudence, nonetheless it seems odd that an interpretation should be made which was patently at variance with the intentions of an electorate only nine years previously. This criticism is reinforced by the fact that in the next major abortion case in Ireland in 1995 a constitutional contradiction within the terms of the newly amended Article 40.3.3° was expressly justified by the Supreme Court by reference to the intentions of the electorate in amending the Constitution in this manner. Thirdly, the interpretation in *X* was radically inconsistent with all other earlier interpretations of Article 40.3.3°.
> Most extraordinarily, however, the interpretation of Article 40.3.3° which the Supreme Court in *X* gave is clearly at variance with the, admittedly impossible terminology of equal rights used therein. Finlay CJ criticised the balancing test which Costello J had employed in the High Court on the basis that it would mean that in practical terms the right to life of the unborn would always receive priority over that of the mother. Nonetheless there is a strong argument for the view that if the rights in question are indeed equal, then the only legitimate approach for a court charged with balancing them when they are in direct conflict (and there is a case for saying that in *X* the rights were not in direct conflict in that the threat to the mother's life derived not from the unborn but from herself), is to assess the comparative magnitude of the respective threats. The net result reached by the Supreme Court in *X*—namely that the young girl in the case should not be forced to carry to term a pregnancy which she did not wish and which was the product of a criminal act—was undoubtedly what was desired by a good deal of public opinion. Moreover, in moral terms it may well be the "right" result. Nonetheless in legal terms, in *X* ... the "right" result was reached by an inappropriate judicial intervention in an area of extreme moral controversy, which struck at the very heart of democratic government. Indeed the judicial activism in *X* is even more insidious ... [when one considers that] ... in *X* the court made an interpretation of a constitutional provision which was in clear and direct violation of the terms of that provision. Abortion politics aside, this is a dangerous approach to constitutional law and one which sets a precedent with breathtaking potential. Neville Cox, "Judicial Activism, Constitutional Interpretation and the Problem of Abortion: *Roe v. Wade* (1973) and *X v. A.G.* (1992)" in Eoin O'Dell ed, *Leading Cases of the Twentieth Century* (Round Hall Sweet & Maxwell, 2000) 237, at 253–254.

Cox's criticism is perhaps unfair. If the terminology of equal rights is indeed "impossible" and given the fact that the unborn's right to life was necessarily contingent on the mother's life—as observed by McCarthy J—an approach that privileged the mother's right to life was justifiable. [5–19]

Following the *X Case*, the people have twice rejected an amendment to Art 40.3 dealing with the substantive issue of abortion, first in 1992 and then in 2002. However, in 1992 amendments were passed allowing for the provision of information and the right to travel. Article 40.3.3° now provides: [5–20]

> This subsection shall not limit freedom to travel between the State and another state. This subsection shall not limit freedom to obtain or make available, in the State, subject to such conditions as may be laid down by law, information relating to services lawfully available in another state.

[5–21] In *A and B v Eastern Health Board* [1998] 1 IR 464, the High Court was again called on to consider an *X Case*-type situation. Here a 13-year-old girl was pregnant as a result of rape. The Health Board had made an application for an interim care order and the District Court ordered that the child be permitted to travel to the United Kingdom for an abortion and that the Health Board be permitted to make the necessary arrangements. The parents of the pregnant girl, who were opposed to an abortion, sought to quash this decision. Geoghegan J refused to quash the District Court direction. He held that there was sufficient psychiatric evidence to substantiate the risk of suicide and, accordingly, that an abortion was permissible under the *X Case* rationale.

[5–22] However, Geoghegan J rejected an argument advanced on the basis of the right to travel. He reasoned that the right to travel was intended to preclude a court from granting injunctions preventing a person from travelling but did not allow the courts to authorise travel outside the jurisdiction for the purposes of obtaining an abortion. As such, the right to travel was more in the character of a freedom than a positive right. The pregnant child in *A and B* was allowed to travel not because she had a right to travel but rather because her abortion was lawful as a matter of Irish law, on account of the threat to her life posed by possible suicide. This reasoning puts children in the care of the State in a worse position than other children. The State cannot prevent children from travelling for an abortion, but it cannot allow the children for whom it has responsibility to travel for the same reason. This issue resurfaced more recently in *D v HSE*, 9 May 2007 (HC). In this case, a 17-year-old girl in the care of the HSE became pregnant. Tragically her first ante-natal scan confirmed that the foetus suffered from anencephaly, which rendered it non-viable outside the womb. McKechnie J held that Ms D was entitled to exercise her constitutional right to travel to the United Kingdom for the purposes of having an abortion. He held that, even though Ms D was in the care of the State, it was not necessary to obtain the approval of the court to allow her travel. Nor did the HSE have any power to prevent Ms D from travelling for her stated purpose.

[5–23] The right to life of the unborn has now also been considered by the courts in a context other than abortion. In *R v R* [2006] IEHC 359, the High Court considered the application of Art 40.3.3° of the Constitution to embryos created *in vitro*. The plaintiff was married to the first defendant. In 2002 the plaintiff underwent IVF treatment. In preparation for this, the plaintiff agreed to the removal of eggs from her ovaries and a mixing of the eggs with the sperm of her husband. Both signed a document in which they consented to the cryo preservation (freezing) of their embryos and undertook full responsibility on an ongoing basis for those embryos. The first defendant also signed documents in which he consented to the fertilisation of his wife's eggs and the implantation of three embryos. He acknowledged that he would become the father of any resulting child. As a result of the IVF treatment, six viable embryos were created and three were implanted in the plaintiff's womb, the other three being frozen. As a result of this process, the plaintiff gave birth to a daughter. Towards the end of the pregnancy, marital difficulties arose and the plaintiff and her husband separated. The issue came before the court because the plaintiff wished to have the three frozen embryos implanted in her uterus. Her husband did not want this to happen and did not wish to become the father of any child that might be born as a result of the implantation of the frozen embryos.

McGovern J directed a trial of a preliminary issue. This established that there was no agreement between the husband and wife as to what should happen to the frozen embryos and that the husband had given neither express nor implied consent to the implantation of the frozen embryos. If there had been agreement or consent to implantation on the part of the husband, there would have been no possible conflict between the wishes of the parties and constitutional requirements. However, as there was no consent to implantation on the part of the husband, the court was required to assess whether there was any constitutional reason why the embryos should be implanted. This turned largely on an interpretation of Art 40.3.3° of the Constitution. [5–24]

In approaching this issue, McGovern J relied largely on the historical approach. He noted Murray CJ's comments in *Curtin v Dáil Éireann* that it was reasonable, where there was no textual guidance, to consider the history or background to the enactment of the Constitution in order to elucidate what was in the contemplation of the framers. On this basis and given the lack of any definition of "unborn" in Art 40.3.3°, McGovern J had regard to the history and background to the amendment of the Constitution. In this regard, McGovern J referred to a number of cases decided after the enactment of Art 40.3.3° which suggested that that constitutional amendment was intended to prevent the legalisation of abortion. The cases referred to were *Attorney General (SPUC) v Open Door Counselling Limited* [1988] IR 593, *Attorney General v X* [1992] 1 IR 1 and *Baby O v Minister for Justice* [2002] 2 IR 169. McGovern J drew the following conclusion: [5–25]

> These remarks seem to further confirm the linking of Article 40.3.3° with the abortion issue. If this is correct then it equates "unborn" with an embryo which has implanted in the womb, or a foetus.... What clearly emerges from the authorities that I have referred to is that the Courts have declared that the Eighth Amendment to the Constitution giving rise to the wording in Article 40.3.3° was for the purpose of making secure the prohibition on abortion expressed in section 57 and 58 of the Offences Against the Person Act, 1861 and not to permit abortion or termination of pregnancy except where it is established as a matter of probability that there is a real and substantial risk to the life of the mother if such termination were not effected. The Courts have never, thus far, considered whether the word "unborn" in Article 40.3.3° includes embryos in vitro.... If Article 40.3.3° and the 1861 Act are concerned with the termination of pregnancy this does not mean that they are concerned with embryos *in vitro*. There has been no evidence adduced to establish that it was ever in the mind of the people voting on the Eighth Amendment to the Constitution that "unborn" meant anything other than a foetus or child within the womb. To infer that it was in the mind of the people that "unborn" included embryos outside the womb or embryos in vitro would be to completely ignore the circumstances in which the amendment giving rise to Article 40.3.3° arose. While I accept that Article 40.3.3° is not to be taken in isolation from its historical background and should be considered as but one provision of the whole Constitution, this does not mean that the word "unborn" can be given a meaning which was not contemplated by people at the time of the passing of the Eighth Amendment and which takes it outside the scope and purpose of the amendment.

[5-26] It is questionable whether McGovern J's unequivocal conclusion on the scope and purpose of the Eighth Amendment is consistent with his recognition of the fact that no court had ever considered whether the word "unborn" in Article 40.3.3° includes embryos *in vitro*. In this regard, it is noteworthy that McGovern J did not cite any pre-1983 source to support his view on the meaning of Article 40.3.3°. Cases post-1983 that concerned abortion and explained the purpose of Article 40.3.3° in relation to its impact on abortion law scarcely count as reliable support for the proposition that the purpose and scope of Article 40.3.3° concerned abortion and only abortion. In considering the purpose of Article 40.3.3°, it is perhaps significant that the framers of that amendment did not simply enact a ban on abortion (similar to the constitutional offence of blasphemy) but rather sought to articulate a statement of rights, a philosophical basis as to why abortion was prohibited. That philosophical basis—explicitly stated in the Constitution—was the right to life of the unborn. McGovern J avoided the need to explore what was meant by the right to life of the unborn essentially by concluding that the Constitution did not so much protect the right to life of the unborn as prohibit abortion. This is an insecure basis for such a far-reaching judgment.

[5-27] Towards the end of his judgment, McGovern J returned to the distinction between law and morality:

> The fact that something is not prohibited by the law does not of itself mean that it is morally acceptable to carry out that act. There may be many people who, because of their moral or religious outlook regard the process of IVF as unacceptable even though it is permitted by the law. There are others who see this a great advance in medical science giving the opportunity to infertile couples to have children. In issues such as this there may well be a divide between Church and State, and between one religion and another. It is not for the Courts to weigh the views of one religion against another, or to choose between one moral view point and another. All are entitled to equal respect provided they are not subversive of the law, and provided there are no public policy reasons requiring the Courts to intervene. Moral responsibility exists even in the absence of law and arises out of the freedom of choice of the individual. People have many different ideas of morality. Society is made up of people of various religious traditions and none. If the law is to enforce morality then whose morality is it to enforce? The function of the Courts is to apply the law, which are the rules and regulations that govern society. Where these rules and regulations are to be found in articles of the Constitution they are approved of by the people, and where they are to be found in legislation they are passed by the Houses of the Oireachtas. Laws should, and generally do, reflect society's values and will be influenced by them. But at the end of the day it is the duty of the Courts to implement and apply the law, not morality.

[5-28] Insofar as this extract suggests that the law can avoid making moral decisions, it is questionable. McGovern J paints a picture of the law allowing people to make their own moral choices in certain respects. This limited role for law would be supported both by those of a liberal persuasion (who value the autonomy of the individual very highly) and by those of a natural law persuasion (who view the moral role of the state as subsidiary to the moral responsibility of the individual). On either account, the law—in leaving certain moral choices to individuals—is itself making a moral decision. A belief in individual autonomy and/or the subsidiary role of the state are both moral beliefs. Where the state allows individuals to make their own moral decisions it does so on the basis of a moral belief that those sorts of decisions are best made by individuals.

This idea is well captured by the first part of the extract quoted above: just because the state—assume for the sake of argument—allows the destruction of non-implanted embryos, does not mean that it is morally correct to destroy such embryos. This is an area in which the law has chosen (for moral reasons) to allow people make their own moral choices. However, has Irish law really made that choice? Is it really the case that in guaranteeing the right to life of the unborn, the Irish Constitution takes the view that it is legally (if not necessarily morally) permissible to destroy unborn life that was conceived *in vitro*? For this was the effect of McGovern J's decision, as he himself recognised. In holding that the word "unborn" was unclear, he ultimately came to the conclusion that the unborn outside the womb had no constitutional right to life. As such, it was a matter for the Oireachtas to determine the legal status of embryos *in vitro*. Pending such determination, however, those embryos had no legal status and could be destroyed. This was a result consistent only with a view that unborn life does not include embryos *in vitro*, a point the judge purported not to be deciding.

The Right to a Good Name

In *Re Haughey* [1971] IR 217, the Supreme Court identified a number of procedural safeguards that apply where an investigation is taking place that may affect a citizen's right to a good name. Section 3(4) of the Committee of Public Accounts (Privilege and Procedures) Act 1970 provided that any witness before the Committee who refused to answer questions to which the Committee might legally require an answer could be certified as having committed an offence. The High Court, having taken such steps as it considered appropriate, might punish or take steps for the punishment of the person as if she had been guilty of contempt of the High Court. Mr Padraic Haughey was questioned by the committee in relation to the moneys being passed to an account in Northern Ireland. He refused to answer questions and was certified to the High Court. The Supreme Court construed the legislation as requiring a trial of the person in the High Court. However, as it did not allow for a trial by jury but allowed for punishments that could only be imposed subsequent to a jury trial, it was unconstitutional. Of more relevance for present purposes, the Supreme Court laid down certain requirements to be followed where the State was—in some form—making inquiries that bore on the good name of a person:

[5–29]

> Therefore, the position of Mr. Haughey was that at a public session of the Committee held on the 9th February, 1971, he had been accused of conduct which reflected on his character and good name and that the accusations made against him were made upon the hearsay evidence of a witness who asserted that he was not at liberty, and therefore was not prepared, to furnish the Committee with the names of Mr. Haughey's real accusers. The question which arises in these circumstances is what rights, if any, is Mr. Haughey entitled to assert in defence of his character and good name? It should be noted that, in the statement which he read to the Committee on the 17th February, 1971, he denied on oath that he had been connected, in any way, with the expenditure of moneys issued out of Subhead J of Vote 16. [1971] IR 217, at 262.

In circumstances such as these, Ó Dálaigh CJ stated that a person had the following rights:

[5–30]

(a) that he should be furnished with a copy of the evidence which reflected on his good name;

(b) that he should be allowed to cross-examine, by counsel, his accuser or accusers;
(c) that he should be allowed to give rebutting evidence;
(d) that he should be permitted to address, again by counsel, the Committee in his own defence.

These rights have spawned a vast body of case law dealing with rights to fair procedures, particularly—but not exclusively—in relation to tribunals. An examination of this case law lies beyond the scope of this book.

The Right to Bodily Integrity

[5–31] As noted in chapter 4, the courts recognised that the right to bodily integrity was constitutionally protected in *Ryan v Attorney General* [1965] IR 294. A number of attempts have been made to expand the negative right to bodily integrity (conceived as a protection against physical intrusion on a person's body) into a positive right to a certain minimum health care. In *State (C) v Frawley* [1976] IR 365, for example, the applicant objected to the conditions in which he was being detained in prison. He suffered from a sociopathic personality disturbance and had made repeated and ill-fated escape attempts; he also had a record of swallowing metal objects. As a result of these difficulties, he was generally kept either in solitary confinement or handcuffed. He was deprived of all metal objects. The evidence was that there was no facility in the State that was suitable for restraining and treating the small number of people who had the psychiatric difficulties of the applicant.

[5–32] Finlay CJ accepted that the right to bodily integrity included a right to freedom from torture and inhuman or degrading treatment. However, he held that this right had not been infringed as the measures to which the applicant objected were neither punitive nor malicious, instead being designed for the prisoner's own benefit or simply to prevent escape. Finlay CJ also accepted that the right to bodily integrity did carry with it some positive obligations but that these had not been breached:

> The right of bodily integrity as an unspecified constitutional right is clearly established by the decision of the Supreme Court in *Ryan v The Attorney General* by which I am bound and which I accept. Even though it was there laid down in the context of a challenge to the constitutional validity of a statute of the Oireachtas which, it was alleged, forced an individual to use water containing an additive hazardous to health, I see no reason why the principle should not also operate to prevent an act or omission of the Executive which, without justification, would expose the health of a person to risk or danger.
>
> When the Executive, in exercise of what I take to be its constitutional right and duty, imprisons an individual in pursuance of a lawful warrant of a court, then it seems to me to be a logical extension of the principle laid down in *Ryan's Case* that it may not, without justification or necessity, expose the health of that person to risk or danger. To state, as Mr MacEntee submits, that the Executive has a duty to protect the health of persons held in custody as well as is reasonably possible in all the circumstances of the case seems to me no more than to state in a positive manner the negative proposition which I have above accepted. Therefore, I am satisfied that such a proposition is sound in law.
>
> The vital question, however, is whether the Executive has failed in that duty in this case on the facts as I find them. I am satisfied that the medical requirements of the prosecutor, as distinct from his psychiatric needs, have at all material times been adequately met by the respondent. The prosecutor has been regularly visited and examined by the medical officer of Mountjoy Prison and, when specialised surgical treatment has been required, that treatment has been afforded in the Mater Hospital by a

> senior consultant surgeon. In my view, the restraints of which the prosecutor most vehemently complains have been designed and implemented to eliminate or diminish, so far as is reasonably practical, the possibility of the prosecutor harming himself by swallowing foreign bodies, by self injury or by injury arising from his climbing and escaping activities.
>
> The real failure in this duty alleged against the respondent is that he has failed to provide the special type of institution and treatment which was recommended by Dr. McCaffrey as a long-term treatment and that, to an extent, imprisonment in any other form is directly harmful to the progress of the prosecutor's condition of personality disturbance. A failure on the part of the Executive to provide for the prosecutor treatment of a very special kind in an institution which does not exist in any part of the State does not, in my view, constitute a failure to protect the health of the prosecutor as well as possible in all the circumstances of the case. If one were to accept in full all the assumptions upon which Dr. McCaffrey's opinion is based, it could be shown that there was a failure of an assumed absolute duty to provide the best medical treatment irrespective of the circumstances. I am satisfied, as a matter of law, that no such absolute duty exists.
>
> It has been urged on behalf of the prosecutor that the respondent cannot be excused from his duty to provide this very specialised type of psychiatric treatment on the grounds of the non-availability of the appropriate facilities since that non-availability flows from an unconstitutional failure on the part of his superiors to provide this specialised type of institution with appropriate staff. Even though the number of persons suffering from a condition even generally akin to that of the prosecutor may be as low as six, not all of whom are in custody, a description of the progress and consequence of the prosecutor's disturbance and the nature of his life in prison would make the availability of appropriate long-term treatment most desirable as a matter of compassion.
>
> However, it is not the function of the Court to recommend to the Executive what is desirable or to fix the priorities of its health and welfare policy. The function of the Court is confined to identifying and, if necessary, enforcing the legal and constitutional duties of the Executive. I cannot conscientiously hold, no matter where my sympathy might lie, that an obligation to provide for prisoners in general the best medical treatment in all the circumstances can be construed as including a duty to build, equip and staff the very specialised unit which Dr. McCaffrey has recommended and which might be appropriate to the needs of the prosecutor and four or five other persons. [1976] IR at 365, at 373.

This reflects the general reluctance of the courts to become overly involved in the enforcement of positive rights that carry resource implications. It is consistent with the position more recently adopted by the Supreme Court in *TD v Minister for Education* [2001] 4 IR 249 and in particular the comments of Murphy J—noted in chapter 4—to the effect that the courts should not enumerate socioeconomic rights under Art 40.3. In *State (Richardson) v Governor of Mountjoy Prison* [1978] IR 131, Barrington J held that the prison authorities had breached the right to bodily integrity in providing for a slopping out process that rendered it likely for human faeces to end up in the sinks in which prisoners had to wash themselves. [5–33]

The Right to Work and Earn a Livelihood

In *Murtagh Properties v Cleary* [1972] IR 330, the plaintiffs sought an interlocutory injunction to restrain the picketing of their premises by members of a trade union who objected to the plaintiffs employing women as bar staff. The trade union claimed that this was in breach of a collective agreement with the plaintiffs. Kenny J granted the interlocutory injunction on the basis that the plaintiffs had a reasonable prospect of success in their argument that the picket would infringe a constitutionally protected [5–34] right to work and earn a livelihood. It has become accepted that this is a constitutionally protected right. However, it does not extend to an absolute right to earn any particular livelihood. In *Attorney General v Paperlink* [1984] ILRM 373, the Attorney sought to preclude the defendant from operating a postal service as this breached the statutory monopoly. Costello J rejected the argument that the right to earn a livelihood entitled the defendants to operate a postal service:

> What then falls for consideration is whether the State monopoly established by the 1908 Act is (a) an "*attack*" on the defendants' right to earn a livelihood and (b) whether it is an "*unjust*" attack on that right. As the defendants' submissions are largely based on conclusions which they say can be drawn from Article 45 the first matter which I must consider is whether I am permitted to have regard to this Article for the purposes of this case. Article 45 has an introductory paragraph which states that the principles of social policy set forth in it are intended for the general guidance of the Oireachtas and that the application of those principles in the making of laws shall be the care of the Oireachtas exclusively "*and shall not be cognisable by any court under any of the provisions of this Constitution*". Notwithstanding the apparently all-embracing exclusion of *Article 45* from the purview of the courts Kenny J considered that he could have regard to it for the purpose of ascertaining what unspecified personal rights were included in the guarantees contained in Article 40.3.1° (see *Murtagh Properties v AG* [1972] IR 335) and Finlay J held that he could look at Article 45.4.2° for the purpose of "*reaching a general conclusion as to what may fairly be embraced by the expression 'the exigencies of the common good'*" — a phrase used in Article 43 in connection with the State's power to delimit the exercise of private property rights (see *Landers v AG* 109 ILTR 1). I respectfully agree. I consider therefore, that I am not precluded by the introductory words of the Article from considering the principles of social policy set out in it for a limited purpose, namely, for assisting the court in ascertaining what personal rights are included in the guarantees contained in Article 40.3.1° and what legitimate limitations in the interests of the common good the State may impose on such rights.
>
> The defendants' arguments are based on Article 45.3.1° which provides that:
>
> The State shall favour and, where necessary, supplement private initiative in industry and commerce.
>
> It is urged that this principle of social policy means that the Constitution contains an ideological preference in favour of private enterprise and private initiative in commerce. The first conclusion they say to be drawn from this interpretation is that the onus is on the State to justify any interference with private initiative in matters of commerce. Having made this submission in opening the defendants' case the defendants' counsel at the close of the case submitted that as the plaintiffs had failed to discharge the onus on them of justifying the State monopoly contained in the 1908 Act the court should declare the Act inconsistent with the Constitution.
>
> There are, it seems to me, two main objections to this first submission. Firstly, the defendants are, in my view, reading a great deal more into the Article than its provisions justify. Article 45 contains provisions to guide the legislature in its law-making activity and by Article 45.3.1° the Oireachtas is told that the State is required to favour and where necessary supplement private initiative in industry and commerce. This guideline is couched in most general language. Undoubtedly it demonstrates a view, found in other Articles of the Constitution, that the social order should not be based on a system in which all the means of production are owned by the State and a preference for one in which, in the main, industry and commerce are carried on by private citizens rather than by State agencies. But it does not follow from this very general guideline that the Oireachtas could not pass laws establishing State trading corporations or public utilities and I do not consider that it is proper to infer from its provision that the State is called

upon in legal proceedings to justify the existence of a State monopoly either in the form of a public utility or a trading corporation.

Secondly, the submission that the onus of proof rests on the plaintiffs ignores the views of the Supreme Court as explained by the Chief Justice in *Norris v AG*.... [1984] ILRM 373, at 386.

In *Rogers v ITGWU* [1978] ILRM 51, Finlay P accepted that a compulsory retirement age was not a breach of the right to earn a livelihood.

The Right to (Marital) Privacy and Autonomy

As was seen in chapter 4, the courts have recognised a right to (marital) privacy. In *McGee v Attorney General* [1974] IR 284, Walsh J relied on a right to marital privacy to strike down the ban on the importation or sale of contraceptives. Henchy J relied on a more individualistic right to privacy, deriving from the human personality. Henchy and McCarthy JJ relied on that same right to privacy to maintain that the ban on anal sex and on same-sex activity between men was unconstitutional in *Norris v Attorney General* [1984] IR 36. In his dissenting judgment in *Norris v Attorney General* [1984] IR 36, at 71, Henchy J explained that the right of privacy included:

[5–35]

> A complex of rights, varying in nature, purpose and range, each necessarily a facet of the citizen's core of individuality within the constitutional order.... There are many other aspects of the right of privacy, some yet to be given judicial recognition. It is unnecessary for the purpose of this case to explore them. It is sufficient to say that they would all appear to fall within a secluded area of activity or non-activity which may be claimed as necessary for the expression of an individual personality, for purposes not always necessarily moral or commendable, but meriting recognition in circumstances which do not endanger considerations such as State security, public order or morality, or other essential components of the common good.

A majority of the Supreme Court, however, considered that there was no right to privacy protected by the Constitution that would extend to prohibiting the Oireachtas from enacting such legislation.

An individual right to privacy was not definitively recognised until *Kennedy v Ireland* [1987] IR 587, in which the plaintiffs successfully sued the state for damages arising out of the bugging of their telephones. Hamilton P quoted from the minority judgments in *Norris* and continued:

[5–36]

> The nature of the right to privacy must be such as to ensure the dignity and freedom of an individual in the type of society envisaged by the Constitution, namely, a sovereign, independent and democratic society. The dignity and freedom of an individual in a democratic society cannot be ensured if his communications of a private nature, be they written or telephonic, are deliberately, consciously and unjustifiably intruded upon and interfered with. I emphasise the words "deliberately, consciously and unjustifiably" because an individual must accept the risk of accidental interference with his communications and the fact that in certain circumstances the exigencies of the common good may require and justify such intrusion and interference. No such circumstances exist in this case.
>
> There has been, as is admitted on behalf of the defendants, a deliberate, conscious and unjustifiable interference by the State through its executive organ with the telephonic communications of the plaintiffs and such interference constitutes an infringement of the constitutional rights to privacy of the three plaintiffs. [1987] IR 587, at 593.

[5–37] In *X v Flynn* 19 May 1994 (HC), Costello J granted an interlocutory injunction retraining journalists from watching and besetting the plaintiff, a rape victim. In *Barry v Medical Council* [1998] 3 IR 387, Costello P held that the right to privacy of a medical practitioner's patients prevailed over any right the practitioner might have to a public hearing. Thus it is clear that Art 40.3.2° protects a right to privacy in the sense of a right to confidentiality.

[5–38] The right of privacy, in the sense of autonomy, was recognised by a majority of the Supreme Court in *Re a Ward of Court (Withholding Medical Treatment) (No 2)* [1996] 2 IR 79, at 156, in the context of a patient's right to refuse medical treatment. Denham J put the matter as follows:

> Medical treatment may not be given to an adult person of full capacity without his or her consent. There are a few rare exceptions to this, *eg* in regard to contagious diseases or in a medical emergency where the patient is unable to communicate. This right arises out of civil, criminal and constitutional law. If medical treatment is given without consent, it may be trespass against the person in civil law, a battery in criminal law and a breach of the individual's constitutional rights. The consent which is given by an adult is a matter of choice. It is not necessarily a decision based on medical considerations. Thus, medical treatment may be refused for other than medical reasons, or reasons most citizens would regard as rational, but the person of full age and capacity may make the decision for their own reasons.

[5–39] Denham J recognised that the difference of capacity between the ward and a sentient person might justify a difference in treatment, but concluded that the difference in situation did not extend beyond the recognition that a person may not be able to exercise a right. Article 40.1 was a positive proposition that obliged the Court to try to provide to the ward the same rights as those of a sentient person:

> The State has due regard to the difference of capacity and may envisage a different process to protect the rights of the incapacitated. It is the duty of the Court to uphold equality before the law. It is thus appropriate to consider if a method exists to give to the insentient person, the ward, equal rights with those who are sentient. [1996] 2 IR 79, at 159.

[5–40] Whatever one's views about the ultimate decision that withdrawal of treatment was not unconstitutional, the use made of Art 40.1 was perplexing. Seldom can a difference in capacity have been so pronounced. Admittedly, the case raised no question of deference to legislative judgment so the Court was more free to make its own assessment of the appropriate response to the difference of capacity. Nevertheless, the autonomy-related rights under consideration made no sense in the case of an almost insentient person. Although one should of course treat people in the unfortunate position of the Ward as equal human persons, worthy of respect, it does not follow that that they have an equal right to self-determination. Autonomy exercised on your behalf by another is not autonomy; it is paternalism. Such paternalism may or may not be justified, but it should not be equated with autonomy.

The Right of Access to the Courts and the Right to Litigate

[5–41] In *State (Quinn) v Ryan* [1965] IR 70, the applicant challenged the constitutionality of s 29 of the Petty Sessions (Ireland) Act 1851 which allowed for the immediate removal from the jurisdiction of the Irish courts of any person who was arrested and detained under a British warrant in Ireland. The applicant had been released from custody due to a defect in an earlier extradition warrant. However, five or 10 minutes later while separated from his legal advisors, he was arrested pursuant to a subsequent warrant and immediately driven to the border with Northern Ireland where he was handed over to the RUC and transferred to Britain. Ó Dálaigh CJ described the events in the following terms:

> From this survey of the evidence it becomes clear that a plan was laid by the police, Irish and British, to remove the prosecutor after his arrest on the new warrant from the area of jurisdiction of our Courts with such dispatch that he would have no opportunity whatever of questioning the validity of the warrant. It is also clear that the applicant's solicitor was refused information (and in one instance supplied with misinformation) as to his client's whereabouts while his client was still within the jurisdiction, and that this refusal was persisted in while the prosecutor was still in Northern Ireland.
>
> It should be pointed out that in zeal for celerity of action the plan provided for sending the prosecutor into Northern Ireland where on no view of the law he was authorised to be sent. The authority of the warrant (if authority it had) was to transmit him to Britain. To have done this would, however, have involved delay in Dublin while the departure of aeroplane or ship was awaited. But any delay within the jurisdiction might have afforded the prosecutor's solicitor an opportunity to challenge the validity of the new warrant in the Courts and this would have set at nought the whole purpose of this plan.
>
> In plain language the purpose of the police plan was to eliminate the Courts and to defeat the rule of law as a factor in Government. [1965] IR 70, at 117–118.

The Supreme Court unanimously agreed that there was a right of access to the High Court to challenge the legality of one's detention and, furthermore, that the courts had whatever powers were necessary to ensure that constitutional rights were vindicated. In *Macauley v Minister for Posts and Telegraphs* [1966] IR 345, Kenny J held that the requirement that a person get the permission of the Attorney General before instituting proceedings against a government Minister was a breach of the right of access to the courts. [5–42]

In *Tuohy v Courtney* [1994] 3 IR 1, the plaintiff sought to sue the defendant, his former solicitor, in relation to the purchase of the plaintiff's home. The plaintiff alleged that his solicitor had acted negligently in various respects but was statute barred by s 11 of the Statute of Limitations 1957, which provides that an action in tort shall not be brought after the expiration of six years from the date on which the cause of action accrued. The plaintiff challenged the constitutionality of this section. Finlay CJ, delivering the judgment of the Court, held that the right of access to courts was not implicated by the provision, as the Statute of Limitations did not preclude a person from initiating a claim. Rather, a defendant could plead the Statute as a defence to a claim. However, the Court held that Article 40.3.1° also protected a right to litigate and that this was *prima facie* infringed by s 11. Finlay CJ then considered whether s 11 was constitutionally permissible: [5–43]

> It has been agreed by counsel, and in the opinion of the Court, quite correctly agreed, that the Oireachtas in legislating for time limits on the bringing of actions is essentially engaged in a balancing of constitutional rights and duties. What has to be balanced is the constitutional right of the plaintiff to litigate against two other contesting rights or duties, firstly, the constitutional right of the defendant in his property to be protected against

unjust or burdensome claims and, secondly, the interest of the public constituting an interest or requirement of the common good which is involved in the avoidance of stale or delayed claims.

The Court is satisfied that in a challenge to the constitutional validity of any statute in the enactment of which the Oireachtas has been engaged in such a balancing function, the role of the courts is not to impose their view of the correct or desirable balance in substitution for the view of the legislature as displayed in their legislation but rather to determine from an objective stance whether the balance contained in the impugned legislation is so contrary to reason and fairness as to constitute an unjust attack on some individual's constitutional rights.

It is in accordance with these principles that the Court approaches the ultimate task of deciding upon the constitutional validity of these impugned statutory provisions.

It cannot be disputed that a person whose right to seek a legal remedy for wrong is barred by a statutory time limit before he, without fault or neglect on his part, becomes aware of the existence of that right has suffered a severe apparent injustice and would be entitled reasonably to entertain a major sense of grievance.

So to state however does not of itself solve the question as to whether a statute which in a sense permits that to occur is by that fact inconsistent with the Constitution.

Statutes of limitation have been part of the legal system in Ireland for very many years and were a feature of the system of law operating in force in Ireland apparently both before and after the Act of Union and have continued from 1922 up to the present (*cf* the judgment of Griffin J in *Hegarty v O'Loughran* [1990] 1 IR 148, at 157).

The primary purpose would appear to be, firstly, to protect defendants against stale claims and avoid the injustices which might occur to them were they asked to defend themselves from claims which were not notified to them within a reasonable time.

Secondly, they are designed to promote as far as possible expeditious trials of action so that a court may have before it as the material upon which it must make its decision oral evidence which has the accuracy of recent recollection and documentary proof which is complete, features which must make a major contribution to the correctness and justice of the decision arrived at.

Thirdly, they are designed to promote as far as possible and proper a certainty of finality in potential claims which will permit individuals to arrange their affairs whether on a domestic, commercial or professional level in reliance to the maximum extent possible upon the absence of unknown or unexpected liabilities.

The counter-balance to these objectives is the necessity as far as is practicable, or as best it may, for the State to ensure that such time limits do not unreasonably or unjustly impose hardship. Any time limit statutorily imposed upon the bringing of actions is potentially going to impose some hardship on some individual. What this Court must do is to ascertain whether the extent and nature of such hardship is so undue and so unreasonable having regard to the proper objectives of the legislation as to make it constitutionally flawed.

It has been suggested that the facts of this case are almost unique and that what is described as a saver inserted in the time limiting provisions to meet those facts would, if it had been inserted, make no significant difference to the protection which the Act of 1957 affords to potential defendants.

It has also been suggested that the jurisdiction of the courts as laid down in *Ó Domhnaill v Merrick* [1984] IR 151 and *Toal v Duignan and others* [1991] ILRM 135 to dismiss as unconstitutionally unjust, claims which are brought even within a statutorily permitted time but which are in fact grossly delayed is a "safety net" to protect the defendant sufficient to permit of a saver to protect the plaintiff who within the statutory time limit is unaware of his right of action. Such a "saver", it is urged, would not in any way significantly diminish the certainty or finality of the time limit.

The Court does not accept that either of these contentions is of such strength as would make an inflexible time limit of six years for breach of contract and tort causing damage other than personal injuries clearly unconstitutional.

The period of six years is, objectively viewed, a substantial period. Historically, it has remained unchanged for this type of action since the Common Law Procedure (Ireland) Act, 1853, and no shortening of it has been legislatively created notwithstanding the very significant increase in literacy, understanding of legal rights and sophistication which has as a matter of common knowledge occurred in the years since that time.

The Act of 1957 contains in Part III thereof extensions of the periods of limitation in cases of disability, acknowledgment, part payment, fraud and mistake. These extensions constitute a significant inroad on the certainty of finality provided by the Act.

The right of a defendant having been sued within a permitted time limit to plead a gross or unreasonable delay sufficient to lead to the dismiss of the action against him as an exercise by the courts of its inherent jurisdiction renders him much less secure and much less protected against loss than a fixed time limit subject to the extensions only which are already contained in the Act of 1957. To mount such a plea in an action of substance is a burdensome and expensive process leading as it has done in some of the cases which have been decided by this Court to a trial in the High Court and an appeal to this Court. The time scale of such proceedings is quite extensive and the period of anxiety and uncertainty for the defendant even if eventually he or she is successful will frequently be very great unless in cases (which may not be frequent) where the plaintiff has substantial assets such a proceeding which the defendant must mount to protect his position will be done completely at his own expense.

These considerations are but some of the matters which the Oireachtas could properly consider in reaching a decision which is the real nub of this case as to whether it should or should not add to the grounds of extension of limitation periods already contained in the Act of 1957 a ground of discoverability of the cause of action. Together with those considerations of course must go the consideration of examples of injustice such as appear to have occurred in this case.

For the Oireachtas to reach a decision either to add or not to add to the extensions of limitation periods contained in Part III of the Act of 1957 an extension relating to discoverability with regard to this particular time limit imposed by that Act, is a decision which in the view of this Court can be supported by just and reasonable policy decisions and is not accordingly a proper matter for judicial intervention. [1994] 3 IR 1, at 47–50.

In *Re Article 26 and sections 5 and 10 of the Illegal Immigrants (Trafficking) Bill 1999* [2000] 2 IR 360, the Supreme Court upheld a 14-day time limit for seeking judicial review of certain immigration decisions, but emphasised that the Bill gave the Court a power to extend time for good and sufficient reason. In *White v Dublin City Council* [2004] 1 IR 545, the Supreme Court struck down a rigid time limit of two months for challenging certain planning decisions, given the absence of any possibility for extending time. [5–44]

The State has enacted a scheme providing for civil legal aid. In *O'Donoghue v Legal Aid Board* [2004] IEHC 413, Kelly J placed the right to civil legal aid on a constitutional footing: [5–45]

> [T]he unfortunate circumstances of the plaintiff in the present case are such that access to the courts and fair procedures under the Constitution would require that she be provided with legal aid. That view is reinforced by the fact that she fell squarely within the entitlements to such under the Act and the regulations but was denied it for a period of 25 months because of the manifest failure of the State. The delay in granting the certificate for legal aid, in my view, amounted to a breach of the constitutional

entitlements of the plaintiff and if she can demonstrate loss as a result she is entitled to recover damages in respect thereof.

It is not enough to set up a scheme for the provision of legal aid to necessitous persons and then to render it effectively meaningless for a long period of time. The State must ... ensure that the scheme "is implemented fairly to all persons and in a manner which fulfils its declared purpose".

The purpose of the 1995 Act is that persons who meet the necessary criteria shall receive legal aid. That carries the implication that the entitlement to legal aid will be effective and of meaning. How can it be if a delay of 25 months is encountered? Equally, how can the scheme be fair if a qualified person cannot get to see a solicitor for such a lengthy period?

The Act of 1995 gives substance, in many ways, to the constitutional entitlement to legal aid for appropriate persons. The legislature is entitled to define reasonable limits to that right. But the right cannot be effectively set at nought for years in the manner that it was here. [2004] IEHC 413, at [103]–[106].

Contents – Chapter 6

Property Rights

Introduction. . . . .[6–01]
Early Case Law and the Interaction Between Art 40.3.2° and Art 43. . . . . [6–08]
What is Property?. . . . . [6–15]
    Constitutionally Protected Property. . . . . [6–15]
    Economic Value Created by Law . . . . [6–19]
Standing to Invoke Property Rights. . . . . [6–33]
Testing the Legitimacy of Restrictions of Property Rights . . . . [6–35]
    Introduction . . . . [6–35]
    The Proportionality Test. . . . . [6–36]
    Regulation of Ownership Rights. . . . . [6–44]
    Regulation of Land Use . . . . [6–49]
    Taxation. . . . . [6–52]
    Retrospective Restrictions of Property Rights. [6–55]
    Imposing the Cost of Achieving a Public Good on One Section of the Community [6–57]
    Anomalous Legislation as Distinct from Clearly Focused Legislation . . . . [6–62]
Compensation . . . . [6–64]
Postscript. . . . . [6–72]

Overview

Both Art 40.3 and Art 43 of the Constitution protect private property rights. The courts have interpreted these provisions together as a protection both of the institution of private property and of the rights of particular individuals over the things that they happen to own. In general, the courts have treated all aspects of economic value (such as land, objects, money, legal actions) as property that may be constitutionally protected. However, the position of economic value that is created by legal regulation is less clear. The courts have developed a proportionality test to assess the legitimacy of restrictions of property rights. This test requires that the restriction be rationally connected to the objective of the legislation, impair the right as little as possible and be such that its effects on rights are proportionate to the objective. However, it is not always easy to discern precisely how this test is applied by the courts. Other factors affect the courts' willingness to strike down legislation as being in breach of property rights. These factors include whether the legislation is anomalous or clearly targeted, whether the legislation imposes a disproportionate burden on a particular section of the community in order to achieve a general good, whether compensation is provided and whether the legislation is retrospective.

CHAPTER 6

Property Rights

Introduction

Rights to private property are protected in two different constitutional articles. Article 40.3.2° provides: [6–01]

> The State shall, in particular, by its laws protect as best it may be from unjust attack and, in the case of injustice done, vindicate the life, person, good name, and property rights of every citizen.

Unusually, private property rights are also protected in another constitutional provision, Article 43 providing a more detailed rationale and defence of the institution of private property: [6–02]

> 1.1° The State acknowledges that man, in virtue of his rational being, has the natural right, antecedent to positive law, to the private ownership of external goods.
> 2° The State accordingly guarantees to pass no law attempting to abolish the right of private ownership or the general right to transfer, bequeath, and inherit property.
> 2.1° The State recognises, however, that the exercise of the rights mentioned in the foregoing provisions of this Article ought, in civil society, to be regulated by the principles of social justice.
> 2° The State, accordingly, may as occasion requires delimit by law the exercise of the said rights with a view to reconciling their exercise with the exigencies of the common good.

The protection of private property is seen as central to the functioning of a liberal democratic society as it gives individuals a stake in the world and the space within which to develop their life plans reasonably free from state intrusion. In *Re Article 26 and the Health (Amendment) (No 2) Bill 2004* [2005] IESC 7, at [120], the Supreme Court stated: [6–03]

> The right to the ownership of property has a moral quality which is intimately related to the humanity of each individual. It is also one of the pillars of the free and democratic society established under the Constitution.

The Supreme Court thus focused on the role of property rights in providing people with security in their lives: those things that they hold cannot (at least without good reason) be taken away from them by the State. This protection may, however, be of greater benefit to those who hold more things. For this reason, Kingston has been critical of the constitutional protection of private property rights: [6–04]

> [R]egarding property as a fundamental right gives rise to many difficulties, both conceptually and in practical terms. Perhaps if property was regarded as an economic, rather than a civil, right some of these difficulties would be resolved, although the fact

that the right is premised on inequality could still give rise to conflict with directly countervailing values, such as the right to equality.... [O]f course, rich people have rights, those rights shared by all human beings, such as freedom from torture, freedom to express themselves, freedom from hunger and from negative discrimination; however, it is not at all clear that they have the right to be rich too. James Kingson, "Rich People Have Rights too? The Status of Property as a Fundamental Human Right" in Liz Heffernan ed, *Human Rights: A European Perspective* (Round Hall, Dublin, 1994), at 296–297.

[6–05] The actual origins of Art 43 drew on a philosophical understanding of property very different from that suggested by Kingston but also quite different from that suggested by the Supreme Court in *Re Article 26 and the Health (Amendment) (No 2) Bill 2004* [2005] IESC 7. Article 43 reflected the teaching of the Roman Catholic Church on property rights, as laid down in the two encyclicals of *Rerum Novvarum* and *Quadragesimo Anno*. In *Rerum Novarum* (1891), Pope Leo XIII responded to the opposing challenges of communism and laissez-faire capitalism by positing a view of private property as being in accordance with the natural law but as permitting considerable state intervention on the grounds of the common good. For general discussion, see Dermot Keogh and Andrew McCarthy, *The Making of the Irish Constitution 1937* (Mercier, 2007), at 117–118.

[6–06] The interaction of Art 40.3.2° and Art 43 initially posed problems for the courts, although a reasonably clear position has emerged over the past 20 to 30 years. The core of this position is that the Constitution protects both the institution of private property and the prima facie rights of citizens to the particular things which they happen to possess. The courts have been fairly expansive in identifying the things over which people can have property rights. In general, every economic interest is (at least prima facie) protected. However, the issue of economic interests arising as a result of actions by the State has posed difficult conceptual issues, as yet unresolved. The courts have developed increasingly structured tests for assessing whether a property right has been illegitimately infringed. There is a burgeoning body of case law determining what restrictions of property rights are legitimate. It is, however, difficult to derive general principles from this case law, although some broad trends are discernible. Finally, the relevance of compensation in rescuing an otherwise illegitimate restriction of property rights remains unclear.

[6–07] Although the courts' understanding of the constitutional protection of property rights has crystallised considerably in the last 15–20 years, it is still necessary to have some understanding of the earlier cases in order to appreciate the position at which the courts have arrived.

Early Case Law and the Interaction Between Art 40.3.2° and Art 43

[6–08] *Buckley v Attorney General* [1950] IR 67 is an early example of robust, judicial activism on the part of the Supreme Court. The case arose out of a dispute in relation to the distribution of certain funds belonging to Sinn Féin. In 1924, the honorary treasurers of Sinn Féin held a sum of over £8,500 as trustees. Disputes subsequently arose between them as to who was entitled to the money. Accordingly, they lodged the money in the High Court under the Trustee Act 1893. After the trustees died, the plaintiffs, who were members of Sinn Féin, brought an action against the Attorney General (as representative of the public) seeking a declaration that the money belonged to the Sinn

Property Rights

Féin organisation and an order that the money be paid out to two of the plaintiffs as honorary treasurers of that organisation. While the action was pending before the High Court, the Oireachtas passed the Sinn Féin Funds Act 1947. Section 10 of that Act provided that all proceedings pending before the High Court in relation to the money should be stayed and that, upon application being made by the Attorney General, the High Court should strike out such proceedings. The Act also provided that the funds should be distributed in a particular way. The Attorney General duly applied to the High Court, but Gavan Duffy P struck out his application on the basis of the separation of powers. On appeal, the Supreme Court considered both the separation of powers argument and the property rights argument. The judgment of the Court was delivered by O'Byrne J:

> We do not feel called upon to enter upon an inquiry as to the foundation of natural rights or as to their nature and extent. They have been the subject-matter of philosophical discussion for many centuries. It is sufficient for us to say that this State, by its Constitution, acknowledges that the right to private property is such a right and that this right is antecedent to all positive law. This, in our opinion, means that man by virtue, and as an attribute, of his human personality is so entitled to such a right that no positive law is competent to deprive him of it and we are of opinion that the entire Article is informed by, and should be construed in the light of, this fundamental conception. Consistently with, and as an adjunct to, this recognition, the Constitution proclaims (1) that in a civil society, such as ours, the exercise of such rights should be regulated by principles of social justice, and (2) that, for this purpose, the State may pass laws delimiting the exercise of such rights so as to reconcile their exercise with the requirements of the common good.
>
> It was contended by counsel for the Attorney General that the intendment and effect of Article 43.1.2°, was merely to prevent the total abolition of private property in the State and that, consistently with that clause, it is quite competent for the Oireachtas to take away the property rights of any individual citizen or citizens. We are unable to accept that proposition. It seems to us that the Article was intended to enshrine and protect the property rights of the individual citizen of the State and that the rights of the individual *are* thereby protected, subject to the right of the State, as declared in clause 2, to regulate the exercise of such rights in accordance with the principles of social justice and to delimit the exercise of such rights so as to reconcile their exercise with the exigencies of the common good.
>
> Clause 2 of this Article introduces a principle of paramount importance. It recognises in the first instance, that the exercise of the rights of private property ought, in a civil society such as ours, to be regulated by the principles of social justice and, for this purpose, (*ie* to give effect to the principles of social justice) the State may, as occasion requires, delimit by law the exercise of such rights so as to reconcile their exercise with the exigencies of the common good. In particular cases this may give rise to great difficulties. It is claimed that the question of the exigencies of the common good is peculiarly a matter for the Legislature and that the decision of the Legislature on such a question is absolute and not subject to, or capable of, being reviewed by the Courts. We are unable to give our assent to this far-reaching proposition. If it were intended to remove this matter entirely from the cognisance of the Courts, we are of opinion that it would have been done in express terms as it was done in Article 45 with reference to the directive principles of social policy, which are inserted for the guidance of the Oireachtas, and are expressly removed from the cognisance of the Courts.
>
> Article 15.4 of the Constitution provides (1) that the Oireachtas shall not enact any law which is in any respect repugnant to the Constitution or to any provision thereof, and (2) that every law enacted by the Oireachtas which is in any respect repugnant to the Constitution or to any provision thereof, shall, to the extent only of such repugnancy, be

invalid. Where it is alleged that a law is repugnant to the Constitution, the jurisdiction and duty to determine such question is expressly conferred on the High Court by Article 34.3.2°, with appeal in all such cases to this Court (Article 34.4.4°). This is a duty of fundamental importance which must be discharged in every case where such a question arises, however onerous that duty may be.

In the present case there is no suggestion that any conflict had arisen, or was likely to arise, between the exercise by the plaintiffs of their rights of property in the trust moneys and the exigencies of the common good, and, in our opinion, it is only the existence of such a conflict and an attempt by the Legislature to reconcile such conflicting claims that could justify the enactment of the statute under review. [1950] IR 67, at 82–84.

[6–09] The Court's decision is a robust defence of the judicial role. In two particular respects, the Court rejected arguments that would have led to a very minimalist protection of private property rights, with probable knock-on effects for the interpretation of other constitutional provisions. First, the Court rejected the contention that the Constitution protected only private property in general but not the actual property rights of particular citizens. If the Court had accepted such a contention, the Oireachtas would have been authorised to interfere with private property to any extent short of establishing a communist state. Secondly, the Court rejected the contention that the scope of the exceptions in Art 43 was exclusively a matter for the Oireachtas. Again, if the Oireachtas had accepted such a contention, it would have excluded itself from all future assessment of whether private property rights had been breached: in each case it would instead have been exclusively a question for the Oireachtas to determine whether property rights should be restricted.

[6–10] That said, O'Byrne J can perhaps be criticised for going too far in asserting the role of the Court to review the assessment of the Oireachtas in relation to the exigencies of the common good. A requirement that the exercise of property rights be actually in conflict with the common good before the Oireachtas can intervene overlooks the extent to which the Oireachtas could better serve the common good by restricting property rights. In the context of planning law, for example, the building of a house by one person might not necessarily conflict with the common good. Nevertheless, the general regulation of building can serve the common good. This issue of establishing the appropriate level of deference to the Oireachtas remains one of the most contentious in constitutional law. It is scarcely surprising that one of the Supreme Court's first forays into this domain failed to produce a sophisticated account of the issue.

[6–11] The robustness of *Buckley* did not persist, as demonstrated by *Attorney General v Southern Industrial Trust* (1961) 109 ILTR 161. The defendant was a hire purchase company and were the owners of a car that was rented, under a hire purchase agreement, to a Mr Simons. Mr Simons violated customs rules by bringing the car from Ireland to the UK. He subsequently returned the car to Ireland. The Attorney General applied to the High Court for the forfeiture of the car pursuant to s 5(1) of the Customs (Temporary Provisions) Act 1945. The defendant questioned the constitutional validity of that provision. In effect, the Act required that the owner of the car (Southern Industrial Trust), not itself guilty of any wrongdoing, should have its property forfeited on account of the wrongdoing of another party. Lavery J laid down the approach which, in his view, the courts should adopt to such legislation:

> ... [B]y positive provision, which indeed might have been considered unnecessary, that the Oireachtas has the primary function in securing that the laws enacted by it have regard to "the requirements of the common good" and are "regulated by the principles of 'social justice'". It is necessary to state this obvious fact as it was contended that the Courts had the peculiar and exclusive jurisdiction of examining legislation to determine whether it was in accordance with the constitutional limitations.
>
> The Oireachtas as the elected representatives of the people have the function of legislating so as to promote the objects laid down in the preamble and to determine social and economic policy. It is not the function of the Courts to determine these matters or to criticise or invalidate the decisions of the Oireachtas.
>
> It *is* the function of the Courts, when its jurisdiction is invoked, to determine "the validity of any law having regard to the provisions of the Constitution" (Article 34.4.4°).
>
> The importance of this function is not to be minimised. While the Courts are not the critics or the overlords of the Oireachtas, they have the solemn duty of acting as the guardians of the rights of the people, whether the majority or minorities and in so doing to examine legislation to ascertain whether it, through error or (which happily has not happened) by deliberate action, the Government or the Oireachtas has infringed the guaranteed rights. (1961) 109 ILTR 161, at 176–177.

Although the Court's reasoning was not—to put it charitably—a model of clarity, its conclusion that the legislation was constitutional was consistent with its relaxed attitude to the courts' role in reviewing the judgment of the Oireachtas.

In many of the early cases, the effect of the dual protection provided by Art 40.3.2° and Art 43 was not adverted to. However, in *Blake v Attorney General* [1982] IR 117, the Supreme Court attempted to explain the differences between Art 40.3.2° and Art 43. O'Higgins CJ explained the distinction as follows: **[6–12]**

> Article 43 is headed by the words "private property." It defines the attitude of the State to the concept of the private ownership of external goods and contains the State's acknowledgement that a natural right to such exists, antecedent to positive law, and that the State will not attempt to abolish this right or the associated right to transfer, bequeath and inherit property. The Article does, however, recognise that the State "may as occasion requires delimit by law the exercise of the said rights with a view to reconciling their exercise with the exigencies of the common good." It is an Article which prohibits the abolition of private property as an institution, but at the same time permits, in particular circumstances, the regulation of the exercise of that right and of the general right to transfer, bequeath and inherit property. In short, it is an Article directed to the State and to its attitude to these rights, which are declared to be antecedent to positive law. It does not deal with a citizen's right to a particular item of property, such as controlled premises. Such rights are dealt with in Article 40 under the heading "personal rights" and are specifically designated among the personal rights of citizens. Under Article 40 the State is bound, in its laws, to respect and as far as practicable to defend and vindicate the personal rights of citizens.
>
> There exists, therefore, a double protection for the property rights of a citizen. As far as he is concerned, the State cannot abolish or attempt to abolish the right of private ownership as an institution or the general right to transfer, bequeath and inherit property. In addition, he has the further protection under Article 40 as to the exercise by him of his own property rights in particular items of property. [1982] IR 117, at 135.

It quickly became clear, however, that such a rigid distinction between Art 40.3.2° and Art 43, despite its conceptual attractiveness, was difficult to maintain. In *Dreher v Irish Land Commission*, Walsh J commented: **[6–13]**

I think it is clear that any State action that is authorised by Article 43 and conforms to that Article cannot by definition be unjust for the purpose of Article 40.3.2°. [1984] ILRM 94, at 96.

[6–14] In *Re Article 26 and the Health (Amendment) (No 2) Bill 2004* [2005] IESC 7, at [114], the Supreme Court stated that this was "a correct statement of the close relationship" between the two Articles. It is thus clear that constitutional law both guarantees that Ireland cannot abolish private property and (of greater contemporary relevance) restricts the actions that the State is entitled to take in respect of particular items of property. The general concepts of the common good and social justice inform the circumstances in which the Oireachtas is allowed to restrict the exercise of property rights.

What is Property?

Constitutionally Protected Property

[6–15] As noted above, the courts have been expansive in their determination of what property falls within the constitutional guarantees. As a rule of thumb, one can state that all economic interests are protected, subject to certain exceptions. *Buckley v Attorney General* itself is authority for the proposition that the property guarantee applies to moneys. *Southern Industrial Trust* establishes that moveable property (such as a car) is protected. In *Central Dublin Development Association v Attorney General* (1975) 109 ILTR 69, it was held that the constitutional guarantee applied both to land and to the rights related to the ownership of land.

[6–16] Rights to intangible things are also protected. In *Phonographic Performance (Ireland) Ltd v Cody* [1998] 4 IR 504, Keane J held that intellectual property rights were protected by the Constitution. In *Re Article 26 and the Employment Equality Bill 1996* [1997] 2 IR 321, the Supreme Court accepted that the right to carry on a business and earn a livelihood was a constitutionally protected property right. In *Chestvale Properties Ltd v Glackin* [1992] ILRM 221, Murphy J accepted that mutual contractual obligations could amount to constitutionally protected property.

[6–17] The courts have not been entirely clear as to whether the right to litigate is protected as a property right, as an aspect of the right of access to the courts, or as an unenumerated right in its own terms. In *Re Health (Amendment) (No 2) Bill 2004* [2005] IESC 7, the Supreme Court considered that the right of patients to recover money unlawfully charged for nursing home care (a *chose in action*) was constitutionally protected property. This was consistent with a view stated in *O'Brien v Manufacturing Engineering Co Ltd* [1973] IR 334 and *O'Brien v Keogh* [1972] IR 144 to the effect that the right to litigate was a constitutionally protected property right. However, some doubt was cast on this in *Moynihan v Greensmith* [1977] IR 55, in which the plaintiff challenged the constitutionality of the limitation period provided by s 9 of the Civil Liability Act 1961 where the alleged tortfeasor has died. The Supreme Court questioned whether the two *O'Brien* cases had been correctly decided, although this appears to have been the first sign of concern at the working out of the relationship between Art 40.3.2° and Art 43, a concern that no longer preoccupies the courts. In *Tuohy v Courtney* [1994] 3 IR 1, another statute of liability was challenged. Given the facts of the case, the Supreme Court felt that there was no material difference in the constitutional protection afforded to the right to litigate as a personal right from that afforded to the right as an aspect of property rights. In truth, it is difficult to see how there could ever be a difference. Although property rights are rights over things (not rights against persons), they are constitutionally protected as the personal rights of the property-owner. Accordingly, there is no structural difference between the constitutionally protected personal property right and other personal rights. Given the property implications of the right to litigate, however, and the preference for connecting rights to a textual basis rather than the vagueness of Art 40.3.1°, it may be that the courts follow the trend of the *Health Amendment Bill Case* in declaring that all aspects of the right to litigate are protected as property rights.

Although shareholdings themselves would appear to be protected property, the courts have resisted attempts to rely on the property guarantee to expand the rights of shareholders. Thus in *Kerry Co-Operative Creameries Ltd v An Bord Bainne* [1990] ILRM 664, Costello J rejected the plaintiff's claim that it was entitled, as a shareholder to a share in the net value of the defendant's underlying assets. In *O'Neill v Ryan* [1993] ILRM 557, the plaintiff claimed that the defendant had damaged a company in which the plaintiff had shares. The Supreme Court held that the plaintiff could not bring a personal action claiming that his property rights had been infringed by reason of the damage to the company. Those who own shares are thus deemed to own them subject to the legal requirements of company law, which requirements may over time lead to an increase or diminution in their economic value. While a retrospective, legislative alteration of company law might be an attack on property rights, a diminution in value due to the normal workings of company law is not. Hogan and Whyte observe that these cases are not fully consistent with earlier cases, such as *Private Motorists Provident Society v Attorney General* [1983] IR 339, in which shareholders were considered to have property rights protected by Art 40.3 against unjust legislative attack. It may be, however, that these cases are explicable by reference to an uncertainty over whether limited companies could invoke property rights. This uncertainty was addressed by the judgment of Keane J in the High Court in *Iarnród Éireann v Ireland* [1996] 3 IR 321, considered below. [6–18]

Economic Value Created by Law

The issue of whether economic value created by law should be constitutionally protected raises issues that go to the core of why property is protected in the first place. It is thus unsurprising that the courts have found it difficult to grapple with the issue. In a number of cases, the courts have held that economic value created by law can be constitutionally protected property. For instance, in *Lovett v Minister for Education* [1997] 1 ILRM 89, at 100, Kelly J held that the entitlement to a pension, contained in a scheme made under s 3 of the Teachers' Superannuation Act 1928, was a constitutionally protected property right. It thus appears that where an economic entitlement is directly provided by statute, that economic entitlement has prima facie constitutional protection as property. [6–19]

The issue becomes more difficult when one seeks to characterise the impact of regulatory schemes. On first impression, a regulatory scheme appears to restrict one's property rights (although of course such restriction may well be justified). Absent the regulatory scheme, one would be entitled to build a house, run a pub, or operate a taxi. However, the differential impact of a regulatory scheme itself appears to convey value. [6–20]

The house one was allowed to build is probably more valuable as a result of the general requirement to obtain planning permission, as such a requirement limits the ability of one's neighbours to develop their land in a way that would adversely affect the value of one's own land. The pub which one has been licensed to run is probably more profitable because it is difficult for someone else to have another pub licensed next door. One can go even further with this analysis and suggest that, as one needs planning permission or a pub licence to build a house or operate a pub, the permission or licence itself enhances the value of one's land. But if a planning permission or licence represents economic value and is thus, along the lines of the decision in *Lovett*, constitutionally protected property, can the requirement to apply for planning permission or a licence still fairly be characterised as a restriction on property rights?

[6–21] The courts' approach to this issue has not been a model of clarity. The courts' attitude to regulatory schemes was illustrated by the Supreme Court's decision in *State (FPH Properties SA) v An Bord Pleanála* [1987] IR 698. At issue was the interpretation of s 26(2) of the Local Government (Planning and Development) Act 1963, which indicated the types of condition that could be attached to a grant of planning permission. McCarthy J held that the legitimate types of condition had to be strictly construed as "the requirement for planning permission constitutes an encroachment on property rights." ([1987] IR 698, at 710). This views the regulatory scheme itself as a restriction of property rights, implying that the regulatory authorisation (the planning permission) cannot be constitutionally protected property as it merely allows one to do what one would have been entitled to do if the general planning system had not already restricted your rights. Viewed in this way, the planning permission is a restoration of the *status quo ante*.

[6–22] A different view was taken in the slightly earlier case of *Pine Valley Developments v Minister for the Environment* [1987] IR 23. A Mr Thornton had received a grant of outline planning permission from the Minister in relation to lands which he subsequently sold to the plaintiff. However, the County Council then refused to grant full planning permission in the terms of the outline permission. The plaintiff challenged this refusal but was unsuccessful as the Supreme Court held that the initial grant of outline permission had been *ultra vires*. The plaintiff then instituted subsequent proceedings claiming, *inter alia*, that its property rights had been unconstitutionally restricted, essentially on the basis that it had paid a development land price for land which no longer had such value. In assessing the property rights claim, Finlay CJ commented:

> What the Minister was doing in making his decision in 1977 to grant outline planning permission to the then owner of these lands was not intended as any form of delimitation or invasion of the rights of the owner of those lands but was rather intended as an enlargement and enhancement of those rights. [1987] IR 23, at 37.

[6–23] For this reason, the plaintiff's property rights had not been infringed by the subsequent quashing, by the courts, of the outline planning permission as that planning permission had increased the value and the plaintiff's rights. Implicitly, what the State gave, the State could take away. It is difficult to square the view that the grant of planning permission is an enlargement of rights with the view that the requirement to obtain planning permission is a restriction of rights. Moreover, Finlay CJ appears—although this is not entirely clear—to have viewed the enlargement of rights effected by planning permission as a reason why any alteration or revocation of the planning permission would not constitute a restriction of property rights.

In *Re Article 26 and Part V of the Planning and Development Bill 1999* [2000] 2 IR 321, the Supreme Court assessed the constitutionality of legislation which, in essence, allowed planning authorities to require developers to provide up to 20 percent of the land in a development at agricultural use value rather than market value. This land would then be used for social and affordable housing. Keane CJ, delivering the judgment of the Court, upheld this provision: [6–24]

> In the present case, as a condition of obtaining a planning permission for the development of lands for residential purposes, the owner may be required to cede some part of the enhanced value of the land deriving both from its zoning for residential purposes and the grant of permission in order to meet what is considered by the Oireachtas to be a desirable social objective, namely the provision of affordable housing and housing for persons in the special categories and of integrated housing. Applying the tests proposed by Costello J in *Heaney v Ireland* [1994] 3 IR 593 and subsequently endorsed by this court, the court in the case of the present Bill is satisfied that the scheme passes those tests. They are rationally connected to an objective of sufficient importance to warrant interference with a constitutionally protected right and, given the serious social problems which they are designed to meet, they undoubtedly relate to concerns which, in a free and democratic society, should be regarded as pressing and substantial. At the same time, the court is satisfied that they impair those rights as little as possible and their effects on those rights are proportionate to the objectives sought to be attained. [2000] 2 IR 321, at 354.

This again suggests a view of the regulation of planning and development (in this case the zoning decision rather than the permission decision) as an enhancement of rights rather than a restriction of rights. However, it differs somewhat from *Pine Valley* in that Keane CJ explicitly considered whether the loss of economic value effected by the legislation was justified. This suggests that the increase in value of land attributable to a planning permission is constitutionally protected property. However, as the Court was prepared to accept that compensation at agricultural use value rather than market value was adequate, the level of constitutional protection afforded to economic value created by regulation is not that great. [6–25]

Although the courts thus appear to accept that the value created by a legislative authorisation can be constitutionally protected property (albeit not very strongly protected), they have not accepted that all value produced by economic intervention in the market is constitutionally protected. In *Maher v Minister for Agriculture, Food and Rural Development* [2001] 2 IR 139, the Supreme Court considered whether milk quotas were constitutionally protected property. The milk quotas scheme was part of the European Community's Common Agricultural Policy. Milk producers were assigned a quota of milk production. If they produced more milk than their quota, they had to pay a super levy on the excess. Although the quotas were initially tied to the land, changes to the scheme allowed quota-holders to lease an unused part of the quota in a particular year to another milk producer. Therefore, the quota system had created a thing—the quota—which had an economic value. The European Communities (Milk Quota) Regulations 2000 changed the scheme so that only persons actively engaged in milk production could sell on their quotas at full value. Other persons could [6–26] only sell at a price fixed by the Minister. This change adversely affected the applicants because their milk quotas were now worth less to them than they had been in the past.

[6–27] The Supreme Court rejected the contention that the milk quotas were property. Keane CJ put the matter in the following way:

> There remains the question as to whether the Regulations of 2000 also constituted an unjust attack on the alleged property rights of the applicants in contravention of Articles 40.3.1° and 2° and 43 of the Constitution. I have no doubt that the regulations do not violate any property rights within the meaning of the relevant articles of the Constitution. Even if one were to adopt the most expansive view of what is meant by a right of property within the meaning of those Articles and extend it beyond the well accepted species of property under our law, real and personal property, including, under the latter category, choses-in-action, it could still in no sense be equated to a right of property.
>
> It seems to me unnecessary in this context to consider whether rights in the nature of licences conferred by the law in relation to particular property, such as planning permissions or licences for the sale of alcohol, constitute property rights. The quotas to which the applicants were entitled in this case are not licences or permits which may enhance the value of property which they own or occupy. The applicants may produce as much milk as they please and require no licence from any authority so to do.
>
> The attempts by the European Economic Community to redress the consequences of the policy of guaranteeing the price of milk in the Community led to the super levy scheme, a regulatory regime intended to redress the imbalance in the market brought about by the guaranteed price policy. That in turn resulted in milk producers, including the applicants, being entitled to sell their milk up to a specified level without incurring the super-levy which would make production uneconomic. Manifestly, such a regulation of the market in milk products could always be altered to the economic disadvantage of those who, like the applicants, had previously benefited from it, but it is a singularly inapt use of language to describe that result as a violation of property rights.
>
> The fact that the right in question may effectively be disposed for cash does not mean that it is a property right. A person who is standing in a queue to buy a particular commodity and gives up his place to someone else for cash would not appear to be doing anything unlawful, but he is most assuredly not disposing of a property right, merely his right to occupy that particular place on public or private land at that particular time. Nor do I find that any assistance is to be derived from comparisons with patents, trademarks or copyright rights, which under our legal system are nowadays generically described as "intellectual property rights". Systems of law in developed societies invariably protect those who produce such intangible assets in the expectation of reward by creating a discrete structure of legal protection, embodied in our case in the relevant statutes. They are not remotely comparable in my view to the opportunities for profit presented by a regulatory scheme designed for the benefit of subsidised producers. [2001] 2 IR 139, at 186–187.

[6–28] For Keane CJ, the mere fact that the quota was of economic value to the farmer did not render it constitutionally protected property. It was different from an authorisation, because it did not add value to the land. It was different from rules of intellectual property law apparently because the purpose of those rules was to grant economic value to creative work whereas the economic value of the quota was more the accidental by-product of a regulatory scheme. It was part of a regulatory scheme which was always susceptible of change to the advantage of some and the disadvantage of others. Murray J, with whom Fennelly J agreed on the property rights issue, focused more on this aspect of the quota system:

Property Rights

It seems to me that when changes are effected to a regime regulating the organisation of a product market, such as that which we have here, which are *internally* rational to the regime and the objectives to be achieved by it, those who participate as economic operators in that market must, in principle, accept such changes as an inherent element in that market in which they participate provided, at least, those changes do not affect other substantive rights independent of the regime and do not offend against fundamental principles such as non- discrimination.

If a person's rights or activities under such a regulatory regime were to be abridged or limited for purposes *external* or *extraneous* to those of the regulatory regime, any question of compensation which might arise would have to be approached from a different perspective. Such could arise, for example, where a state authority compulsory acquired a portion of a farmer's lands for public road or public housing to the extent that his entitlement to be attributed or ability to use a quota was reduced or eliminated altogether. Obviously this does not arise in this case....

In my view the adjustments implemented by the Regulations of 2000, are internally rational to the objectives to be achieved by the regulatory regime. There is no forfeiture. There is no interference with a substantive right, such as property right.

The foregoing measures are no more than regulatory adjustments which are an inherent part of a particular organisation of any market. Clearly no economic operator who participates in such a market can legitimately expect it to remain in a static or frozen form and must accept the consequences of such inherent internal adjustment as governing his or her participation in that market....

It is clear that the price fixed by the first respondent is internally and rationally related to the functioning and the continuing existence of the common organisation of the milk market with a view to achieving its objectives. Non-active milk producers, such as the applicants who have a quota and who, for reasons personal to them, do not wish to or cannot resume actual production of milk, are allowed an opportunity to sell at a maximum price which takes account, on the one hand, of the needs of such persons, and on the other of persons who wish to enter the system, acquire a quota or an additional quota and actively produce milk. The so called "market value" relied upon by the applicants is also an artificial product of the organised market in milk. The potential opportunity to sell at the "market price" generated by the functioning of the quota system to the exclusion of the regime now established by the Regulations of 2000 (including the price fixed by the first respondent under those Regulations) is not a property right. Property rights generate notions of proprietorship and dominion. In the context of this scheme I do not consider that the applicants had a proprietary interest in the selling at the particular "market price" which they seek to rely on. For the reasons stated I consider that the first respondent, in fixing the price which he did, has acted within the ambit of the common organisation of the milk market and a quota regime and if there can be said to be a market price, it is that governed by the maximum price fixed by the first respondent. To hold otherwise it would be to deny the first respondent his right and duty to exercise his lawful regulatory powers to ensure the proper functioning of the system. It would also wrongfully attribute to the applicants some proprietorial right to determine how the regulatory system in which they have participated, should be operated. [2001] 2 IR 139, at 229, 232–234.

Although it may seem odd to accord milk quotas the status of (prima facie) constitutionally protected property, the difficulty lies in identifying a sure means of distinguishing between this form of economic value and the other forms of economic value which the courts do accept as being constitutionally protected. For instance, it appears from *Maher* that the courts are inclined to accept the view that authorisations which add value to land are constitutionally protected property. But are applicants for and recipients of such authorisations not also participating in a regulated market? [6–29]

Indeed, this point can be taken somewhat further. To say that I *own* the copyright in this book is another way of saying that the law will visit bad consequences on anyone who does things that the law deems to be an infringement of my copyright. To say that you *own* this book is to say that the law will visit bad consequences on anyone who does something that the law deems to be inconsistent with your ownership of the book. We are both participating in a regulated market in which the law determines the legal consequences of ownership. Yet because we have constitutional property rights in the book or the copyright to the book, the State is precluded from making certain alterations to that market.

[6–30] A sceptic might argue that the courts' attitude to property rights, highlighted by the distinction drawn between milk quotas and other forms of property, is an attempt to naturalise the ownership of things and thus shield from scrutiny the justice of the distribution of property in society. If you *own* this book and are characterised as naturally having *dominion* and *proprietorship* over it, there is then no call to question the factors that have put you in a position to afford this (most reasonably priced!) book. It is just the way things are. On the other hand, if your ownership of this book were characterised in the same way as the milk quotas in *Maher* (a result of a positive decision by the State to visit bad consequences on anyone who should act in a way deemed inconsistent with your ownership of the book), all sorts of questions would need to be answered: Why should the State allow you to keep this book? Is it fair that you should be in a position to "buy" and "own" this book simply because your ancestors did well out of the plantations, while a homeless person, whose need to know about her constitutional rights or indeed whose need for paper to light a fire at night may be greater than yours, is not in a position to "buy" and "own" this book? While there is some merit to this criticism, it must function as a criticism not of the courts but of the Constitution. For it is Art 43 that naturalises the ownership of property: it is Man's natural right—antecedent to all positive law—to own privately external goods. The question that remains, however, is as follows: if the Constitution requires us to naturalise the ownership of certain external goods—ignoring the extent to which ownership is constituted by legal regulation—why must we not also naturalise the ownership of milk quotas?

[6–31] This is not to argue in favour of the ultimate claim in *Maher*. There seem to be good grounds for contending, given that the quota is awarded annually, that any prospective alteration to the quota scheme is justifiable by reference to the common good. One can, however, imagine retrospective changes to the system (such as the Minister drastically lowering the price at which she would purchase back quotas) that raise some justice concerns that can best be characterised as relating to private property rights.

[6–32] This is somewhat similar to the position reached by Costello J in *Hempenstall v Minister for the Environment* [1994] 2 IR 20. In this case, the applicants challenged the constitutionality of SI 172/1992 Road Traffic (Public Service Vehicles) (No 2) Regulations 1992. These regulations lifted a moratorium on the issuing of new hackney taxi licences. The applicants, themselves taxi-drivers, argued that the issuing of new licences would decrease the value of their own existing licences. The Minister accepted that the applicants' licences were valuable, constitutionally protected property, but contended that the applicants' constitutional rights had not been unjustly attacked. Costello J accepted the Minister's contention, concluding on this point:

> [E]ven if it were established that the making of the Regulations of 1992 resulted in a diminution in the value of the applicants' taxi-plates this would not as a matter of law amount, in my opinion, to an attack on the applicants' property rights. Property rights arising in licences created by law (enacted or delegated) are subject to the conditions created by law and to an implied condition that the law may change those conditions. Changes brought about by law may enhance the value of those property rights (as the Regulations of 1978 enhanced the value of taxi-plates by limiting the numbers to be issued and permitting their transfer) or they may diminish them (as the applicants say was the effect of the Regulations of 1992). But an amendment of the law which by changing the conditions under which a licence is held, reduces the commercial value of the licence cannot be regarded as an attack on the properly right in the licence-it is the consequence of the implied condition which is an inherent part of the property right in the licence. [1994] 2 IR 20, at 28.

Standing to Invoke Property Rights

In a number of cases, the courts had expressed the view that non-natural persons, such as companies, could not invoke constitutional property rights. See, for instance, the judgment of Carroll J in *Private Motorists' Provident Society v Attorney General* [1983] IR 339. This problem can usually be avoided by including a shareholder in the company as a plaintiff. The value of a shareholder's shareholding would be reduced if the company's property were reduced. However, this tactic is not available in the case of publicly owned companies, both because the shareholder (usually a government Minister) has only a nominal interest in the company and also because that shareholder is unlikely to challenge the constitutionality of legislation. This situation arose in *Iarnród Éireann v Ireland* [1996] 3 IR 321. Keane J (in the High Court) held that companies could invoke constitutional property rights, notwithstanding the individualistic, natural law tone of Art 43:

[6–33]

> Undoubtedly, some at least of the rights enumerated in Article 40.3.2°-the rights to life and liberty-are of no relevance to corporate bodies and other artificial legal entities. Property rights are, however, in a different category. Not only are corporate bodies themselves capable in law of owning property, whether movable or immovable, tangible or intangible. The "property" referred to clearly includes shares in companies formed under the relevant companies' legislation which was already a settled feature of the legal and commercial life of this country at the time of the enactment of the Constitution. There would accordingly be a spectacular deficiency in the guarantee to *every* citizen that his or her property rights will be protected against "unjust attack", if such bodies were incapable in law of being regarded as "citizens", at least for the purposes of this Article, and if it was essential for the shareholders to abandon the protection of limited liability to which they are entitled by law in order to protect, not merely their own rights as shareholders but also the property rights of the corporate entity itself, which are in law distinct from the rights of its members.
>
> Article 43 undoubtedly treats the general right of private property, the abolition of which in its entirety is expressly prohibited, as one inhering in "man in virtue of his rational being" and, in that sense, as being "antecedent to positive law", including the Constitution itself. But it does not necessarily follow that the property rights of the individual citizens which are protected against "unjust attack" by Article 40.3 are confined to rights enjoyed by human persons. Had the framers of the Constitution wished

to confine the comprehensive guarantee in Article 40.3 in that manner, there was nothing to prevent them including a similar qualification to that contained in Article 40.1.

The present case demonstrates that the restriction on the property rights of the citizen which would logically result from confining the protection of Article 40.3 to individual citizens would not necessarily be eased in every case by joining the shareholders as plaintiffs in the proceedings. If this case were to depend on the *locus standi* of the second plaintiff, it would appear that his property rights as an individual arising out of his ownership of one share in the first plaintiff are of so nominal a nature as not to afford him any such *locus standi*. It is unnecessary at this point to consider how many other corporate bodies would be in a similarly impotent state, although they would clearly include some in the private sector, such as companies limited by guarantee. It is sufficient to say that, although the strategy adopted in *Private Motorists' Provident Society v. Attorney General* [1983] IR 339 of joining the shareholder as a plaintiff was accepted by the Supreme Court as obviating any constitutional difficulty that might have arisen in that case, it is of critical importance that the Court expressly refrained from holding that the corporate plaintiff had no *locus standi* . In the result, I consider that I am not bound to hold that where, as here, it is not possible to make effective use of such a strategy, the claim of a corporate plaintiff must necessarily fail.

I am satisfied that the expression "every citizen" is not confined in Article 40.3.2 to citizens in their individual capacity as human persons and that artificial legal entities must also be protected by the laws of the State against unjust attacks on their property rights. [1996] 3 IR 321, at 345.

[6–34] O'Neill has advanced some criticisms of Keane J's reasoning:

> Keane J indicates some support for extending whatever personal rights and guarantees a company is capable of enjoying to the company. Thus, his starting point is the fact that companies are capable in law of holding property. Of course, the mere fact that a person – artificial or human – has a statutory or common law right to something does not mean that that right is automatically deserving of constitutional protection – capacity in law does not translate into constitutional protection in every case. Keane J makes this point in order to highlight the fact that constitutional protection of this type of right is possible. Its justification, however, lies in the fact that shares are protected property. From this, he extrapolates that it is necessary for the Constitution to protect the property rights of the company. In the case before him, of course, there was no shareholder whose rights were infringed so that his basing of the company's rights on those of a hypothetical shareholder is somewhat unconvincing.
>
> He does make some attempt to ground his conclusion that the company can rely on the Constitution in the actual text, drawing a distinction between the wording in Article 40.1 and Article 40.3.2°. It scarcely needs pointing out that the fact that Article 40.1 guarantees that "All citizens shall, as human persons, be held equal before the law..." does not alter the fact that Article 40.3.2° refers to "citizens" and gives no indication that this includes artificial persons. Ailbhe O'Neill, *The Constitutional Rights of Companies* (Thomson Round Hall, 2007), at [8.25] to [8.26].

Although the Supreme Court expressly reserved its decision on this point in the appeal, it now seems to be generally accepted that non-natural persons can invoke constitutional property rights.

Testing the Legitimacy of Restrictions of Property Rights

Introduction

Both Art 40.3 and Art 43 clearly envisage that the Oireachtas may restrict property rights. Article 40.3 prohibits only *unjust* attacks. Article 43 accepts that the exercise of property rights ought to be regulated by the principles of social justice so that such exercise is consistent with the exigencies of the common good. As noted above, the Supreme Court made clear in *Buckley* that the courts will review the assessment of the Oireachtas as to what the common good requires. This is a difficult and politically contentious task. In recent years, the courts have developed more sophisticated tests that have introduced greater predictability into the case law. Nevertheless, it remains difficult to predict with confidence how the courts will react to particular restrictions of property rights. That said, it is possible to observe certain trends that can be of some predictive assistance. Some of these trends relate to the subject-matter of the restriction (what type of property is being affected?), while others relate to the manner of the restriction (in what way is the owner's rights over the thing affected?). In this section, we shall first consider the tests which the courts use to test the legitimacy of restrictions. We shall then consider the various trends. [6–35]

The Proportionality Test

The courts have developed the proportionality test in relation to a number of constitutional rights, including property rights. In *Iarnród Éireann v Ireland* [1996] 3 IR 321, Irish Rail challenged the constitutionality of ss 12 and 14 of the Civil Liability Act 1961. Under these sections, where two defendants are held concurrently liable for wrong suffered by a plaintiff, that plaintiff is entitled to enforce its full award of damages against either defendant, notwithstanding the level of fault of that defendant. That defendant is then entitled to claim back from the other defendant the proportion of the award for which that other defendant was liable. A Mr Gaspari, having been injured in a train accident caused by a collision with a herd of cattle on the line, sued Irish Rail, and the owner of the cattle. Irish Rail was held 30 percent responsible for the accident, the cattle owner being held 70 percent responsible. As the cattle owner was of inadequate means, Mr Gasapari sought the full amount from Irish Rail. [6–36]

Keane J held that the proportionality test should be applied to assess the legitimacy of the interference with property rights: [6–37]

> If the State elects to invade the property rights of the individual citizen, it can do so only to the extent that this is required by the exigencies of the common good. If the means used are disproportionate to the end sought, the invasion will constitute an "unjust attack" within the meaning of Article 40.3.2°.
>
> The criteria which the court should employ in determining whether the means used in the case of any particular enactment are disproportionate to the end sought were defined as follows by Costello J (as he then was) in *Heaney v Ireland* [1994] 3 IR 593, at 607:—
>> "The objective of the impugned provision must be of sufficient importance to warrant overriding a constitutionally protected right. It must relate to concerns pressing and substantial in a free and democratic society. The means chosen must pass a proportionality test.
>> They must:—
>>> (a) be rationally connected to the objective and not be arbitrary, unfair or based on irrational considerations,

(b) impair the right as little as possible, and
(c) be such that their effects on rights are proportional to the objective." [1996] 3 IR 321, at 361–362.

[6–38] Despite stating a proportionality test, Keane J decided the case more by means of an inquiry into the justice of the legislation. He noted that, if the legislation were held unconstitutional, it was tort victims who would pay the price as they would not be able to recoup their full damages:

> If the plaintiffs' arguments in the present case are well founded, it means that the defendant whose conduct has been blameworthy in this sense will escape liability for a significant part of the damage which he has brought about, solely because another person was also to blame and is impecunious. The effect of the Constitution will thus have been to exonerate to that extent the blameworthy at the expense of the blameless. I am satisfied that it cannot have been the intention of the framers of the Constitution, in providing protection for the property rights of the citizen, that the Constitution should be the source of a significantly greater injustice than is involved in the abridgement of those rights which was the necessary consequence of a civilised and humane system of tortious liability. [1996] 3 IR 321, at 368.

[6–39] Although this conclusion validly describes the differing impact of different regimes for joint and several liability, it sheds little light on the application of the proportionality test. Keane J did not rigorously evaluate those differing impacts against the various criteria of the proportionality test. The case does, therefore, indirectly make the important point that the recitation of the proportionality test by a court does not necessarily mean that a proportionality test is being applied.

[6–40] In *Daly v Revenue Commissioners* [1995] 3 IR 1, the proportionality test was more closely applied. The applicant challenged the constitutionality of s 18 of the Finance Act 1987, as amended by s 26(1) of the Finance Act 1990. The 1987 Act had introduced a system whereby the public services, in paying people for professional services, deducted tax from the payment at the standard rate and paid that sum of money directly to the Revenue. As originally enacted, s 18 allowed the amount deducted to be set off as a credit against the tax due by the professional person for the same tax period. However, in 1990 the tax system changed so that self-employed people had to pay tax for the year of assessment rather than the year after the assessment. This would have given a windfall benefit to professional persons who received the tax credit. Accordingly, s 18 was amended to provide that the tax credit could only be claimed in the year following assessment. This had the potential to produce very harsh results as a taxpayer could have the tax deducted at source, then pay the full amount of tax and only receive the credit for deducted tax the following year. In the applicant's case, he had had to borrow from the bank to meet his income tax liabilities. This had had considerable knock-on effects in his personal life in terms of stress and strain. Costello P applied the proportionality test in the following way:

> The objective of Part III of the Finance Act, 1987, is, like all legislation permitting the collection of tax at source, to assist the collection of tax and to prevent avoidance. In addition it had a specific objective, namely to minimise the difference in the way employed professionals (who are subject to the PAYE system) and self-employed professionals are treated in the tax system. But the withholding tax regime as enacted

by Part III is not challenged in these proceedings-it is only the amendment to section 18 brought about by section 26 of the Act of 1990. It seems to me therefore that the court is not concerned with considering the general objectives of Part III of the Act of 1987 but must focus on the specific objective sought to be achieved by the amendment. As pointed out already, the object of the amendment was to avoid the payment of a windfall gain to established taxpayers arising from the change in the basis of assessment from a previous year's basis to a current year's basis which sections 14 and 15 of the Act had effected. If it can be shown that the means chosen to achieve that end fail to pass a test of proportionality then the court must conclude that the infringement with the applicant's constitutionally protected rights is impermissible. However, in applying this test the court must take into account the context in which the amendment was made as the effect of the means employed to obtain the section's objective will be influenced by the other provisions of the regime in which the amendment is made.

Conclusions

I think the section 26 amendment fails the proportionality test for two reasons. First, the effect of section 26 of the Act of 1990 is to alter the credit arrangements contained in section 18 of the Act of 1987 so that the withholding tax deducted is not available as a credit against liability for the income tax payable in the year of assessment in which it was deducted. This seems to me to produce results which are manifestly unfair to established taxpayers. It causes them hardship in that:—
1. (a) the collection of withholding tax reduces their ability to pay the income tax which it has been collected to discharge, and
2. (b) it requires double payment of tax.

This unfairness is not mitigated by the interim refund provisions which inadequately deal with the anticipated hardships which the regime imposes and indeed it is exacerbated by the fact that withholding tax collected over a period may exceed the taxpayer's total liability for tax. Secondly, the effects on the taxpayer's property rights is not proportional to the objective to be achieved. The section was designed to deal with a *transitional* situation (namely a windfall gain arising in one year from the change in the basis on which the self-employed were taxed) but in doing so it has imposed a *permanent* measure which involves a permanently unfair method of collecting tax. And this effect is borne not only by established taxpayers who might have enjoyed the windfall gain if the amendment was not enacted but also by new entrants to the regime who would have obtained on benefits in 1991.

The respondents accept that the problem posed by the creation of a windfall gain could have been dealt with differently but urge that this was a matter for the Oireachtas and not for the courts to decide. I agree. This court has neither the jurisdiction nor the competence to say whether or not the taxpayers should have been allowed to enjoy a windfall gain in 1991 or how the objective envisaged by section 26 could best be achieved. But it can examine the measure actually adopted and decide whether or not the interference with property rights has been brought about by means which are unfair to individual taxpayers or affect property rights in a manner out of proportion to the objective which the measure is designed to achieve. As I have reached a conclusion on these matters unfavourable to the amendment I must declare section 26(1) of the Act of 1990 to be invalid having regard to the provisions of the Constitution. I will hear counsel on what further orders (if any) the applicant is entitled to consequential on this declaration. [1995] 3 IR 1, at 11–13.

Costello P's judgment involves a detailed consideration of the mechanism of interfering with property rights, emphasising the extent to which the courts are prepared to assess the exigencies of the common good. Ultimately, it was the disproportion between the effect on the applicant—and similarly situated people—and the end sought to be achieved that led Costello P to hold the provision as unconstitutional. This is of some [6–41] importance, because there has been an increasing tendency of the courts to assess not the proportionality between effects and objectives, but rather the proportionality between the means and the objective.

[6–42] The advantage of the proportionality test is that it provides some structure to the analysis of whether a property right has been legitimately restricted. Rather than the one, amorphous and quite emotive question of whether there was an unjust attack, there is a series of more particular, less emotive questions. If this process is rigorously followed, it may be easier to secure agreement on the outcome: *ie* is the restriction legitimate? The proportionality test has been approved by the Supreme Court in *Re Article 26 and Part V of the Planning and Development Bill 1999* [2000] 2 IR 321, at 349, discussed above. However, the application of the test by the Court was somewhat lacking:

> In the present case, as a condition of obtaining a planning permission for the development of lands for residential purposes, the owner may be required to cede some part of the enhanced value of the land deriving both from its zoning for residential purposes and the grant of permission in order to meet what is considered by the Oireachtas to be a desirable social objective, namely the provision of affordable housing and housing for persons in the special categories and of integrated housing. Applying the tests proposed by Costello J in *Heaney v Ireland* [1994] 3 IR 593 and subsequently endorsed by this court, the court in the case of the present Bill is satisfied that the scheme passes those tests. They are rationally connected to an objective of sufficient importance to warrant interference with a constitutionally protected right and, given the serious social problems which they are designed to meet, they undoubtedly relate to concerns which, in a free and democratic society, should be regarded as pressing and substantial. At the same time, the court is satisfied that they impair those rights as little as possible and their effects on those rights are proportionate to the objectives sought to be attained. [2000] 2 IR 321, at 354.

[6–43] The Court thus concluded that the various elements of the proportionality test were satisfied, but gave no reasoned analysis of the "rational connection" to the "objective of sufficient importance" or of how the measures impaired rights as little as possible and had effects that were proportionate to the objectives sought to be attained. This may have been a function of the absence of facts in an Article 26 reference, but the blithe conclusion that the legislation impaired the rights as little as possible and that their effects were proportionate to the objectives sought to be attained is more a formulaic recitation of the test rather than an application of the test. And if one does not assess what the effects of the legislation actually are, it is difficult to come to a conclusion as to whether those effects are proportionate to the objectives being achieved. It is questionable whether the proportionality test, applied in this way, offers any greater rigour than the old test of "unjust attack".

Separate from the proportionality test, it is possible to identify various trends in the case law. Some of these trends relate to the subject-matter being regulated; others relate to the form and effect of the regulation.

Regulation of Ownership Rights

[6–44] Perhaps because land is so obviously property, the courts have been quite interventionist in protecting property rights in this area. In *Blake v Attorney General* [1982] IR

117, the plaintiffs challenged the constitutionality of certain provisions of the Rent Restrictions Act 1960. This Act was the latest version of a scheme of rent restrictions that had existed, initially on a temporary basis, since 1915. In effect, a cap was placed on the rent that was payable by the tenants of controlled dwellings. There were also provisions which made it unusually difficult for a landlord to regain possession of a controlled dwelling. The Supreme Court held the provisions unconstitutional, O'Higgins CJ delivering the judgment of the Court:

> [I]t should first be noted that, in accordance with its long title, the Act of 1960 makes provision for restricting rents only "in certain cases." As already indicated, these cases comprise lettings of houses or dwellings within specified valuation limits which were built or constructed prior to 7th May, 1941. No reason for this selection is apparent from the impugned legislation and, apart from the fact that rent control existed only in such cases in the previous temporary legislation, no reason was advanced by counsel for the Attorney General. The result is that lettings of all houses and dwellings outside the specified valuation limits and of all such houses and dwellings, irrespective of valuation, built after 1941 are free of any form of rent control.
>
> Further, the legislation expressly excludes all lettings of dwellings made under the Labourers Acts, 1883-1958 or the Housing of the Working Classes Acts, 1890-1958 (to be read in conjunction with section 120 of the Housing Act, 1966) and thereby excludes the many thousands of lettings made by local authorities to persons in need of housing assistance.
>
> It is further to be noted that the statutory provisions contained in Part II of the Act of 1960 operate in respect of the house or dwelling controlled, irrespective of the means of the tenant. Neither the means of the tenant nor the lack of means of, or possible hardship to, the landlord may be considered in determining the permitted rent. Therefore, it is apparent that in this legislation rent control is applied only to some houses and dwellings and not to others; that the basis for the selection is not related to the needs of the tenants, to the financial or economic resources of the landlords, or to any established social necessity; and that, since the legislation is now not limited in duration, it is not associated with any particular temporary or emergency situation....
>
> Once basic rents are determined under section 7 or section 9 of the Act of 1960, no review thereof is now permitted. The temporary revival of the power to review under section 7 in certain cases, provided by the Act of 1971, has long since expired. This means that all owners whose rents are controlled are restricted in their income to the amount of the basic rent and to such lawful additions as may be related to increases in rates and to a percentage of actual expenditure on maintenance, repair or improvement. This absence of any power to review such rents, irrespective of changes in conditions, is in itself a circumstance of inherent injustice which cannot be ignored. When this is coupled with the absence of any provision for compensating the owners whose rental incomes are thus permanently frozen, regardless of the significant diminution in the value of money, the conclusion that injustice has been done is inevitable.
>
> In the opinion of the Court, the provisions of Part II of the Act of 1960 (as amended) restrict the property rights of one group of citizens for the benefit of another group. This is done, without compensation and without regard to the financial capacity or the financial needs of either group, in legislation which provides no limitation on the period of restriction, gives no opportunity for review and allows no modification of the operation of the restriction. It is, therefore, both unfair and arbitrary. These provisions constitute an unjust attack on the property rights of landlords of controlled dwellings and are, therefore, contrary to the provisions of Article 40.3.2°, of the Constitution. [1982] IR 117, at 138–140.

[6–45] The Court also held that the restrictions on repossession were inextricably linked to the arbitrary and unfair scheme of rent control, and were therefore also unconstitutional. Following the Supreme Court's decision in *Blake*, the Oireachtas enacted the Housing (Private Rented Dwellings) Bill 1981. Section 9 of the Bill provided (in effect) that the difference between the controlled rent and the fair market value would be bridged over the course of five years. This Bill was referred by the President to the Supreme Court under Art 26 and was also held unconstitutional. O'Higgins CJ again delivered the judgment of the Court:

> The effect of the rebates permitted by section 9 is that, for a period of five years after the enactment of the Bill as law, landlords are to receive an amount which will be substantially less than the just and proper rent payable in respect of their property. In the absence of any constitutionally permitted justification, this clearly constitutes an unjust attack upon their property rights. The Bill offers no such justification for depriving the landlord of part of his or her just rent for the period specified in the Bill. This Court has already held that the pre-existing rent control constituted an unjust attack upon property rights. In such circumstances, to impose different but no less unjust deprivations upon landlords cannot but be unjust having regard to the provisions of the Constitution. [1983] IR 181, at 191.

[6–46] Both these cases suggest a concern, on the part of the courts, for the rights of landowners. More recently, however, the courts have upheld the constitutionality of legislation that benefited the rights of tenants at the expense of those of landlords. In *Shirley v AO Gorman & Company Ltd* [2006] IEHC 27, the High Court upheld the constitutionality of s 8 of the Ground Rents (No 2) Act 1978 and s 7(4) of the Landlord and Tenant (Amendment) Act 1984. The 1978 Act allowed certain tenants to acquire the landlord's freehold interest in the land, while the 1984 Act provided that the price to be paid to the landlord was, in effect, one eighth of the market value. Peart J accepted that the legislation had the social justice objective of redistributing wealth from the advantaged land-owning class to the disadvantaged tenant class. He was notably slow, however, to review the extent to which the legislation was required by the exigencies of the common good:

> Of course the Courts enjoy an ultimate supervisory role in ensuring that legislation passed by the Oireachtas is constitutional, but the Courts should be slow to in any way substitute its own view of what may or may not be required in order to reconcile the exercise of property rights with the exigencies of the common good. Until some point of absolute extremity is reached where legislation is patently and manifestly not in pursuit of any possible common good exigency, the Court should abstain from interfering with the role of the legislature in deciding what measures are needed. The present case is not such a situation. The Oireachtas can be seen over many decades by now as having in mind a social justice objective in the area of the relationship between landlord and tenant. The fact that a measure or a series of measures as part of an overall scheme has a consequence in some cases, such as the present one and other Shirley properties, where some persons already prosperous and even wealthy, are entitled to purchase at a fair price the residual interest of the landlord, as well as poorer persons, does not take the scheme outside of a common good exigency. I certainly have received no evidence to suggest that in anything like a very large number of cases, not to mention even the majority of cases, such a situation arises. The common good does not mean the good of all in the sense of every person without exception. In other words, the fact that some anomaly is thrown up by the

scheme, such as where the first named defendant is a wealthy entity, does not mean that the legislation does not meet the exigencies of the common good in a broad sense.

Peart J's willingness to accept the anomalies produced by the scheme is in some tension with *Blake*. It may be that the 1978 Act generally performed its legitimate function of redistributing land interests from the wealthy to the poor, whereas the legislation impugned in *Blake* was wholly anomalous. Nevertheless, Peart J seems, at the very least, to have been considerably more sanguine about the potential for inequity in the system. Peart J also upheld the constitutionality of the compensation provision in the 1984 Act. He considered that the compensation provided was fair when one considered that, given the possibility of a tenant gaining a reversionary lease, the landlord was unlikely ever to regain possession. Accordingly, one eighth of market value was fair compensation for the reversionary leasehold interest. [6–47]

In *Representatives of Chadwick and Goff v Fingal County Council* [2007] IESC 49, some of the claimants' land had been compulsorily acquired for the purposes of building a motorway. The claimants had sought compensation not simply for the injury caused by the use of the motorway on the lands taken from them, but also for injury caused by the use of the motorway on other lands not taken from them. This would amount to a re-interpretation of s 63 of the Land Clauses Consolidation Act 1845 and the claimants asserted their constitutionally protected property rights to support this reinterpretation. The Supreme Court unanimously rejected this argument, Fennelly J reasoning: [6–48]

> It is common case that the appellants are entitled under the section to be compensated for the value of the property taken, for the effects (if any) of severance and for injurious affection of their retained lands by anticipated use by the Council of the lands acquired from them. It is also common case that, if no land had been taken, there would have been no right to compensation for the damage, inconvenience or loss of amenity caused by the future operation of the motorway. No neighbour of the appellants has any such right, unless land is taken and used for that purpose. The appellants' claim is premised on the proposition that the acquisition has affected or will adversely affect some property right, which is entitled to constitutional protection. What is at stake is the non-tortious effect of activities on land not taken. The injurious affection here in contemplation is the alleged damaging effects to the retained lands of acts which would not give rise to any cause of action at law, particularly the law of nuisance, and does not entail any injury to any existing property right. I find it impossible to discern any unfairness or injustice in this scheme of compensation which could give rise to any issue as to whether, to use the language of Article 40.3.2° of the Constitution, there was an "*unjust attack*" on property rights. It follows, as a corollary, that the claimants' right to sue the Council or any other user either of the land taken or any other lands is undisturbed. [2007] IESC 49, at [36].

Regulation of Land Use

The courts have accepted wholesale regulation of the use of land. In *Central Dublin Development Association v Attorney General* (1975) 109 ILTR 69, the plaintiffs challenged a number of provisions of the Planning and Development Act 1963, including the two most basic provisions: the power of a planning authority to make a development plan (outlining the planning objectives for its functional area) and the requirement to obtain planning permission for the development of land. In relation to the development plan, Kenny J made the following points: [6–49]

> I do not think that the giving of power to a planning authority to make a development plan after they have considered and heard objections to the draft is an unjust attack on property rights....
>
> The making of a plan will necessarily decrease the value of some property but I do not think that the Constitution requires that compensation should be paid for this as it is not an unjust attack on property rights. (1975) 109 ILTR 69, at 90.

[6–50] In relation to the requirement to obtain planning permission, Kenny J reasoned as follows:

> [Article 43.2.1°] does not require that the exercise of the rights of property must in all cases be regulated by the principles of social justice. It recognises that the exercise of these rights ought to be regulated by these principles and that the State *accordingly* may delimit (which I think means restrict) by law the exercise of the said rights with a view to reconciling it with the exigencies of the common good. If there is to be planning development, someone must decide whether new or altered buildings are to be allowed in a specified place and whether land should be retained as an unbuilt space. The very nature of town and regional planning requires restriction in the sense that building in a particular area may not be appropriate or that the proposed buildings are not suitable or that buildings may not be used for some purposes. Town and Regional planning is an attempt to reconcile the exercise of property rights with the demands of the common good and Part IV defends and vindicates as far as is practicable the rights of the citizens and is not an unjust attack on their property rights. (1975) 109 ILTR 69, at 90.

[6–51] This acceptance of fairly significant restrictions of property rights in the context by means of land use control is also illustrated by in *Re Article 26 and Part V of the Planning and Development Bill 1999*, in which—as noted above—the Supreme Court upheld the requirement that a developer cede up to 20% of the land in a particular development at agricultural use value rather than market value. More recently, in *Clinton v An Bord Pleanála* [2005] IEHC 84, the High Court has upheld the constitutionality of compulsory purchase legislation.

Taxation

[6–52] The courts have articulated a slowness to intervene in taxation matters. In *Madigan v Attorney General* [1986] ILRM 136, the Supreme Court upheld the constitutionality of residential property tax. The tax was levied annually at 1½ percent of the amount by which the property exceeded £65,000. Homes where there was an aggregate income of less than £20,000 were excluded from the tax. O'Higgins CJ expressed the reticence of the courts in inquiring into taxation legislation:

> This tax is correctly described as a tax on owners who occupy and enjoy their residential property. It does not relate to the treatment of citizens as human persons and is not cognisable under *Article 41*. As counsel for the defendants have submitted, the reasoning contained in this Court's decision in *Brennan v Attorney General* and in the passage quoted from the judgment, apply to this case. Further, in the opinion of the court, the decision to impose such a tax must be presumed to have been taken for the purpose of contributing to the revenue required by the State and for the purpose of exacting that contribution from the better off and the well-to-do who can be presumed to occupy the more valuable houses. This accords with the clear duty imposed on the Government and on Dail Eireann by *Articles 28 and 17* of the Constitution. It is not for the court to question the choice of imposition which has been made, nor to enquire into the extent to which the desired contribution to the revenues of the State will be achieved. These are

matters which belong to the political arena and are for consideration and discussion in the National Parliament. So far as the courts are concerned this is a tax measure. As such it necessarily interferes with the property rights of affected citizens. However, such interference cannot be challenged as being unjust on that account, if what has been done can be regarded as action by the State in accordance with the principles of social justice and having regard to the exigencies of the common good as envisaged by *Article 43.2* of the Constitution. [1986] ILRM 136, at 161.

This circumspection in relation to taxation legislation does not apply solely when the right invoked is a property right. In *MhicMhathúna v Ireland* [1995] 1 IR 484, the Supreme Court indicated the special deference that was due in the context of taxation legislation: [6–53]

> [Given that] the Oireachtas was specifically charged under the Constitution with legislating for the nation's finances it is the Oireachtas which decides what kind of taxes should be imposed, what rates should apply, and what allowances would be given and that that was not a function which the courts in the administration of justice should carry out. [1995] 1 IR 484, at 495.

Notwithstanding this reticence, however, the courts have struck down taxation legislation. As seen in *Daly v Revenue Commissioners* [1995] 3 IR 1, the courts are prepared to hold taxation legislation unconstitutional where it operates in an anomalous way or so as to impose a very particular burden on certain individuals. The concern with anomalous legislation, clearly expressed in *Blake*, is also reflected in *Brennan v Attorney General* [1983] ILRM 449 (HC); [1984] ILRM 355 (SC). The plaintiffs challenged the constitutionality of the Valuation Acts 1852–1918 which provided a valuation system for agricultural land based on prices in the 1850s. The plaintiffs also challenged s 11 of the Local Government Act 1946 which used this valuation system as the basis for local taxation. The Supreme Court struck down the legislation for the following reasons: [6–54]

> With regard to *Article 40.3* the court is of opinion that the plaintiffs' complaints that this Article has not been observed are justified and should be upheld. In the opinion of the court the complaints are proper to be considered primarily under the provisions of *Article 40.3.2°*. The evidence and the facts as found by the learned trial judge was that the use of the 1852 valuations was continued as a basis for agricultural rates, long after the lack of uniformity, inconsistencies and anomalies had been established and, long after methods of agricultural production had drastically changed. This in itself was an unjust attack on the property rights of those who like the plaintiffs found themselves with poor land paying more than their neighbours with better land. When this injustice had become obvious the State had a duty to take action in protection of the rights involved. This it failed to do. In continuing by means of *section 11 of the Local Government Act 1946* the same system without revision or review the State again, in the opinion of the court, failed to protect the property rights of those adversely affected by the system from further unjust attack. In the assessment of a tax such as a country rate reasonable uniformity of valuation appears essential to justice. If such reasonable uniformity is lacking the inevitable result will be that some ratepayer is required to pay more than his fair share ought to be. This necessarily involves an attack upon his property rights which by definition becomes unjust. The plaintiffs have established such injustice in this particular case. [1984] ILRM 355, at 365.

The position thus appears to be that the courts will not query the decision to impose any tax, but that the operation of the tax must be fair and reasonably consistent.

Retrospective Restrictions of Property Rights

[6–55] In *Re Article 26 and the Health (Amendment) (No 2) Bill 2004* [2005] IESC 7, the Supreme Court considered the constitutionality of legislation that retrospectively abrogated property rights. In 2004, it had emerged that old people had been unlawfully charged for public nursing home care since the 1970s. Faced with the possibility of legal actions to recover monies that had been collected without lawful authority, the Oireachtas enacted the Health (Amendment) (No 2) Bill 2004. The President referred the Bill to the Supreme Court, which characterised the effect of these retrospective provisions as follows:

> [T]o deem the combined imposition and payment of the unlawful charges concerned to be lawful, and always to have been lawful, for the purpose of enabling the State to successfully resist any claim brought after 14 December 2004 insofar as such a claim is for the recovery of the charges in question on the ground that they had, at least from 1976, been unlawfully imposed. [2005] IESC 7, at [78].

[6–56] In assessing whether the legislation was constitutionally valid, the Court adopted a very stringent test:

> Where a statutory measure abrogates a property right, as this Bill does, and the State seeks to justify it by reference to the interests of the common good or those of general public policy involving matters of finance alone, such a measure, if capable of justification, could only be justified as an *objective* imperative for the purpose of avoiding an extreme financial crisis or a fundamental disequilibrium in public finances. [2006] IESC 7, at [132].

This dictum is, on its face, difficult to square with other dicta of the courts (noted above) in relation to the primacy of the Oireachtas in the financial sphere. In assessing taxation legislation, which arguably abrogates property rights over certain amounts of money, the courts do not require that the financial stability of the State be at stake. What could explain this dictum, however, is the fact that the property rights were being retrospectively abolished. The old people who had unlawfully been charged the money were having a pre-existing, vested right abrogated. Such legislation is more likely to be struck down.

Imposing the Cost of Achieving a Public Good on One Section of the Community

[6–57] The courts have also expressed particular concern about legislation that imposes the cost of achieving a general social good on one section of the community. This concern was somewhat evident in *Blake v Attorney General* where certain landlords bore the cost of subsidising the accommodation of certain tenants. The concern was more forcibly and directly expressed in *Re Article 26 and the Employment Equality Bill 1996* [1997] 2 IR 321. The Bill imposed an obligation on employers not to discriminate on the grounds of disability, but this obligation was subject to a number of exceptions. Section 34(4) of the Bill—as interpreted by the Court—relieved the employer of the obligation not to discriminate where the employee had special needs or would require special facilities to participate in employment and either (a) the employer had done all that was reasonable to accommodate those special needs or (b) it would have imposed undue hardship on the employer to make such accommodation.

The Court held that, notwithstanding the provisions of s 34(4), the obligations imposed on employers breached the property rights provisions of the Constitution: [6–58]

> The Court is satisfied that the provisions under consideration constitute a delimitation of the exercise by employers of a right protected by that Article, *ie* the right to carry on a business and earn a livelihood. It is also satisfied that these limitations have been imposed by the Oireachtas with a view to reconciling the exercise of the rights in question with a specific aspect of the common good, *ie* the promotion of equality in the workplace between the disabled and their more fortunate fellow citizens. The issue which the Court has to resolve is as to whether the abridgement of those rights effected by these provisions constitutes an "unjust attack" on those rights in the case of individual employers, having regard to the manner in which it has been effected....
>
> The Bill has the totally laudable aim of making provision for such of our fellow citizens as are disabled. Clearly it is in accordance with the principles of social justice that society should do this. But, *prima facie*, it would also appear to be just that society should bear the cost of doing it. It is important to distinguish between the proposed legislation and legislation to protect the health and safety of workers. It is entirely proper that the State should insist that those who profit from an industrial process should manage it as safely, and with as little danger to health, as possible. The cost of doing the job safely and in a healthy manner is properly regarded as part of the industrialist's costs of production. Likewise it is proper that he should pay if he pollutes the air the land or the rivers. It would be unjust if he were allowed to take the profits and let society carry the cost. Likewise it is just that the State, through its planning agencies, should insist that the public buildings and private buildings to which the general public are intended to have access for work or play should be designed in such a way as to be accessible by the disabled as well as by the able-bodied.
>
> But the difficulty with the section now under discussion is that it attempts to transfer the cost of solving one of society's problems on to a particular group. The difficulty the Court finds with the section is not that it requires an employer to employ disabled people, but that it requires him to bear the cost of all special treatment or facilities which the disabled person may require to carry out the work unless the cost of the provision of such treatment or facilities would give rise to "undue hardship" to the employer.
>
> There is no provision to exempt small firms or firms with a limited number of employees, from the provisions of the Bill. The wide definition of the term "disability" in the Bill means that it is impossible to estimate in advance what the likely cost to an employer would be. The Bill does provide that one of the matters to be taken into consideration in estimating whether employing the disabled person would cause undue hardship to the employer is "the financial circumstances of the employer" but this in turn implies that the employer would have to disclose his financial circumstances and the problems of his business to an outside party.
>
> It therefore appears to the Court that the provisions of the Bill dealing with disability, despite their laudable intention, are repugnant to the Constitution for the reasons stated. [1997] 2 IR 321, at 366–368.

This case involves a very strongly stated principle against the imposition on one section of the community of the cost of achieving a public good. Yet the precise parameters of the principle are difficult to judge. The court clearly considers it acceptable that certain economic externalities (such as the costs of pollution) be [6–59] considered part of a business's production costs. Accordingly, laws restricting pollution could not be unconstitutional. Moreover, laws requiring that buildings accessible to the public be accessible to people with disabilities are also considered acceptable. Yet a law effectively requiring businesses to make accommodation for employees or potential employees with disabilities is deemed to be unconstitutional. If such a law had contained no exemptions, one could easily see how it would have restricted property rights too much. However, given that obligation was limited by the concepts of "reasonable accommodation" and "undue hardship"—both of which, by reason of the presumption of constitutionality, would have to be interpreted by a decision-maker in a manner consistent with the Constitution—it is difficult to see how this provision went too far.

[6–60] A somewhat specialised application of this principle can be seen in *Re Article 26 and the Health (Amendment) (No 2) Bill 2004*. As discussed above, the Supreme Court articulated a very onerous standard of justification (threat to the financial stability of the State) in the context of the retrospective abrogation of property rights affected by that Bill. However, the Court also articulated a somewhat different basis for its decision. Those whose rights to recover money unlawfully charged were being restricted were effectively being asked to pay for the cost of nursing home care that should—on the basis of legislation in force—have been borne by the community at large. Indeed, it was a particularly vulnerable section of the community that was being asked to bear this cost. The Court characterised the people affected in the following terms:

> [T]he property rights to be abrogated in their entirety by the Bill belong to the most vulnerable members of society. While the extension of full eligibility to all aged seventy or over, regardless of means, in 2001 means that a number will not be of limited means, the reality is that a great many will still be among the poorest in our society. Whatever exceptions may exist, it is an undoubted fact that the Bill will affect very many people who are old, or poor or disabled, mentally or physically, or all of these. As already stated, persons so situated will almost certainly have had little or no capacity to understand their rights under the legislation or to protest at the unlawfulness of the charges. [2005] IESC 7, at [123].

[6–61] The vulnerability of the people targeted was part of the reason why the legislation was unconstitutional:

> The Court does not exclude the possibility that, in certain cases, the delimitation of property rights may be undertaken in the interests of general public policy. However, the invocation of these Articles in circumstances where rights such as arise in this case, rights very largely of persons of modest means, are to be extinguished in the sole interests of the State's finances would require extraordinary circumstances. [2005] IESC 7, at [130].

This suggests that the courts should, in the future, be particularly careful to protect the property rights of the vulnerable.

Anomalous Legislation as Distinct from Clearly Focused Legislation

[6–62] One point that clearly emerges from many of the cases cited above is that anomalous legislation is difficult to justify. The courts have been prepared, perhaps quite appropriately, to accept fairly draconian restrictions on property rights. *Central Dublin*

Development Association v Attorney General and in *Re Article 26 and Part V of the Planning and Development Bill 1999* both demonstrate the courts' willingness to accept severe restrictions of property rights where a compelling social objective is at least articulated and ostensibly served by the legislation. This point is also illustrated by *BUPA Ireland Ltd v Health Insurance Authority*, 23 November 2006 (HC). The applicant challenged the constitutionality of the risk equalisation scheme that operated in the health insurance market, having been established by the Minister for Health under s 12 of the Health Insurance Act 1994. The government had decided that the Irish health insurance market should adopt the community rating principle. This means that applicants for health insurance pay the same premium, regardless of their age. This is despite the fact that older people represent a greater risk for insurance companies as they are more likely to have health problems. Given that people tend to be slow to change their health insurer, newer entrants into the health insurance market are likely to have a younger subscriber base than the existing dominant insurer, the VHI. That younger insurer base could, given community rating, allow the newer entrants generally to offer lower premiums and thereby compete unfairly with the VHI. To offset this danger, the state introduced risk equalisation the effect of which was to require newer entrants, such as BUPA, to make substantial payments to the VHI in order to equalise their risk base. McKechnie J accepted that this would impose a significant financial liability on BUPA (BUPA estimated the sum as €100 million over three years) and was a *prima facie* interference with property rights. However, he accepted that the interference with property rights was justified:

> The Government has decided that a core principle of private health insurance in this country should be community rating across the market. In addition it has legislated for open enrolment, lifetime cover and minimum benefits. The belief is that this system is for the general good and will result in all persons, irrespective of health status, age or gender, being able to obtain cover at affordable prices. The objective of risk equalisation, as has been repeatedly stated, is to support this community rating -across the market. It does so by way of inter generational solidarity. The State's belief is that without a risk equalisation scheme there are potential vices which could seriously disturb the ordinarily functioning of this type of system. In fact, full support for the attachment of a risk equalisation scheme, with such a system is forthcoming from several international studies as well as from a variety of other expert opinion. The report of the Advisory Group is clear-cut in the necessity for a risk equalisation scheme. As referred to earlier in this judgment, the report also quoted similar supporting views which it had received from many of those who made submissions to it during the course of its work. The White Paper comprehensively endorses the Government's position on this regulatory framework. Mr. Barrett in his affidavit evidence repeated the objective of the scheme and the justification therefor. He referred to the danger of cherry picking which in my view is a real danger and is capable of leading to the existence of a significant difference in risk profile between insurers. Community rating and open enrolment are not in themselves sufficient to guard against this. Risk selection, consciously or sub consciously can lead to this undesirable result. Such a situation is not sustainable even in the immediate term. It can lead to practices such as shadow pricing, excessive profits and more sinisterly a death spiral resulting in market instability. For the purposes of this case it is not essential to determine the precise academic parameters of what constitutes a death spiral. In my view there is sufficient evidence of a compelling nature to support this possibility occurring. There cannot be an obligation on the State to defer corrective action until the presence of a worst case scenario is established. In my opinion therefore, the availability of a risk equalisation scheme, which depending on circumstances may or may not be activated, has

> been in principle justified as being a necessary measure to underpin the operation of the regulatory regime in this country. There is no doubt in my mind but that a collapse of the private market would heavily impact on the availability of public health services. Therefore the creation of a risk equalisation scheme, pursuant to section 12, is in my view a pressing and substantial need in a free and democratic society. I believe that the provision of such a scheme, (in a regulated market) and its impact on the property rights of BUPA is a regulation of the exercise of those rights in accordance with the principles of social justice and that the limitations placed on such rights are essential in the common good. Such rights are not absolute and their exercise may be curtailed when balanced against the common good. 23 November 2006 (HC), at [293].

Notwithstanding the significant restriction of property rights, the clearly articulated and compelling policy basis for the measure made it easy for the Court to conclude that the measure was justified. (The Supreme Court subsequently struck down the risk equalisation scheme on a narrower basis without considering the property rights issues. [2008] IESC).

[6–63] However, where the legislation is so anomalous that it becomes difficult to identify the objective being served, the courts have been far less willing to uphold the restriction. In *Blake*, the scheme of controlled rents did not apply to buildings constructed after 1941 nor to buildings above a certain rateable valuation. In *Brennan*, the system of local taxation for farm land turned on a valuation survey carried out over the course of the 1850s which, as a result of the Great Famine, valued land in the south of the country more highly than land in the north where the survey had commenced. Anomalous legislation of this type serves the common good in such a haphazard way that the courts have been less prepared to tolerate the individual restrictions on property rights that exist under such a system. This is not to say, however, that the effects of legislation must be perfectly coherent. As *Shirley* demonstrates, the existence of some anomalous results will not, of itself, render legislation unconstitutional.

Compensation

[6–64] The payment of compensation by the State to the property owner is one way in which a restriction of property rights can be rendered legitimate. However, not every interference with property rights requires compensation in order to be legitimate. Kenny J identified a useful principle in *Central Dublin Development Association v Attorney General* (1975) 109 ILTR 69, at 83–84:

> The word "ownership" in the English test is, I think, misleading because there is no known legal right of ownership. There is a bundle of rights which, for brevity, is called ownership....
>
> The State has pledged itself by Article 40.3.2° by its law to protect as best it may from unjust attack the property rights of every citizen and while some restrictions on the exercise of some of the rights which together constitute ownership do not call for compensation because the restriction is not an unjust attack, the acquisition by the State of all the rights which together make up ownership without compensation would in almost all cases be such an attack.

[6–65] This suggested that compensation would be required for expropriation (or near expropriation) of property, but that lesser interferences with the right to private property would not require compensation. In that case, Kenny J upheld Part VI of the Local Government (Planning and Development) Act 1963, which provided that compensation would not be paid where property was devalued by reason of the refusal of planning permission for certain specified reasons or by reason of the attachment of certain types of conditions to planning permissions. In Kenny J's view, these were restrictions of property rights and did not come close to the sort of appropriation of property that would require compensation.

However, it is not always easy to distinguish between a restriction of property rights and an expropriation. In *Electricity Supply Board v Gormley* [1985] 1 IR 129, the Supreme Court held that the ESB's power to erect power lines over land without compensating the owner was unconstitutional. Finlay CJ delivered the judgment of the Court: [6–66]

> Section 53 of the [Electricity (Supply) Act 1927], as amended, must be interpreted as granting to the plaintiff a power compulsorily to impose a burdensome right over land.
>
> That is, in the instant case, the right to place below and above the land of the defendant three large structures connected by wires carrying electricity; to keep them there permanently, if necessary, and to enter the lands from time to time for the purpose of repairing and maintaining them.
>
> The results of the exercise of that power are, firstly, that the use of the land for agriculture is permanently interfered with to a greater or lesser extent, depending on whether, at any time, the area in which the masts are situated is used for grazing or tillage; secondly, that in the case of any particular landowner who wished to erect a building or other structure on the portion of land occupied by one of these masts he would be prevented from doing so; and thirdly, that in the case of this defendant's land, at least, there is major permanent damage to the amenity of the lands surrounding the house.
>
> Whether the granting of such powers to the plaintiff without the provision of any obligation to pay adequate compensation constitutes a failure as far as practicable to respect, defend or vindicate the property rights of the defendant in these lands in breach of Article 40, s. 3, sub-s. 1, of the Constitution or a failure, as best the State may, to protect those rights from unjust attack, in breach of Article 40, s. 3, sub-s. 2, is a question which falls to be decided in accordance with the principles laid down by this Court in *Dreher v. Irish Land Commission* [1984] I.L.R.M. 94, where, in his judgment, with which all the other members of the Court agreed, Walsh J. at p. 96, states:—
>
> > "The State in exercising its powers under Article 43 must act in accordance with the requirements of social justice but clearly what is social justice in any particular case must depend on the circumstances of the case. In Article 40.3.2 'the State undertakes by its laws to protect as best it may from unjust attack, and in the case of injustice done, vindicate ... (the) property rights of every citizen.' I think it is clear that any State action that is authorised by Article 43 of the Constitution and conforms to that Article cannot, by definition, be unjust for the purpose of Article 40.3.2. It may well be that in some particular cases social justice may not require the payment of any compensation upon a compulsory acquisition that can be justified by the State as being required by the exigencies of the common good."
>
> Having regard to the social benefits of electricity and its contribution to the economic welfare of the State, the uncontradicted evidence adduced in this case of the necessity for and value of this transmission line to the national supply system leads to an inescapable conclusion that the power to lay it compulsorily is a requirement of the common good.
>
> The vital question remains, however, as to whether the requirements of social justice or of the common good make this one of the "particular cases" referred to by Walsh J. in *Dreher v. Irish Land Commission* [1984] I.L.R.M. 94, where payment of compensation is not necessary.
>
> The Court does not accept the contention that the payment of compensation, *ex gratia*, in an amount determined by the plaintiff is to be equated with a right to

compensation, lacking, as it does, the essential ingredient of the ultimate right to have the amount assessed by an independent arbiter or tribunal.

[6–67] The Court concluded that s 53 of the Act was unconstitutional because it did not specifically provide a right to compensation. In more recent cases, however, the courts have not taken such a categorical approach to the need to provide compensation, instead viewing the provision of compensation as a factor to be taken into account. In *Re Article 26 and the Health (Amendment) (No 2) Bill 2004* [2005] IESC 7, at [118], Murray CJ commented:

> [W]here an Act of the Oireachtas interferes with a property right, the presence or absence of compensation is generally a material consideration when deciding whether that interference is justified pursuant to Article 43 or whether it constitutes an *"unjust attack"* on those rights. In practice, substantial encroachment on rights, without compensation, will rarely be justified.

[6–68] Of course, sometimes the payment of compensation would defeat the whole purpose of the restriction of the property right. If the State had to pay compensation where it levied taxes, there would be no point in levying taxes. Even outside this situation, though, the courts have not insisted on a strong right to compensation.

For instance, in *Re Article 26 and Part V of the Planning and Development Bill 1999* [2000] 2 IR 321, the Supreme Court upheld the constitutionality of requiring a developer to cede up to 20 percent of the lands in a development, receiving compensation at only agricultural use value. However, it is perhaps significant that the Court in that case characterised the value of developers' lands as being enhanced by the general scheme of land use regulation; once the value is characterised as being *enhanced* by State regulation, it is easier to come to the conclusion that the owner should be compensated for loss of only some of that value.

[6–69] In *O'Callaghan v Commissioners of Public Works* [1985] ILRM 364, the plaintiff challenged the constitutionality of s 8 of the National Monument Act 1931 on the grounds that it failed to provide for compensation for the owners of lands on which national monuments were designated. Such a designation could severely limit the uses to which a landowner could put the land. The Supreme Court rejected this argument:

> The plaintiff complains of the absence of a provision for the payment of compensation to him in respect of the limitation placed upon his user of the lands; in the view of the court the absence of such a provision for the payment of compensation to him in respect of a limitation of use of which he was substantially on notice before his purchase and which is a requirement of what should be regarded as the common duty of all citizens — to preserve such a monument, can be no ground for suggesting that the prohibition or limitation is an unjust attack on his property rights. [1985] ILRM 364, at 368.

[6–70] The Court's point about notice is a telling one: if a person buys land with notice that a restriction attaches—or is likely to attach—to that land, the price will reflect that restriction. Why should such a person get the added bonus of compensation for that restriction? The Court's point about every citizen's duty being to protect national monuments slightly misstates the point in that the duty only affects those citizens who happen to have a national monument on their land. In this light, the Court's point again raises the issue considered above: why is the protection of national monuments a burden that is fair to impose on a particular section of society while the reasonable accommodation of persons with disabilities is not?

All told, the courts' case law on the role of compensation is both confused and confusing. Strong statements about the need for compensation are often not matched by judgments striking down legislation for a want of compensation. In the end, the role of compensation is scarcely more determinative of cases than any of the factors mentioned in the previous section. Only two relatively limited statements may be made: the provision of compensation renders legislation less likely to be struck down as constitutional; the greater the interference with property rights (expropriation being the greatest interference), the more likely that the absence of compensation will lead to legislation being struck down. [6–71]

Postscript

The courts' interpretation of Arts 40.3 and 43 is a case study in how a relatively coherent corpus of constitutional law can be developed in a manner that does not pay particular attention to the historical or philosophical antecedents of the guarantees that it interprets. Hogan has drawn attention to this phenomenon. [6–72]

> If we attempt to sum up these developments, it seems clear that we have arrived at the position whereby the actual language of Article 40.3.2° and Article 43 does not really matter. Certainly, even if Article 43 was inspired by Catholic social teaching, the case-law has long since broken loose of that particular inspirational source. Instead, the courts have sought to employ a workable judicial methodology and this is why the adoption of the proportionality doctrine is so significant. While we have seen that it would be wrong to regard this principle as a solution to every such difficulty, the advantage of this new doctrine is that it will help to provide a badly needed analytical framework and, hence, reduce otherwise subjective judicial appraisals in important areas of constitutional law. But we must also not lose sight of the fact that the reason why this doctrine was adopted with such enthusiasm by the judiciary was because they had quietly acknowledged the limitations of the text of Art 40.3.2° and Art 43. Indeed, it might not be too much to say that the courts have now jettisoned all but the most superficial reliance on the actual text.
>
> In fact, the emergence of this essentially European doctrine only serves to demonstrate Fr Cahill's extraordinary prescience back in 1937. [Fr Edward Cahill SJ had predicted to Éamonn de Valera that the courts, not well schooled in the social teaching of the Catholic Church, would over-emphasise the individualistic aspect of Art 43 at the expense of the social obligations that attach to private property.] Certainly, despite the language of Art 43.1.1°, natural law thinking has played almost no role in the development of this jurisprudence. And while there is nothing in these developments to suggest that the courts have sought to apply doctrinaire free market values in their interpretation of the property rights, the entire thrust of the proportionality doctrine as formulated in cases such as *Heaney*—with its emphasis on, e.g., impairing individual rights as little as possible—is to focus on the rights of the individual. This, perhaps, is only to be expected, since the nature of judicial review is that the courts are required to focus on the operation of the law as it affects the individual plaintiff and do not, generally speaking, have the capacity to examine how such a law impacts on the public at large. Gerard Hogan, "The Constitution, Property Rights and Proportionality" (1997) 32 *Irish Jurist* 373, at 396.

CONTENTS – CHAPTER 7

Liberty and the Dwelling Place

Introduction.	[7–01]
Procedural or Substantive Guarantee	[7–02]
Illegalities Leading to Unconstitutional Detention	[7–13]
Rights of Prisoners.	[7–19]
Liberty and the Legality of Detention Powers	[7–27]
Preventive Detention.	[7–36]
Inviolability of the Dwelling	[7–39]

Overview

Article 40.4.1° of the Constitution provides that no citizen shall be deprived of his liberty save in accordance with law. This provision was initially given a purely procedural interpretation, ensuring only that deprivations of liberty were in accordance with law. Subsequently, the courts started to review the constitutionality of legislation that restricted liberty. The courts generally consider that the legality of a person's detention is not affected by the conditions experienced during that detention. Although the rights of prisoners have been recognised, the courts have generally been quick to conclude that the rigours of prison life militate against the assertion of constitutional rights while in gaol. The courts have upheld significant deprivations of liberty in both the criminal justice context and the mental health context, emphasising the procedural protections that apply in each case. However, the courts took a sceptical view of preventive detention, limiting the grounds on which bail could be refused. This position was effectively reversed by constitutional amendment in 1997.

CHAPTER 7

Liberty and the Dwelling Place

Introduction

Article 40.4.1° of the Constitution provides: [7–01]

> No citizen shall be deprived of his liberty save in accordance with law.

Article 6 of the Irish Free State Constitution of 1922 contained a similar provision: "The liberty of the person is inviolable, and no person shall be deprived of his liberty save in accordance with law." Article 40.4.2° provides the detailed procedure for habeas corpus applications which end the unlawful custody of a person.

Procedural or Substantive Guarantee

An issue arises as to whether Art 40.4.1° is a purely procedural guarantee, permitting all restrictions of liberty that have been authorised by law, or whether it posits a substantive guarantee of liberty that, prima facie at least, cannot be restricted by laws. This issue was first considered in respect of Art 6 of the 1922 Constitution. In *State (Ryan) v Lennon* [1935] IR 170, the Supreme Court considered Art 2A of that Constitution. Originally, the 1922 Constitution allowed for amendment by ordinary legislation for a period of eight years. However, prior to that period running out, the Constitution was amended (again by ordinary legislation) to allow for amendment by ordinary legislation to continue for a further eight years. [7–02]

Subsequent to this provision, Art 2A was inserted into the Constitution. This was a lengthy provision that effectively came into operation by order of the Executive Council. This order could be made whenever, in the opinion of the Executive Council, circumstances existed which rendered it expedient. The Article established a tribunal, staffed by military personnel, to try certain offences and also granted a number of powers to police officers in relation to the arrest and detention of persons. The Article also provided that, in the event of an inconsistency between its provisions and other provisions contained in the Constitution, its own provisions took precedence. The prosecutors were detained under the provisions of the Article and sought their release. The Court considered a number of arguments in relation to whether Art 2A was a valid amendment of the Constitution, a majority concluding that it was. [7–03]

The Court also considered whether Art 6 of the 1922 Constitution precluded the restriction of liberty authorised by Art 2A. Kennedy CJ reasoned: [7–04]

> In the Constitution ... the Constituent Assembly also enunciated certain propositions, containing statements of fundamental principle in the constitutional sphere so expressed as to convey clearly the intention that they are to be accepted for the purposes of the Constitution as immutable and absolute, subject only to the specific qualifications

expressed in certain cases.... A ... declaration of principle is contained in Article 6, which lays it down that the liberty of the person is inviolable, flowing from which there follows the concrete case, "no person shall be deprived of his liberty" with the specific qualification "except in accordance with law." An enactment to the general effect that a citizen may be taken and detained in custody, without being charged with any offence known to the law but just whenever and for as long as a soldier or policeman deems it expedient, would conflict with the principle laid down in Article 6, and, in my opinion, whether purporting to be an ordinary law, or an amendment of the Constitution, would be invalid and void and could not be sustained under the power of amendment. On the other hand, ordinary laws may be enacted validly specifying the cases in which, the causes for which, the times during which, and the persons by whom, a person may in accordance with the ordinary law be deprived of his liberty. [1935] IR 170, at 208.

[7–05] However, a majority of the Court disagreed with the Chief Justice, adopting a narrower interpretation of the phrase "in accordance with law". Fitzgibbon J put the matter as follows:

In Article 6 it is declared that "the liberty of the person is inviolable," but that is not a law of universal application, for the Article proceeds: "and no person shall be deprived of his liberty *except in accordance with law*." The law may, therefore, make provisions in accordance with which a person may be deprived of his liberty. It is for the Legislature to prescribe those provisions, and for the Courts to enforce them, and even if, under Amendment No. 17, a person has been deprived of his liberty by the mere caprice of an Executive Minister (section 24(2), and Appendix, clause 7), or the unfounded suspicion, "incapable of being rebutted or questioned by cross-examination, rebutting evidence, or otherwise," "of any member of the Gárda Síochána" (sections 13 and 29), "or of the Defence Forces of Saorstát Éireann" (section 13), such a deprivation would be "in accordance with law," and the prisoner would have no redress. [1935] IR 170, at 229.

[7–06] This case illustrates a disagreement as to the proper meaning of "save in accordance with law". Under Fitzgibbon J's reasoning, the phrase "save in accordance with law" renders Art 6 a procedural guarantee for the legality of administrative action and not a guarantee that allows legislation to be tested against a constitutionally endorsed notion of liberty. Although Kennedy CJ did not explicitly address this argument, he must be taken to have viewed some substantive content in the phrase "in accordance with law" which could be offended by a legislative restriction of liberty. Under Fitzgibbon J's approach, legislation could never be found unconstitutional under Art 6; under Kennedy CJ's approach, that possibility would have remained open.

[7–07] Some commentators have referred to the difference between these two approaches as the difference between an "ordinary legislation" or "positivist" view and a "higher law" view. See Hogan and Whyte, *Kelly: the Irish Constitution* (4th ed, Butterworths LexisNexis, 2003), at [7.4.01]–[7.4.17]. Although this may be a helpful description of the unusual issues that arose in *State (Ryan) v Lennon* where the authorisation of liberty was constitutionally authorised, it is somewhat less helpful in relation to the cases that have arisen under the 1937 Constitution. To describe as non-positivist an interpretation of the Constitution that gives substantive (as distinct from procedural) force to Art 40.4.1° raises more questions about the character of law and legal propositions than it answers. For this reason, it is more helpful to analyse the cases under the 1937 Constitution using the terminology of "procedural" and "substantive".

The issue arose quickly in *State (Burke) v Lennon* [1940] IR 36 in which a prisoner challenged the legality of his detention under s 55 of the Offences Against the State Act 1939. This provision effectively allowed for internment without trial for as long as that part of the Act remained in force. The Minister for Justice was empowered to issue a warrant for the detention where he was satisfied that a person was engaged in activities calculated to prejudice the preservation of the peace, order or security of the State. In habeas corpus proceedings in the High Court, Gavan Duffy J held that this power was unconstitutional: [7–08]

> In my opinion, the saving words in the declaration that "No citizen shall be deprived of his liberty save in accordance with law" cannot be used to validate an enactment conflicting with the constitutional guarantees. The opinion of Mr Justice FitzGibbon in *Ryan's Case* is relied upon by Mr Maguire, but it does not apply, in my judgment, to a Constitution in which fundamental rights and constitutional guarantees effectively fill the *lacunae* disclosed in the polity of 1922. The Constitution, with its most impressive Preamble, is the Charter of the Irish People and I will not whittle it away. There is nothing novel in the solemn recognition of the right to personal freedom as an essential basis of the social structure of a society of free men. In my opinion, the Constitution intended, while making all proper provisions for times of emergency, to secure his personal freedom to the citizen as truly as did Magna Charta in England. Whatever abuses were perpetrated in this country, despite the Magna Charta Proclamation for Ireland of 1216, in England Magna Charta was taken to mean what it said.... In my opinion, the right to personal liberty and the other principles which we are accustomed to summarise as the rule of law were most deliberately enshrined in a national Constitution, drawn up with the utmost care for a free people, and the power to intern on suspicion or without trial is fundamentally inconsistent with the rule of law and with the rule of law as expressed in the terms of our Constitution. [1940] IR 136, at 155–156.

It is somewhat odd that Gavan Duffy J relied on the assertion that the 1937 Constitution contained fundamental rights and personal guarantees that filled the *lacunae* disclosed in the polity of 1922, to conclude that Article 40.4.1° which is in the same terms as Article 6 of the 1922 Constitution should be interpreted in a different way. [7–09]

The Oireachtas then enacted the Offences Against the State (Amendment) Bill 1940, which was referred to the Supreme Court by the President under Art 26 of the Constitution. This Bill substantially re-enacted the provisions that had been found unconstitutional by Gavan Duffy J. The Supreme Court upheld the constitutionality of the provisions, Sullivan CJ giving the opinion of the Court:

> The phrase "in accordance with law" is used in several Articles of the Constitution, and we are of opinion that it means in accordance with the law as it exists at the time when the particular Article is invoked and sought to be applied. In this Article, it means the law as it exists at the time when the legality of the detention arises for determination. A person in custody is detained in accordance with law if he is detained in accordance with the provisions of a statute duly passed by the Oireachtas; subject always to the qualification that such provisions are not repugnant to the Constitution or to any provision thereof.
>
> Accordingly, in our opinion, this Article cannot be relied upon for the purpose of establishing the proposition that the Bill is repugnant to the Constitution—such repugnancy must be established by reference to some other provision of the Constitution. [1940] IR 470, at 482

Thus in 1940, the settled view of the Supreme Court was that the protection afforded by Art 40.4.1° was purely procedural. A number of subsequent cases, without explicitly [7–10] addressing the distinction between procedural and substantive interpretations of the phrase "in accordance with law", appeared to suggest a move away from the purely procedural interpretation. In *Re Philip Clarke* [1950] IR 235, for instance, a person detained pursuant to s 165(1) of the Mental Treatment Act 1945 challenged his detention by way of habeas corpus proceedings. This provision allowed a Garda to take a person "believe to be of unsound mind" into custody if he was of the opinion that such a step was necessary for the public safety or the safety of the person himself. The Supreme Court upheld the constitutionality of this provision but did not refer to the procedural interpretation of Art 40.4, instead offering a substantive justification for the provision. This justification turned largely on a paternalistic concern for the well-being of mentally ill people. What is relevant for present purposes, however, is that the Supreme Court chose to provide a substantive justification for the provision. This implied that a restriction on liberty without substantive justification might be found unconstitutional, effectively the position preferred by Kennedy CJ and Gavan Duffy J, but rejected by a majority of the Supreme Court in *State (Ryan) v Lennon* and the majority of the Supreme Court in *Re Article 26 and the Offences Against the State (Amendment) Bill 1940*.

[7–11] This shift from the procedural interpretation to the substantive interpretation was confirmed in *People (Attorney General) v O'Callaghan* [1966] IR 501. In this case, the defendant was refused bail by Murnaghan J in the High Court and appealed to the Supreme Court. The Supreme Court laid down a number of constitutional criteria that would have to be met before bail could be refused; these shall be considered below. For present purposes, it suffices to note the interpretation of Art 40.4.1° given by some members of the Court. Walsh J put the matter thus:

> In this country it would be quite contrary to the concept of personal liberty enshrined in the Constitution that any person should be punished in respect of any matter upon which he has not been convicted or that in any circumstances he should be deprived of his liberty upon only the belief that he will commit offences if left at liberty, save in the most extraordinary circumstances carefully spelled out by the Oireachtas and then only to secure the preservation of public peace and order or the public safety and the preservation of the State in a time of national emergency or in some situation akin to that. [1966] IR 501, at 516.

[7–12] Following this decision, the State ceased to rely on the procedural interpretation of Art 40.4.1° to defend legislative restrictions of liberty. See, for instance, *Re Article 26 and the Emergency Powers Bill 1976* [1977] IR 159. In *King v Attorney General* [1981] IR 233, the Supreme Court struck down on several grounds s 4 of the Vagrancy Act 1824 which attached heightened criminal liability to a "suspected person or reputed thief". Henchy J reasoned that the phrase "save in accordance with law" meant "without stooping to methods which ignore the fundamental norms of the legal order postulated by the Constitution." [1981] IR 233, at 257.

Illegalities Leading to Unconstitutional Detention

[7–13] Even under the procedural approach, an illegal deprivation of liberty would amount to an unconstitutional deprivation of liberty as it would not be "in accordance with law". Article 40.4.2° provides the habeas corpus procedure by which the High Court can swiftly end an illegal detention. However, the courts have been slow to hold that every and any illegality in the process leading to detention renders the detention itself illegal. Moreover, the courts have on occasion held that the habeas corpus procedure is an inappropriate way of determining complex issues of law or fact that may arise in relation to the legality of detention. There appears to be a judicial preference for such matters to be determined by way of appeal or judicial review, although whether the jurisdiction of Art 40.4.2° can be ousted in this way is constitutionally questionable.

In relation to irregularities of form, the courts have been slow to find a detention illegal. In *State (McDonagh) v Frawley* [1978] IR 131, at 136, O'Higgins CJ held that the phrase "in accordance with law" did not mean that a convicted person had to be released merely because some defect or irregularity attached to the detention. There would, in his view, have to be "a default of such fundamental requirements that the detention may be said to be wanting in due process of law". In *State (McKeever) v Governor of Mountjoy Prison*, 19 December 1966 (SC), Ó Dálaigh CJ had stipulated that the irregularity must be such that "would invalidate any essential step in the procedures leading to detention". This begs the question of what is a fundamental requirement or an essential step. In *McDonagh*, O'Higgins CJ suggested that the imposition of a sentence of imprisonment for life where there was legal authorisation for a sentence of penal servitude for life would be so technical a default as not to render the detention illegal. At the other end of the scale, the imposition of a sentence of imprisonment where the statute creating an offence authorised only a fine would presumably be a default of a fundamental requirement. However, it is far more difficult to identify where the line should be drawn between those two points. [7–14]

In *Re Article 26 and the Emergency Powers Bill 1976* [1977] IR 159, the Supreme Court upheld the constitutionality of the Bill which, *inter alia*, granted the Gardaí a fairly extensive arrest power. Although the Supreme Court held that the Bill had duly been adopted pursuant to Art 28 of the Constitution and could not therefore be constitutionally challenged, it emphasised that the provisions of the Constitution would be relevant to the construction of the Act once enacted and to the legality of actions taken pursuant to the Act: [7–15]

> In this context it is important to point out that when a law is saved from invalidity by Article 28.3.3°, the prohibition against invoking the Constitution in reference to it is only if the invocation is for the purpose of invalidating it. For every other purpose the Constitution may be invoked. Thus, a person detained under section 2 of the bill may not only question the legality of his detention if there has been non-compliance with the express requirements of section 2, but may also rely on provisions of the Constitution for the purpose of construing that section and of testing the legality of what has been done in purported operation of it. A statutory provision of this nature which makes such inroads upon the liberty of the person must be strictly construed. Any arrest sought to be justified by the section must be in strict conformity with it. No such arrest may be justified by importing into the section incidents or characteristics of an arrest which are not expressly or by necessary implication authorised by the section.
>
> While it is not necessary to embark upon an exploration of all the incidents or characteristics which may not accompany the arrest and custody of a person under that section, it is nevertheless desirable, in view of the submissions made to the Court, to state that the section is not to be read as an abnegation of the arrested person's rights (constitutional or otherwise) in respect of matters such as the right of communication, the right to have legal and medical assistance, and the right of access to the Courts. If the section were used in breach of such rights the High Court might grant an order for release

under the provisions for *habeas corpus* contained in the Constitution. It is not necessary for the Court to attempt to give an exhaustive list of the matters which would render a detention under the section illegal or unconstitutional. [1977] IR 159, at 173.

[7–16] This appeared to open up the possibility that a detention which was originally lawful might become unlawful by reason of the treatment of the prisoner, in particular by reason of the denial of the prisoner's rights. The Courts have, however, proven slow to order the end of detentions on this basis. In *State (McDonagh) v Frawley* [1978] IR 131, for instance, the prisoner, who had been convicted and sentenced to two years' imprisonment, argued that he was not receiving proper treatment for backache. O'Higgins CJ, with whom the other members of the Court agreed, suggested that a convicted person was in a different situation to a person arrested under the Emergency Powers Act. Many of a convicted person's normal constitutional rights were, he reasoned, abrogated or suspended while in prison; prison discipline had to be accepted and the prisoner's detention could not be deemed illegal simply because he was not receiving the sort of treatment for backache which he considered would be appropriate.

[7–17] A more extreme situation had been posed by the prisoner in *State (C) v Frawley* [1976] IR 365. The prisoner suffered from a severe sociopathic disorder which led him to make repeated escape attempts, involving hazardous climbing feats, and had a recorded history of swallowing metal objects which then had to be removed from his stomach by surgical intervention. The prison governor subjected the prisoner to a strict regime, for his own protection, whereby he was generally kept in solitary confinement, handcuffed when not in such confinement, and kept out of any contact with metal objects. It was accepted that the prisoner's condition would best be met by detention in a specialist psychiatric unit with suitable outlets for his physical and mental abilities. However, no such facility existed in the country at the time and Finlay P held that the right to bodily integrity did not go so far as to oblige the State to provide such a facility. Finlay P then considered whether the treatment of the prisoner rendered his detention unlawful:

> The question which has given me the most trouble in this case is whether the conditions under which the prosecutor has been and is detained in prison constitute a failure to protect him from torture or from inhuman or degrading treatment and punishment-thus making his detention unlawful. Notwithstanding the harshness of the privations which he has undergone and, to a lesser extent, continues to suffer, I have finally come to the conclusion that those conditions do not constitute such failure.
>
> I am quite satisfied that the purpose and intention of the restrictions and privations surrounding the prosecutor's detention are neither punitive nor malicious. The strongest confirmation of this would appear to be that the restrictions have been somewhat relaxed since the improvement in his condition noted by Dr McCaffrey in the last six or seven months. There was no evidence before me of any privation or hardship which does not appear related to one or other of the main purposes of keeping the prosecutor from escaping and preventing him from injuring himself. In seeking to achieve these two purposes, the respondent is discharging two duties which appear to me to be constitutional in origin.
>
> I must construe the entire concept of torture, inhuman and degrading treatment and punishment as being not only evil in its consequences but evil in its purpose as well. It is most commonly inspired by revenge, retaliation, the creation of fear or improper interrogation. It is to me inconceivable to associate it with the necessary discharge of a duty to prevent self-injury or self-destruction. [1976] IR 365, at 374.

In *State (Comerford) v Governor of Portlaoise Prison* [1981] ILRM 86, Barrington J **[7–18]**
accepted that there was a legal obligation to treat remand prisoners differently from
convicted prisoners. However, the transfer of a remand prisoner to a high security
section of the gaol did not render his detention illegal.

It is difficult to ascertain how extreme the circumstances of detention must be in
order for a prisoner's detention to be deemed illegal. It may be that there was no reality
to the Supreme Court's suggestion in the *Emergency Powers Bill Reference* that the
conditions of detention could render such detention illegal. The Court's statement may
instead have been an *obiter dictum* intended to lessen the blow of upholding such
draconian legislation. In any event, there are good reasons not to grant release to a
prisoner who suffers maltreatment in prison. Why should a prisoner, even one whose
rights are being infringed, gain the windfall benefit of an end to such detention? Would
it not be more appropriate to rectify the infringement of rights but keep the prisoner in
custody? Or would proven torture justify an end to such imprisonment?

Rights of Prisoners

Although the courts have been slow to order the release of a convicted prisoner based **[7–19]**
on an infringement of rights while in prison, different issues apply in relation to claims
of convicted prisoners that the prison authorities should respect their rights while in
prison. In *Murray v Ireland* [1985] IR 532, the prisoners were a husband and wife each
sentenced to life imprisonment for the murder of a Garda. They asserted that they
enjoyed a right to procreate and that the prison authorities had unconstitutionally
restricted this right by denying them conjugal visits, given that the wife would in all
likelihood be too old to procreate when she was released. Costello P held that the right
asserted was protected by Art 40.3.1° of the Constitution but proceeded to consider
whether the restriction on the right in the present case was justified:

> Prisoners have liberty to exercise certain constitutionally protected rights, (and enjoy
> other negative rights such as the right not to be tortured) not because they are in some
> way superior in a scale of values to the right to liberty – the right to life is clearly superior
> to the right to liberty, but the right to fair procedures clearly is not. When the State
> lawfully exercises its power to deprive a citizen of his constitutional right to liberty many
> consequences result, including the deprivation of liberty to exercise many other
> constitutionally protected rights, which prisoners must accept. Those rights which may
> be exercised by a prisoner are those (a) which do not depend on the continuance of his
> personal liberty (so a prisoner cannot exercise his constitutional right to earn a
> livelihood) or (b) which are compatible with the reasonable requirements of the place
> in which he is imprisoned, or to put it another way, do not impose unreasonable demands
> on it....
>
> I do not think that the plaintiffs' claim, that they be permitted to leave prison from
> time to time to exercise their right to beget children, is a valid one as it is clearly
> incompatible with the restriction on their liberty, which is constitutionally permitted by
> their imprisonment. What remains then to consider is the claim to exercise this right in
> prison and the practical consequences involved in it. For if the plaintiffs' right to beget
> children cannot now be exercised without putting unreasonable demands on the prison
> service, the restriction on its exercise cannot be constitutionally invalid as it is a
> reasonable consequence of the lawful exercise of the power of the State to imprison them.
>
> There are as I have said 1,100 to 1,200 married prisoners at present serving sentences
> in 11 different institutions and the practical problems of according to all these prisoners
> facilities to beget children, are obviously very great. The reasonable requirements of the

prison service would not, in my judgment, permit the exercise by all married prisoners of their right to beget children and so the concession made in this connection was properly made. This means that the fact of imprisonment does not in itself amount to an unconstitutional infringement of a prisoner's rights. But the plaintiffs, in effect, claim to be in a special category arising from the combination of circumstances to which I have referred and they say these super-added facts make the present restrictions invalid. But, in considering this submission it must be borne in mind, as I have already pointed out, that if they, as a married couple without children, can validly claim to exercise this right during their imprisonment, so too can all married prisoners with children who can establish that at the end of their imprisonment his or her chances of begetting a child are small or non-existent. Whilst no attempt has been made to establish the number involved, I cannot conclude that it would be inconsiderable. It, therefore, seems to me that it would place unreasonable demands on the prison service, to require prison authorities to make facilities available, within the confines of the prison, to enable all prisoners who fall within this category to exercise their right to beget children. If this is so, then prisoners in this category, including the plaintiffs, cannot validly complain that the exercise of their rights has been unconstitutionally restricted. [1985] IR 532, at 542–543.

[7–20] The Supreme Court upheld this judgment on appeal, although McCarthy J, with whom Hamilton P, Keane and O'Flaherty JJ concurred, put the matter somewhat differently, observing:

The unenumerated right to procreate children, like all unenumerated rights, must be given a rational meaning. It may be lost temporarily as a result of any form of detention, arrest or imprisonment for a criminal offence; detention for a contempt of court; detention pursuant to mental treatment procedures. The suspension or abeyance of the right does not depend upon practical considerations but because of the nature of a constitutional right. If a person is deprived of liberty in accordance with law, then that person loses, for instance, the express right to vote (*Article 16*); the person loses the non-expressed or unenumerated right to travel, to earn a livelihood, the right to be let alone, to give some examples. [1991] ILRM 465, at 477.

Costello J appears to have identified two types of rights which cannot be denied to prisoners: (a) those which do not depend on the continuance of liberty and/or (b) those which are compatible with the reasonable demands of the place of imprisonment. Category (b) might better be characterised as a condition that must be satisfied before a right can be exercised by a prisoner. As such, it requires an assessment of the implications for the prison regime of the prisoner exercising that right. In contrast, McCarthy J's approach is more conceptual and abstract: the very fact of being in prison results in a suspension of rights.

[7–21] In *Breathnach v Ireland* [2001] 3 IR 230, the Supreme Court rejected a prisoner's claim that his right to vote had been unconstitutionally infringed. Article 16.1.2° of the Constitution provides that all citizens without distinction of sex who have reached the age of 18 years who are not disqualified by law and comply with the provisions of the law relating to the election of members of Dáil Éireann, shall have the right to vote at an election for members of Dáil Éireann. A difficulty arose for the applicant as he had not challenged the constitutionality of the Electoral Acts; if they were presumed to be constitutional, the only way in which his right to vote could be exercised would be if he were escorted to the relevant polling station on voting day—a requirement that would be onerous in the extreme if applied to all prisoners. Nevertheless, the Supreme Court considered and rejected the argument that the State was obliged to provide appropriate facilities, whether by means of postal voting or polling stations within the prison, to allow the applicant exercise his right to vote.

Keane CJ addressed the different formulations put forward by Costello and McCarthy JJ in *Murray* and concluded: [7–22]

> [McCarthy J's *dictum*] is in accord with the principles explained by Costello J in the High Court and Finlay CJ in his judgment in the same case. I do not read this passage as suggesting that the right to vote is "lost" in the full sense in consequence of the imprisonment: rather that it cannot be exercised unless, for example, the prisoner is on temporary release. The learned judge did not speak of the right as being permanently "lost", but as being in suspension or abeyance. That, as was found in that case, is a necessary consequence of the voluntary acts of the applicant/respondent, resulting in the loss of his liberty. No doubt the provision of facilities to enable the applicant to exercise his rights by post or in the precincts of the prison would not be wholly impractical, although it would undoubtedly require legislation. For the reasons stated, however, there is no obligation on the State to provide the machinery, since the right remains in suspension or abeyance during the period of the applicant's imprisonment. [2001] 3 IR 230, at 239.

Denham J reasoned:

> The applicant has no absolute right to vote under the Constitution. As a consequence of lawful custody many of his constitutional rights are suspended. The lack of facilities to enable the applicant vote is not an arbitrary or unreasonable situation. The absence of such provisions does not amount to a breach by the State of the applicant's right to equality.
>
> The words of McCarthy J, cited previously, in Murray v Ireland [1991] ILRM 465, at 477, correctly state the law. If a person is lawfully deprived of their liberty and is in prison then that person loses certain constitutional rights including the right to vote. That does not exclude the legislature from deciding in the future to legislate for a scheme whereby prisoners could vote. [2001] 3 IR 230, at 249.

If Keane CJ was correct that there was no difference between McCarthy J's view of rights in suspension and Costello J's view of rights that were incompatible with the reasonable demands of the place of imprisonment, this could only be so because those rights suspended are those which are incompatible with the reasonable demands of the place of imprisonment. However, Keane CJ relies on the proposition that the right to vote is suspended to remove any obligation on the State to facilitate an exercise of that right, without scrutinising how difficult it would be for the State to do so. Indeed, Keane CJ explicitly accepts that such an approach would not be "wholly impractical". This is much closer to McCarthy J's approach than to that of Costello J. [7–23]

In *Holland v Governor of Portlaoise Prison* [2004] 2 IR 573, the applicant challenged a blanket policy on communication with the media on the basis that his right to communication was thereby infringed. He was seeking access to the media, by way of visits and letters, for the purpose of highlighting what he claimed to have been a miscarriage of justice in his criminal case. The prison governor argued that the censorship of the applicant's communications was justified by the demands of the security and good discipline of the prison. The applicant, however, did not challenge the general power to censor communications but rather the way in which that power [7–24] was being applied to him by reason of the blanket ban on communication with the media.

[7–25] McKechnie J applied a proportionality analysis to the restriction in a manner that seems considerably stricter than the approach adopted by the Supreme Court in *Breathnach*:

> Given that the right in issue in this case is constitutionally based, it can I think be taken that any permissible abolition, even for a limited period, or any interference, restriction or modification on that right should be strictly construed with the onus of proof being on he who asserts any such curtailment. In addition, the limitation should be no more than what is necessary or essential and must be proportionate to the lawful objective which it is designed to achieve. That a test of proportionality, where relevant, is now applied when considering constitutional rights is beyond doubt. [2004] 2 IR 573, at 594.

[7–26] McKechnie J then relied on principles of administrative law to establish that the prison governor had invalidly fettered his discretion by adopting and acting on a blanket policy against contact with the media. Nevertheless, McKechnie J, at the request of the parties, proceeded to consider the constitutional principles that might apply were the prison governor to give individual consideration to the applicant's request for media contact. He summarised the principles as follows and then considered their application:

> 1. that when serving a prison sentence, lawfully imposed, a prisoner must suffer a diminution or compromise on the exercise of certain constitutional rights;
> 2. the rights so affected, the "affected rights" for the duration of the sentence, are in the first instance his right to liberty and secondly certain other rights (i) which are affected by the loss of this right and (ii) which are consequential on the convicted prisoner having to serve his sentence in a place of detention, namely a prison;
> 3. these "affected rights" are not, in my view, capable of exhaustive definition but will depend on the circumstances of each case;
> 4. to be lawful, any limitation, either complete or partial, or the exercise of these "affected rights" must have as their objective:-
>   (i) the incarceration of the prisoner so as to serve his sentence; and
>   (ii) the maintenance of security, discipline and good order within the prison; these being the basis of the justification advanced in this case;
> 5. the objective underpinning the restriction must be of such significance or value in a democratic society so as to warrant the position of overriding a right which is constitutionally based;
> 6. the interference on restriction:-
>   (i) must be rationally connected to the said objective and must not be arbitrary, unfair or based on irrational considerations;
>   (ii) must be necessary or essential in order to achieve the legitimate aim to which it is addressed;
>   (iii) must be not more extensive than the minimum required to achieve its intended aim; and
>   (iv) must otherwise be proportionate to that objective;
> 7. each application by a prisoner must be individually considered by the respondent or his deputed officer and must be decided upon by reference to the above criteria, which is general in character and outline;

8. the respondent, when applying rules 59 and 63, is vested with a discretion derived from statute, and as such, while he may have regard to a policy or guidelines, he cannot rely upon either in such a way as to deprive him or otherwise fetter the exercise of this discretion.

If the above summary accurately represents the position, then the commencement point in any consideration of the issues which arise in this case is whether or not the respondent can restrict, either partially or fully, the applicant's right to communicate with the media. In my view, there is no doubt whatsoever but that this right can be the subject matter of limitation, which can have varying consequences ranging from minimal interference to outright prohibition. What will legally justify any form of restriction, up to a complete ban, will have to depend on the circumstances of each case, though in my view any decision which is or is equivalent to a total denial must surely be capable of justification only in acute circumstances. Do such circumstances exist in this case? Or to put it more formally, is a complete bar necessary so as to enable the respondent to maintain discipline and good order within his prison and is such a ban proportionate to the attainment of these objectives, the legitimacy of which is not denied?

In my humble view, the answer is no. The only evidence advanced on behalf of the respondent is that set forth in paragraph 7 of the affidavit of the deputy governor which is quoted above. Such evidence constitutes no more than broad propositions of potential disruption without any details being offered by way of specific security problems which either have previously occurred or, as a matter of probability, would arise either from correspondence or from face to face meetings. These undefined potentialities, in my view, cannot be allowed to undermine substantially the constitutional rights of the applicant. Accordingly, I do not believe that the respondent has satisfied this court as to a necessity for such a blanket ban which, in my view, is entirely disproportionate to the penal objective which he seeks to maintain. This objective is one which I think is properly legitimate but, it is the means adopted to achieve its results which, in my view, are unlawful. Therefore, I remain of the opinion that this ban cannot be justified. [2004] 2 IR 573, at 600–601.

McKechnie J distinguished *Breathnach* on the basis that the background statutory provisions and the factual events and circumstances in that case were very different. Given that both Keane CJ and Denham J in *Breathnach* were prepared to consider that case effectively as if it were a challenge to the constitutionality of the legislation, it cannot be so easily distinguished. The close attention paid by McKechnie J to the implications for the prison regime is far more similar to Costello J's approach in *Murray* than to the Supreme Court in *Breathnach*.

Liberty and the Legality of Detention Powers

As noted above, the courts have adopted a substantive interpretation of the phrase "save in accordance with law" in Art 40.4, with the result that legislatively authorised detentions can be tested against the substantive concept of personal liberty endorsed by the Constitution. In addition, detentions that have no legal authorisation are unconstitutional as they cannot be regarded as in accordance with law, whether under the procedural or substantive understanding of that term. Notwithstanding that the courts scrutinise the constitutionality of detentions in these two ways, they have been slow to find legislatively authorised detentions unconstitutional. [7–27]

In *DPP (Stratford) v Fagan* [1994] 3 IR 265, the Supreme Court considered the operation of s 109 of the Road Traffic Act 1961. This provision obliges a person driving a car to stop if required to do so by a Garda. In this case, Garda Stratford, without [7–28] having formed a suspicion that that the defendant had committed an offence, required him to stop. He then smelt the defendant's breath, breathalysed him and charged him with driving while under the influence of alcohol, contrary to s 49 of that Act. A question arose as to whether this evidence was admissible. If the Garda had no legal authorisation to stop, it would follow that the detention was otherwise than in accordance with law and therefore unconstitutional. Under the authority of *People (DPP) v Kenny* [1990] 2 IR 110, unconstitutionally obtained evidence is inadmissible, unless there are extraordinary, excusing circumstances. There was no explicit legislation authorising a Garda to stop cars in this manner. A majority of the Supreme Court nevertheless held that the Garda had legal authority to stop and detain the defendant. Blayney J reasoned that the Gardaí have a common law duty to prevent and detect crime. Accordingly, if they find it necessary to stop drivers for the purposes of doing so, the common law gives them power to stop drivers. Finlay CJ broadly agreed with this reasoning, commenting:

> I do not see any logical difference in principle between these clearly accepted examples of a common law right on the part of the Garda Síochána to stop a car or cars travelling on a particular route or at a particular place and the right which is claimed on behalf of the Garda Síochána in this case to stop cars travelling at a particular time and on a particular route in the belief that it is probable that one or more of them is being driven in a manner which constitutes an offence, namely, being driven by a person who has in their body an excess of alcohol.
>
> To set up a road check in the vicinity of a licensed premises at a time of night when the premises are being closed for the purpose of attempting to identify persons who may be committing the very serious offence of driving while drunk seems to me a proper exercise of the common law duties of the Garda Síochána in their policing activities.
>
> I have carefully considered whether the fact that, in more recent times, in many instances, certain powers of stopping vehicles have been specifically granted by statutes, examples of which are referred to in the judgment about to be delivered by Denham J, is inconsistent with the existence of the common law right which appears to me to exist to create a road check under the circumstances on which it was done on this occasion. I am satisfied that there is not such an inconsistency, and that in all the instances which are referred to there are a series of powers such as powers of arrest and search which go together, as it were, as a package, and flow from the stopping of the vehicle.
>
> Apart from that consideration, the fact that the legislature may decide at any time to set out in a very particular and specific manner a power for such a body as the Garda Síochána is not in my view to be taken as a reason for concluding that the common law right of the same type did not already exist if there are other grounds for so deciding. [1994] 3 IR 265, at 269–270.

Denham J strongly dissented, addressing the issue of the Garda's common law duty in the following way:

> The term "duty", it was argued, includes every matter that is the business of the gardaí and includes the Road Traffic Acts. Mr Hardiman referred to Parker LJ's definition in *Rice v Connolly* [1966] 2 QB 414 of the obligations and duties of a constable as set out previously in this judgment. He submitted that if a garda acts in accordance with those obligations, while on duty, and stops a person, he is entitled so to do.
>
> If the very broad sweep of Parker LJ's definition were used to empower a member of the gardaí to stop a person, then logically they could also be the foundation for other impingements on fundamental rights of persons, for example search, detention, arrest. Yet these infringements of liberty are carefully set out in statute, and common law, and

founded on the concept of a reasonable suspicion, for we do not have an inquisitorial system of law.

Broadly, the garda is given powers, such as a right to stop, arrest, search, which are activated by the member's reasonable suspicion. That is the foundation of the constitutional protection of individual's rights and the rule of law.

If there is to be an invasion of a person's fundamental rights, for good social reasons, for the benefit of the community, then it should be set out in a clear and certain fashion in law. The formula submitted by counsel to ground the right to stop here would lead to a very uncertain foundation on which a garda would base his right while "on duty". It would lead to uncertainty on all sides. It is as much in the interest of the Garda Síochána as the public that the authority of the garda to stop a person in a vehicle or to restrict liberty in any way, should be clear and certain.

The approach proposed by the Director of Public Prosecutions would be a major alteration in principle in the relationship between the gardaí and the public. It proposes that, rather than have gardaí act in accordance with the ordinary power of citizens together with a specific authority, the gardaí could simply call in aid the fact that they are "on duty". When "on duty" in the terms of the definition of Parker LJ in *Rice v Connolly* [1966] 2 QB 414, any consequential act would, following the logic of the complainant's submission, be lawful. Thus, rather than seeking an authority for an action of a garda, the simple issue would become as to whether he was "on duty". Garda duties and obligations are wide. Thus, the reach of garda power if it depended only on him acting in the course of the obligations and duties of a garda as set out in *Rice v Connolly*, would be very broad and unclear, and have further detrimental consequences.

I am satisfied that the submission of the Director of Public Prosecutions is incorrect, and consider that the fundamental approach in law and under the Constitution is to seek to find the precise authority for the power of the gardaí to stop a person in the circumstances of this case. It is a matter of balance between an individual's rights and an ordered community. That balance has to be established with certainty and clarity. To hold that the general duty of a garda under common law gives an entitlement to stop vehicles without suspicion is contrary to long established principles of giving to the garda authority specific rights to stop a person, in a precise statutory form, or in common law, where the member has a reasonable suspicion.

It is for the Oireachtas to determine if a law should be passed, as it has in other areas, providing for the right to stop persons in vehicles and in what circumstances. That is a matter for the legislature, not this Court. [1994] 3 IR 265, at 286–287

In reaching these conclusions as to the interpretation of statute and common law, Denham J placed some reliance on the concept of personal liberty protected by the Constitution. If the gardaí have an implicit legal power to do whatever they consider necessary for the purposes of preventing and detection of crime, is there any substance to the Constitution's guarantee that a person shall not be deprived of her liberty save in accordance with law? [7–29]

In *State (Trimbole) v Governor of Mountjoy Prison* [1985] IR 550, the Supreme Court adopted a more stringent approach. Mr Trimbole had been arrested purportedly pursuant to s 30 of the Offences Against the State Act 1939 on suspicion of possession of a firearm. The original 24-hour period of detention was extended for a further 24 hours. He initiated habeas corpus proceedings which were due to be heard that evening. However, prior to the hearing of the habeas corpus proceedings, the Minister for Justice made an order applying the relevant provisions of the Extradition Act 1965 to Australia, thereby allowing for his extradition to Australia. The arrest under the 1939 Act had merely been a pretext to keep the applicant in custody until the Minister for [7–30]

Justice brought the Extradition Act into force in respect of Australia. The High Court held that there was no basis for Mr Trimbole's arrest and detention, ordering his release. However, he was immediately re-arrested in the precincts of the Four Courts pursuant to a provisional arrest warrant to facilitate his extradition to Australia. Mr Trimbole then challenged this detention by way of habeas corpus proceedings. In the High Court, Egan J upheld Mr Trimbole's application and this was affirmed on appeal by the Supreme Court. Finlay CJ reasoned as follows:

> The Courts have not only an inherent jurisdiction but a positive duty: (i) to protect persons against the invasion of their constitutional rights; (ii) if invasion has occurred, to restore as far as possible the person so damaged to the position in which he would be if his rights had not been invaded; and (iii) to ensure as far as possible that persons acting on behalf of the Executive who consciously and deliberately violate the constitutional right of citizens do not for themselves or their superiors obtain the planned results of that invasion....
>
> It is clear that not every unlawful arrest, even though it may be classified as conscious and deliberate, gives to a person so arrested, after his necessary release from illegal detention, any immunity from the proper enforcement of due processes of law or makes him unamenable to answer to criminal offences in our courts.
>
> It is equally clear that a person wanted for extradition in this country as the result of a valid request for extradition under lawful treaty or reciprocal arrangements could not by reason only of the fact that he was subjected in the first instance to an unlawful arrest gain any long-term or permanent immunity from extradition.
>
> The finding of the learned trial judge in this case, however, is of quite a different situation and is, in effect, a finding, that the unlawful arrest was part and parcel of a planned operation prompted by delay in bringing into operation the reciprocal extradition agreements, and therefore the application of the Act of 1965 as between Australia and Ireland. [1985] IR 550, at 573–577.

[7–31] In *People (DPP) v Quilligan (No 3)* [1993] 2 IR 305, the Court directly considered the constitutionality of s 30 of the Offences Against the State Act 1939, the provision under which Mr Trimbole had originally been arrested. This provision allows the Gardaí to arrest a person on suspicion of committing an offence scheduled under that Act and then detain that person for an initial period of 24 hours which can be extended by a further 24 hours. The provision was challenged by reference to the equality guarantee, the right to silence and the liberty guarantee, which is the present concern. The Supreme Court, the judgment of which was given by Finlay CJ, approved the comments of Walsh J from *People (DPP) v Quilligan (No 1)* [1986] IR 495, at 509 as to the purpose of s 30:

> The object of the powers given by s. 30 is not to permit the arrest of people simply for the purpose of subjecting them to questioning. Rather is it for the purpose of investigating the commission or suspected commission of a crime by the person already arrested and to enable that investigation to be carried on without the possibility of obstruction or other interference which might occur if the suspected person were not under arrest. Section 30 is part of the statute law of the State permanently in force and it does not permit of any departure from normal police procedure save as to the obligation to bring the arrested person before a court as soon as reasonably possible.

Finlay CJ then noted the various protections that were afforded to an accused person under s 30 and concluded that the provision was constitutional:

Where a person has been arrested pursuant to section 30 of the Act of 1939 he has got, in the view of this Court, the following protections.

1. If the arresting garda does not have a *bona fide* suspicion based on reason of one or other of the matters provided for in the section the arrest is unlawful and he may be released by an order pursuant to Article 40 of the Constitution-*The State (Trimbole) v The Governor of Mountjoy Prison* [1985] IR 550.
2. At the time of the arrest the suspect must be informed, if he does not already know, of the offence pursuant to the Act of 1939 or scheduled for its purposes, of which he is suspected, otherwise his arrest will be unlawful- *The People (Director of Public Prosecutions) v Walsh* [1980] IR 294.
3. The person detained has, during his detention, a right to legal assistance, and the refusal to grant it to him when reasonably requested can make his detention unlawful- *In re The Emergency Powers Bill, 1976* [1977] IR 159, and *Director of Public Prosecutions v Healy* [1990] ILRM 313.
4. The right to medical assistance- *In re The Emergency Powers Bill, 1976* [1977] IR 159.
5. The right to access to the courts-*In re The Emergency Powers Bill, 1976* [1977] IR 159.
6. The right to remain silent and the associated right to be told of that right-*The People (Director of Public Prosecutions) v Quilligan* [1986] IR 495.
7. The Judges' Rules with their provisions in regard to the giving of cautions and the abstention from cross-examination of a prisoner apply to a person in detention under section 30- *The People (Director of Public Prosecutions) v Quilligan* [1986] IR 495.
8. A person detained under section 30 must not, in the words of Walsh J in *The People (Director of Public Prosecutions) v Quilligan* [1986] IR 495, "be subject to any form of questioning which the courts would regard as unfair or oppressive, either by reason of its nature, the manner in which it is conducted, its duration or the time of day or of its persistence into the point of harassment, where it is not shown that the arrested person has indicated clearly that he is willing to continue to be further questioned".
9. If the detention of a person arrested under section 30 is extended by a Chief Superintendent for a further period after the first period of twenty-four hours, he must entertain also the necessary *bona fide* suspicion of the suspect that justified his original arrest and must be satisfied that his further detention is necessary for the purposes provided for in the section- *The People (Director of Public Prosecutions) v Eccles, McPhillips and McShane* (1986) 3 Frewen 36.

The Court having considered all these protections, any of which can be made effective either by, where appropriate, the release of the person detained from his detention, pursuant to an order made under Article 40 of the Constitution or can be given effect to by the exclusion of evidence obtained in violation of any of these rules applicable to detention under section 30, is satisfied that having regard to the purposes of the section as outlined in the judgment of Walsh J in *The People (Director of Public Prosecutions) v Quilligan* [1986] IR 495, to which reference has already been made, that section 30 has not been established as constituting a failure by the State as far as practicable by its laws to defend and vindicate the personal right of immediate liberty of the citizen.

This reasoning is not particularly convincing. Much has been made of the shift from a procedural to substantive interpretation of Art 40.4. However, Finlay CJ's reasoning suggests that a legislative deprivation of liberty will be substantively justified if it is trammelled by a range of procedural protections for other rights of the accused person. [7–32]

Deprivations of liberty are also legislatively authorised in non-criminal contexts. As noted above, in *Re Philip Clarke* [1950] IR 235, the Supreme Court upheld the constitutionality of s 165 of the Mental Treatment Act 1945 which allows a Garda to take a person of unsound mind to a Garda station where she believes that the person should for her own safety or the safety of the public be taken under care and control. Once the person is in the Garda station, an authorised medical officer can make a recommendation for the reception and detention of the person in a district mental hospital. In *Re Philip Clarke*, the applicant's complaint focused on the absence of any judicial intervention and determination between the arrest of the person and his subsequent detention. O'Byrne J, who delivered the judgment of the Court, rejected this contention:

> The impugned legislation is of a paternal character, clearly intended for the care and custody of persons suspected to be suffering from mental infirmity and for the safety and well-being of the public generally. The existence of mental infirmity is too widespread to be overlooked, and was, no doubt, present to the minds of the draughtsmen when it was proclaimed in Article 40, 1, of the Constitution that, though all citizens, as human beings, are to be held equal before the law, the State may, nevertheless, in its enactments, have due regard to differences of capacity, physical and moral, and of social function. We do not see how the common good would be promoted or the dignity and freedom of the individual assured by allowing persons, alleged to be suffering from such infirmity, to remain at large to the possible danger of themselves and others.
>
> The section is carefully drafted so as to ensure that the person, alleged to be of unsound mind, shall be brought before, and examined by, responsible medical officers with the least possible delay. This seems to us to satisfy every reasonable requirement, and we have not been satisfied, and do not consider that the Constitution requires, that there should be a judicial inquiry or determination before such a person can be placed and detained in a mental hospital.
>
> The section cannot, in our opinion, be construed as an attack upon the personal rights of the citizen. On the contrary it seems to us to be designed for the protection of the citizen and for the promotion of the common good.
>
> In our opinion the section in question is not repugnant to either the letter or spirit of the Constitution and, accordingly, we are of opinion that this ground of appeal fails. [1950] IR 235, at 247–248.

The Court adopted a paternalistic attitude that places considerable faith in the medical profession. It is questionable whether this adequately respects the rights to individual autonomy of those who are alleged to be mentally ill.

[7–33] In *Croke v Smith* [1998] 1 IR 101, the Supreme Court considered the constitutionality of a further provision of the Mental Treatment Act 1945. Section 162 of the Act allows a designated person to apply to a medical practitioner for a recommendation for the detention and reception of a person of unsound mind in a district mental hospital. Section 171 allows the resident medical superintendent of the hospital to make or refuse a chargeable patient reception order. If such an order is made, various persons connected with the hospital have the power to detain the patient and, if she escapes, to retake her within 28 days. The Act allows for patients who have recovered to be discharged. Further, a patient can be discharged where a friend or relative applies to take care of the patient. However, a patient cannot be discharged where the resident medical superintendent certifies that the patient is dangerous or otherwise unfit for discharge. This is subject to the right of the patient to appeal the certificate to the

Minister for Health who may require the Inspector of Mental Hospitals to examine the patient. Having considered the report of the Inspector, the Minister may order the discharge of the patient. On the application of any person, the Minister may have a patient examined by two medical practitioners. If they certify that the patient can be released without any risk to himself or others, the Minister may order the discharge of the patient. There are various provisions that allow the Inspector raise issues as to the detention of patients. Further, the President of the High Court can order the Inspector to examine and report on the condition of a particular patient.

The applicant again argued that the lack of judicial oversight—in some form— rendered the original detention unconstitutional. The Court did not accept this proposition, essentially adopting the reasoning from *Re Philip Clarke*: [7–34]

> Though the decision made by the registered medical practitioner to make a recommendation for a reception order may, and the decision of the medical superintendent to make a chargeable patient reception order will, result in the deprivation of the liberty of the person to whom they relate, such decisions cannot be regarded as part of the administration of justice but are decisions entrusted to them by the Oireachtas in its role of providing treatment for those in need, caring for society and its citizens, particularly those suffering from disability, and the protection of the common good. These decisions can only be made when it is established that the person to whom they relate is a person of unsound mind and is a proper person to be taken in charge and detained under care and treatment. These decisions can be set aside in the appropriate circumstances by the court upon an application for judicial review or upon complaint made to the High Court in accordance with Article 40.4.2 of the Constitution but this does not mean that the decisions are part of the administration of justice....
>
> The Court is satisfied that the original detention of a person considered to be of unsound mind and a proper person to be taken charge of and detained under care and treatment pursuant to a chargeable patient reception order made in accordance with the provisions of section 171 of the Act is not part of the administration of justice and does not require a judicial inquiry or determination and that the sections which permit of such detention do not constitute an attack upon the personal rights of the citizen but rather vindicate and protect the rights of the citizens concerned by providing for their care and treatment and are not repugnant to the Constitution on this ground. [1998] 1 IR 101, at 115–116.

However, the Court gave separate consideration to the issues that arose from the continued detention of persons. In this regard, the Court placed considerable emphasis on the various review safeguards and the presumption of constitutionality: [7–35]

> There is no doubt that the provisions of section 172 of the Act empowers the persons, set forth in sub-section (2) thereof, to deprive a person, in respect of whom a chargeable patient reception order has been made, of his liberty. By virtue of the provisions of Article 40 of the Constitution, the State, however, in its enactments is obliged to have due regard to differences of capacity, physical and moral, and of social function.
>
> The Mental Treatment Act, 1945, was, as stated in the preamble thereto, "An Act to provide for the prevention and treatment of mental disorders and the care of persons suffering therefrom..." As stated by the Supreme Court in *In re Philip Clarke* [1950] IR 235, the legislation was "of a paternal character, clearly intended for the care and custody of persons suspected to be suffering from mental infirmity and for the safety and well-being of the public generally".

> The purpose of section 172 of the Act was to provide for the detention of persons of unsound mind and certified to be proper persons for detention under care and treatment.
>
> The State, including the Oireachtas, is obliged by virtue of the provisions of Article 40.3.1 in its laws to respect, and as far as practicable by its laws to defend and vindicate the personal rights of the citizen but in its laws is entitled to have due regard to differences of capacity and the particular requirements of citizens, particularly those suffering from incapacity including mental disorders.
>
> Do the provisions of section 172 of the Act, having regard to the citizen to whom it is applicable, constitute a failure by the Oireachtas to respect and, as far as practicable, defend and vindicate the personal rights of such citizens? In view of the requirements set forth in sections 163 and 171, which do not of themselves constitute an attack upon the personal rights of the citizen affected thereby or a failure to defend and vindicate such rights, the Court is satisfied that it has not been established that the provisions of section 172 constitutes a failure by the Oireachtas to respect and, as far as practicable, to defend and vindicate the right of such citizens affected thereby.
>
> In being so satisfied, the Court has had regard to the presumption of constitutionality which the Act is entitled to enjoy and in particular the presumption that the Oireachtas intended that the proceedings, procedures, discretions and adjudications by the resident medical superintendent, the Inspector of Mental Hospitals and the Minister permitted by the Act are to be conducted in accordance with the principles of constitutional justice and in particular with regard to the principle thereof that no person should be unnecessarily deprived of his liberty even for a short period.
>
> This requirement places a heavy responsibility on these officers to ensure that no person detained pursuant to the provisions of section 172 of the Act is detained for any period longer than is absolutely necessary for his proper care and treatment and that the safeguards provided for in the Act be stringently enforced. The necessity for the continued detention of a patient, to whom section 172 of the Act applies, must be regularly reviewed to ensure that he or she is not being unnecessarily detained. Decisions made in this regard are not decisions made in the administration of justice but the decision makers are obliged to act in accordance with the principles of constitutional justice and to have regard to the constitutional right to liberty. [1998] 1 IR 101, at 132–133.

This decision approves the reasoning of O'Byrne J in *Re Philip Clarke*. Again it relies on a paternalistic attitude to persons with mental illnesses and a high level of faith in the medical profession.

Preventive Detention

[7–36] As noted above, *People (Attorney General) v O'Callaghan* [1966] IR 501 was the case that marked the decisive shift away from the procedural interpretation of Art 40.4. It also constitutionalised the bail laws. The accused was charged with various offences largely relating to a burglary and sought bail. The Attorney General opposed bail. In the High Court, Murnaghan J listed a wide range of factors which could be considered by a judge on a bail application including the likelihood of the commission of further offences while on bail. Mr O'Callaghan successfully appealed to the Supreme Court. In allowing the appeal, Ó Dálaigh CJ relied principally on the presumption of innocence. However, Walsh J also relied on Art 40.4:

> The learned Judge goes on to add that in certain cases the likelihood of personal danger to the prisoner—from the hands of persons injured or incensed by the crime, may in itself be a ground for refusing bail. This proposition is quite unsustainable. If an accused wants protective custody he need not ask for bail or accept it. A bail motion cannot be used as a vehicle to import into the law the concept of protective custody for an unwilling

recipient. An accused person on bail is entitled to as much protection from the law as may be required.

Of the matters enumerated by the Judge [some] are ... matters relevant to the fundamental test in that they are guides to a decision on the probability of the accused evading justice in that they may all ... constitute to some degree an inducement to the accused to flee justice....

Ground number 4 of the learned Judge, that is to say, the likelihood of the commission of further offences while on bail, is a matter which is in my view quite inadmissible. This is a form of preventative justice which has no place in our legal system and is quite alien to the true purposes of bail. It is true that in recent years a number of decisions in England on the question of bail appear to have admitted this concept of preventative justice being applied by the refusal of bail. It has also been stated in English cases that a professional criminal, knowing that he is guilty and the probability of conviction, may be tempted to commit some more offences before imprisonment in the belief that it will probably make little difference to his ultimate sentence having regard to his record and the meanwhile may offer some present profit.

In this country it would be quite contrary to the concept of personal liberty enshrined in the Constitution that any person should be punished in respect of any matter upon which he has not been convicted or that in any circumstances he should be deprived of his liberty upon only the belief that he will commit offences if left at liberty, save in the most extraordinary circumstances carefully spelled out by the Oireachtas and then only to secure the preservation of public peace and order or the public safety and the preservation of the State in a time of national emergency or in some situation akin to that....[1966] IR 501, at 515–519.

In *Ryan v DPP* [1989] IR 399, the Director asked the Supreme Court to reconsider the principles laid down in *O'Callaghan*. The Supreme Court, however, approved *O'Callaghan*. In 1996, the people inserted Art 40.4.6° into the Constitution: [7–37]

> Provision may be made by law for the refusal of bail by a court to a person charged with a serious offence where it is reasonably considered necessary to prevent the commission of a serious offence by that person.

In *Gregory v Windle* [1994] 3 IR 613, O'Hanlon J upheld the constitutionality of the courts' power to bind a person over to keep the peace. This power is not dependent on a person being convicted of any offence and it may result in a person's imprisonment for a defined period. O'Hanlon J reasoned as follows: [7–38]

> [T]he power vested in the courts to bind a person to keep the peace and/or be of good behaviour for a fixed period of time, with the requirement that he enter into a bond and provide sureties to ensure his compliance with the undertaking, is a beneficial and necessary jurisdiction, which, if exercised prudently and with discretion, does not give rise to any conflict with the constitutional guarantee of personal liberty.
>
> A person who is the victim of abusive or intimidating or violent language or behaviour on the part of another person should be able to invoke the protection of the legal process without waiting for an actual assault to take place, and without having to embark on costly legal proceedings in search of an injunction. It seems to be reasonable and proper that a person who has been guilty of some form of outrageous behaviour or language should be asked to give guarantees in appropriate form that it will not be repeated in the future, and this has, in fact, been the course adopted by the courts for so many centuries that the origin of the jurisdiction is buried in the mists of the common law.

The liberty of the subject is, in my opinion, sufficiently safeguarded by the supervisory role exercised by the superior courts in respect of the orders made by courts of limited and local jurisdiction. [1994] 3 IR 613, at 622–623.

It is questionable whether this judgment is consistent with the principle against preventive detention established by *O'Callaghan* and approved in *Ryan*. O'Hanlon J refers to the procedural safeguards established by the supervisory role of the superior courts. As noted above, the courts have upheld the constitutionality of provisions of the Mental Treatment Act 1945 that seek to prevent a person of unsound mind from harming herself or [TU1]others. Is that a form of preventive detention that should be unconstitutional on the basis of the *O'Callaghan* principles?

Inviolability of the Dwelling

[7–39] Article 40.5 of the Constitution provides:

> The dwelling of every citizen is inviolable and shall not be forcibly entered save in accordance with law.

In *Ryan v O'Callaghan* 22 July 1987 (HC), Barr J confirmed that the phrase "in accordance with law" should be interpreted in the same way as that phrase in Art 40.4.1°, *ie* as authorizing only those interferences with the dwelling that did not breach the fundamental norms of the Constitution.

[7–40] In *People (Attorney General) v O'Brien* [1965] IR 142, the accused's house had been searched pursuant to a warrant that wrongly gave the address as 118 Cashel Road, Crumlin instead of 118 Captain's Road, Crumlin. The accused argued that evidence obtained pursuant to the search should not have been admitted in evidence, it having been obtained in breach of his constitutional rights. This case is most significant as the initiation of the unconstitutionally obtained evidence doctrine; however, the Supreme Court also considered whether Art 40.5 of the Constitution had been breached. Kingsmill Moore J described any infringement of the Constitution in this case as having been accidental and unintentional. Walsh J gave greater consideration to the meaning of Art 40.5:

> That does not mean that the guarantee is against forcible entry only. In my view, the reference to forcible entry is an intimation that forcible entry may be permitted by law but that in any event the dwelling of every citizen is inviolable save where entry is permitted by law and that, if necessary, such law may permit forcible entry. In a case where members of a family live together in the family house, the house as a whole is for the purpose of the Constitution the dwelling of each member of the family. If a member of a family occupies a clearly defined portion of the house apart from the other members of the family, then it may well be that the part not so occupied is no longer his dwelling and that the part he separately occupies is his dwelling as would be the case where a person not a member of the family occupied or was in possession of a clearly defined portion of the house. In this case the appellants are members of a family living in the family dwelling-house and also appear to have their own respective separate bedrooms. Each of the appellants would therefore have a constitutional right to the inviolability of No. 118 Captain's Road. [1965] IR 142, at 169–170.

[7–41] In *DPP v McMahon* [1986] IR 393, the Supreme Court held that the protection of Art 40.5 only extended to such part of the premises that is a dwelling. Accordingly, the entry of a Garda as a trespasser onto licensed premises that were part of a building which also comprised a dwelling did not breach Art 40.5.

In *People (DPP) v Lawless* 3 Frewen 30, the Court of Criminal Appeal held that only the person whose dwelling it is can invoke the guarantee. In *DPP v Corrigan* [1986] IR 290, it was held that the term "dwelling" does not include the garden and driveway of the premises. (However, in *DPP v McCreesh* [1992] 2 IR 239, the Supreme Court held that there must be express statutory authority to allow a Garda arrest a person on that person's own land).

As noted above, in *Ryan v O'Callaghan* 22 July 1987 (HC) Barr J confirmed that Art 40.5 was a substantive guarantee of the dwelling. In that light, he assessed the constitutionality of the procedure set out in s 42 of the Larceny Act 1916, whereby a member of An Garda Síochána could obtain a search warrant from a Peace Commissioner. Barr J noted that the procedure: [7–42]

> ... contains important elements for the protection of the public.... The investigating police officer must swear an information that he has reasonable cause for suspecting that stolen property is to be found at the premises to be searched and he must satisfy a Peace Commissioner, who is an independent person unconnected with criminal investigation per se, that it is right and proper to issue the warrant. 22 July 1987 (HC), at 5.

Similar to the courts' jurisprudence on Art 40.4.1°, therefore, it appears that legislatively authorised interferences with the dwelling place will generally be justified where there are procedural safeguards.

CONTENTS – CHAPTER 8

Freedoms of Expression, Assembly and Association

Introduction. . . . .[8–01]
Public Order and Morality . . . . [8–02]
Freedom of Expression . . . . [8–03]
    Rationale . . . . [8–03]
    The Freedom to Express What? . . . . [8–04]
    The Freedom of Whom? . . . . [8–10]
    Restrictions on Freedom of Expression. [8–13]
    Blasphemy . . . . [8–24]
Freedom of Assembly . . . . [8–27]
Freedom of Association . . . . [8–28]
    Trade Unions. . . . . [8–29]
    Political Parties . . . . [8–38]
    Sports Clubs . . . . [8–39]
    Restrictions on Freedom of Association . . . . [8–42]
    The Extent of the Freedom . . . . [8–49]

Overview

Article 40.6 of the Constitution protects the three freedoms of expression, assembly and association, all subject to public order and morality. The courts initially drew a distinction between the freedom to express opinions and the freedom to communicate information (protected by Art 40.3) but this distinction has faded. The courts apply a proportionality test to the restriction of free speech. The general right of the media to report court proceedings has been strongly upheld, and the courts have been slow to grant prior restraint orders. However, the courts have upheld restrictions on the means of communication and have upheld a broad restriction on religious and political speech. Although blasphemy is a constitutional crime, the courts have indicated that it requires to be defined by the Oireachtas before it can be prosecuted. Much of the earlier case law in relation to freedom of association occurred in the context of trade unions. The courts delivered a series of decisions that emphasised the rights of unions to refuse members and the rights of individuals not to be forced to join unions. More recently, the courts have held that the right of freedom of association is not absolute and can be restricted to support other constitutional values, such as equality in the context of a discriminating golf club.

CHAPTER 8

Freedoms of Expression, Assembly and Association

Introduction

Article 40.6 of the Constitution provides: [8–01]

> 1° The State guarantees liberty for the exercise of the following rights, subject to public order and morality:
> i. The right of the citizens to express freely their convictions and opinions. The education of public opinion being, however, a matter of such grave import to the common good, the State shall endeavour to ensure that organs of public opinion, such as the radio, the press, the cinema, while preserving their rightful liberty of expression, including criticism of Government policy, shall not be used to undermine public order or morality or the authority of the State.
> The publication or utterance of blasphemous, seditious, or indecent matter is an offence which shall be punishable in accordance with law.
> ii. The right of the citizens to assemble peaceably and without arms. Provision may be made by law to prevent or control meetings which are determined in accordance with law to be calculated to cause a breach of the peace or to be a danger or nuisance to the general public and to prevent or control meetings in the vicinity of either House of the Oireachtas.
> iii. The right of the citizens to form associations and unions. Laws, however, may be enacted for the regulation and control in the public interest of the exercise of the foregoing right.
> 2° Laws regulating the manner in which the right of forming associations and unions and the right of free assembly may be exercised shall contain no political, religious or class discrimination.

The Article thus guarantees liberty for the exercise of three freedoms: expression, assembly and association. Each liberty is guaranteed, however, subject to public order and morality. In addition, different specific restrictions are envisaged in respect of the different liberties. An issue arises as to whether the broad authorisation for public order and morality restrictions in the first sentence implies that the restrictions authorised by the other sentences are more limited. This issue has arisen most forcibly in the context of freedom of association and so will be considered in that section.

Public Order and Morality

In *State (Lynch) v Cooney* [1982] IR 337, the Supreme Court considered the constitutionality of s 31 of the Broadcasting Authority Act 1960, as amended, which allowed the Minister for Posts and Telegraphs to direct RTÉ not to broadcast certain matters if he was of the opinion that it would undermine the authority of the State. The Minister made an order under the section directing RTÉ not to broadcast any matter, [8–02] whether being a party political broadcast or not, made by or on behalf of or inviting support for the Sinn Féin organisation. In the High Court, O'Hanlon J held that the meaning of s 31 was that where the Minister held a bona fide opinion, the basis for that opinion could not be reviewed by the High Court. Largely on this basis, he concluded that the section infringed Art 40.6.1°(i) too greatly. On appeal, however, the Supreme Court held that the presumption of constitutionality required s 31 to be construed in such a way as to allow the courts review the basis for the Minister's opinion. On this basis, the Supreme Court considered that the freedom of expression of the applicant had not been unduly restricted:

> The legislation deals with, amongst other things, the control of freedom of expression and free speech within the powers granted by [Article 40.6.1] of the Constitution. This provision enables the State, in certain instances, to control these rights and freedoms. The basis for any attempt at control must be, according to the Constitution, the overriding considerations of public order and public morality. The constitutional provision in question refers to organs of public opinion and these must be held to include television as well as radio. It places upon the State the obligation to ensure that these organs of public opinion shall not be used to undermine public order or public morality or the authority of the State. It follows that the use of such organs of opinion for the purpose of securing or advocating support for organisations which seek by violence to overthrow the State or its institutions is a use which is prohibited by the Constitution. Therefore, it is clearly the duty of the State to intervene to prevent broadcasts on radio or television which are aimed at such a result or which in any way would be likely to have the effect of promoting or inciting to crime or endangering the authority of the State. These, however, are objective determinations and obviously the fundamental rights of citizens to express freely their convictions and opinions cannot be curtailed or prevented on any irrational or capricious ground. It must be presumed that when the Oireachtas conferred these powers on the Minister it intended that they be exercised only in conformity with the Constitution. [1982] IR 337, at 361.

Freedom of Expression

Rationale

[8–03] As with most of the rights in the Constitution, one can rationalise freedom of expression in terms of personal dignity and autonomy. To preclude an individual from speaking her mind offends her dignity and restricts her autonomy. However, freedom of expression also plays a more instrumental role in supporting a democratic culture. Boyle has described this role in the following terms:

> Democracy as a means of government is in part designed to ensure popular control of governmental and collective decision making on an on-going basis. The ideal democracy might be direct decision-making by all citizens but the Greek city state experience is not replicable in modern political systems by reason of their size and by reason of time. Therefore we have evolved the idea of representatives to carry out the democratic wishes of the people. The role of a democratic system is to ensure that such representatives are accountable not only at election times but on a permanent basis to those they represent. At the same time democratic society can encourage greater participation by its members over a wide field of social and communal activity.
>
> Freedom of expression is clearly a centre of freedom within such a model. It enables people to be informed about and to debate ideas. It enables the political parties who in practice emerge to represent the popular will to persuade people about their policies and

to oppose each other's policies. The media, newspapers and electronic media, are a critical means to ensure that citizens are informed and in a position to ensure that government activity is accountable to them at all times. Greater participation by citizens at all levels of decision-making requires that they are informed or able to inform themselves about public issues.

The major justification for granting freedom of expression a special status is precisely that it performs these democratic functions. It is true that it performs other functions, from education to entertainment, but it is the role in linking citizen to representative and ensuring accountability of administration and government on an on-going basis, which justifies its special character. In this connection media are a partner in the democratic process. Media freedom is not something that belongs or is of concern only to the press; it is a public freedom in which we all have an interest. In examining the national and international regulation within which freedom of expression these considerations should inform the critique. In particular the public function of media in sustaining and deepening democracy needs to be highlighted. Kevin Boyle, "Freedom of Expression and Democracy" in Liz Heffernan ed, *Human Rights: A European Perspective* (Round Hall, Dublin, 1994) 211, at 216–217.

The very fact that the rights of the media are specifically protected, combined with the fact that freedom of expression is protected in the same context as two other political freedoms—association and expression—suggests that the instrumental, political justification for free expression is, in the Irish context, the most compelling. That said, the Irish courts have not fashioned a constitutional jurisprudence that is especially protective of free speech in the public realm.

The Freedom to Express What?

The courts have adverted to a distinction between two types of expression protected by Art 40.6.1°(i): the expression of opinion and the communication of information. In *Attorney General v Paperlink Ltd* [1984] ILRM 373, Costello J had held that the right to communicate was protected as an unenumerated right under Art 40.3.1°, but not under Art 40.6.1°(i). In *Oblique Ltd v Promise Production Company* [1994] 1 ILRM 74, Keane J drew the distinction as follows: [8–04]

> Article 40.6.1° is concerned not with the dissemination of factual information, but the rights of the citizen, in formulating or publishing convictions or opinions, or conveying an opinion; and the rights of all citizens, including conveying information, arises in our law, not under Article 40.6.1° but under Article 40.3.1°.

Although the concept of expression of opinions provided some justification for this division of constitutional protection, it was still difficult and somewhat artificial to divide the constitutional protection of free speech into two separate provisions. Perhaps recognising this, the Supreme Court has since held that the division between the two forms of expression is not so rigid. Thus in *Irish Times Ltd v Ireland* [1998] 1 IR 539, at 404–405, Barrington J reasoned: [8–05]

> Article 40.6.1 (i) is unique in conferring liberties and rights upon the "organs of public opinion".... These rights must include the right to report the news as well as the right to comment on it. A constitutional right which protected the right to comment on the news but not the right to report it would appear to me to be a nonsense. It therefore appears to me that the right of the citizens "to express freely their convictions and opinions" guaranteed by Article 40 of the Constitution is a right to communicate facts as well as a

right to comment on them. It appears to me also that when the European Convention on Human Rights states that the right to freedom of expression is to include "freedom ... to receive and impart information" it is merely making explicit something which is already implicit in Article 40.6.1 of our Constitution.

[8–06] The Supreme Court endorsed this position in *Murphy v Independent Radio and Television Commission* [1999] 1 IR 12, at 24–25. It could be argued that Barrington J was considering the press, an organ of public opinion, which has its own guarantee of liberty of expression, perhaps a broader guarantee than that afforded to citizens by the first sentence. However, Barrington J explicitly addressed the right of citizens "to express freely their convictions and opinions"; moreover, the whole tenor of his judgment is to remove artificial distinctions. It therefore appears almost certain that both the right to communicate information and the right to express opinions, of both media and the citizens, are protected by Art 40.6.1°(i). If there is any shortfall in the protection offered by this provision, however, it is covered by the right to communicate information implicitly recognised by Art 40.3.1°. This approach of minimising the differences between freedom of expression and the right to communicate was approved by Fennelly J in *Mahon v Post Publications Ltd* [2007] IESC 15, at [51]:

> Clearly, the Constitution, unequivocally guarantees both the right to express convictions and opinions and the right to communicate facts or information. These rights are inseparable. It matters little, at least for present purposes, which Article of the Constitution expresses the guarantee. The right of a free press to communicate information without let or restraint is intrinsic to a free and democratic society.

[8–07] The courts thus appear to be less concerned to categorise a claim rigidly as one of freedom of expression or the right to communicate. In *Holland v Governor Portlaoise Prison* [2004] 2 IR 573, the applicant, a prisoner, challenged a blanket policy on communication with the media on the basis that his right to communication was thereby infringed. He was seeking access to the media, by way of visits and letters for the purpose of attempting to secure their support, by public media presentation, in order to highlight what he claimed to have been a miscarriage of justice in his criminal case. The prison governor argued that the censorship of the applicant's communications was justified by the demands of the security and good discipline of the prison. McKechnie J characterised the interaction of Art 40.3.1° and Art 40.6.1°(i) in the following way:

> It, therefore, seems quite clear that depending on the circumstances of any particular case, a claimant or plaintiff may be able to rely, not only on Article 40.3 of the Constitution but also on Article 40.6.1°. In the instant proceedings, it appears to me that, in all probability, the applicant can rely upon both sub-articles in furtherance of his claim. His attempts to communicate with R.T.É involved apparently a mixture of fact, information, convictions and opinions and with the result that, by seeking to influence the media to bring to the attention of the public what he describes as a miscarriage of justice, he was undoubtedly, in a most direct way attempting to influence public opinion. Consequently, I believe that both sources of protection are available in principle to him.
>
> If, however, I should be incorrect in this view it seems to me that for practical purposes, in the particular circumstances of this case, there is no valid distinction in the consequences which would follow from confining reliance to one or other but not both of these sub-articles. No issue on the facts of this case arises which could be said to involve "public order or morality or the authority of the State" as that phrase is contained in Article 40.6.1°. Therefore, in my opinion, it is not necessary to conclusively decide on the preferment of one sub-article to the exclusion of the other. [2004] 2 IR 573, at 590.

Setting aside the distinction between the communication of information and the [8–08] expression of opinions, it is beyond doubt that Art 40.6.1°(i) protects political speech. The reference to "criticism of Government policy", if nothing else, implies that speech linked to the political process is protected by the Article. The courts have not restricted the guarantee to narrowly political speech, holding that speech in general in the public domain is protected. In *Murphy v IRTC* [1999] 1 IR 12, the applicant challenged the constitutionality of s 10(3) of the Radio and Television Act 1988, which prohibits the broadcast of any advertisement "which is directed towards any religious or political end or which has any relation to an industrial dispute." Under this section, the IRTC prevented a radio station from broadcasting the applicant's advertisement concerning an evening presentation of the evidence of the resurrection of Christ. Barrington J, delivering the judgment of the Court, commented:

> The Court agrees, however, with counsel for the second respondent when he submits that the learned trial judge was perhaps unduly restrictive in denying to the applicant any right to rely on Article 40.6.1° because he was not attempting to influence public opinion. The Court doubts if the guarantee of freedom of expression contained in Article 40.6.1° is confined to those who wish to influence public opinion. A politician who addresses the nation over the airwaves is clearly attempting to influence public opinion. But an advertisement, though apparently directed at an individual consumer, may also be intended to influence consumers generally. One could not say that the advertisement in the present case, with its opening question "What think ye of Christ?", is directed exclusively at individuals and not at the citizenry at large.
>
> The Court is not suggesting that to invoke the protection of Article 40.6.1° a person must be attempting to influence the citizens at large. But, on the facts of the present case, it would appear that the applicant is *prima facie* entitled to invoke the protection of Article 40.6.1° as well as the protection of Article 40.3. [1999] 1 IR 12, at 25.

It thus appears that any attempt to engage in public speech is prima facie protected by [8–09] Article 40.6.1°(i). Barrington J also explicitly left open the possibility that purely private speech would be protected by the free expression guarantee. Notwithstanding its focus on public speech, *Murphy* cannot be taken as authority for the proposition that private speech receives any less protection.

The courts have not yet had cause squarely to consider whether purely commercial speech is protected by the guarantee. The form of speech in *Murphy* was commercial (a paid advertisement) but the content was assuredly non-commercial. That the Court regarded the freedom as being prima facie infringed in *Murphy* cannot, therefore, count as firm authority for the proposition that commercial speech is protected by Art 40.6.1°(i). That said, the trend in other jurisdictions—as well as under the European Convention on Human Rights—has been to afford at least some level of protection to commercial speech. Given the general expansiveness of the Court's comments in *Murphy* and, indeed, *Irish Times*, it seems likely that the Irish courts will reach a similar conclusion in respect of commercial speech. In *Irish Times* itself, there was some suggestion from Barrington J that the commercial conveyance of information might still be protected under Art 40.3.1° as an aspect of the unenumerated right to communicate.

The Freedom of Whom?

The first sentence of Art 40.6.1°(i) makes clear that citizens benefit from the [8–10] guarantee. The second sentence indicates that organs of public opinion, such as the radio, the press and the cinema, also benefit from the guarantee. As this is an illustrative list, it seems unarguable but that newer organs of public opinion, such as television and the internet, would be considered to be organs of public opinion. Insofar as the internet is used for personal communication, citizens would presumably have the same freedom as guaranteed by the first sentence of Art 40.6.1°(i). In *Irish Times Ltd v Ireland* [1998] 1 IR 539, at 404, Barrington J observed that "organs of public opinion" could not have rights; accordingly, the rights accorded by the second sentence of the guarantee had to be held by the persons, natural or artificial, who controlled those organs. If non-natural persons are covered by the second sentence of the guarantee, there seems to be a strong argument for the proposition that non-natural persons are covered by the first sentence of the guarantee also. That is, it is probably the case that non-natural persons, unconnected with the media, have rights of free expression guaranteed by the first sentence of Art 40.6.1°(i). However, this point has yet to be decided by the courts.

[8–11] An issue that has attracted academic attention, but has not yet been addressed by the courts, is whether the separate mention of the media in the second sentence affects the level of protection afforded to media expression. McDonald has argued that media speech is entitled to a greater level of protection under Art 40.6.1(i):

> [T]he second sentence in Article 40.6.1° also covers factual and comment expressions by the media.... While it is true that the word "moreover" in the second sentence does suggest a reference to what is referred to in the first sentence, the sub-clause reference in the second sentence, "while preserving their rightful liberty of expression", goes outside any subordinate context to make an independent assertion about media entitlements. This is borne out by a comparison of the second sentence with and without the sub-clause. If read without the sub-clause, it is clear the organs of public opinion could only enjoy whatever right was given to them by the first sentence. But, when we include the sub-clause, it becomes immediately apparent that its inclusion does nothing to further the qualification of the first sentence and that therefore the people were intending a reference to something more than was mentioned in the first sentence. What is that extra? Again, if one construes this as the only reference in the entire document to a fundamental feature of democratic life, then one has to interpret it as a reference which extends to the full range of media speech. This is also borne out by the words of the sub-clause itself. The term "expression" clearly denotes, in this context, the overall output of the media. There is absolutely no reason to read "expression" as somehow focusing just on opinions, and to do so is to ignore the fact that "expression" was in the context a perfectly proper way to succinctly refer to the totality of media output....
>
> When we are looking at media speech and individual speech what we have to be looking at are the nature of these activities, what it is that is separate and distinct about them and not where they may overlap. The intrinsic tendency of media speech is to speak to the public for public consumption. It cannot do anything else. The intrinsic tendency of individual speech is not to speak to the public since an individual may also speak privately. Of course, the individual may speak publicly as well, but he is not inevitably bound to do so. The media is....
>
> The point remains and can be put as follows. If media and individual speech are intrinsically different activities, then it must follow that the specific reference in Article 40.6.1° to media liberty of expression must mean that appropriate and balanced legal protections which recognise the unique features of media speech activities are mandated by the Constitution and that any legislation which purports to offer less than that is unconstitutional.... Marc McDonald, "Defamation Reform: A Response to the LRC Report" (1992) 10 *ILT* 270, at 274.

McDonald's careful parsing of Art 40.6.1(i) may provide a basis for affording greater protection to media speech. However, is questionable whether it is desirable to introduce further distinctions into a case law that has already been marred by unnecessary distinctions such as that between the communication of factual material and the expression of opinion. With the continued development of the internet and the collapsing distinction between broadcasting and narrowcasting, it would not be helpful to require the courts to draw a rigid distinction between speech made through established media and other forms of speech. [8–12]

Restrictions on Freedom of Expression

As with all constitutional rights, the right to free expression may legitimately be restricted. In *Murphy v IRTC* [1999] 1 IR 12, at 26, Barrington J, delivering the judgment of the Supreme Court, confirmed that the proportionality test should be applied to restrictions of free expression. As the cases below illustrate, however, the courts have generally—though not universally—been fairly tolerant of restrictions on free expression. [8–13]

Court Proceedings: In *Irish Times Ltd v Ireland* [1998] 1 IR 359, the *Irish Times*—as well as a number of other newspapers—challenged an order made by a Circuit Court Judge restricting the contemporaneous coverage of a criminal trial. The Supreme Court struck down these restrictions. While some of the judges relied on the requirement, in Art 34.1, that justice be administered in public, other judges relied on Art 40.6.1°(i). Barrington J commented: [8–14]

> The freedom of expression guaranteed by Article 40.6.1° of the Constitution includes criticism of government policy. *A fortiori* it includes criticism of other aspects of State activity including the working of the courts. [1998] 1 IR 359, at 406.

In this vein, O'Flaherty J commented:

> The press are entitled to report, and the public to know, that the administration of justice is being conducted fairly and properly. This is not to satisfy any idle curiosity of the public. The public have both a right and a responsibility to be kept informed of what happens in our courts. Since the proper administration of justice is of concern to everyone in the State, the press has a solemn duty to assure the public by fair, truthful and contemporaneous reporting of court proceedings whether or not justice is being administered in such a manner as to command the respect and the informed support of the public. As it was put by Fitzgerald J, in an Irish case of the last century, one of the many securities for the due administration of justice is "the great security of publicity": *R v Gray* (1865) 10 Cox CC 184, at 193.
>
> In my judgment the blanket ban imposed by the trial judge went too far. It was not justified. It was an order to prevent what was only a possibility of harm though made, I have no doubt, from the best of motives. The risk that there will be some distortion in the reporting of cases from time to time must be run. The administration of justice must be neither hidden nor silenced to eliminate such a possibility. The light must always be allowed shine on the administration of justice; that is the best guarantee for the survival of the fundamental freedoms of the people of any country. [1998] 1 IR 359, at 396.

This decision was more recently followed in *Independent Newspapers of Ireland Ltd v Judge Anderson* [2006] IEHC 62, in which the newspaper challenged an order made by a District Judge restraining media outlets from reporting the name of an accused [8–15] person charged with offences in relation to the possession of child pornography. Clarke J held that the only basis on which such an order could be made was if it was necessary to ensure a fair trial. In this case, the District Judge had erred by making an order on the basis of the likely effect to the good name of the accused person. Clarke J approved a procedure whereby the District Judge could make an order without hearing argument from the media outlets concerned. However, having made such an order, a District Judge had to have the power to reconsider the order having heard argument from the media outlets concerned. In assessing what circumstances would justify the grant of such an order, Clarke J relied on the principle of proportionality:

> If any restrictive order is justified under *Irish Times Limited* principles then, in order to amount to a justified interference with Article 34.1, such an order must, in my view, comply with principles analogous to those which have been developed under the doctrine of proportionality.
> Such an order should, therefore:-
> i.   be designed only to restrict the publication of material which, it is adjudged, would cause serious prejudice leading to a real risk to a fair trial; and
> ii. should do so in a manner which interferes as little as possible with the entitlement to report fully on all aspects of the administration of justice; and
> iii. should do so in a way which is proportionate.
>
> Against such a test it seems to me that the restrictive orders in this case fail. The orders seem more designed to protect the anonymity of the first named notice party rather than preventing the publication of any material that would not be admissible at a trial and where publication might, therefore, be prejudicial to such trial. The orders of themselves do not prevent the publication of material which makes any accusations against the first named notice party but which do not specify that he stands charged with offences now before the courts. The jury at the trial will, of course, know the identity of the accused.

[8–16] *Prior Restraint Orders*: The courts have generally been slow to grant injunctions to restrain publication of material, absent legislative authorisation or some compelling justification. In *M v Drury* [1994] 2 IR 8, the High Court refused to grant an order restraining a number of newspapers from publishing material relating to her married and family life, in particular allegations that she had been having an affair with a priest. O'Hanlon J reasoned:

> In the present case the court is asked to intervene to restrain the publication of material, the truth of which has not as yet been disputed, in order to save from the distress that such publication is sure to cause, the children of the marriage who are all minors. This would represent a new departure in our law, for which, in my opinion, no precedent has been shown, and for which I can find no basis in the Irish Constitution, having regard, in particular, to the strongly-expressed guarantees in favour of freedom of expression in that document. [1994] 2 IR 8, at 17.

[8–17] In *Reynolds v Malocco* [1999] 2 IR 203, however, Kelly J granted an interlocutory injunction restraining publication of an allegedly defamatory article. Although he accepted that, given the importance of the freedom of expression, such an injunction should rarely be granted, Kelly J reasoned that the slim likelihood of the plaintiff recovering damages from any of the defendants warranted the grant of an injunction. Nevertheless, it still seems rare that such an injunction will be granted. In *Foley v Sunday Independent Ltd* [2005] IEHC 14, Kelly J refused an interlocutory injunction to the plaintiff who feared that an article would mark him out as a police informant, thereby putting his life and bodily integrity in danger. In *Aherne v RTÉ* [2005] IEHC 180, Clarke J refused an order restraining RTÉ from broadcasting a report in relation to the Leas Cross Nursing Home, run by the applicants. Assessing the privacy interest involved, Clarke J held that while the applicants had raised an arguable case that their privacy had been infringed, the filming related to the applicants in their capacity as the managers of a nursing home and not in relation to their own private life. As such, it did not infringe to a great extent on their privacy. In addition, there were real issues of public interest and concern raised by the programme. Bearing in mind the general principle against prior restraint orders, Clarke J held that it would be inappropriate to make the order sought.

In *Attorney General for England and Wales v Brandon Books* [1986] IR 597, Carroll J refused to grant an injunction restraining publication of a work concerning the British secret service. There was no copyright or confidentiality issue and, as the state security invoked was not Ireland's, there was no basis for granting an injunction. However, such injunctions have been granted in the commercial context. In *Oblique Financial Services Ltd v The Promise Production Company Co Ltd* [1994] 1 ILRM 74, Keane J held that the right to communicate factual information could be subjected to confidentiality interests. That said, in *National Irish Bank v RTÉ* [1998] 2 IR 465, a majority of the Supreme Court held that the public interest in publication outweighed the confidentiality of the information, where the publication of the information could help expose and defeat wrongdoing. [8–18]

Most recently, in *Mahon v Post Publications ltd* [2007] IESC 15, the Supreme Court refused an application by the Mahon Tribunal to restrain the publication of confidential material that the Tribunal was circulating to witnesses prior to public hearings of the tribunal. The Court held that such a prior restraint would have to be clearly authorised by law; no such clear authorisation existed. The reasoning of Fennelly J, with whom three other members of the Court agreed, was perhaps more sympathetic to freedom of expression than has traditionally been the case with the Irish courts: [8–19]

> The Tribunal seeks, in the form of an injunction, a general order restraining future publication by the media. That form of order is called prior restraint. That is axiomatic and must be recognised before proceeding further in the discussion.
>
> Freedom of expression is, of course, guaranteed both by the Constitution and by the Convention, but, even without those guarantees and simply on the basis of the common law, it is elementary that any party asking a court to impose prior restraint of publication must justify it.
>
> It is no function of the Court to adjudicate on the dispute agitated in the affidavits as to whether future publication by the media of material regarded as confidential by the Tribunal would be in the public interest, as the defendant claims, or would be aimed at boosting circulation, as Ms Griffin has stated on behalf of the Tribunal. The courts do not pass judgment on whether any particular exercise of the right of freedom of expression is in the public interest. The media are not required to justify publication by reference to any public interest other than that of freedom of expression itself. They are free to publish material which is not in the public interest. I have no doubt that much of the material which appears in the news media serves no public interest whatever. I have equally no doubt that much of it is motivated, and perfectly permissibly so, by the pursuit of profit. Publication may indeed be prompted by less noble motives. So far as the facts of the present case are concerned, the decision of Mr O'Kelly to publish the names of three TD's

in direct defiance of the wishes of the Tribunal was disgraceful and served no identifiable public interest. On the other hand, that does not mean that it was unlawful.

The right of freedom of expression extends the same protection to worthless, prurient and meretricious publication as it does to worthy, serious and socially valuable works. The undoubted fact that news media frequently and implausibly invoke the public interest to cloak worthless and even offensive material does not affect the principle. Like Kelly J, I cite the following passage from the judgment of Hoffmann L.J., as he then was, in *R. v Central Independent Television PLC* [1994] Fam. 192; [1994] 3 WLR 20:

> "Newspapers are sometimes irresponsible and their motives in a market economy cannot be expected to be unalloyed by considerations of commercial advantage. Publication may cause needless pain, distress and damage to individuals or harm to other aspects of the public interest. But a freedom which is restricted to what judges think to be responsible or in the public interest is no freedom. Freedom means the right to publish things which government and judges, however well motivated, think should not be published. It means the right to say things which 'right thinking people' regard as dangerous or irresponsible. This freedom is subject only to clearly defined exceptions laid down by common law or statute."

For the purposes of the present appeal, it is the last sentence of that passage which is important. The Tribunal needs to point to an exception clearly defined by law. [2007] IESC 15, at [40]–[44]

What is significant is Fennelly J's recognition of the value in freedom of expression itself, even where what is expressed is worthless. This recognition may lead to the courts developing a more robust protection of free expression in the future.

[8–20] *Defamation Law*: In *Hynes-O'Sullivan v O'Driscoll* [1988] IR 436, Henchy J commented that the law on qualified privilege ought to reflect a due balancing of the constitutional right to freedom of expression and the constitutional protection of every citizen's good name. More recently the courts have indicated a willingness to rethink the law of defamation in light of constitutional principles. The effective incorporation of the European Convention on Human Rights into Irish law has stimulated this process. For instance, in *Hunter v Duckworth* [2003] IEHC 81, Ó Caoimh J reasoned:

> I am satisfied that no essential difference exists between the provisions of the Convention and the provisions of Article 40.6.1° of the Constitution. What is relevant is how they should be interpreted. It is clear that the Convention does not provide as such for the protection of one's reputation. However, Article 10 recognises that the protection given to freedom of expression may be curtailed and may be subject to restrictions as a prescribed by law and as are necessary in a democratic society for a variety of interests including the protection of the reputation or rights of others. It is, however, necessary to assess whether the common law of defamation as traditionally interpreted in this jurisdiction meets the requirements of the Constitution. In interpreting the Constitution this Court can have regard to the interpretation of the Convention insofar as it indicates how Article 40.6.1° may be interpreted.

As the main impetus for development in this area derives from Art 10 of the European Convention on Human Rights, particularly as interpreted by the UK courts, and as legislative reform of the area is now proposed by the government, it is not appropriate to consider the matter further here.

[8–21] *Methods of Communicating Information*: In *Carrigaline Community Television Broadcasting Co Ltd v Minister for Transport, Energy and Communications (No 2)* [1997] 1

ILRM 241, the plaintiffs challenged the constitutionality of ss 3, 4 and 6 of the Wireless and Telegraphy Act 1926 and ss 3 and 4 of the Broadcasting, Wireless and Telegraphy Act 1988. Essentially, the plaintiffs' complaint was that they were precluded, as a result of ministerial decisions taken under those Acts, from operating a system whereby they rebroadcast television signals from the United Kingdom to an area of Cork and west Waterford. The Minister had made a policy decision that another rebroadcasting mechanism should be used; accordingly, the plaintiffs' operation was unlicensed and unlawful. Keane J (in the High Court) held in favour of the plaintiffs on certain grounds, but rejected the constitutional arguments. In relation to the freedom of expression argument, he reasoned as follows:

> That the enactment of a licensing scheme by the Oireachtas in order to ensure the orderly use of the airwaves was a constitutionally permissible regulation of the constitutional rights already referred to is conceded by the plaintiffs. Their submission, however, that this was the limit of the powers of the Oireachtas and that a licensing scheme which permitted the minister to take into account other matters could not be validly provided for in legislation is not, in my view, well founded.
>
> The Oireachtas was entitled to legislate on the basis that the minister would not be confined in the exercise of his licensing powers to ensuring that levels of mutual interference were kept to a minimum and that emergency and life saving transmissions were protected. They were also entitled to provide a licensing scheme which would accommodate relevant policy objectives enshrined in other legislation, *eg* the establishment and development of indigenous sound radio and television programme services and the encouragement of the use of the Irish language. They could also have legitimately envisaged that the minister would make use of his licensing powers to protect and vindicate the constitutional rights of the citizens to express their opinions and the opinions of others and to communicate information.
>
> If, in the light of the technical evidence available to him, the minister could reasonably conclude that the licensing of a particular form of transmission such as MMDS was the most efficient means of ensuring the greatest range of diversity of opinion and information while at the same time accommodating other legitimate policy objectives, then the fact that the relevant legislation permitted the minister to license that system to the exclusion of others would not of itself, in my judgment, render the legislation as a result invalid. [1997] 1 ILRM 241, at 288–289.

Religious and Political Speech: Even in the context of religious and political speech, surely close to the core of what the expression guarantee seeks to protect, the courts have been tolerant of legislative restrictions of free speech. As seen above, in *Murphy v IRTC* [1999] 1 IR 12, the applicant challenged the constitutionality of section 10(3) of the Radio and Television Act 1988, which prohibits the broadcast of any advertisement "which is directed towards any religious or political end or which has any relation to an industrial dispute." Under this section, the IRTC prevented a radio station from broadcasting the applicant's advertisement concerning an evening presentation of the evidence of the resurrection of Christ. Barrington J, applying the proportionality test, reasoned as follows: [8–22]

> It seems to the Court important to stress that there are three kinds of advertisements which are totally banned. These are:-
> 1. advertisements directed towards any religious end,
> 2. advertisements directed towards any political end,
> 3. advertisements which have any relation to an industrial dispute.

203

One can best glean the policy of the Act of 1988 by looking at the three kinds of prohibited advertisement collectively. One might get a false impression by singling out one kind of banned advertisement and ignoring the others. All three kinds of banned advertisement relate to matters which have proved extremely divisive in Irish society in the past. The Oireachtas was entitled to take the view that the citizens would resent having advertisements touching on these topics broadcast into their homes and that such advertisements, if permitted, might lead to unrest. Moreover the Oireachtas may well have thought that in relation to matters of such sensitivity, rich men should not be able to buy access to the airwaves to the detriment of their poorer rivals....

In the present case the limitation placed on the various constitutional rights is minimalist. The applicant has the right to advance his views in speech or by writing or by holding assemblies or associating with persons of like mind to himself. He has no lesser right than any other citizen to appear on radio or television. The only restriction placed upon his activities is that he cannot advance his views by a paid advertisement on radio or television....

Counsel for the applicant, argued that it would have been possible to have had — instead of a blanket ban on religious advertising — a more selective administrative system whereby inoffensive religious advertisements would be permitted, and religious advertisements likely to cause offence, banned. No doubt this is true. But the Oireachtas may well have decided that it would be inappropriate to involve agents of the State in deciding which advertisements, in this sensitive area would be likely to cause offence and which not. In any event, once the Statute is broadly within the area of the competence of the Oireachtas and the Oireachtas has respected the principle of proportionality, it is not for this Court to interfere simply because it might have made a different decision.

It therefore appears to the Court that the ban on religious advertising contained in section 10(3) of the Act of 1988 is rationally connected to the objective of the legislation and is not arbitrary, unfair or based on irrational considerations. It does appear to impair the various constitutional rights referred to as little as possible and it does appear that its effects on those rights are proportional to the objective of the legislation. [1999] 1 IR 12, at 22, 26–27.

[8–23] This judgment well illustrates the limited protection offered by Art 40.6.1°(i). If the State may restrict religious speech on the grounds of divisiveness or possible unrest, there seems little basis on which the State could not restrict speech. Hogan and Whyte have been critical of this decision:

> [O]ne might well question whether the Supreme Court has succeeded in this case in striking a proper balance between the plaintiff's freedom of expression and the interests of the common good. Apart from the contention that the Court may have placed an excessive value on the perceived need to protect the listening public from advertisements of this nature, the Court failed to take into account the fact that the ban infringed the right to communicate of at least that section of that public that would welcome the provision of this type of information. Nor is it necessarily the case that the ban on religious advertising protects poorer rivals from their wealthier counterparts as it could be argued that larger (and wealthier) denominations, because of their existing, extensive network of contacts, have less need of radio advertising than less established (and possibly poorer) churches. Gerard Hogan and Gerry Whyte, *Kelly: The Irish Constitution* (4th ed, LexisNexis Butterworths, Dublin, 2003), at [7.5.120].

The political ban in s 10 of the Radio and Television Act 1988 was subsequently challenged in *Colgan v Independent Radio and Television Commission* [2000] 2 IR 490. In this case, the defendant had banned the broadcast of an advertisement relating to abortion on the ground that it constituted advertising with a political end. O'Sullivan J held that he was bound to follow the decision in *Murphy*. The Supreme Court had seen no distinction in the degree of sensitivity of religious and political advertisements. That being the case, the same result had to be reached.

Blasphemy

Article 40.6 makes blasphemy a criminal offence: [8–24]

> The publication or utterance of blasphemous, seditious, or indecent matter is an offence which shall be punishable in accordance with law.

This provision received little judicial attention for many years, presumably because there existed comprehensive censorship laws. As this regime was dismantled, it seemed likely that the constitutional offence of blasphemy would come into sharper focus. In *Corway v Independent Newspapers (Ireland) Ltd* [1999] 4 IR 484, the applicant sought the leave of the High Court (as required by s 8 of the Defamation Act 1961) to institute criminal proceedings against the defendant in respect of an allegedly blasphemous cartoon. In the Supreme Court, Barrington J described the cartoon in the following terms:

> [The] cartoon ... depicted on the right a plump and comic caricature of a priest. The priest was holding a host in his right hand and a chalice in his left hand. He appears to be offering the host to three figures on the left hand side of the cartoon. The three figures are the prominent politicians Mr. Prionsias de Rossa, Mr. Ruarí Quinn and Mr. John Bruton. But they are turning away and appear to be waving goodbye. At the top of the cartoon are printed the words "Hello progress-bye bye Father" followed by a question mark.
>
> The words at the top of the cartoon are clearly meant to be a play upon a phrase used during the referendum campaign by some of the campaigners against divorce. That is to say "Hello divorce-bye bye daddy".
>
> The applicant maintains that the cartoon picture and caption appear calculated to insult the feelings and religious convictions of readers generally by treating the sacrament of the eucharist and its administration as objects of scorn and derision. [1999] 4 IR 484, at 493–494.

Barrington J, with whom all other members of the Court agreed, reasoned that [8–25] although blasphemy was clearly a crime, it could not be prosecuted in the absence of a statutory definition:

> The Constitution of Ireland re-enacted the provisions of the Constitution of the Irish Free State guaranteeing freedom of conscience and the free profession and practice of religion. It also re-enacted the provision prohibiting the State from imposing any disability or making any discrimination on the ground of religious profession, belief or status. It did however, add a new section in the following terms:-
> Article 44
> 1. 1 The State acknowledges that the homage of public worship is due to Almighty God. It shall hold His Name in reverence, and shall respect and honour religion.
>   2 The State recognises the special position of the Holy Catholic Apostolic and Roman Church as the guardian of the Faith professed by the great majority of the citizens.
>   3 The State also recognises the Church of Ireland, the Presbyterian Church in Ireland, the Methodist Church in Ireland, the Religious Society of Friends in Ireland, as well as the Jewish Congregations and the other religious denominations existing in Ireland at the date of the coming into operation of this Constitution.

In 1972, the fifth amendment to the Constitution removed the second two sub-sections quoted above leaving the religious guarantee in effect, as it had been under the Constitution of the Irish Free State, but subject to the significant addition of the first sub-section quoted above.

The Constitution also introduced (in Article 40.1) a specific guarantee of equality before the law to all citizens as human persons. The effect of these various guarantees is that the State acknowledges that the homage of public worship is due to Almighty God. It promises to hold his name in reverence and to respect and honour religion. At the same time it guarantees freedom of conscience, the free profession and practice of religion and equality before the law to all citizens, be they Roman Catholics, Protestants, Jews, Muslims, agnostics or atheists. But Article 44 goes further and places the duty on the State to respect and honour religion as such. At the same time the State is not placed in the position of an arbiter of religious truth. Its only function is to protect public order and morality....

It is difficult to see how the common law crime of blasphemy, related as it was to an established church and an established religion could survive in such a constitutional framework.... There is no doubt that the crime of blasphemy exists as an offence in Irish law because the Constitution says so. It says that the publication or utterance of blasphemous matter "is an offence which shall be punishable in accordance with the law". Yet the researches of the Law Reform Commission would appear to indicate that the framers of the Constitution did not intend to create a new offence. This may explain why there is no statutory definition of blasphemy. The Censorship of Films Act, 1923 s. 7(2) and s. 13(1) of the Defamation Act, 1961, assume that the crime exists without defining it. It would appear that the legislature has not adverted to the problem of adapting the common law crime of blasphemy to the circumstances of a modern State which embraces citizens of many different religions and which guarantees freedom of conscience and a free profession and practice of religion.

From the wording of the Preamble to the Constitution it is clear that the Christian religion is one of the religions protected from insult by the constitutional crime of blasphemy. But the Jewish religion would also appear to be protected as it seems quite clear that the purpose of the fifth amendment to the Constitution was certainly not to weaken the position of the Jewish congregations in Ireland but to bring out the universal nature of the constitutional guarantees of freedom of religion. What then is the position of the Muslim religion? Or of polytheistic religions such as Hinduism? Would the constitutional guarantees of equality before the law and of the free profession and practice of religion be respected if one citizen's religion enjoyed constitutional protection from insult but another's did not? ...

[I]n the absence of any legislative definition of the constitutional offence of blasphemy, it is impossible to say of what the offence of blasphemy consists. As the Law Reform Commission has pointed out neither the *actus reus* nor the *mens rea* is clear. The task of defining the crime is one for the legislature, not for the courts. In the absence of legislation and in the present uncertain state of the law the Court could not see its way to authorising the institution of a criminal prosecution for blasphemy against the respondents. [1999] 4 IR 484, at 500–502.

[8–26] Barrington J then considered the cartoon in question and concluded that it was not blasphemous. This judgment has been criticised by Cox:

> This is a problematic conclusion for a number of reasons. First, the court concluded that it was unable to give definition to the crime of blasphemy, yet it had already referred to the definition given in Murdoch's *Dictionary of Irish Law*, without any suggestion that the definition therein offered was deficient. It is unclear why, having been cited with apparent approval it was then rejected. Secondly, the court *was* able to conclude that this particular cartoon *was not* blasphemous—a curious feat if the *actus reus* of the crime could not be defined.

Most importantly, Barrington J. was essentially announcing that the Court would not apply a constitutional clause where interpretation of the wording of that clause posed conceptual problems. This is, however, an unusual admission for a Supreme Court, charged with the interpretation of the constitution to make....

It might be argued in defence of the Supreme Court that the basis for the decision was a respect for the constitutionally required separation of the powers of government. After all, Article 40.6.1(i) refers to blasphemy being a crime punishable *by law* and under Article 15 of the Constitution, the legislature is deemed to be the sole lawmaking body in the state. This, however, is the basis for the final major criticism of the case, namely that such reluctance to judicial activism is entirely inconsistent with the traditional approach of the Supreme Court. Article 40.3.3. of the Constitution, for example, protects the right to life of the unborn (in terms far vaguer than those used in the straightforward blasphemy clause) and requires that the state respect and vindicate that right *through its laws*. Yet the Irish High and Supreme Courts have used this clause to resolve intricate problems in respect of abortion, covering issues of travel, information and the practice of abortion itself. Similarly, from a silent Constitution the court has found a right to have a feeding tube removed from a patient in a near permanent vegetative state, thereby allowing her to die.... Why, with such a history of activism behind it, the Supreme Court suddenly felt the need to defer to the law making power of the legislature in respect of arguably one of the clearest phrases in the constitution is uncertain.

It might be suggested that the difference between these situations and the blasphemy case, is that in respect of the latter what is at issue is the use of criminal sanction and that the Supreme Court quite rightly does not want to create crimes, preferring to leave this to the legislature. This argument, however, ignores the obvious fact that it is the constitution that has created the crime and the court is merely required to apply this aspect of criminal law, just as it is asked to apply corresponding statutory provisions of criminal law. If this scenario is unusual as a matter of constitutional interpretation it is because, being the only constitutional crime, there is no analogous situation available.

It may well be that blasphemy as a crime should not exist at Irish law, being an unwarranted restriction on the right to freedom of expression.... This, however, is not the point. The people endorsed a constitution that *did* require that blasphemy be a crime. The courts, as guardians of the Constitution are bound to enforce the terms of that constitution without fear or favour and in a spirit of political and social independence. The failure of the Supreme Court to do so in *Corway*, on the grounds that a constitutional term was of uncertain definition, was passive judicial activism in stark form and amounted to a subtle yet telling attack on the grounding principles of constitutional democracy. Neville, Cox, "Constitutional Law-Constitutional Interpretation-Passive Judicial Activism-Constitutional Crime of Blasphemy" (2000) 22 *DULJ* 21.

Freedom of Assembly

The courts have not considered the meaning of this provision in any case in which it was in issue. [8–27]

Freedom of Association

This is the last of the three political freedoms guaranteed by Art 40.6.1°. It is explicitly a guarantee to form both associations and unions, a particular form of association. While most of the case law (and all the early case law) involved trades unions, the guarantee has also been invoked in relation to political parties and—more recently—sports clubs. Specific doctrinal issues have arisen as to whether the guarantee protects certain activities incidental to the association itself and the legitimate bases on which freedom of association can be restricted. Before considering these, however, it is helpful to examine how the freedom has been interpreted in different contexts. [8–28]

Trade Unions

[8–29] The guarantee has been considered in a number of cases involving the membership of trade unions, where workers have sought to assert rights to leave unions, join a different union or work without being a member of a particular union. In *Murphy v Stewart* [1973] IR 97, the plaintiff sought to leave the National Union of Vehicle Builders (NUVB) in order to join the Irish Transport and General Workers Union (ITGWU). The ITGWU would have accepted the plaintiff as a member, but the NUVB refused to consent to the plaintiff leaving its union in order to join the ITGWU; as a result, the plaintiff could not—under the rules of the Irish Congress of Trade Unions—be accepted as a member of the ITGWU. In the High Court, Murnaghan J held that the actions of the NUVB violated the constitutional right of the plaintiff to join the union of his choice. However, this decision was overturned on appeal. Walsh J, with whom the other members of the Court agreed, reasoned:

> In the ordinary sense, there is no constitutional right to join the union of one's choice. The constitutional guarantee is the guarantee to form associations or unions, but in ordinary circumstances before a person can join an existing union or association he must be entitled to do so either by law, or by the rules of that association or union, or by the consent of its members. This is, broadly speaking, the effect of the decision in *Tierney v Amalgamated Society of Woodworkers* [1959] IR 254; but it is not a completely unqualified statement of the constitutional position. It has been submitted in this Court on behalf of the plaintiff, and not really contested by the defendants, that among the unspecified personal rights guaranteed by the Constitution is the right to work; I accept that proposition. The question of whether that right is being infringed or not must depend upon the particular circumstances of any given case; if the right to work was reserved exclusively to members of a trade union which held a monopoly in this field and the trade union was abusing the monopoly in such a way as to effectively prevent the exercise of a person's constitutional right to work, the question of compelling that union to accept the person concerned into membership (or, indeed, of breaking the monopoly) would fall to be considered for the purpose of vindicating the right to work. That, however, is not the position in the present case and it is unnecessary to devote further attention to that topic. [1973] IR 97, at 117–118.

If the Court had ordered that the plaintiff be allowed to join the ITGWU, the members of that union would have been forced to associate with someone with whom they did not wish to associate. If freedom of association is to be fully protected, it seems to require that people also be free to dissociate. This point had been clarified in an earlier case.

[8–30] In *Educational Company of Ireland v Fitzpatrick* [1961] IR 345, the defendants were members of a trade union and most of them worked for the plaintiff. They went on strike and picketed the plaintiffs' premises with a view to forcing the plaintiff to require its other workers to join the union. An issue arose as to the constitutionality of ss 2 and 3 of the Trade Disputes Act 1906, which effectively authorised such picketing where there was a trade dispute, as defined in the Act. A majority of the Supreme Court found for the plaintiff. Kingsmill Moore J reasoned:

> The first step in the constitutional argument of the plaintiffs was an attempt to show that the Constitution guaranteed the right of citizens not to join associations or unions if they did not so desire, and the right not to be coerced into so joining. The Constitution does not give such a guarantee in express terms, but I think it does so by necessary implication.

> The right to express freely convictions and opinions, guaranteed by Article 40.6.1°(i), must include the right to hold such convictions and opinions and the right not to be forced to join a union or association professing, forwarding, and requiring its members to subscribe to contrary opinions. The undertaking in Article 40.3.2°, to protect the property rights of every citizen may perhaps include an undertaking to protect his right to dispose of his labour as he wills, and would include impliedly a right not to be forced against his will into a union or association which exacts from him a regular payment. Moreover I think a guarantee of a right to form associations and unions is only intelligible where there is an implicit right to abstain from joining such associations or unions or, to put it another way, to associate and unite with those who do not join such unions. In *National Union of Railwaymen and Others v Sullivan and Others* [1947] IR 77 Murnaghan J, giving the judgment of the Court, emphasised at 102 the constitutional right of the citizen to a free choice of the persons with whom he would associate and the decision seems to me to establish that a person shall not be coerced, at any rate by legislative action, into joining an association which he is not willing to join. Accordingly I hold that there is an implicit guarantee in the Constitution that citizens shall not be coerced to join associations or unions against their will. [1961] IR 345, at 395–396.

Maguire CJ dissented reasoning that the defendants were associating together and taking actions—permitted by the 1906 Act—to strengthen their association. This difference of approach as between Kingsmill Moore J and Maguire CJ identifies a fundamental disagreement as to the meaning and purpose of the association guarantee. If the association guarantee is intended as a strong guarantee of trade union activity, it would probably permit of the tactics employed by the Educational Company. The actual strength of unions would be more important that the freedom of individuals. In contrast, if the association guarantee is intended as a strong protection of individual freedom, the freedom of dissociation must trump the needs of a strong union. The majority clearly endorsed this latter view. [8–31]

Having established that the freedom of association included a freedom of dissociation, Kingsmill Moore J proceeded to address the generally important issue of when that freedom could be said to have been interfered with. For there was no rule or statement of law preventing the employees from dissociating. Rather they were being put under pressure to join the Union. Kingsmill Moore J's comments on this point, therefore, have application to other situations where the State (or, indeed, private parties) act not through clear legal statements but rather through pressure. Kingsmill Moore J stated the point as follows: [8–32]

> I have used the word "coerced" (which does not appear in the Constitution) and it is necessary to explain the sense in which I use that word, and also to indicate the nature of the coercion which the law may restrain as violating the exercise of the rights granted by the Constitution. I am unable to accept the view of Lord Watson that a person cannot properly be said to be coerced if, having two courses open to him, he follows the course which he considers conducive to his own interests. Coercion to my mind consists in forcing a person by action or threat of action to do or abstain from doing something which he is unwilling to do or abstain from doing, and which, but for such action or threats of action, he would not do or abstain from doing. Attempted coercion is the attempt (which may not be successful) by action or threat of action to produce a similar result. If a highwayman presents a pistol to my head and says, "Your money or your life," he attempts to coerce me, though he gives me a choice of two courses. I may, indeed, adopt a heroic attitude and say, "Shoot away," but, if discretion or pusillanimity prevail and I disgorge my money, it seems to me idle to say that I have not been coerced into so

doing. Similarly if I give money to a blackmailer, under threat of exposure, I may properly be said to have been coerced.

It seems to me that any form of pressure which compels me to act in a way in which I would not have acted but for such pressure is a form of coercion and any such pressure designed to deprive me of a right given me by the Constitution is against the spirit of the Constitution; but certain forms of pressure do not come within the province of the law to restrain. Unpopularity or social ostracism may be coercive to prevent me from exercising a right guaranteed to me, but the law has no concern with them, nor will it, in general, interfere with economic pressure exercised by another person in pursuance of his own legitimate interests. The Constitution guarantees my right to join an association, no matter how extreme its tenets may be, provided it is not illegal. Nevertheless my membership may involve me in unpopularity, loss of friendship, social ostracism, all designed to make me forgo my right. An employer may hesitate to engage me anticipating that my membership will cause trouble. These forms of pressure may coerce me to resign my membership against my desires, but they are not restrainable by the law.

It is a very different matter when the Legislature intervenes to authorise or facilitate coercion by attempting to legalise acts, directed to that end, which previously were illegal and restrainable. [1961] IR 396–397.

[8–33] Kingsmill Moore J is surely correct to hold that coercion does not imply an absence of choice. It should not be possible to pressurise people unduly into not exercising their constitutional rights. However, once one concedes this point, it becomes difficult to identify the dividing line between legitimate and illegitimate pressure. Many factors are relevant to the decisions that one makes. Not every factor that might encourage one not to exercise a constitutional right should be characterised as illegitimate pressure or unconstitutional coercion. That said, the campaign of picketing in this instance appears to have been sufficiently serious as to qualify as coercion.

[8–34] In *Meskell v CIE* [1973] IR 121, the Supreme Court followed *Education Company of Ireland* in awarding damages to the plaintiffs for actionable conspiracy where the defendant agreed with its unions to terminate the contracts of all employees and offer re-employment only on the condition that the worker join and remain in one of the unions.

[8–35] In a number of cases, the courts have derived from Art 40.6.1°(iii) a right to fair procedures on the part of union members. In *Rodgers v ITGWU* [1978] ILRM 51, the defendant had advertised a meeting for workers concerning wages. However, the advertisement did not state that the meeting would consider a proposal for compulsory retirement at the age of 65. The plaintiff—who was approaching that age—was late for the meeting and missed the discussion on the retirement proposal. Finlay P observed that *Education Company of Ireland* had established a right to join or not join a union. A necessary corollary of this right was a right to participate in the democratic process provided by the union and in particular to take part in its decision-making process within the rules of that trade union. Finlay P held that the plaintiff had not had adequate notice of the meeting; however, there had also been a subsequent meeting of which he had had sufficient notice. In Finlay P's view, the courts should ensure fair procedures in this context, but should not interfere too much as the union was a sophisticated decision-making body. Given *Murphy v Stewart*, Finlay P was incorrect to state that the *Educational Company of Ireland* case established a right to join or not join a union. That case established a right to not join, but not a right to join as such a right would interfere with the freedom of association of the other members of the

Union. Given the absence of a right to join a union, it is difficult to derive a right to fair procedures from that source. If one's membership of the union depends on the free choice of other members to associate with you, perhaps the terms of one's membership are also dependent on the views of the other members. That said, it may be possible to derive the right to fair procedures from other sources, such as the general protection of fair procedures implicit in Art 40.3.1°.

In *Doyle v Croke* (1988) 7 JISLL 170, the plaintiffs complained that inadequate notice had been given of meetings at which a strike committee took a decision that—if there were a settlement—money would be distributed only to those members who had participated in the picket. Costello J followed *Rodgers* in accepting that there was right to fair procedures. He also reasoned that if the right to form unions was to be effective, it had to include the right of a member to be protected from internal procedures that might be unfair to them. As such, notice of the meeting should have been given to each member (the notice here had only been pinned up in the factory) and it should have indicated the rights of which they might be deprived. Again, however, it is unclear precisely why the right to form unions requires internal rules of fair procedures in order to be effective. Such fair procedures may be desirable but it is, at least, contentious to maintain that organisations cannot be effective unless they have fair internal procedures for their members. [8–36]

In *Dublin College ASA v City of Dublin VEC* 31 July 1981 (HC), it was held that the right to associate does not imply any duty on the part of an employer to recognise that association and negotiate. [8–37]

Political Parties

In *Loftus v Attorney General* [1979] IR 221, the Supreme Court considered the constitutionality of s 13(2) of the Electoral Act 1963 which establishes that the registrar of political parties shall register as a political party any political party that in his opinion is a genuine political party and is organised to contest a general or local election. Parties already represented in the Dáil at the time of the Act were automatically registered. The main benefit of registration was that it allowed the name of the party to appear beside the candidate's name on the ballot paper. The registrar refused to register the plaintiff's political party, "the Christian Democratic Party of Ireland." The plaintiff challenged the validity of this decision and the constitutionality of s 13(2) on several grounds. The Supreme Court, *per* O'Higgins CJ, rejected the challenge to section 13(2) based on Article 40.6.1°(iii) on the following grounds: [8–38]

> It seems proper and in the public interest to regulate such statutory rights and facilities as are given by this legislation. If some control and regulation were not provided, genuine political action might be destroyed by a proliferation of bogus front organisations calling themselves political parties but with aims and objects far removed from the political sphere. [1979] IR 221, at 242.

This decision has been strenuously criticised by Hogan and Whyte:

> [N]o serious public interest is capable of being served by the ponderous machinery of a "Register" of parties just to control and restrict the use of party labels on ballot papers. A restriction such as to exclude labels that are confusing, offensive or prolix could easily be

defended as being in the interest of order; but what business is it of the State's if a candidate, being a member of a tiny localised group of eccentrics, or even of a "bogus front organisation", chooses to offer himself for election under a grandiloquent party title? The Supreme Court's apprehension that without such control "genuine political action might be destroyed" seems a small compliment to the discernment of the electorate, and to overestimate its susceptibility to fine words. Gerard Hogan and Gerry Whyte eds, *Kelly: The Irish Constitution* (4th ed, LexisNexis Butterworths, Dublin, 2003), at [7.5.197].

Sports Clubs

[8–39] In *O'Donohoe v Ó Baróid*, 23 April 1999 (HC), McCracken J followed *Murphy* in holding that there was no constitutional right to join a sports club. In the conjoined cases of *Equality Authority v Portmarnock Golf Club* and *Portmarnock Golf Club v Ireland* [2005] IEHC 235, the High Court considered the correct interpretation and constitutionality of s 8 of the Equal Status Act 2000. The golf club had a rule that all its members would be gentlemen. The Equality Authority took a case under s 8 of the Act, seeking a declaration that the club was a "discriminating club" within the meaning of the Act. The effect of such a declaration was that the club could lose its club licence which in turn would prevent the club from selling intoxicating liquor on its premises. The District Court had concluded that the club was a discriminating club. The club appealed this ruling by way of case stated and also instituted separate proceedings that in effect challenged the constitutionality of s 8 of the Equal Status Act should the club be found to be in breach of it. O'Higgins J allowed the club's appeal, reasoning that it benefited from an exception in the Act which provided that a club would not be a discriminating club if its principal purpose was to cater for persons of a particular gender. O'Higgins J held that the principal purpose of the club was to cater for the needs of male golfers.

[8–40] However, O'Higgins J also considered the club's constitutional challenge. Although *obiter*, his comments provide further guidance as to the meaning of Art 40.6.1°(iii). O'Higgins J rejected the club's argument that s 8 of the Act (if it applied to the club) amounted to an unconstitutional coercion of the club's members to associate in a particular way:

> In my view the provisions of the Equal Status Act 2000 do not amount to actions authorising or facilitating coercion in relation to the right of freedom of association. The members' right to associate with each other is unchanged. The right to carry on the main activities of the Club is not affected by the legislation. The right to exclude women from membership is unchanged. The restrictions which would be imposed on the Club by an interpretation other than that contended for by the Golf Club would not strike at the core of freedom of association but would constitute a permissible control and regulation in the public interest of an ancillary activity of the Club. This is still true even if the deprivation of what is loosely termed a Club licence and what have been called the "naming and shaming" provisions are regarded as sanctions, a point which I do not have to decide. The restrictions on activities in this case are—if not peripheral—at least incidental to the purposes of the Club in marked contrast to the regulation held to be permissible in the *PMPS v Moore* and the *Aughey v Attorney General* cases where regulations which impinged on essential purposes of the associations were involved.
>
> The activity prohibited *ie* the holding of what is termed a Club licence—is not a primary or core activity of the Club, and it has not been argued otherwise. Likewise no argument was advanced as to necessity, or even the advantages on a financial level of

holding such a Club licence. The right of association is a constitutionally protected right but the right to hold a social Club licence is not. The right to hold such a licence is dependant on the existing statutory regime.

In my view a statute such as the Equal Status Act 2000—even if it were to have the effect of depriving the golf Club of its Club licence in circumstances contemplated by section 8 of the Equal Status Act 2000—could not be said to be contrary to the constitutionally protected right of association unless its provisions were unjustified as being disproportionate to the goals of the legislation. No such argument has been pursued in this case.

[8–41] In *Educational Company of Ireland*, the coercion involved the picketing of the employer's premises. The alleged coercion in *Portmarnock Golf Club* was the withdrawal of the facility to sell alcohol; this was clearly of a different order, although its intention was presumably to encourage clubs to cease to be "discriminating clubs". This again raises the question of where the dividing line lies between legitimate coercions (gentle encouragement) and illegitimate coercions. Perhaps it depends, as Higgins J, suggests on how closely it impacts on the core activity of the association. Following this line of reasoning, it would presumably—absent sufficient justification—be unconstitutional to prohibit a discriminating club from playing golf. Would it be unconstitutional to prohibit a discriminating club from participating in inter-club competitions?

Restrictions on Freedom of Association

[8–42] An issue arises on account of the way in which Art 40.6 authorises two different bases for the restriction of the right of freedom of association. The first sentence guarantees liberty for the exercise of the right, subject to public order and morality. However, Art 40.6.1°(iii) itself states that exercise of the right can be regulated and controlled in the public interest. Two textual points emerge: on the one hand, the latter restriction appears broader as it refers generally to the "public interest" as distinct from "public order or morality". On the other hand, the latter restriction may be narrower in that it only permits *regulation* of the exercise of the right, whereas the former restriction may imply that – where public order and morality so require—there may be no liberty for the exercise of the right at all.

[8–43] These points were made by the Supreme Court at a relatively early stage. In *NUR v Sullivan* [1947] IR 77, the Court, *per* Murnaghan J, struck down s 26 of the Trade Union Act 1941 which set up a tribunal to determine which unions would be allowed to organise in relation to which trades:

> There is no doubt that a law may be made dealing with the exercise of the right of forming associations and unions if that law can properly be called a law regulating the exercise of such right.
>
> Similarly a law may be made dealing with the exercise of the right of forming associations and unions if that law can properly be called a control of the exercise of the right.... The Trade Union Act, 1941, moreover, does not prohibit all association, but it purports to limit the right of the citizen to join one or more prescribed associations, *ie* the Union or Unions in respect of which a determination has been made. Any such limitation does undoubtedly deprive the citizen of a free choice of the persons with whom he shall associate. Both logically and practically, to deprive a person of the choice of the persons with whom he will associate, is not a control of the exercise of the right of association, but a denial of the right altogether. It was stressed, in argument, that control, in the public

interest, was given to the Oireachtas and that such control might extend to depriving the citizen of all freedom of choice of his associates, provided he could join a prescribed association for the particular object. The Constitution states the right of the citizens to form associations or unions in an emphatic way, and it seems impossible to harmonise this language with a law which prohibits the forming of associations and unions, and allows the citizen only to join prescribed associations and unions.

In the opinion of this Court, a law which takes away the right of the citizens, at their choice, to form associations and unions, not contrary to public order or morality, is not a law which can validly be made under the Constitution, and Part III of the Trade Union Act, 1941, is, in its main principles, repugnant to the Constitution. [1947] IR 77, at 101–102.

[8–44] Given the differences between the public order and morality ground, on the one hand, and the public interest ground, on the other hand, there is some textual justification for the Supreme Court's approach to this issue. However, it may be that the Court paid too close attention to the text. The courts have generally been quick to conclude that constitutional rights may be limited. In respect of other constitutional provisions, such as Art 40.1, where specific grounds of restriction are identified, the courts have not limited the grounds of restriction to those explicitly stated in the text.

[8–45] The Supreme Court adopted the *NUR v Sullivan* distinction in *PMPS v Attorney General* [1983] IR 339. Section 5 of the Industrial and Provident Societies Act 1978 provided that the plaintiff—and others—were not to accept or hold deposits after a period of five years after the enactment of the Act. This was challenged on a number of grounds. Under Art 40.6.1°(iii), the plaintiff alleged that this amounted to a complete frustration of the purpose for the association. The Supreme Court rejected this argument, accepting the *NUR* distinction between prohibitions on association and regulation of the exercise of association. The law in question merely regulated what the association could do; it did not impact on the association. Accordingly, it could be and was justified by reference to the general public interest. This decision highlights the tension introduced into the case law as a result of *NUR v Sullivan*. In *Educational Company of Ireland*, Kingsmill Moore J had considered that the picketing amounted to an unconstitutional interference with the freedom to dissociate. In *PMPS*, however, a legislative restriction that would have had the effect of forcing PMPS into liquidation (*ie* forced dissociation) was deemed not to be an abrogation of the liberty to associate but merely an interference with the exercise of that liberty. It is *NUR v Sullivan* that requires these distinctions to be drawn. If the public interest (as distinct from public order and morality) were sufficient justification to prohibit some associations, then it would not have been necessary in *PMPS* to characterise coerced dissociation as a mere regulation of association.

[8–46] In *Aughey v Ireland* [1989] ILRM 87, two detective Gardaí felt that they were not adequately represented by either the Garda Representative Association or the Association of Garda Sergeants and Inspectors. Section 1 of the Garda Síochána Act 1977 imposed limits on the freedom of Gardaí to form representative associations where the objects of the association were to control or influence the pay, pensions or conditions of service of any police force. Accordingly, the plaintiffs sought the permission of the Garda Commissioner to form their own union. The Commissioner refused permission. In the Supreme Court, Walsh J upheld both the decision and the legislation on which it was based. He characterised the restriction on association as not being a prohibition but rather as being a regulation: associations could be formed, just not if their object was to control or influence pay, etc. Accordingly, it could be justified by reference to general public interest concerns. Walsh J also interpreted Art 40.6.1° as meaning that if there was "no threat to public order or to public morality there [was] a guaranteed right to form associations and unions". [1989] ILRM 87, at 91. He expressly rejected an invitation to overrule *NUR v Sullivan* as it was unnecessary to do so for the purposes of deciding the case, as the law in issue was a regulation not a prohibition. Although Walsh J was correct to characterise the law in question as a regulation, it is questionable whether it is acceptable to regulate a union in a manner that prevents it from representing its members in relation to pay and conditions. Arguably, a union is a specific type of association and the express protection of the freedom to form unions implies a freedom to undertake the tasks characteristic of a union. This argument is explored further below.

In *Portmarnock Golf Club*, it appears that O'Higgins J implicitly rejected the *NUR* line of authority. The Club argued that s 8 of the Equal Status Act 2000, if it operated against the Club, amounted to a restriction on the membership decision and not just a restriction on the exercise of association. Accordingly, the Club argued, it could only be justified by reference to public order or morality, and not by reference to the general public interest. O'Higgins J rejected this argument: [8–47]

> There is no basis in either the structure or the language of the Article for the contention that there are separate aspects of the exercise of the right to association, firstly the membership decision, untrammelled by considerations other than those of public order or morality, and secondly, the activities of the Club, to which additional considerations apply. Both the "subject to public order and morality" proviso, and the provision allowing for the regulation and control of the right are expressed to be in relation to "the exercise of the foregoing right" *ie* the right to form associations. A proper reading of the provision specifically allows for the enactment of laws regulating the exercise of the right of association itself and not merely the activities in which the association engages.

This decision cannot be reconciled with *NUR v Sullivan*. Whereas the Supreme Court in *NUR v Sullivan* focused on the fact that the very liberty to exercise the right could be restricted by public order and morality, O'Higgins J overlooks the word "liberty" and focuses instead on the fact that the concept of exercise of the right is common to both restrictions. On a close textual reading, *NUR v Sullivan* would appear to be correct. However, the outcome reached by O'Higgins J would both avoid the sorts of distinction raised by *Aughey* and render Art 40.6 more consistent with other constitutional provisions, where general aspects of the common good are always allowed to justify restrictions of rights. [8–48]

Indeed O'Higgins J also noted the general proposition of constitutional law that it is not necessary for the Constitution explicitly to authorise derogations from a right in order for such derogations to be permissible. Even if restrictions on association decisions could only be justified by reference to public order or morality, it is arguable that the promotion of equality is an aspect of public morality.

The Extent of the Freedom

These cases implicitly raise another issue that has not received that much attention: to what extent does Art 40.6.1°(iii) protect other freedoms that are incidental to the core [8–49] freedom of association. As noted above, in *Doyle v Croke* (1988) 7 JSILL 170, Costello J suggested that for the freedom of association to be effective it should not be construed restrictively. In that case, he held that a member of a union was entitled to fair procedures in relation to the conduct of a strike. However, Costello J did not suggest that the freedom of association guaranteed a right to strike. Nevertheless, the proposition that the freedom of association guarantees other incidental freedoms—necessary in order to make the core freedom effective—is an interesting one.

[8–50] As noted above, in *Irish Times Ltd v Ireland* [1998] 1 IR 359, Barrington J held that for freedom of expression to be effective, a journalist would have to be able to write about facts as well as opinions. He compared this with the freedoms of assembly and association:

> [I]t would be absurd to suggest that the press enjoys constitutional protection under Article 40.6.1°(i) when criticising government policy but not when reporting the facts on which its criticism is based.
>
> The sister rights guaranteed by Article 40.6.1° are the right of the citizens "to assemble peaceably and without arms" and the right of the citizens "to form associations and unions" but it would be absurd to suggest that the right of the citizens "to assemble peaceably and without arms" guaranteed the right of the citizens to assemble but not their right actually to hold a meeting or that the right of the citizens "to form associations and unions" guaranteed the right of the citizens to "form" associations but not their right to manage or run them for any particular purpose. Likewise it seems to me absurd to suggest that the constitutional right of the citizens to express freely their convictions and opinions does not also protect, subject to constitutional exceptions, their right to state facts. In this context it is important to remember that we are construing, not a revenue statute, but a constitution. [1998] 1 IR 359, at 406.

[8–51] Barrington J suggested that Art 40.6.1°(iii) extends to a right to "manage or run" associations (and unions) "for any particular purpose". The emphasis in this proposition, however, must rest on the phrase "manage or run" rather than "for any particular purpose". There is no reason in principle to suppose that the freedom of association confers a right to pursue purposes which would otherwise be illegal. However, there is reason in principle to suppose that the freedom of association should allow effective association, provided that the purpose is legal. Put another way, provided that an activity is in itself lawful (such as golf), people should prima facie be allowed to be associate together—on their own terms—to pursue that activity. Where an activity is unlawful if performed by an individual (such as murder or the violent overthrow of the State), there is no reason why even prima facie constitutional protection should be obtained simply because two or more people associate together to achieve that objective.

[8–52] This general position is subject to the caveat that Art 40.6.1°(iii) protects both associations in general and unions. Unions are a particular type of association dedicated to a particular purpose (broadly speaking, the protection of workers' interests). The explicit protection for unions must count as implicit protection for at least some of their purposes. This suggests that some activity that would be unlawful if conducted by an individual may have constitutional protection if conducted by a Union. What purposes of unions obtain prima facie constitutional protection is another matter, but there do at least seem to be grounds for arguing that there is a constitutional right to strike.

This line of reasoning points to a slightly different resolution of the issues in *PMPS* [8–53] and *Aughey*. It is unlawful—generally speaking—to accept and hold deposits. Individuals cannot be banks. There was thus no interference—not even *prima facie*—with PMPS's freedom of association. The freedom to associate does not imply a freedom to undertake activity as an association that would be unlawful if undertaken as an individual. The position with unions, however, is different. Accordingly, it is difficult to support Walsh J's assertion that the restriction at issue in *Aughey* was a regulation of purposes rather than a restriction of association. The first sentence of Art 40.6.1° guarantees liberty specifically for the formation of associations with worker protection objectives. If this is correct, the result in *Aughey* could then only be achieved by accepting O'Higgins J's view in *Portmarnock Golf Club* that the very liberty of association itself can be restricted on the basis of the general public interest, and not just on the basis of public order and morality. For the reasons explored above, this would be a welcome development.

If the courts were to adopt this schema, the final point turns again on the question of [8–54] coercion. In line with *Educational Company of Ireland* and *Portmarnock Golf Club*, if an activity is lawful if carried out by an individual, it would amount to an unconstitutional restriction of the freedom of association if that activity were to be made unlawful (or radically unappealing) when performed by an association of people. Drawing the line between acceptable and unacceptable coercion remains difficult.

CONTENTS – CHAPTER 9

Family and Education

Introduction	[9–01]
Marital Families and Recognition for Other Types of Family Unit	[9–05]
Definition of "Marriage" and "Family"	[9–05]
Legislative Recognition of Non-Marital Families	[9–11]
The Right to Marry	[9–25]
The Rights of Married Couples and Families	[9–30]
Family Rights	[9–30]
Rights of Married Couples	[9–32]
The Position of Non-Marital Families	[9–33]
The Limits of Art 41	[9–33]
Alternative Means of Constitutional Protection	[9–35]
Standing of Non-Nationals to Invoke Arts 41 and 42	[9–42]
Derivative Rights to Reside in Ireland	[9–46]
The Right of a Child Citizen to Reside in the State	[9–51]
The Child Citizen's Right to the Care and Companionship of her Parents in the State	[9–54]
Species of Common Good that can Override the Right	[9–56]
Woman's Life Within the Home	[9–62]
Legitimising Discrimination by Reference to Art 41.2	[9–63]
Attempts to Expand Art 41.2	[9–65]
Proposals for Change	[9–69]
The Autonomy of Married Couples	[9–70]
Children's Rights and Family Autonomy	[9–73]
Children's Rights	[9–73]
Parental Autonomy in the Custody Context	[9–76]
Parental Autonomy in the Health Context	[9–86]
Parental Autonomy in the Education Context	[9–102]
Primary Education	[9–114]
The Meaning of (Primary) Education	[9–114]
Parental Choice in Primary Education	[9–124]
At Risk Children	[9–127]

Overview

Articles 41 and 42 of the Constitution protect family and education rights. The courts have limited the protection of Art 41 to families based on the institution of opposite sex marriage. The courts have recognised a right to marry but this right is limited to opposite sex couples. However, the courts have recognised certain rights for members of non-marital families under Art 40.3 of the Constitution. The courts have recognised a far stronger set of rights for non-marital mothers than for non-marital fathers. The courts have emphasised that the rights contained in Arts 41 and 42 derive from the natural law leading the courts to allow a wide range of foreign nationals invoke those rights where the foreign nationals concerned have some connection with Ireland.

The courts have recognised that Irish citizens have a limited right to have their family members reside with them within the State. Initially, the courts interpreted this right in a strong way. However, the courts have now held that the right is no more than a procedural entitlement that the Minister for Justice consider the family relationship and the rights of the child when making any deportation decision. Factors of the common good, including maintenance of the asylum system, justify restrictions of the right. Somewhat controversially, Art 41.2 recognises the role played by women in the home. The courts have relied on this provision principally to uphold legislation that discriminates against husbands and fathers in favour of mothers.

The courts have strongly upheld the autonomy of married couples, holding unconstitutional legislation that might interfere with decisions jointly made by spouses. The courts have also strongly upheld the autonomy of marital families, protecting from State intervention the decisions of parents over their children in the contexts of custody, health and education. Art 42.4 guarantees a right to free primary education. This right has been interpreted to include education for those with considerable learning difficulties. However, the right is time-limited and expires when the child reaches the age of 18. The courts have also fashioned case law that requires the State to step in and assist vulnerable children where their parents have failed.

CHAPTER 9

Family and Education

Introduction

Articles 41 and 42 of the Constitution, dealing with the family and education, are among the most contentious provisions of the Constitution. They reflect a natural law understanding of civil society, proper family units and parental autonomy that is—at the very least—not as widely shared today as it was in 1937. As a result, many arguments about what sort of country Ireland should be take place within the context of Arts 41 and 42. [9–01]

In *Northwestern Health Board v HW* [2001] 3 IR 622, at 686–687 Keane CJ considered the natural law ethos of Arts 41 and 42: [9–02]

> Article 41.1 acknowledges the primary role of the family in society. In philosophic terms, it existed as a unit in human society before other social units and, in particular, before the unit of the State itself. The philosophical origins of the modern system of democracy are to be found in the beliefs of Locke and Rousseau that civil government is the result of a contract between the people and their rulers: the family existed before that unit and enjoys rights which, in the hierarchy of rights posited by the Constitution, are superior to those which are the result of the positive laws created by the State itself. As the trial judge noted, this is an express recognition by the framers of the Constitution of the natural law theory of human rights, but the belief that the family occupies that philosophic status in contrast to the role of the State is by no means confined to those thinkers who subscribe to that particular philosophy.
>
> What is beyond argument is that the emphatic language used by the Constitution in Article 41 reflects the Christian belief that the greatest of human virtues is love which, in its necessarily imperfect human form, reflects the divine love of the creator for all his creation. Of the various forms which human love can take, the love of parents for their children is the purest and most protective, at least in that period of their development when they are so dependant on, and in need of, that love and protection. I believe that Article 41, although couched in the language of "rights", should not be seen as denying the truth to be derived from the experience of life itself, that parents do not pause to think of their "rights" as against the State, still less as against their children, but rather of the responsibilities which they joyfully assume for their children's happiness and welfare, however difficult the discharge of those responsibilities may be in the sorrows and difficulties almost inseparable from the development of every human being. The rights acknowledged in Article 41 are both the rights of the family as an institution, and the rights of its individual members, which also are guaranteed in Article 42, under the heading "Education", and which also derive protection from other articles of the Constitution, most notably Article 40.3.
>
> Again, the Article speaks, not of the authority of parents, but of the authority of the family. While the family, because it derives from the natural order and is not the creation of civil society, does not, either under the Constitution or positive law, take the form of a juristic entity, it is endowed with an authority which the Constitution recognises as being

superior even to the authority of the State itself. While there may inevitably be tensions between laws enacted by the State for the common good of society as a whole and the unique status of the family within that society, the Constitution firmly outlaws any attempt by the State in its laws or its executive actions to usurp the exclusive and privileged role of the family in the social order.

Contrast this with the views of Denham J expressed in the same case [2001] 3 IR 622, at 718:

> The fact that the family is the fundamental unit group of society is a constitutional principle. Whatever historical origin or origins may be given for this principle it is a principle of the Constitution. In this case the family is one recognised and protected by the Constitution. The responsibility and authority of the family is exercised by the defendants. The child is a member of the family and has the benefit of being a part of that unit. The child is the responsibility of the parents. The rights of the parents in exercising their responsibility are not absolute; the child has personal constitutional rights. The child has rights both as part of the unit of the family and as an individual. Legislation has long recognised the welfare of the child as paramount.

[9–03] The views of Keane CJ and Denham J are markedly different. Whereas Keane CJ viewed the primacy of the family as stemming from the fact that the family pre-existed civil society—its existence and primacy is thus recognised by the Constitution. In contrast, Denham J viewed the primacy of the family as being established by the Constitution—a fact of positive law. Although one might think that a person committed to the former natural law view might be slower to countenance State intervention in the family than a person committed to the positivists' view, that has not transpired to be the case, as the decisions in *NWHB* itself (discussed below) make clear.

The natural law ethos also pervades Art 42. Glendenning has explained this influence as follows:

> In Ireland in the 1920s, the Catholic Social Movement presented an alternative to socialism in Europe and this movement gradually grew in importance prior to 1937. The Papal encyclical *Quadragesima Anno* (1931) viewed State activity in education with suspicion, and promulgated the principle of subsidiarity which perceives the State as playing a restricted role in family life and in the education of children. This doctrine became one of the main principles of Catholic social teaching which later emerged as a political doctrine. While the Catholic Church states that it does not contest the educational role of the State in relation to its citizens, it clearly views such role as subsidiary; its duty being to protect the rights of the child only in cases of parental default, incapacity or misconduct. These principles became the upholding pillars of Articles 42 and 44 as the system of education envisaged would be a State-aided system in which the State's role would be subsidiary and the family/parents would be the primary educators. (Dympna Glendenning, *Education and the Law* (Butterworths, Dublin, 1999), at [3.22].)

[9–04] An approach that gives parents the primary role in relation to education ensures that the State cannot assume an overly powerful position. For instance, there is less chance of political indoctrination of the young by the State. On the other hand, some parents may be misguided as to what their children's best interests are; an approach that favours parental primacy runs the risk of vulnerable children being left behind. Much of the case law can be read as an attempt to balance these competing considerations, albeit a balance that leans far more in favour of parental primacy.

Some have argued, however, that the theory of parental primacy in education has masked a reality of religious primacy and state control. Whyte has put the matter as follows:

> However the praxis of Irish education arguably does not conform to a literal interpretation of the constitutional provisions in two significant respects. First, looking at what one may call the "Catholic" strand of these provisions, the Family rarely exercised its right and duty to educate directly through the parents; in the majority of cases it was happy to assign this responsibility to schools controlled by religious interests who did not involve parents in the management structures. This, while not necessarily unconstitutional, gave rise to a situation which is not easily reconciled with a literal reading of Article 42 which, after all, does not even refer to the position of the school owners. Furthermore, despite the apparently subordinate role allocated to the State by the Constitution, the system actually developed in a very centralised manner.... Thus, in practice, parents ended up at the base of a pyramidal structure whose other constituent parts were the State and school-owners. Gerry Whyte, "Education and the Constitution: Convergence of Paradigm and Praxis" (1990–1992) 25–27 *Ir Jur* 69, at 69–70.

Articles 41 and 42 specifically deal with the position of women/mothers in the family as well as the position of children within the family unit. Men/fathers are not specifically identified. Flynn has commented on this absence of specific references to men:

> The text of the Constitution says less directly about men than it does about women. While the Articles which provide that rights relating to the franchise and to citizenship are to be extended without discrimination on grounds of sex apply equally to men and to women, there is no counterpart in the Constitution of the provisions which contain a vision of women's contribution to society or which specify certain categories of women, such as widows, who are to be the special objects of social protection. However, this silence does not mean that there is nothing being said by the Constitution about men. When the Constitution's text is read by the courts, it becomes apparent that a very definite paradigm of masculinity is at play within the Irish legal order. In some ways the contours of masculinity as imagined under the Constitution can be drawn in opposition to those of femininity. (Leo Flynn, "To be an Irish Man: Constructions of Masculinity in the Constitution" in Tim Murphy and Patrick Twomey eds, *Ireland's Evolving Constitution 1937–1997* (Hart, 1998), at 138.)

With this sense of the ethos of Arts 41 and 42 established, it is now possible to begin examining the specific doctrinal issues that have arisen.

Marital Families and Recognition for Other Types of Family Unit

Definition of "Marriage" and "Family"

The term "family" is not directly defined in the Constitution. However, Art 41.3 pledges the State to guard the "institution of Marriage, on which the Family is founded." This suggested at least some link between the Article 41 family and marriage. The Supreme Court considered this issue in *State (Nicolaou) v An Bord Uchtála*. Here the appellant was the unmarried father of a child. The child's mother wished to place the child for adoption. However, ss 14(1) and 16(1) of the Adoption Act 1952 effectively excluded the father from the adoption process; most importantly,

[9–05]

his consent to the adoption was not required. He challenged this exclusion, partly on the basis that his family rights under Art 41 were infringed. The Supreme Court, *per* Walsh J, rejected this argument on the basis that the unit of unmarried parents and child did not constitute a family protected by Art 41:

> It is quite clear from the provisions of Article 41, and in particular section 3 thereof, that the family referred to in this Article is the family which is founded on the institution of marriage and, in the context of the Article, marriage means valid marriage under the law for the time being in force in the State. While it is quite true that unmarried persons cohabiting together and the children of their union may often be referred to as a family and have many, if not all, of the outward appearances of a family, and may indeed for the purposes of a particular law be regarded as such, nevertheless so far as Article 41 is concerned the guarantees therein contained are confined to families based upon marriage. This, in the opinion of the Court, is of itself sufficient to render the appellant's submissions in respect of this Article of the Constitution unsustainable and the Article avails him nothing.
>
> For the same reason the mother of an illegitimate child does not come within the ambit of Articles 41 and 42 of the Constitution. Her natural right to the custody and care of her child, and such other natural personal rights as she may have (and this Court does not in this case find it necessary to pronounce upon the extent of such rights), fall to be protected under Article 40, section 3, and are not affected by Article 41 or Article 42 of the Constitution. [1966] IR 567, at 643–644.

[9–06] In this way, the Supreme Court excluded non-marital families from the protection of Art 41, while holding out the possibility of some constitutional protection for non-marital family-type relations under other constitutional provisions. This will be explored further below. *Nicolaou* clarified the restrictive character of Art 41. Although this restrictive character was unremarkable in 1937, it has become a bone of contention for many. The effects of the limitation of constitutional protection to married families are threefold: (a) it precludes unmarried families from availing themselves of protections contained in Art 41 (as Mr Nicolaou sought to do); (b) it provides constitutional authorisation for legislative discrimination against unmarried families (see *O'Brien v Stoutt* [1984] IR 316; [1985] ILRM 86, discussed below); and (c) it implicitly deems non-marital families to be less worthy of recognition than marital families.

[9–07] In 1996, the Constitution Review Group recommended that Art 41 be amended to provide, in effect, recognition for marital and non-marital families. However, in 2006 the All Party Oireachtas Committee on the Constitution recommended no change, commenting that an "amendment to extend the definition of the family would cause deep and long-lasting division in our society and would not necessarily be passed by a majority." (*The All Party Oireachtas Committee on the Constitution: 10th Progress Report: The Family*, 2006, at 122). Instead the Committee recommended primarily legislative change to improve the situation of unmarried family units. Although such an approach could deal with the practical problems caused by discrimination against non-marital families, it would leave unaffected the three issues identified above: *ie* the inability of such families to rely on Art 41, the authorisation for legislative discrimination in the future, and the implication that non-marital families are less worthy than marital families. For this reason, a purely legislative approach is likely to leave many people dissatisfied.

It is thus clear that marriage is a necessary condition for a group of persons to constitute a family unit protected by Art 41. But is it a sufficient condition? In *Murray v Ireland* [1985] IR 532, at 537, Costello J held that a married couple need not have children in order to constitute a marital family protected by Art 41. Conversely, in *G v An Bord Uchtála* [1980] IR 32, at 70 Walsh J suggested that the orphaned children of married parents constituted an Art 41 family, even after their parents' death. Therefore, provided that there was at some stage a married couple, the non-production of children and/or the subsequent death of one or both the parents do not affect the status of the unit as a constitutionally protected unit. Marriage is both a necessary and sufficient condition for constitutional protection under Art 41. [9–08]

As the definition of "family" turns on "marriage", it is of crucial importance to ascertain the meaning of "marriage". Again this term is not defined in the Constitution. In *Murphy v Attorney General* [1982] IR 241, at 286, the Supreme Court, *per* Kenny J, referred to "marriage" as a "permanent, indissoluble union of man and woman." In *N v K*, McCarthy J put the matter as follows: [9–09]

> Marriage is a civil contract which creates reciprocating rights and duties between the parties but, further, establishes a status which affects both the parties to the contract and the community as a whole. The contract is unique in that it enjoys, as an institution, a pledge by the State to guard it with special care and to protect it against attack, with a prohibition against the enactment of any law providing for the grant of a dissolution of marriage (Article 41, s. 3, of the Constitution). This constitutional prohibition emphasises the durability that is peculiar to the contract of marriage and the consequent need for a full appreciation of what that contract entails and that one is wholly free to enter into it or not. [1985] IR 733, at 754.

In *CT v DT*, Murray J somewhat altered the earlier understanding of marriage to allow for the fact that divorce was now constitutionally permissible:

> Of course society, as always, evolves and continues to evolve and there are a far greater number of committed partnerships established outside marriage than was heretofore the case. Nonetheless, marriage itself remains a solemn contract of partnership entered into between man and woman with a special status recognised by the Constitution. It is one which is entered into in principle for life. It is not entered into for a determinate period. [2003] 1 ILRM 321, at 374.

Marriage is a more complex juristic entity than is the family. Based on these dicta in the cases, there appear to be three aspects to it. First, it is a contract. Secondly, that contract is regulated by law. Thirdly, all legal regulation of marriage is ultimately subject to the Constitution. For example, prior to the removal of the constitutional ban on divorce, it would clearly have been unlawful for legislation to allow for divorce. This would not necessarily have been in breach of a particular person's rights (although a person divorced by their spouse would probably have had standing to challenge any divorce legislation); it would simply have been in breach of the Constitution for the Oireachtas to legislate for divorce. It is arguable that the same position now applies with regard to same-sex marriage. If marriage, as constitutionally defined by the courts, is the union of a man and a woman, it would be unconstitutional for the Oireachtas to legislate for gay marriage in just the same [9–10] way as it would have been unconstitutional for the Oireachtas to legislate for divorce.

Legislative Recognition of Non-Marital Families

[9–11] However, it may still be possible for the Oireachtas to provide legislative recognition (short of marriage) for non-marital families. As we have seen, the All-Party Oireachtas Committee on the Constitution recommended that legislative provision be made for non-marital family units. There is some debate as to whether this is permissible under Art 41. Although the Oireachtas has never sought to provide legislative recognition to forms of partnership other than marriage, it has traditionally provided different treatment to individuals depending on whether they are married or not. The treatment afforded to married couples has generally been better than that afforded to unmarried couples. However, occasionally tax and social welfare provisions have impacted more harshly on married couples than on unmarried couples. In a number of cases, challenges have been made to the constitutionality of legislation that affords worse treatment to married couples than to individuals who are not married. In such cases, the comparison put before the courts has been between a married couple and an unmarried couple. The principles laid down in these cases thus provide some guidance as to the constitutional limits on how well partnerships other than marriage can be legislatively treated. That said, as the cases did not involve the courts in examining a systematic partnership scheme, one needs to be careful about too readily drawing inferences from these cases to apply to the currently contentious issue of partnership recognition.

[9–12] The Income Tax Act 1967 aggregated the incomes of wife and husband in order to determine their liability for income tax. The result of this was that many married persons with two incomes paid significantly more in tax than they would have paid if they were single. In *Murphy v Attorney General* [1982] IR 241, the Supreme Court held that this system of taxation breached "the pledge of the State to guard with special care the institution of marriage and to protect it against attack". The precise reason why the provision breached Art 41 was unclear from Kenny J's reasoning and was only clarified in a later case, *Muckley v Ireland* [1985] IR 472. Immediately following *Murphy*, the Supreme Court had acceded to the State's request to limit the retrospective effect of its judgment so as to preclude people from instituting claims for the repayment of unconstitutionally levied taxes. In order to give legislative effect to this concession, the Oireachtas then enacted ss 18–21 of the Finance Act 1980. Section 21 provided for a system under which tax collected from married persons in the tax years prior to 1979/1980 would not be any less than would have been collected under the provisions struck down in *Murphy*. This went somewhat further than the concession to retroactivity allowed by the Court in *Murphy*. In *Muckley*, however, the plaintiffs sought to offset an underpayment of tax in 1979/1980 against the overpayments they had made in previous years pursuant to the legislation deemed unconstitutional in *Murphy*. The State sought to defend s 21 on the grounds that:

> [T]he new system is not an attack on the family or the institution of marriage as, being retrospective in effect, taxpayers cannot avoid the incidence of the new tax by not getting married or, in the case of married couples, by separating. Article 41 of the Constitution cannot therefore be invoked .... [1985] IR 472, at 481.

Family and Education

This gist of this argument was that Art 41 simply prohibited inducements not to marry. As the Muckleys were already married, no retrospective legislation could induce them not to marry. However, both the High Court and the Supreme Court rejected that this was the correct interpretation of Art 41. Finlay CJ, for the Supreme Court, held that such an interpretation of Art 41 misunderstood the essential basis of the *Murphy* decision: [9–13]

> Essentially the decision [in *Murphy* was] to the effect that the invalid sections penalised the married state. Section 21 of the Act of 1980 has the same effect, and does not escape invalidity merely on the basis that, though imposing an identical tax burden, the effect is retrospective and not continuing or prospective. It still contains the fatal flaw in common with the invalidated sections of imposing on the married couples to whom it applies a greater burden of taxation than that imposed on a man and woman living together outside of marriage. [1985] IR 472, at 485.

Essentially, in *Muckley* the Supreme Court held that Art 41 prohibited the penalisation of marriage, irrespective of whether that penalisation would or could induce people not to marry. This decision has been uncontroversially applied in a number of other cases: *Hyland v Minister for Social Welfare* [1989] IR 629 (discrimination against married couples in the context of unemployment benefits); *H v EHB* [1988] IR 747 (discrimination against married couples in the context of disability benefits); *Greene v Minister for Agriculture* [1990] 2 IR 17 (discrimination against married couples in the context of eligibility for headage payments). [9–14]

The position is somewhat clouded, however, by *MhicMhathúna v Ireland* [1989] IR 504 (HC); [1995] 1 IR 484. The plaintiffs questioned the constitutionality of tax legislation that provided a tax-free allowance to single parents who had a child or children living with them. The plaintiffs also challenged the constitutionality of social welfare legislation that provided an unmarried mother's allowance. This case raised similar issues to *Murphy*, *Muckley* and *Hyland*, in that it appeared that married couples were being treated less well than unmarried people. In the High Court, Carroll J rejected the plaintiffs' claims. The crucial question for present purposes is whether, in so doing, she resuscitated the inducement test that had been rejected by the Supreme Court in *Muckley*. To answer this, it is necessary to set out her reasoning in some detail: [9–15]

> The plaintiffs allege that the State has failed to protect the family and that there is an "inducement" not to get married because of the benefits given to the unmarried. The onus on the plaintiffs is to establish "a clear breach by the State of its pledge to guard with special care the institution of marriage and protect it against attack" (see *Murphy v. Attorney General* [1982] I.R. 241 per Kenny J. at page 286).
>
> In my opinion the plaintiffs have failed to discharge this onus. I find it impossible to accept that a woman would choose, in preference to marriage, to have a baby so that she could draw the unmarried mother's allowance, knowing that she could not cohabit and that she would have to qualify for the means test. I find it equally impossible to accept that an unmarried working woman would choose to have a baby outside marriage so that she could get an additional tax-free allowance which could only be claimed if she was not cohabiting. I am completely satisfied that no such inducements not to marry exist.
>
> The plaintiffs suggest that the State has made it more advantageous to be an unmarried mother than to be married with children and therefore the State has failed in its duty to protect the institution of marriage.

I do not accept this argument. It is not more advantageous to be alone in bringing up children. The burden and responsibility of parenthood is heavier on a single parent than on a married couple living together. The extra support directed by the State to single parents (including unmarried mothers) is child centred and cannot, in my opinion, be designated as an attack on the institution of marriage.

Where couples are concerned, an unmarried couple, with children, living together are worse off, in relation to allowances, than a married couple living together. An unmarried couple with children living apart are the same in relation to allowances as a married couple living apart. There can be no incentive there to avoid matrimony.

[9–16] Carroll J essentially rejected two arguments put forward by the plaintiffs: the inducement argument and the penalisation argument. She rejected the penalisation argument on the basis of a direct/indirect discrimination point and a justification point. That is, she characterised the measures as discriminating not as between married couples and unmarried couples but rather as between cohabiting couples and non-cohabiting couples. (Now it could be argued that a measure that discriminates directly against cohabiting couples discriminates indirectly against married couples as such couples are more likely to be cohabiting. However, Carroll J did not address this point, implicitly deciding that the indirect discrimination was not a concern). In any event, she also held that there was a justification for the discrimination: it was more difficult to bring up a child on one's own and the legislation merely tried to alleviate the burden of this.

She rejected the inducement test for similar reasons: as married couples living together were treated better than unmarried couples living together and as married couples living apart were treated the same as unmarried couples living apart, there could be no inducement not to marry. Essentially, as there was no (direct) penalisation of the married state, there could be no inducement not to marry.

[9–17] On appeal, the Supreme Court, *per* Finlay CJ, expressly approved of Carroll J's reasoning, although it noted that the inducement argument had not been argued so strongly on appeal. Finlay CJ also reasoned that the courts should be particularly deferential to legislative judgment in the context of taxation and social welfare payments. He considered that a total removal of support for the family could constitute a breach of the constitutional duty under Art 41. However, when what was alleged was only a partial removal of support, it was legitimate to take into account the other supports offered to the family. The Court was not prepared to overturn the legislative judgment in this regard.

[9–18] *Murphy*, *Muckley* and *MhicMhathúna* all arose in the context of a discrete legislative advantage or disadvantage that impacted unfavourably on married couples. In this context, there is considerable judicial support for a penalisation test and some judicial support for an inducement test. These judicial dicta are cast in a new light, however, when one considers the constitutionality of a legislative scheme granting marriage-like status to non-marital unions, whether same-sex or opposite-sex. In this context, Mee provides a different perspective on the inducement test:

Another way to argue the point is to contend that creating a competing state-sponsored institution, which will prove more attractive to some couples than marriage, amounts to an inducement not to marry.... It is submitted that *Muckley* establishes only that the creation of an inducement not to marry is not a *necessary* aspect of an unconstitutional attack on marriage. The case leaves open the possibility that, given that there is more than one way to skin a constitutionally-protected institution, the creation of an inducement not to marry would be *sufficient* to violate the constitution. The issue was explored further in *Mhic Mhathúna v Ireland*, where the claimants argued *inter alia* that the existence of social welfare and taxation supports for single parents and unmarried mothers amounted to an inducement not to marry and therefore constituted an unconstitutional attack on the institution of marriage. In the High Court, Carroll J held that the impugned provisions did not, in fact, create any inducement or incentive not to marry. Carroll J's decision was upheld by the Supreme Court on appeal and her stated reasons for judgment were regarded as "correct". Thus, the Supreme Court expressed no difficulties with Carroll J's willingness to engage with the "inducement" argument which had been advanced by the claimants. The authors of *Kelly* comment that "Carroll J did not refer to *Muckley* and consequently offered no justification for the resurrection of the inducement test" which had been "rejected by the Supreme Court in *Muckley*". It is perhaps somewhat harsh to suggest that Carroll J "resurrected" the inducement question, when clearly she was responding to an argument by the claimant expressly based on inducement and when, as already pointed out above, the Supreme Court in *Muckley* had rejected only the argument that the existence of an inducement was invariably necessary. It is also not surprising that the Supreme Court made no specific comment on the inducement argument in *Mhic Mhathúna*, given Finlay CJ's comment that this argument had been less clearly relied upon by the claimants when the case moved to the Supreme Court. It should also be noted that the authors of *Kelly* are not hostile to "Carroll J's inducement test", stating that there is "much to be said for [it]" in the context of the issues considered in *Mhic Mhathúna*.

To sum up, it is submitted that there is a strong argument that the creation of a registered partnership scheme for heterosexual couples (whether it carried the same consequences as marriage or a less extensive set of rights and duties) would be unconstitutional as infringing Article 41.3.1°. The legislation creating such a scheme would, of course, enjoy the presumption of constitutionality and, as Kenny J stated in *Murphy v Attorney General*, the onus would be on anyone seeking to challenge its constitutionality to establish "a clear breach by the State of its pledge to guard with special care the institution of marriage and to protect it against attack". In this connection, it may be useful to make one final point relating to the existing case law in this area.

The decided cases generally involve a comparison between the position of married couples and cohabiting couples. Logically, the existence of the state of being married presupposes its opposite, the state of being unmarried. The position which our courts have reached—that there is nothing impermissible in treating both sets of couples on a par in relation to specific matters—was really unavoidable. It could hardly be contended that married couples must be treated more favourably than cohabiting couples in absolutely every respect by the law. The issues are different if the legislature takes it upon itself to create a new institution, comparable to marriage, which gives some of the same privileges as marriage but overall carries a less extensive set of legal consequences than marriage. In the nature of people's preferences, the difference between the legal consequences of the two institutions will encourage some couples to choose the rival institution over marriage. Since there was no obligation on the state to set up the rival institution in the first case, it is much harder from a constitutional point of view for the state to defend its actions than in the type of cases which have thus far arisen. (John Mee, "Cohabitation, Civil Partnership and the Constitution" in Oran Doyle and William Binchy eds, *Committed Relationships and the Law* (Four Courts Press, Dublin, 2007), at 205–206.)

Mee is surely correct to note the difficulty of extrapolating principles from the early cases that apply to the quite different issue of legislative recognition for non-marital partnerships. However, it may be that he overstates the level of support that the inducement test has (and is likely to have) in the case law. To establish that a law was an

[9–19]

inducement not to marry, presumably a court would have to undertake empirical research into how that law affected the state of mind of couples not before the court. The difficulty of undertaking such a task is indirectly demonstrated by the judgment of Carroll J herself in *MhicMhathúna*. Carroll J decided that there was no inducement simply because there was no penalisation. If the courts were to adopt this approach, an inducement test would—outside the rather special circumstances of *Muckley*—be no different from a penalisation test.

[9–20] Mee concludes that partnership recognition for opposite sex couples could be unconstitutional for providing an inducement not to marry. However, he suggests that the same argument would not apply in relation to same-sex couples, as such couples could never marry anyway. As such, any legislation providing a scheme of recognition for same-sex partnerships could not be said to induce people not to marry. Mee then considers and rejects a counter-argument:

> The counter-argument could be raised that there are some people whose sexual preferences make it possible for them to have a committed relationship with someone of either sex and that introducing a civil partnership for same sex couples (which could carry the same benefits as marriage) would remove the incentive for such people to choose a marital relationship with someone of the opposite sex. However, it does not seem that the institution of marriage is benefited if the fiscal and other societal benefits associated with marriage induce a person to marry someone other than (and of a different gender from) the person to whom he or she would otherwise have committed himself or herself. Rather, as is evidenced by the experience of Irish society over past decades, the institution of marriage appears to be harmed by the painful breakdown of opposite sex marriages where one of the parties is homosexual and would not have entered into the marriage if society had been willing to recognize same sex civil partnership. John Mee, "Cohabitation, Civil Partnership and the Constitution" in Oran Doyle and William Binchy eds, *Committed Relationships and the Law* (Four Courts Press, Dublin, 2007), at 208.

[9–21] There is much sense in this proposition; however, it presupposes a qualitative rather than a quantitative approach to protecting the institution of marriage. That is, it takes seriously the risk that the institution might be qualitatively harmed by corralling quantitatively more homosexuals into opposite-sex marriage. If this is the case, might the institution not also be qualitatively harmed by corralling quantitatively more heterosexuals into marriage when they are only choosing marriage grudgingly as the only possible State recognition for their relationship?

[9–22] A different perspective on the whole issue of legislative partnership recognition is gleaned from *Ennis v Butterly* [1996] 1 IR 426. The plaintiff and defendant were married but not to each other. However, they lived together. When the relationship broke down, the plaintiff asserted that they had an agreement to marry and an agreement to cohabit pending that marriage. The plaintiff claimed, *inter alia*, that the defendant had breached both agreements. The defendant brought an application seeking to have the plaintiff's claim struck out as disclosing no cause of action. Section 2(1) of the Family Law Act 1981 provides that an agreement between two people to marry each other does not have the force of law in the State and cannot be sued upon. In striking out the plaintiff's claim based on contract, but not her related claim based on misrepresentation, Kelly J considered the permissibility of agreements to marry and cohabitation agreements. The provisions of the Family Law Act 1981 determined the first question. In addressing cohabitation agreements, Kelly J reasoned as follows:

> [The public policy of this State] is to be found in the first instance in the Constitution and, in particular, Article 41 thereof. In that Article, the State recognises the family as the natural primary and fundamental unit group of society and as a moral institution possessing inalienable and imprescriptible rights antecedent and superior to all positive law. The State pledges itself to guard with special care the institution of marriage, on which the family is founded and protect it against attack....
>
> Given the special place of marriage and the family under the Irish Constitution, it appears to me that the public policy of this State ordains that non-marital cohabitation does not and cannot have the same constitutional status as marriage. Moreover, the State has pledged to guard with special care the institution of marriage. But does this mean that agreements, the consideration for which is cohabitation, are incapable of being enforced? In my view it does since otherwise the pledge on the part of the State, of which this Court is one organ, to guard with special care the institution of marriage would be much diluted. To permit an express cohabitation contract (such as is pleaded here) to be enforced would give it a similar status in law as a marriage contract. It did not have such a status prior to the coming into effect of the Constitution, rather such contracts were regarded as illegal and unenforceable as a matter of public policy. Far from enhancing the position at law of such contracts the Constitution requires marriage to be guarded with special care. In my view, this reinforces the existing common law doctrines concerning the non-enforceability of cohabitation contracts. I am therefore of opinion that, as a matter of public policy, such agreements cannot be enforced.
>
> I am strengthened in this view by the fact that, notwithstanding the extensive reform of family law which has taken place in this country over the last 20 years, nowhere does one find any attempt on the part of the legislature to substantially enhance the legal position of, or to confer rights akin to those of married persons upon the parties to non-marital unions e.g. a right to maintenance. This absence of intervention on the part of the legislature suggests to me that it accepts that it would be contrary to public policy, as enunciated in the Constitution, to confer legal rights on persons in non-marital unions akin to those who are married. [1996] 1 IR 426, at 438–439.

The important aspect of Kelly J's reasoning was his suggestion that enhanced legal rights for cohabitation contracts would be a breach of the State's obligation to guard the institution of marriage with special care. Although he was fortified in his view by the fact that the legislature had not attempted to make such contracts enforceable, it seems implicit in what he says that it would not be open for the Oireachtas to make such contracts enforceable.

[9–23] In reaching his conclusion, Kelly J relied partly on a sentence taken from the judgment of Henchy J in *Nicolaou v An Bord Uchtála* [1966] IR 567. If one considers the whole paragraph from which the sentence was taken, however, it becomes clear that the comments of Henchy J, while they may support Kelly J's decision in *Ennis v Butterly*, do not support his suggestion that it would be unconstitutional for the Oireachtas to provide recognition to partnership contracts other than marriage. Henchy J reasoned as follows:

> Article 41 deals with only one kind of family, namely, a family founded on the institution of marriage. Article 41, 1, 1°, accords the recognition of the State to such family as "the natural primary and fundamental unit group of Society, and as a moral institution possessing inalienable and imprescriptible rights, antecedent and superior to all positive

law"; and Article 41, 1, 2°, gives the guarantee of the State to protect it in its constitutional authority, as the necessary basis of social order and as indispensable to the welfare of the nation and of the State. I am satisfied that no union or grouping of people is entitled to be designated a family for the purposes of the Article if it is founded on any relationship other than that of marriage. If the solemn guarantees and rights which the Article gives to the family were held to be extended to units of people founded on extra-marital unions, such interpretation would be quite inconsistent with the letter and the spirit of the Article. It would be tantamount to recognition of such units "as the necessary basis of social order and as indispensable to the welfare of the Nation and the State" (Article 41, 1, 2°). For the State to award equal constitutional protection to the family founded on marriage and the "family" founded on an extra-marital union would in effect be a disregard of the pledge which the State gives in Article 41, 3, 1°, to guard with special care the institution of marriage. [1967] IR 567, at 622.

[9–24] Henchy J was clearly addressing an issue of judicial interpretation rather than legislative action. The claim being advanced by the prosecutor, which he rejected, was that Art 41 protected both marital and non-marital families. As such, Henchy J's comments concern the rights granted by Art 41 not whether Art 41 precludes rights from being granted by the Oireachtas. In this regard, the last sentence of the paragraph quoted must be read in the following way. The only two bodies that can "award" constitutional protection are the people (by referendum) and the courts (by interpretation, the issue before Henchy J). The last sentence cannot be read as a restriction on the Oireachtas providing legislative protection to non-marital families but can only be read as a direction as to the correct judicial interpretation of Art 41. Indeed, Henchy J did not seem to have any difficulty with the rights afforded to the non-marital mother in the adoption process. In short, Henchy J's comments do not support Kelly J's suggestion that it would be unconstitutional for the legislature to recognise cohabitation contracts.

The Right to Marry

[9–25] In *Ryan v Attorney General* [1965] IR 294, at 313, Kenny J suggested that the right to marry was one of those unenumerated rights protected by Art 40.3.1° of the Constitution. Although it might appear more sensible to protect the right to marry under Art 41, that might preclude unmarried people from invoking the right, a "Catch-22" situation. The right to marry itself did not come sharply into focus until 2006. In *O'Shea v Ireland*, 17 October 2006 (HC), Laffoy J declared unconstitutional s 3(2) of the Deceased Wife's Sisters Marriage Act 1907 as amended by s 1(2)(b) of the Deceased Brother's Widow's Marriage Act 1921. The relevant bar in s 3(2) was a prohibition on a man from marrying the divorced wife of his brother during the lifetime of such brother. Having divorced her husband, the first plaintiff sought to marry her former husband's brother. Laffoy J held that the prohibition contained in s 3(2) was a prima facie restriction of the constitutional right of each of the plaintiffs to marry, commenting, "It is an impairment of the essence of the right of each because it prevents each marrying her and his chosen partner." The question was whether the plaintiffs had established that the restriction was not justified.

[9–26] Laffoy J did not perceive a factual basis for any defence of the statutory bar. The State simply had not adduced evidence to support the proposition that the statutory prohibition would provide a strong emotional barrier by encouraging the feeling that siblings-in-law are in the same relationship as natural brothers and sisters. Moreover, the bar would not stop the relationships occurring. As the plaintiffs' circumstances demonstrated, the prohibition on marriage had not stopped them forming their relationship in the first place. The fact that the relationships would occur anyway, however, was only relevant because the supposed purpose of the marriage bar was to preclude the relationships. The mere fact that people will form relationships does not oblige the State to recognise those relationships. This point is well illustrated by a case decided very shortly after *O'Shea*.

In *Zappone v Revenue Commissioners* [2006] IEHC 404 the plaintiffs were two women who were Irish citizens, although Dr Zappone was originally Canadian. They had lived together as a cohabiting couple since their relationship began in 1981. On 13 March 2003, the plaintiffs married each other in Vancouver, British Columbia in Canada. In April 2004, the plaintiffs wrote to the Revenue Commissioners requesting that they should be allowed to claim their allowances as a married couple under the Taxes Consolidation Acts. The Revenue Commissioners refused to do so on the basis that the relevant Acts referred to "husband" and "wife" and the Oxford English Dictionary defined those terms in gender-specific ways. Accordingly, the Revenue Commissioners' view was that the plaintiffs could not be treated as a married couple for the purpose of the tax laws. Between the initiation of proceedings and the hearing of the case, s 2(2)(e) of the Civil Registration Act 2004 came into force. This provision precludes marriage by same-sex couples. Although no declaration of unconstitutionality was sought in respect of that provision, the case effectively turned on whether the plaintiffs had an entitlement to marry as a matter of Irish law. [9–27]

The Court accepted that there was a right to marry, but held that the discrimination was justified by reference to Art 41 of the Constitution:

> I accept the arguments made by the defendants in relation to the issue of discrimination on the basis that the right to opposite sex marriage is derived from the Constitution and thus that this is a justification for any distinction between the position of the plaintiffs and married couples....
>
> The final point I would make on this topic is that if there is in fact any form of discriminatory distinction between same sex couples and opposite sex couples by reason of the exclusion of same sex couples from the right to marry, then Article 41 in its clear terms as to guarding [with special care the institution of marriage] provides the necessary justification. (At 129 of the unreported judgment.)

The reference to Art 41 of itself does not support the conclusion that discrimination against same-sex couples is constitutionally warranted. For that begs the question of whether same-sex marriage is protected by Art 41. In this regard, Dunne J referred to many of the cases above—such as *CT v DT*—to demonstrate that the marriage protected by Art 41 was opposite-sex marriage. Accordingly, the State was entitled to discriminate against opposite sex couples. The plaintiffs sought to argue that those cases involved *obiter dicta*, as the issue of gay marriage was not at stake, and moreover that the interpretation of the Constitution should be amended to reflect changing values. Dunne J rejected this argument on a number of grounds. Most convincingly, she questioned whether society's values really were changing: [9–28]

> Having regard to the clear understanding of the meaning of marriage as set out in the numerous authorities opened to the Court from this jurisdiction and elsewhere, I do not

see how marriage can be redefined by the Court to encompass same sex marriage. The Plaintiffs referred frequently in the course of this case to the "changing consensus" but I have to say that there is little evidence of that. The consensus around the world does not support a widespread move towards same sex marriage. There has been some limited support for the concept of same sex marriage as in Canada, Massachusetts and South Africa together with [Spain, Belgium and the Netherlands] but, in truth, it is difficult to see that as a consensus, changing or otherwise. (At 127.)

[9–29] Although the meaning of marriage is contested now in a way that that would have been inconceivable in 1937, it is not the case that the meaning of marriage has unequivocally shifted. Accordingly, even if one accepts that the Constitution's protection of marriage is a values issue and requires a present tense interpretation, it does not necessarily follow that the constitutional meaning of marriage should be expanded to include same-sex marriage. This does raise questions of the role that the courts should play in social change: should they lead change by lending their weight to the questioning of traditional concepts (such as marriage) or should they reflect change by only adapting constitutional interpretations where there has been an unequivocal shift in how the term is understood? A constitution with a strong egalitarian guarantee could require a court to lend its weight to the questioning of traditional concepts. However, given the limited force that has been accorded to Art 40.1 and the explicit approval of legislative discriminations against non-marital families, it is (at least) fully consistent with existing case law for the courts to rely on a traditional, albeit now contested, understanding of marriage in order to exclude same-sex couples from that institution. This decision is under appeal to the Supreme Court.

The Rights of Married Couples and Families

Family Rights

[9–30] Article 41 describes the rights of the family as being "inalienable and imprescriptible," words interpreted by Kenny J in *Ryan v Attorney General* [1965] IR 294, at 308 as meaning "cannot be given away" and "cannot be lost through passage of time" respectively. That "inalienable and imprescriptible" in no way connote "absolute" is clear from the Supreme Court opinion in *Re Article 26 and the Adoption (No 2) Bill 1987* [1989] IR 656. The bill at issue allowed for the adoption of marital children in exceptional circumstances where their parents had failed them. The precise circumstances in which the State is allowed to interfere with parents' authority over the children will be considered in more detail below. It is that protection of the family, as an autonomous unit, from outside interference that is probably the most significant aspect of Art 41. However, the courts have considered a number of other family rights. In *PH v J Murphy & Sons Ltd* [1987] IR 621; [1988] ILRM 542, the plaintiffs' father had suffered severe personal injury during the course of his employment; the plaintiffs asserted a cause of action against the employers derived from Art 41. Costello J, however, held that Art 41 protected the family from legislation or deliberate state acts that interfered with its constitution or authority. Art 41 did not, however, confer a protection on the family against a negligent act that might interfere with its constitution or authority. Costello J appeared to accept, however, that Art 41 might impose some obligations on private citizens.

[9–31] There have been conflicting dicta from the courts as to whether Art 41 can grant rights to some family members as against other family members. On the one hand, in *People*

(DPP) v T (1988) 3 Frewen 141, the Court of Criminal Appeal relied on Art 41 in holding unconstitutional any common law rule or provision of the Criminal Justice (Evidence) Act 1924 which might prevent the accused's spouse giving evidence against him. The accused was charged with a number of offences relating to the sexual abuse of his daughter. The Court reasoned that Art 41 included an obligation to enforce its protective provisions against members of the family who were guilty or alleged to be guilty of injuries to other members of the family. On the other hand, in *L v L* [1992] 2 IR 77, at 108, where a wife sought to rely on Art 41.2 to establish that her husband owned the home on trust for her, Finlay CJ commented that Art 41.2 did not purport "to create any particular right within the family, or to grant to any individual member of the family rights, whether of property or otherwise, against other members of the family, but rather deals with the protection of the family from external forces." it was not the purpose of Art 41 to create property rights for one family member as against another family member.

Rights of Married Couples

We have already considered the case law arising from *Murphy v Attorney General* [1982] IR 241 that considered whether certain legislation amounted to an unjust attack on marriage. There are, however, a few other cases in which the courts have considered the rights of married couples. In *ER v JR* [1981] ILRM 125, Carroll J relied on Art 41 in holding that the relationship of a marriage guidance counsellor to his clients gave rise to confidentiality. She considered that this was a practical support for the institution of marriage. In *Murray v Ireland* [1985] IR 532, Costello J held that married couples had the right to procreate. However, this right was not absolute and had been permissibly restricted by the State in the case of the two plaintiffs, who were both in prison. In *TF v Ireland* [1995] 1 IR 321, the plaintiff challenged the constitutionality of the Judicial Separation Act 1989, in particular s 3 which allows the courts to grant a decree of judicial separation where a normal marital relationship has not existed for at least a year. The Supreme Court, *per* Hamilton CJ, rejected the plaintiff's contention that this contravened Art 41 of the Constitution, reasoning that although it was "an important element in marriage that the spouses live together", cohabitation had to be based on consent and could not be enforced. It thus appears that one of the rights of married couples is the right to separate. [1995] 1 IR 321, at 375. Article 41.3.2 now allows the courts, in limited circumstances, to grant a divorce.

[9–32]

The Position of Non-Marital Families

The Limits of Art 41

As we saw above, in *State (Nicolaou) v An Bord Uchtála* [1966] IR 567; (1968) 102 ILTR 8, the Supreme Court held that the family protected by Art 41 is the family based on marriage. The most obvious consequence of this is that the members of non-marital families (mothers, fathers and children) cannot rely on Art 41 to protect them from certain types of State action. A second consequence is that Art 41 is taken by the courts to legitimise legislative discrimination against the members of non-marital families. In *O'Brien v Stoutt* [1984] IR 316; [1985] ILRM 86, the Supreme Court upheld the constitutionality of s 67(3) of the Succession Act 1965 which provides that, where a deceased dies intestate and is survived by "issue" and no spouse, her estate is distributed between her issue. Having decided that "issue" referred solely to marital

[9–33]

children, Walsh J (for the Court) upheld this legislative discrimination between marital and non-marital children:

> Having regard to the constitutional guarantees relating to the family, the Court cannot find that the differences created by the Act of 1965 are necessarily unreasonable, unjust or arbitrary. Undoubtedly, a child born outside marriage may suffer severe disappointment if he does not succeed to some part of his parents' property on intestacy, but he can suffer the same disappointment if the parent or parents die testate and leave that child no property—an event which could occur even if the Act of 1965 did enable intestate succession on the part of such child. [1984] IR 316, at 336.

[9–34] This latter point seems to be of dubious relevance. The mere fact that the Succession Act 1965 allows unmarried parents to exclude their children from their will in circumstances where married parents would not be allowed to do so scarcely counts as support for the Succession Act 1965 also discriminating against unmarried children in the context of intestate succession. It is a manifestation of the same discriminatory policy, not an independent justification for that policy.

Alternative Means of Constitutional Protection

[9–35] Non-marital mothers and (but to a far lesser extent) non-marital fathers have had some success in relying on other provisions of the Constitution to protect their relationships with their children. In *Nicolaou* itself, the Supreme Court seemed to accept that the non-marital mother had some constitutional rights in relation to her child, albeit not under Art 41. Walsh J reasoned as follows:

> [T]he mother of an illegitimate child does not come within the ambit of Articles 41 and 42 of the Constitution. Her natural right to the custody and care of her child, and such other natural personal rights as she may have (and this Court does not in this case find it necessary to pronounce upon the extent of such rights), fall to be protected under Article 40, section 3, and are not affected by Article 41 or Article 42 of the Constitution. There is no provision in Article 40 which prohibits or restricts the surrender, abdication, or transfer of any of the rights guaranteed in that Article by the person entitled to them. The Court therefore rejects the submission that the Adoption Act, 1952, is invalid in as much as it permits the mother of an illegitimate child to consent to the legal adoption of her child, and lose, under the provision of s. 24 (*b*) of the Act, all parental rights and be freed from all parental duties in respect of the child.

[9–36] The effect of the natural mother's rights being protected under Art 40.3 rather than Art 41 was that they were "alienable." Accordingly, a non-marital mother could consent to the adoption of her child; marital parents could not. This issue was important in *G v An Bord Uchtála* [1980] IR 32: a non-marital mother gave her child up for adoption, fearing that she did not have the resources to raise the child properly. She subsequently informed her family of the birth and of her decision to place the child for adoption and they offered to help her bring up the child. She then informed the Adoption Board that she was withdrawing her consent to the adoption. Her child had already been placed with the prospective adopters. Section 14 of the Adoption Act 1952 provided that an adoption could not be made without the consent of the mother of the child. However, s 3 of the Adoption Act 1974 provided that, where a consent was withdrawn, the prospective adopters could apply to court seeking to have the need for consent dispensed with. The mother instituted proceedings seeking to have her child returned to her; the prospective parents sought to have the need for the mother's consent dispensed with. Walsh J relied on the constitutional rights of the natural mother to impose a very stringent consent requirement:

> I am satisfied that, having regard to the natural rights of the mother, the proper construction of the provision in s. 3 of the Act of 1974 is that the consent, if given, must be such as to amount to a fully-informed, free and willing surrender or an abandonment of these rights. However, I am also of opinion that such a surrender or abandonment may be established by her conduct when it is such as to warrant the clear and unambiguous inference that such was her fully-informed, free and willing intention. In my view, a consent motivated by fear, stress or anxiety, or a consent or conduct which is dictated by poverty or other deprivations does not constitute a valid consent....
>
> So far as the constitutional rights of the plaintiff are concerned, the findings of the President do not indicate that she has surrendered or abandoned her constitutional rights by a fully informed, free and willing surrender or abandonment of these rights, or at all, nor did the President so find. Before anybody may be said to have surrendered or abandoned his constitutional rights, it must be shown that he is aware of what the rights are and of what he is doing. Secondly, the action taken must be such as could reasonably lead to the clear and unambiguous inference that such was the intention of the person who is alleged to have either surrendered or abandoned the constitutional rights. The facts of the present case do not support any such conclusion. Less than eight weeks after the birth of her child, the plaintiff had already signed a form consenting to the placing of the child for adoption. Prior to that she had been subject to several representations urging her that it was in the best interests of the child and herself to have the child placed for adoption. When the representations were initially made to her, they were made to her within one week of the birth of her child and while she was still in hospital. It is not difficult to imagine the anxieties and troubled state of mind of this lonely young girl, who was but a short time past her twenty-first birthday and who, unknown to friend or family, had given birth to her child far from home. [1980] IR 32, at 74, 80.

[9–37] Henchy and Kenny JJ agreed with Walsh J's conclusion, but for somewhat different reasons. O'Higgins CJ and Parke J dissented, concluding that the consent was valid. Walsh J took the view that the best interests of the child should only be considered if a mother surrenders her rights. Such an approach suggests that the custody of children should be determined first by reference to the rights of adults and only secondarily by reference to the needs of the child.

[9–38] Non-marital fathers have had much greater difficulty in persuading the courts of their constitutional rights in relation to their offspring. In *State (Nicolaou) v An Bord Uchtála* [1966] IR 567, the Supreme Court rejected an unmarried father's claim to the custody of his child. In a memorable passage, Walsh J explained the difficulty of giving rights to unmarried fathers:

> When it is considered that an illegitimate child may be begotten by an act of rape, by a callous seduction or by an act of casual commerce by a man with a woman, as well as by the association of a man with a woman in making a common home without marriage in circumstances approximating to those of married life, and that, except in the latter instance, it is rare for a natural father to take any interest in his offspring, it is not difficult to appreciate the difference in moral capacity and social function between the natural

father and the [natural mother, as well as other persons with rights in the adoption process.] [1966] IR 567, at 641.

[9–39] This approach classified all natural fathers together and reasoned that, as a group, they deserved the level of rights appropriate to a rapist or a callous seducer. However, it scarcely seems fair that fit fathers should suffer simply because there are unfit fathers. This unfairness has become more acute as births outside marriage have become more common.

The position of natural fathers has improved somewhat. In *K v W* [1990] 2 IR 437, a non-marital father asserted a constitutional right to the care and custody of his child. Section 6A of the Guardianship of Infants Act 1964 (inserted by s 12 of the Children Act 1987) allowed a non-marital father to apply to court to be appointed a guardian of the infant. In this case, the mother wished to place the child for adoption. The father applied to be appointed a guardian under s 6A. If appointed a guardian, he would have had a good claim to custody as against the prospective adopters who were not guardians (s 10(2) of the Guardianship of Infants Act 1964). On a case stated from the High Court, Finlay CJ (with whom Walsh, Griffin and Hederman JJ agreed) reasoned as follows:

> Section 6A gives a right to the natural father to apply to be appointed guardian. It does not give him a right to be guardian, and it does not equate his position *vis-à-vis* the infant as a matter of law with the position of a father who is married to the mother of the infant. In the latter instance the father is the guardian of the infant and must remain so, although certain of the powers and rights of a guardian may, in the interests of the welfare of the infant, be taken from him.
>
> The right to apply to be appointed guardian of the infant under s. 6A of the Act of 1964 (as inserted by the Act of 1987) is a right to apply pursuant to a statute which specifically provides that the court in deciding upon such application shall regard the welfare of the infant as the first and paramount consideration.
>
> To construe s. 6A of the Act of 1964 as has been done in the case stated as giving to the father a right to guardianship which cannot be denied unless (a) he is not a fit person, or (b) there are circumstances or good reasons involving the welfare of the child which require that he should not be appointed is incorrect, in my view, for two reasons. It presumes a right to guardianship, whereas s. 6A creates merely a right to apply for guardianship.
>
> A right to guardianship defeasible by circumstances or reasons "involving the welfare of the child" could not possibly be equated with regarding the welfare of the child as the first and paramount consideration in the exercise by the court of its discretion as to whether or not to appoint the father guardian. The construction apparently placed by the learned trial judge in the case stated upon s. 6A to a large extent would appear to spring from the submission made on behalf of the applicant on this appeal that he has got a constitutional right, or a natural right identified by the Constitution, to the guardianship of the child, and that the Act of 1987 by inserting s. 6A into the Act of 1964 is thereby declaring or acknowledging that right.
>
> I am satisfied that this submission is not correct and that although there may be rights of interest or concern arising from the blood link between the father and the child, no constitutional right to guardianship in the father of the child exists. This conclusion does not, of course, in any way infringe on such considerations appropriate to the welfare of the child in different circumstances as may make it desirable for the child to enjoy the society, protection and guardianship of its father, even though its father and mother are not married.

> The extent and character of the rights which accrue arising from the relationship of a father to a child to whose mother he is not married must vary very greatly indeed, depending on the circumstances of each individual case.
>
> The range of variation would, I am satisfied, extend from the situation of the father of a child conceived as the result of a casual intercourse, where the rights might well be so minimal as practically to be non-existent, to the situation of a child born as the result of a stable and established relationship and nurtured at the commencement of his life by his father and mother in a situation bearing nearly all of the characteristics of a constitutionally protected family, when the rights would be very extensive indeed. [1990] 2 IR 437, at 446–447.

The language of "rights of interest or concern" is considerably more favourable than the primary characterisation in *Nicolaou* of unmarried fathers as rapists and casual seducers. However, the practical position of unmarried fathers has not changed greatly. Whereas—in relation to natural mothers—the best interests of the child are only considered if the mother surrenders her rights, in relation to natural fathers, the father only has a right if the best interests of the child require it. [9–40]

The All-Party Oireachtas Committee on the Constitution recommended that a new section should be introduced into Art 41 as follows:

> All children, irrespective of birth, gender, race or religion, are equal before the law. In all cases where the welfare of the child so requires, regard shall be had to the best interests of that child.

By "irrespective of birth," the committee presumably means "irrespective of the marital status of one's parents at the time of birth." This might address the injustice in *O'Brien v Stoutt*, if legislation were to attempt to draw such a distinction in the future. The Committee declined to recommend any explicit recognition for the rights of the non-marital father. However, it considered that this amendment would assist the plight of non-marital fathers: [9–41]

> The committee's decision not to seek an extended definition of the family means that the natural or birth father will not have constitutional rights *as such* vis-à-vis his child. The committee nevertheless believes that its proposed amendment in respect of the rights of children will indirectly improve the rights the status of the natural or birth father. Thus, for example, if no child could henceforth be discriminated against on grounds of birth, this would surely oblige the courts to refashion a line of (highly controversial) jurisprudence since the Supreme Court's decision in [*Nicolaou*]. If the Constitution were to contain an express guarantee of non-discrimination on the grounds of birth and to have regard to the best interests of the child, this would mean that some of the *Nicolaou* rationale would disappear. The child under those circumstances would have the same right to the company and care of his or her father as would a child born within marriage. In any event, the welfare and best interests of the child (which considerations would, if the committee's proposals were to be accepted, now be elevated to constitutional status) would generally mean that the child had a constitutional right to have the company and care of his or her father and to ensure that the father played a part in decision-making concerning his or her welfare. *Report of All Party Oireachtas Committee*, at 124.

This reasoning is not particularly convincing. Much of the concern that unmarried fathers have in relation to the courts is based on a belief (right or wrong) that gendered attitudes to child-rearing count against them when decisions are being made. It is difficult to see why the elevation of a best interests test from legislative status to constitutional status would alter the gendered way in which that term is interpreted, if that is indeed the case.

Standing of Non-Nationals to Invoke Arts 41 and 42

[9–42] As noted above, the language of Art 41 suggests a recognition by the State of pre-existing, universal family rights, antecedent and superior to all positive law. This raises the interesting issue of whether one has to be Irish to invoke Art 41. In *Northants County Council v ABF* [1982] ILRM 64, a child, who had been born in England to married parents, was taken into care by the Council. The child's father abducted the child and travelled to Ireland. The father sought to rely on Art 41 of the Constitution; the Council argued that only Irish citizens could rely on Art 41. Hamilton J rejected this argument for the following reasons:

> It seems to me however that non-citizenship can have no effect on the interpretation of Article 41 or the entitlement to the protection afforded by it.
>
> What Article 41 does is to recognise the Family as the natural primary and fundamental unit group of society and as a moral institution possessing inalienable and imprescriptible rights antecedent and superior to all positive law, which rights the State cannot control. In the words of Walsh J already quoted, "these rights are part of what is generally called the natural law" [*McGee v Attorney General* [1974] IR 284, at 317] and as such are antecedent and superior to all positive law.
>
> The natural law is of universal application and applies to all human persons, be they citizens of this State or not, and in my opinion it would be inconceivable that the father of the infant child would not be entitled to rely on the recognition of the Family contained in *Article 41* for the purpose of enforcing his rights as the lawful father of the infant the subject matter of the proceeding herein or that he should lose such entitlement merely because he removed the child to this jurisdiction for the purpose of enforcing his said rights.
>
> These rights are recognised by Bunreacht na h-Éireann and the courts created under it as antecedent and superior to all positive law: they are not so recognised by the law or the courts of the jurisdiction to which it is sought to have the infant returned.
>
> Consequently it is for these reasons that I have at this stage refused to grant the orders sought by the applicant herein viz. that the child be returned to them or their agent. [1982] ILRM 164, at 166.

[9–43] Hamilton J accepted, however, that the child also had rights and that a separate hearing would be necessary to determine whether those rights were being breached. A somewhat different emphasis is apparent from *Saunders v Midwestern Health Board*, 23 June 1987 (SC) (*ex tempore*). Finlay CJ reasoned:

> Where ... parents having no connection with Ireland bring their children unlawfully from the country in which they are, into the jurisdiction of this court, in breach of an order made by the court in the jurisdiction in which they are domiciled and in which the children were being reared, I do not accept that they can by that act alone confer on themselves and their children constitutional rights under Articles 41 and 42 of the Constitution. (Quoted in Hogan and Whyte eds, *Kelly: The Irish Constitution* (4th ed, LexisNexis Butterworths, Dublin, 2003), at [7.6.42].)

[9–44] Despite the apparent restrictiveness of the approach in *Saunders*, O'Flaherty J in *Eastern Health Board v An Bord Uchtála* [1994] 3 IR 207 appeared to endorse a more expansive approach. In this case, Irish parents had—with the consent of the Indian authorities—removed an Indian child from India for adoption in Ireland. The child had been left at an orphanage and it was unclear who its parents were. However, a preliminary issue arose as to whether the Adoption Acts 1952–1988, which by this stage allowed for the adoption of marital children, applied to non-citizen children born outside the State. The Supreme Court held that the Acts did apply to non-citizen children born outside the State. Finlay CJ, with whom Hederman, Egan and Blayney JJ agreed, reached this conclusion on the basis of statutory interpretation. O'Flaherty J, however, also relied on the Constitution, commenting that the references in Art 42.5 to "parents" and "children" were not confined to parents and children within the State.

In a sense, the difficulties articulated here are symptoms of the issue identified at the start of the chapter. If the Irish Constitution merely recognises pre-existing family rights (that are antecedent and superior to all positive law), then non-nationals should be allowed to invoke those rights in Irish courts. On the other hand, the Irish courts must surely be conscious of the risk of over-reaching themselves. If the child in *Northants* had not been brought to Ireland, should the courts still have allowed the father to rely on Article 41 and 42? It is impractical for the Irish courts to give judgments with extra-territorial effect, but should the enforcement of one's natural rights (if that is what they are) depend on mere geographical happenstance? [9–45]

Derivative Rights to Reside in Ireland

If an Irish citizen has a right to reside in the State and has a right to the care and companionship of her family members, the question arises whether she has a right to the care and companionship of those family members in the State. This question is acute where the family members in question have no other right to remain in the State. Despite their superficial similarities, this issue should not be confused with the question of standing to invoke Arts 41 and 42. The constitutional right asserted here is one that can only be asserted by the Irish citizen. However, non-citizen family members of that citizen can gain an incidental right to reside in the State, which they otherwise would not have. Everything, however, pivots on the rights of the Irish citizen, usually (but not always) a child. [9–46]

This issue was first considered in a number of High Court cases in the 1980s. In *Pok Sun Shun v Ireland* [1986] ILRM 593, the plaintiff married an Irish citizen after a deportation order was issued against him. When the deportation order was sought to be enforced against him, he claimed that his wife had a right to the care and companionship of her husband in the State. Costello J refused this claim, reasoning that as the Minister for Justice was entitled to deport an alien from the state, the family rights of the wife did not extend so far as to restrict any such deportation. All that was necessary was for the Minister to consider the fact that she was married. In *Osheku v Ireland* [1986] IR 733, the plaintiff again sought leave to remain in Ireland on the basis that he was married to an Irish citizen, with whom he had a son. Again this right to reside was argued to be derived from the wife and son's right to the society of their husband and father. Gannon J refused this application, again relying on the power of the State to control immigration. However, he also commented that citizens had no obligation to reside within the State but that the State had no obligation to provide a place of residence within the State for citizens. This suggests that the State is entitled, as a matter of Irish constitutional law, to deport its own citizens. The issue eventually came before the Supreme Court in *Fajujonu v Minister for Justice* [1990] 2 IR 151; [9–47]

[1990] 1 ILRM 234. The plaintiffs were two non-nationals who married in the UK prior to moving to Ireland, where they had three children. They did not comply with their legal obligation to notify the immigration authorities of their arrival in the State. Some three years after they arrived in the State, the plaintiffs came to the attention of the authorities. They were requested to leave the State and then sought to restrain the Minister for Justice from issuing a deportation order against them. In the High Court, Barrington J found for the Minister for Justice, relying on grounds slightly more sophisticated than those advanced in *Osheku* and *Pok Sun Shun*. He reasoned that the control of immigration was a matter peculiarly within the competence of the Government and that the courts should be slow to intervene in that area. He considered that the parents could not, by positing a wish to remain in Ireland on their children, confer on themselves a derivative right to remain in the State. The Supreme Court, however, took a different view, granting a greater weight to the rights of the child citizen and (in effect) remitting the matter to the Minister for reconsideration. Finlay CJ and Walsh J delivered judgments which, although they agreed on the need for the Minister to reconsider the case, differed in emphasis. Griffin, Hederman and McCarthy JJ agreed with both judgments. In relation to the right at issue, Finlay CJ reasoned as follows:

> I have come to the conclusion that where, as occurs in this case, an alien has in fact resided for an appreciable time in the State and has become a member of a family unit within the State containing children who are citizens, that there can be no question but that those children, as citizens, have got a constitutional right to the company, care and parentage of their parents within a family unit. I am also satisfied that *prima facie* and subject to the exigencies of the common good that that is a right which these citizens would be entitled to exercise within the State.
>
> I am also satisfied that whereas the parents who are not citizens and who are aliens cannot, by reason of their having as members of their family children born in Ireland who are citizens, claim any constitutional right of a particular kind to remain in Ireland, they are entitled to assert a choice of residence on behalf of their infant children, in the interests of those infant children. [1990] 2 IR 151, at 162.

Walsh J, on the other hand, reasoned as follows:

> It is abundantly clear that citizens of this State may not be deported. The third plaintiff is one of three children of the first two plaintiffs, all of which children are citizens of Ireland. If the first two plaintiffs, being the parents of the infant children, are deported, the effect must be that their children who are Irish citizens are faced with the choice of remaining within this State as they are entitled so to do and therefore being in effect compulsorily separated from their parents, or having to leave the State with their parents and thus ceasing to have the benefit of all the protection afforded by the laws and the Constitution of this State. In my view, the first two plaintiffs and their three children constitute a family within the meaning of the Constitution and the three children are entitled to the care, protection and the society of their parents in this family group which is resident within the State. There is no doubt that the family has made its home and residence in Ireland.
>
> In view of the fact that these are children of tender age, who require the society of their parents and when the parents have not been shown to have been in anyway unfit or guilty of any matter which make them unsuitable custodians to their children, to move to expel the parents in the particular circumstances of this case would, in my view, be inconsistent with the provisions of Article 41 of the Constitution guaranteeing the integrity of the family. [1990] 2 IR 151, at 164 and 166.

Whereas Finlay CJ had emphasised the "appreciable time" spent by the non-national in the State, Walsh J emphasised the "tender age" of the children and their consequent need for the companionship of their parents. As the right is the right of the child, Walsh J's focus on the position of the child, rather than the position of the parent, seems more appropriate. [9–48]

Finlay CJ and Walsh J also differed in emphasis as to how the right could be restricted. Finlay CJ put the matter as follows:

> In these circumstances, I am satisfied that the protection of the constitutional rights which arise in this case require a fresh consideration now by the Minister for Justice, having due regard to the important constitutional rights which are involved, as far as the three children are concerned, to the question as to whether the plaintiffs should, pursuant to the Act of 1935, be permitted to remain in the State. I am, however, satisfied also that if, having had due regard to those considerations and having conducted such inquiry as may be appropriate as to the facts and factors now affecting the whole situation in a fair and proper manner, the Minister is satisfied that for good and sufficient reason the common good requires that the residence of these parents within the State should be terminated, even though that has the necessary consequence that in order to remain as a family unit the three children must also leave the State, then that is an order he is entitled to make pursuant to the Act of 1935. [1990] 2 IR 151, at 163.

Walsh J put the matter as follows:

> I agree with the opinion expressed by the Chief Justice that there is nothing to suggest that the Minister had applied his mind to any of these considerations, and the matter will have to be reconsidered by the Minister, bearing in mind the constitutional rights involved. In my view, he would have to be satisfied, for stated reasons, that the interests of the common good of the people of Ireland and of the protection of the State and its society are so predominant and so overwhelming in the circumstances of the case, that an action which can have the effect of breaking up this family is not so disproportionate to the aim sought to be achieved as to be unsustainable. [1990] 2 IR 151, at 166.

Both Finlay CJ and Walsh J thus accepted that the Minister needed to reconsider the rights of the citizen child, but that common good factors could justify a deportation order. However, Walsh J referred to the factors of the common good having to be "predominant and overwhelming", whereas Finlay CJ spoke only of "good and sufficient reason". The approach of Finlay CJ is considerably more open to deportation. [9–49]

The decision in *Fajujonu* came to be regarded as conferring a strong, derivative right of residence on non-citizens who had family members living in Ireland. As the number of non-nationals entering the country grew, many people became concerned that *Fajujonu* undermined the immigration system by providing an alternative means of residence outside of the normal system. The Supreme Court (sitting with seven judges) revisited the issue in *Lobe and Osayande v Minister for Justice* [2003] 1 IR 1. In both cases, the parents claimed that the child citizens, to whom they were related, had a right to the care and companionship of their family in Ireland. The parties agreed that *Fajujonu* correctly stated the law, but disagreed over what *Fajujonu* meant. The Supreme Court was thus faced with the unenviable task of reconciling the inconsistencies between the judgments of Finlay CJ and Walsh J in *Fajujonu* itself. [9–50]

In doing so, they addressed three separate issues: the right of a citizen child to reside in the State; the right of a citizen child to the care and company of her parents in the State; and the species of common good that can override such a right. The applicants lost on all three counts.

The Right of a Child Citizen to Reside in the State

[9–51] Keane CJ, Hardiman, Geoghegan and Murray JJ appeared to agree that a child citizen could not assert her own right to reside in the State and that no such right could be asserted on her behalf by parents who were not independently entitled to remain in the State. Hardiman J put the matter as follows:

> I do not consider that a parent in taking a decision in relation to the welfare, education or residence of a child can realistically be described as exercising the child's choice for it. On the contrary, such parent is making his or her own decision for or on behalf of the child. This, however, is a parental decision, made in the ordinary course of the care and custody of a child and not a delegated exercise of some notional authority of the child. The myriad decisions, ranging from crucial to banal, which parents habitually take in relation to children are not usually so analysed as to their legal character and would not be here unless there was some point to be gained. In the case of an infant of about one year, it is wholly unrealistic to regard a decision as to place of residence as being anything but the parents' decision. As such, it is constrained by the parents' capacities: they are not at large in the decisions they can take but constrained by their material circumstances, their own needs and entitlements and the laws which apply to them. I believe that what the parents have done in this case was aptly described by Barrington J. in *Fajujonu v. Minister for Justice* [1990] 2 I.R. 151: they have posited on the child a wish to remain in Ireland. But this wish is wholly notional: the only persons at present capable of wishing or electing anything in relation to residence are the parents: the decision is theirs, subject only to their capacity and the laws applying to them....
>
> What is unusual about the present case is that the child has a right, which is not shared by the parents, which he is at present incapable of exercising. Accordingly, he will be bound by whatever decision the parents may lawfully make in his regard. A decision about a child's medical treatment is, *prima facie*, within the authority of his family. A decision about an alien parent's desire to live in the State is not. [2003] 1 IR 1, at 158–159.

[9–52] If a child citizen cannot assert her right to reside in the state and that right cannot be asserted on her behalf by her parents (unless they have some independent right to reside), it does not seem accurate to say that the child citizen has a right to reside in the State. Moreover, this approach is inconsistent with Finlay CJ's statement in *Fajujonu* that parents are entitled to assert a choice of residence on behalf of their infant children and Walsh J's view that citizens of the State may not be deported. People over the age of 18 have no constitutional entitlement to free primary education. On the basis of Hardiman J's reasoning, does this mean that parents cannot assert a child's right to free primary education?

[9–53] A similar argument to that of Hardiman J was made by Ireland before the European Court of Justice in Case C-200/02 *Chen v Secretary of State for the Home Department* [2004] ECR I-9925, where a non-EU national sought to gain a derivative right to reside in the United Kingdom based on the rights of her Irish (and therefore) EU citizen child, born in Belfast. The Advocate General rejected the Irish Government's argument to the effect that a child cannot have rights which it is incapable of independently asserting:

41. In that connection, the Irish Government appears to object that, as a matter of principle, Catherine could not invoke the rights of movement and residence provided for by the Treaty.
42. If I have correctly understood that government's reasoning, it considers that, given her tender age, Catherine is not in fact capable of independently exercising the right to choose a place of residence and establish herself there. Consequently, she cannot be regarded as a person entitled to the rights accorded to nationals of a Member State by Directive 90/364.
43. I do not agree with that reasoning. I think it derives from a confusion between the capacity of a person to be the subject of rights and obligations (legal personality) and the capacity of that person to take action which produces legal effects (legal capacity).
44. The fact that a minor cannot exercise a right independently does not mean that he has no capacity to be an addressee of the legal provision on which that right is founded.
45. The line of reasoning should instead follow the opposite course. Because, according to a general principle which is common to the legal systems of the Member States (and not only to them), legal capacity is acquired at birth, even a minor is a subject of law and, as such, is therefore a holder of the rights conferred by law.
46. The fact that he is not in a position to exercise those rights independently does not detract from his status as the holder of those rights. On the contrary, it is precisely because he has that status that other persons, appointed by operation of law (parents, guardian, etc.), will be able to give effect to his rights and will be able to do so not because they are the holders of those rights but because they are acting on behalf of the minor, that is, they are acting on behalf of the sole and actual holder of those rights

It is arguable that the Supreme Court in *Lobe* confused legal personality and legal capacity in the same way.

The Child Citizen's Right to the Care and Companionship of her Parents in the State

Keane CJ, Denham, Murray, Hardiman and Geoghegan J agreed that the child citizen had no substantive right to the care and companionship of her parents within the State. They reconciled this conclusion with *Fajujuonu* by emphasising the fact specificity of that case. For instance, Denham J observed that the length of time the parents were in the State was an "important factor" for the Court ([2003] 1 IR 1, at 53–54). However, this factor appears to have been more important for Finlay CJ than for Walsh J. In contrast, the minority judges (McGuinness and Fennelly JJ) considered that length of residence, although a factor recited by Finlay CJ, was not part of the ratio of the case [2003] 1 IR 1, at 120.

[9–54]

Addressing the issue on the basis of first principles, Murray J reasoned as follows:

> In my view the arguments advanced on behalf of the applicants in essence amount to a false syllogism. It was submitted that infants who are citizens have a constitutional right of residence. Such infants have a constitutional right to the care, company and parentage of their parents within the State. Therefore, the parents have a right to remain in the State. For the reasons outlined in this judgment, this conclusion is not validated by the preceding premises. In my view the arguments advanced on behalf of the applicants in essence amount to a false syllogism. It was submitted that infants who are citizens have a constitutional right of residence. Such infants have a constitutional right to the care, company and parentage of their parents within the State. Therefore, the parents have a right to remain in the State. For the reasons outlined in this judgment, this conclusion is not validated by the preceding premises. [2003] 1 IR 1, at 90.

[9–55] Although Murray J may have been correct to characterise the applicants' argument as a false syllogism, it does not necessarily follow from the failure of the syllogism that there is no basis on which the applicants' argument can be supported. Estelle Feldman and I have argued elsewhere as follows:

> Most people would accept, as a general proposition, that constitutional rights should be secured within the State. For instance, imagine an unlikely law authorising intrusive medical experiments on all children born to non-national parents once they reach their first birthday. It would scarcely count as a defence of this law that the children could exercise their right to reside in the State or their right to bodily integrity outside the State, but that there was no constitutional requirement that they be allowed to exercise both rights simultaneously. Although it does not deductively follow from one's right to residence and one's right to bodily integrity that one should be able to exercise the two simultaneously, the *prima facie* assumption is that one should be able to exercise them simultaneously. The same *prima facie* assumption should apply to the rights asserted in [*Lobe*]. Byrne and Binchy eds, *Annual Review of Irish Law 2003* (Thomson Round Hall, Dublin, 2004), at 154.

In the end, the majority concluded that the child citizen had a procedural right. This was well summarised by Finlay Geoghegan J in the later case of *Ojo v Minister for Justice,* 8 May 2003 (HC), at 33:

> Where there is an Irish born child, the Minister is obliged to consider the facts of each case by an appropriate inquiry in a fair and proper manner as to the facts and factors affecting the family. If the Minister is satisfied for good and sufficient reason that the common good requires that the residence of the parents within the State should be terminated even though that has the necessary consequence that in order to remain a family unit the child who is an Irish citizen must also leave the State then that is an order he is entitled to make.

Species of Common Good that can Override the Right

[9–56] The court again divided on this point, the majority judges concluding that generalised injury to the common good could justify a deportation. Murray J put the matter as follows:

> [The Minister] had regard to two matters which are material to promoting the interests of the common good, namely the application of the Dublin Convention [which established a system for determining which EU Member State was responsible for any particular asylum seeker] and the protection of the integrity of the immigration and asylum systems. Each of the families who comprise the applicants in this case were in this State for a relatively short period before the deportation orders were made. The grounds upon which they seek to challenge the respondent's deportation orders stem from the birth of children in this State some months after their arrival. It seems to me entirely reasonable to conclude that the circumstances relating to the applicants are not unique but on the contrary that it is a situation that could apply or would apply to a substantial proportion of applicants for asylum. In these circumstances, it seems to me entirely reasonable that the respondent would consider whether a refusal to make a deportation in such circumstances could call in question the integrity of the immigration and asylum systems including their effective functioning. That is a matter for him. It has not been contested that the circumstances of each of the families are such that the respondent may require that their applications for asylum be examined in another state pursuant to the Dublin Convention. [2003] 1 IR 1, at 91–92.

The minority judges, on the other hand, required evidence of specific damage to the common good, related to the particular applicants. McGuinness J put the matter as follows:

> It seems to me to be necessary for the respondent to have before him in his consideration of the case some specific evidence of the danger to the common good which is related to the illegal immigrants concerned, whether as individuals or as members of a class or group. [2003] 1 IR 1, at 122.

If generalised common good factors may be considered by the Minister, it becomes difficult to foresee any circumstances in which the procedural right *(ie* the right to have one's case considered) lead to a substantive decision in favour of the child. The integrity of the asylum system will always weigh against the child. This may count against allowing the consideration of such a general and omni-present factor. On the other hand, it could be argued that the control of immigration is a constitutional necessity. It is not something that the Executive *may choose* to do but rather is something that the Executive *must* do. If this is the case, one may have to accept the interference with family rights. Article 9 of the Constitution has since been amended with the result that children born in Ireland to non-national parents are not constitutionally entitled to Irish citizenship unless their parents resided in Ireland for three years prior to their birth. In the light of this amendment, it is questionable whether the integrity of the asylum system still counts as a good reason for overriding the constitutional right. [9–57]

As seen above, the All Party Oireachtas Committee has recommended that the following be inserted in the Constitution:

> All children, irrespective of birth, gender, race or religion, are equal before the law. In all cases where the welfare of the child so requires, regard shall be had to the best interests of that child.

The Committee believes that this provision will provide indirect uplift in the rights of non-marital fathers. If this is the case, it is possible that the explicitly stated equality of children irrespective of race might oblige the Supreme Court to revise its view that the children of non-nationals have fewer rights than children of nationals.

Following the *Lobe* decision, the citizenship referendum in 2004 and alterations to the patterns of births to non-Irish parents within Ireland, the Minister for Justice decided that "rather than engaging in a case by case analysis, as a gesture of generosity and solidarity to the persons concerned, a general policy would be adopted of granting those persons (the non-Irish parents of Irish born children) permission to remain in the State provided that they fulfilled certain criteria." For this reason, the Minister established IBC/05. A number of persons refused residence under the scheme challenged those refusals in *Bode v Minister for Justice, Equality and Law Reform* [2006] IEHC 341 (and related cases). The Minister accepted that, in administering the Scheme and deciding on particular applications, no consideration had been given by him or on his behalf to the position or rights of the Irish born child. Whereas the right asserted in *Lobe* had been the right of the child to have the care and companionship of its parents within the State, the right most strongly asserted in *Bode* was the right of the child to be reared and educated with due regard to her welfare including a right to [9–58] have her welfare considered in the sense of what was in her best interests in decisions affecting her. The Minister did not contend that there were common good reasons that justified him in not taking into account the rights of the child, nor that there were common good reasons that required him to refuse an application where continuous residency had not been established.

[9–59] Finlay Geoghegan J reasoned that a positive decision on an IBC/05 application is one which has a considerable impact on a child's life. It prima facie defends and vindicates the personal rights of the citizen child to live in the State and to be reared and educated with due regard to her welfare. It was therefore a breach of the rights of the citizen child for a decision to be taken in relation to IBC/05 without any consideration of the rights of that child. She put the position as follows:

> Applying the above to the rights identified herein and the IBC/05 application the position appears to be as follows. The citizen child of the non-national parent has, *prima facie*, a right to remain in the State. While in the State (at least) the citizen child has a right to be educated and reared with due regard to his/her welfare and in a decision affecting this, to have considered what is in his/her best interests. These are qualified rights in the sense that the respondent having had due regard to these rights and taking account of all relevant factual circumstances may decide for good and sufficient reason, in the interests of the common good, that the parent be refused permission to remain in the State even if this is a decision which is not in the best interests of the child. In deciding whether there is such good and sufficient reason in the interests of the common good to refuse the application of the parent on IBC/05 for permission to remain in the State the respondent should ensure that his decision, in the particular circumstances of the citizen child and parent is not disproportionate to the ends sought to be achieved. (At 34 of the Unreported Judgment.)

The Supreme Court unanimously allowed the State's appeal, taking a very different view of the IBC/05 scheme. Denham J, with whom the other members of the Court agreed, characterised the scheme in the following terms:

> The scheme was introduced by the Minister, exercising the executive power of the State, to address in an administrative and generous manner a unique situation which had occurred in relation to a significant number of foreign nationals within the State. However, those who did not succeed on their application under this scheme remained in the same situation as they had been prior to their application. They were still entitled to have the Minister consider the Constitutional and Convention rights of all relevant persons.
> The scheme enabled a fast, executive decision, giving a benefit to very many people. However, a negative decision in the IBC 05 Scheme did not affect any substantive claim for permission to remain in the State. In other words, an adverse decision to an applicant under the IBC 05 Scheme left the applicant in no worse position than he or she was prior to the application as no decision had been made on any substantive rights [2007] IESC 62.

[9–60] For this reason, there was no obligation on the Minister to consider the rights of the child when making a decision under the IBC/05 scheme. In other words, as a negative decision under the scheme would not put the child in any worse position than she would have been in had the scheme not existed—and as the scheme was an act of Executive generosity—there was no need to consider the rights of the child at that stage. The rights of the child could be considered at the other statutory stages in the decision-making process, for instance when a deportation order was being made. This left open the possibility that the Minister is under an obligation to consider the Irish child's right to have its welfare taken into account when deportation decisions are made about its non-Irish parents.

In the subsequent case of *Dimbo v Minister for Justice* [2008] IESC 26, the Supreme Court quashed a deportation decision on the basis that the Minister had not given adequate consideration to the rights of the child. Denham J, with whom the other members of the Court agreed, outlined the sort of consideration that the Minister ought to give to these issues: [9–61]

> I would affirm the decision that the consideration should be fact specific to the individual child, his or her age, current educational progress, development and opportunities. This consideration relates not only to educational issues but also involves the consideration of the attachment of the child to the community, and other matters referred to in s.3 of the Act of 1999.
> The extent of the consideration will depend on the facts of the case, including the age of the child, the length of time he or she has been in the State, and the part, if any, he or she has taken in the community. Thus, his or her education, and development within the State, within the context of his or her family circumstances, may be relevant. If the child has been in the State for many years, and in the school system for several years, and taken part in the community, then these and related facts may be very pertinent. However, if the child is an infant then such considerations will not arise.
> However, I respectfully disagree with the learned trial judge, and I believe the High Court erred, in holding that the Minister was required to inquire into and take into account the educational facilities and other conditions available to the Irish born child of a proposed deportee in the country of return, in the event that the child accompany the deportee. I am satisfied that while the Minister should consider in a general fashion the situation in the country where the child's parent may be deported, it is not necessary to do a specific analysis of the educational and development opportunities that would be available to the child in the country of return. The Minister is not required to inquire in detail into the educational facilities of the country of the deportee. This general approach does not exclude a more detailed analysis in an exceptional case. The decision of the Minister is required to be proportionate and reasonable on the application as a whole, and not on the specific factor of comparative educational systems.

Woman's Life Within the Home

Article 41.2 is probably the most contentious provision in the Constitution. It recognises the role of woman within the home and provides that the State will endeavour to ensure that "mothers shall not be obliged by economic necessity to engage in labour to the neglect of their duties in the home." Many object to the constitutional endorsement to such a gendered division of labour. Any considered view of Art 41.2 must set it alongside Art 45.2(i) (which speaks of the equal right of men and women to an adequate means of livelihood) and Art 45.4 which explicitly recognises women workers. For this reason, Art 41.2 cannot be understood as intended to preclude women from the world of work. However, it does clearly envisage women (particularly mothers) as the appropriate home-makers and carers, with all that implies for a gendered division of labour. [9–62]

Legitimising Discrimination by Reference to Art 41.2

The courts have, at times, relied on Art 41.2 to justify certain sex discriminations. In *de Búrca v Attorney General* [1976] IR 38; (1977) 111 ILTR 37, O'Higgins CJ relied on Art [9–63]

41.2 to uphold the constitutional validity of s 5 of the Juries Act 1927 which exempted women from jury service, unless they specifically opted in under s 16 of that Act. O'Higgins CJ considered that such an exclusion was nearly mandated by Art 41.2. (The other members of the Court disagreed with O'Higgins CJ and struck down s 5.) In *O'G v Attorney General* [1985] ILRM 61, the plaintiff challenged the constitutionality of s 5(1) of the Adoption Act 1974 which precluded adoption orders being made in favour of childless widowers. McMahon J rejected the State's arguments based on Art 41.2, noting that although the article recognised the value of a mother's work in the home, it did not involve a "denial of the capacity of widowers as a class to be considered on the merits as suitable adopters." [1985] ILRM 61, at 65.

[9–64] The State has more successfully relied on Art 41.2 in the socioeconomic context. In *Dennehy v Minister for Social Welfare*, 24 July 1984 (HC), Barron J upheld the constitutional validity of various social welfare provisions that discriminated in favour of deserted wives as against deserted husbands. The Supreme Court took a similar approach in the later case of *Lowth v Minister for Social Welfare* [1998] 4 IR 321, at 341; [1999] 1 ILRM 5, at 13, commenting, "the provisions of the Constitution dealing with the family recognise a social and domestic order in which married women are unlikely to work outside the family home."

Attempts to Expand Art 41.2

[9–65] A number of judges have attempted to expand the reach of Art 41.2, but these attempts have not yet found general favour. In *L v L* [1989] ILRM 528 (HC); [1992] 2 IR 77 (SC); [1992] ILRM 115 (SC), the plaintiff claimed that her husband owned part of the family home on a resulting trust for her. Under ordinary, equitable principles, to establish a resulting trust, one must have made a contribution in money or money's worth to the purchase price. As a full-time housewife, the plaintiff had not earned the money to make such a contribution and thus found herself prejudiced by the equitable principles. Both the High Court and the Supreme Court accepted that these principles were incompatible with Art 41.2. However, whereas Barr J (in the High Court) was prepared to develop the equitable principles so as to render them consistent with Art 41.2, the Supreme Court considered that such an approach would amount to the creation of new law and went beyond the judicial role.

[9–66] In *Sinnott v Minister for Education* [2001] 2 IR 545, an autistic man successfully sued the State for its failure to provide for his free primary education up to the age of 18. His mother also sued the State, claiming that her constitutional rights had also been infringed. A majority of the Supreme Court held that Mrs Sinnott had no recognisable cause of action; they were particularly concerned by the possibility of derivative causes of action (*ie* Mrs Sinnott having her own cause of action out of precisely the same facts as gave rise to Jamie Sinnott's right of action). Denham J, however, held in favour of Mrs Sinnott. She distinguished *L v L* on the grounds that it concerned a balance of property rights as between spouses, not a protection of the family from the outside. Denham J reasoned as follows:

> [Mrs Sinnott] has rights as part of the unit of the family and duties as a parent within that family unit. If there is a breach by the State of a right of one of the members of the unit as, for example, here the child the first plaintiff, then because of the nature of the right breached this may have an impact on the family as a unit and the parent in the family. The

> negative impact on the family and [Mrs Sinnott] was fully documented by the learned High Court judge.... [This case] is grounded on a fundamental concept ... that our society is built on the family. Further, that within the family the special benefit given by women in the home, is recognised. It is acknowledged that that benefit is not just for the particular home, family and children, but for the common good.
>
> This special recognition is of the 21st century and belongs to the whole of society. It is not to be construed as representing a norm of a society long changed utterly. Rather it is to be construed in the Ireland of the Celtic Tiger. As important now as ever, is the recognition given. It is a recognition for all families—of whatever religion or none.
>
> Thus, in Ireland, in relation to the family and the home, women have a constitutionally recognised role which is acknowledged as being for the common good. This gives to women an acknowledged status in recognition not merely of the physical aspect of home making and family building, but of the emotional, social, physical, intellectual and spiritual work of women and mothers. The undefined and valuable role of the father was presumed and remained unenumerated by the drafters of the Constitution.
>
> Article 41.2 does not assign women to a domestic role. Article 41.2 recognises the significant role played by wives and mothers in the home. This recognition and acknowledgement does not exclude women and mothers from other roles and activities. It is a recognition of the work performed by women in the home. The work is recognised because it has immense benefit for society. This recognition must be construed harmoniously with other Articles of the Constitution when a combination of Articles fall to be analysed. [2001] 2 IR 545, at 662–665.

Denham J held that, given the way in which education rights are stitched into family rights and the constitutionally approved role of mothers within families, the breach of her son's education rights amounted to a breach of Mrs Sinnott's own rights.

Article 8 of the European Convention on Human Rights has been interpreted by the European Court of Human Rights as imposing some positive obligations on states to protect family life. See, for instance, *Botta v Italy* (1998) 26 EHRR 241. Setting aside the majority's concerns in *Sinnott* over derivative actions, it is possible that Denham J's reasoning may provide the seeds of a positive rights interpretation of Art 41. That said, given the courts' current wariness of positive rights, such seeds may take a long time to germinate.

[9–67]

Mullally has commented on *Sinnott* as follows:

> Denham J highlighted the relational nature of rights and responsibilities within the family. She noted that Kathy Sinnott had rights and duties as a parent within the family unit. A breach by the state of the rights of one member of the family could have a negative impact on the family, and particularly on the person charged with the primary care of the family—in this case, Kathy Sinnott. Denham J also attempts to rescue Article 41.2, which she argues, does not assign women to a domestic role, but rather seeks to give recognition to the work performed by women in the home. In this case, she concluded, the state had failed to give due recognition to the work performed by Kathy Sinnott, work, Denham J noted, that was of "immense benefit for society". Denham J's arguments stand in marked contrast to the reluctance of the majority of the judiciary to inquire into relations within the family and to give legal recognition to the work of carers within the home. The majority of the Supreme Court acknowledged the work undertaken by Kathy Sinnott, but refused to acknowledge any rights arising from her role as a carer. The transformative potential of rights is blocked by a deeply gendered division between the public and the private spheres and a presumption that the tests of justice that normally apply within the

public sphere do not extend to domestic relations. Siobhán Mullally, *Feminist Jurisprudence* in Tim Murphy ed, *Western Jurisprudence* (Thomson Round Hall, Dublin, 2004), at 365.

[9–68] Article 41.2 has traditionally been a feminist bugbear. However, perhaps by focusing the courts' attention on private life within the home (where care has traditionally been provided by women) it forces the state to ponder the justice of care arrangements. From a feminist perspective, does this possibility offset the detriment of having textual, constitutional endorsement for gendered care roles?

In *DT v CT* [2003] 1 ILRM 321, at 376, Murray J made the following *obiter* comments about Art 41.2:

> The Constitution views the family as indispensable to the welfare of the State. Article 41.2.1° recognises that by her life in the home the woman gives to the State a support without which the common good cannot be achieved. No doubt the exclusive reference to women in that provision reflects social thinking and conditions at the time. It does however expressly recognise that work in the home by a parent is indispensable to the welfare of the State by virtue of the fact that it promotes the welfare of the family as a fundamental unit in society. *A fortiori* it recognises that work in the home is indispensable for the welfare of the family, husband, wife and children, where there are children.... I would observe in passing that the Constitution, as this court has stated on a number of occasions, is to be interpreted as a contemporary document. The duties and obligations of spouses are mutual and, without elaborating further since nothing turns on this point in this case, it seem to me that it implicitly recognises similarly the value of a man's contribution in the home as a parent.

It is difficult to identify a canon of interpretation that allows the references in Art 41.2 to be extended to men and fathers.

Proposals for Change

[9–69] The Constitution Review Group recommended the retention of Art 41.2, but in gender-neutral form:

> The State recognises that home and family life gives to society a support without which the common good cannot be achieved. The State shall endeavour to support persons caring for others within the home.

The All Party Oireachtas Committee recommended a different gender-neutral form of Art 41.2:

> The State recognises that by reason of family life within the home, a parent gives to the State a support without which the common good cannot be achieved.
> The State shall, therefore, endeavour to ensure that both parents shall not be obliged by economic necessity to work outside the home to the neglect of their parental duties.

The Oireachtas committee's suggestion clearly covers only parental carers, excluding non-parental carers. Whatever the importance of work done by non-parental carers, recognition of such a role would not fit easily with the nuclear family ethos of Art 41. That said, given that ethos, is it consistent to have a gender-neutral version of Art 41.2?

The Autonomy of Married Couples

We have seen how the courts have on occasion characterised Arts 41 and 42 as protecting the family from outside interference. This aspect of family rights comes into sharp focus in the context of the autonomy of married couples to make decisions for themselves without State interference. Partially in response to the situation identified in *L v L*, the Oireachtas enacted the Matrimonial Home Bill 1993. Section 4 of the Bill provided that where either or both spouses owned a legal or beneficial interest in the matrimonial home, a beneficial interest would vest in both spouses as joint tenants. Section 7, however, provided that such a beneficial interest would not vest where a spouse or person intending to marry excluded the application of the Bill, having previously obtained independent legal advice. Section 6 of the Bill provided a further exception where a court, upon application being made to it by the owning spouse, could order that it would be unjust to deem that the property was jointly owned. The Supreme Court, on an Art 26 reference, decided that the Bill was repugnant to Art 41: [9–70]

> The Court accepts that the provisions of this Bill are directed to encourage the joint ownership of matrimonial homes and that such an objective is clearly an important element of the common good conducive to the stability of marriage and the general protection of the institution of the family. In this context it relies upon the views expressed in the judgments of the Court in *L. v. L.* [1992] 2 I.R. 77.
>
> It is the opinion of the Court that the right of a married couple to make a joint decision as to the ownership of a matrimonial home is one of the rights possessed by the family which is recognised by the State in Article 41, s. 1, sub-s. 1 of the Constitution as antecedent and superior to all positive law and its exercise is part, and an important part, of the authority of the family which in Article 41, s. 1, sub-s. 2 the State guarantees to protect.
>
> The provisions of the Bill apply the automatic ownership as joint tenants to every instance of a dwelling occupied by a married couple on or after the 25th June, 1993, other than dwellings already owned equally. The interference with decisions which may have been jointly made by spouses with regard to the ownership of the matrimonial home effected by this universal application does not therefore depend in any way on instances where the decision arrived at constitutes something which is injurious to or oppressive of the interests of a spouse or of members of the family or which constitutes a failure on the part of one of the spouses to discharge what might fairly be considered as his or her family obligations.
>
> The mandatory creation of joint equal interests in the family home also applies to every dwelling occupied as a family home irrespective of when it was first acquired by the married couple concerned and irrespective therefore of the time at which a freely arrived at decision between them may have been made as to the nature of the ownership and in whom it should vest. The provisions of the Bill do not seek to apply to particular categories of cases only, or to particular instances of the acquisition and ownership of matrimonial homes only, but rather are applied to each and every category and instance falling within the time scale provided for in the Bill, with a right of defeasance.
>
> This right of defeasance consists in the first instance in the provisions of s. 7 of the Bill which permit a non-owning spouse who would benefit by virtue of the provisions of s. 4, sub-s. 2 by becoming an equal owner with the owning spouse to declare in writing after having obtained legal advice that he or she does not wish that the section should apply to the home.
>
> In the case of joint decisions which may have been made, possibly many years before and succeeded by other arrangements of family assets and possessions founded on the original agreed decision concerning the ownership of the family home, this means that the entire matter must again be reviewed between the spouses and that if a decision which has

already existed in favour of ownership by one of them is to be continued, that the non-owning spouse must register the declaration under section 7.

In the event that such a joint decision has been made a considerable number of years ago, even though freely and fully agreed at that time, it may be that upon the passing of this Bill a non-owning spouse on grounds which could be reasonable or could be wholly unreasonable would not be willing to make the declaration under section 7.

In those circumstances section 6 of the Bill comes into operation and forces a couple who may well have been content though not enthusiastic about the arrangements which they had made and by which a substantial part of their married life had been governed to become involved in the litigation contemplated by section 6.

In some instances the net effect of these legislative proposals would be automatically to cancel a joint decision freely made by both spouses as part of the authority of the family and substitute therefor a wholly different decision unless the spouses can agree to a new joint decision to confirm the earlier agreement or unless the owning spouse can succeed in obtaining a court order pursuant to section 6.

Having regard to the extreme importance of the authority of the family as acknowledged in Article 41 of the Constitution and to the acceptance in that Article of the fact that the rights which attach to the family including its right to make decisions within its authority are inalienable and imprescriptible and antecedent and superior to all positive law, the Court is satisfied that such provisions do not constitute reasonably proportionate intervention by the State with the rights of the family and constitute a failure by the State to protect the authority of the family.

The Court accepts, as it has indicated, the advantages of encouraging, by any appropriate means, joint ownership in family homes as being conducive to the dignity, reassurance and independence of each of the spouses and to the partnership concept of marriage which is fundamental to it. It is not, however, satisfied that the potentially indiscriminate alteration of what must be many joint decisions validly made within the authority of the family concerning the question of the ownership of the family home could reasonably be justified even by such an important aspect of the common good. [1994] 1 IR 325–327.

[9–71] This decision marks a very strong protection of marital autonomy. Although the Supreme Court accepted that the Oireachtas could seek to protect the more vulnerable spouse (typically the wife) where marital relationships broke down, it reasoned that marital autonomy had not been sufficiently protected by the Bill. The Court was unimpressed with the exceptions provided by the Oireachtas to cater for marital autonomy. In this regard, the Court set a very high threshold. The Oireachtas had provided an exception, under s 7, whereby a spouse could, having obtained legal advice, opt out of joint ownership. There was also a discretion for a court to declare that it would be unjust for co-ownership applied. Taken together, these exceptions would have allowed a court to hold spouses to a genuine joint decision as to the ownership of their home. For the Supreme Court, however, the very fact that a court application might be required to vindicate such a joint decision meant that marital autonomy had been unduly interfered with. If this is the case, it becomes difficult to see how any retrospective scheme of joint ownership could ever be legislatively imposed, notwithstanding the Supreme Court's dictum that such a scheme was an aspect of the common good that could be pursued by the Oireachtas. This shows very little, if any, deference to the Oireachtas's choice of means for pursuing a legitimate objective. A prospective-only scheme might avoid these difficulties; however, as houses bought by spouses since 1993 have tended to be co-owned in any event, such legislation might serve little purpose.

The Court speaks of the "extreme importance of the authority of the family." When [9–72] one protects the autonomy of a group, one protects the authority of those who are powerful within the group, i.e. the authority of those who (in reality) make the decisions for the group. Although the rationale of the Supreme Court's decision was to protect decisions taken jointly by husband and wife, its most significant effect was presumably to protect decisions taken by husbands to benefit themselves. It is probably reasonable to assume that significantly more marital decisions (both as regards ownership of the marital home and generally) are now taken jointly than was the case prior to 1993. For that reason, the Court's decision poses fewer practical concerns. However, the same dynamics can be seen at play in relation to children's rights. In this context, the questions become: who makes decisions or asserts rights on behalf of children? In what circumstances can the State intervene?

Children's Rights and Family Autonomy

Children's Rights

Children do have constitutional rights. One can assume that children have the rights [9–73] stated in the Constitution, unless those rights are explicitly (or implicitly) age-limited, such as the right to vote under Art 16.2. Thus in *Landers v Attorney General* (1975) 109 ILTR 1, the High Court implicitly accepted that Art 40.1 prima facie applied to children. The plaintiff was a young child with a good singing voice. It was argued that ss 2(b) and 2(c) of the Prevention of Cruelty to Children Act 1904, which restricted the hours at which the plaintiff could perform, were unconstitutionally discriminatory. Finlay J rejected these arguments on the basis that the discrimination could not be described as invidious.

Children, however, have also been held to have a number of specific rights. Article 42.5 [9–74] refers to the rights of the child in requiring the State, when taking the place of parents, to act "always with due regard for the natural and imprescriptible rights of the child". Given its textual position—as a saver to an exception allowing intervention in the marital family—the most obvious meaning of this phrase would be that the State, when interfering in a marital family, must always have due regard to the rights of the child to be part of that family. However, the courts have given this phrase a considerably more expansive reading. In *State (Nicolaou) v An Bord Uchtála* [1966] IR 567, at 643 Walsh J commented that such rights included "the right to religious and moral, intellectual, physical and social education."

In *G v An Bord Uchtála* [1980] IR 32, at 55–56, O'Higgins CJ described the rights of the child in the following terms:

> The child also has natural rights. Normally, these will be safe under the care and protection of its mother. Having been born, the child has the right to be fed and to live, to be reared and educated, to have the opportunity of working and of realising his or her full personality and dignity as a human being. These rights of the child (and others which I have not enumerated) must equally be protected and vindicated by the State. In exceptional cases the State, under the provisions of Article 42, s. 5, of the Constitution, is given the duty, as guardian of the common good, to provide for a child born into a family where the parents fail in their duty towards that child for physical or moral reasons. In the same way, in special circumstances the State may have an equal obligation in relation to a child born outside the family to protect that child, even against its mother,

if her natural rights are used in such a way as to endanger the health or life of the child or to deprive him of his rights. In my view this obligation stems from the provisions of Article 40, s. 3, of the Constitution.

[9–75] This is a list of rights with which few, if any, could disagree. Indeed, it provides little that is not provided to all people (such as the right to life and the right to work) or that is not reasonably implicit in other provisions of the Constitution (such as the right to be educated). However, the right to be fed might have some novel implications. The real controversy, however, lies not in the enumeration of rights but rather in the question of who asserts those rights on behalf of the child. In outline, the position adopted by the courts has been that parents have the primary role in relation to the assertion of their children's rights (and of making decisions generally for their children), but that the State can intervene in exceptional circumstances. This position has been developed in three separate contexts: custody, health care and education.

Parental Autonomy in the Custody Context

[9–76] In *M v An Bord Uchtála* [1977] IR 287, an unmarried mother placed her son for adoption. However, it transpired that there had been a flaw with the adoption process in that, contrary to ss 14 and 15 of the Adoption Act 1952, the Adoption Board had not satisfied itself that the natural mother understood the nature and effect of her consent and of the adoption order. The adoption order was therefore void. In the meantime, the child's mother had married the child's father. As the adoption order was void, the Supreme Court was faced with a custody dispute between the natural and married parents of the child and proposed adoptive parents. A majority of the Supreme Court held that the child should be returned to his natural and married parents, notwithstanding that he had lived the first six years of his life with his adoptive parents, O'Higgins CJ reasoning:

> I must now consider the position of the plaintiffs, the child and the adopting parents. It has been argued by counsel for the Board that the plaintiffs' failure to take action earlier than they did, with the consequent effect on the child in relation to his surroundings, renders it unjust and contrary to the child's interests to remove him now from the care of the adopting parents. No one can be unmoved by such a plea or feel anything but compassion for all of those involved in this human drama. However, in coming to a just conclusion one must not allow compassion to confuse, or permit sympathy to conceal, fundamental rights. [1977] IR 287, at 296.

[9–77] This approach explicitly placed the fundamental rights of the parents above the question of the child's best interests. Henchy J dissented, partly on the basis of the culpable delay on the part of the child's natural parents in instituting legal proceedings, and partly on the basis of the welfare of the child:

> The child, a boy now six years old, has been growing up in an Irish provincial setting. He has never known his parents. His father has never seen him. His mother last saw him when he was about five weeks old. For the whole of his sentient life he has been with the adoptive parents. The plaintiffs' case simply is that, because the adoption order was made without jurisdiction the child should now be sundered from the adoptive parents and, regardless of how damaging it might be to the child or to the adoptive parents, be sent out to a foreign country to take his place in the plaintiffs' home as their legitimated child. If

> the plaintiffs' case is accepted, this would be done without hearing any representations on behalf of either the child or the adoptive parents. No account would be taken of the possible ill-effects of the sudden and drastic transfer of this six-year-old boy to strange parents in a strange home in a far-away country.
>
> For my part, I am satisfied that the orders asked for in the statement of claim are discretionary orders and that, in the light of what has happened with the passage of time, the plaintiffs have now no standing to apply for those orders. In my opinion, the discretion of the Court should not be exercised in their favour for that reason and, more particularly, because it has not been shown that those orders would be compatible with the welfare of the child. [1977] IR 287, at 301.

[9–78] The judgments in *M* present an apparent conflict between the rights and welfare of the child, on the one hand, and the rights of the natural parents on the other. In subsequent cases, the substance of O'Higgins CJ's decision has been maintained but the underlying rationale has been adjusted. Accordingly, the issue is now framed in terms of a presumption that the welfare of a child is best served by living with her married parents and that the married parents make the best decisions on behalf of a child.

[9–79] In *Re JH* [1985] IR 375, the Supreme Court considered the situation of a child who had been placed for adoption. Prior to the adoption order being made final, the mother withdrew her consent to the adoption and married the father of the child. This again raised the issue of a dispute as to custody between natural, married parents and proposed adoptive parents. However, the child had only been with its proposed adoptive parents for two years. In this case, unlike in *M*, reliance was placed on s 3 of the Guardianship of Infants Act 1964, which requires the court to have regard to the welfare of the infant as the first and paramount consideration. Having regard to that test, Lynch J—in the High Court—held that custody of the child should remain with the adoptive parents because the evidence presented to the court as to the risk of long term psychological harm if custody was awarded to the natural parents was sufficiently proximate to outweigh the contrary factors such as the anomalous legal position of the infant as the legitimised child of the natural parents.

[9–80] The Supreme Court allowed the appeal on the part of the child's married, natural parents. Finlay CJ relied on Art 42.5 to hold that the State could not supplant the role of the parents save in exceptional circumstances where there was a physical or moral failure of duty on the part of the parents. It was necessary to read s 3 of the Guardianship of Infants Act 1964 in a manner compatible with this constitutional principle:

> In the case, therefore, of a contest between the parents of a legitimate child—who with the child constitute a family within the meaning of Articles 41 and 42 of the Constitution—and persons other than the parents as to the custody of the child, as this case is, it does not seem to me that s. 3 of the Act of 1964 can be construed as meaning simply that the balance of welfare as defined in s. 2 of the Act of 1964 must be the sole criterion for the determination by the Court of the issue as to the custody of the child. To put the matter in another way, it does not appear to me that this is a case, as would be the situation in a contest between the parents of a legitimate child as to which of them should have general custody, where the Court could or should determine the matter upon the basis of the preferred custody, having regard to the welfare of the child as defined in s. 2 of the Act....
>
> I would, therefore, accept the contention that in this case s. 3 of the Act of 1964 must be construed as involving a constitutional presumption that the welfare of the child, which is defined in s. 2 of the Act in terms identical to those contained in Article 42, s. 1, is

to be found within the family, unless the Court is satisfied on the evidence that there are compelling reasons why this cannot be achieved, or unless the Court is satisfied that the evidence establishes an exceptional case where the parents have failed to provide education for the child and to continue to fail to provide education for the child for moral or physical reasons. [1985] IR 375, at 394–395.

[9–81] Finlay CJ thus identified a primary rule that married parents should have custody of their child, subject to two exceptions. First, if there are compelling reasons as to why the child's welfare cannot be secured with her married parents, the Court may deprive those parents of custody. Secondly, if the parents have failed and continue to fail to provide education for their child, then the Court may award custody to other persons. This latter exception turns on culpability: parents who fail in their parental duties can lose custody. The first exception is less normatively loaded, in that it appears to turn on some conception of the child's best interests. However, the presumption identified by Finlay CJ is not merely an evidential presumption that simply requires the adoptive parents to show that the best interests of the child lie with them. Such an approach was advanced by Lynch J and explicitly rejected by the Supreme Court. Instead, it is a legal, counter-factual presumption. The Court presumes that the welfare of the child lies with the married parents, notwithstanding evidence in a particular case that this is not so. The presumption can only be displaced by compelling evidence that the welfare of the child *cannot* be secured with the married family.

[9–82] In 2006, this issue again arose for consideration by the courts. In *N v HSE* [2006] IEHC 278, the applicants sought the return to them of their daughter. Their daughter had been born to them in July 2004 while they were unmarried. She was placed for adoption and since November 2004 was in the care of the proposed adoptive parents. The applicants got married in January 2006 and six weeks later instituted habeas corpus proceedings to secure the return of their daughter. The High Court gave its judgment in June 2006. As with the earlier cases, no final adoption order had been made at this stage so their daughter had not yet become the child of the constitutional family of the proposed adoptive parents. The High Court held that the adoptive parents should retain custody of the child. This decision was quickly appealed to the Supreme Court, which unanimously reversed the High Court's decision, thus re-establishing the orthodoxy of *Re JH*.

[9–83] Hardiman J provided a cogent justification for the primacy given to parental rights by the Constitution. He endorsed the test in *Re JH*, emphasising that there was a constitutional presumption that the welfare of the child is to be found within the family; accordingly, state intervention can only be justified if it is established that there are compelling reasons why the welfare of the child *cannot* be secured in the custody of the parents. Responding to the general public debate on the issue of parental authority, he offered the following defence of this constitutional position:

> I do not regard the constitutional provisions summarised above, or the jurisprudence to which they have given rise, as in any sense constituting an adult centred dispensation or as preferring the interests of marital parents to those of the child. In the case of a child of very tender years, as here, the decisions to be taken and the work to be done, daily and hourly, for the securing of her welfare through nurturing and education, must of necessity be taken and performed by a person or persons other than the child herself. Both according to the natural order, and according to the constitutional order, the rights and

duties necessary for those purposes are vested in the child's parents. Though selflessness and devotion towards children may easily be found in other persons, it is the experience of mankind over millennia that they are very generally found in natural parents, in a form so disinterested that in the event of conflict the interest of the child will usually be preferred....

There are certain misapprehensions on which repeated and unchallenged public airings have conferred undeserved currency. One of these relates to the position of children in the Constitution. It would be quite untrue to say that the Constitution puts the rights of parents first and those of children second. It fully acknowledges the "natural and imprescriptible rights" and the human dignity, of children, but equally recognises the inescapable fact that a young child cannot exercise his or her own rights. The Constitution does not prefer parents to children. The preference the Constitution gives is this: it prefers parents to third parties, official or private, priest or social worker, as the enablers and guardians of the child's rights. This preference has its limitations: parents cannot, for example, ignore the responsibility of educating their child. More fundamentally, the Constitution provides for the wholly exceptional situation where, for physical or moral reasons, parents fail in their duty towards their child. Then, indeed, the State must intervene and endeavour to supply the place of the parents, always with due regard to the rights of the child.

If the prerogatives of the parents in enabling and protecting the rights of the child were to be diluted, the question would immediately arise: to whom and on what conditions are the powers removed from the parents to be transferred? And why?

[9–84] Applying the "compelling reasons" test and having reviewed the evidence, Hardiman J held that a phased and gradual transfer of custody from the adoptive parents to the natural, married parents would mitigate any concerns as to long-term psychological damage to the child. The Court could not take into account any inability on the part of the adoptive parents to participate in such a process. There were, therefore, no compelling reasons why the welfare of the child could not be achieved with the married parents. Applying the "failure of duty" test, Hardiman J held that participation in the adoption process (i.e. the taking of steps that could lead to a child's adoption) could not constitute a failure of duty.

[9–85] Hardiman J's judgment is consistent with *Re JH* and effectively restores the constitutional status quo that was unsettled by McMenamin's judgment in the High Court. However, his rationalisation and statement of the constitutional position raises a broader issue that perhaps suggest some shift in constitutional thinking. His judgment referred repeatedly to the constitutional presumption that the welfare of the child is to be found in her natural family. However, this is not what was held in *Re JH*. In that case, Finlay CJ's comments were explicitly referenced to a context where there was "a contest between the parents of a legitimate child—who with the child constitute a family within the meaning of Articles 41 and 42 of the Constitution—and persons other than the parents as to the custody of the child". Thus Hardiman J's judgment effectively replaces a presumption in favour of the marital family with a presumption in favour of the natural family. This raised few issues in *Re JH* itself as the natural family had got married, but it is not difficult to see how it could pose difficulties. At an ideological level, it is clearly inconsistent with the whole ethos of Arts 41 and 42. From *State (Nicolaou)* onwards, the courts have been consistent in their view that Arts 41 and 42 protect the marital family, not natural families. While natural mothers have many rights in respect of their children, natural fathers do not. This points up the second difficulty with Hardiman J's presumption in favour of natural families: what happens where the natural parents do not agree on the custody of the child? Thirdly, consider the situation where the adoption had been completed and the child had become part of the adoptive parents' marital and constitutionally protected family before her natural parents got married. On the basis of Hardiman J's presumption in favour of the natural family, the child would have to be returned to her natural parents. On the basis of the *Re JH* presumption, however, the child would have to remain with her married adoptive parents. The courts will have to resolve this conflict in a future case.

Parental Autonomy in the Health Context

[9–86] Over time, the courts have come to a very similar position in relation to parental autonomy in relation to health care decisions. Here, however, the disagreement is not between two sets of parents but rather between the married parents and the State acting to preserve what it regards as the best interests of the children. In *Ryan v Attorney General* [1963] IR 294, the plaintiff objected to plans to fluoridate the water supply. One of her arguments was that this undermined her parental authority to make decisions about the best way to care for the health of her children. The Supreme Court rejected this argument, reasoning that there was nothing in the Constitution "which recognises the right of a parent to refuse to allow the provision of measures designed to secure the health of his child when the method of avoiding injury is one which is not fraught with danger to the child and is within the procurement of the parent." [1963] IR 294, at 350. In many ways, *Ryan* was a difficult case in that it would not have been possible to provide unfluoridated water to Mrs Ryan's family without denying the health benefits of fluoridation to the rest of the population.

[9–87] The issue of parental autonomy in health decisions came much more sharply into focus in *Northwestern Health Board v HW* [2001] 3 IR 622. Since 1979, health boards have carried out PKU tests on newly born children. This tests whether the child has a number of diseases. The prevalence of these diseases in Ireland is quite high; if diagnosed early, the diseases can be controlled by a combination of diet and medication; if undiagnosed, the diseases can all lead to severe mental handicap. The test consists of slightly puncturing the skin of the infant, usually in its heel, so as to procure a few drops of blood. This blood is then sent for analysis. In *NWHB*, the parents of an infant child refused their consent for the carrying out of this test. The Health Board applied to court for orders empowering it to carry out the test. In the High Court, McCracken J refused the orders sought, a position that was upheld by a majority of the Supreme Court on appeal.

Murphy J reasoned as follows:

> The position is different in the present case where the court is invited, to exercise, not the jurisdiction conferred upon it by particular legislation or in wardship matters, but the power and duty of the State in a role which is clearly subsidiary to that of the parents. In relation to the education of their children the relationship between the State and the family is clearly and expressly dealt with in Article 42. The corresponding rights and duties of the State in relation to matters of general medical welfare are unenumerated and ill defined but the subsidiarity of the State to the parents is clearly established. Clearly, it would be incorrect to suggest that the State could, or should, intervene merely because by doing so it could advance significantly the material interests of a child. If such a crude test were permitted then children of less well off parents might be given readily in fosterage to

others who, it could be demonstrated, had the capacity to advance the material and, even, moral welfare of the child.

The Thomistic philosophy—the influence of which on the Constitution has been so frequently recognised in the judgments and writings of Walsh J.—confers an autonomy on parents which is clearly reflected in these express terms of the Constitution which relegate the State to a subordinate and subsidiary role. The failure of the parental duty which would justify and compel intervention by the State must be exceptional indeed. It is possible to envisage misbehaviour or other activity on the part of parents which involves such a degree of neglect as to constitute abandonment of the child and all rights in respect of it. At the other extreme, lies the particular decision, made in good faith which could have disastrous results. In the present case the parents did not present a refusal to the proposed P.K.U. test. Indeed, they positively agreed to the test provided it could be carried out on hair or urine samples. The objection of the parents centres exclusively upon the invasion or puncture—as they see it—of the blood cells of the child. No reasoning based on any scientific view or any religious doctrine or practice was cited in support of this firmly stated objection. Nevertheless, I do not accept that a particular ill advised decision made by parents (whose care and devotion generally to their child was not disputed) could be properly categorised as such a default by the parents of their moral and constitutional duty so as to bring into operation the supportive role of the State.

If the State had an obligation in the present case to substitute its judgment for that of the parents, numerous applications would be made to the courts to overrule decisions made by caring but misguided parents. Such a jurisprudence and particular decisions made under it would tend to damage the long term interests of the child by eroding the interest and dedication of the parents in the performance of their duties. In my view the subsidiary and supplemental powers of the State in relation to the welfare of children arise only where either the general conduct or circumstances of the parents is such as to constitute a virtual abdication of their responsibilities or alternatively the disastrous consequences of a particular parental decision are so immediate and inevitable as to demand intervention and perhaps call into question either the basic competence or devotion of the parents. [2001] 3 IR 622, at 732–733.

Murphy J's reasoning suggests a similar approach to the role of parents as that seen in the custody cases. Provided decisions are taken in good faith, the State will not intervene, even though there may be disastrous consequences. Before the State can intervene, there must either be a virtual abdication of parental responsibility or disastrous consequences that are so immediate and inevitable as to demand intervention. Although the latter situation appears to focus more on the best interests of the child than on the bona fides of the parents, it is subject to the qualification that the disastrous consequences "perhaps call into question either the basic competence or devotion of the parents". This again shifts the focus away from the situation of the children onto the rights of the parents, rights that can only be lost through culpable behaviour. [9–88]

Murray J took a similar view:

What is in issue here is whether the defendants have acted in such a manner that exceptional circumstances arise by reason of a breach of duty on their part which would justify the State overriding their personal decision with regard to their child in this case. If the State had a duty or was entitled to override any decision of parents because it concluded, established or it was generally considered that that decision was not objectively the best decision in the interest of the child, it would involve the State and ultimately the courts, in a sort of micro-management of the family. Parents with unorthodox or unpopular views or lifestyles with a consequential influence on their children might for that reason *alone* find themselves subject to intervention by the State or by one of the agencies of the State. Similar consequences could flow where a parental decision was simply considered unwise. That would give the State a general power of intervention and would risk introducing a method of social control in which the State or its agencies would be substituted for the family. That would be an infringement of liberties guaranteed to the family. Decisions which are sometimes taken by parents concerning their children may be a source of discomfort or even distress to the rational and objective bystander, but it seems to me that there must be something exceptional arising from a failure of duty, as stated by this court in *The Adoption (No. 2) Bill, 1987* [1989] I.R. 656, before the State can intervene in the interest of the individual child. [2001] 3 IR 622, at 740.

[9–89] Murray J's concern over the micro-management of the family is similar—at least in form—to the concern expressed by the Supreme Court in *Re Article 26 and the Matrimonial Home Bill 1993* in relation to valid, joint decisions being overridden. In each case, concerns over particular vulnerable persons, whether young children or brow-beaten spouses, is subordinated to a more general and long-term concern over the effect of State intervention in family relations. One's views on the appropriateness of the Supreme Court's decisions in these cases probably turn on which one views as the more pressing social problem: the relatively small number of particularly vulnerable people who could suffer a lot, or the relatively large number of people generally (but not extremely) affected by increased State intervention.

[9–90] Keane CJ dissented. His judgment focuses less on the unitary family governed by parental decision and more on the position of individuals within the family, in particular the position of children:

> Article 41 speaks, not of the authority of parents, but of the authority of the family. While the family, because it derives from the natural order and is not the creation of civil society, does not, either under the Constitution or positive law, take the form of a juristic entity, it is endowed with an authority which the Constitution recognises as being superior even to the authority of the State itself. While there may inevitably be tensions between laws enacted by the State for the common good of society as a whole and the unique status of the family within that society, the Constitution firmly outlaws any attempt by the State in its laws or its executive actions to usurp the exclusive and privileged role of the family in the social order.
>
> The family as a concept is, of course, meaningless divorced from the individuals of which it is composed....
>
> The intervention of the High Court in this case was sought by the plaintiff in order, as it claimed, to protect and vindicate the personal rights of Paul under Article 40.3, including the unenumerated rights referred to in that passage. Specifically, it was said that the court had an inherent jurisdiction to protect those rights which was not dependent on any statutory provision.
>
> That such a jurisdiction exists is, I think, clear. The cases in which it may be invoked will, of course, be unusual and perhaps even exceptional, since in the vast majority of cases it can safely be left to the parents to protect their children's rights. It is not the law, however, that the courts are powerless to protect those rights in cases where, for whatever reason, they cannot be afforded that protection by the other organs of State or where—as here—it is said that they are not being upheld by the parents.
>
> I have no doubt that the passage I have cited already from the judgment of Waite L.J. in the English Court of Appeal in *In re T. (A Minor) (C.A.)* [1997] 1 W.L.R. 242, also represents the law in this jurisdiction. I do not accept the submission advanced on behalf of the defendants that, because of the particular provisions of the Constitution upholding the authority and constitution of the family, the court, in a case such as this, is obliged to

allow the wishes of the parents, however irrational they may be, to prevail over the best interests of Paul, which must be the paramount concern of the court under the Constitution and the law. Far from giving effect to the values enshrined in Article 42, such an approach would gravely endanger his right, so far as human endeavours can secure it, to a healthy and happy life and would be a violation of those individual rights to which he is entitled as a member of the family and which the courts are obliged to uphold. It seems to me that the wise and humane observations of Waite L.J. in *In re T. (A Minor) (C.A.)* [1997] 1 W.L.R. 242, are completely in harmony with the philosophy which informs our Constitution since they lay proper emphasis on the weight that must be given, where appropriate, to the wishes of the parents. It is, indeed, noteworthy that, in that case, the court set aside the order at first instance requiring the operation to be carried out and, on one view, the case could be regarded as being at the outer limits of the area in which the wishes of parents may outweigh what, on another view, might have appeared to be, on balance, in the best interests of the child. That the same considerations apply to the compulsory application of a particular test—as distinct from a purely medical procedure—is clear from the decision in *In re C. (A Child) (H.I.V. Testing) (Fam. D.)* [2000] Fam. 48, with which I would respectfully agree....

The trial judge was concerned in this case with what he saw as a rapid progression towards the "Brave New World" in which the State always knows best. I think that this, with respect, is a mistaken view. The plaintiff in this case, as an administrative body charged with promoting the welfare of children in its area, who may be regarded as an emanation of the State, ultimately does not claim to know best. It undoubtedly, however, approaches this case on the basis that the scientists know best. It can, of course, be said with some truth that not all the advances of science in our time have been beneficial, although the scientists would doubtless argue that this was because of the misuse which states and other organisations have made of their discoveries and inventions. No doubt, scientists, in common with other groups in society, can also be arrogant and complacent. The fact remains that in our daily lives we constantly proceed on the basis that they do indeed know best. When we board an aircraft, we like to think that the captain is guided by his or her technical manuals and not by what he or she has been told by an astrologer. If we have to undergo brain surgery, we would hope that the surgeon conducts the operation in accordance with the latest state of scientific knowledge and not in accordance with the requirements of some arcane religious cult.

It is also a mistaken belief, in my view, to equate the parents' refusal to allow this test to be carried out with the multitude of decisions parents make in their daily lives concerning the education and upbringing of their children. Every sensible parent recognises that they cannot hope to protect their children from the risks which are an inevitable part, of everyday existence and that, for example, to allow a child to play a particular game which on occasions has resulted in injury to those who take part is a decision which may, depending on the age of the child, have to be made by its parents and which could not conceivably, in any civilised society, be made by the State. None of those considerations apply to the test under consideration in the present case: a conscientious weighing by a properly informed parent of the dangers consequent on not having the test as against the minimally invasive nature of the procedure involved could in this case result in one conclusion only.

Nor can any useful analogy be drawn, in my view, with cases in which parents may decline to have their children inoculated or immunised against the risk of contracting specific diseases. It is common knowledge that there are cases in which at least some doctors question the desirability of the procedures involved and a court in such cases might well be reluctant to interfere with the conscientious decision of the parents concerned. That does not arise in this case.

Paul is not a party to these proceedings, but the High Court and this court is in the fortunate position that the arguments of someone appearing on his behalf would have been the same as those put forward by the plaintiff. What is beyond doubt is that, if this test is not administered and in the course of the next few years, he suffers death or serious brain damage as a result, the responsibility will not be that of the defendants alone. In this case, the defendants have refused to protect and vindicate, so far as practicable, the constitutional right of Paul to be guarded against unnecessary and avoidable dangers to his health and welfare. The courts, in my view, can and should. [2001] 3 IR 622, at 687, 690 and 706–707.

[9–91] The approach of Waite LJ in *Re T (A Minor) (CA)* [1997] 1 WLR 242, endorsed by Keane CJ as also being the correct constitutional position in Ireland, is as follows:

All these cases depend on their own facts and render generalisations—tempting though they may be to the legal or social analyst—wholly out of place. It can only be said safely that there is a scale, at one end of which lies the clear case where parental opposition to medical intervention is promoted by scruple or dogma of a kind which is patently irreconcilable with principles of child health and welfare widely accepted by the generality of mankind; and that at the other end lie highly problematic cases where there is genuine scope for difference of view between parent and judge. In both situations it is the duty of the judge to allow the court's own opinion to prevail in the perceived paramount interests of the child concerned, but in cases at the latter end of the scale, there must be a likelihood (though never of course a certainty) that the greater the scope for genuine debate between one view and another the stronger will be the inclination of the court to be influenced by a reflection that in the last analysis the best interests of every child include an expectation that difficult decisions affecting the length and quality of its life will be taken for it by the parent to whom its care has been entrusted by nature.

[9–92] It is questionable whether a principle that the Court's own opinion always prevail "in the perceived paramount interests of the child concerned" is consistent with the Thomistic view that the State can only overturn parental decisions about their children in exceptional circumstances where the parents have failed. Whatever one's views about the circumstances in which the State should be allowed to intervene, it seems unarguable that the Constitution establishes a system in which the State can seldom intervene. Despite the intrinsic merits of Keane CJ's approach, it seems difficult to square it with the Constitution.

[9–93] The most compelling articulation of parental autonomy is that provided by Hardiman J in *N v HSE*. This account stresses that children do have rights; the question is simply one of who should exercise those rights. As parents generally make the best decisions for their children, the State should be very slow to intervene. In the long run, parental decision-making is more likely to secure the best interests of the child. Even adopting such an approach, however, one can query whether the decision in *NWHB v HW* goes too far. If the reason why we protect parental autonomy is because we believe it to be the best way of securing parental rights, then it would seem to follow that the basis for state intervention should turn on the best interests of the child. Adopting this approach, it is permissible to operate a presumption (even a strong presumption) that the best interests of the child are best served by parental decision-making. However, the rebuttal of the presumption must also turn on some assessment of the child's best interests. The difficulty with the approach of the majority judgments in *NWHB v HW* was that the best interests of the child were practically irrelevant to the rebuttal of the presumption. The presumption could only be rebutted by evidence that the parents were bad people, not by evidence that the child was at risk of suffering disastrous consequences. No reasonable parent, conscientiously assessing and balancing the risks involved in the PKU test, could possibly come to a decision that their child should not have the test. Yet the decision was allowed to stand as the parents were—in general—good parents. Although such a decision may well have been required by Art 41, it gives pause for thought as to the wisdom of the balance struck by Art 41.

The majority judges were also concerned that there was no legislation requiring the test to be carried out. They reasoned that, if they were to require the test in this case, it would effectively be making the test compulsory in all cases. Such a decision should be made by the Oireachtas, if it were to be made at all. That said, there was little in the majority judgments to suggest that their conclusion would have been different had the PKU test been legislatively authorised. Keane CJ noted the concern over the separation of powers but reasoned that his duty was to protect the best interests of the child. Another important issue that may arise in future cases is the question of the common good. The diseases for which the PKU test screens are not infectious. Were the State to introduce a compulsory vaccination programme for an infectious disease, such as measles, a court would have to consider not only the question of parental autonomy but also the question of the common good. The efficacy of such a programme would depend on the participation of a large proportion of the population. [9–94]

NWHB concerned an infant child: it is unclear what happens where a child is not old enough legally to make decisions for herself but yet could have a meaningful input into the decision-making process. Mills has made the following points: [9–95]

> The court has taken the decision that, unless there are "exceptional circumstances", parents are the arbiters of whether a child will undergo a medical procedure (in this case, a diagnostic test). The court has made clear it envisages the extreme scenario as being one where the child's life is threatened, but offers no further guidance. It is clear that the courts in other circumstances recognise no distinction in the medical "process" between diagnosis and treatment, so what happens when a child less than 16 expresses a wish to avail himself of a medical course of action to which his parents are opposed. This might be termed the *Gillick* scenario and the possibility of it arising in this jurisdiction demands some clarity on the rights that will be afforded to a minor who is mature enough to express his consent to medical treatment, and who wishes to do so in defiance of the wishes of his parents for "religious and moral, intellectual, physical [or] social" reasons. The law as it stands in Ireland is at a crossroads. The direction indicated by Keane CJ points towards a scenario where the "competent" minor might be able to exercise his personal Constitutional autonomy and have that autonomy recognised by the courts. The signpost held by Hardiman J—and by default, the rest of the Supreme Court—hints at a hard path for the child wishing for cogent and mature reasons to escape the "inalienable and imprescriptible" rights inherent in the clutches of the family. Simon Mills, *"PKU: Please Keep Unclear?"* (2001) 23 *DULJ* 180, at 187.

The position of the competent child is directly addressed by neither the paternalistic state envisaged by Keane CJ nor the state deferential to family authority envisaged by the majority judges.

Both *NHWB* and *Lobe* (above) involved parents making choices on behalf of their children. Compare and contrast the judicial attitude to the choices made by W's parents and the choices made by Lobe's parents. Mullally has put the concern in the following way: [9–96]

The findings of the Supreme Court in the *L* and *O* cases stand in marked contrast to the Court's deference to the family unit in previous cases. Just one year earlier, in the *NWHB* case, Keane CJ had held that because it derives from the "natural order", the family was endowed with an authority that the Constitution recognised as being superior even to the authority of the State. He went on to argue that the Constitution outlawed any attempt by the State to usurp "the exclusive and privileged role of the family in the social order." In the same case, Murphy J noted that the express terms of the Constitution relegated the State to a subordinate and subsidiary role. Therefore, the circumstances that could justify intervention by the State in the family unit must be exceptional indeed. . . . In the *L* and *O* cases, however, this line of reasoning was turned on its head, with the State's interest in immigration control invoked to challenge the exercise of parental authority and to undermine the children's best interests. Siobhán Mullally, "Defining the Limits of Citizenship: Family Life, Immigration and Non-Nationals in Irish Law" (2004) 39 *Ir Jur* 334, at 340.

[9–97] It is difficult to identify what factors explain the change between *NWHB* and *Lobe*. In particular, it is difficult to square Hardiman J's views in *Lobe* that the non-national parents of Irish children cannot assert that child's right of residence on her behalf with his views in *N v HSE*:

> In the case of a child of very tender years, as here, the decisions to be taken and the work to be done, daily and hourly, for the securing of her welfare through nurturing and education, must of necessity be taken and performed by a person or persons other than the child herself. Both according to the natural order, and according to the constitutional order, the rights and duties necessary for those purposes are vested in the child's parents.

[9–98] There is much concern that Art 42.5 requires the State to be too deferential to parental autonomy. The Constitution Review Group recommended that Art 42 be amended to include an express requirement that "in all actions concerning children, whether by legislative, judicial or administrative authorities, the best interests of the child shall be the paramount consideration." They also recommended that Art 42.5 be amended expressly to permit State intervention either where parents have failed in their duty or where the interests of the child require such intervention and a re-statement of the State's duty following such intervention. The All Party Oireachtas Committee on the Constitution has recommended a different amendment:

> All children, irrespective of birth, gender, race or religion, are equal before the law. In all cases where the welfare of the child so requires, regard shall be had to the best interests of the child.

[9–99] Is there a sense in which both proposed amendments miss the point? Presumably, nearly everyone now agrees that a child's best interests are the paramount concern. The question that then arises is whether a child's best interests are better served by having decisions on its behalf made by the State or made by its parents. Presumably everyone also agrees that the initial decision-maker should be the parents, but that there should be some circumstances in which the State can intervene to overturn bad parental decisions. The question that arises is: in which circumstances can the State intervene? Article 42.5, as currently drafted, at least has the merit of squarely addressing that question: the State can intervene in the exceptional circumstance of parental failure.

[9–100] Neither the Constitution Review Group's report nor the Oireachtas committee's report directly addresses this question, both preferring to focus on the level of importance of the welfare of the child. By stating that the best interests of the child shall always be the paramount consideration, the CRG implicitly states that parental autonomy only lasts until the State decides that the parents have made a mistake. By requiring regard to be had to the best interests of the child, the Oireachtas committee requires only a process of consideration.

More recently, the Government proposed that Art 42.5 be deleted and that the following Art 42A be inserted into the Constitution: [9–101]

> 1. The State acknowledges and affirms the natural and imprescriptible rightsof all children.
> 2.1° In exceptional cases, where the parents of any child for physical or moral reasons fail in their duty towards such child, the State as guardian of the common good, by appropriate means shall endeavour to supply the place of the parents, but always with due regard for the natural and imprescriptible rights of the child.
> 2.2° Provision may be made by law for the adoption of a child where the parents have failed for such a period of time as may be prescribed by law in their duty towards the child, and where the best interests of the child so require.
> 3. Provision may be made by law for the voluntary placement for adoption and the adoption of any child.
> 4. Provision may be made by law that in proceedings before any court concerning the adoption, guardianship or custody of, or access to, any child, the court shall endeavour to secure the best interests of the child. (Article 42A.5 has not been reproduced here as it is not relevant to the issues raised by this chapter.)

Article 42A.2.1° reproduces Art 42.5, with the sole change that it now applies to "any child". This would acquire for the unmarried parents of children the same level of State deference as is required in respect of the married parents of children. However, it would potentially raise issues as to which parent the State should defer. Apart from this change, however, the proposed Art 42A.2.1° would not require the courts to reassess their determination of *NWHB v HW*. However, Art 42A.4 would provide explicit constitutional authorisation for the "best interests" test in adoption, guardianship, custody and access cases, thereby removing the need for the constitutional presumption identified in *Re JH*.

Parental Autonomy in the Education Context

Article 42 contains a number of statements that emphasise the primacy of the family in the context of education. Article 42.1 refers to the family as "the primary and natural educator of the child." Article 42.2 provides that parents shall be free to provide the education in their homes or in private schools or in schools established by the State. Article 42.3.1° again emphasises the secondary role of the State by guaranteeing that the State will "not oblige parents in violation of their conscience and lawful preference to send their children to schools established by the State, or to any particular type of school designated by the State." Article 42.3.2°, however, provides an exception that performs a similar function in the education context to that performed more generally by Art 42.5. It provides as follows: [9–102]

> The State shall, however, as guardian of the common good, require in view of actual conditions that the children receive a certain minimum education, moral, intellectual and social.

[9–103] This provision was first considered in *Re Article 26 and the School Attendance Bill 1942* [1943] IR 334. Section 4 of the Bill allowed the Minister for Education to grant certificates to parents who were educating their children at home, certifying that the children were receiving a suitable education other than by attending school. The Court considered that this provision was repugnant to the Constitution for the following reasons:

> What is the meaning and extent of [Article 42.3.2°]? What is referred to as "a certain minimum education" has not been defined by the Constitution and accordingly, we are of opinion that the State, acting in its legislative capacity through the Oireachtas, has power to define it. It should, in our opinion, be defined in such a way as to effectuate the general provisions of the clause without contravening any of the other provisions of the Constitution. Subject to these restrictions, it seems to us that the State is free to act, so long as it does not require more than a "certain minimum education" which expression, in the opinion of this Court, indicates a minimum standard of elementary education of general application.
>
> If the standard contemplated by the section which has been referred to us exceeds these limits we do not think it can be justified under the Constitution.
>
> Sect. 4 of the Bill deals with the granting of certificates by the Minister certifying that children are receiving suitable education otherwise than by attending school. We must construe that section as we find it and try to ascertain its meaning and effect. We assume that the powers conferred upon the Minister by the section if passed into law will be exercised in a reasonable, conscientious and temperate manner. But, making this assumption, we are nevertheless of opinion that a Minister, construing the section in a reasonable manner, might require a higher standard of education than could be properly be prescribed as a minimum standard under Article 42 (3) (2) of the Constitution. We are further of opinion that the standard contemplated by the section might vary from child to child, and, accordingly, that it is not such a standard of general application as the Constitution contemplates. In these respects we are of opinion that the proposed legislation exceeds the limits permitted by the Constitution and is repugnant to it....
>
> We are of opinion that the section is open to objection from a constitutional point of view in one other respect. Under sub-s. 1 not only the education, but also *the manner in which such child is receiving it* must be certified by the Minister. We do not consider that this is warranted by the Constitution. The State is entitled to require that children shall receive a certain minimum education. So long as parents supply this general standard of education we are of opinion that the manner in which it is being given and received is entirely a matter for the parents and is not a matter in respect of which the State under the Constitution is entitled to interfere. [1943] IR 334, at 345–346.

[9–104] The Supreme Court interpreted "certain minimum" as meaning a very low standard. Although this is a permissible interpretation of Art 42.3.2°, the word "minimum" does not necessarily mean that the standard must be low. It could be argued that "minimum" merely requires that it is a standard which must be met. That said, such a reading would make the word "certain" superfluous. As the State may require "a certain minimum education", the Court's interpretation is probably correct. The Court deemed s 4 repugnant to the Constitution on the basis that the Minister might exercise his power to require a level of education greater than a certain minimum education. Given the evolution of the presumption of constitutionality, it is unlikely that a court would come to such a conclusion today. Instead, the Court would presume that the Minister would exercise her power in a constitutional manner.

More controversial still is the distinction between manner and content. This distinction is not explicitly stated in the text of Art 42.3.2° and thus must depend on one's understanding of education. It is not necessarily the case that education connotes merely the imparting of content.

Article 42.3.2° was again considered in *DPP v Best* [2000] 2 IR 17. The defendant was prosecuted under s 17 of the School Attendance Act 1926 for not sending her children to school without reasonable excuse. The defendant submitted that she did have a reasonable excuse as she was providing "suitable elementary education" to her children at home. The District Judge stated a case for the opinion of the High Court as to whether she was precluded from convicting the defendant in the absence of a statutory definition of "suitable elementary education." The Supreme Court held that the absence of a statutory definition did not preclude a conviction. They held that the statutory phrase "suitable elementary education" could not be interpreted so as to require an education that exceeded the "certain minimum education, moral, intellectual and social" referred to in Art 42.3.2°. However, they held that the onus of proof was on the defendant to satisfy the District Judge, on the balance of probabilities, that the required level of education was being provided. In the course of their judgments the five judges made certain observations about what constitutes "a certain minimum education." These comments are of general assistance. [9–105]

Denham J reasoned as follows: [9–106]

> The common good is evoked in Article 42. The State as guardian of the common good shall require (in view of actual conditions) that the children receive a certain minimum education, moral, intellectual and social. The actual conditions referred to in the Article must refer to conditions in the community, not only the family, otherwise personal situations would negate the common good. The personal situation of the parents has already been taken into account (*per* Article 42.1) in the requirement to consider parental rights and duties according to their means.
>
> The common good places the children's right to receive a certain minimum education, moral, intellectual and social as a priority. It does not require a high standard of education—but it is a mandatory minimum standard. The standard is a question of fact, which must be decided in view of factors including actual conditions in the community and having regard to, *inter alia*, the physical and intellectual capacity of the children. The minimum education must be conductive to the child achieving intellectual and social development and not such as to place the child in a discriminatory position....
>
> The fact that the legislature has not defined what constitutes a "suitable elementary education" does not prevent the District Judge from pronouncing a formal order of conviction or acquittal, as the case may be. There should be expert evidence before the District Judge as to suitable elementary education. Having heard the evidence the District Judge should make findings of fact. She should determine whether the education the children are receiving is suitable elementary education. In construing "suitable elementary education" it must not exceed "a certain minimum education, moral, intellectual and social." This is a minimum standard of elementary education of a general character but should have regard to the intellectual and other capacities of the child. It is not necessarily equivalent to the primary school curriculum. It is a minimum education, moral, intellectual and social which must be considered in light of factors, including those previously reviewed, such as the time the issue is determined, the family, the parents, their means, the child, the geographical situation, the actual circumstances and the common good. In balancing these factors, which is not an exhaustive list, the District Judge should, whilst recognising the parental and family rights, at the same time acknowledge the child's constitutional rights and the duty of the State as guardian of the common good. An education which creates a discriminatory situation for the child may establish

circumstances where the rights of the child and the interest of the common good outweigh considerations of the family and parental rights.

If, on the evidence, the District Judge finds as a fact that the parent is not providing a suitable elementary education she should convict. If the District Judge finds as a fact that the parent is providing a suitable elementary education she should acquit. According to the Act the onus rests on the parent to provide a reasonable excuse. [2000] 2 IR 17, at 49–50.

[9–107] Keane J reasoned as follows:

As to the question of Irish being included in any curriculum or system of home education, it would be going too far to say that its absence would, of itself, mean that the constitutional standard had not been reached, since that standard is to be determined in view of "actual conditions".... But given the status of Irish as the first official language and the fact that a knowledge of it is a precondition to at least some forms of employment, it could not be said that its absence from a curriculum cannot be taken into account in determining whether the education of the child reaches the constitutional standard.

When the District Judge is giving her decision in the present case, she will, of course, be doing so in the light of the evidence tendered to her, including that of the respondent and the inspector, as to the nature of the education being given to the children. But, as in any other case, she will also be in a position to bring to bear on the decision her experience of the world and her common sense. The fact that the Oireachtas has not embodied the minimum constitutional standard in legislation will not in any way prevent her, in my view, from arriving at a fair and objective decision in the case....

It is necessary to emphasise again that the phrase "suitable elementary education" is not to be interpreted so as to require the giving of an education which exceeds the "certain minimum education, moral, intellectual and social" referred to in Article 42.3.2°. So interpreted, it would certainly require the education of the children, in intellectual terms, to a basic level of literacy and numeracy. But since the standard is to be determined in the light of "actual conditions"—and, for that matter, "suitable" must also be similarly construed—the minimum education to which the children are entitled may, in today's world, require more than those basic constituents. It is also to be noted that the minimum education is not necessarily to be equated to the present primary school curriculum which, it was said on behalf of the prosecutor and the Attorney General, was above the constitutional minimum.

It is undoubtedly desirable that the minimum standard of elementary education which it is the policy of the Act of 1926 to ensure that all children receive should be a standard of general application. However, the right of children recognised by Article 42.3.2° is to "receive" the certain minimum education. It follows that those providing the education, whether they be schools or parents, must ensure that it is designed to meet the needs of, and develop to the fullest possible extent the capacities of, the particular children concerned. Thus, while it does not arise in this case, it can be readily envisaged that children with some degree of learning difficulties may be entitled to a form of education which takes account of those difficulties.

That brings me to one final matter. It would appear from the report of the inspector that he was not satisfied with the teaching methods being employed by the respondent and that it was not simply the subject matter which gave him concern. Counsel for the respondent, in submitting that such an approach was not consistent with Article 42.2.3°, relied on the following passage in the judgment of Sullivan CJ in *In re Article 26 and the School Attendance Bill 1942* [1943] IR 334, at 346:

We are of opinion that the section is open to objection from a constitutional point of view in one other respect. Under sub-s. 1, not only the education, but also *the manner in which such child is receiving it* must be certified by the Minister. We do not consider that this is warranted by the Constitution. The State is entitled to require that children shall receive a certain minimum education. So long as parents supply this general standard of education we are of opinion that the manner in which it is being given and received is entirely a matter for the parents and is not a matter in respect of which the State under the Constitution is entitled to interfere.

... [I]t seems to me that the view of the court in that case that the State is not in any way entitled to interfere in the manner in which education is being given to children rests on an unduly narrow construction of Article 42.2.3° and should not now be followed. It would seem to me that the right of the child to be educated, given such emphasis in the decisions in *G v An Bord Uchtála* [1980] IR 32; *Crowley v Ireland* [1980] IR 102 and *O'Donoghue v Minister for Health* [1996] 2 IR 20, would be seriously violated if the State could not intervene, although satisfied that teaching methods were patently inadequate, simply because the curriculum purported to be taught approximated, for example, to the primary school curriculum. [2000] 2 IR 17, at 60–62.

Murphy J, however, took a more restrictive view: [9–108]

I can only express my own tentative view that the common good as referred to in Article 42.3.2° is the interest of the community—rather than the particular individual—in having a population which is educated to a standard which would be recognised throughout the country as the minimum needed to function in a civilised society. It might be described as the lowest common denominator in educational standards. The moral, intellectual and social education which the State may require under Article 42.3.2° is something which Article 42.2 recognises parents could provide in their homes. It is understandable that a moral education could be so provided but one might have thought that the social input would require the type of intercourse or relationships which would develop with other children in a school environment. That cannot be so. The Supreme Court on the reference to it of the School Attendance Bill, 1942 in *In re Article 26 of the Constitution and the School Attendance Bill, 1942* [1943] IR 334, established two important propositions which are relevant to the present case. First, the court held that the "certain minimum education" referred to in the Article "indicates a minimum standard of elementary education of *general application*" (emphasis added) and secondly, that "the manner in which [education] is being given and received is entirely a matter for the parents and is not a matter in respect of which the State under the Constitution is entitled to interfere."

Of what then does this "minimum standard of elementary education of general application" consist? As Kenny J pointed out in the High Court in *Ryan v The Attorney General* [1965] IR 294, at 310, the education referred to in the Constitution was such that it could be provided in schools and must therefore be given a limited interpretation extending only to education of a scholastic nature. Since the State cannot dictate the method or manner of education it would seem to follow that it is the only subject matter in relation to which the State may prescribe minimum standards. The fact that these are standards of "general application" suggests, as I say, a very modest standard indeed.

Insofar as it falls to me to do so I would conclude that the expression "a certain minimum education, moral, intellectual and social" used in Article 42.3.2° indicates a very basic standard indeed. The underlying objective is to provide young people with a basic education so that they can communicate orally and in writing within society and record, organise and deal with ordinary social and business matters involving communication, enumeration and arithmetic. The common good also requires that children should be encouraged to develop a sense of responsibility and the capacity to live within a civilised society.

It is within the parameters of that modest standard that the expression "a suitable elementary education" must be interpreted. Whether a child is receiving a suitable elementary education can be tested in one or other of two ways. First, the judge of the District Court can arrange to interview the child and hopefully satisfy herself that the proficiency of the child in the core subjects to which I referred is such that he or she must be in receipt of a suitable elementary education. Alternatively, the judge may be satisfied by the evidence of the parents—supported where necessary by evidence of experts—that the course of education being pursued in the home is such that, having regard to its manner, duration and subject matter, it may be considered in all of the circumstances "a suitable elementary education."

[9–109] Lynch J gave a more expansive account of what was required by Art 42.3.2°:

Children are citizens and persons within the meaning of those terms as used in the Constitution and the law. They have added rights given to them by the Constitution and by law for their well being and protection during infancy. The persons primarily responsible for ensuring their well-being and protection during infancy are their parents. As part of their well-being and protection children are entitled to, and parents are under an obligation to provide within their means for, an education to qualify their children for such reasonable standard of life as adults as is clearly within their competence if given appropriate education.

In these circumstances the primary school curriculum might well amount to no more than "suitable elementary education of a general nature" and/or "a certain minimum education, moral, intellectual and social" in the case of a bright child well capable of coping with and benefiting from the primary school curriculum. In such a case the parents would be quite entitled, if they could afford it, to "provide" such education in their home by engaging and paying qualified teachers. It seems most unlikely, however, that the parents in the present case could "provide" suitable education and/or "a certain minimum" education by undertaking the task of tuition themselves, having regard to their own limited educational history and lack of qualifications. If either of the boys the subject matter of this prosecution is bright enough to be well capable of coping with and benefiting from the primary school curriculum, it is clear and has been so found by the District Judge that the parents are not providing an education which is equal to or comparable with the primary school curriculum. That standard, in the case of an intellectually bright and physically sound and healthy child, might be held by the District Judge to equate with "suitable elementary education of a general nature and/or a certain minimum education, moral, intellectual and social." [2000] 2 IR 17, at 71–72.

[9–110] Barron J reasoned as follows:

With this in mind, the court must consider the actual education being provided, curricular subjects as well as non-curricular subjects, and the quality of the teaching and the response of the child to that teaching so as to ensure that the right of the child to develop its potential is not being infringed.

In the past, a certain minimum education might well have been regarded as having been provided if the child concerned could read and write and have reasonable numeracy together with a smattering of knowledge in other disciplines. Such would not be so regarded today. There may be too much pressure on children to obtain success in State examinations, but it is a fact of life that in this competitive world progress in the form of entry to higher education and entry to gainful employment is measured in terms of academic success in national examinations. Any form of education which takes a child, who would otherwise have been in such mainstream, out of it cannot today be regarded as being a certain minimum.

It is obviously too narrow a test to equate a certain minimum as enabling the child concerned to achieve its potential in the national examinations. Not all children reach that standard nor sit such examinations nor derive the same benefit from that form of education. The need to provide a certain minimum education must be considered in the light of the right of the parents to educate their children at home. This right cannot be abused to the detriment of the child. The parents alone cannot say what is best for their child.

The concept of a certain minimum education indicates that this is a basic minimum. In practical terms, it requires that the core subjects in a school curriculum should be provided to the same standard. Since it is the right of the child which is being protected its welfare must be considered. As in other circumstances affecting children what is being done must be shown to be for the child's benefit. It is clear from the wide field of subjects provided for in national examinations that it is recognised that
what suits one child might not suit another. So the certain minimum is the provision of tuition in those subjects which suit the particular child and at the same time will not deprive that child of future opportunities.

In general it seems to me that the intellectual portion of the constitutional requirement is more likely to be satisfied at a school. On the contrary it seems to me that the moral and social requirements are more likely to be satisfied at home. In all cases it remains a question of fact. Clearly, a difficult one since it is probably easier to say that the certain minimum is not being provided rather than to say that it is. [2000] 2 IR 17, at 76–77.

It is difficult to distil any general principles from these dicta, all of which differ subtly in emphasis. Some dicta, however, stretch considerably what is constitutionally permissible. If social education requires socialisation, it could be argued that home education is never permissible. However, given that the Constitution explicitly permits home education, it is surely impermissible to build into the standard of "certain, minimum education" something which cannot be achieved at home. Lynch J seems to imply that only fully qualified teachers would be capable of home schooling "bright" children. However, it seems likely that professional teaching ability would be even more crucial with regard to less "bright" children. The differences between Keane J and Murphy J broadly parallel their differences in *NWHB*. Questions again arise as to whether Keane J's view that minimum education must "develop to the fullest possible extent the capacities of the particular children concerned", however admirable, is really consistent with the minimalist approach of Art 42.3.2°. [9–111]

Writing in 1967, Kelly identified the State interest in compulsory education as follows: [9–112]

The interest of the individual and of the family, their right to autonomy, is clear enough. Where is the State interest which conflicts, or might conflict with it in the sphere of education? This State interest is not an absolute one, I feel sure; it might not exist at all in a simple and primitive society in which governmental functions were minimal and the economic and industrial apparatus of the country very elementary. But when we are dealing with a state in the modern Western world, the situation is quite different. The complication of life on every front, along with the multiplication of governmental activities, makes an educated population an absolute necessity; scarcely any economic activity, scarcely any industrial process, even the humblest, scarcely any administrative function can be conducted today by an illiterate or by a man who cannot perform simple arithmetical tasks; and an increasing number of such activities, processes and functions require an increasing degree of literacy and other kinds of training from an increasing number of persons.... Citizens [without intellectual training] would represent a serious social burden as well as an economic handicap; and it seems to me that the State, one of whose functions today is taken to be the duty of spreading prosperity and the opportunity of happiness, derives its right to compel the education of children from this likelihood. (Reprinted in Gerry Whyte, "Education and the Constitution: Convergence of Paradigm and Praxis" (1990) 25 *Ir Jur (ns)* 69, at 84–85.)

[9–113] Kelly provides an exceptionally utilitarian justification for Art 42.3.2°. It is the general needs of society, rather than any desire to allow children develop and flourish, that provides the justification for State intervention. By restricting state interference to where the *common good* requires it, Art 42.3 arguably suppresses still further the child's own interest in being educated. This distinguishes Art 42.3 from Art 42.5 where the (admittedly limited) interference that is permitted is predicated on the rights of the child, not the common good. Effectively, under Article 42.3, a child can only be educated to the extent either that her parents decide or that the common good requires. Little value is placed by the State on the child's right to education for its own sake. Ryan comments on Art 42:

> What strikes one immediately is the largely parent-centred focus of this constitutional scheme. The dichotomy posed is one of parent and State, the emphasis being very much on the entitlements of adults *vis-à-vis* the State rather than on the best interests of the child. The centrepiece of this constitutional philosophy focuses on family autonomy, the main purpose being to limit State intervention in the family. The result of this philosophy is a legal framework that in its most fundamental form views children simply as an adjunct of the family, the object of an ideological struggle between the family, on the one hand, and the State on the other. (Fergus Ryan, "Children, One-Parent Families and the Law" [2006] 1 *IJFL* 3, at 5–6.

Could Art 42.5, which at least mentions children's rights, provide a wider basis for intervention to secure the education rights of children in the face of parental neglect?

Primary Education

The Meaning of (Primary) Education

[9–114] Article 42 of the Constitution envisages a three-way relationship between parent, child and State. We have already seen the limits to parents' power over their children. However, there are also certain obligations on the State in relation to education—services that both parents and children can demand from the State. For Art 42.4 contains one of the few explicit, socio-economic rights in the Constitution:

> The State shall provide for free primary education and shall endeavour to supplement and give reasonable aid to private and corporate educational initiative, and, when the public good requires it, provide other educational facilities or institutions with due regard, however, for the rights of parents, especially in the matter of religious and moral formation.

It is the first clause of this guarantee that is most significant as it is phrased in mandatory language and admits of no exceptions. The obligation on the State in relation to other forms of education is only to "endeavour to supplement." The final phrase of the guarantee ensures that the State does not use its education-providing role to oust the autonomy of parents, especially in religious and moral matters.

[9–115] In *Crowley v Ireland* [1980] IR 102, the Supreme Court emphasised that the State's obligation was to *provide for* free primary education. The State did not have to provide that education itself directly. Accordingly, the State had not breached its obligations where teachers in a particular national school refused to teach. Despite this decision, Art 42.4 has become one of the most frequently invoked and effective rights in the

Constitution. As it is the only explicit, socio-economic right, there is a strong incentive for those who seek services from the State to phrase their claims in terms of "education" and, more specifically, "primary education." The courts have generally adopted an expansive approach to the meaning of "education". In *Ryan v Attorney General* [1965] IR 294, at 310, Kenny J interpreted education (in Art 42 generally) as being of a scholastic nature, as Art 42.2 envisaged education being provided in schools. The Supreme Court, *per* Ó Dálaigh CJ, took a broader view:

> Education essentially is the teaching and training of a child to make the best possible use of his inherent and potential capacities, physical, mental and moral. To teach a child to minimise the dangers of dental caries by adequate brushing of his teeth is physical education for it induces him to use his own resources. To give him water of a nature calculated to minimise the danger of dental caries is in no way to educate him, physically or otherwise, for it does not develop his resources. [1965] IR 294, at 350.

During the 1990s, there was a significant attempt to use Art 42.4 to oblige the State to provide education to children with mental and intellectual disabilities. This led to a very expansive interpretation of "primary education" on the part of the High Court, followed by a partial retrenchment on the part of the Supreme Court. In *O'Donoghue v Minister for Health* [1996] 2 IR 20, the applicant, who was physically disabled and profoundly mentally handicapped, sought an order compelling the State to provide him with free primary education. There had been no place for him in any suitable school and so he had been cared for at home by his mother who had him educated privately at her own expense. The State claimed that he was ineducable and that the education referred to in Art 42.4 was only scholastic education. O'Hanlon J rejected these contentions:

[9–116]

> The first contention of the respondents in response to the claim brought on behalf of the applicant is the assertion that, however deeply one may feel for his plight, and that of his mother who has to look after him, he must be regarded as ineducable.
> Kenny J in *Ryan v The Attorney General* [1965] IR 294 considered that the word "education" when used in Article 42 of the Constitution was not wide enough to include the concept of "rearing and nurturing." Because it was to be education of a kind which could be provided by parents in their homes, or alternatively in schools established or recognised by the State, he considered that it must be one that could be defined as being "of a scholastic nature."
> If, in using that expression, he had in mind what has been traditionally referred to in this country as "book learning," then one would have to agree that it is virtually certain that education in this narrow sense will never be of any benefit to the applicant because of his mental and intellectual disabilities. Kenny J's real purpose, however, was to say that "education" was not wide enough in this context to include "rearing and nurturing" and Ó Dálaigh CJ, in delivering the judgment of the Supreme Court in the same case, and in agreeing with that decision of Kenny J, enlarged upon the definition of "education" as given in the judgment of the High Court. For the purposes of the present case I consider that the longer definition is more useful:—
>> Education essentially is the teaching and training of a child to make the best possible use of his inherent and potential capacities, physical, mental and moral. To teach a child to minimise the dangers of dental caries by adequate brushing of his teeth is physical education for it induces him to use his own resources.
> What the Chief Justice there stated is in harmony with the dramatic advances which have been made since that judgment was delivered in seeking to alleviate the lot of the mentally handicapped through education, initially focusing on the mild and moderate

cases of mental handicap, and in more recent times including all children, however serious their handicap, in the educational system. The whole momentum, as evidenced in the declarations emanating from the Vatican, from the United Nations, and in the protocol to the European Convention on Human Rights, has been towards the provision for every individual of such education as will enable him or her—in the words of the Chief Justice—"to make the best possible use of his [or her] inherent and potential capacities, physical, mental and moral"—however limited those capacities may be.

Counsel for the respondents, in closing their case, urged me to hold that it still remained uncertain whether the efforts put in to the education of the severely and profoundly mentally handicapped were of any real and lasting benefit to these children, and whether any advances made were not lost again as soon as the stimulus of the teacher was withdrawn.

I am led to believe, however, by evidence of Professor Hogg, of the applicant's mother and of the other mothers of handicapped children who were witnesses in the case, and by other evidence in the case, that this contention by the respondents is not well-founded.... I find against the respondents in relation to the first contention that the applicant must be regarded as "ineducable."

Assuming the applicant is "educable," should such education as can be provided for the applicant at the present stage of his development be regarded as "primary education" within the meaning of that phrase as used in Article 42 of the Constitution? [O'Hanlon J quoted from Article 42 of the Constitution and continued.]

A corresponding, but much shorter, provision was contained in the Constitution of the Irish Free State, as follows:—

"All citizens of the Irish Free State (Saorstát Éireann) have the right to free elementary education." (Article 10)....

Some dictionary definitions of the terms used in Article 42 read as follows:—

    Education: "Bringing up or training, as of a child; instruction; strengthening of the powers of body or mind; culture."

    Educate: "To bring up and instruct; to teach; to train."

    Primary: "First; original; of the first order; first-formed; chief; elementary; fundamental; belonging to the first stages of education, elementary."

(Chambers "Twentieth Century Dictionary", 1981)

At first sight, the word "primary" as used in Article 42, s. 1 ("The State acknowledges that the primary and natural educator of the child is the Family...") and as used in Article 42, s. 4 ("The State shall provide for free primary education...") would appear to be synonymous, but the Irish text of the Constitution leads to a different conclusion. The adjective given as equivalent to "primary" in Article 42, s. 1 is "príomhdha," meaning "principal" or "foremost" while "primary education" in Article 42, s. 4 is rendered in the Irish text as "bun-oideachas."

Fr. Dineen's Dictionary gives the following meanings for the Irish terms which arise for consideration:—

    Bun—:   "(as prefix) Principal, basal, foot—."

    Oideachas: "Advice, instruction, teaching (rec. in this sense)."

    Príomhdha: "Primitive, chief, primary."

I conclude, having regard to what has gone before, that there is a constitutional obligation imposed on the State by the provisions of Article 42, s. 4 of the Constitution to provide for free basic elementary education of all children and that this involves giving each child such advice, instruction and teaching as will enable him or her to make the best possible use of his or her inherent and potential capacities, physical, mental and moral, however limited these capacities may be. Or, to borrow the language of the United Nations Convention and Resolution of the General Assembly—"such education as will be conducive to the child's achieving the fullest possible social integration and individual development; such education as will enable the child to develop his or her capabilities and skills to the maximum and will hasten the process of social integration and reintegration".

This process will work differently for each child, according to the child's own natural gifts, or lack thereof. In the case of the child who is deaf, dumb, blind, or otherwise physically or mentally handicapped, a completely different programme of education has to be adopted and a completely different rate of progress has to be taken for granted, than would be regarded as appropriate for a child suffering from no such handicap....

I believe that it has now come to be accepted that trained teachers and the school environment can make a major contribution to this process which cannot — with the best will in the world — be provided as effectively or as successfully by parents and family in the home. This seems to me to get over whatever difficulty might otherwise arise in reconciling the present claim with the view expressed by Kenny J in *Ryan v The Attorney General* [1965] IR 294 that "education" as used in Article 42 of the Constitution was intended to mean "education of a kind which could be provided by parents in their homes, or alternatively in schools established or recognised by the State", and therefore "of a scholastic nature."

I therefore come to the conclusion that the education to which the applicant in the present case lays claim in reliance on rights derived from the provisions of Article 42 of the Constitution can be correctly described as "primary education" within the meaning of that phrase as used in Article 42, section 4. [1996] 2 IR 20, at 61–67.

O'Hanlon J's account of education was refreshingly expansive and holistic. A sceptic, however, could argue that the applicant was not educable. However broadly one interprets education, it is arguable that a child who will make progress provided that the education continues, but will regress if the education is removed, is not educable.

In *Comerford v Minister for Education* [1997] 2 ILRM 134, McGuinness J held that the State had breached its obligations under Art 42.4 in failing to provide appropriate educational services to a disadvantaged boy who had been diagnosed with attention deficit disorder. However, as much of the failure in this case was attributable to the boy's parents and given the high threshold for State interference with parental decisions, McGuinness J held that the State was only in default of its obligations once it initiated the procedures of the School Attendance Act 1926 in respect of the child. [9–117]

Sinnott v Minister for Education [2001] 2 IR 545 witnessed a partial retrenchment on the part of the Supreme Court. Mr Sinnott was a 23 year old profoundly autistic man. Up until the trial of the action, he had received no more than two years primary education and training from the State. He instituted proceedings seeking damages for the failure to provide him with the education in the past and also declarations and injunctions relating to his ongoing entitlement to such education. In the High Court, Barr J awarded damages to Mr Sinnott and granted a mandatory injunction requiring the State to provide primary education and ancillary services for Mr Sinnott for as long as such education and services were reasonably required by him. It was an aspect of Mr Sinnott's condition that he would regress if the services were withdrawn. The orders granted, therefore, effectively required that the services be provided for the rest of his life. The State appealed to the Supreme Court, not contesting that the services sought by Mr Sinnott were primary education but contending that the right to free primary education, under the Constitution, ended when a person reached the age of 18. Six of the seven judges accepted this contention. Denham J reasoned as follows: [9–118]

> It is clear from the wording of Article 42 that education is grounded in the family sphere. The family consists of children and parents. The primary educator is the family, which is

expressly protected. Both the parents and children have rights. A balance is created. Whilst the family remains the primary educator, the State, as guardian of the common good, shall require a certain standard. This standard is described as a certain minimum education, moral, intellectual and social. It is certainly not a high standard.

Into this formation the right to have provided free primary education is placed. I am satisfied that counsel for the first plaintiff was correct when he described it as a promise to the people. It is reflective of community values. It is reflective of the approach of the people of Ireland to education.

Article 42.4 is placed in an Article redolent of the family, where children are addressed as part of a family, where the primary educator is acknowledged as the family. It paints a picture of a family of two parents, mother and father, and children learning from their parents.

The term "child" falls to be construed in light of the plain language of Article 42. The word "child" in general use describes a young person. It is a term used in a context where the focus is on the family, parents and children. The Article anticipates the teaching of young children. The Article makes reference to schools—of different types. The Article specifically refers to children. The Article speaks of a certain minimum education. The Article addresses the rights of parents. The Article stresses education in a context of schools. The article is not addressing issues such as, for example, succession where the term "child" might be used in a different sense. It would be rewriting the Constitution to construe the term "child" as meaning a childish person. Consequently, the meaning of the words "child" and "children" is clear. There is no ambiguity. The child is described within a family where the parents are the educator. It is addressed to a young person. It is age related.

I am reinforced in this view by the fact that Article 42 follows Article 41 which relates to the family. The family is acknowledged as the natural primary and fundamental unit group of society. The words of Article 42, including those relating to the family, parents and children, continue the theme.

The essence of Article 42 is the concept of the family, and a child growing up in the heart of the family. Article 42 describes the situation of the education of a young person within the family unit, a young person who is growing and learning. It also makes provision for intervention for the common good to require that children receive a certain minimum education. A person who has achieved adulthood is no longer subject to parental authority or decisions such as are envisaged in Article 42.

For all these reasons I am satisfied that Article 42 does not relate to adults. It does not give to adults the right to free primary education. This right is reserved for children. This is not to limit in any way other rights which may be extant in the Constitution relating to adults, whether they be able bodied or disabled. Thus as the right provided for in Article 42.4 runs for children only, the next question is to what age the right runs.

In general primary school is completed when a child is under 14 years of age. This case deals with particular facts. It is conceded that the first plaintiff has the right until he is 18. The choice of 18 years of age is somewhat arbitrary. The choice is based on the fact that a young person becomes an adult in the eyes of the community in many aspects at the age of 18. He or she may vote, *inter alia*.

Most children finish primary education, as it is understood in a general sense, between the ages of 12 and 14 years of age. Thus on first impression it would appear that 14 is a more logical age than 18. However, the right to have free primary education provided is a fundamental and important right established by the Constitution. It is a right with which certain individuals or groups may encounter physical, mental or social difficulties in exercising. Therefore, the norm may not cover minorities. The right is given to all children. It is appropriate that the construction of the Article should ensure that all children may get the benefit of the right. Consequently, it is fitting that the age at which the right ceases to exist is when the person is no longer a child. Therefore it is reasonable to take the age at which society treats a young person as an adult as the age when the right ceases to exist. The State's case that the first plaintiff is recognised as an adult when he reaches 18 years of age is reasonable. [2001] 2 IR 545, at 653–655.

Hardiman J took a slightly different approach: [9–119]

> It is thus manifest that, whether one reads the Constitution in its Irish or English text, the primary provider of education is seen as the parent, and the recipient as a child of such parent. This appears to me plainly to involve the consequence that the recipient of primary education would be a person who is not an adult and in respect of whom the primary educator, according to the natural order, is his family.
>
> In making the contrary case, counsel for the first plaintiff suggested that the word "child" where it occurs in Article 42 should be interpreted as meaning merely "offspring" or "descendant", terms which, they said, might apply to a person of any age. This view does not appear to me to be tenable. Firstly, it entirely ignores the language and structure of the Article, where the term "child" is never used in isolation but always with a correlative of "parent" or "family". Secondly, it is even more difficult to maintain the construction contended for if one has regard to the primary (Irish) text, where that connotation would be expressed in a term such as "sliocht" rather than "leanbh".
>
> The correlatives used for the term "child" ("leanbh") are "Family" ("Teaghlach"), and "parents" ("tuistí"). Moreover, the word "clann" is used as a synonym for the recipients of education, meaning the children of a family.
>
> Accordingly, I cannot accept the artificial construction advanced on behalf of the first plaintiff: that the word "child" or its equivalent in the national language should be interpreted as extending to a person of any age who has an ongoing need for education. Apart altogether from the analysis of the language and of the structure of the Article offered above, the first plaintiff's contention simply does violence to the ordinary meaning of the word....
>
> [I]t is submitted [that] there is no age specified in the Article at which the condition of being a child ceases. This point appears to have weighed particularly heavily with the learned trial judge who referred to it on several occasions. On the basis of the omission to specify an end to the status of childhood, he equated the term "child" to "citizen" (at p. 40) and envisage that "a child" might require education into adulthood.
>
> This appears to me to empty the term "child" or its Irish equivalent of all meaning and treat it as synonymous with "person" or "citizen". Indeed, counsel for the first plaintiff specifically submitted that Article 42.4 should be read "as though primary education were guaranteed to the *citizen*". This is plainly not the intention of the Constitution. Both of these terms are used elsewhere in the text of the Constitution; the use of the term "child", rather than either of them in Article 42 must therefore be given significance. For example, the term "citizen" is widely used in Article 40 and, in Article 40.1., emphasis is laid on the status of each "citizen" as human persons....
>
> It is clear that the recipients of education under Article 42 fall into the restricted category of "children" and not the broader category of "citizens" or "persons". I believe that in equating children with "citizens" the learned trial judge fell into error and unwarrantedly extended the category of recipients of that form of education which is required by the Constitution. Article 42.1 to Article 42.5 have to be read together: it is clear on such a reading that those for whom the State provides for free primary education and/or supplements and gives aid to private and corporate educational initiative, or, when the public good provides it provides other educational facilities or institutions, are the children of the parents whose right and duty is preserved in the last phrase of Article 42.4 having been earlier recognised as "inalienable". Article 42.4 is a single sentence requiring due regard for the rights of parents in the doing of any of the things required or permitted to be done in the same sub-article. It cannot in my view be read otherwise without doing violence to the ordinary meaning of words, and ignoring its context in Article 42, and in the Constitution generally. It is not permissible, in my view, to read the final words of

Article 42.4, referring to "the rights of parents" as qualifying only the obligation of the State to give aid to non-State educational initiatives and to provide educational facilities themselves in certain circumstances. If regard is to be had for the rights of parents "especially in the matter of religious and moral formation" in relation to these obligations, it would be strange indeed if there was no obligation to have regard to those rights in relation to free primary education. This is the educational service availed of by the great majority of children, both at the present time and in 1937. To construe Article 42.4 as meaning that the State had to have regard for the rights of the parents in the matter of assisting private educational initiative (which at primary school level only ever served the minority of children), but not in providing for free primary education (which was always availed of by the great majority) would require one to ignore the spirit and historical context of the Constitution. An obligation to have regard to the rights of parents is consistent only with a view of the recipients of primary education as children. The fact that some children are unfortunately without parental guidance does not in any way detract from this analysis: their position is specifically envisaged in Article 42.5 and they are still persons in respect of whom the primary educator, according to the natural order, would be their family.

Obviously, the obligation to provide for free primary education, does not restrict the State to that provision. By statute, the State has provided for free secondary education for the last 34 years and more recently has provided for free undergraduate university education as well. It is clear from the terms of Article 42.4 that the State may also provide "other educational facilities or institutions"; other, that is, than primary schools or institutions provided by "private and corporate educational initiative". If the term "primary education" is construed on a historic basis it is clear that what was in the mind of the drafters of the Constitution was the ordinary, scholastically oriented primary education represented by the ministerially prescribed National School curriculum. The contrary was not submitted. The highly specialised services which, according to the witnesses called on behalf of the first plaintiff at the trial he stands in need seem quite different from the ordinary content of "primary education" either in 1937 or today. Apart from anything else, conventional primary education is progressive and teleological in the sense of leading a child through a predetermined course to the end of one level of education and the beginning of the next. It is painfully clear that the services required by the first plaintiff are at a much more basic level. This is a level which the normal child achieves before starting the ordinary process of primary education and include such very basic features as continence, mobility and the ability to talk. Moreover, it is clear from the evidence that, in so far as the first plaintiff can achieve any of the things it would be at a modest level, requiring constant reinforcement because of the ever present risk of "unlearning". The first plaintiff's counsel expressed with great clarity his client's needs. He said:—

"The first plaintiff is not capable of learning much more than toilet training, preserving his mobility and responding to simple instructions, and perhaps a few words."

It must be doubted whether a child who was immobile or largely so, incontinent and almost unable to talk or communicate would be likely to benefit from primary education in the ordinary sense of that term, or whether indeed he would be accepted into the primary education system. It may be, therefore, that facilities for such a child might be provided in "other education facilities or institutions", to use the wording of Article 42.4. But this case was not made, even as an alternative. This, presumably, was on the basis that the duty to provide such institutions was qualified by the words "when the public good requires it". These words, it may be thought, import a level of executive discretion, which the first plaintiff says is entirely absent from the first eight words of the sub-article. In any event, no case was made based on any other part of the sentence which constitutes Article 42.4. [2001] 2 IR 545, at 690–693.

[9–120]   Given that Art 42.4 does not limit the provision of education to "children", it is questionable whether Hardiman and Denham JJ were correct to limit the State's provision of primary education to "children". Does "child" necessarily mean a person under the age of 18? Denham and Hardiman JJ focused on the child/parent context of Art 42.4. However, the juxtaposition of child with parent does not necessarily imply that child means young person. You do not cease to be your parent's child when you reach the age of 18. The context of Art 42.4 is admittedly one of parents providing for and making choices about their children's education. Although this context might suggest that child means "young person", it could equally mean someone who is incapable of making her own educational choices. In this regard, Jamie Sinnott would seem to be the paradigm of a person who needs decisions to be made on his behalf by his parents.

Keane CJ dissented, providing a very different view of what was meant by "child": [9–121]

> [A] significant part of the argument in the case was directed to a meticulous parsing of both the Irish and English texts of these provisions with a view to ascertaining whether they lend support to the view that the only beneficiaries of the right acknowledged in those opening words are "children" who had not yet reached the age of 18. As it happens, while it is not of critical importance in this case, those opening words contain no reference whatever to children, whether in family units or otherwise, and do not differ substantially from the plain unvarnished text of the 1922 Constitution. It would also seem clear that the closing words, with their reference to "the rights of parents" were intended to qualify the obligation on the State to give reasonable aid to other initiatives and to provide educational facilities themselves. As noted in *Crowley v. Ireland* [1980] I.R. 102, the use of the words "provide *for*" in the opening words were sufficient to safeguard the rights of parents to have their children educated in schools of their own choice rather than State schools.
>
> It is clear, accordingly, that while the principal beneficiaries of the right to free primary education recognised and protected in Article 42.4 are children in family units, they were not intended to be the only beneficiaries. Children without parents, natural or adoptive, whether they grow up in the care of institutions, foster parents or older relatives, are equally entitled to the right protected in Article 42.4. The issue with which the High Court and this court is concerned is whether the rights of the beneficiaries, whether they are children in family units or otherwise, cease when they reach a particular age, irrespective of the fact that they might still be reasonably regarded as being in need of primary education....
>
> I do not think that any useful guidance can be derived from dictionary definitions as to what is meant by the expression "primary education". Its meaning, in the vast majority of cases, is clear. It denotes the stage of a child's education lasting from ages six to twelve and does not extend to the kind of training and human development that takes place from birth to age four. The latter normally takes place in the home and not in a school setting. The primary school curriculum in this country has since 1831 had as its central component education in literacy and numeracy, and now includes as already noted, in addition, mathematics, social and environmental studies, music and physical education. In addition, Irish is a compulsory subject in the primary school curriculum. It should be noted, however, as pointed out in *Director of Public Prosecutions v. Best* [2000] 2 I.R. 17 that the curriculum, as it now exists, represents more than the "minimum education, moral, intellectual and social" which it is the State's duty to ensure that children receive pursuant to Article 42.3.2°.
>
> That is not the form of "primary education" to which the first plaintiff was found to be entitled in *O'Donoghue v. Minister for Health* [1996] 2 I.R. 20 by O'Hanlon J. and to which Barr J. found the first plaintiff in this case to be entitled. The latter's needs at this stage of his life still do not extend significantly beyond the basic skills which more fortunately endowed children acquire in the home between birth and four....
>
> Even if it were open to this court to treat as incorrect the finding in the High Court that the first plaintiff was entitled to free primary education up to the age of 22, the defendants would encounter serious difficulties in acknowledging the constitutional right

of the first plaintiff to free primary education up to the age of 18, because of his special needs, but not thereafter. If a person is in receipt of education on the eve of his 18th birthday, it is in the vast majority of cases a total misuse of language to describe that as primary education in the normal sense. However, it is properly regarded as primary education in the case of a person such as the first plaintiff, even though in chronological and physical terms he has ceased to be a person who would normally be regarded as being in receipt of such education.

If it is the law that a person in the position of the first plaintiff ceases to be entitled to free primary education at the stage in his life when he becomes an adult, it is for the courts alone, in the absence of any specific age limit to be found in Article 42, to determine when that stage would be reached. The contention on behalf of the first plaintiff is that he has not yet become an adult in terms of his educational needs and may never reach that stage. The contention on behalf of the Minister is that the age is fixed at 18 years. While that, as it happens, is the age fixed by legislation as the age of majority for a number of important legal purposes, it was not within the competence of the Oireachtas to subject the first plaintiff's constitutional right to such an age limitation and they have not attempted so to do in the Act of 1998. *A fortiori*, it is certainly not the function of the Minister to determine the age at which the constitutional right of a person in the position of the first plaintiff ceases. As the whole history of this litigation from beginning to end eloquently demonstrates, that is the function of the courts and the courts alone.

All those who survive that period of their life, which is properly and unarguably described as childhood, begin to pass certain legal and societal milestones. At the age of 14, they are capable of committing criminal offences. At the age of 16, they are no longer required to attend school and may, if the opportunity arises, enter the adult world of work. (The school leaving age was fixed at this level by s. 2(1) of the Education (Welfare) Act, 2000.) At the age of 17, their parents cease to be responsible for their welfare. (It should be noted, however, that s. 2(1) of the Child Care Act, 1991, defines a "child" as "a person under the age of 18 years other than a person who is or has been married".) Between the ages of 15 and 17, they are classified by the criminal law as "young persons" and may suffer what amounts to a form of imprisonment. At that stage, consensual sexual intercourse with them by a person of the same age or older ceases to be a criminal offence. At the age of 18, they are entitled to marry, to vote and to incur legal obligations under the civil law. Although the age of 21 is no longer the significant legal watershed that it once was, the custom of treating it as a form of entry into adult life does not seem to have entirely vanished. The Constitution itself does not recognise persons who have not reached the age of 35 as of sufficient maturity to be eligible to be President of Ireland.

Where in this spectrum can it be said with any semblance of truth that the first plaintiff passed from childhood to adulthood? So far as the evidence in this case goes, virtually none of these stages is of any significance in his case. He is one of a relatively small category of people in our society who, because of their mental handicap, can never enjoy life in all its diversity and richness but to whom at least a measure of happiness may be available. The uncontested evidence in this case is that, to attain even that low plateau, the first plaintiff requires continuing access to what, in his case, is education, as defined by Ó Dálaigh C.J., albeit often extremely basic in character. No principled basis exists either in law or in the evidence for the contention advanced by the defendants that a person in his position ceases to be in need of primary education at age 18, at age 22 or at any age in the future which can now be identified with any precision. [2001] 2 IR 545, at 629–630, 637–639.

[9–122] Keane CJ's approach can be described as the "functional child" approach. Although it would have secured education for Mr Sinnott, it is questionable whether it is consistent with the constitutional meaning of "child". Can the word "child" be extended to include anyone who requires services that are generally required by the paradigmatic child, the young person? The State did not contest, before the Supreme Court, that the services sought by Mr Sinnott were "education". Accordingly, the authority of *O'Donoghue v Minister for Education* was not expressly challenged. However, some of the comments of Hardiman J (similar to views expressed by Murphy J) suggested scepticism as to whether the services sought were education.

In this regard, more recent cases have suggested, at the very least, a reluctance to raise the standard of education that is constitutionally guaranteed. For instance, in *O'Carolan v Minister for Education* [2005] IEHC 296, the applicant was a profoundly autistic child seeking to have the State fund his education in a centre in Wales, on the basis that placement being offered to him in Dublin was not suitable to meet his needs. McMenamin J held that the legal test was whether the education offered by the State was "appropriate". Having reviewed the evidence, McMenamin J concluded that the education offered by the State was appropriate. O'Mahony has argued that the legal test was incorrect. Based on *O'Donoghue* and indeed *Ryan*, he has suggested that the correct test requires an assessment of whether the education would allow a child "to make the best possible use of his or her inherent and potential capacities." (See Conor O'Mahony, "The Right to Education and 'Constitutionally Appropriate' Provision" (2006) 28 *DULJ* 422.) Such an approach would necessarily involve a comparison between the provision offered by the State and the provision sought by a child in order to determine which is better. The fact that McMenamin J did not adopt such an approach suggests a possible retrenchment on the principle identified in *O'Donoghue* but certainly—at the very least—an unwillingness further to extend the scope of court intervention in this area. [9–123]

Parental Choice in Primary Education

In *O'Sheil v Minister for Education* [1999] 2 IR 321, the plaintiffs wished to educate their children on the basis of Steiner principles. They sought to compel the State to provide funds for a school that would operate on the basis of these principles. This form of education would certainly meet the standard of a "certain minimum education" under Art 42.3.2°. Accordingly, the parents were fully entitled to educate their children in this way at their own expense. The question was whether the State, under Art 42.4, had an obligation to fund such education. Laffoy J reasoned as follows: [9–124]

> When one adopts a global approach to the interpretation of Article 42 the values enshrined in it become obvious. It is concerned with education in a broad sense—religious and moral, intellectual, physical and social. In its entirety it is imbued with the concept of parental freedom of choice. While parents do not have the choice not to educate their children, it recognises that all parents do not have the same financial capacity to educate their children. It is in this overall context that the obligation is imposed on the State to "provide for free primary education". In my view it would pervert the clear intent of the Constitution to interpret that obligation as merely obliging the State to fund a single system of primary education which is on offer to parents on a "take it or leave it" basis. In the case of parents of limited or modest means unable to afford, or to afford without hardship, fees charged by private schools, it would render worthless the guarantee of freedom of parental choice, which is the fundamental precept of the Constitution. If the defendants' stance—that it has discharged its constitutional obligations to the plaintiffs by providing financial aid for fifteen denominational schools within a twelve mile radius of Cooleenbridge School—were tenable, it would render meaningless the guarantee of

parental freedom of choice in the case of the parent plaintiffs. It is not tenable. Moreover, it is clear from the evidence that it is not the stance adopted by the Minister in practice, as the past recognition of multi-denominational schools and Gaelscoileanna indicates.

In order to fulfil its constitutional obligation to provide for free primary education, in my view, the State must have regard to and must accommodate the expression of parental conscientious choice and lawful preference. However, this does not mean that the State must accede to an application for financial aid from any group of parents who are united in their choice of primary education which establishes that what is being provided by it is education, that it is being provided in a school and that it meets a standard of what can reasonably be defined as primary education, as the plaintiffs contended. As was pointed out by the Supreme Court judgments in *Crowley v. Ireland* [1980] I.R. 102, the State's constitutional obligation is to make arrangements for the availability of free primary education. Those judgments identified the main features of the arrangements then in place: subsidisation of provision of school buildings and facilities by means of capital grants; meeting the day-to-day costs of running the schools by payment of teachers' salaries and by means of capitation grants; and prescribing and enforcing standards, through provision of a curriculum and supervision. It is also implicit in Article 42.4, in my view, that the scheme by which the arrangements are put in place, involving as it must, the disbursement of public money, be rational. Even though the State must have regard to the constitutional guarantee of parental freedom of choice in framing such a scheme, nonetheless it is proper for the State and, indeed, I would say incumbent on the State, to incorporate in the scheme measures to ensure that need and viability are properly assessed and that there is accountability.

In summary, therefore, I reject the defendants' contention that they have discharged their constitutional obligation to the plaintiffs by provision of funded denominational national schools in East Clare. I also reject the plaintiffs' contention that once the parent plaintiffs, being a group of parents exercising a similar lawful preference as to the manner in which they educate their children, establish in this Court that they are providing education for their children in a school which meets the standard which can be reasonably defined as primary education, this Court can direct that they be funded on the same basis as primary schools recognised by the State are funded. The correct constitutional position is somewhere between the two polarised positions adopted by the parties in these proceedings. Fulfilment of the State's constitutional obligation under Article 42.4 must take account of the parental freedom of choice guaranteed by Article 42, but it must be based on arrangements which have a rational foundation and prescribe proper criteria for eligibility which accord with the purpose of Article 42 and of the provisions of the Constitution generally. [1999] 2 IR 321, at 346–348.

[9–125] Assessing the criteria actually employed by the State to decide whether to fund a form of primary education, Laffoy J held that the teacher qualification criteria were not unreasonable. Further, she held that it was permissible—given Art 8 of the Constitution—to require that Irish be taught in order for a particular form of primary education to be funded. She emphasised that "primary education" envisaged a higher standard than "certain minimum education." Accordingly, while it was permissible for parents not to teach their children Irish, it was also permissible for the State to require the teaching of Irish as a pre-requisite for the funding of primary education.

[9–126] Laffoy J implicitly held that the State may provide a level of primary education that is greater than the certain minimum education that may be required under Art 42.3.2°. Writing in 1967, Kelly took a different view, reasoning that such a course of action would induce parents not to provide for their children's education outside the State system, thereby subverting the idea of parental choice that imbues Art 42:

It is no answer to this point of view to say (which is perfectly true) that the State does not actually compel parents to send their children to a State primary school, nor to submit their children to the primary certificate examination now being abolished, so that parents who dislike the curriculum of the State primary schools are quite free to provide an alternative primary education in their own home or in private schools. It is no answer, because although there is no theoretical compulsion, we know that for the vast bulk of the people, either for geographical or economical reasons, there is no practical alternative, I might say no alternative at all, to the local national school. (Reprinted in Gerry Whyte, "Education and the Constitution: Convergence of Paradigm and Praxis" (1990) 25 *Ir Jur (ns)* 69, at 84–5.)

Laffoy J's view seems preferable. Although it may lead to pressure on parents to send their children to primary schools, as opposed to providing education themselves at home, this is surely preferable to the alternative. Kelly's approach—particularly given the limited interpretation of "certain minimum education"—would lead to a race to the bottom in terms of educational provision. Such a race to the bottom could not be reversed by strengthening the standard of "certain minimum education" as such would also lead to the pressure on parents which Kelly wished to avoid.

At Risk Children

We have seen in *Comerford v Minister for Education* how Art 42.4 may require the State to make special provision for the educational needs of disadvantaged children. A similar, but broader, use has been made of Art 42.5. We have seen in *NWHB v HW* how the State is only entitled to intervene in parental decisions in the rather limited circumstances of Art 42.5. However, Art 42.5 does not just allow the State to intervene. It obliges the State to intervene. In *FN v Minister for Education* [1995] 1 IR 409, the High Court derived from Art 42.5 a right, on the part of at risk children, to be cared for by the State. The applicant was a 12 year old child whose father was unknown and whose mother, now dead, had had no contact with him since an early age. After a period of time with foster parents, an "out of control" order had been obtained by the notice party, which had subsequently provided various types of accommodation for him. He was ultimately diagnosed as suffering from a hyperkinetic conduct disorder by a consultant psychiatrist who recommended a period of time in a secure unit which could contain him safely while confronting his behaviour. Geoghegan J addressed his claim as follows:

[9–127]

> [W]here there is a child with very special needs which cannot be provided by the parents or guardian there is a constitutional obligation on the State under Article 42, s. 5 of the Constitution to cater for those needs in order to vindicate the constitutional rights of the child. It is not necessary for me to determine how absolute that duty is; conceivably there may be very exceptional circumstances where there is some quite exceptional need of the child which the State cannot be expected even under the Constitution to provide.... But it would seem to me that on the balance of probabilities the provision of such necessary accommodation, arrangements and services by the State as might meet the necessary requirements of this applicant is not so impractical or so prohibitively expensive as would come within any notional limit on the State's constitutional obligations. There may be differences of opinion among the experts as to the level of staffing arrangements which would be required, even on a temporary basis, for the proper care of F.N. but I am not convinced at present that even the more extreme view taken by Doctor Byrne as to staff ratio is prohibitively expensive. He has given evidence that similar facilities are available in Canada and other countries. I would have thought that in considering questions of

expense and practicality, the State would have regard not merely to the immediate cost but to a possible long term saving of cost if the special treatment of recalcitrant children led in the long term to a reduction of crime and drug abuse. But these are obviously to some extent areas of policy. I advert to them merely to indicate why it is not self-evident to me that the more elaborate requirements suggested by Doctor Byrne fall outside the ambit of any constitutional duty owed by the State. [1995] 1 IR 409, at 416.

[9–128] It is difficult to argue that children, such as FN, should not receive the sort of services which he sought. It also seems unarguable that the court cases concerning FN and similarly placed children succeeded, if nothing else, in focusing political and public attention on the issue. However, one wonders how suited the language of constitutional rights was to FN's situation. Is it meaningful to speak of a right to be locked up (presumably against your will) in a secure unit?

[9–129] Following *FN*, many rights of this type were asserted on behalf of children. Frustration with the State's response led to mandatory orders being granted. In *TD v Minister for Education* [2001] 4 IR 259, the Supreme Court held that such orders could not be granted, save in the most exceptional of circumstances. However, the right itself still exists and may be vindicated by way of declaratory relief. In *ED v Health Services Executive* 28 April 2005 (SC) *ex tempore*, Murray CJ emphasised that parental failure was a pre-requisite to state intervention under Art 42.5. Accordingly, although the child in that case required a psychiatric assessment, he could not rely on Art 42.5 to obtain it as he had been cared for very well by his mother. It is perhaps unsettling that one's constitutional entitlement to certain services depends on points of constitutional interpretation of this type and not on need. However, this is perhaps an inevitable by-product of the attempt to shoehorn socio-economic claims into constitutional rights to which they are not particularly suited (primary education in Mr Sinnott's case, parental failure in ED's case).

CONTENTS – CHAPTER 10

Religion

Introduction. . . . . [10–01]
Freedom of Conscience and Free Practice and Profession of Religion . . . . [10–02]
Non-discrimination. . . . . [10–07]
Non-endowment. . . . . [10–15]
Overview of Case Law on Art 44 . . . . [10–22]

Overview

Article 44 provides a number of protections and freedoms in relation to religion. Freedom of conscience and the free practice and profession of religion are all protected. The courts have held that the freedom of conscience protected is religious conscience. However, this protection is subject to public order and morality. In this light, the courts have upheld a ban on religious advertising. Article 44 also precludes the State from discriminating on the grounds of religion. However, the courts have held that this guarantee is subordinate to the provision guaranteeing free practice of religion. Accordingly, the courts have concluded that the State must discriminate on the basis of religion where necessary to give full effect to the free practice clause. Article 44 also precludes the State from endowing any religion, although the courts have held that this does not prevent the State from funding the salaries of school chaplains.

Chapter 10

Religion

Introduction

Article 44.2 contains a set of guarantees, relating to religion, that would be fairly typical in liberal democracies. Article 44.2.1°–4° offers a number of protections to individuals. On the one hand, freedom of conscience and the free profession and practice of religion are guaranteed. On the other hand, the State cannot endow any religion, nor can the State discriminate on the grounds of religious, profession, belief or status. Moreover, the State cannot discriminate between schools under the management of different religious denominations and children attending a school receiving public money cannot be obliged to attend religious instruction at that school. Article 44.2.5°–6° protect the religious denominations themselves from State interference. Taken together, these provisions would suggest a position whereby the State respects religion, but is strictly neutral as between religions and (as importantly) as between believers and non-believers. An examination of the case law, however, reveals that this is far from the case. This perhaps reflects the ringing declaration of Art 44.1 (the State shall respect and honour religion) and, more practically, the endorsement given by Art 42 to the Roman Catholic model of education. Whatever its inspiration, the result is a case law that is anything but neutral on the question of religion. [10–01]

Freedom of Conscience and Free Practice and Profession of Religion

In *McGee v Attorney General* [1974] IR 284, the plaintiff sought a declaration that the law banning the importation of contraceptives was unconstitutional. One of her arguments was that the law infringed her freedom of conscience under Art 44.2.1°. The Supreme Court rejected this contention, Walsh J reasoning as follows: [10–02]

> [T]he plaintiff says that, so far as her conscience is concerned, the use of contraceptives by her is in accordance with her conscience and that, in using them, she does not feel that she is acting against her conscience. It was submitted that social conscience, as distinct from religious conscience, falls within the ambit of Article 44. I do not think that is so. The whole context in which the question of conscience appears in Article 44 is one dealing with the exercise of religion and the free profession and practice of religion. Within that context, the meaning of s. 2, sub-s. 1, of Article 44 is that no person shall directly or indirectly be coerced or compelled to act contrary to his conscience in so far as the practice of religion is concerned and, subject to public order and morality, is free to profess and practise the religion of his choice in accordance with his conscience. Correlatively, he is free to have no religious beliefs or to abstain from the practice or profession of any religion. Because a person feels free, or even obliged, in conscience to pursue some particular activity which is not in itself a religious practice, it does not follow that such activity is guaranteed protection by Article 44. It is not correct to say, as was submitted, that the Article is a constitutional guarantee of a right to live in accordance with one's conscience subject to public order and morality. What the Article guarantees is

the right not to be compelled or coerced into living in a way which is contrary to one's conscience and, in the context of the Article, that means contrary to one's conscience so far as the exercise, practice or profession of religion is concerned. [1974] IR 284, at 316–317.

Walsh J held in favour of the plaintiff on the grounds that it infringed her right to marital privacy for the State effectively to preclude her from using contraception. Given that conclusion, what end is served by limiting the conscience protected by Art 44 to religious conscience?

[10–03] The limitation of Art 44 in this way makes it crucially important to be able to determine what is a religion. Article 44.1.2° and 44.1.3° (deleted by referendum in 1972) recognised the Roman Catholic Church, the Church of Ireland, the Presbyterian Church in Ireland, the Methodist Church in Ireland, the Religious Society of Friends and the Jewish Congregation, so presumably they qualify as religions for the purpose of Art 44. These articles also recognised "the other religious denominations existing in Ireland at the date of the coming into operation of this Constitution", but it would be question begging to use that to identify what constitutes a religion. Is Islam protected by Art 44? Buddhism? Scientology? How should the courts address this issue? Given Walsh J's insistence that the freedom of conscience protected is religious conscience, it presumably follows that world-views or value systems that define themselves (to some extent) in opposition to religion cannot be characterised as religions. On this basis, secular humanism cannot be characterised as a religion.

[10–04] In *Murphy v IRTC* [1999] 1 IR 12, the applicant challenged the constitutionality of s 10(3) of the Radio and Television Act 1988, which prohibits the broadcast of any advertisement "which is directed towards any religious or political end or which has any relation to an industrial dispute." Under this section, the IRTC prevented a radio station from broadcasting the applicant's advertisement concerning an evening presentation of the evidence of the resurrection of Christ. The applicant contended that this infringed his rights under Art 44. The Supreme Court, *per* Barrington J, rejected this claim:

> One can best glean the policy of the Act of 1988 by looking at the three kinds of prohibited advertisement collectively. One might get a false impression by singling out one kind of banned advertisement and ignoring the others. All three kinds of banned advertisement relate to matters which have proved extremely divisive in Irish society in the past. The Oireachtas was entitled to take the view that the citizens would resent having advertisements touching on these topics broadcast into their homes and that such advertisements, if permitted, might lead to unrest. Moreover the Oireachtas may well have thought that in relation to matters of such sensitivity, rich men should not be able to buy access to the airwaves to the detriment of their poorer rivals....
>
> There is no question of any form of discrimination or distinction being made by s. 10(3) on the grounds of religious profession belief or status. The ban contained in sub-s. (3) is directed at material of a particular class and not at people who profess a particular religion. All people in the same position are treated equally. The fact that people who wish to advertise motor cars or tinned beans may be treated differently is not relevant. It appears to the Court that the prohibition on advertising contained in s.10(3) is broad enough to cover not only advertisements tending to favour any or all religions but also advertisements tending to attack all or any religion. It cannot therefore be regarded as an attack on the citizen's right to practise his religion. It may however constitute a limitation on the manner in which the citizen can profess his religion.

It appears to the Court that it is not sufficient to say, in reply to this argument, that religion is a private affair and that the citizen's right to profess his religion is not affected by denying him access to the airwaves. Religion is both a private and a public affair and a citizen, convinced of the truth of his own religion, will naturally wish not only to convert his fellow citizens, but to influence the evolution of society....

It is sufficient to admit that the ban on religious advertising is a restriction, however limited, on the freedom of the citizen to profess, express or practise his religion and to inquire whether, in the circumstances of the case, the restriction is justified. In the present case the limitation placed on the various constitutional rights is minimalist. The applicant has the right to advance his views in speech or by writing or by holding assemblies or associating with persons of like mind to himself. He has no lesser right than any other citizen to appear on radio or television. The only restriction placed upon his activities is that he cannot advance his views by a paid advertisement on radio or television....

Counsel for the applicant argued that it would have been possible to have had—instead of a blanket ban on religious advertising—a more selective administrative system whereby inoffensive religious advertisements would be permitted, and religious advertisements likely to cause offence, banned. No doubt this is true. But the Oireachtas may well have decided that it would be inappropriate to involve agents of the State in deciding which advertisements, in this sensitive area would be likely to cause offence and which not. In any event, once the Statute is broadly within the area of the competence of the Oireachtas and the Oireachtas has respected the principle of proportionality, it is not for this Court to interfere simply because it might have made a different decision.

It therefore appears to the Court that the ban on religious advertising contained in s. 10(3) of the Act of 1988 is rationally connected to the objective of the legislation and is not arbitrary, unfair or based on irrational considerations. It does appear to impair the various constitutional rights referred to as little as possible and it does appear that its effects on those rights are proportional to the objective of the legislation. [1999] 1 IR 12, at 22–23, 26–27.

Does the fact that some might find religious speech offensive justify the restriction of religious speech? Barrington J observed that there was no question of discrimination once all religious speech treated the same, but this only means that there was no discrimination as between religions, not as between religious speech and other speech. Barrington J described the restriction of speech as "minimalist" but it was an absolute prohibition in a particular context. In that light, can the legislation fairly be described as proportional? **[10–05]**

Religious freedom is only guaranteed, subject to "public order and morality". The Supreme Court did not rely on this specific exception in *Murphy* but it was relied on by the Court of Criminal Appeal in *People (DPP) v Draper,* 24 March 1988, *The Irish Times.* Hogan and Whyte describe the case as follows: **[10–06]**

> [T]he Court of Criminal Appeal dismissed an appeal against conviction in the case of a man convicted on two counts of malicious damage to religious statues. Referring to the man's motivation – he believed that he had been sent by God – McCarthy J said that the court was not questioning the sincerity of his beliefs. However the guarantee of freedom of conscience and the free profession and practice of religion was expressly subject to public order and morality. In the instant case, there was no question of morality but rather one of public order. There was a requirement that the property of citizens must be protected. The defendant had damaged property and the law said that this was an offence. Gerard Hogan and Gerry Whyte, *Kelly: the Irish Constitution* (4th ed, LexisNexis Butterworths, 2003), at [7.8.43].

Although this is not the easiest of cases from which to derive general principles, the public order and morality exception appears to have a significant effect on the religious freedom guarantee. If religious freedom is to be protected only to the extent that it does not offend public morality, what exercises of religious freedom are likely to be protected from State interference? Is the delineation of an act as an offence by the criminal law sufficient to determine that it offends public morality and hence cannot be protected as an exercise of religious freedom?

Non-discrimination

[10–07] The flip side of the State's guarantee of religious freedom is the State's eschewal of endowment and discrimination. The non-discrimination guarantee received its first significant consideration in *Quinn's Supermarket v Attorney General* [1972] IR 1. Article 2 of the Victuallers' Shops (Hours of Trading on Weekdays) (Dublin, Dun Laoghaire and Bray) Order 1948 effectively exempted Kosher butcher shops from a ban on evening opening. The plaintiffs challenged the constitutionality of this provision, partly on the grounds of Art 40.1 and partly on the grounds of Art 44.2.3°. The Supreme Court, *per* Walsh J, held that although the plaintiffs did not suffer a disability on the ground of their religion, the preferential treatment for Kosher butcher shops did amount to a discrimination on the ground of religious profession, belief or status:

> It was submitted on behalf of the defendants here that "discrimination" should be construed as if it read "discrimination against". In my view the learned High Court judge was quite correct in rejecting that submission. If the provision had read "discrimination against" — meaning distinguishing unfavourably on the grounds of religious profession, belief or status — it would also mean that the test would have been related to the religious profession, belief or status of the person discriminated against. It is the omission of the word "against" which confirms me in my view that this portion of the constitutional provision should be construed as meaning that the State shall not make any "distinction" on the ground of religious profession, belief or status. This is confirmed by the Irish text which says "*ná aon idirdhealú do dhèanamh...*" To discriminate, in that sense, is to create a difference between persons or bodies or to distinguish between them on the ground of religious profession, belief or status; it follows, therefore, that the religious profession, belief or status does not have to be that of the person who feels he has suffered by reason of the distinction created. Indeed it is wide enough to enable the person who might be thought to have profited from the distinction but who did not accept the validity of such distinction, to challenge it by showing that it was based upon the religious profession, belief or status of the suffering party. In such instance the suffering party could avail of the remedies open to him under the "disability" provision, as well as under the "discrimination" provision, if in fact he was suffering a disability.
>
> Therefore, I am of opinion that the exception made in relation to the sale of meat killed according to the Jewish ritual is a discrimination on the ground of religious profession, belief or status within the meaning of sub-s. 3 of s. 2 of Article 44 and that it is, prima facie at least, unconstitutional on its face. However, the matter does not end there. Certain questions of fact in this case are of vital importance. Evidence was given orally in the High Court by witnesses of the Jewish religion and further evidence was offered in this Court, at the request of the Court, by the Chief Rabbi of Ireland. None of this evidence is contradicted as a question of fact and, so far as the Court is concerned, the question of what are the beliefs or professions of the Jewish religion is a question of fact.
>
> The facts are that it is an essential element of the Jewish religion that only meat killed and authorised by the Jewish ritual method should be eaten by persons practising the

Jewish religion, and that the shops dealing in the sale of meat killed by the Jewish ritual method are owned, and were owned at; the date the order was made, by members of the Jewish religion who, by the tenets or rules of their religion, would be compelled to close their shops before the hours of sunset on Friday afternoons and would be prohibited from re-opening before sunset on Saturdays. This was so even though many, if not all, of the employees of these shops would not be of the Jewish religion. For the sake of convenience, I shall refer to meat "killed and prepared by the Jewish ritual method" as kosher meat. It also appears that over 90% of all the Jewish families in Ireland accept these rules as the binding rules of their religion and acknowledge that the required duty of Judaism is to observe these rules regarding meat and other kosher foods. Such observance is a strict commandment in the code of Jewish law. It is also a fact that, in any case where in special circumstances it might be unavoidable that the supply of kosher meat might be conducted by one who was not a practising member of the Jewish faith, it was essential that a religiously observant Jewish representative, fully cognisant of all the requirements regarding the meat, should at all times supervise the supply and sale of such meat.

The conclusion of fact is that between the hours of sunset on Friday afternoons and sunset on Saturday afternoons it would not be possible for any practising member of the Jewish religion to obtain any meat for consumption save that which, by the commandments of his religion, he is forbidden to eat; between those hours such person would be left with the choice of observing his religion's commandments and in consequence going without meat, or of being compelled to act in breach of his religion's commandments by buying the type of meat that he is forbidden to buy. If by law the hours of trading in kosher meat is confined to hours which present a member of the Jewish religion with the choice I have mentioned, then that law interferes with the free profession and practice of that religion.

Therefore, there arises a conflict between the constitutional guarantee of the free profession and practice of religion and the constitutional guarantee against discrimination on the ground of religious profession, belief or status....

Our Constitution reflects a firm conviction that we are religious people. The preamble to the Constitution acknowledges that we are a Christian people and Article 44, s. 1, sub-s. 1, acknowledges that the homage of public worship is due to Almighty God but it does so in terms which do not confine the benefit of that acknowledgment to members of the Christian faith. In Article 44, s. 1, of the Constitution [removed by referendum in 1972] the State recognises the existence of the several religious denominations there named, including the Jewish Congregations, as well as all other unnamed ones existing at the date of the coming into operation of the Constitution. This declaration is an express recognition of the separate co-existence of the religious denominations, named and unnamed. It does not prefer one to the other and it does not confer any privilege or impose any disability or diminution of status upon any religious denomination, and it does not permit the State to do so.

Section 2, sub-s. 1, of Article 44 of the Constitution guarantees freedom of conscience and the free profession and practice of religion in terms which do not confine these to Christianity and Judaism. It appears to me, therefore, that the primary object and aim of Article 44, and in particular the provisions of s. 2 of that Article, was to secure and guarantee freedom of conscience and the free profession and practice of religion subject to public order and morality; and to ensure that the practice of religion and the holding of particular religious beliefs shall not subject the person so practising religion or holding those beliefs to any disabilities on that account, or permit distinctions on the ground of religious profession, belief or status between persons in the State who are free to profess and practise their religion. If, however, the implementation of the guarantee of free profession and practice of religion requires that a distinction should be made to make possible for the persons professing or practising a particular religion their guaranteed right to do so, then such a distinction is not invalid having regard to the provisions of the Constitution. It would be completely contrary to the spirit and intendment of the provisions of Article 44, S. 2, to permit the guarantee against discrimination on the ground of religious profession or belief to be made the very means of restricting or preventing the free profession or practice of religion. The primary purpose of the guarantee against discrimination is to ensure the freedom of practice of religion. Any law which by virtue of the generality of its application would by its effect restrict or prevent the free profession and practice of religion by any person or persons would be invalid having regard to the provisions of the Constitution, unless it contained provisions which saved from such restriction or prevention the practice of religion of the person or persons who would otherwise be so restricted or prevented.

In my view, the provisions of s. 25 of the Shops (Hours of Trading) Act, 1938, did not require that all orders or regulations made by the Minister for Industry and Commerce pursuant to the powers there granted should be of such strict or general application that no provision could be made to exempt the person or persons whose practice of religion would be restricted or prevented without such exemption. In my view, the section, if it had so intended, would itself have been invalid.

It is quite clear that the exemption which was achieved by way of definition of the term "victualler's shop" in the Order of 1948 was intended to avoid any such restriction upon the practice of their religion by members of the Jewish religion in the trading area mentioned in the Order. The fact that it might cause less hardship in the year 1968 than in the year 1948, because of the improvements in the method of keeping meat for a period in refrigerators, does not affect the issue. To hold otherwise would be to penalise those members of the Jewish religion who have not got such facilities in their homes.

So long as the present dietary laws remain a binding part of the Jewish religion, then a sufficient exemption of the type under review would be not merely not invalid but would be necessary if the hours of trading were regulated as at present. If, however, at some future date there is a change in these dietary laws to the extent that they are no longer binding upon members of the Jewish religion, as indeed there have been some changes in respect of members of the Catholic religion, then the position alters and such an exemption might no longer be justifiable having regard to the provisions of the Constitution. As in *Ryan v. The Attorney General* the validity of the exempting provision would depend upon the existing state of fact, which in this case would be that these dietary laws are a binding part of the Jewish religion. What I have said about the laws of religion is not to be construed in any way as saying that a similar exemption would be valid in respect of pious customs or practices which linger on after they have ceased to be a binding part of religion and, *a fortiori*, in respect of purely secular activities or restrictions which historically had their origins in religious observance.

Finally, I come to the plaintiffs' complaint that the discrimination is more than is necessary as it results in shops in which the only business carried on is the sale of kosher meat being open without restriction as to hours on every weekday as well as on Sundays. All shops are permitted to be open for the sale of meat on Sundays. Up to the outbreak of the last war, it was the practice in the Jewish Community for shops engaged in the sale of kosher meat to open only for a short time on Saturday night after the end of the period of the Jewish Sabbath, so as to cater for the needs of people buying meat for Sunday. It appears that this practice ceased during the war years because shops tended to close down after dark and it appears that the practice has not been revived at any time since then, though of course it might be revived at any time if the need for its revival existed. It always was and still is the practice for these shops to open for a period on Sunday mornings. Shopkeepers engaged in the sale of other meat do not apparently avail themselves of the right to trade on Sunday. Sunday then is usually the first occasion after the previous Friday that members of the Jewish religion are able to purchase the only meat which, according to their religion, they may lawfully consume. Even if the former practice of opening the shops after dark on Saturdays still continued, the time of day might prove to be very inconvenient to many Jewish people and the provision of the Order of 1948 which excludes such shops from the definition of "victualler's shop" would not be a justification for closing them on Sundays. Without the Sunday opening, the very pressures upon the practice of the Jewish religion which the Order of 1948 sought to avoid would not have been removed. Furthermore if, for the sake of maintaining a balance of trading hours, the Order of 1948 had sought by a special provision to make it unlawful for the proprietor of any shop in which the only business carried on was that of selling kosher meat to keep such shop open for the serving of customers on Sundays, it would have the very infirmity which the plaintiffs have contended for in this case in relation to the exclusion. Such a distinction could not at all be justified on the grounds that it was necessary to permit the free exercise of anyone's religious practice or belief, even if it did result in all butchers' shops having the same number of trading hours each week.

In my opinion the plaintiffs are justified in their complaint that the discrimination is more than is necessary in so far as it relates to weekdays other than Saturdays. There is no evidence whatsoever to suggest that the free practice of the Jewish religion would be hampered in any way by the application of the fixed hours to the koshermeat shops on those days, and no such ground has been advanced by the Attorney General in support of his appeal against the order of the High Court. For the reasons I have already given, a discrimination on Saturdays would not be invalid. However, the words of the exemption in Article 2 of the Order of 1948 gives exemption for every day, and by its terms is incapable of being modified by deletion so as to confine it to Saturdays. Therefore, in my view it is invalid although an exemption from the trading hours on Saturdays would not be invalid even if in practice such an exemption was not availed of. Such an exemption would avoid the possibility of a member of the Jewish Community having to choose between the practice of his religion and the sale or purchase of meat on that day. [1972] IR 1, at 15–17, 23–27.

Walsh J refers to a number of factual matters in identifying the practices of the Jewish religion. Which is more important: the tenets of the religion or the actual practice of persons who would identify themselves as adherents to the religion? Given the subsequent proliferation of refrigerators, should this case be decided in the same way today? In holding that any religious discrimination that is necessary to guarantee the free practice of religion could not be unconstitutional, Walsh J effectively elevated the free practice guarantee over the non-discrimination guarantee. Could one not equally have argued that any restriction of religious freedom that is necessary to ensure non-discrimination could not be unconstitutional? However, the State's commitment in Art 44.1 to respect and honour religion may provide a basis for preferring the free practice guarantee over the non-discrimination guarantee. On Walsh J's reasoning, it appears that if the law on butcher shop opening had not made an exception for Kosher butcher shops, it would have been unconstitutional. Such an approach—requiring legislative exceptions to be made for religious reasons—would impose an onerous duty on the Oireachtas. It appears to be inconsistent with the tenor of the much less reasoned decision in *Draper* (above). Walsh J ultimately concluded, however, that the measure was invalid because (by allowing Kosher shops to open late every night of the week) it went further than was necessary to ensure the free profession and practice of the Jewish religion. Kenny J dissented on this ground, refusing to hold the Order unconstitutional. Is the greater level of precision required by Walsh J's approach justified by the fact that there are two competing constitutional rights at issue? [10–08]

In *Re Article 26 and the Employment Equality Bill 1996* [1997] 2 IR 321, the Supreme Court endorsed Walsh J's approach of upholding religious discriminations that are necessary to secure the free practice of religion. Section 37(1) of the Bill provided an exception from the general prohibition of discrimination on proscribed grounds by [10–09] allowing a religious institution, *inter alia*, to provide more favourable treatment to an employee or prospective employee on a proscribed ground. The Court considered that this was a proportional restriction of both Art 40.1 and Art 44.2.3°.

[10–10] In a sense, the Bill sought to copper-fasten the decision in *McGrath v Trustees of Maynooth College* [1979] ILRM 166. The plaintiffs in that case were both priests employed by Maynooth College. They sought laicisation and wore non-clerical garb; following a disciplinary process, they were dismissed. At the time, Maynooth College, which received funding from the State, was both a seminary and a college for non-religious people. The Supreme Court considered a number of issues relating to disciplinary procedures but also focused on Art 44 of the Constitution. O'Higgins CJ did not accept that the fact that Maynooth College received funding from the State rendered it subject to the ban on religious discrimination. In any event, even if Maynooth were subject to Art 44.2.3°, the freedom of every religious denomination to manage its own affairs protected the action taken by the college authorities in this instance. Henchy J provided an analysis more similar to that offered by Walsh J in *Quinn's Supermarket*:

> The constitutional provision invoked here must be construed in terms of its purpose. In proscribing disabilities and discriminations at the hands of the State on the ground of religious profession, belief or status, the primary aim of the constitutional guarantee is to give vitality, independence and freedom to religion. To construe the provision literally, without due regard to its underlying objective, would lead to a sapping and debilitation of the freedom and independence given by the Constitution to the doctrinal and organisational requirements and proscriptions which are inherent in all organised religions. Far from eschewing the internal disabilities and discriminations which flow from the tenets of a particular religion, the State must on occasion recognize and buttress them. For such disabilities and discriminations do not derive from the State; it cannot be said that it is the State that imposed or made them; they are part of the texture and essence of the particular religion; so the State, in order to comply with the spirit and purpose inherent in this constitutional guarantee, may justifiably lend its weight to what may be thought to be disabilities and discriminations deriving from within a particular religion.
>
> That is what happened here. The *raison d'être* of the college, whatever academic or educational accretions it may have gathered over the years, has been that it has at all times been a national seminary where students are educated and trained for the Roman Catholic priesthood. This inevitably means that at least some of its academic staff must not alone be priests but priests with particular qualifications and with a required measure of religious orthodoxy and behaviour. It is part of the purpose of the statutes (which, incidentally, were drawn up by the trustees, who are all bishops of the Roman Catholic Church, and were not imposed by the State) that due standards are to be observed by those of the academic staff who are priests. Even if it be said that the statutes are, by recognition or support, an emanation of the State, the distinctions drawn in them between priest and layman, in terms of disabilities or discriminations, are no part of what is prohibited by *Article 44.2.3*. They represent no prejudicial State intrusion where priest is advanced unjustifiably over layman, or vice versa, as was the case in *Molloy v Minister for Education* [1975] IR 88. On the contrary, they amount to an implementation of the guarantee that is to be found in *subs. 5* of the same section that 'every religious denomination shall have the right to manage its own affairs, own, acquire and administer property, movable and immovable, and maintain institutions for religious or charitable purposes'. These statutes are what the designated authorities of the Roman Catholic Church in Ireland have deemed necessary for this seminary. Their existence or their terms

cannot be blamed on the State as an unconstitutional imposition, particularly at the suit of these two plaintiffs who as priests formally and knowingly undertook to be bound by them. I would therefore uphold the conclusion reached in the High Court that the plea that the relevant college statutes are repugnant to *Article 44.2.3* fails. [1979] ILRM 166, at 187–188.

Henchy J followed the reasoning of Walsh J in *Quinn's Supermarket* in concluding that the purpose of the prohibition on religious discrimination was to protect the free practice of religion. Given that Art 44.2.1° already protects the free practice of religion, this interpretation of Art 44.2.3° appears to render it redundant. Might not the purpose of a prohibition on religious discrimination be to prohibit religious discrimination? On the other hand, the plaintiffs in this case did agree to be bound by the statutes of the College in accepting employment in the first instance. Is this sufficient to deprive them of their constitutional rights? Although few would quibble with the right of religious institutions to manage their own affairs, should they be able to do so while receiving large sums of money from the State? [10–11]

The non-discrimination guarantee was successfully invoked in *Mulloy v Minister for Education* [1975] IR 88. The Minister for Education established a scheme for the payment of teachers that recognised the teaching work done by non-religious teachers abroad but not such work done by religious teachers. The plaintiff was a priest who had taught on the missions for some time and was prejudiced salary-wise as a result. The Supreme Court upheld the High Court's decision that the scheme was unconstitutional. Walsh J reasoned as follows: [10–12]

> As explained in the judgment given in this Court in *Quinn's Supermarket* v. *The Attorney General*, it is not permissible to create differences between persons or bodies or to distinguish between them on the ground of religious profession, belief or status, irrespective of whether the difference is to their benefit or to their disadvantage—save where it is necessary to do so for the implementation of the constitutional right to the full and free practice of religion. That consideration does not arise at all in the present case. There may be many instances where, in order to implement or permit of the full and free exercise of the freedom of religion guaranteed by the Constitution, the law may find it necessary to distinguish between ministers of religion or other persons occupying a particular status in religion and the ordinary lay members of that religion or the rest of the population; but this is not one of those cases.
>
> The present case concerns the disposition of public funds on a basis which, if sustainable, enables a person who is not a religious to obtain greater financial reward than a person who is a religious and is otherwise doing the same work and is of equal status and of length of service, or recognised service in the case of a teacher. If that were constitutionally possible it would enable the State to prefer religious to lay people, or vice-versa, in a matter which is in no way concerned with the safeguarding or maintenance of the constitutional right to free practice of religion or freedom of conscience or of profession of religion. In my view, the State is not permitted by the Constitution to do this. The reference to religious status, in both the Irish text and the English text of the Constitution, relates clearly to the position or rank of a person in terms of religion in relation to others either of the same religion or of another religion or to those of no religion at all. Thus it ensures that, no matter what is one's religious profession or belief or status, the State shall not impose any disabilities upon or make any discrimination between persons because one happens to be a clergyman or a nun or a brother or a person holding rank or position in some religion which distinguishes him from other persons whether or not they hold corresponding ranks in other religions or whether or not they

297

profess any religion or have any religious belief, save where it is necessary to do so to implement the guarantee of freedom of religion and conscience already mentioned. [1975] IR 88, at 96–97.

[10–13] Although Art 44.2.3° was successfully invoked, Walsh J emphasises that the free practice of religion was not in any way served by the discrimination in question. His insistence that the only basis on which a religious discrimination can be legitimised is the need to secure free practice of religion has a further interesting effect. Whereas Art 44.2.3° is on its face neutral as between believers and non-believers, its subjugation to Art 44.2.1° ensures that it is permissible to discriminate against non-believers in order to protect believers' free practice of religion but not to discriminate against believers in order to protect non-believers' freedom not to practice religion.

[10–14] Article 44.2.3° was also successfully invoked in *M v An Bord Uchtála* [1975] IR 81. Here the plaintiffs challenged the constitutionality of s 12 of the Adoption Act 1952 which provided that an adoption order could only be made if the adoptive parents were of the same religion as the child's parents or, if the child was born out of wedlock, its mother. The second plaintiff had a child out of wedlock and subsequently married the first plaintiff who was not the child's father. The child lived with the two plaintiffs, who sought to adopt the child. The Adoption Board, however, refused to make the adoption order on the basis that the mother's husband was of a different religion from the child's mother; as such, s 12 prohibited an adoption. In effect, s 12 would have precluded a couple with different religions from adopting a child, save in the unlikely event of there being an orphaned child of parents with the same two different religions. Pringle J struck down s 12 as a breach of Art 44.2.3°.

Non-endowment

[10–15] The guarantee against the endowment of religion raises similar issues as to the State's neutrality between religious believers and non-believers. In *Campaign to Separate Church and State v Minister for Education* [1998] 3 IR 321, the plaintiffs challenged the constitutionality of the system whereby the salaries of chaplains in community schools were paid from public funds. The chaplains exercised a pastoral role but also made provision for religious worship and instruction in accordance with the wishes of the parents and local bishop. The basis for this arrangement was a model trust deed entered into by the Minister and the trustees of the relevant school; however, the monies for the payment of chaplains were voted on annually by the Oireachtas in Appropriation Acts. Both the High Court and the Supreme Court upheld the constitutionality of this funding scheme. The plaintiffs argued that this amounted to an unconstitutional endowment of religion. Barrington J rejected this contention:

> [T]he Court's decision in *The Employment Equality Bill, 1996* [1997] 2 I.R. 321, has a wider significance for the resolution of the problem presented in this case. As was pointed out in the Court's judgment on the reference the system of denominational education was well known to the framers of the Constitution. We know this because they refer to it. Article 44.2.4° prescribes that legislation providing State aid for schools shall not discriminate between schools under the management of different religious denominations nor be such as to affect prejudicially the right of any child to attend a school receiving public money without attending religious instruction at that school.
>
> These references appear to me to establish two facts. First, the Constitution does not contemplate that the payment of monies to a denominational school for educational purposes is an "endowment" of religion within the meaning of Article 44.2.2° of the

Constitution. Secondly, the Constitution contemplated that if a school was in receipt of public funds any child, no matter what his religion, would be entitled to attend it. But such a child was to have the right not to attend any course of religious instruction at the school. As was pointed out in *The Employment Equality Bill, 1996* each denominational school has its own ethos. Teachers of a particular religious persuasion do not convey their ideas merely through formal instruction but tend to organise the schools in such a way as best to promote the religious values which they themselves embrace. The framers of the Constitution were clearly aware of this when they contemplated the provision of funds for denominational education. They cannot therefore have regarded such provision as an "endowment" of any religion or religions.

The archbishops admit to an indirect benefit received by the churches through the payment of the salaries of school chaplains in the sense that they admit that if the State did not pay the salaries of school chaplains the churches would feel obliged to raise the monies themselves and would thereby be at a loss. I do not think, however, that this argument can be decisive because the exact same argument could be advanced concerning the payment of the salaries of teachers in denominational schools. No doubt had the State refused to subsidise the payment of the salaries of teachers in denominational schools, the churches would have been at a very significant loss. Notwithstanding this fact clearly the framers of the Constitution did not consider such payments an endowment of religion or religions.

But the matter does not end there. Article 42 of the Constitution acknowledges that the primary and natural educator of the child is the family and guarantees to respect the inalienable right and duty of the parents to provide for the religious and moral, intellectual, physical and social education of their children. Article 42.2 prescribes that the parents shall be free to provide "this education" (*i.e. religious,* moral, intellectual, physical and social education) in their homes or in private schools or "in schools recognised or established by the State". In other words the Constitution contemplates children receiving religious education in schools recognised or established by the State but in accordance with the wishes of the parents.

It is in this context that one must read Article 44.2.4° which prescribes that:-

"Legislation providing State aid for schools shall not discriminate between schools under the management of different religious denominations, nor be such as to affect prejudicially the right of any child to attend a school receiving public money without attending religious instruction at that school."

The Constitution therefore distinguishes between religious "education" and religious "instruction"-the former being the much wider term. A child who attends a school run by a religious denomination different from his own may have a constitutional right not to attend religious instruction at that school but the Constitution cannot protect him from being influenced, to some degree, by the religious "ethos" of the school. A religious denomination is not obliged to change the general atmosphere of its school merely to accommodate a child of a different religious persuasion who wishes to attend that school.

The community and the comprehensive schools are an attempt to make post-primary education available to all the children of Ireland irrespective of their means. They involve a vast increase in the number of children receiving post-primary education and a corresponding increase in the number of post-primary teachers most of whom are lay people. In community schools it is no longer practicable to combine religious and academic education in the way that a religious order might have done in the past. Nevertheless parents have the same right to have religious education provided in the schools which their children attend. They are not obliged to settle merely for religious "instruction". The role of the chaplain is to help to provide this extra dimension to the religious education of the children. The evidence establishes that, besides looking after the pastoral needs of the children, the chaplain helps them with counsel and advice about their day to day problems. It therefore appears to me that the present system whereby the salaries of chaplains in community schools are paid by the State is merely a manifestation, under modern conditions, of principles which are recognised and approved by Articles 44 and 42 of the Constitution.

The evidence goes to establish that the work of the chaplains is highly valued by parents. Nevertheless it may be worthwhile entering two *caveats*. First, this judgment proceeds upon the basis that the system of salaried chaplains is available to all community schools of whatever denomination on an equal basis in accordance with their needs. Secondly, while it is obviously right and proper that a chaplain should counsel and advise any child who may consult him about its problems it would be constitutionally impermissible for a chaplain to instruct a child in a religion other than its own without the knowledge and consent of its parents. [1998] 3 IR 321, at 356–358.

[10–16] Having reviewed the historical background to the relevant constitutional provisions—in particular the existence of a scheme whereby religious institutions received state funding to provide education—Keane J reasoned as follows:

Article 44.2.2° was thus intended to render unlawful the vesting of property or income in a religion *as such* in perpetual or quasi-perpetual form. It was not designed to render unlawful the comprehensive system of aid to denominational education which had become so central a feature of the Irish schools system and the validity of which was expressly acknowledged by the Constitution. But while a provision of this nature had originally been prompted by a fear that the religion of the majority would be endowed in preference to the others, the wording of the Article makes it clear that it was also intended to prohibit in any form the "concurrent endowment" which had been proposed by the House of Lords during the disestablishment controversy.

It is true that in *The Employment Equality Bill, 1996* [1997] 2 I.R. 321 Hamilton C.J., delivering the judgment of this Court, said at p.354:-

"This system [of aid to denominational schools] does not involve the endowment of any religion. The endowment of a religion implies the selection of a favoured State religion for which permanent financial provision is made out of taxation or otherwise. This kind of endowment is outlawed by Article 44.2.2° of the Constitution."

That passage undoubtedly reflects, as I have indicated, the historical background against which Article 44.2.2° was enacted. It should not, however, be treated as authority for the proposition that the concurrent endowment of various religions is constitutionally permissible. Counsel for the plaintiffs and the defendants were, I think, in agreement that such concurrent endowment was not sanctioned by the Constitution. [1998] 3 IR 321, at 365–366.

[10–17] The Supreme Court concluded that the payments did not constitute endowment because endowment involves the vesting of property or income in a religion *as such* in perpetual or quasi-perpetual form. In contrast, any support given to religions here was indirect, in that it relieved them of the burden of providing salaries for priests who happened to be chaplains. Barrington J counters any objection to this indirect benefit on the grounds that the same indirect benefit is given to religious orders by the state's payment of the salaries of teachers in denominational schools. Such a system was clearly endorsed by the Constitution; by extension the indirect benefit provided by the payment of chaplains' salaries could not be unconstitutional. But are the two situations truly comparable? There seems to be an important ground of differentiation. Chaplains provide an explicitly religious service. It is one thing to allow a religious institution to gain an indirect benefit from its provision of a non-religious service, but quite another to allow it gain such an indirect benefit from its provision of a religious service. On the basis of Barrington J's reasoning, it would seem permissible for the State to pay the salaries of diocesan priests, as the only benefit to religious orders would be the indirect one of not having to pay the salaries themselves. Surely the truth of the matter is that in this situation there is also a direct benefit to the religious institution: their core religious mission is being advanced. Similarly with regard to school chaplains: religious orders receive the indirect benefit of not having to pay salaries to the chaplains, *but also* the direct benefit of having chaplains proselytise young people.

In the High Court, Costello P provided further reasons as to why this form of payment, even if it were an endowment, remains constitutional. These reasons were endorsed on appeal by Keane J (with whom Hamilton CJ and O'Flaherty J agreed). Costello P reasoned as follows: [10–18]

> The Irish Constitution has developed the significance of these parental rights and in addition has imposed obligations on the State in relation to them. It declares (in Article 42.2) that parents are to be free to provide for the education of their children in their homes, or in private schools or in schools recognised or established by the State; that the State shall not oblige parents in violation of their conscience to send their children to schools established or designated by the State; and that the State shall require (in view of the actual conditions) that children receive a certain minimum education, moral, intellectual and social. The Article contains a final section (s. 4) as follows:-
>
> "The State shall provide for free primary education and shall endeavour to supplement and give reasonable aid to private and corporate educational initiative, and, when the public good requires it, provide other educational facilities or institutions with due regard, however, for the rights of parents, especially in the matter of *religious and moral formation.*"
>
> I have emphasised the words "religious and moral formation" to draw attention to the fact that this Article recognises that parents have rights not only to provide for the religious *education* of their children (s. 1) but also rights in the matter of their religious *formation* (s. 4) and that it specifically enjoins the State when providing educational facilities to have regard to both these distinct rights. The difference between the ordinary meaning of these two concepts is not difficult to identify; broadly speaking, the religious *education* of a child is concerned with the teaching of religious doctrine, apologetics, religious history and comparative religions, whilst the religious *formation* of a child involves familiarising the child not just with religious doctrine but with religious practice (by attendance at religious services) and developing the child's spiritual and religious life by prayer and bible reading and I think that the Constitution should be construed so as to reflect this meaning. In the case of parents who profess the catholic faith, the religious formation of their children involves ensuring that their children attend mass and that they pray and receive the sacraments on a regular basis.
>
> Turning then to the issue in this case, it is clear that one of the important reasons why *chaplains* as well as *teachers of religion* are appointed to the staff of community schools is for the purpose of assisting the religious formation of the children attending the school (assistance which, *inter alia*, is given by the celebration of mass in the school). In effect, the State by paying the salaries of chaplains is having regard to the rights of parents *vis-à-vis* the religious formation of their children and enabling them to exercise their constitutionally recognised rights. If this is the purpose and effect of the payment, how can it be said that it is unconstitutional? [1998] 3 IR 321, at 340–341.

In effect, Costello P sought to avoid an interpretation of Art 44.2.2° that would prohibit something that was apparently supported by another constitutional provision. There is strong judicial support for this method of harmonious constitutional [10–19] interpretation, *ie* the idea that constitutional articles should be read together so as to identify a harmonious meaning. The advantage of such an approach is that it avoids a result whereby two provisions of the Constitution are given mutually inconsistent meanings. However, it raises the question of which article is to be given interpretative precedence. Here Costello J delimited the scope of Art 44.2.2° by reference to Art 42.4. In that way, the non-endowment guarantee was rendered subordinate to the obligation on the State to assist parents in relation to the moral formation of their child. But why should the constitutional provisions not be structured in the opposite manner? It is—at the very least—arguable that no constitutional provision should be interpreted to permit something that is expressly prohibited by another constitutional provision. If one gives interpretative precedence to Art 44.2.2°, one would have to conclude that the obligation on the State to assist parents in the moral formation of their children cannot go so far as to allow the State to endow a religion. Indeed, in the present context there may well be more support for this structuring of the two provisions. For the obligation in Art 44.2.2° is bald and clear-cut ("The State guarantees not to endow any religion"). On the other hand, the obligation in Art 42.4 is both aspirational ("endeavour to supplement and give reasonable aid") and involves a further interpretative move from the explicit negative obligation on the State to respect the rights of parents in relation to religious and moral formation to an implied positive obligation on the State to assist parents in that regard. Although that interpretative move from negative obligation to positive obligation is not in itself problematic, it becomes so when it is employed in such a way as to override the clearly worded constitutional guarantee of non-endowment.

[10–20] A final difficulty with the decision in *Campaign to Separate Church and State* is its support for the integrated curriculum. In 1937, religion was taught as a stand-alone subject. It was thus practically possible for a non-believer to attend a publicly funded religious school without being exposed to religious instruction. This facility was guaranteed by Article 44.2.4°:

> Legislation providing State aid for schools shall not discriminate between schools under the management of different religious denominations, nor be such as to affect prejudicially the right of any child to attend a school receiving public money without attending religious instruction at that school.

[10–21] Since 1971, however, the Department of Education has encouraged the integration of religious instruction into the whole school curriculum. As Clarke notes, "it is currently impossible in practice to attend most publicly funded denominational schools without attending religious instruction". Desmond Clarke, "Education, the State and Sectarian Schools" in Tim Murphy and Patrick Twomey eds, *Ireland's Evolving Constitution 1937-1997: Collected Essays* (Hart, 1998), at 74. The Supreme Court endorsed this practice in *Campaign to Separate Church and State*, Barrington J observing:

> The Constitution therefore distinguishes between religious "education" and religious "instruction"—the former being the much wider term. A child who attends a school run by a religious denomination different from his own may have a constitutional right not to attend religious instruction at that school but the Constitution cannot protect him from being influenced, to some degree, by the religious "ethos" of the school. A religious denomination is not obliged to change the general atmosphere of its school merely to accommodate a child of a different religious persuasion who wishes to attend that school.

It is questionable whether "religious instruction" (Art 44.2.4°) can be so easily distinguished from religious education in this way. If this is a valid distinction, where should one locate the dividing line between instruction and education? For instance, would it be permissible for a school to require a student to participate in a religious choir?

Overview of Case Law on Art 44

At the outset of this chapter, it was contended that, taken together, the provisions of Art 44 would suggest a position whereby the State respects religion, but is strictly neutral as between religions and (as importantly) as between believers and non-believers. An examination of the case law reveals that this is not the case. It is helpful to reconsider the broad outlines of the case law. Despite the guarantee of non-discrimination, it is always permissible for the State to discriminate on the grounds of religion, provided it is necessary to secure the free practice of religion. On the other hand, it is never permissible for the State to discriminate on the grounds of religion in order to secure the rights of non-believers. Despite the guarantee against endowment, it is permissible for the State to fund religious institutions to fulfil their core religious functions, provided this is done on an ongoing cash basis, rather than the provision of a lump sum from which the institution could then derive an income. Moreover, although non-believers are entitled to opt out of religious instruction in a publicly funded school, they cannot be shielded from the religious ethos of the school and must participate in the religiously educative mission of the school. [10–22]

All told, these cases suggest a constitutional situation that is far more pro-religion than the bare text of Art 44.2 would suggest. As noted at the outset, however, some support for this position can be found in Art 44.1 by which the State undertakes to respect and honour religion. Moreover, the overtly religious sentiments of the Preamble arguably provide some basis for the pro-religion interpretation of Art 44.2. There is, however, an alternative way of understanding the courts' interpretation of Art 44.2. The approach of the courts has generally been deferential, upholding various legislative schemes that deal favourably with religions. Apart from the narrowly based unconstitutionality in *Quinn* and the discriminations in *Mulloy* and *M*, the courts have generally deferred to legislative judgment. Nevertheless, the *dictum* of Walsh J in *Quinn* to the effect that the Oireachtas is constitutionally required to make exceptions to facilitate the free practice of religion points up a pressure point on this issue. With an increasingly diverse society, it becomes more likely that Irish citizens will have religious practices that are not catered for by particular legislative schemes. It is therefore highly likely that some citizens will find their religious freedom restricted by legislation. When such a restriction is constitutionally challenged (as it surely will be), the courts will have to decide which is more important: religion or deference? [10–23]

Clarke has been particularly critical of the interaction of religion and education in Ireland: [10–24]

> According to Roman Catholic theology, the dominant objective in any human enterprise is the "salvation of souls". There is one true Church, and the salvation of souls is conditional on membership of this Church.... This evangelical motive is translated into a policy on schools by imposing a moral duty on members of the Catholic Church to send their children to exclusively Catholic schools, if they are available.... The moral pressure

on members to proselytise the next generation is transformed into a claim that Roman Catholics have a *right* to send their children to such schools. However, the alleged right is based on nothing more than the theology of a particular church. Assuming a theologically-based right, Roman Catholics then look to the state to secure their rights. They are encouraged by Canon Law to press their theological rights until the State provides them, at public expense, with the kind of schools which their Church requires them to attend....

The evangelical objectives of the various Churches are not objectionable as such. It is perfectly reasonable for each Church to try to persuade new members to join and to encourage current members to remain active. Freedom to pursue such objectives—on condition that the means used are unobjectionable—is exactly what is meant by freedom of thought and freedom of expression. But, it is not the role of the State to co-operate in the evangelical missions of competing Churches. By adapting its educational policy to the theologies of competing churches, the State reinforces the divisive and sectarian theologies of the churches in the civil life of citizens.

It should be acknowledged immediately that there is no reasonable basis for the claim that the state should have exclusive control of the management, curriculum, funding or philosophy of educational institutions, including schools. Therefore, the provisions of the Constitution which permit parents to arrange for the education of their children in a variety of different types of school are, in this respect, beyond reproach and are consistent with an enlightened philosophy of education. No State should establish one uniform style of school and attempt to force all children, by law or otherwise, to attend a "state school"....

But it does not follow, just because the State should not coerce all young citizens into state schools, that parents have a right to demand that the State provide them with precisely the kind of schools that they prefer. In particular, there is no good reason why the State should provide parents, at public expense, with schools for their children from which other children are excluded simply because of their religion. Canon Law does not request merely that the State establish schools in which the religious beliefs of young Catholics are respected. That is a perfectly reasonable request. Instead it demands that the State finance schools from which children and teachers of other religious denominations are excluded because, by their presence in any given school in sufficiently large numbers, the ethos of the school is changed....

The constitutional provision which forbids discrimination on religious grounds in the admission of children to publicly funded schools is inconsistent, in principle and now in practice [because of the integration of religious teaching into the whole curriculum], with a public policy to finance sectarian schools which discriminate against student applicants on religious grounds and against qualified teachers on religious or life-style grounds. More fundamentally, an educational policy which supports, protects and finances the sectarian theological divisions of the churches is inconsistent with the constitutional requirement to treat all citizens equally and to provide publicly funded services, such as healthcare or education, through institutions which treat all citizens in a non-discriminatory manner. The State should therefore refuse to support from public funds educational institutions which discriminate against citizens on the basis of their religious or philosophical convictions.

This proposal is sometimes caricatured as a proposal that education in schools should be value-free. It is also misdescribed as a suggestion that the State should impose a uniform system of secular schooling on all young people and coerce them to attend state schools in preference to the legitimate preferences of their parents. It is even understood by others as part of a conspiracy to disseminate a form of irreligious liberalism which is subversive of the religious values which many parents wish their children to acquire through education. None of these claims stands up to scrutiny. There is no suggestion here that education is, or ought to be, value-free, or that it should be exclusively secular. Nor is it suggested that the State should coerce young citizens into any particular type of school or education. The proposal is much simpler and narrower in scope: in providing educational services from public finances, the State should not discriminate, in principle or in practice, against any citizen on the basis of their religious or philosophical convictions. Desmond Clarke, "Education, the State and Sectarian Schools" in Tim Murphy and Patrick Twomey eds, *Ireland's Evolving Constitution 1937-1997: Collected Essays* (Hart, 1998), at 69–76.

Clarke's reasoning may be dependent for its force on the particular context of Irish education. He notes before the extracted paragraphs that in 1937 almost all education at primary level and most education at secondary level was provided in schools which were owned and managed by religious denominations and that the majority of such schools were Roman Catholic. As such, the system of state funded support for parental choice effectively buttressed Roman Catholic control of education and has under-written its continued existence, even in the face of diminishing adherence to the Catholic faith. But is Clarke correct to argue that all funding for religious education is objectionable? In *O'Sheil v Minister for Education*, Laffoy J commented that for parental choice of education to be meaningful, the state must fund a number of options. Provided that several options are funded and available (denominational, multi-denominational and secular), it is arguable that no-one's rights of religious freedom (including freedom from religion) are infringed. [10–25]

Clarke rejects the idea that the form of education he envisages would be value-free or exclusively secular. However, it seems to follow from his reasoning that (whatever about privately funded education) state-funded education would have to be exclusively secular in its values. There are two problems with this. First, why should non-secular education be available only to those who can afford to pay for it? Secondly, on what basis does the State choose secular values? Writing in the context of a slightly different debate, Whyte argues as follows: [10–26]

> Nor is it clear that state neutrality is capable of ensuring equality as between believers and non-believers insofar as there may be no neutral territory for the State to occupy between belief and non-belief. Hitchcock argues that such neutrality is impossible to attain inasmuch as all public policy is based on value-judgments and the rejection of religion by the state is itself a value-judgment:
>
>> To maintain that such neutrality is possible seems to require postulating that public policy is somehow arrived at in a "value-free" manner. Yet it would be difficult to show any policies which are in fact completely neutral....
>
> A related problem here is that the idea of State neutrality presupposes that it is possible to distinguish between religious and secular belief. This in turn raises the very difficult question of how to define religion. Buddhism is generally recognised as a religion and yet, insofar as it is predominantly non-theistic, this would suggest that the term "religion" cannot be restricted to systems of belief in God. In that case, is transcendental meditation a religion? Is scientology a religion? And, more germane to the present discussion, is secular humanism a religion? For if it is, then that surely makes a nonsense of any attempt by the State to be neutral as between religious and secular belief. Gerry Whyte, "The Role of Religion in the Constitutional Order" in Tim Murphy and Patrick Twomey eds, *Ireland's Evolving Constitution 1937-1997: Collected Essays* (Hart, 1998), at 56–57, quoting Hitchcock, "Church, State and Moral Values: the Limits of American Pluralism [1981] *Law and Contemporary Problems*, at 14–18.

In light of these comments, is the State is entitled to fund only secular education? I suggested above that, given the decision in *McGee*, secular humanism could not be [10–27] viewed as a religion. Nevertheless, it is a world-view and value system. Is it less troubling for the State to use its funding influence to ensure that children are taught secular humanism than to use that influence to ensure that children are taught a religious world-view?

CONTENTS – CHAPTER 11

The Legislative Power and the Oireachtas

Introduction...[11–01]
Delegated Legislation..[11–06]
Henry VIII Clauses: the Interaction of the Non-delegation
    Doctrine and the *Ultra Vires* Doctrine..........................[11–31]
Primary Legislation as a Deliberative Process.......................[11–41]
Investigative Powers of the Oireachtas..............................[11–49]

Overview

Article 15 vests the legislative power of the State in the Oireachtas. Nevertheless, the courts have upheld the constitutionality of primary legislation that delegates a legislative power to another body. The test stated by the courts requires that the primary legislation deal with all matters of principle and policy and leave only matters of detail to the secondary legislation. The courts have not applied this test in a strict way, however, only striking down primary legislation that dealt with no matters of principle or policy. The courts have prohibited primary legislation that delegates a power to amend primary legislation. Although the courts have not struck down many laws on the basis of Art 15, they have used Art 15 to narrow the grant of legislative power made by primary legislation, thereby leading to specific instances of secondary legislation being struck down as *ultra vires*. The courts have held that it is permissible for the Oireachtas to legislate by reference.

Chapter 11

The Legislative Power and the Oireachtas

Introduction

Article 6 of the Constitution provides: [11–01]

1. All powers of government, legislative, executive and judicial, derive, under God, from the people, whose right it is to designate the rulers of the State and, in final appeal, to decide all questions of national policy, according to the requirements of the common good.
2. These powers of government are exercisable only by or on the authority of the organs of State established by this Constitution.

This establishes a separation of powers whereby three governmental powers—legislative, executive, judicial—are exercised by three branches of government established by the Constitution. Legislation is the stipulation of generally applicable rules and standards that are, in the first instance, used by persons to guide and regulate their own behaviour and, in the second instance, used by official bodies (such as courts) to determine whether persons have behaved lawfully. The legislative power is thus the power to lay down these generally applicable standards. The Constitution assigns this power to the Oireachtas, Art 15.2.1° providing:

> The sole and exclusive power of making laws for the State is hereby vested in the Oireachtas: no other legislative authority has power to make laws for the State.

Although the origin of this provision may have most to do with the Oireachtas asserting legislative competence as against the Imperial Parliament in Westminster, its contemporary relevance lies in the way in which it precludes the other constitutionally established branches of government (the courts and the Government) from exercising legislative power. Article 15.2.2° empowers the Oireachtas to create or recognise subordinate legislatures. This provision was designed to allow for the creation or recognition of a devolved Northern Ireland Parliament in the event of re-unification. The Oireachtas has never exercised its powers pursuant to this provision and, as such, it has had no bearing on the case law that has developed. [11–02]

In *State (Walshe) v Murphy* [1981] IR 275, the High Court considered the character of the legislative power: [11–03]

> The sole and exclusive power of making laws for the State is vested in the Oireachtas by Article 15.2.1°. Prima facie, such power of legislation is absolute and all-embracing, subject to the qualifications imposed upon it by the Constitution.

309

The qualifications imposed upon the exercise of that power fall into two main categories. First, there is the general qualification contained in Article 15.4.1°, that the Oireachtas "shall not enact any law which is in any respect repugnant to this Constitution or any provision thereof." Secondly, there are to be found throughout the Constitution specific prohibitions against the enactment of laws with a particular effect or particular purpose. Examples of those are contained in Article 15.5, which provides: "The Oireachtas shall not declare acts to be infringements of the law which were not so at the date of their commission." Article 40.6.2° provides that laws regulating the manner in which the right of forming associations and unions and the right of free assembly may be exercised "shall contain no political, religious or class discrimination." Article 41.3.2° provides that "no law shall be enacted providing for the grant of a dissolution of marriage." Article 43.1.2° provides: "The State accordingly guarantees to pass no law attempting to abolish the right of private ownership or the general right to transfer, bequeath, and inherit property."

In addition, there is the category of prohibition arising from specific rights or inhibitions contained in the Constitution; in a sense, this category is a sub-classification of the general prohibition against the enactment of laws repugnant to the Constitution. One example, in the context of the matters arising in this case, is the provision of Article 35.5, whereby the remuneration of a judge "shall not be reduced during his continuance in office" which provision would inhibit the Oireachtas from enacting legislation to that effect.

Further, it seems to me there are to be found in the Constitution several instances where the Oireachtas is actively obliged to regulate certain matters by law; in other words, to enact statutory provisions to provide for them. One example is the obligation of the Oireachtas under Article 36.1 to provide by statute for the number of the judges of the Supreme Court and of the High Court, and for the remuneration, age of retirement and pensions of such judges. Another example is the example under debate in this case, *ie*, the obligation of the Oireachtas to provide by statute the number of judges of all other courts and their terms of appointment.... The effect of these provisions seems to me to be that the Oireachtas, while retaining a discretion as to the details of the legislation concerned and as to the precise regulations created thereby, has a constitutional obligation to make some regulations or some provisions.

Then there is the fifth category of the legislative powers of the Oireachtas which seems to me to consist of all other areas or topics or matters in respect of which legislation might be enacted and in which, subject to the overall obligation not to enact a statute repugnant to the Constitution and subject to the other specific prohibitions against the enactment of laws having a particular effect or consequence, the Oireachtas may enact legislation. [1981] IR 275, at 284–286.

[11–04] It can be seen from this that the legislative power, although broad, is not absolute. The Oireachtas cannot legislate inconsistently with the Constitution. Unlike the Westminster Parliament, for instance, the Oireachtas is not sovereign. Article 34.3.2° of the Constitution provides that the High Court is responsible for assessing whether the Oireachtas has legislated in accordance with the Constitution. (The scope of the judicial power will be addressed in chapter 13.) In *Murphy v Attorney General* [1982] IR 237, Henchy J spelt out the effect of these limitations in the following way:

> The Constitution, therefore, as part of its inbuilt checks and balances, has made it abundantly clear that the delegated power of legislation given to the Oireachtas (a power which may in turn be sub-delegated by the Oireachtas pursuant to Article 15.2.2°) is a power which, regardless of any interim presumption of constitutionality that may attach to its enactments, cannot be exercised save within the constitutionally designated limitations of that power; and once it has lost the presumption of constitutionality as a

result of a judicial condemnation on the ground of unconstitutionality, it must, in accordance with Article 15.4.2°, be held to "be invalid"—not, be it observed, to have "become invalid." It is to be deemed null and void from the moment of its purported enactment, no less than if it had emanated from a person or body with no power of legislation. In my judgment, the constitutional disposition of the powers of the State in this respect falls into line with the general principle that, when a constitution or a constitutional statute gives a specifically confined power of legislation to a legislature, laws found to have been enacted in excess of that delegation are *ultra vires* and therefore void *ab initio*. This is a principle which is inherent in the nature of such limited powers, but it is unequivocally spelled out in some constitutions and constitutional statutes. [1982] IR 237, at 309–310.

Although the more recent decision in *A v Governor of Arbour Hill Prison* [2006] IESC 45 (see chapter 16) has added considerable nuances—to say the least—to Henchy J's judgment in *Murphy*, this passage remains a good description of the extent of legislative competence under the Constitution.

The reservation of the legislative power of government to one constitutional organ helps to secure the rule of law. For rules of general application can (presumptively) only be laid down by the national parliament. (The courts have allowed the Oireachtas to delegate some legislative powers to other bodies, an issue that will be addressed in detail below). The democratic participation in the enactment of those rules, as well as the important requirements as to promulgation, ensure that the rules are, if not known, at least knowable. Moreover, the other organs of government (the courts and the Government) as well as various public bodies established by statute can only act within the general framework established by the rules laid down by the Oireachtas—although there may be executive powers vested in the Government and judicial powers vested in the courts that allow for some independent scope of action. Fennelly J explained this system in *Kennedy v Law Society of Ireland (No 3)* [2002] 2 IR 458, at 486. Mr Kennedy, a solicitor, complained that the Law Society's investigation of him was *ultra vires* (beyond its powers) as it was not clearly authorised by the legislation governing the Law Society. As the Society had acted without legal authority, their action could have no legal effect. The Supreme Court accepted this contention, Fennelly J observing:

[11–05]

> The issue is essentially one of *ultra vires*. The delegatees of statutory power cannot be allowed to exceed the limits of the statute or, as here, the secondary legislation conferring the power. The rationale for this is simple and clear. The Oireachtas may, by law, while respecting the constitutional limits, delegate powers to be exercised for stated purposes. Any excessive exercise of the delegated discretion will defeat the legislative intent and may tend to undermine the democratic principle and, ultimately, the rule of law itself. Secondly, the courts have the function of review of the exercise of powers. They are bound to ensure respect for the laws passed by the Oireachtas. A delegatee of power which pursues, though in good faith, a purpose not permitted by the legislation by, for example, combining it with other permitted purposes is enlarging by stealth the range of its own powers. These principles, in my view, must inform any test for deciding whether a power has been exercised *ultra vires*. Henchy J stated in *Cassidy v Minister for Industry and Commerce* [1978] 1 IR 297, at 310:
>
>> The general rule of law is that where Parliament has by statute delegated a power of subordinate legislation, the power must be exercised within the limitations of that power as they are expressed or necessarily implied in the statutory delegation. Otherwise it will be held to have been invalidly exercised for being *ultra vires*.

It is through this system that the rule of law is protected in Ireland. Since public bodies can only act within the scope of powers legally assigned to them, citizens are governed by legal rules and not by the whims of the powerful.

Delegated Legislation

[11–06] The assignment of an exclusive legislative power to the Oireachtas poses many practical difficulties. Given the regulatory society in which we live, it would scarcely be feasible for the Oireachtas to be involved in the promulgation of all generally applicable standards. For instance, in the context of planning law the detailed rules establishing whether particular developments require planning permission now run to 43 pages, setting out very specific categories many of which are subject to equally specific conditions and limitations. These categories are frequently amended in the light of experience. This is only one small area of regulation; there are many others. It would probably be impossible to have such detailed regulations all enacted by the Oireachtas, a rather cumbersome 166-person assembly. Moreover, it is difficult to see how democracy would be enhanced by requiring the input of all national representatives on such issues.

[11–07] For these reasons, the courts have been prepared to allow the Oireachtas to delegate some of its legislative power to other persons. However, it would be clearly inconsistent with Art 15.2 to allow the Oireachtas delegate all its legislative power. Accordingly, the courts have developed a test that allows the Oireachtas to delegate some legislative power but not too much legislative power. Before addressing that test, however, it is necessary to consider a preliminary issue that sometimes causes confusion. Not all the powers assigned by the Oireachtas to other bodies are legislative powers. Frequently, the Oireachtas will assign an administrative power to a statutory authority (such as the power to decide on planning appeals that is assigned to An Bord Pleanála by the Planning and Development Act 2000). As administrative power is not constitutionally vested in the Oireachtas, there can be no constitutional objection to the assignment (not "delegation") of this power. Accordingly, where a statutory provision is challenged as being an unconstitutional delegation of power, the first question to address is whether the power assigned is a legislative power at all. In *Re Article 26 and the Health (Amendment) (No 2) Bill 2004* [2005] IESC 7, it was argued that the power delegated to the chief executive officer of a health board to remit nursing home charges amounted to an illegitimate delegation of legislative power. The Court held that this argument was unfounded:

> As regards the criticism made of the discretionary power conferred on the chief executive officer to waive or reduce a charge in a case of individual hardship, the court considers that counsel for the Attorney General were correct in pointing out that that does not constitute the exercise of a delegated power to legislate but rather is the exercise of an administrative discretion to address the particular circumstances of an individual case. When public officials are charged with administering a statutory scheme it may be difficult, if not impossible, for the Oireachtas to prescribe in legislation for every special circumstance of individuals who find themselves on the margins of such a scheme. In this instance the task of the administrator is to avoid undue hardship in individual cases in the general application of the scheme. That is simply an administrative function. A subsidiary argument of counsel assigned by the court was that judicial review of the decision of a chief executive officer in the exercise of such a discretion would not be an adequate remedy to a person who felt they had been wrongly refused a waiver or reduction of a

charge. The court does not accept this argument. The criterion (undue hardship) according to which the chief executive officer should exercise his or her discretion is adequately set out in the Act and there is no reason to consider that an arbitrary decision or other unlawful misuse of his or her powers by a chief executive officer could not be subject to judicial review in the ordinary way. [2005] IESC 7, at [54].

Although the Court did not identify the precise distinction between administrative and legislative power, the distinction surely turns on the power to lay down generally binding rules. As the chief executive officer's power was limited to making discretionary decisions in individual cases (as distinct from laying down the criteria against which discretionary decisions could be made), it was an administrative power not a legislative power. As such, there could be no constitutional objection to the Oireachtas assigning the power. [11–08]

Bearing this distinction in mind, it is now possible to address the test that has been developed by the courts to establish whether a delegation of legislative power is permissible. This test has been easy to state but not so easy to apply. In *Cityview Press v An Comhairle Oiliúna* [1980] IR 381, the plaintiff challenged a levy imposed on it by AnCO, a corporate body established under the Industrial Training Act 1967. The Act sought to make better provision for the training of persons involved in any activity or industry. Section 21 of the Act allowed AnCO to impose a levy on employers within an industry designated by AnCO under section 23 of the Act. The plaintiff challenged this as an unconstitutional delegation of legislative power. O'Higgins CJ laid down the "principles and policies" test: [11–09]

> In the view of this Court, the test is whether that which is challenged as an unauthorised delegation of parliamentary power is more than a mere giving effect to principles and policies which are contained in the statute itself. If it be, then it is not authorised; for such would constitute a purported exercise of legislative power by an authority which is not permitted to do so under the Constitution. On the other hand, if it be within the permitted limits – if the law is laid down in statute and details only are filled in or completed by the designated Minister or subordinate body – there is no unauthorised delegation of legislative power. [1980] IR 381, at 399.

This test posits a distinction between, on the one hand, principles and policies and, on the other hand, details. Principles and policies should be dealt with by primary legislation of the Oireachtas; however, details may be filled in by secondary legislation. Adopting the example given above, it would be permissible for primary legislation to stipulate that minor development does not require planning permission while leaving to secondary legislation the task of enumerating what exactly constitutes minor development. This test addresses both the practical difficulties of having the Oireachtas address every matter of detail and the democratic desirability of having the Oireachtas deal with matters of principle and policy. [11–10]

Applying the test to the matter in hand, O'Higgins CJ reasoned:

> In this instance, in the opinion of the Court, there has not been any unconstitutional delegation of authority. The Act of 1967 contains clear declarations of policies and aims and it establishes machinery for the carrying out of these policies and the achievement of these aims. In particular, the fact that there will be a levy is provided for in section 21 and the obligation to pay it is laid down. The only matter which is left for determination by

AnCO is the manner of calculating this levy in relation to a particular industry. This is doing no more than adding the final detail which brings into operation the general law which is laid down by the section. In addition, the Oireachtas has taken care to provide a manner whereby a levy order made under that section will continue to be under the supervision of either House of the Legislature itself. This is done under the provisions of [section 21(6)] whereby a levy order may be annulled by a resolution of either House of the Oireachtas. [1980] IR 381, at 399.

[11–11]   It is apparent from this extract that the principles and policies test is not applied with stringent rigour. As David Gwynn Morgan has noted, the Act provided no indication as to the principles to be used in fixing the amount of the levy—whether it is to be based on turnover, profit, number of employees requiring training, *etc*. See David Gwynn Morgan, *The Separation of Powers in the Irish Constitution* (Round Hall, Sweet & Maxwell, 1997), at 239. It is thus questionable whether the Oireachtas could fairly be said to have left only matters of detail to AnCO.

[11–12]   *McDaid v Sheehy* [1991] 1 IR 1 provides a rare example of a court applying the principles and policies test in a manner that leads to a declaration of unconstitutionality. Section 1(d) of the Imposition of Duties Act 1957 allowed the Government to "impose, whether with or without qualifications, limitations, allowances, exemptions or preferential rates, an excise duty on any particular matter or thing as from any specified day and, for the purpose of the duty, require the taking out of a licence for the doing of any particular thing." The plaintiff objected to the Imposition of Duties (No 221) (Excise Duties) Order 1975 which imposed a duty in respect of certain hydrocarbon oils. In the High Court, Blayney J applied the principles and policies test to hold that s 1(d) was unconstitutional:

> When this test is applied to the provisions of the Act of 1957 giving the Government power to impose customs and excise duties, and to terminate and vary them in any manner whatsoever, I have no doubt that the only conclusion possible is that such provisions constitute an impermissible delegation of the legislative power of the Oireachtas. The question to be answered is: Are the powers contained in these provisions more than a mere giving effect to principles and policies contained in the Act itself? In my opinion they clearly are. There are no principles or policies contained in the Act. Section 1 states baldly that "the Government may by order" do a number of things one of which is to impose a customs duty or an excise duty of such amount as they think proper on any particular description of goods imported into the State. In my opinion the power given to the Government here is a power to legislate. It is left to the Government to determine what imported goods are to have a customs or excise duty imposed on them and to determine the amount of such duty. And the Government is left totally free in exercising this power. It is far from a case of the Government filling in only the details. The fundamental question in regard to the imposition of customs or excise duties on imported goods is first, on what goods should a duty be imposed, and secondly, what should be the amount of the duty? The decision on both these matters is left to the Government. In my opinion, it was a proper subject for legislation and could not be delegated by the Oireachtas. I am satisfied accordingly that the provisions of the Act of 1957 which I cited earlier are invalid having regard to the provisions of the Constitution. [1991] 1 IR 1, at 9.

[11–13]   However, the terms of the 1975 Order had been confirmed by s 46 of the Finance Act 1976. Blayney J held that this conferred retrospective validity on the Order, with the consequence that it ought not to be struck down. On appeal, the Supreme Court agreed that the Finance Act 1976 retrospectively conferred validity on the Order but concluded that it was, as a result, unnecessary and inappropriate for the Court to consider whether s 1(d) of the 1957 Act was unconstitutional. For this reason, the Supreme Court did not engage in an application of the *Cityview* test.

Blayney J's reasoning appears to have been that it was unconstitutional for the Oireachtas simply to delegate an area of regulation. This reasoning also underpinned the Supreme Court decision in *Laurentiu v Minister for Justice* [1999] 4 IR 26, the one case in which legislation has actually been struck down as a breach of Art 15.2.1°. Here the applicant challenged the constitutionality of s 5(1)(e) of the Aliens Act 1935: [11–14]

> The Minister may, if and whenever he thinks proper, do by order (in this Act referred to as an aliens order) all or any of the following things in respect either of all aliens or of aliens of a particular nationality or otherwise of a particular class, or of particular aliens, that is to say:
> (e) make provision for the exclusion or the deportation and exclusion of such aliens from Saorstát Éireann and provide for and authorise the making by the Minister of orders for that purpose.

Pursuant to this provision, the Minister had made the Aliens Order, 1946, art 13(1) of which provided: [11–15]

> Subject to the restrictions imposed by the Aliens Act, 1935 (No. 14 of 1935), the Minister may, if he deems it to be conducive to the public good so to do make an order (in this Order referred to as a deportation order) requiring an alien to leave and to remain thereafter out of the State.

The applicant had been refused both asylum and leave to remain in the State on humanitarian grounds. He challenged the deportation order made against him on the basis that the parent statutory provision—s 5(1)(e) of the Aliens Act 1935—was unconstitutional. A majority of the Supreme Court held this provision unconstitutional on the grounds that it breached the principles and policies test. Keane J, with whom Hamilton CJ concurred, reasoned: [11–16]

> The central issue in the case, however, is as to whether section 5(1)(e) of the Act of 1935 infringes Article 15.2 because the principles and policies, if any, which are to be given effect to by orders made by the Minister in exercise of his powers under the provision are not set out in the statute itself.
>
> In considering that question, it is helpful to examine more closely the expression "principles and policies". The "policy" of a particular legislative provision is presumably an objective of some sort which parliament wishes to achieve by effecting an alteration in the law. To take a clear cut example, the policy of legislation concerning rented property was initially to prevent the exploitation of tenants by drastically abridging freedom of contract. In more recent times, the Oireachtas took the view, prompted by the courts (see *Blake v Attorney General* [1982] IR 117) that the law was, in some areas at least, unduly weighted in favour of the tenants. Accordingly, the pre-existing law was altered so as to give effect to a different objective. However, as the use of the expression "principles and policies" in the plural by O'Higgins CJ indicates and the example I have given illustrates, one can have different policies underlying various provisions in the same legislation or legislative code.
>
> In the present case, accordingly, it is necessary to identify first the alterations in the law, if any, effected by the relevant provisions and, secondly, the objective which was intended to be thereby achieved.

In considering what was the state of the law when the Act of 1935 was enacted, I shall leave out of account, for reasons which will become apparent later, the legislation which was then in force and which was repealed by the Act of 1935 itself. It is clear that, altogether apart from the provisions of the Act of 1935 and any preceding legislation, Saorstát Éireann as a sovereign state enjoyed the power to expel or deport aliens from the State for the reasons set out in the judgment of Gannon J in *Osheku v Ireland* [1986] IR 733. It is, of course, the case that in modern times, both here and in other common law jurisdictions, the exercise of the power is regulated by statute, but that does not affect the general principle that the right to expel or deport aliens inheres in the State by virtue of its nature and not because it has been conferred on particular organs of the State by statute.... It is sufficient to say that, in the light of the authorities to which I have referred, it is clear that, at the time the Act of 1935 was enacted, the power of Saorstát Éireann to expel or deport aliens was, in the absence of legislation, vested in the Crown acting on the advice of the Executive Council.

The change, accordingly, effected in the law by section 5(1)(e) was not the conferring on the State of an absolute and unrestricted power to deport aliens: that power was already vested in the State. But it was now to be exercised by the Minister in whatever manner he chose, subject only to the restrictions imposed elsewhere in the Act in the case of diplomatic and consular representatives and aliens who had been resident in the State for at least five years. In short, the objective of section 5(1)(e) was to enable the Minister to exercise, at his absolute and uncontrolled discretion, the power of deporting individual aliens or categories of aliens or, if he considered it a preferable course, to spell out himself in the form of regulations the restrictions or qualifications which should be imposed on the exercise of the power. The Minister in effect opted for the first course in making the Order of 1946....

That was certainly an alteration in the law; but to describe it as a "policy" begs the question, since it assumes that such an alteration can properly be so described. The *policy* of the legislation was not to enable the State to deport aliens at its pleasure, subject only to whatever qualification, by legislation or otherwise, it elected to impose on the exercise of the power: that power was already vested in the State. The effect of the alteration was to enable the Minister, and not the Oireachtas, to determine, not merely the aliens or classes of aliens who should be deported, but also the modifications, if any, to which the exercise of the power should be subjected. Undoubtedly, the designation of categories of aliens as being either immune from, or subject to, deportation at the discretion of the State and the delineation in legislative form of modifications on the exercise by the State of its powers in the area of deportation were policy decisions; but they were decisions which could henceforth be taken by the Minister. The Oireachtas had, in effect, determined that policy in this area should be the responsibility of the Minister, subject only to the restrictions to which I have already referred and, of course, to the power of annulment vested in either House. As Geoghegan J [in the High Court] succinctly put it, at 42:—

> The Oireachtas of Saorstát Éireann did not legislate for deportation. It merely permitted the Minister for Justice to legislate for deportation.

The situation in this case is in some ways analogous to that which arose in *McDaid v Sheehy* [1991] 1 IR 1. The central role in the raising of effectively delegated in that case to the Government and, as Blayney J found, such a delegation could not of itself be properly described as a "policy". It is difficult to see how the similar assignment in this case of the State's power to deport aliens to a minister could properly be regarded as a "policy".

It is quite usual to find that the exercise of the rule making power is subject to annulment by either House and I do not underestimate the value of such a provision. However, even in the hands of a vigilant deputy or senator, it is something of a blunt instrument, since it necessarily involves the annulment of the entire instrument, although parts only of it may be regarded as objectionable. In any event, I do not think that it could be seriously suggested that a provision of this nature was sufficient, of itself, to save an enactment which was otherwise clearly in breach of Article 15.2. [1999] 4 IR 26, at 90–93.

Denham J reached the same conclusion for much the same reasons. The minority (Barrington and Lynch JJ) dissented, but not on grounds that directly questioned the *City View* test or the manner in which it was applied. Barrington J reasoned that as non-nationals had no right to enter the State, the principles and policies test (designed to protect the Irish polity) ought not be applied in their favour. Lynch J reasoned that as the Government possessed the immigration control power in the absence of legislation, it was permissible for the Oireachtas to nominate a member of the Government, the Minister for Justice, to exercise that power. (This issue is explored further in chapter 12). [11–17]

Laurentiu is a stark case. If one sets aside the concerns of Barrington and Lynch JJ and merely applies the principles and policies test, it is difficult to see how the principles and policies test could be satisfied. For s 5(1)(e) simply provided no principles and policies whatsoever; it abdicated the role of the Oireachtas in regulating the exclusion and deportation of non-nationals. However, *Laurentiu* has not led to other legislation being struck down on the basis of Art 15.2.1°. [11–18]

A case that well illustrates the relaxed manner in which the principles and policies test is generally applied is *Leontjava v DPP and Chang v DPP* [2004] 1 IR 591. The applicants were before the District Court on charges pursuant to arts 5(6) and 15 of the Aliens Order 1946 as amended. Article 5(1) of the 1946 Order provides that an immigrant must, on arrival in the State, present herself to an immigration officer for leave to land. Article 5(6) provides that an immigration officer may attach conditions as to the duration of stay and the business in which such an immigrant may engage. Article 15 of the 1946 Order provides that every immigrant shall produce on demand her registration certificate (if registered) or a valid passport or other such document, unless she can give a satisfactory explanation of the circumstances which prevent her from doing so. The applicants were prosecuted for offences in connection with these provisions. [11–19]

The applicants then sought, by way of judicial review, to prohibit their trials on the grounds, *inter alia*, that s 5(1)(h) of that Act was inconsistent with Art 15.2 of the Constitution. The other grounds of challenge are considered later on in this chapter. Section 5(1)(h) of the Aliens Act 1935, as amended, provides, *inter alia*: [11–20]

> The Minister may, if and whenever he thinks proper, do by order (in this Act referred to as an aliens order) all or any of the following things in respect either of all aliens or of aliens of a particular nationality or otherwise of a particular class, or of particular aliens, that is to say:—
> (h) require such aliens to comply, while in Saorstát Éireann, with particular provisions as to registration, change of abode, travelling, employment, occupation, and other like matters.

In the High Court, Finlay Geoghegan J held that s 5(1)(h) fell foul of the *Cityview* test for much the same reasons as given by Keane J in *Laurentiu*: [11–21]

> [T]he Act of 1935 does not set out any policies and principles according to which the power given to the Minister under section 5(1)(h) to require aliens to comply whilst in the

> State in relation to the matters set out therein with "particular provisions" should be exercised.... Further, there is no indication, even in relation to the specific matters referred to in paragraph (h), as to the policies according to which the Minister should determine either those aliens to which any requirements should apply or the "particular provisions" with which such aliens should be required to comply in any order made under section 5(1)(h). The broad nature of the "particular provisions" purported to be authorised (as already concluded) intrinsically requires a policy decision for their determination. Hence, as was concluded by the Supreme Court in *Laurentiu v Minister for Justice* [1999] 4 IR 26 in relation to section 5(1)(e), section 5(1)(h) simply gives to the Minister the power to determine such policies and principles. [2004] 1 IR 591, at [38].

[11–22] The Supreme Court, however, overturned this conclusion on appeal. Keane CJ, with whom the other members of the Court agreed on this point, reasoned that the policy enunciated in s 5(1)(h) was plain: "the desirability of regulating the registration, change of abode, travelling, employment and occupation of aliens while in the State and the further desirability of regulating 'other like matters.'" [2004] 1 IR 581, at [34]. Keane CJ did not consider problematic the use of phrases such as "particular provisions" or "other like matters", reasoning that they were wholly consistent with a legislative scheme whereby primary legislation dealt with matters of broad scope and secondary legislation filled in the details. However, it is difficult to see how the "desirability of regulating registration, change of abode, travelling, employment and occupation" provides much more guidance than the "desirability of regulating immigration", which was arguably the policy of s 5(1)(e) as struck down in *Laurentiu*. At the very least, can it really be said that s 5(1)(h) dealt with *all* matters of principle and policy leaving *only* matters of detail to be filled in by way of secondary legislation?

[11–23] Estelle Feldman and I have argued elsewhere:

> [T]he courts have tended to draw from the fact that the primary legislation deals with some matters of principle and policy the false inference that the primary legislation deals with all matters of principle and policy, thus satisfying the *Cityview* test. This is what the Supreme Court did in *Leontjava and Chang*. The Court noted the legislative policy that it was desirable to regulate certain aspects of an immigrant's life in the State and concluded that the legislative power had not been constitutionally delegated. However, the Court did not advert to the absence of any principles and policies capable of informing the way in which those aspects of an immigrant's life should be regulated. If the Supreme Court, as it indicated, was applying the *Cityview* test, it made the false inference of concluding that the primary legislation dealt with all matters of principle and policy, simply because that legislation dealt with some matters of principle and policy. Finlay Geoghegan J, on the other hand, applied the *Cityview* test correctly, holding that the primary legislation did not deal with all matters of principle or policy.
>
> It may be that the *Cityview* test is too restrictive. To preclude secondary legislation from dealing with any matters of principle or policy may be to reduce it to the level of administrative action, thereby depriving it of any legislative character. Against this, however, the trenchant statement in Article 15.2 that the Oireachtas is the sole legislative authority in the State perhaps supports such a limited role for secondary legislation. In any event, given that the courts, with the exception of Finlay Geoghegan J in *Leontjava and Chang*, have consistently applied the *Cityview* test in this emasculated way, a judicial restatement of that test to reflect the real position would be welcome. Raymond Byrne and William Binchy, *Annual Review of Irish Law 2004* (Thomson Round Hall, 2005), at 183–184.

This relaxed application of the principles and policies test is apparent in other cases. In *Re Article 26 and the Health (Amendment) (No 2) Bill 2004* [2005] IESC 7, it was contended that the prospective scheme for nursing home charges was unconstitutional partly because it breached Art 15.2.1°. Section 1 of the Bill delegated to the Minister for Health a power to set the charge for nursing home fees, subject to the limit that it could not be greater than 80 percent of the old age (non-contributory) pension. Counsel assigned by the Court argued that, subject to the upper limit on charges (80 percent of the non-contributory old-age pension) and the exclusion from charges of certain persons, the Minister had no guidance as to how the charges should be imposed or what the level of those charges should be. However, the Court considered that the Minister's discretion was limited by (a) the maximum level of weekly charges and (b) the policy that the charges should not in general cause undue hardship. The Court concluded:

[11–24]

> [T]he imposition of charges pursuant to the section in question would be no more than the implementation of the principles and policies contained in the Act and the power delegated to [the Minister] to make the regulations is compatible with the Constitution. [2005] IESC 7, at [53].

This conclusion, however, does not follow from the restrictions on the Minister's power noted by the Court. For it does not follow from the fact that the primary legislation specifies certain principles and policies that no principles and policies are left for the determination of the Minister. In order to satisfy the *Cityview* test, it is necessary to show not simply that the primary legislation lays down principles and policies but also that the primary legislation lays down *all* the principles and policies that are necessary for the exercise of the secondary legislation.

[11–25]

It is questionable whether this test was met by the referred legislation, particularly if one considers the remarks of the Court in relation to the socio-economic rights issue. In assessing Counsel's claim that a socio-economic right had been infringed, the Court made the following observations:

[11–26]

> In this instance the Oireachtas has been careful to insert into the Bill a cap on the maximum charge which the Minister can impose.... In doing so it is clear that it sought to avoid causing undue hardship generally to persons who avail of the in-patient services. No doubt it can be said that the State could or should have been more generous, or less so with regard to persons of significant means, but that is the kind of debate which lies classically within the policy arena and is not a question of law. [2005] IESC 7, at [42].

It is difficult to see how, as the Court implies with regard to people of significant means, it would be a policy matter to decide on a charge of greater than 80 percent of the non-contributory pension, but not a policy matter to decide on whether to impose a charge of 1 percent or 80 percent of the non-contributory pension. The other limiting factor suggested by the court—avoidance of undue hardship—provides no guidance on this question as those with significant means are, by definition, unlikely to suffer undue hardship by a charge of 80 percent of the non-contributory pension. The Minister's decision as to whether to impose charges of 1 percent or 80 percent (or somewhere in between) thus, on the Court's account of the character of these decisions, involves policy decisions, the sort of decisions that the *Cityview* test purports to preclude the Oireachtas from delegating.

[11–27]

[11–28] Gerry Whyte and I have argued elsewhere as to how the *Cityview* test should be reformulated to reflect its actual application:

> The most plausible interpretation of the case law on this point is that the test stated by the Supreme Court in *Cityview* does not accurately represent the courts' position. The real test is not whether the Oireachtas has dealt with all matters of policy and principle, but rather whether the Oireachtas has dealt with no matters of principle or policy. Only in *Laurentiu v Minister for Justice* did the courts strike down primary legislation as being in breach of Article 15.2.1°. In *Laurentiu*, the legislation contained no principles or policies, leaving everything to the Minister by delegating to the Minister the power to "make provision for the deportation or exclusion of aliens". In other cases, such as *Lovett v Minister for Education*, the courts have employed the double construction rule to preclude delegates of legislative power from implementing principles and policies that were not envisioned by the primary legislation. However, in cases such as *Cityview* and the *Health Bill Reference case*, where the grant of legislative power on its face *requires* the delegate to make decisions of principle or policy, the courts seem prepared to uphold the validity of the legislation, provided that the primary legislation deals with *some* matters of principle and policy. Oran Doyle and Gerry Whyte, "The Separation of Powers and Constitutional Egalitarianism" in Eoin O'Dell ed, *Older People in Modern Ireland: Essays on Law and Policy* (Firstlaw, 2005), 391, at 401.

[11–29] However, it has been argued that a stricter application of the non-delegation doctrine would transfer power from the unelected delegated law-makers to the unelected judiciary. If one's rationale for the non-delegation doctrine is a liberal democratic preference for laws to be made by elected representatives, this may not be such a desirable outcome:

> The most obvious response to the identified weaknesses in the doctrine is to suggest the development of a more rigorous standard of review.... However, the indeterminacy inherent in any exposition of the doctrine mitigates against calls for its re-invigoration. There is an obvious risk with any abstract standard of review that it will serve as the pretext for the assumption of power by the courts – power which could be exercised on the basis of subjective judicial preferences. A revised, and reinforced, version of the doctrine would simply replace a system without scrutiny with one under which unelected judges would wield enormous, and unpredictable, supervisory powers. For the liberal democrat, rule by judicial discretion is just as objectionable as rule by faction. Eoin Carolan, "Democratic Control or High-Sounding 'Hocus-Pocus'? – A Public Choice Analysis of the Non-Delegation Doctrine" (2007) 29 *DULJ* 111, at 131.

[11–30] Carolan argues that the emergence of the administrative state, which the *Cityview* test attempts to facilitate, cannot be conceptually accommodated within the traditional, tripartite separation of powers. Nevertheless, the administration (as a fourth arm of government) could contribute to liberal democratic ideals. Carolan sketches how this might work in an Irish context:

> The liberal democratic demand for the legitimation of any exercise of public power, for example, would not be satisfied by the simple substitution of a system of judicial dominance for one of executive control. Judicial scrutiny, therefore, would have to employ criteria reflecting its role as the guardian of the interest of the individual citizen. The courts, reflecting the public choice theories of electoral representation, could not simply defer to the legislature's choice of political program as normatively superior. Rather, the judges would have to examine measures for traces of interest-group influence. The

practical details of doing so might be difficult to elaborate but some requirement of evidence that the demands of public welfare have been considered would be an advance in this direction.

Similarly, the administration would have to be regarded as a more independent entity in our governing structures. Administrative discretion would become an opportunity to counteract or expose interest group control of the executive or legislature. This could be achieved by a variety of means, the efficacy or appropriateness of which require further examination. A greater judicial insistence on the giving of reasons, for example, or on the entitlement of citizens to participate in the discretionary process, would represent such an improvement. The courts already regard the administration as subject to greater scrutiny than the elected organs of government. However, the judiciary deferentially regulates its involvement to reflect the premise that the legislature retains pre-eminent control of the policy-making process. This notion, as this article has argued, has been undermined by contemporary political theories which cast the legislature as the captured agent of organised interest groups. The courts should therefore take account of these theories by refusing to unquestioningly accept the pre-eminence of the legislative branch. Neither can the courts take responsibility for setting society's policies. It can however ensure that the administration functions as an obstacle to factional control by first, recognising the potentially beneficial role of an administration with greater independence from legislative or executive control, and secondly, by insisting on an enhanced level of procedural and substantive scrutiny of that administrative process. This more vigorous involvement on the part of the courts would, from the perspective of a post-public choice liberal democrat, provide the individual citizen with an enhanced safeguard against the control of public power by organised sectional interests. *ibid*, at 137.

Henry VIII Clauses: the Interaction of the Non-delegation Doctrine and the *Ultra Vires* Doctrine

As the analysis of the previous cases has demonstrated, non-delegation issues tend to arise in a context in which a person objects to how she has been treated by a public body. She objects to the action of the public body on the basis that it depends for its validity on the exercise of a power unconstitutionally delegated in breach of Art.15.2. Another important restriction on public bodies is that each must act in accordance with the power actually assigned to them by legislation. It was this restriction on the powers—or *vires* —of a public body to which Fennelly J was principally referring in *Kennedy v Law Society*. These two restrictions (the non-delegation doctrine and the *ultra vires* doctrine) interact in a powerful way to protect individuals from the arbitrary exercise of public power. [11–31]

In *East Donegal Co-operative Ltd v Attorney General* [1970] IR 317, the Supreme Court relied on the presumption of constitutionality to endorse the double construction rule. It followed from a presumption that all post-1937 statutes were constitutional that, where two or more interpretations of a statutory provision are open and only one of which is constitutional, the court ought to adopt the constitutional reading. In the context of Art 15.2, it is likely that the constitutional reading will limit the scope of the public authority's power to act. However, if the public power is restricted in this way, it becomes more likely that a public authority will have acted beyond the scope of the power, *ie, ultra vires*. In this way, the non-delegation doctrine and the *ultra vires* doctrine can combine to protect the interests of people affected by the exercise of public power. This position can be represented by the following diagram: [11–32]

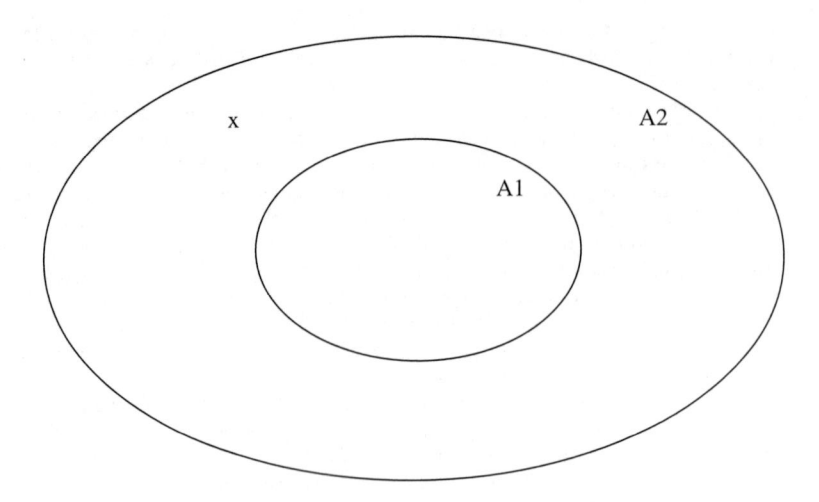

[11–33] A statute assigns a legislative power (A) to a public body. Pursuant to that power, the body makes delegated legislation (x) which affects an individual. The individual wishes to convince a court that (x) was *ultra vires* the public body. She can achieve this in one of two ways: either by showing that the parent legislation itself (A) is unconstitutional (thereby removing the entire power) or by showing that (x) was beyond the scope of what is permitted by (A), properly interpreted. This latter argument works in the following way. The large circle marked (A2) represents an expansive reading of the statutory power (A) that would be unconstitutional. The smaller circle marked (A1) represents an alternative reading of the statute that would be constitutional. The small (x) marks out the action taken by the public body pursuant to the power (A) that is being construed by the court. The double construction rule requires that the court adopt reading A1 over reading A2: the reading that preserves the constitutionality of the statute must be adopted. However, action (x) lies within the scope of reading (A2) but outside the scope of reading (A1). Accordingly, the presumption of constitutionality requires that the court uphold the constitutionality of the legislation by adopting reading (A1); the court must then strike down the impugned action (x) on the basis that it is *ultra vires* the (narrowly interpreted) scope of power delegated to the public body (A1).

[11–34] This approach has been taken by the courts in a number of cases, a good illustration of which is *Cooke v Walshe* [1984] IR 710, in which the plaintiff had suffered serious injuries in a car accident. The Health Act 1970 provided that health services should be provided for free to those with inadequate means. Section 72 authorises the Minister for Health to regulate how such services are provided free of charge in the Act. Purportedly under s 71, the Minister had made the Health Services Regulations 1971, art 6(3) of which provided that health services would not be available for free to a person injured in a car accident, unless that person can establish that she is not entitled to damages or compensation for her injuries from a third person. The plaintiff, a person with full eligibility under the Act, was injured in a car accident. The defendant in the personal injuries action sought to challenge the constitutionality of s 71, and the validity of art 6(3), by reference to Art 15.2 of the Constitution. The High Court directed that the Attorney General defend the *vires* and constitutionality of the legislation. The High Court upheld the legislation, but the Supreme Court allowed the appeal. O'Higgins CJ reasoned as follows:

> The defendant has challenged the validity of the regulation. He mounts this challenge on two distinct grounds. In the first place he questions whether the regulation is properly made within the powers conferred on the Minister by section 72. Obviously, if he succeeds on this ground the regulation will be held to be *ultra vires* the Minister and on that account to be void. If, on the other hand, the regulation is held to be within the apparent authority conferred on the Minister by the section, then the Court must consider whether the section itself is valid having regard to the provisions of the Constitution. It is well settled that the consideration of any question involving the validity of a statute or a section thereof should, in appropriate circumstances, be postponed to the consideration of any other question, the resolution of which will determine the issue between the parties. It is, therefore, proper in this case that the question of *ultra vires*, apart from any question of constitutionality, should first be considered. In the consideration of such question, however, the validity of the section must be presumed and it must be interpreted in accordance with the existence of such a presumption. This means that if the section is capable of being interpreted in two ways, one of which would give a meaning which is consistent with what is permitted by the Constitution and the other of which would not, that meaning which is so consistent must be adopted.
>
> The interpretation of the section is a prerequisite to a determination of whether what purports to be done by the regulation is, in fact, within the Minister's powers under the section. What then is permitted by section 72? The first sub-section applies only to health boards and clearly relates to the manner in which these boards are to administer the health services provided for under the section. While it refers to the making of regulations "regarding the manner in which and the extent to which the board or boards shall make available services," this must not be taken as meaning that such regulations may remove, reduce, or otherwise alter obligations imposed on health boards by the Act. To attach such a meaning, unless compelled to do so by the words used, would be to attribute to the Oireachtas, unnecessarily, an intention to delegate in the field of lawmaking in a manner "which is neither contemplated nor permitted by the Constitution." (See this Court's judgment in *Cityview Press v An Chomhairle Oiliúna* [1980] IR 381.) Accordingly, these words must be taken as applying only to standards, periods, places, personnel or such other factors which may indicate the nature and quality of the services which are to be made available. However, it is not so much on this sub-section as on sub-section 2, that reliance was placed in justification of the regulation. I again quote this subsection:—
>
>> Regulations under this section may provide for any service under this Act being made available only to a particular class of the persons who have eligibility for that service.
>
> Here, again, it is necessary to seek a meaning for these words which absolve the National Parliament from any intention to delegate its exclusive power of making or changing the laws. Needless to say, if such a meaning is not possible then the invalidity of the sub-section would be established. *Prima facie*, therefore, these words are to be interpreted in such a manner as to authorise only exclusions which the Act itself contemplates. Such exclusions may be possible in relation to particular services for persons with limited eligibility. Those with such eligibility are classified under section 46 and the Minister, by sub-section 3, is given power to change or alter this classification. The obligation imposed on health boards is to provide, not all the services, but, such services as are specified, for persons with limited eligibility. While I do not find it necessary to come to a final decision in this regard it seems to me possible that regulations under the sub-section could excuse a particular health board or health boards from the obligation to provide a particular service for a particular class of those with limited eligibility, while the obligation to provide

that service for others with limited eligibility remained. I am, however, satisfied that the sub-section is not to be interpreted as permitting by regulation the cancelling, repeal or alteration of anything laid down in the Act itself unless such is contemplated by the Act.

Having said this, I turn to what the regulation purports to do. It, in effect, seeks to add new sub-sections to section 52 and 56 of the Act which exclude, from the benefit of these sections and the statutory entitlement thereby afforded, a category of persons whose exclusion is in no way authorised or contemplated by the Act. Included in this category must, necessarily, be persons who by the Act are given full eligibility and full statutory entitlement to avail of the services provided for by the two sections without charge. This is, in reality, an attempt to amend the two sections by ministerial regulation instead of by appropriate legislation. In my view, the National Parliament could not and did not intend to give such a power to the Minister for Health when it enacted section 72 of the Health Act, 1970. Accordingly, in my view, the regulation is *ultra vires* the Minister and is void. [1984] IR 710, at 728–729.

[11–35] This illustrates the general approach outlined above. On one interpretation of s 72, art 6(3) was impermissible (interpretation A1). On another interpretation of s 72, art 6(3) was permissible (interpretation A2). All other things being equal, a court would adopt the interpretation that upheld the exercise of public power, *ie* interpretation A2. However, interpretation A2 was considered unconstitutional as it delegated to the Minister a power to reverse the principle/policy choice of full eligibility made by the primary legislation. For this reason, the Supreme Court had to adopt the narrower interpretation A1, thereby striking down art 6(3) as *ultra vires* the powers of the Minister, properly interpreted. (In *Harvey v Minister for Social Welfare* [1990] 2 IR 232, the Supreme Court came to the same conclusion on a similar set of facts).

[11–36] The Court's precise reason for opting for interpretation A1 over interpretation A2 is worthy of consideration. The Court effectively held that it would be unconstitutional for the Oireachtas to delegate to a Minister the power either to amend primary legislation or to act inconsistently with primary legislation. Such a legislative provision is commonly referred to as a Henry VIII clause. The effect of *Cooke* and *Harvey* appears to be to outlaw Henry VIII clauses. Some have emphasised that this is distinct from the general principles and policies test:

> A significant feature of *Harvey* is that it demonstrates that there are, in fact, two separate – if inter-related – strands to the case-law on Article 15.2.1°, mainly:
>
> (i) the "principles and policies" criteria and
> (ii) the principle that the Oireachtas may not delegate the power to make, repeal or amend legislation.
>
> While these strands are related, they are mutually exclusive criteria in that, for example, a statute which contained clear principles and policies might yet fall to be condemned under Article 15.2.1° if it purported to give the relevant Minister power to amend its provisions by regulation. Gerard Hogan and Gerry Whyte eds, *Kelly: The Irish Constitution* (4th ed, LexisNexis Butterworths, 2003), at [4.2.27].

[11–37] Although Hogan and Whyte are correct to highlight the differences between the two tests, the "principles and policies" concern does appear to lie behind the prohibition on Henry VIII clauses. Primary legislation that delegates to a Minister the power to amend that legislation appears very explicitly to have left open principle and policy choices to the Minister. Only where the Minister's power to amend is limited to matters of detail would the prohibition on Henry VIII clauses proscribe legislation that passed muster on the principles and policies test. Morgan has considered this scenario:

> Let us take some examples of the different types of situation in which a Henry VIII clause might be desirable. In the first place, there may be unknown pearls lurking in the unplumbed depths of pre-Independence statutes. Moreover, the question of which legislation came over to post-Independence Ireland is not always clear. Accordingly the possibility of a Henry VIII clause would, in certain circumstances, be a useful arrow in the draftsman's quiver. The second category consists of a number of provisions by which the legislation has enabled a Minister to "index-link" a monetary limit contained in a statute and (in contrast to certain earlier statutes of this type) the draftsman has gone out of his way to attempt to proof the legislation against an attack based on Article 15.2.1° by enunciating the principle which is to govern any increase. For example, section 16(1) of the Courts Act 1991 fixes monetary limits for the civil jurisdiction of the District and Circuit Courts; but then – empowers the Government to amend these limits by order. Then it goes on to state that any such order must have regard "to changes in the value of money, generally, in the State since the said monetary amount was so specified". But this caution does not meet the point that the provision may be unconstitutional on the ground that it is a Henry VIII clause, in that it confers power to amend primary legislation by varying the monetary amount fixed in the parent Act. This suggestion stems from the principle, being criticized here, namely that, in the case law decided so far, a Henry VIII clause has been regarded as automatically unconstitutional. It is suggested that this is neither a desirable result nor one which is required by Article 15.2.1°, in each case for the same reason. For in making such an order, the Government is not laying down a new principle but merely implementing a principle laid down by the Oireachtas, namely that the limits on jurisdiction should be adjusted in line with inflation.
>
> As an example of a third category – attempting to cater for teething troubles in the introduction of a complicated scheme – take section 4 of the Building Societies Act 1989. Notwithstanding its being confined to the first three years of the Act's operation, it seems to be unconstitutional. This section provides:
>
>> If, in any respect, any difficulty arises in bringing any provision of this Act into operation or in relation to the operation of any such provision, the Minister may by regulations do anything which appears to him to be necessary or expedient for removing that difficulty, for bringing that provision into operation, or for securing or facilitating its operation, and any such regulations may modify any provision of this Act so far as may be necessary or expedient for carrying such provision into effect for the purposes aforesaid but no regulations shall be made under this section in relation to any provision of this Act after the expiration of 3 years commencing on the day on which the relevant provision of this Act came into operation.

(See, similarly, the Canals Act 1986, section 13; Valuation Act 1988, section 4; Companies Act 1990, section 24.) Contradicting the criticism advanced here, there are two policy-constitutional arguments which tell against Henry VIII clauses. The first of these proceeds from the basis that a Henry VIII clause may be the parent of delegated legislation which contradicts some principle which has been settled by the Oireachtas. The short answer to this is that, *ex-hypothesis*, we are concerned here with Henry VIII clauses which *do not* authorise any delegated legislation which could introduce a novel principle: this feature was illustrated by the earlier discussion of *Harvey*. Secondly, it may be said that some person may read an act of the Oireachtas and not be aware that one of more of its provisions has been reversed by the progeny of a Henry VIII clause and thus not be in force. But a form of this argument can of course be made against delegated legislation of any type in that, by definition, it is legislation which cannot be discovered by surveying the acts of the Oireachtas. The solution, in either case, lies in the provision of adequate publicity, for delegated legislation; coupled with the fact that the existence of a Henry

VIII clause (especially if it is a precise type, like the specimen in *Harvey*) should put any person interested on notice of the possible existence of delegated legislation which might reverse principal legislation.

Unfortunately, this line of criticism has not been judicially considered, perhaps because it has not been admitted that the taboo on Henry VIII clauses involved any extension of the precept banning new principles in delegated legislation. David Gwynn Morgan, *The Separation of Powers in the Irish Constitution* (Round Hall, Sweet & Maxwell, 1997), at 248–250.

[11–38] Although Morgan's points are well made, the absolute character of the prohibition on Henry VIII clauses is—in some respects—reassuring. Given the relaxed manner in which the principles and policies test has been applied by the courts, there are grounds for scepticism about how the courts might apply a rule that Henry VIII clauses are impermissible unless they relate to matters of detail.

[11–39] *Lovett v Minister for Education* [1997] 1 ILRM 89 provides a further illustration of the ways in which the non-delegation doctrine and the *ultra vires* doctrine can interact. The Teachers Superannuation Act 1928 empowers the Minister for Education to make and apply a pension scheme for teachers. Section 3 of the Act sets out certain matters which may be contained in the scheme. Paragraph 8(1) of the Secondary Teachers Superannuation (Amendment) Scheme 1935 provides, *inter alia*, that where any person in receipt of a pension under the scheme is, during the continuance of the scheme, convicted of a crime or offence and sentenced to imprisonment with hard labour for any term or to imprisonment for a term exceeding 12 months or to penal servitude for any term, such pension shall be forfeited as from the date of such conviction. Mr Lovett, a teacher, was held by the Minister to have forfeited his entitlements under the pension scheme after he received a suspended sentence of two years for crimes of dishonesty. Kelly J, citing *Cityview Press*, held that this provision in the scheme was *ultra vires* the power conferred by s 3 of the 1928 Act:

> Applying the test formulated in this quotation from the judgment of O'Higgins CJ, I am of opinion that the provisions of paragraph 8(1) of the scheme go far beyond the principles and policies which are contained in the 1928 Act. That Act had as its object the formulation and carrying out of schemes for the provision of pensions and gratuities for teachers and former teachers. It does not appear to me that it has anything to do with deterring the commission of criminal offences whether by teachers or retired teachers. If it had, one would expect to find some mention of this either in the long title or in the body of the Act. There is none.
>
> It is, I think, significant that although section 3 contains a non-exclusive list of what may be contained in a scheme, nowhere is there mentioned any entitlement to include a forfeiture, or indeed any other provision, in such a scheme by reference to criminal wrongdoing.
>
> Paragraph 8(1) of the scheme, in my view, goes very much further than giving effect to principles and policies which are contained in the statute itself. I am of opinion that the 'forfeiture' provision contained in paragraph 8(1) of the scheme cannot be regarded as the mere filling in or completion of a detail by the minister.
>
> The very use of the term 'forfeiture' is indicative of something penal. The justification given for it by the minister is that it is a deterrent against the commission of crime. But the 1928 Act has nothing to do with the enforcement of the criminal law even in an indirect way. [1997] 1 ILRM 89, at 96.

[11–40] In one sense, there was no need to rely on Art 15.2 to reach this conclusion. Secondary legislation that exceeds the power actually delegated is, under the normal principles of administrative law, *ultra vires* and invalid. Strictly speaking, the citation of Art 15.2 adds nothing to this analysis. That said, Art 15.2 and the *Cityview* test (as formulated if not as applied) articulate a powerful constitutional and political basis for the *ultra vires* doctrine: decisions of principle and policy should be the preserve of democratically elected legislators. The identification of this rationale may ensure that the *ultra vires* doctrine is applied with the requisite force.

Primary Legislation as a Deliberative Process

The final piece of the jigsaw in *Chang and Leontjava* was s 2 of the Immigration Act 1999, enacted in the aftermath of *Laurentiu*, which provided: [11–41]

> (1) Every order made before the passing of this Act under section 5 of the Act of 1935 other than the orders or provisions of orders specified in the Schedule to this Act shall have statutory effect as if it were an Act of the Oireachtas.
> (2) If subsection (1) would, but for this subsection, conflict with a constitutional right of any person, the operation of that subsection shall be subject to such limitation as is necessary to secure that it does not so conflict but shall be otherwise of full force and effect.

The intention of the Oireachtas in enacting this provision seems to have been to ensure that the provisions of the Aliens Order 1946 (other than those provisions directly invalidated as a result of *Laurentiu*) had legal force and effect independent of the validity or otherwise of the original enabling provision under which it was made. A second and less obvious effect, however, was that a provision of the 1946 Order would have been rendered valid, notwithstanding that it was *ultra vires* its enabling statute. In *Chang and Leontjava*, the High Court had held that s 5(1)(h) was unconstitutional. Although the Supreme Court overruled this point, it had held that Art 5(6) of the Aliens Order 1946 was *ultra vires* the 1935 Act. If s 2 was constitutionally valid, therefore, Art 5(6) would have been valid, notwithstanding that it was *ultra vires* s 5 of the 1935 Act, and Art 15 would have been valid, notwithstanding whether the delegation of legislative power in s 5(1)(h) was itself constitutional. For these reasons, it was necessary for both Finlay Geoghegan J and the Supreme Court to examine the constitutionality of s 2 of the 1999 Act. [11–42]

The constitutionality of s 2 turns on whether the Oireachtas is procedurally constrained by the Constitution from enacting primary legislation that either purports to confer the status of primary legislation on some other provision not enacted pursuant to the procedures established by the Constitution for primary legislation or purports to incorporate such a provision by reference. In the High Court, the State argued that the 1946 Order remained a statutory rule and, as such, did not become an Act of the Oireachtas. Finlay Geoghegan J accepted this contention. However, the State also argued that the 1946 Order, although secondary legislation, had as part of its legal status characteristics of an Act of the Oireachtas: these special characteristics were, as noted above, that the 1946 Order did not depend on the 1935 Act for its validity or effect. Finlay Geoghegan J summarised the effect of s 2 in the following way: [11–43]

> The clear and unambiguous meaning of section 2(1), insofar as is relevant to these proceedings, is that the substantive provisions of the Aliens Order 1946 ... are to have statutory effect as if they are an Act of the Oireachtas but whilst not being contained in an Act of the Oireachtas. [2004] 1 IR 591, at [52].

[11–44] Finlay Geoghegan J then referred to a number of provisions of the Constitution that led her to conclude that there was a procedural constraint on the law-making powers of the Oireachtas. In particular, she concluded that Art 25.4.3° and Art 25.4.5° required that the text of any provision which is to be treated as a "law" or as an "Act of the Oireachtas" must be contained in the Bill signed by the President and must be enrolled in the office of the registrar of the Supreme Court. This was further confirmed, in her view, by Art 26.1.1°:

> This [Article] appears to require that every provision which may subsequently have the status of a "law" made by the Oireachtas pursuant to Article 15.2 of the Constitution be capable of being referred to the Supreme Court as a Bill or as a specified provision of a Bill for a decision on its constitutionality prior to its signature by the President. Neither articles 5(6) or 15 of the Aliens Order 1946, at issue in these proceedings nor any other provision of any Aliens Order referred to in section 2(1) of the Act of 1999 could have been referred by the President to the Supreme Court pursuant to Article 26. [2004] 1 IR 581, at [77].

[11–45] From her consideration of these constitutional provisions, she reasoned that a "law" in Art 25 was exclusively an Act of the Oireachtas and that, therefore, "law" in Art 15.2 referred solely to an Act of the Oireachtas. Accordingly, she ruled that s 2 of the 1999 Act was unconstitutional as it purported to deem something a statutory law which could not be such a law.

[11–46] The Supreme Court allowed the State's appeal. Keane CJ noted that the Constitution was silent as to the form of legislation. He further noted a widespread practice of incorporation by reference, whereby primary legislative status had been conferred on such diverse sources of law as international conventions and secondary legislation. He concluded:

> [T]he Constitution affords a strikingly wide latitude to the Oireachtas in adopting whatever form of legislation it considers appropriate in particular cases. Under Article 15 it enjoys the sole and exclusive power of making laws for the State and where, as here, it has expressed its clear and unequivocal intention that particular instruments should have the force of law in the State, it is difficult to see on what basis it can be asserted that it has exceeded or abused its exclusive legislative role. In the view of the court, the choice by the Oireachtas to incorporate the instruments in question by reference rather than by setting out their text *verbatim* in the body of the Act was one which they were entitled to make, unless it can be clearly established that the result was in conflict with specific provisions of the Constitution. [2004] 1 IR 591, at [82].

[11–47] Addressing the more particular constitutional provisions mentioned by Finlay Geoghegan J, the Supreme Court held that the purpose of Art 25 was to ensure that an official and authoritative text of every Act passed by the Oireachtas and signed by the President was available in the office of the Supreme Court: those requirements had been met in this case. The Court also rejected the contention that the requirements of the Art 26 reference procedure mitigated against the constitutional validity of this type of legislation:

> If the President, after consultation with the Council of State, was of the view that a reference was desirable because one or more of the provisions contained in the orders being of statutory effect were of questionable constitutional validity, there was nothing to

prevent her from referring section 2 of the Bill to this court for a decision as to its constitutionality. That would be the reference of a "specified provision" within the meaning of Article 26.1.1° and the fact that only part of the specified provision was, in the view of the President, of questionable validity would not in the slightest degree affect her power to make such a reference. Holders of the Office of President have, in the past, referred an entire Bill to this court for a decision as to its constitutionality, although it was inconceivable that every single provision in the Bill was regarded as of questionable validity: see, for example, *The Employment Equality Bill, 1996* [1997] 2 IR 321. [2004] 1 IR 581, at [88].

The Court concluded that the applicant had not successfully rebutted the presumption of constitutionality. Estelle Feldman and I have argued elsewhere that Finlay Geoghegan J's conclusion is to be preferred to that of the Supreme Court: [11–48]

> Although the Supreme Court's interpretation of Article 25 was at least as convincing as that of Finlay Geoghegan J ... its interpretation of Article 26 was not so convincing. Keane CJ implied that the Supreme Court, if section 2 of the 1999 Act had been referred pursuant to Article 26 reference, could consider the constitutional validity of the provisions of the Aliens Order 1946. In this way, he reasoned, Article 26.1.1° was satisfied. However, Keane CJ's acceptance that section 2 alone could have been referred by the President implied two further points. First, the President would not have been able to refer the provisions of the 1946 Order independently of section 2 of the 1999 Act. Secondly, the President would, if she wanted to refer any provision of the 1946 Order, have to refer all the provisions of that Order, under the guise of referring section 2 of the 1946 Act. This appears inconsistent with Article 26 of the Constitution, which clearly envisages that the President be able to specify the provisions of a Bill which she wants the Supreme Court to assess the constitutionality of:
>> The President may, after consultation with the Council of State, refer any Bill to which this Article applies to the Supreme Court for a decision on the question as to whether such Bill or any specified provision or provisions of such Bill is or are repugnant to this Constitution or to any provision thereof.
> In *Re Article 26 and the Employment Equality Bill 1996*, the Supreme Court interpreted Article 26.1.1° in the following way:
>> It would have been possible for the President to specify some specific provision or provisions of the Bill on which she needed the Court's decision but she was not obliged to do that. [1997] 2 IR 321, at 331.
> Keane CJ's observation – that Presidents in the past had referred a whole bill even though it was inconceivable that all provisions of the Bill were considered to be of questionable validity – failed to address the issue of whether it was legitimate for the Oireachtas to deprive the President of the facility to refer specific provisions of a Bill.
> Thus the Supreme Court's decision in *Leontjava and Chang*, to the effect that the 1946 Order was validly incorporated into the 1999 Act, deprived (albeit retrospectively and hypothetically) the President of certain of her powers under Article 26, principally her power to specify certain provisions of that Order to be referred to the Supreme Court. This deprivation, although retrospective and hypothetical in *Leontjava and Chang*, operates prospectively and really for future legislation that adopts the technique of incorporation by reference. If it is a constitutionally necessary feature of a Bill that the President be able to refer specified provisions of that Bill to the Supreme Court, it was unconstitutional for section 2 of the 1999 Act to deprive the President of this power. If that is the case, it follows that the attempt of section 2 to make those provisions part of the 1999 Act should have been held constitutionally invalid.
> On the other hand, the State's argument in the High Court (to the effect that the provisions of the Order were not part of the Act but were nevertheless accorded the status

of primary legislation) would also have been inconsistent with Article 26. For on this argument, none of the provisions of the Order could have been referred, even indirectly and en masse, to the Supreme Court. Therefore, those provisions would have the status of primary legislation without having been subject to all the procedural requirements for the enactment of primary legislation.

Even if the Supreme Court was correct in its interpretation of Article 26, its general reasoning raises concerns for future cases. The Court, in upholding the capacity of the Oireachtas to adopt this type of legislation, emphasised both the procedural freedom accorded to the Oireachtas as to the form of legislation and the prevalence of the legislative technique of incorporation by reference. The question is whether each of these rationales stands on its own. It seems clear that procedural freedom cannot, of itself, justify the Court's decision. For there are legislative exercises of procedural freedom that the Court would presumably not countenance. Most obviously, the Court would presumably, if pushed, require that the incorporation by reference device be confined to existing legal provisions that could meaningfully be "ratified" by the Oireachtas. If the Oireachtas were allowed to incorporate into primary legislation all future Orders issued pursuant to the 1935 Act, that would set at nought Article 15.2.1°, as interpreted by the courts in assessing delegation of legislative power. For this reason, procedural freedom could not, of itself, have been a sufficient basis for the Court's decision. Raymond Byrne and William Binchy, *Annual Review of Irish Law 2004* (Thomson Round Hall, 2005), at 186–188.

Investigative Powers of the Oireachtas

[11–49] *Maguire v Ardagh* [2002] 1 IR 385 addressed the question of whether the Oireachtas has any inherent investigative powers. In April 2000, a man had been shot by members of the Gardaí at Abbeylara. The Garda Commissioner prepared a report on the incident which was presented to the Minister for Justice who in turn placed it before the Oireachtas. A joint committee of both Houses proposed that a sub-committee would inquire into the incident. The sub-committee issued directions to a number of persons to attend and give evidence. The sub-committee also proposed a process whereby cross-examination would occur on the final day of the inquiry along with submissions. Moreover, persons would have to apply to the sub-committee for leave to cross-examine. A number of Gardaí who had been called to give evidence objected to these procedures; they applied to court to quash the sub-committee's directions. In several wide-ranging judgments, both a divisional High Court and the Supreme Court addressed both the power of the Oireachtas to hold investigations at all and the limits that might apply to that power.

[11–50] A majority of the Supreme Court held that the Oireachtas had no inherent, general power to conduct an investigation. It was accepted by all parties that there was no explicit power to conduct investigations, but the respondents contended that there was an implicit power as such a power was necessary for the Oireachtas to function as a representative parliament. The majority accepted that it would be constitutionally permissible for the Oireachtas to undertake certain types of inquiry (so as to better inform itself of matters relevant to its functions), but not one of the type proposed for Abbeylara, which would have significant effects for the rights of those persons appearing before it. Murray J put the matter as follows:

> The freedom to inquire and be informed on matters relevant to the exercise of their functions by members of the Oireachtas is in a sense neutral, once it does not impinge on the rights of third parties or the functions of other constitutional organs such as the courts.

But the Houses of the Oireachtas are creatures of the Constitution. That is their sole source of governmental authority which, according to Article 6 of the Constitution, is derived from the people. If it acts so as to affect the rights of citizens, this cannot be compared to a simple search for knowledge. If an organ of State acts so as to affect the rights of citizens, it can only be justified in doing so pursuant to a governmental power conferred on it by the Constitution. When the Oireachtas exercises its authority in a manner which may affect the rights of others, it acts with the aura and authority of a constitutional organ of State. To adjudicate, in the sense that the term is used here, on the culpability of citizens in their conduct cannot in my view be equated with the everyday search for knowledge of facts or expert opinions. That is a governmental power which it seems to me can only be exercised by virtue of power conferred by the Constitution.

Accordingly, different considerations must arise when the Houses of the Oireachtas assert a constitutional power to embark upon an adjudicative process, in the secondary sense, which has as one of its objects or functions to make findings of fact or reach conclusions which may impugn the good name of a citizen. As I have already pointed out earlier in this judgment this is a very great power capable of affecting the rights of citizens with potentially disastrous consequences. I would note in passing that the courts themselves do not have such an extensive power, there being no investigatory role attributed to them....

The task of the court is a cognitive one. It is to ascertain whether there has resided in the Constitution an inherent power of the Oireachtas to conduct inquiries which may lead to adverse findings impugning the good name of a citizen. It is an interpretation which must be mandated by the Constitution. The question must also be approached in the light of other rights, in particular personal rights, guaranteed and protected by the Constitution as well as concurrent powers of the Oireachtas....

The fundamental and intrinsic value of the right to one's good name and reputation, long recognised by the common law, is expressly raised to constitutional status by Article 40. As I have already pointed out, the Constitution was drafted and adopted so as to give express powers in specific circumstances to the Houses of the Oireachtas to make findings of culpability of certain persons or officeholders for wrongdoing which would inevitably have the gravest consequences for their good name and reputation. The contrasting silence of the Constitution on the question of a power vested in the Houses of the Oireachtas to exercise its authority so as to make findings of fact involving personal culpability for wrongdoing, in this case one of unlawful killing, on the part of individuals so as to impugn their good name and reputation, is one reason why I cannot conclude that the existence of an inherent power is mandated by the terms of the Constitution itself....

There are further considerations which lead me to conclude that the Constitution of Ireland does not permit, let alone mandate, that there is to be found in its provisions an unexpressed inherent power of the Oireachtas to conduct inquiries of this nature concerning the personal culpability of individuals, leading to findings which may impugn their good name.

Committees of inquiry are, by virtue of their role and function, part of the political process. Evidently, they are composed of public representatives answerable to their constituents, public opinion and with a day to day interest in the cut and thrust of everyday politics. I do not say that a public representative by virtue of his or her political role is incapable of acting fairly and objectively. Nonetheless, there is the underlying fact that they each have an ever present interest, from one perspective or another, in the political issues of the day including the ever present one of the standing or otherwise of the Government in office and its ministers. Constitutionally the Government is answerable to members of the Dáil and in a different, but substantive way, may be the subject of support or opposition by members of the Seanad. Unlike other forms of inquiry, Oireachtas committees are not independent of the political process. The question arises whether the Constitution, although silent on the matter, intended that personal culpability of citizens for serious wrongdoing with consequential implications for their good name should be decided in the course of an inquiry which was part of the political process.... [T]here is at least a real risk that the integrity or objectivity of parliamentary inquiries could be compromised by purely political considerations. It was the reality of such frailties that brought the parliamentary committee system in Britain into disrepute. It is difficult to imagine that the framers of the Constitution of 1922 would not have been aware of this factor. Nor could one suppose that it was not considered by the drafters of the Constitution of 1937. The views expressed in the document of the Office of the Attorney General appears to envisage that in certain circumstances, particularly where there is the risk of bias or of a parliamentary committee being perceived as being open to political bias, that the Oireachtas, in the exercise of its own discretion, would resort to the option of an independent statutory tribunal *in lieu* of an inquiry conducted by a committee of the Oireachtas. I find it highly improbable that the Constitution was intended to confer an inherent power of this nature on the Oireachtas without expressly doing so or that, in the face of potential frailties to which the two texts which I have just cited refer, it would have been impliedly left to the Oireachtas to exercise its own exclusive discretion as to whether an inquiry which may result in findings of fact impugning the good name of a citizen should be conducted by an Oireachtas committee or an independent statutory tribunal. [2002] 1 IR 385, at 595–601.

[11–51] Although the decision of the Court was limited to the inherent jurisdiction of the Oireachtas to conduct inquiries of this type, several of the dicta of the majority suggest that it might well be unconstitutional for the Oireachtas to legislate to allow itself conduct inquiries that might impugn the good names of individual citizens, who were not members of the Oireachtas.

CONTENTS – CHAPTER 12

The Executive Power and the Government

Introduction.	[12–01]
Implicit Executive Powers	[12–03]
Explicit Executive Power Over External Relations	[12–19]
Composition of the Government	[12–30]
Cabinet Confidentiality	[12–32]

Overview

Article 28 vests the executive power of the State in the Government. While some executive powers, such as the power over external affairs, are explicitly stated in the Constitution, the courts have accepted that there are other executive powers that vest in the Government. It appears that the implicit governmental powers of the State that are not explicitly vested in any other organ of government (such as the immigration control power) vest, at least presumptively, in the Government. The courts have held that they have a power to review the Government's exercise of the executive power where it acts in clear disregard of the Constitution. The courts have held that the Government cannot fetter its power to conduct foreign affairs by legally committing itself in advance to reach agreements with other States. In all other respects, however, the courts have shown notable deference to the Government in its exercise of the foreign affairs power. The confidentiality of Government discussions is now protected by the Constitution, subject to certain limited exceptions.

CHAPTER 12

The Executive Power and the Government

Introduction

Article 28 of the Constitution provides: [12–01]

> The Government shall consist of not less than seven and not more than fifteen members who shall be appointed by the President in accordance with the provisions of this Constitution.
>
> The executive power of the State shall, subject to the provisions of this Constitution, be exercised by or on the authority of the Government.

There is very little textual guidance, however, as to what the executive power actually consists of. Articles 28 and 29 do assign specific powers to the Government, implicitly deeming them to be aspects of the executive power. For instance, Art 28.3.2° assigns to the Government the responsibility of protecting the State in a time of invasion. Article 28.4.4° provides that the Government shall prepare estimates of the receipts and estimates of the expenditure of the State for each financial year and present them to the Dáil. This suggests that the Government, overseen by the Dáil, has the primary responsibility in relation to state finances. Article 29.4.1° provides:

> The executive power of the State in or in connection with its external relations shall in accordance with Article 28 of this Constitution be exercised by or on the authority of the Government.

It is thus clear that the conduct of foreign affairs is a matter for the Government. [12–02] However, beyond these tasks, it is not immediately clear what else falls within the executive power assigned to the Government. Both the legislative and the judicial power clearly identify certain tasks by reference to their character: the legislative power is about legislating—the laying down of general rules. The judicial power is about the administration of justice—applying those rules and resolving disputes. In contrast, there is no obviously clear core of the executive power. In this chapter, consideration will first be given to what other aspects of state activity might fall within the executive power. Then the case law on the Government's clear power in relation to external affairs will be examined. Finally, some consideration will be given to the structure and functioning of the Government.

Implicit Executive Powers

Not every power that happens to be exercised by members of the Government is part [12–03] of the executive power of the State. This point was made by Walsh J in *Murphy v Dublin Corporation* [1972] IR 215, in which the Supreme Court rejected a claim by the

Minister for the Environment to executive privilege over a document prepared in the context of the compulsory purchase proceedings under the Housing Act 1966. Walsh J commented as follows:

> Up to this I have been dealing with the case on the basis that the claim made was a claim of executive privilege not to produce a document. Such a claim is, of course, one made with reference to a document brought into being in the course of the carrying out of the executive functions of the State. It does not appear to me that this is such a document.
>
> The Housing Act, 1966 (at article 5 of the third schedule) constitutes the Minister for Local Government as the adjudicating authority upon the dispute which arises between the owner of the land which is made the subject of a compulsory purchase order and the local authority making such order. The executive powers of government of the State are vested in the Government: Article 28.2 of the Constitution. Different Departments of State are set up to deal with the business of executive government which are assigned to these Departments: see Article 28.12. The Government is collectively responsible for the Departments of State administered by the members of the Government assigned as Ministers over particular Departments (Article 28.4.2), and the powers, duties and functions of the Department are assigned to and administered by the Minister named.
>
> The function which is given to the Minister by article 5 of the third schedule of the Act of 1966 is not an executive power of the State assigned to his Department or a power which vested in the Government as an executive power from the State. He is *persona designata* in that the holder of the office of the Minister for Local Government is the person designated for that function. If the Oireachtas had so enacted, the Act could just as easily have assigned the function to the chairman of Córas Iompair Éireann, or to the chairman of the Electricity Supply Board, or to the head of any other State-controlled or semi-State corporation; if it had done so, there could be no question of such person seeking or being granted the executive privilege of non-production of the document in question. The fact that the Minister for Local Government was the person chosen by the Oireachtas to carry out this function does not *per se* confer upon the function the character of the exercise of the executive power of the State. The Act does not require that the person appointed by the Minister to conduct an inquiry should be a member of the Civil Service and, by choosing a member of the Civil Service to perform this function, the Minister cannot thereupon confer upon the function all the privileges or protections, if any, which hedge a civil servant in the business of the State assigned to him. [1972] IR 215, at 237–238.

[12–04] It is thus clear that just because a particular power happens to be exercised by a member of the Government does not make it an executive power. The Minister in question could be acting as a *persona designata* under some legislation. In contrast, executive powers—being powers that are envisaged by the Constitution—cannot depend for their existence on a legislative grant of power. Therefore, in order to identify what constitutes an implicit executive power, one cannot simply focus on the person who exercises that power. Not all powers exercised by the Government are executive powers. On the other hand, it would clearly be unconstitutional for a body other than the Government to exercise something that is an executive power.

[12–05] In *Haughey v Moriarty* [1999] 3 IR 1, at 32, the Supreme Court recognised the existence of implicit executive powers, Hamilton CJ commenting:

> Having regard to the sovereign and democratic nature of the State, each of the organs of government enjoy the powers normally exercised by such organs in a sovereign and democratic state and are not restricted to the powers expressly set forth in the provisions

of the Constitution. They are, however, subject to the provisions of the Constitution and in the exercise of such powers, are obliged to have regard to such provisions.

Casey has noted the suggestion that the legislative power is what is left of State power when legislative and judicial powers are subtracted. (James Casey, *Constitutional Law in Ireland* (3rd ed, Round Hall, Sweet & Maxwell, 2000), at 230–231). The suggestion referred to by Casey appears to be that of Halsbury to the effect that executive functions are "merely the residue of functions of government after legislative and judicial functions have been taken away". (*Halsbury's Laws of England* (4th ed, 1988, Vol 8, at [814]). This requires an answer to the question of what constitutes a function of government in the first place. For unless one knows what all the functions of government are, one cannot know what constitutes the residue left behind after legislative and judicial functions have been subtracted. It appears to follow from *Murphy v Dublin Corporation* [1972] IR 215 that not all functions that happen to be performed by organs of government are government functions. So some other method is required of working out what government functions are. [12–06]

Another method of identifying the parameters of the executive power is to adopt a broadly historical approach: a function that has traditionally been vested in the executive arm of government may be regarded as part of the executive power of the State. Morgan has considered both these approaches: [12–07]

> Is there any way in which one can offer more precise guidelines to determine the bounds "the executive power of the State." One suggestion – attractive by reasons of its apparent simplicity – is to reason that because there are ideas about what constitutes the legislative function and, more vaguely, the judicial function, one should simply subtract these from the total power of the State: "Other constitutions are equally laconic in this regard [*sc* a definition] and it has been suggested that so indefinite is the notion of executive power that it amounts to what is left when the legislative and judicial powers are subtracted." The difficulty with this suggestion is that, first, it merely moves the difficulty one place on, in that it shifts the problem on to a determination of what is a "power of government" Secondly, at the policy level, it would lead to an unrealistically wide concept of "the executive power of the State": for it would mean no "fourth" administrative arm of government (to use US parlance). In other words, it entirely overlooks the more difficult question of where the border-line runs, which marks off the executive power of the State from the remainder of the executive function.
>
> A more promising basis may be the broadly historical approach which is appealing in the case of the executive function because, as explained above in part I, the executive function is such barren ground for any analytical approach. This means simply that if a function has been traditionally vested in the executive arm of government, then this is some warrant for saying that it is to be regarded as coming within "the executive power of the State." And as regards whether a function has been traditionally vested in the executive, some assistance may be obtained from the British Prerogative. The Prerogative has always been said to embrace "those rights and capacities which the King alone enjoys in contradistinction to others." In other words, it is a specialised and reasonably well-defined compartment of the law (mainly the common law). David Gwynn Morgan, *The Separation of Powers in the Irish Constitution* (Round Hall, Sweet & Maxwell, 1997), at 271–272.

Morgan is correct to assert that the residual functions of government approach does not, in and of itself, answer the question as to the extent of executive power. As pointed out above, this approach raises an anterior question as to what constitute the functions [12–08] of government in the first place. This does not mean that it is a futile inquiry, however, because the question as to what constitute the functions of government may be answerable. If one can ascertain what the functions of government are, it does become possible to derive the parameters of the executive power. The functions of government would seem to be those powers that some organ must have in order for the community in question properly to be called a state. A community without a rule-making body or without an adjudicating body would not be considered a state. By the same token, a community must have certain other powers in order to be a state—control over its own external relations, for instance. These other powers that are neither legislative nor judicial in character are—presumptively at least—executive. This approach, which may be termed an "inherent state powers" approach, dovetails to a certain extent with Morgan's historical approach. For one's sense of what powers a state must have in order to be a state will necessarily be informed by the sorts of powers that have traditionally been accorded to the state, whether in the form of prerogatives or otherwise. To answer the question, therefore, of what constitutes an implicit executive power, one would ask oneself (a) is this a power which a state must have in order to be a state? (b) if so, has the Constitution failed to assign this power explicitly to any other organ of government? (c) if so and by way of confirmation, is this a power that was traditionally accorded to the executive arm of the state?

[12–09] The jurisprudence on immigration law is the closest that the courts have come to addressing these issues. In *Osheku v Minister for Justice* [1986] IR 733, the High Court considered the State's role in relation to immigration in the context of a challenge to the constitutionality of the Aliens Act 1935, as well as to certain orders made thereunder. Gannon J rejected this claim, in the process making the following observations about the State's power in relation to aliens:

> The control of aliens which is the purpose of the Aliens Act, 1935, is an aspect of the common good related to the definition, recognition, and the protection of the boundaries of the State. That it is in the interests of the common good of a State that it should have control of the entry of aliens, their departure, and their activities and duration of stay within the State is and has been recognised universally and from earliest times. There are fundamental rights of the State itself as well as fundamental rights of the individual citizens, and the protection of the former may involve restrictions in circumstances of necessity on the latter. The integrity of the State constituted as it is of the collective body of its citizens within the national territory must be defended and vindicated by the organs of the State and by the citizens so that there may be true social order within the territory and concord maintained with other nations in accordance with the objectives declared in the preamble to the Constitution. [1986] IR 733, at 746.

[12–10] Although Gannon J's judgment identified the power to deport aliens as being inherent in the State, it failed to specify in which organ of State the power resided. In *Re Article 26 and the Illegal Immigrants (Trafficking) Bill 1999* [2000] 2 IR 360, the Supreme Court characterised immigration control as "an inherent element of State sovereignty over national territory long recognised in both domestic and international law." This idea was further elaborated on by Hardiman J in *FP v Minister for Justice* [2002] 1 IR 164, at 168–169:

> The inherent nature of these powers in a state is demonstrated by their assertion over a vast period of history from the very earliest emergence of states as such, and its existence

in all contemporary states even though these vary widely in their constitutional, legal and economic regimes, and in the extent to which the rule of law is recognised.

In Ireland, the other common law jurisdictions, the member states of the European Union and elsewhere, this power is the subject of detailed regulation both by domestic law and by international instruments. There is a detailed provision directed at ensuring the constitutional and human rights of applicants for asylum.

All these cases clearly demonstrate that the control of immigration is a power of government, irrespective of whether it is explicitly mentioned in the Constitution or in statutory legislation. As the Constitution does not explicitly assign the function to any organ of government, one would expect—following the residual powers analysis developed above—that this power should be characterised as an executive power and vest in the Government. [12–11]

This question was addressed by a number of judges in *Laurentiu v Minister for Justice* [1999] 4 IR 26. Denham J, with whom Hamilton CJ agreed, characterised the separation of powers in the Constitution as being overlapping but, in general, function-driven. The control of aliens was historically a matter for the Government. The executive of a state, as an incident of sovereignty, had power and control over aliens. Denham J thus appears to have concluded that power and control over aliens was part of the executive power of the State. Keane J, again with whom Hamilton CJ agreed, provided a slightly different and more elaborate account of immigration-related powers. He characterised the power in the following way: [12–12]

> It cannot be too strongly emphasised that no issue arises in this case as to whether the sovereign power of the State to deport aliens is executive or legislative in its nature: it is clearly a power of an executive nature, since it can be exercised by the executive even in the absence of legislation. But that is not to say that its exercise cannot be controlled by legislation and today is invariably so controlled: any other view would be inconsistent with the exclusive law making power vested in the Oireachtas. The Oireachtas may properly decide as a matter of policy to impose specific restrictions on the manner in which the executive power in question is to be exercised: what they cannot do, in my judgment, is to assign their policy making role to a specified person or body, such as a Minister. [1999] 4 IR 26, at 93.

More recently, the Supreme Court has confirmed this characterisation of the executive power. Following the *Lobe* decision, the citizenship referendum in 2004 and alterations to the patterns of births to non-Irish parents within Ireland, the Minister for Justice decided that "rather than engaging in a case by case analysis, as a gesture of generosity and solidarity to the persons concerned, a general policy would be adopted of granting those persons (the non-Irish parents of Irish born children) permission to remain in the State provided that they fulfilled certain criteria." For this reason, the Minister established IBC/05, a scheme to allow otherwise unqualified immigrants seek leave to remain in the State. (For a full discussion of these issues, see chapter 9). For present purposes, it suffices to note how the Supreme Court characterised the scheme in *Bode v Minister for Justice, Equality and Law Reform* [2007] IESC 62, at 29–30: [12–13]

> The scheme was introduced by the Minister, exercising the executive power of the State, to address in an administrative and generous manner a unique situation which had occurred in relation to a significant number of foreign nationals within the State. However, those who did not succeed on their application under this scheme remained in the same

situation as they had been prior to their application. They were still entitled to have the Minister consider the Constitutional and Convention rights of all relevant persons.

The scheme enabled a fast, executive decision, giving a benefit to very many people. However, a negative decision in the IBC 05 Scheme did not affect any substantive claim for permission to remain in the State. In other words, an adverse decision to an applicant under the IBC 05 Scheme left the applicant in no worse position than he or she was prior to the application as no decision had been made on any substantive rights.

[12–14] The courts' case law on the immigration control power is consistent with the general analysis of the executive power suggested by Casey and Morgan. Traditionally, the immigration control power was exercised by the executive as a prerogative. Moreover, it is the sort of power that a state must have in order to be a state. It is thus an inherent state power which does not depend on positive legislation for its existence. As the Constitution has not expressly assigned the power to any organ of government (and as it is clearly neither legislative nor judicial in character), it must be part of the executive power, exercisable by the Government.

[12–15] However, it seems that implicit executive powers, such as the immigration control power, are only presumptively assigned to the Government: the Oireachtas can assume and exercise the immigration control power. In *Laurentiu v Minister for Justice* [1999] 4 IR 26, a majority of the Supreme Court held that s 5(1)(e) of the Aliens Act 1935 breached Art 15.2 of the Constitution in delegating legislative power to the Minister for Justice:

> The Minister may, if and whenever he thinks proper, do by order (in this Act referred to as an aliens order) all or any of the following things in respect either of all aliens or of aliens of a particular nationality or otherwise of a particular class, or of particular aliens, that is to say:
> (e) make provision for the exclusion or the deportation and exclusion of such aliens from Saorstát Éireann and provide for and authorise the making by the Minister of orders for that purpose.

[12–16] The Court's consideration of the delegated legislative power issue is addressed in chapter 11. In discussing the immigration control power, both Denham and Keane JJ made several references to how that power was regulated by legislation, without any suggestion that such legislation was illegitimate. Denham J referred to the legislature having "grasped the power over aliens from the executive" (at 63), without indicating that there was anything wrong in the Oireachtas assuming that function. Keane J said of the power to deport:

> It is clearly a power of an executive nature, since it can be exercised by the executive in the absence of legislation. But that is not to say that its exercise cannot be controlled by legislation and today is invariably so controlled: any other view would be inconsistent with the exclusive law making power vested in the Oireachtas. *ibid*, at 93.

[12–17] There are two possible justifications for this position. First, as implicit executive powers have not (by definition) been explicitly constitutionally assigned to any organ of government, there is less need for the courts to ensure that the Oireachtas does not assume control of the power. Secondly, as the Government is politically answerable to Dáil Éireann, it perhaps follows that it not legally as objectionable for the Oireachtas to assume powers that presumptively were assigned to the Government. In this regard, Morgan quotes an Australian commentator:

> It has been seen that the judicial power is subject to considerations different from those affecting the other two powers; the fact that the Constitution separated judicial power from legislative and executive powers does not mean that it separated the latter powers from each other. If, as the Constitution must have contemplated in introducing responsible government, Parliament can control the executive politically, there is little logic in maintaining that the executive retains a sphere of action legally independent from parliamentary control. Indeed, shortly after the passage quoted, the High Court in *Boilermakers* noted that the character of the separated powers 'is determined according to traditional British conceptions' and added: 'So understood difficulties as between executive and legislative power are not to be expected and none has arisen. Lane, *The Australian Federal System* (1979), at 65–66 quoted in David Gwynn Morgan, *The Separation of Powers in the Irish Constitution* (Round Hall, Sweet & Maxwell, 1997), at 278.

Somewhat more controversially, it appears that if the Oireachtas asserts (or even unsuccessfully attempts to assert) a legislative power over an area presumptively assigned to the Government, the executive power over that area is extinguished. This proposition appears to follow from the Supreme Court majority decision in *Lauretinu*. The Court's decision that s 5(1)(e) of the Aliens Act 1935 was unconstitutional implied that s 5(1)(e) became void in 1937. On one analysis, this could have resurrected the presumptive executive power over immigration control. However, the majority held that the proposed deportation of Mr Laurentiu by the Minister for Justice was invalid because of a lack of legislative authority. This suggests that the failure of the legislative power did not lead to the resurrection of the executive power. On the other hand, s 5(1)(e) was but one of a number of legislative provisions that purported to assume control over immigration and then delegate aspects of that control to the Minister for Justice. It may be that if the courts were faced with a total failure of the legislative power they might allow an executive power to be resurrected. To hold otherwise would— arguably—be to deprive the State of one of its inherent rights. [12–18]

Explicit Executive Power Over External Relations

The Government's power over external relations has received a reasonable amount of consideration from the courts. In *Boland v An Taoiseach* [1974] IR 338, the Supreme Court considered a challenge to the Sunningdale Agreement. By clause 5 of this agreement with the British Government, the Irish Government fully accepted and solemnly declared that there could be no change in the status of Northern Ireland until a majority of the people of Northern Ireland desired a change in that status. Mr Boland challenged this as a breach of Arts 2 and 3 of the Constitution which, at that stage, made a territorial claim to the whole island of Ireland. The Supreme Court rejected this argument, Budd J reasoning: [12–19]

> Viewing what is said by the Irish Government in clause 5 in the light of what is said in clause 3, it would appear to me that what is stated on behalf of the Irish Government is a statement of a matter of policy. It is for the Executive to formulate matters of policy. The judiciary has its own particular ambit of functions under the Constitution. Mainly, it deals with justiciable controversies between citizen and citizen or the citizen and the State and matters pertaining thereto. Such matters have nothing to do with matters of State

policy. Viewing the matter from another angle, as to the nature of any relief that could properly be claimed in proceedings of this nature, I ask whether it could be said that the Courts could be called upon to pronounce adversely or otherwise on what the Government proposed to do on any matter of policy which it was in course of formulating. It would seem that that would be an attempted interference with matters which are part of the functions of the Executive and no part of the functions of the judiciary. From a practical standpoint alone, what action would be open to the Courts? The Courts could clearly not state that any particular policy ought not to be pursued. [1974] IR 338, at 366.

The Court thus demonstrated its unwillingness to get involved where the issue raised concerned foreign policy, notwithstanding the apparent inconsistency between the Agreement and the Constitution.

[12–20] Some years later, however, the courts did exercise their power of judicial review over the Government's exercise of foreign policy, albeit in somewhat unusual circumstances. In *Crotty v An Taoiseach* [1987] IR 713, Mr Crotty objected to Ireland's proposed ratification of the Single European Act (the SEA). The SEA, a Treaty entered into by the then 12 Members of the European Economic Community, was the first significant amendment to the Treaty of Rome. (Further consideration is given to *Crotty* in chapter 14). Of relevance to present purposes, Mr Crotty objected to Title III of the SEA which essentially committed Ireland to endeavouring to formulate and implement a European foreign policy. The actual obligations, however, tended to be aspirational and consultative in character. A majority of the Supreme Court held that it would be unconstitutional for the Government to sign up to Title III. Walsh J reasoned as follows:

> [Title III impinges] upon the freedom of action of the State not only in certain areas of foreign policy but even within international organisations such as the United Nations or the Council of Europe. That latter effect of the Treaty could amount to the establishment of combinations within these organisations. In touching upon the maintenance of the technological and industrial conditions necessary for security the Treaty impinges upon the State's economic, industrial and defence policies. The obligation on the High Contracting Parties after five years to examine whether any revision of Title III is required does not give the Treaty a temporary character.
>
> I mentioned earlier in this judgment that the Government is the sole organ of the State in the field of international relations. This power is conferred upon it by the Constitution which provides in Article 29.4 that this power shall be exercised by or on the authority of the Government. In this area the Government must act as a collective authority and shall be collectively responsible to Dáil Éireann and ultimately to the people. In my view it would be quite incompatible with the freedom of action conferred on the Government by the Constitution for the Government to qualify that freedom or to inhibit it in any manner by formal agreement with other States as to qualify it....
>
> In enacting the Constitution the people conferred full freedom of action upon the Government to decide matters of foreign policy and to act as it thinks fit on any particular issue so far as policy is concerned and as, in the opinion of the Government, the occasion requires. In my view, this freedom does not carry with it the power to abdicate that freedom or to enter into binding agreements with other States to exercise that power in a particular way or to refrain from exercising it save by particular procedures, and so to bind the State in its freedom of action in its foreign policy. The freedom to formulate foreign policy is just as much a mark of sovereignty as the freedom to form economic policy and the freedom to legislate. The latter two have now been

curtailed by the consent of the people to the amendment of the Constitution which is contained in Article 29.4.3 of the Constitution. If it is now desired to qualify, curtail or inhibit the existing sovereign power to formulate and to pursue such foreign policies as from time to time to the Government may seem proper, it is not within the power of the Government itself to do so. The foreign policy organ of the State cannot, within the terms of the Constitution, agree to impose upon itself, the State or upon the people the contemplated restrictions upon freedom of action. To acquire the power to do so would, in my opinion, require a recourse to the people "whose right it is" in the words of Article 6 "... in final appeal, to decide all questions of national policy, according to the requirements of the common good." In the last analysis it is the people themselves who are the guardians of the Constitution. In my view, the assent of the people is a necessary prerequisite to the ratification of so much of the Single European Act as consists of title III thereof. [1987] IR 713, at 782–784.

Finlay CJ and Griffin J dissented, on the basis that Title III did not amount to the sort of "clear disregard" of the Constitution that would be necessary to justify court intervention. Finlay CJ reasoned: [12–21]

I do not consider that it has been established that adherence by the State to the terms of Article 30 of the SEA amounts, in the words of FitzGerald CJ, "to a clear disregard by the Government of the powers and duties conferred on it by the Constitution." Furthermore, I interpret the decision of Griffin J in *Boland v An Taoiseach* [1974] IR 338 as being consistent with the view already expressed by me that where an individual person comes before the Courts and establishes that action on the part of the Executive has breached or threatens to breach one or other of his constitutional rights that the Courts must intervene to protect those rights but that otherwise they can not and should not....

It was submitted that, whereas the plaintiff acknowledged that the Courts had no function to intervene with the Executive in the formation or statement of policy, either in external relations or in any other part of Government activity, a difference arose where the declaration of policy involved, as it is stated Article 30 of the SEA involves, a commitment to other states for consultation, discussion and an endeavour to coincide policies. I cannot accept this distinction. It appears probable that under modern conditions a state seeking cooperation with other states in the sphere of foreign policy must be prepared to enter into not merely vague promises but actual arrangements for consultation and discussion. I can find no warrant in the Constitution for suggesting that this activity would be inconsistent with the Constitution and would, as is suggested, presumably in each individual instance, require a specific amendment of the Constitution. [1987] IR 713, at 774–775.

The disagreement between the majority and the minority in *Crotty* largely turned on whether Title III really involved the Government ceding its power over foreign relations. Both the majority and the minority appeared to agree that it would be unconstitutional for the Government to cede its foreign relations power. This establishes an important principle of the separation of powers. It is ordinarily impermissible for one organ of government to cede its governmental power either to another organ of government or to an outside agency. The constitutionally authorised recipient of a power cannot give it away. [12–22]

The activist approach taken by the Supreme Court in *Crotty* did not lead to a generally activist approach in reviewing the executive power over external affairs. Shortly afterwards in *McGimpsey v Ireland* [1990] 1 IR 110, the Supreme Court was asked to strike down aspects of the Anglo-Irish Agreement; this Agreement included provisions [12–23] affirming the existing status of Northern Ireland and recognising that this status would only be changed with the consent of the majority of the population of Northern Ireland. Interestingly, the case was taken by two Northern Ireland Unionists who objected to the Agreement on Unionist grounds but sought to argue that it was inconsistent with Arts 2 and 3 of the Constitution. Finlay CJ summarised the effect of those Articles and rejected the plaintiffs' claim:

> With Articles 2 and 3 of the Constitution should be read the preamble, and I am satisfied that the true interpretation of these constitutional provisions is as follows:—
>
> 1. The re-integration of the national territory is a constitutional imperative (*cf* Hederman J in *Russell v Fanning* [1988] IR 505).
> 2. Article 2 of the Constitution consists of a declaration of the extent of the national territory as a claim of legal right.
> 3. Article 3 of the Constitution prohibits, pending the re-integration of the national territory, the enactment of laws with any greater area or extent of application or extra-territorial effect than the laws of Saorstát Éireann and this prohibits the enactment of laws applicable in the counties of Northern Ireland.
> 4. The restriction imposed by Article 3 pending the re-integration of the national territory in no way derogates from the claim as a legal right to the entire national territory.
>
> The provision in Article 3 of the Constitution contained in the words "and without prejudice to the right of the Parliament and Government established by this Constitution to exercise jurisdiction over the whole of that territory" is an express denial and disclaimer made to the community of nations of acquiescence to any claim that, pending the re-integration of the national territory, the frontier at present existing between the State and Northern Ireland is or can be accepted as conclusive of the matter or that there can be any prescriptive title thereby created and an assertion that there can be no estoppel created by the restriction in Article 3 on the application of the laws of the State in Northern Ireland. This is of course quite distinct from the extra-territorial effect of the laws of the State in respect of matters occurring outside the State for which persons are made answerable in the courts of the State.
>
> *The decision*
>
> With regard to these three main grounds of appeal I have come to the following conclusions.
>
> 1. *Inconsistency of the Agreement with Articles 2 and 3 of the Constitution*
>
> The main source of this submission was article 1 of the Anglo-Irish Agreement. In the course of his judgment Barrington J, after considering the details of that and other provisions of the Agreement, reached the following conclusion:—
>
>> "It appears to me that in article 1 of the agreement the two Governments merely recognise the situation on the ground in Northern Ireland, (paragraph (b)), form a political judgment about the likely course of future events, (paragraph (a)), and state what their policy will be should events evolve in a particular way (paragraph (c))."
>
> I find myself in agreement with this economical but precise analysis of the provisions of article 1. The learned trial judge then concluded that on any interpretation of the provisions of Articles 2 and 3 of the Constitution, these provisions of the Anglo-Irish Agreement were not in any way inconsistent with either of those two Articles. With that conclusion I am in complete agreement. There can be no doubt but that the only reasonable interpretation of article 1, taken in conjunction with the denial of derogation from sovereignty contained in article 2(b), of the Anglo-Irish Agreement is that it constitutes a recognition of the *de facto* situation in Northern Ireland but does so expressly without abandoning the claim to the re-integration of the national territory. These are essential ingredients of the constitutional provisions in Articles 2 and 3.

> This interpretation is not affected by the provisions of article 4(c) or article 5(c) nor are either of these two articles capable of any separate inconsistent interpretation. In so far as they accept the concept of change in the *de facto* status of Northern Ireland as being something that would require the consent of the majority of the people of Northern Ireland these articles of the Agreement seem to me to be compatible with the obligations undertaken by the State in Article 29.1 and 29.2 of the Constitution, whereby Ireland affirms its devotion to the ideal of peace and friendly co-operation and its adherence to the principles of the pacific settlement of international disputes. [1990] 1 IR 110, at 119.

The Court also rejected a *Crotty*-type claim that the Agreement fettered the Government's power to conduct foreign policy: [12–24]

> The submission made on this issue was that the terms of the Anglo-Irish Agreement were of similar character to the terms of the Single European Act which the decision of this Court in *Crotty v An Taoiseach* held to be inconsistent with the provisions of Article 29 of the Constitution.
>
> I am satisfied that this analogy is quite false. The Anglo-Irish Agreement is an agreement reached between two governments, both of whom have an acknowledged concern in relation to the affairs of Northern Ireland. It acknowledges that the Government of Ireland may make representations, put forward proposals, and try to influence the evolution of peace and order in Northern Ireland.
>
> The frameworks contained in the Agreement and structures created by it provide methods of carrying out these activities, it can be argued, in the manner most likely to make them effective and acceptable, namely, constant mutual discussion. The Government of Ireland at any time carrying out the functions which have been agreed under the Anglo-Irish Agreement is entirely free to do so in the manner in which it, and it alone, thinks most conducive to the achieving of the aims to which it is committed. A procedure which is likely to lead to peaceable and friendly co-operation at any given time must surely be consistent with the constitutional position of a state that affirms its devotion not only to the ideal of peace and friendly co-operation but to that ideal founded on international justice and morality.
>
> The basis of the decision of this Court in *Crotty v An Taoiseach* was that the terms of the Single European Act could oblige the Government in carrying out the foreign policy of the State to make the national interests of the State, to a greater or lesser extent, subservient to the national interests of other member states. I have no doubt that there is a vast and determining difference between the provisions of this Agreement and the provisions of the Single European Act as interpreted by this Court in *Crotty v An Taoiseach*. [1990] 1 IR 110, at 121–122.

In two more recent cases, litigants have sought to challenge the State's provision of Shannon airport as a stopover for US military aircraft. In *Horgan v Ireland* [2003] 2 IR 468, the plaintiff first argued that the provision of Shannon airport breached rules of customary international law on neutrality. In this regard, he relied on Art 29.3 of the Constitution which provides that Ireland accepts the generally recognized principles of international law as its rule of conduct in its relations with other states. Kearns J accepted that such customary rules could form part of Irish law simply by virtue of Art 29.3. This was in contrast to treaties which, according to Art 29.6, could only be part of domestic law if approved by the Oireachtas. Kearns J approved previous case law to the effect that principles of international law could only enter national law to the extent that they were not inconsistent with any constitutional, statutory or judge-made law. However, Kearns J took a deferential view as to the force any such customary rules might have in national law. He first followed the judgment of Fennelly J in *Kavanagh v* [12–25]

Governor of Mountjoy Prison [2002] 3 IR 97 in holding that the plaintiff did not gain justiciable rights under Art 29. He then considered an alternative argument:

> The court must nonetheless consider whether, in the event of its conclusion under (a) being found to be incorrect, the provisions of Articles 29.1 to 29.3 create binding obligations on the State whereby it must act in accordance with generally recognised principles of international law if and when same are identified.
>
> Obviously the Constitution must be given a harmonious interpretation, so that consideration of this issue of necessity involves considering not merely Article 29 of the Constitution but those other provisions of the Constitution which bear on the topic. These include Article 5: "Ireland is a sovereign, independent, democratic State". Article 6.1 provides that "all powers of government, legislative, executive and judicial, derive, under God, from the people ..." and Article 6.2 that "these powers of government are exercisable only by or on the authority of the organs of State established by this Constitution". Article 15 provides that the sole and exclusive power of making laws for the State is vested in the Oireachtas and that no other legislative authority has power to make laws for the State. Article 28 provides that the executive power of the State shall, subject to the provisions of the Constitution, be exercised by or on the authority of the government. Under Article 28.4.1 the Government is responsible to Dáil Éireann. Article 29.5.1 provides that "every international agreement to which the State becomes a party shall be laid before Dáil Éireann" and section 6 of that Article provides "no international agreement shall be part of the domestic law of the State save as may be determined by the Oireachtas".
>
> These Articles demonstrate that the Government, and the Government alone, can exercise the executive power of government. Its freedom and discretion is limited only by those exceptions as provided for in the Constitution.... [Kearns J then reviewed a number of dicta from *Crotty v An Taoiseach*.]
>
> The defendants attach considerable significance, and I think correctly, to the fact that nowhere in this portion of his judgment does Walsh J suggest that the executive is inhibited in its international relations or in the exercise of sovereign power by anything contained in Article 29.1 to 29.3. On the contrary, Walsh J emphasises repeatedly that the executive cannot be told, either externally or internally, how to conduct its relations with other states....
>
> If executive powers conferred on the executive by the Constitution can only be depleted or removed by referendum, can it ever be said that the wide discretion so accorded to it in foreign policy and conduct in international relations can be curtailed by the operation of some general principle of customary law? In my view, the answer can only be in the negative.
>
> In reaching this conclusion, I am mindful that the implications of holding to a contrary view would inevitably include the following:—
>
> (a) the conduct of international relations, normally characterised by discretion, flexibility and the ability to adapt to changing circumstances, would now be constrained by constitutional rules, the content of which would be impossible to determine without a court ruling;
>
> (b) the generally recognised principles of international law themselves are not defined by the Constitution, are not discernible by any process of interpretation of it and are liable to disputes;
>
> (c) although the conduct of international relations sometimes requires urgent action, there could be no certainty that any step would be consistent with the Constitution without prior declarations from the courts;
>
> (d) while it is acknowledged that the generally recognised principles of international law may change if the practice of states changes, Ireland alone would be freeze-bound by the pre-existing principles. It could not itself be a participant in any such

> change. Ireland would thus have to conform to a norm established by the practice of other states, but could not become one of the states whose conduct could change such a norm;
>
> (e) interpretation of the constitutional principles as argued for by the plaintiff would clearly permit a challenge to a war declared by the executive even with the approval of the Dáil under Article 29.3, on the grounds that it was a war that did not comply with justice and morality, or the principle of pacific settlement of disputes, under Articles 29.1 and 29.2.
>
> I accept and hold with the submission of the defendants that the provisions of Articles 29.1 to 29.3 are to be seen therefore as statements of principle or guidelines rather than binding rules on the executive....
>
> I accept the submission of the defendants that the Constitution is not to be treated like an ordinary statute. While it has precise legal provisions, it also has less precise provisions, such as those relating to fundamental freedoms. It also includes aspirational or declaratory provisions which cannot be made the subject matter of binding legal norms. The declarations contained in Articles 29.1 to 29.3 seem to me to fall into this last category. [2003] 2 IR 468, at 509–513.

Kearns J also rejected the plaintiff's claim that the provision of Shannon Airport amounted to participation in a war without the consent of Dáil Éireann: [12–26]

> The judicial organ does not decide an issue of "participation" in this context as a primary decision-maker. Under the Constitution, those decisions are vested in the Government and Dáil Éireann respectively. This is not a situation where the court can approach the matter on a "clean sheet" basis, ignoring decisions made by those constitutionally designated to do so within their own special areas of competence.
>
> The issue of "participation" is not a black and white issue. It may well ultimately be, as stated by the first defendant, a matter of "substance and degree". However, that is quintessentially a matter for the Government and the elected public representatives in Dáil Éireann to determine and resolve. In even an extreme case, the court would be still obliged to extend a considerable margin of appreciation to those organs of State when exercising their functions and responsibilities under Article 28.
>
> The plaintiff is effectively asking that the Dáil be told by this court to resolve afresh on a matter on which it has already resolved on the presumed basis that the court is better suited than the Dáil for deciding what constitutes "participation" in a war. The court cannot without proof of quite exceptional circumstances, accept this contention and accordingly, the plaintiff's claim under Article 28 of the Constitution also fails. [2003] 2 IR 468, at 515–516.

This judgment again marks out a high level of judicial deference to the Government's role in foreign affairs. In the light of this decision, the Supreme Court's conclusion in *Crotty* appears quite exceptional.

The meaning of Art 28.3 was again considered in *Dubsky v Government of Ireland* [2005] IEHC 442, in which Mr Dubsky challenged the Government's decision to allow US aircraft involved in the military action in Afghanistan to overfly the State and/or refuel in Shannon. Mr Dubsky argued that the assent of the Dáil was required for this activity. Macken J addressed the meaning of this provision: [12–27]

> On the question of the scope of the Article, I find that this is both wide and narrow. It is required to be met, in conformity with the constitutional process therein envisaged, on each and every occasion on which there is an intended declaration of war on the part of

the State or when there is an intended participation by the State in a war, whether declared by it or not. In that sense it is very wide. It is narrow in the sense that it requires such an assent only in those two circumstances, and not otherwise, as is clear from its wording. In the event there is no declaration of war, or no participation in a war, there is no requirement for any assent. The Article does not require that the Dáil determine that the State has not declared war. Equally it does not require that the Dáil determine that the State is not participating in a war.

[12–28] Mr Dubsky relied on the statement in Art 28.3.3° that—in that subsection—"time of war" includes a time when there is taking place an armed conflict in which the State is not a participant but in respect of which each of the Houses of the Oireachtas shall have resolved that, arising out of such armed conflict, a national emergency exists affecting the vital interests of the State. He contended that this demonstrated that "an armed conflict" was "a war". Macken J rejected this argument, on the basis that the purpose of the definition in Art 28.3.3° was to allow the Oireachtas to declare a state of emergency. Accordingly, the definition could not be carried across to the quite different context of Art 28.3.1°, nor used to determine the general meaning of "war".

[12–29] Macken J held that neither Mr Dubsky nor the Government had established that there was or was not a war in Afghanistan. As Mr Dubsky bore the onus of proof, however, he could not be successful in his claim. Nevertheless, she considered the issue of "participation" for the sake of completeness. She adopted Kearns J's statement in *Horgan* to the effect that there would have to be an "egregious disregard of constitutional duties" before the courts should intervene on the grounds of Art 28. Applying this exacting test, she was not satisfied that Mr Dubsky had demonstrated that Ireland was participating in the conflict in Afghanistan, even if that conflict were to be constitutionally characterised as a war.

Composition of the Government

[12–30] Article 28.1 provides that the Government shall consist of not fewer than seven but not more than 15 members. Article 28.5 provides that the Head of the Government, or Prime Minister, is called the "Taoiseach". The Taoiseach is obliged to keep the President generally informed on matters of domestic and foreign policy. The Taoiseach must nominate a member of the Government to be Tánaiste. Article 28.6.2° and Art 28.6.3° provide:

> 2° The Tánaiste shall act for all purposes in the place of the Taoiseach if the Taoiseach should die, or become permanently incapacitated, until a new Taoiseach shall have been appointed.
> 3° The Tánaiste shall also act for or in the place of the Taoiseach during the temporary absence of the Taoiseach.

[12–31] This provision was judicially considered in *Riordan v An Taoiseach* [1997] 3 IR 502, in which Mr Riordan objected to the fact that the Taoiseach and the Tánaiste had been out of the State simultaneously. The Supreme Court rejected this argument, O'Flaherty J reasoning:

> The applicant urges that the effective stewardship of the country requires that when the Taoiseach leaves the State then the Tánaiste automatically must act in the place of the

Taoiseach and take on his duties. In my view, it is manifestly absurd to suggest that with modern communications and the speed of travel by aircraft, it is necessary for the Taoiseach to hand over his duties as head of Government whenever he leaves these shores.

The duties of the Taoiseach outlined in the Constitution are to appoint and dismiss Ministers and to communicate between the Government and the President with regard to the summoning or dissolution of Dáil Éireann, the presentation of Bills for signing, Bills for an Article 24 procedure and general information on policy matters. Aside from these specific tasks, the Ministers and Secretaries Act, 1924, gives the Taoiseach's Department responsibility for all public services not allocated to another department. It should also be borne in mind that Article 28.4.2 of the Constitution declares that "the Government shall meet and act as a collective authority, and shall be collectively responsible for the Departments of State administered by the members of the Government". With such collective responsibility, the extent of the Taoiseach's specific legal powers and responsibilities are not that extensive. No doubt in practice he does have a vital role to play as the leader of the Government. With modern telecommunications and sensible delegation of authority combined with collective responsibility, the Taoiseach can exercise leadership of the Government while abroad in most instances.

The proper construction of Article 28.6.3 is that it authorises the Tánaiste to assume the functions of the Taoiseach on those occasions when the Taoiseach is "absent" in the sense of being temporarily unable to fulfil his functions either through illness, incapacity or because of his being incommunicado whether at home or abroad. It follows from this that as long as the Tánaiste is not himself absent in this specific sense during this time, he is complying with his constitutional duty regardless of whether he happens to be within the geographical confines of the State or not. Accordingly, the applicant's claim must be dismissed.

In upholding the judgment of the learned High Court judge, it is only requisite to say that the Constitution does not expressly prohibit the Tánaiste from leaving the State if the Taoiseach is also outside the State. This is to be contrasted with the situation of the President, who is the only citizen who requires the permission of any other body to leave the State since Article 12.9 of the Constitution provides: "The President shall not leave the State during his term of office save with the consent of the Government".

Further, I agree with the submission advanced on behalf of the respondent that there is no logic in implying a geographical or territorial dimension to the term "absence" (of the Taoiseach) in the sub-section in question. In circumstances where the Taoiseach is simply uncontactable, then the lawfulness and constitutionality of the Tánaiste's action *qua* the Taoiseach cannot depend on whether or not the Taoiseach is incommunicado within or without the territorial limits of the State. [1997] 3 IR 502, at 507–508.

Cabinet Confidentiality

In contrast to the very detailed procedures laid out for the Oireachtas, the Constitution is largely silent as to how the Government should function. One important issue that did arise for judicial consideration was the confidentiality of Cabinet discussions. The Beef Tribunal sought to question a former Government Minister about discussions in the Cabinet. The Attorney General objected to this line of questioning and sought a court injunction. In *Attorney General v Hamilton (No 1)* [1993] 2 IR 250, a narrow majority of the Supreme Court accepted that Cabinet discussions were absolutely confidential. Finlay CJ reasoned: [12–32]

> Article 28.4, subsections 1 and 2 of the Constitution impose upon the members of the Government separate though clearly related obligations, and these are:
>
> 1. They must meet as a collective authority.
> 2. They must act as a collective authority.

3. They must be collectively responsible for all the Departments of State and not merely the one which each of them administers.
4. They have as a Government a responsibility to Dáil Éireann.

These obligations involve some obvious, necessary, consequential duties. The first of those relevant to the issues arising in this appeal is the necessity for full, free and frank discussion between members of the Government prior to the making of decisions, something which would appear to be an inevitable adjunct to the obligation to meet collectively and to act collectively. The obligation to act collectively must, of necessity, involve the making of a single decision on any issue, whether it is arrived at unanimously or by a majority. The obligation to accept collective responsibility for decisions and, presumably, for acts of government as well, involves, as a necessity, the non-disclosure of different or dissenting views held by members of the Government prior to the making of decisions....

This somewhat extended analysis of the real meaning of the constitutional imperatives contained in Article 28.4.1 and 28.4.2 of the Constitution points, in my view, with very great force indeed, to the extreme desirability of the protection of complete confidentiality for the discussions of members of the Government meeting as such. To state that, however, does not of itself lead to a conclusion that the Constitution must be interpreted as affording such a protection. The obligation, however, to construe the Constitution in its entirety in the manner most likely to make it an effective instrument for the ordering of society and the governing of the Nation lends significant support to such a conclusion. [1993] 2 IR 250, at 266–267.

In 1997, the Constitution was amended to allow for some exceptions to this judicially enumerated principle of cabinet confidentiality:

28.4.3° The confidentiality of discussions at meetings of the Government shall be respected in all circumstances save only where the High Court determines that disclosure should be made in respect of a particular matter —

i. in the interests of the administration of justice by a Court, or
ii. by virtue of an overriding public interest, pursuant to an application in that behalf by a tribunal appointed by the Government or a Minister of the Government on the authority of the Houses of the Oireachtas to inquire into a matter stated by them to be of public importance.

[12–33] This Amendment, however, not only recognised exceptions to the principle of cabinet confidentiality but elevated that principle from a contested judicial interpretation to a textually stated constitutional rule. In 2003, the All Party Oireachtas Committee on the Constitution recommended that Art 28.4.3° be deleted and replaced with:

The confidentiality of discussions at meetings of the Government shall be respected save in such limited cases as may be prescribed by law.

This proposal has never been put to the People.

Contents – Chapter 13

The Judicial Power and the Courts

Introduction.	[13–01]
The Character of the Judicial Power.	[13–02]
The Reservation of the Judicial Power to the Courts	[13–10]
Oversight of Other Governmental Powers as an Aspect of the Judicial Power	[13–17]
The Majority's View of the Separation of Powers: A High Constitutional Value	[13–21]
The Majority's View on when the Courts may make a Mandatory Order	[13–25]
The Minority's View of the Separation of Powers: A Framework for Government	[13–32]
The Minority's View on when the Courts may make a Mandatory Order?	[13–35]
Difficulties in Both the Majority and Minority Positions	[13–39]
The Distinction between Commutative and Distributive Justice	[13–48]
The Separation of Powers and Competing Visions of Democracy	[13–52]
Judicial Impeachment.	[13–59]
The Constitutionality of the Impeachment Process	[13–61]
The Constitutionality of the Power to Compel Judges	[13–68]
The Direction to Produce the Computer.	[13–69]

Overview

Article 34 of the Constitution vests the judicial power in the courts. The courts have characterised the judicial power as involving the determination or ascertainment of the rights and liabilities of persons. On this basis, the courts have held that Tribunals of Inquiry and detentions of the mentally ill do not involve an exercise of the judicial power. Subject to certain exceptions, aspects of the judicial power cannot be taken away from the courts, for instance by the Oireachtas purporting to determine a case that was pending before the courts. The courts have a power to ensure that the other organs of government act constitutionally. However, the courts have held that they do not have the power, except in the most exceptional of cases, to grant mandatory injunctions directing other organs of government to protect constitutional rights in a particular way. In drawing this distinction, the courts have taken the view that the Constitution accords near total responsibility to the Oireachtas and the Government in respect of resource allocation matters. The courts see themselves as committed to ensuring that the process of democracy is fair rather than ensuring that the results of that process are fair. The latter task is better suited to the electorally mandated organs of government.

CHAPTER 13

The Judicial Power and the Courts

Introduction

Article 34.1 of the Constitution provides:

> Justice shall be administered in courts established by law by judges appointed in the manner provided by this Constitution, and, save in such special and limited cases as may be prescribed by law, shall be administered in public.

Thus the judicial power identified in Art 6 of the Constitution is assigned to the courts. The extent of this power is illustrated by Art 34.3.2°:

> Save as otherwise provided by this Article, the jurisdiction of the High Court shall extend to the question of the validity of any law having regard to the provisions of this Constitution, and no such question shall be raised (whether by pleading, argument or otherwise) in any Court established under this or any other Article of this Constitution other than the High Court or the Supreme Court.

The courts, therefore, have the power to ensure that the other organs of government act constitutionally, at least insofar as those organs of government act by passing laws. Three main issues arise for consideration in relation to the judicial power. First, what is meant by judicial power or the administration of justice? Second, what limits apply to the courts' power to ensure that other organs of government act constitutionally? Third, what powers to oversee the courts do the other organs of government possess?

The Character of the Judicial Power

In *McDonald v Bord na gCon* [1965] IR 217, Mr McDonald challenged the constitutionality of s 47 of the Greyhound Industry Act 1958. This provision empowered Bord na gCon to exclude a person from (a) being on any greyhound race track, (b) being at any authorised coursing meeting, (c) being at any public sale of greyhounds. Mr McDonald argued that this provision allowed the Board to exercise a judicial power. In the High Court, Kenny J held in favour of Mr McDonald:

> The relevant provisions of the Constitution restricting the exercise of judicial power by persons other than judges are:—
> Article 6.1: "All powers of government, legislative, executive and judicial, derive, under God, from the people...
> 2. These powers of government are exercisable only by or on the authority of the organs of State established by this Constitution."
> Article 34.1: "Justice shall be administered in public courts established by law by judges appointed in the manner provided by this Constitution."

Article 37: "Nothing in this Constitution shall operate to invalidate the exercise of limited functions and powers of a judicial nature, in matters other than criminal matters, by any person or body of persons duly authorised by law to exercise such functions and powers, notwithstanding that such person or such body of persons is not a judge or a court appointed or established as such under this Constitution."

Every exercise of the judicial power referred to in Article 6 is not an administration of justice for the Courts in this country have jurisdictions and powers the exercise of which is not an administration of justice and new powers and functions may be conferred on Courts and judges although the exercise of these powers and functions is not an administration of justice. Article 26 of the Constitution, dealing with the reference of Bills to the Supreme Court, is an example of this, for if the President refers a Bill to the Supreme Court for a decision as to whether it or any part of it is repugnant to the Constitution, it seems to me that the Supreme Court when deciding the matter is not administering justice but is giving an advisory opinion. Another example is the jurisdiction which the Court possesses over wards of Court...

It seems to me that the administration of justice has these characteristic features:
1. A dispute or controversy as to the existence of legal rights or a violation of the law;
2. The determination or ascertainment of the rights of parties or the imposition of liabilities or the infliction of a penalty;
3. The final determination (subject to appeal) of legal rights or liabilities or the imposition of penalties;
4. The enforcement of those rights or liabilities or the imposition of a penalty by the Court or by the executive power of the State which is called in by the Court to enforce its judgment;
5. The making of an order by the Court which as a matter of history is an order characteristic of Courts in this country...

It seems to me that an exclusion order made by the Board under section 47 of the Act of 1958 possesses all the characteristics I have mentioned of the administration of justice. The Board may make an exclusion order only when they are satisfied that there has been some violation of the code of conduct which should govern greyhound racing and this necessarily involves a controversy. An exclusion order is the imposition of a liability: it is significant that the Control Committee is given power by Article 31 (4) of the Greyhound Race Track (Racing) Regulations, 1960, to impose unlimited fines. The making of an exclusion order involves a determination (not subject to appeal) that the person against whom it is proposed to make it has been guilty of some disreputable behaviour or conduct. It was argued by counsel for the Attorney General that an exclusion order is not an order of the same nature as an injunction because an injunction is enforced by the executive authority of the State while an exclusion order can be enforced only by the licensee of a greyhound racing track or those acting under his authority. It was also said that the administration of justice is characterised by the enforcement of the Court's orders by the Court or by the executive power of the State which the Court invokes. It seems to me, however, that a body or tribunal which may lawfully execute its orders by physical force or authorise others to do so does not differ from a Court in this respect. The effect of an exclusion order is that the licensee of any greyhound race track or those authorised by him may remove by force the person against whom the order is made from the track and may thereby override his contractual rights. Lastly, an exclusion order seems to me to be similar in form and in effect to an injunction against trespass and such an injunction is an order characteristic of Courts in this country.

I am not dealing with a power of exclusion or a power to expel derived from contract but with a power derived solely from an Act of the Oireachtas. A rule deriving its force from contract and similar to that in section 47 of the Act of 1958 would not necessarily be invalid because it authorised the administration of justice by persons who were not Judges.

In my opinion, the Board when making an exclusion order under section 47 of the Act of 1958 is administering justice. [1965] IR 217, at 229–232.

Kenny J rejected the contention that the power conferred on the Board was the sort of limited judicial power that could be delegated in accordance with Art 37 of the Constitution. On appeal, the Supreme Court adopted the criteria suggested by Kenny J but concluded that s 47 had a different ambit. In particular, the Court reasoned that s 47 did not, of itself, operate to exclude a person: such an exclusion could only be validly effected by the appropriate landowner who would in any event have such a power as a landowner. As such, s 47 did not constitute an exercise of the judicial power. [13–03]

The criteria laid down by Kenny J have been applied in many cases, but the courts have been slow to conclude that any investigative or determinative power assigned to a statutory body is actually a judicial power that must be exercised by the courts. *Goodman International v Hamilton (No 1)* [1992] 2 IR 542 illustrates this principle. Following public concern, the Dáil by resolution established a Tribunal of Inquiry to investigate: [13–04]

> (i) Allegations concerning illegal activities, fraud and malpractice in and in connection with the beef processing industry made or referred to
> (a) in Dáil Éireann and
> (b) on a television programme transmitted on May 13th, 1991.
> (ii) Any matters connected with or relevant to the matters aforesaid which the Tribunal considers it necessary to investigate in connection with its inquiries into the matters mentioned at (i) above.

The Minister for Agriculture appointed Mr Justice Liam Hamilton, then President of the High Court, to be the sole member of the Tribunal. The Tribunal compiled a list of allegations, many of which were critical of Goodman International, a beef processing company. Goodman International argued that Dáil and Seanad Éireann could not validly direct the Tribunal to hold an inquiry into allegations the subject matter of current civil proceedings; allegations about private affairs of the parties; allegations relating to crimes already prosecuted in the criminal courts; allegations of criminal conduct. Goodman International contended that these were matters that lay within the scope of the judicial power and therefore could not be exercised by any body other than the courts. Although the Tribunal was chaired by a judge, it was not a court. [13–05]

The High Court and the Supreme Court both rejected these claims. Finlay CJ quoted Kenny J's test from *McDonald* and continued: [13–06]

> I am satisfied that with the possible exception of the first clause in this statement of the characteristics of the administration of justice, where it speaks of a controversy as to the existence of a violation of the law, the activities of this Tribunal of Inquiry fulfils none of the other fundamental conditions or characteristics of the administration of justice as laid down in this case. It can be argued, I suppose, that by reason of the inquisitorial nature of the Tribunal that it is not accurate to speak of a controversy concerning the violation of the law, but even if it is, and I would incline to the view that it would come within that category, that fact alone could not conceivably make the proceedings of this Tribunal an administration of justice within the meaning of Article 34 of the Constitution.
>
> In a sense, a positive test which can be applied, and very strikingly, is that contained in clause 5 of the principles laid down by Kenny J. It is no part, and never has been any part of the function of the judiciary in our system of law, to make a finding of fact, in effect, *in vacuo* and to report it to the Legislature. The courts do not even exercise a function of making, in cases between litigants, a finding of fact which does not have an effect on the determination of a right.

With regard to the suggestion that the findings of the Tribunal, if not an impermissible administration of justice by a body other than a court, is a usurpation of the activities of courts in cases where either civil cases are pending or may be instituted, it seems to me that again this submission arises from a total misunderstanding of the function of the Tribunal. A finding by this Tribunal, either of the truth or the falsity of any particular allegation which may be the subject matter of existing or potential litigation, forms no part of the material which a court which has to decide that litigation could rely upon. It cannot either be used as a weapon of attack or defence by a litigant who in relation to the same matter is disputing with another party rights arising from some allegation of breach of contract or illegal contract or malpractice. I am, therefore, satisfied that the submission under Article 34 must fail. [1992] 2 IR 542, at 589–590.

[13–07] In *Croke v Smith (No 2)* [1998] 1 IR 101, the Supreme Court considered the constitutionality of a provision of the Mental Treatment Act 1945. Section 162 of the Act allows a designated person to apply to a medical practitioner for a recommendation for the detention and reception of a person of unsound mind in a district mental hospital. Section 171 allows the resident medical superintendent of the hospital to make or refuse a chargeable patient reception order. If such an order is made, various persons connected with the hospital have the power to detain the patient and, if she escapes, to retake her within 28 days. The Act allows for patients who have recovered to be discharged. Further, a patient can be discharged where a friend or relative applies to take care of the patient. However, a patient cannot be discharged where the resident medical superintendent certifies that the patient is dangerous or otherwise unfit for discharge. This is subject to the right of the patient to appeal the certificate to the Minister for Health who may require the Inspector of Mental Hospitals to examine the patient. Having considered the report of the Inspector, the Minister may order the discharge of the patient. On the application of any person, the Minister may have a patient examined by two medical practitioners. If they certify that the patient can be released without any risk to himself or others, the Minister may order the discharge of the patient. There are various provisions that allow the Inspector raise issues as to the detention of patients. Further, the President of the High Court can order the Inspector to examine and report on the condition of a particular patient.

[13–08] The applicant again argued that the lack of judical involvement in the detention decision—in some form—rendered the original detention unconstitutional. The Court did not accept this proposition:

> Though the decision made by the registered medical practitioner to make a recommendation for a reception order may, and the decision of the medical superintendent to make a chargeable patient reception order will, result in the deprivation of the liberty of the person to whom they relate, such decisions cannot be regarded as part of the administration of justice but are decisions entrusted to them by the Oireachtas in its role of providing treatment for those in need, caring for society and its citizens, particularly those suffering from disability, and the protection of the common good. These decisions can only be made when it is established that the person to whom they relate is a person of unsound mind and is a proper person to be taken in charge and detained under care and treatment. These decisions can be set aside in the appropriate circumstances by the court upon an application for judicial review or upon complaint made to the High Court in accordance with Article 40.4.2 of the Constitution but this does not mean that the decisions are part of the administration of justice...

The Judicial Power and the Courts

> The Court is satisfied that the original detention of a person considered to be of unsound mind and a proper person to be taken charge of and detained under care and treatment pursuant to a chargeable patient reception order made in accordance with the provisions of section 171 of the Act is not part of the administration of justice and does not require a judicial inquiry or determination and that the sections which permit of such detention do not constitute an attack upon the personal rights of the citizen but rather vindicate and protect the rights of the citizens concerned by providing for their care and treatment and are not repugnant to the Constitution on this ground. [1998] 1 IR 101, at 115–116.

It thus appears that, regardless of what interests or rights may be at stake, there is no constitutional entitlement to judicial intervention. In dealing with another provision of the Act, the Court emphasised that the administrative decisions made under the Act would be subject to judicial review, but that there was no requirement for a judicial decision in order to deprive a person of her liberty: [13–09]

> The Court is satisfied that, in exercising the powers conferred on them by the Act of 1945, the resident medical superintendent and the Minister are not engaged in the administration of justice and that no judicial intervention is necessary or required unless they or either of them fail to comply with the requirements of fair procedures and constitutional justice or fail to have regard to the constitutional right to liberty of the patient.
>
> While it may be desirable that the necessity for the continued detention of the person, in respect of whom a chargeable patient reception order has been made, be subject to automatic review by an independent review board as provided for in the Mental Treatment Act, 1981, which has not, unfortunately, after fifteen years, been brought into force by the Minister, the failure to provide for such review in the Act has not been shown to render the provisions of the Act of 1945, and in particular section 172 thereof, constitutionally flawed because of the safeguards contained in the Act, which have been outlined in the course of this judgment. If, however, it were to be shown in some future case, that there had been a systematic failure in the existing safeguards, and that the absence of such a system of automatic review was a factor in such failure, that might cause this Court to hold that a person affected by such failure was being deprived of his constitutional rights.
>
> If they so fail, their decisions are subject to review by the High Court, whether by way of an application for judicial review or by way of a complaint made to the High Court in accordance with the provisions of Article 40.4.2 of the Constitution.
>
> The Court is further satisfied that the detention of a patient does not require automatic review by an independent tribunal because of the obligation placed on a person in charge of a district mental hospital to discharge a patient who has recovered. Inherent in this section is the obligation placed on the resident medical superintendent to regularly and constantly review a patient in order to ensure that he or she has not recovered and is still a person of unsound mind and is a proper person to be detained under care and treatment. If such review is not regularly carried out, in accordance with fair procedures and rendering justice to the patient then the intervention of the court can be sought because of the obligation placed on the resident medical superintendent to exercise the powers conferred on him by the Act in accordance with the principles of constitutional justice. There is no suggestion that such a review is not carried out. [1998] 1 IR 101, at 131–132.

The Reservation of the Judicial Power to the Courts

Once a power is characterised as a judicial power, however, the courts trenchantly defend the jurisdiction of the courts to exercise that power. This is particularly the case where the courts are already vested with a dispute. *Buckley v Attorney General* [1950] [13–10]

IR 67 is an early example of robust, judicial activism on the part of the Supreme Court. The case arose out of a dispute in relation to the distribution of certain funds belonging to Sinn Féin. In 1924, the honorary treasurers of Sinn Féin held a sum of over £8,500 as trustees. Disputes subsequently arose between them as to who was entitled to the money. Accordingly, they lodged the money in the High Court under the Trustee Act 1893. After the trustees died, the plaintiffs, who were members of Sinn Féin, brought an action against the Attorney General (as representative of the public) seeking a declaration that the money belonged to the Sinn Féin organisation and an order that the money be paid out to two of the plaintiffs as honorary treasurers of that organisation. While the action was pending before the High Court, the Oireachtas passed the Sinn Féin Funds Act 1947. Section 10 of that Act provided that all proceedings pending before the High Court in relation to the money should be stayed and that, upon application being made by the Attorney General, the High Court should strike out such proceedings. The Act also provided that the funds should be distributed in a particular way. The Attorney General duly applied to the High Court, but Gavan Duffy P struck out his application on the basis of the separation of powers:

> This application, made to the High Court of Justice by junior counsel on behalf of the Attorney General, raises a constitutional issue of transcendent importance, because the applicant challenges directly in this Court the primacy of the law in the legal domain, and the High Court of Justice of Ireland is the bastion of the Constitution of Ireland. The plaintiffs, in an action now awaiting trial in the High Court, are asserting a claim to specific funds, a right of property. The pleadings are closed and the action stands for hearing as soon as a Judge can be found, in the now congested state of our legal business, to set aside the necessary time for the hearing. I am not to-day concerned with the merits of the plaintiffs' claim, but with their right to have it tried by a Judge of the High Court. That the plaintiffs are citizens of this State is not disputed and, since the defendants have taken no steps to defeat the action under the Rules of Court as an irregular proceeding, I must assume that the action is properly constituted under the Rules, that it is neither frivolous nor vexatious, and that the statement of claim discloses a cause of action.
>
> Accordingly, this application to dismiss the action is made in an action wherein the plaintiffs appear to be exercising in a regular way their constitutional right of seeking from the High Court of Justice a determination according to law of a claim to property. The Constitution, laying down the fundamental rights, recognises the equality of all citizens before the law and declares that the State guarantees in its laws to respect the personal rights of the citizens; I think their right to hold property individually or collectively is one of the first of those rights. Yet I am solemnly asked in this Court, sitting as a Court of Justice, independent in the exercise of its functions, instead of giving a judicial decision in the action, to make a summary order, dismissing the pending action out of Court, without hearing the plaintiffs on the merits of their claim and without even listening to anything that they may have to say against this unprecedented application.
>
> Now, the Constitution, after declaring all powers of government, legislative, executive and judicial, to derive, under God, from the people, makes those powers exercisable only by or on the authority of the organs of State established by the Constitution. Then, after making provisions, of the type normal in a democracy, for the separation of powers, legislative, executive and judicial, the Constitution entrusts to the Courts of Justice, and to no other organ of State, the general power to administer justice and, subject to a right of appeal to the Supreme Court, it proceeds to invest the High Court of Justice with full original jurisdiction and power to determine all matters and questions; that is, of course, in legal proceedings duly brought before the High Court.
>
> Justice involves due process of law, and that law, to recall the monumental declaration of Daniel Webster, is the general law, a law which hears before it condemns, which

proceeds upon inquiry and renders judgment only after trial, so that every citizen shall hold his life, liberty, and property and immunities under the protection of the general rules which govern society; arbitrary executions of power under the forms of legislation are thus excluded and no organ of the State can deny to the citizens the equal protection of the law.

I assume the Sinn Féin Funds Act, 1947, under which this application is made, to have been passed by the Legislature for excellent reasons, and, as a matter of course, I give to the Oireachtas all the respect due to the legislative assembly of the nation; but I cannot lose sight of the constitutional separation of powers. This Court cannot, in deference to an Act of the Oireachtas, abdicate its proper jurisdiction to administer justice in a cause whereof it is duly seized. This Court is established to administer justice and therefore it cannot dismiss the pending action without hearing the plaintiffs; it can no more dispose of the action in that arbitrary manner at the instance of the Attorney General than it could give judgment for the plaintiffs without hearing the Attorney General against their claim. Moreover, this action is not stayed unless and until it is stayed by a judicial order of the High Court of Justice; the payment out of the funds in Court requires a judicial order of this Court, and under the Constitution no other organ of State is competent to determine how the High Court of Justice shall dispose of the issues raised by the pleadings in this action. [1950] IR 67, at 69–71.

The Supreme Court came to the same conclusion in somewhat less trenchant terms: [13–11]

> There is another ground on which, in our view, the Act contravenes the Constitution. We have already referred to the distribution of powers effected by Article 6. The effect of that article and of Articles 34 to 37, inclusive, is to vest in the Courts the exclusive right to determine justiciable controversies between citizens or between a citizen or citizens, as the case may be, and the State. In bringing these proceedings the plaintiffs were exercising a constitutional right and they were, and are, entitled to have the matter in dispute determined by the judicial organ of the State. The substantial effect of the Act is that the dispute is determined by the Oireachtas and the Court is required and directed by the Oireachtas to dismiss the plaintiffs' claim without any hearing and without forming any opinion as to the rights of the respective parties to the dispute. In our opinion this is clearly repugnant to the provisions of the Constitution, as being an unwarrantable interference by the Oireachtas with the operations of the Courts in a purely judicial domain. [1950] IR 67, at 84.

A similar, albeit less stark, conclusion was reached in *Maher v Attorney General* [1973] [13–12] IR 140, in which the Supreme Court held that s 44(2)(a) of the Road Traffic Act 1968 was unconstitutional. This section provided that a certificate prepared by a designated, registered medical practitioner to the effect that a certain level of alcohol was present in a person's blood would be "conclusive evidence that, at the time the specimen was taken or provided, the concentration of alcohol in the blood of the person from whom the specimen was taken or by whom the specimen was provided was the specified concentration of alcohol." The Court held that this was an impermissible intrusion on the judicial power, Fitzgerald CJ reasoning:

> In the result it precludes the District Justice from forming any other judgment in respect of this vital ingredient of the prosecution's case: he is bound under the terms of the statutory provision to proceed and act as if this had been his own judgment on the matter. It was clearly intended by the Oireachtas that this should be the effect of the evidence because, when one compares it with the phrase "until the contrary is shown" in the following paragraph and the same phrase in the preceding sub-section, it is clear that the object of the statutory provision was to remove this element altogether from the area of

contestable facts. In effect it means that an accused person is not free to contest the determination of the concentration of alcohol set out in the certificate. The best he could hope to do would be to endeavour to show that the procedure prescribed for the making of the analysis had not been followed in accordance with the statute and the regulations made under the statute....

So far as this important element of the offence is concerned, the result is that, provided the regulations have been complied with, the evidence furnished by the certificate from the Bureau is incontestable and therefore the District Justice is precluded from exercising his judgment in respect of this matter and the accused is precluded from challenging it.

The administration of justice, which in criminal matters is confined exclusively by the Constitution to the courts and judges set up under the Constitution, necessarily reserves to those courts and judges the determination of all the essential ingredients of any offence charged against an accused person. In so far as the statutory provision in question here purports to remove such determination from the judges or the courts appointed and established under the Constitution, it is an invalid infringement of the judicial power. This principle has already been clearly established by the decisions of this Court.... As far as this case is concerned, the offending element of the provision is the evidential conclusiveness given to the certificate. If the word "conclusive" had not been in the paragraph, it would not be open to the objection which has now been taken. By giving the certificate this evidential quality, the Oireachtas has invalidly impinged upon the exercise of the judicial power and to that extent the statutory provision is invalid having regard to the provisions of the Constitution. [1973] IR 140, at 145–146.

[13–13] The courts have taken a similar view of the judicial function in relation to sentencing. In *Deaton v Attorney General* [1963] IR 170, the Supreme Court held that s 186 of the Customs Consolidation Act 1876 was unconstitutional insofar as it purported to allow the Revenue Commissioners to elect which of the penalties prescribed by the section was to be imposed by the District Court upon conviction. Ó Dálaigh CJ delivered the judgment of the Court:

There is a clear distinction between the prescription of a fixed penalty and the selection of a penalty for a particular case. The prescription of a fixed penalty is the statement of a general rule, which is one of the characteristics of legislation; this is wholly different from the selection of a penalty to be imposed in a particular case. It is here that the logic of the respondents' argument breaks down. The Legislature does not prescribe the penalty to be imposed in an individual citizen's case; it states the general rule, and the application of that rule is for the Courts. If the general rule is enunciated in the form of a fixed penalty then all citizens convicted of the offence must bear the same punishment. But if the rule is stated by reference to a range of penalties to be chosen from according to the circumstances of the particular ease, then a choice or selection of penalty falls to be made. At that point the matter has passed from the legislative domain. Traditionally, as I have said, this choice has lain with the Courts. Where the Legislature has prescribed a range of penalties the individual citizen who has committed an offence is safeguarded from the Executive's displeasure by the choice of penalty being in the determination of an independent judge. The individual citizen needs the safeguard of the Courts in the assessment of punishment as much as on his trial for the offence. The degree of punishment which a particular citizen is to undergo for an offence is a matter vitally affecting his liberty; and it is inconceivable to my mind that a Constitution which is broadly based on the doctrine of the separation of powers—and in this the Constitution of Saorstát Éireann and the Constitution of Ireland are at one—could have intended to place in the hands of the Executive the power to select the punishment to be undergone by citizens. It would not be too strong to characterise such a system of government as one of arbitrary power. [1963] IR 170, at 182–183.

The implication of this decision appears to be that it is competent for the Oireachtas to stipulate a penalty for a particular offence, but that it is not competent for the Oireachtas to allow the Government (or an administrative organ of state) to select between a range of penalties. Where the Oireachtas has legislated to provide for a range of possible penalties, the choice between those must be a matter for the courts. [13–14]

The courts developed a practice of imposing sentences subject to review. Under this practice, where a person was sentenced to a term of imprisonment, the sentence would include within it a term to the effect that the convict would re-appear before the court on a certain date. At that time, the court would review the situation of the convict and consider whether it was appropriate to suspend some or all of the remainder of the sentence. The difficulty with this approach was that it seemed to involve the courts in commuting or remitting sentences in contravention of Art 13.6 of the Constitution: [13–15]

> The right of pardon and the power to commute or remit punishment imposed by any court exercising criminal jurisdiction are hereby vested in the President, but such power of commutation or remission may also be conferred by law on other authorities.

Section 23 of the Criminal Justice Act 1951 assigned the power to remit or commute sentences to the Minister for Justice. While the practice of reviewing sentences ensured that those convicted did serve some prison sentence and allowed for a review of those on programmes (such as drug treatment programmes) which might be relevant to whether they should be released, there were considerable judicial doubts over the appropriateness of the procedure. In *People (DPP) v Finn* [2001] 2 ILRM 211, the Supreme Court (albeit by way of *obiter dicta*) expressed its firm view that the practice should cease. Keane CJ delivered the judgment of the Court: [13–16]

> There can be no doubt that, in the opinion of some judges, the review procedure is an important mechanism which helps to ensure the rehabilitation of convicted persons. There are, however, two important aspects of such sentences which must be borne in mind in considering their legal validity.
>
> First, there is the factor... that a sentence in this form is, in effect, an invasion by the judicial arm of government of the executive domain which is not authorised by law. The court recognises the force of the view expressed by Walsh J in *Aylmer* that a trial judge, in imposing a sentence in this form, does not in any way interfere with the statutory power of the Minister for Justice to commute or remit the sentence pursuant to section 23 of the Criminal Justice Act 1951. It is undoubtedly the case that, where such a sentence is imposed, there is in law nothing to prevent the Minister for Justice from exercising his power of commutation or remission during the period between the imposition of the sentence and the review date.
>
> However, the essential legal frailty of the review procedure is not that it deprives the executive of its statutory power to commute or remit the sentence during that period. It is that, when the review date arrives and the Central Criminal Court or the Circuit Court, on being satisfied that the relevant conditions have been met, suspends the balance of the sentence and orders the release of the convicted person, it is in substance exercising the power of commutation or remission which the Oireachtas has entrusted exclusively to the government or the Minister for Justice to whom the power may be delegated. The minister cannot, of course, in exercising that power do what the court purports to do at the review stage, *ie* impose a suspended sentence which would normally involve the convicted person being returned to prison on foot of the order of a court in the event of his being convicted of further offences or breaking other conditions attached to the sentence. But if one looks

to the substance of the order made by the court at the review date it is clearly an order which releases the convicted person before the completion of the sentence which the judicial arm of government considered appropriate at the sentencing stage and must, accordingly, be regarded as, in all but name, the exercise by the court of the power of commutation or remission which, during the currency of the sentence imposed by the court, is vested exclusively in the executive.

The making of such orders is not merely inconsistent with the provisions of section 23 of the 1951 Act: it offends the separation of powers in this area mandated by Article 13.6 of the Constitution. That provision expressly vests the power of commutation or remission in the President but provides that the power may also be conferred *by law*, on other authorities. Since under Article 15.2.1° of the Constitution the sole and exclusive power of making laws for the State is vested in the Oireachtas, it was for the legislative arm alone to determine which authorities other than the President should exercise that power. In enacting section 23 of the Criminal Justice Act 1951, the Oireachtas conferred the power of commutation or remission on the government or, where it delegated its power, the minister.... It would seem to follow that the remission power, despite its essentially judicial character, once vested under the Constitution in an executive organ, cannot, without further legislative intervention, be exercised by the courts. That, as has been noted, has been done in the case of certain drug offences by the Criminal Justice Act 1999.

It is also, of course, open to the Oireachtas to provide by legislation, as has been done in other countries, for the regular review of sentences by a parole board and such an approach might well be consistent with modern penological principles. These again, however, are entirely matters for the legislature and not within the competence of the courts, having regard to Art 13.6, to determine. [2001] 2 ILRM 211, at 231.

Oversight of Other Governmental Powers as an Aspect of the Judicial Power

[13–17] As demonstrated by both this chapter and the previous two chapters, discussions of the various governmental powers quickly develop into a discussion about the boundaries between those powers. In relation to the legislative power, the most vexed question is the extent to which that power can be exercised by bodies other than the Oireachtas. *Buckley* is an example of the courts protecting the judicial power from legislative encroachment. It quickly becomes clear, however, that the Irish Constitution does not establish a rigid separation of powers. Instead, certain types of power seem to be presumptively assigned to particular organs of government, but each organ of government has some power to check or balance another organ of government.

[13–18] Thus Art 34.3.2° assigns to the courts the power of ensuring that no law is unconstitutional. This would appear to apply to all laws made by the Oireachtas or by delegated legislative bodies, but what about the actions of the other organs of State that are not "laws"? In *Boland v An Taoiseach* [1974] IR 338, at 362, Fitzgerald CJ identified a power on the part of the courts to review Government action:

> Consequently, in my opinion, the Courts have no power, either express or implied, to supervise or interfere with the exercise by the Government of its executive functions, unless the circumstances are such as to amount to a clear disregard by the Government of the powers and duties conferred on it by the Constitution.

Although this was stated as a negative proposition, it implies that the courts have a power (and perhaps a duty) to intervene where the Government acts in clear disregard of the Constitution, whatever that may mean. This jurisdiction was exercised by a majority of the Supreme Court in *McKenna v An Taoiseach (No 2)* [1995] 2 IR 10, holding that the Government's funding of one side of a referendum campaign was unconstitutional.

The question of the boundaries between the different organs of government came into sharp focus in two cases in 2001: *Sinnott v Minister for Education* [2001] 2 IR 545 and *TD v Minister for Education* [2001] 4 IR 259. An issue that potentially arose in each case was whether the courts had the power to grant a mandatory order to enforce constitutional rights. In *Sinnott*, a majority of the court held that Mr Sinnott's right to education had expired when he was 18. Accordingly, there was no need to consider whether the courts had the power to enforce such a right. Nevertheless, Hardiman J did address that issue, presaging many of his comments in *TD*. In *TD*, the right at issue was derived from Art 42.5 and Art 40.3 of the Constitution: a child's right to positive state intervention where her parents have failed. In the case of Mr TD, the intervention required was a secure detention centre. The High Court had granted an order requiring the Minister for Education to implement his policy to build a particular detention centre. The State appealed to the Supreme Court, conceding the existence of the right but querying the power of the courts to make such mandatory orders. By a majority of four to one, the Supreme Court held that such an order should only be made in the most exceptional of circumstances; the facts of this case did not reach that threshold. The Court addressed a number of issues which shall be considered before the more general academic debate will be canvassed. [13–19]

There is little agreement in *TD* as to the status of the separation of powers. This disagreement is most starkly illustrated by the judgments of Hardiman and Denham JJ. Hardiman J viewed the separation of powers as a superordinate constitutional value, capable of trumping any other constitutional concern, including most pertinently a concern for the efficacy of constitutional rights. Denham J viewed the separation of powers as a subordinate constitutional value, trumped by a concern for the efficacy of constitutional rights. [13–20]

The Majority's View of the Separation of Powers: A High Constitutional Value

Hardiman J, in the leading majority judgment, described the separation of powers as a "high constitutional value", as important as the fundamental rights invoked by the plaintiff in this case. Not only was the separation of powers a high constitutional value, it was, in Hardiman J's view, a precisely delineated constitutional doctrine. He argued that the separation of powers was rigid, not functional. The Constitution created three equal powers and distributed them between the three organs of government. Although the Constitution created a number of mutual checks and balances, it gave to no organ of government a general supervisory power over the other: [13–21]

> I believe that all of the suggested foundations for a jurisdiction to make an order of the kind in question here are based on a misapprehension of the powers of the superior courts in relation to those of the other organs of government. The Constitution, in my view, does not attribute to any of the branches of government an overall, or residual, supervisory power over the others. It creates three equal powers, none of which is generally dominant. Equality of the powers can only operate in practice on the basis that each has its discrete remit. Since each of the powers, legislative, executive and judicial must "fit harmoniously into the general constitutional order and modulation" as Henchy J said in *The People v O'Shea* [1982] IR 384, the Constitution provided specifically for certain mutual checks

and balances. These include the power of the courts to ensure that legislation is consistent with the Constitution, the power of the legislature to remove a judge of the superior courts and the power of the executive to tender binding advice to the President as to the appointment of judges.

The existence of these specific powers does not, in my view, suggest that the separation of powers is in any general sense a porous one, still less that a court, or any other organ of government, can strike its own balance, in a particular case, as to how the separation of powers is to be observed.

I believe, with great respect to the High Court judgment, that its view of the separation of powers is unduly courts centred. The proposition that "The court has to attempt to fill the vacuum which exists by reason of the failure of the legislature and the executive" seems to me to come close to asserting a general residual power in the courts, in the event of a (judicially determined) failure by the other branches of government to discharge some (possibly judicially identified) constitutional duty. If this were accepted I believe it would have the effect of attributing a paramountcy to the judicial branch of government which I do not consider the Constitution vested in it....

The terms of Article 40.3.1° involve the State in a guarantee to "respect, and, as far as practicable, by its laws to defend and vindicate the personal rights of the citizen". This guarantee is given by *the State* and not uniquely by any one of the organs of state. It is a guarantee to respect, vindicate and defend these rights "by its laws". Since the Constitution is the fundamental law of the State, it follows that the solemn task of respecting, vindicating and defending these rights is to be undertaken by all the organs of State, each in its constitutionally mandated and delimited sphere....

In effect, each organ of government shows respect for the others by recognising the boundaries [between them]. I do not believe that the boundaries are porous or capable of being ignored or breached because one organ rightly or wrongly considers that another organ is unwise or inadequate in the discharge of its own duties. It is easy to imagine circumstances in which a hypothetical legislature or executive might be annoyed or frustrated or even outraged by a judicial decision, or even by the very idea that the judiciary would decide a particular issue, as happened in *Buckley and Others (Sinn Féin) v Attorney General and Another*. But it is now an axiom of our constitutional dispensation that, assuming the decision to be properly within the judicial sphere, the other organs cannot remove the matter in issue from that sphere or set aside the decision in a *lis inter partes*. There is an obvious corollary of this in relation to matters properly within the sphere of the legislature or executive....

One of the reasons why recognition of these boundaries is important is that a failure to recognise them can bring the courts into unwarranted and unjustifiable conflict with the political branches of government. If an order of the sort in question here could properly be made, it could properly be enforced by the ordinary procedures for the enforcement of court orders in civil matters including contempt procedures. Assuming the order to be properly made, if a relevant minister changed his or her policy without court sanction, or was tardy in implementing a policy enshrined in a courts order, the court might proceed to consider the question of contempt. But this would be a wholly unwarranted and unconstitutional proceeding because, in the words of Finlay CJ, at 499, of the report in *MhicMhathúna v. Attorney General*:

> "... matters within the field of national policy, to be decided a combination of the executive and the legislature, ... cannot be adjudicated upon by the courts."

Accordingly, the fundamental requirement for constitutional harmony and modulation imperatively requires that the courts, as well as the other branches of government, recognise and observe the boundaries between them. [2001] 4 IR 259, at 367–371.

[13–22] Although Hardiman J's basic idea that the separation of powers is rigid and non-porous was both plausible and coherent, the concepts became somewhat confused when he stipulated that the courts could not determine how the separation of powers was to be observed. If the separation of powers is a constitutional value, it follows that its interpretation is a matter for the courts. In deciding whether a person's constitutional rights have been illegitimately breached, a court must identify the meaning of, *inter alia*, the separation of powers. Of course, a court does not so much "strike its own balance" as interpret the Constitution's balance; nevertheless, the courts do appear to have a residual power as to what the separation of powers requires. Indeed, in determining what the separation of powers required in the context of this case, Hardiman J was exercising just such a power. It therefore seems wrong to assert that the courts have no power to stipulate how the separation of powers should be observed.

A more convincing element of Hardiman J's judgment is his suggestion that the separation of powers precludes any organ of government having a residual power to step into the sphere of another organ of government where it feels that the other organ is failing in its constitutional duties. This conception of the separation of powers requires a reasonably clear understanding of what each power of government entails. Hardiman J provided little guidance in this regard, although he did refer to powers which were quintessentially judicial (such as the power to order habeas corpus). This suggests that he considered what was involved in the legislative, executive and judicial powers respectively to be self-evident or, in more fashionable language, axiomatic.

[13–23]

Hardiman J's conception of the separation of powers is broadly replicated in the decisions of Keane CJ and Murray J. Murray J considered as central to the separation of powers the idea that no one organ of government should have "paramountcy":

[13–24]

> As I have indicated, one of the fundamental objects of the concept of the separation of powers is that no one of the three organs of government is paramount in the exercise of State power.... It follows that in order to avoid the paramountcy of one organ of State, each must respect the powers and functions of the other organs of State as conferred by the Constitution. Each must exercise its powers within the competence which it is given by that Constitution. The Oireachtas cannot exercise a judicial function attributed to the courts, no more than the courts may exercise a function attributed to the Oireachtas. [2001] 4 IR 259, at 331.

In Murray J's view, there was a crucial difference between the courts reviewing how another organ of government exercised its powers and the courts taking on the exercise of that power themselves. The question arises, however, as to whether the courts granting mandatory orders in exceptional circumstances really amounts to the courts assuming another power of government for themselves.

The Majority's View on when the Courts may make a Mandatory Order

It does not necessarily follow from the status of the separation of powers as a high constitutional value, nor even from a conception of the separation of powers as rigid and exhaustively enunciated constitutional rules, that the courts may never grant a mandatory order to enforce a citizen's constitutional rights. The general conception of the separation of powers, as set out by Keane CJ and Hardiman and Murray JJ, needs to ground a more practical test, which test can then be used to assess the legitimacy of mandatory orders in particular circumstances. The most focused consideration of this issue is found in the judgment of Murray J, with whom Hardiman J expressly agrees on this point.

[13–25]

[13–26] For Murray J, the crucial distinction—as outlined above—lies between the courts reviewing another organ's exercise of its power and the courts exercising that other organ's power themselves. In this regard, Murray J rejected the argument, advanced by Kelly J in the High Court and in the earlier case of *DB v Minister for Justice* [1999] 1 IR 29 to the effect that the Court was not making policy but merely requiring the Executive to follow its own policy. Murray J reasoned that the incorporation of a policy programme into a High Court order effectively took the policy out of the hands of the Executive. The Court became the arbiter and final decision-maker of the policy, deciding which variations of the policy might be permitted. For these reasons, the order made by the High Court in this case represented judicial exercise of executive power, rather than judicial review of executive power. The High Court order was thus illegitimate.

[13–27] That said, there could be mandatory orders which did not go so far. Murray J stated a formula to test the legitimacy of such orders:

> [A] mandatory order directing the executive to fulfil a legal obligation (without specifying the means or policy to be used in fulfilling the obligation) *in lieu* of a declaratory order as to the nature of its obligations could only be granted, if at all, in exceptional circumstances where an organ or agency of the State had disregarded its constitutional obligations in an exemplary fashion. In my view the phrase "clear disregard" can only be understood to mean a conscious and deliberate decision by the organ of state to act in breach of its constitutional obligation to other parties, accompanied by bad faith or recklessness. A court would also have to be satisfied that the absence of good faith or the reckless disregard of rights would impinge on the observance by the State party concerned of any declaratory order made by the court. [2001] 4 IR 259, at 337.

[13–28] Hardiman J expressly approved of this test, noting that only "absolutely exceptional circumstances" would justify the making of such an order. He emphasised that a mandatory order might direct the fulfilment of a manifest constitutional obligation, but could not specify the means or policy to be used in fulfilling the obligation. To do so would, presumably, breach Murray J's distinction between review and exercise of another organ's power of government. Finally, Hardiman J reiterated the exceptionally exceptional circumstances in which such an order could be made:

> Such an order, in my view, could only be made as an absolutely final resort in circumstances of great crisis and for the protection of the constitutional order itself. I do not believe that any circumstances which would justify the granting of such an order have occurred since the enactment of the Constitution 64 years ago. I am quite certain that none are disclosed by the evidence in the present case. [2001] 4 IR 259, at 372.

[13–29] The "clear disregard" test is borrowed from other cases in which the courts have reviewed the exercise of executive power. This test, as noted above, was employed in the decision of Fitzgerald CJ in *Boland v An Taoiseach*:

> Consequently, in my opinion, the Courts have no power, either express or implied, to supervise or interfere with the exercise by the Government of its executive functions, unless the circumstances are such as to amount to a clear disregard by the Government of the powers and duties conferred on it by the Constitution. [1974] IR 338, at 362.

[13–30] This formula of words was adopted by Hamilton CJ in *McKenna v An Taoiseach (No 2)* [1995] 2 IR 10. The novelty of *TD* lies not with the formula of words but rather with Murray and Hardiman JJ's interpretation that "clear disregard" meant conscious and deliberate disregard. This interpretation is far from obvious. A less strained interpretation is that "clear disregard" requires the courts to be cautious about reviewing executive action, intervening only where a breach of constitutional requirements has been unambiguously established. The judgments in *TD* do not specify whether this interpretation of "clear disregard" is of general application to the courts' review of executive action or of limited application to the question of whether the courts can grant a mandatory order against the executive.

The majority position may be summarised as follows. The separation of powers is a fundamental constitutional doctrine. Each organ of government exercises its own type of powers and only interacts with other organs of government where it has explicit authorisation from the Constitution to do so. The courts have a power to review how the other organs of government exercise their powers; the courts have no power to exercise those other powers themselves. It follows from this that a mandatory order which determines policy for the executive branch is illegitimate. That said, certain mandatory orders, perhaps orders which identify constitutional goals rather than determine the policy means of achieving those goals, may be legitimate. Nevertheless, even mandatory orders of this type may only be granted in a situation of constitutional meltdown, where another organ of government is deliberately, recklessly and with *mala fides* ignoring declaratory orders of the courts and appears likely to continue to do so. Whether the other organs of government are likely to respect a mandatory order in those circumstances is open to question. [13–31]

The Minority's View of the Separation of Powers: A Framework for Government

Denham J, the sole dissenting judge, provided an account of the separation of powers which differed significantly from that presented by Hardiman J in particular. Although agreeing that no one organ of government could be paramount, they disagreed over whether the doctrine of separation of powers was rigid; they disagreed over whether the checks and balances enumerated in the Constitution were illustrative or exhaustive; they disagreed, most fundamentally, over whether the separation of powers—as a core constitutional value—was an end in itself or a framework for government. These disagreements are well illustrated by Denham J's opening observations on the matter: [13–32]

> Fundamental powers of government are distributed between [the Legislature, Executive and Judiciary]. A separation of powers is described although it is not a strict division or distribution of power. It is not a doctrine applied rigidly in the Constitution. A framework for government is established which includes a functional separation of powers to independent organs of State. It is the separation and independence of the institutions which is important. However, checks and balances are created between the three organs of State, for example, the power given to the superior courts to review legislation, and the power given to the Government to appoint judges and to Dáil Éireann and Seanad Éireann to remove a judge. [2001] 4 IR 259, at 298–299.

Denham J further reasoned that the checks and balances established by the Constitution breached the theoretical lines of the separation of powers. The separation of powers, neither rigid nor absolute, had to be balanced with the duty of the courts to guard constitutional rights. [13–33]

[13-34] Although not on its own sufficient to decide the case, Denham J's general conception of the separation of powers is much more open to the possibility of courts making mandatory orders. Once it is posited that the textually enumerated checks and balances are not exhaustive, it becomes feasible for the courts to take a more expansive attitude to the enforcement of constitutional rights. Whereas Hardiman J's "rigid" conception of the separation of powers allowed little scope for novel constitutional remedies in the enforcement of rights, Denham J's "functional" conception of the separation of powers allowed greater innovation on the part of the courts.

The Minority's View on when the Courts may make a Mandatory Order

[13-35] Denham J noted that the practice of the courts was generally not to make a mandatory order. Such orders ill fitted both the respect which the courts owed to the other organs of government and the dynamics of social deprivation and behavioural difficulty, the particular context of this case. Nevertheless, Denham J reasoned that this general practice did not preclude the courts from making orders which had some impact on policy. In any event, she differed from the majority judges in placing considerable weight on the fact that the courts were not making policy but rather mandating that the respondents follow their own policy. The issue was whether such an order breached the doctrine of the separation of powers. In this regard, two principles were relevant:

> In a situation, thus, where there is a balance to be sought between the application of the doctrine of the separation of powers and protecting rights or obligations under the Constitution, the courts have a specified constitutional duty to achieve a just and constitutional balance. Whilst acknowledging the separation of powers, and the respect which must be paid to all the great organs of State, if it is either a matter of protecting rights and obligations under the Constitution or upholding the validity of a statute then the Constitution must prevail. Similarly in relation to constitutional rights the appropriate institution must exercise its powers in the light of the Constitution. When a court is required to determine such an issue a declaratory order is the preferable procedure. On those very rare occasions when such a declaratory approach is not feasible then the court has the power and indeed the duty and responsibility to uphold the Constitution and to vindicate constitutional rights. This is at the core of the duty and responsibility of the High and Supreme Courts of Ireland. [2001] 4 IR 259, at 307.

[13-36] On the rare occasions when a declaratory order was not feasible, the courts had the power and duty to vindicate constitutional rights by means of a mandatory order. In deciding that a mandatory order would be appropriate on the facts of this case, Denham J mentioned a number of factors, the most important of which seem to be the following:

- The applicants had constitutional rights which are not contested.
- The nature of the constitutional rights in question meant that time was of the essence. Damages at a later stage would not be an adequate remedy.
- There had been culpable delay by the respondents.
- Kelly J, the High Court judge, had been managing this list of cases for some time and had extensive knowledge of all the cases.
- All parties to the cases willingly set out for the judge the plans of the respondents for establishing relevant facilities.

- Counsel for the applicants did not process their cases, in light of the evidence of the respondents as to their plans and the expectation that the plans would be implemented. Thus the applicants had altered their position to their detriment.
- By informing the Court of their plans, the respondents benefited from an absence of litigation individually by each applicant.
- Finally, and perhaps most crucially, the order of the Court was to enforce the policy of the Executive. The Court did not investigate the basis for a policy or establish a new policy.

Denham J, considering that the current case was exceptional, reasoned that where cases involved conflicting rights, a proportionate and balanced decision should be sought. Such a decision, in her view, involved the exercise of judicial discretion, within the parameters of the Constitution, to reach a just decision. Although at the extremity of the courts' jurisdiction, the orders were warranted given the exceptional circumstances of the case and the obligation of all organs of government to serve the common good. The courts' duty to vindicate the constitutional rights of citizens justified any intrusion into areas normally the reserve of the Executive and the Legislature. [13–37]

Denham J's approach may be summarised as follows. The separation of powers is a functional doctrine, facilitating good governance. It is a factor to be considered in all judicial decisions involving judicial review, but it must be balanced against other considerations, most notably the primacy of the Constitution itself. Mandatory orders lie at the extremes of the courts' jurisdiction to vindicate constitutional rights and should only be granted in exceptional circumstances. Given the time-limit on the applicants' enjoyment of the rights at issue and the culpable delay on the part of the respondents, the Court was justified in granting a mandatory order which would only require the respondents to implement their own policy. [13–38]

Difficulties in Both the Majority and Minority Positions

Both the majority and the minority judgments provide a fairly, but not fully, coherent account of the separation of powers. Hardiman J described the separation of powers as a "core constitutional value" and held that the constitutional doctrine of the separation of powers was rigid, not functional. Although the Constitution enumerated a number of checks and balances as between the different organs of government, these were exhaustive and did not suggest a general power on the part of the courts to supervise how the other organs of government exercised their power. Hardiman J ultimately agreed with Murray J that the courts had a power to review how other organs of government exercised their powers but not a power to exercise those powers themselves. Mandatory orders which identified a constitutional goal could be granted but only in a situation of constitutional meltdown, where another organ of government was deliberately, recklessly and with *mala fides* ignoring declaratory orders of the courts and appeared likely to continue to do so. [13–39]

It is difficult to see how Hardiman J's general views on the separation of powers is reconcilable with any power on the part of the courts to supervise actions of the Executive. Although Art 28.2 of the Constitution provides that the executive power shall be exercised by the Government subject to the provisions of the Constitution, no provision of the Constitution identifies which organ of government, if any, decides [13–40] whether the Government has acted constitutionally. Article 34.3.2° grants jurisdiction to the High Court and the Supreme Court to determine the validity of any law having regard to the provisions of the Constitution. This would allow those courts to assess the constitutionality of delegated legislation enacted by members of the Government, but this is not an instance of the executive power. The courts have no express power to assess the constitutional validity of any exercise of the executive power. If such a power of review exists, it must be inferred from the provisions of the Constitution and, in particular, from those provisions which deal with the distribution of powers between different branches of government. It seems reasonable to infer that the courts' power to review legislation is an instance of a general power to assess whether organs of government have acted unconstitutionally. This general power would then include a power to review whether the executive power had been exercised unconstitutionally. This was essentially the inference made by the Supreme Court in *Boland v An Taoiseach* when it decided that the Court could review and interfere with the exercise of the executive function if the circumstances amounted to a clear disregard of the Constitution. The problem is that this inference is impermissible under Hardiman J's logic on the grounds that it treats the specifically enumerated checks and balances in the Constitution as illustrative, not exhaustive. As such, the Court in *Boland* and *a fortiori* the Court in *Sinnott* should not have recognised any power on the part of the courts to review the exercise of the executive function.

[13–41]   The incompatibility between Hardiman J's general view of the separation of powers and his specific doctrinal test for the case in hand created a considerable tension in both his judgment and the judgment of Murray J. This tension can be seen in the meaning attributed to the phrase "clear disregard" by both judges. As noted above, Hardiman and Murray JJ agreed that a mandatory order, identifying a constitutional goal, could be made where the Executive acted in clear disregard of the Constitution. Murray J interpreted "clear disregard" as meaning "a conscious and deliberate decision by the organ of state to act in breach of its constitutional obligation to other parties, accompanied by bad faith or recklessness".

[13–42]   Two points may be made about this definition. First, it does not accord with the natural meaning of the words. In this regard, the word "disregard" is not at issue but rather the qualifying "clear". This suggests that the disregard should be plain, obvious, evident or manifest. In the context of cases such as *Boland*, it suggests that the courts should not intervene unless it is plain, obvious, evident and manifest that the Executive has acted in disregard of the Constitution. The word "clear" does not import any of the *mens rea* type requirements suggested by Murray J. In short, Murray J's interpretation of "clear disregard" had more to do with his views on the undesirability of mandatory orders than it has with any understanding of the words themselves. It was a substantive legal point, not a linguistic point.

[13–43]   Secondly, this interpretation of "clear disregard" is at odds with how the phrase was interpreted in other cases. In *McKenna v An Taoiseach (No 2)* [1995] 2 IR 10, Hamilton CJ adopted the "clear disregard" test and concluded that the Executive had acted unconstitutionally in funding one side of a referendum campaign but not the other. Even if one accepts the conclusion of the Supreme Court, it remains the case that the Executive was acting with the endorsement of the High Court from the earlier case of *McKenna v An Taoiseach (No 1)* [1995] 2 IR 1 (decided in 1992). It can thus hardly be said that the Executive had consciously and deliberately with bad faith or recklessness decided to act in breach of its constitutional obligations. This strengthens the conclusion of the previous paragraph: Murray J's interpretation of "clear disregard" is determined by substantive legal or political reasons, not by the meaning of the words themselves.

In the end, Hardiman and Murray JJ's doctrine of the separation of powers is a strange concoction. It concedes that the courts may review the exercise of Executive power despite the fact that the Constitution enumerates no such power and, more pertinently, despite the fact that their general account of the separation of powers precludes the courts from inferring such a power. In reviewing the exercise of Executive power, it adopts the test of "clear disregard" employed in earlier cases. However, it attributes a meaning to that test which is wholly inconsistent both with the natural meaning of the words and with the way in which the test was applied in the earlier cases. These tensions undermine the coherence and cogency of the position adopted by both judges. These tensions could have been avoided if the judges had followed the logic of their general argument, overruled *Boland* and *McKenna*, and conceded no power on the part of the courts to review the constitutionality of Executive action. That they were not prepared to do so lends credence to Denham J's view that the constitutionally enumerated checks and balances are illustrative, not exhaustive, and that some attempt must be made to infer, from all the provisions of the Constitution, a constitutional theory which takes account of both the separation of powers and the protection of constitutional rights. [13–44]

Denham J's judgment also, however, lacks coherence in certain respects. As noted above, Denham J reasoned that the separation of powers had to be balanced with the obligation to give effect to constitutional rights: [13–45]

> In a situation, thus, where a there is a balance to be sought between the application of the doctrine of the separation of powers and protecting rights or obligations under the Constitution, the courts have a specified constitutional duty to achieve a just and constitutional balance. Whilst acknowledging the separation of powers of powers, and the respect which must be paid to all the great organs of State, if it is either a matter of protecting rights and obligations under the Constitution or upholding the validity of a statute then the Constitution must prevail. Similarly in relation to constitutional rights the appropriate institution must exercise its powers in the light of the Constitution. When a court is required to determine such an issue a declaratory order is the preferable procedure. On those very rare occasions when such a declaratory approach is not feasible then the court has the power and indeed the duty and responsibility to uphold the Constitution and to vindicate constitutional rights. [2001] 4 IR 259, at 307.

The difficulty with this reasoning is twofold. First, Denham J's conclusion that the separation of powers must always, in the case of conflict, give way to the enforcement of constitutional rights is inconsistent with her opening statement that a balance must be struck. The idea of balance is difficult in that it presupposes some standard for assessment of the relative weights of the two concepts; notwithstanding these conceptual difficulties, the idea of balance is surely inconsistent with the view that the separation of powers can be observed only to the extent that it does not prejudice the enforcement of constitutional rights. Secondly and more importantly, Denham J's conclusion to privilege the rights argument over the separation of powers argument [13–46] conflates two concepts, namely the effectiveness of constitutional rights and the supremacy of the Constitution. The reason offered by Denham J for privileging the rights argument over the separation of powers argument was that "the Constitution must prevail". But the Constitution envisages both the protection of rights and the separation of powers. The supremacy of the Constitution cannot be a reason for favouring one constitutional doctrine over another. Upholding the Constitution requires respect for the separation of powers as much as it requires the vindication of constitutional rights.

[13–47] Thus although Denham J's judgment is more coherent than those of the majority judges in its willingness to view the Constitution as a whole and to infer a separation of powers doctrine from all of its provisions, it is less coherent in its ultimate realisation of that doctrine. For Denham J's purported balancing of two constitutional doctrines is in fact an *a priori* privileging of one over the other. That conclusion is grounded solely on the—in reality far from conclusive—observation that the Constitution must be upheld.

The Distinction between Commutative and Distributive Justice

[13–48] Both Hardiman and Murray JJ approved a distinction identified several years previously by Costello J in *O'Reilly v Limerick Corporation* [1989] ILRM 181 in which the plaintiffs sought damages from the Corporation for a breach of their constitutional rights arising out of the conditions in which they had been forced to live. Costello J held that this was an inappropriate matter for consideration by the courts:

> As I understand the plaintiffs' argument it is this. Each individual in society requires a certain minimum standard of basic material conditions to foster and protect his or her dignity and freedom as a human person; the right to be provided with these conditions is one of the unenumerated personal rights embraced by Article 40.3.2° of the Constitution; the State's duty to respect and as far as practicable to defend and vindicate this unenumerated right has been broken by permitting the plaintiffs to live in conditions without water and sanitary services, and the plaintiffs are entitled to damages for this breach....
>
> An analysis of these claims can begin by pointing to the jurisdiction which they require the court to exercise. In actions where plaintiffs assert that they enjoy a constitutionally guaranteed right which is not explicitly enumerated in the Constitution the court is asked to determine either that the asserted right is an 'unspecified right' within the meaning of Article 40.3.1° or that it is a right which can be inferred from a textual analysis of some other article. In both instances it will be submitted that either the asserted right is one of those basic human rights which inhere in the citizen because of the particular concept of man enshrined in the Constitution or because it is one of those fundamental civil or social rights which inhere in the citizen by virtue of the particular political regime which the Constitution has established. Usually the claim relates to a wrongful interference in some activity which the plaintiff seeks to protect. In this case an entirely different kind of claim is advanced; the court is asked to consider a claim that the plaintiffs have a constitutionally protected right to be provided by the State with certain physical resources and services. As all rights which are constitutionally protected involve correlative constitutionally-imposed duties it will help an analysis of the validity of their claim if I look at the duty correlative to the asserted right. It will be then seen that what is involved in the plaintiffs' case is an assertion that the State has a duty to provide them with the resources and services they lack and the adjudication the court is asked to make is that the State has failed in that duty and to award damages because of it. That this

claim raises a problem concerning the court's jurisdiction is, I think, tacitly accepted by the plaintiffs' advisers. The claim for mandatory relief is based on an allegation of breach of statutory duty but although a breach of constitutional duty is also alleged no claim for mandatory relief based on such breach is advanced. This seems to me to imply an admission that the court would not have jurisdiction to make such an order and to raise the question why if the court lacks jurisdiction to make a mandatory order for the present breach of a constitutional duty it has jurisdiction to award damages for past breaches?

Whilst the matter was not broached in argument I will assume for present purposes that if the plaintiffs' claim is sustainable that they are entitled to damages for what they have suffered over the past six years. It is relevant then to point out that if the court has jurisdiction to entertain the present claims then it must have jurisdiction to entertain similar claims not only on behalf of the 150 children of the plaintiffs now living in similar conditions to those of the plaintiffs but also claims by the travellers on the roadside on unofficial and unserviced sites elsewhere throughout the State (numbering 1,149 families in 1980 according to the Report of the Travelling People Review Body). And if the court has jurisdiction to adjudicate on a claim by travellers that the State has breached a duty to make adequate provision for their welfare there is no reason why it should not have jurisdiction to entertain similar claims by other deprived persons in our society.... The question raised by their claim is this; can the courts with constitutional propriety adjudicate on an allegation that the organs of Government responsible for the distribution of the nation's wealth have improperly exercised their powers? Or would such an adjudication be an infringement by the courts of the role which the Constitution has conferred on them?

It will, I think, help to answer these questions if I refer briefly to certain aspects of the traditional academic distinction which is made between the two different types of justice which should exist in a political community, distributive justice and commutative justice and to the different concepts involved in this distinction. There is an important distinction to be made between the relationship which arises in dealings between individuals (a term which includes dealings between individuals and servants of the State and public authorities) and the relationship which arises between the individual and those in authority in a political community (which for convenience I will call the Government) when goods held in common for the benefit of the entire community (which would nowadays include wealth raised by taxation) fall to be distributed and allocated. Different obligations in justice arise from these different relationships. Distributive justice is concerned with the distribution and allocation of common goods and common burdens. But it cannot be said that any of the goods held in common (or any part of the wealth raised by taxation) belong exclusively to any member of the political community. An obligation in distributive justice is placed on those administering the common stock of goods, the common resource and the wealth held in common which has been raised by taxation, to distribute them and the common wealth fairly and to determine what is due to each individual. But that distribution can only be made by reference to the common good and by those charged with furthering the common good (the Government); it cannot be made by any individual who may claim a share in the common stock and no independent arbitrator, such as a court, can adjudicate on a claim by an individual that he has been deprived of what is his due. This situation is very different in the case of commutative justice. What is due to an individual from another individual (including a public authority) from a relationship arising from their mutual dealings can be ascertained and is due to him exclusively and the precepts of commutative justice will enable an arbitrator such as a court to decide what is properly due should the matter be disputed. This distinction explains why the court has jurisdiction to award damages against the State when a servant of the State for whose activity it is vicariously liable commits a wrong and why it may not get jurisdiction in cases where the claim is for damages based on a failure to distribute adequately in the plaintiffs' favour a portion of the community's wealth.

I must of course apply the law of the Constitution to the plaintiffs' claims and if there was anything in the Constitution which would require me to ignore the principles which I have just outlined I should have to do so. But there is not; indeed I think they accord well with the constitutional text. The State (against whom damages are sought) is the legal embodiment of the political community whose affairs are regulated by the Constitution. The powers of Government of the State are to be exercised by the organs of the State established by it. The sole and exclusive power of making laws for the State is vested in the Oireachtas; the executive power of the State is exercised by or on the authority of the Government; and justice is to be administered in courts established by law. In relation to the raising of a common fund to pay for the many services which the State provides by law, the Government is constitutionally responsible to Dáil Éireann for preparing annual estimates of proposed expenditure and estimates of proposed receipts from taxation. Approval for plans for expenditure and the raising of taxes is given in the first instance by Dáil Éireann and later by the Oireachtas by the enactment of the annual Appropriation Act and the annual Finance Act. This means that questions relating to raising common funds by taxation and the mode of distribution of common funds are determined by the Oireachtas, although laws enacted by the Oireachtas may give wide discretionary powers to public authorities and public officials (including Ministers) as to their distribution in individual cases. It is the Oireachtas or officials acting under the authority of the Oireachtas which under the Constitution determine the amount of the community's wealth which is to be raised by taxation and used for common purposes and the Oireachtas or officials acting on its authority determine how the nation's wealth is to be distributed and allotted. The courts' constitutional function is to administer justice but I do not think that by exercising the suggested supervisory role it could be said that a court was administering justice as contemplated in the Constitution. What could be involved in the exercise of the suggested jurisdiction would be the imposition by the court of its view that there had been an unfair distribution of national resources. To arrive at such a conclusion it would have to make an assessment of the validity of the many competing claims on those resources, the correct priority to be given to them and the financial implications of the plaintiffs' claim. As the present case demonstrates, it may also be required to decide whether a correct allocation of physical resources available for public purposes has been made. In exercising this function the court would not be administering justice as it does when determining an issue relating to commutative justice but it would be engaged in an entirely different exercise, namely, an adjudication on the fairness or otherwise of the manner in which other organs of State had administered public resources. Apart from the fact that members of the judiciary have no special qualification to undertake such a function, the manner in which justice is administered in the courts, that is on a case by case basis, make them a wholly inappropriate institution for the fulfilment of the suggested role. I cannot construe the Constitution as conferring it on them. So I must hold that I am not empowered to make the adjudication which the plaintiffs ask me to make. I should add that I am sure that the concept of justice which is to be found in the Constitution embraces the concept that the nation's wealth should be justly distributed (that is the concept of distributative justice), but I am equally sure that a claim that this has not occurred should, to comply with the Constitution, be advanced in Leinster House rather than in the Four Courts. [1989] ILRM 181, at 195.

[13–49] Although Costello J was correct to identify a distinction between distributive and commutative justice, the difficulty lies with finding positive support for that distinction in the Constitution and—more particularly—mapping that distinction onto a rigid theory of the separation of powers. Phelan has made the following points:

> To an extent...the role of the Oireachtas and the government in the future development of social rights depends on the resources available to it, which it will acquire through

taxation and Community transfers. These resources must be redistributed according to the State's moral obligations to seek to provide for the common good, which in this context means the establishment of the conditions necessary for a socially just society, ideas which are informed by the Constitution. The courts have considered themselves bound by the principle of the separation of powers and have been wary of interfering in the choices of redistribution of national resources.

The Constitution expresses the idea of moral obligation on social actors to strive for social justice. In connection with this as an idea, though not as a legal obligation, it is important to recall that non-state charitable action (Charity is mentioned in the Preamble as having to be duly observed) plays an important role in society: a central role in charity and education has been played by religious orders for centuries; families act not only as the fundamental unit of society but also as a support for their individual members in relations with society in general.

The courts have a central role, particularly in the development of constitutional jurisprudence on and affecting social rights. The interpretation and evolution of the Constitution is a continuing process towards the goal of the best framework conditions wherein individuals and families may pursue their fulfilment through the exercise of their personal liberty. This goal is a set of conditions in the State which will best guarantee a socially just liberty. This might be misunderstood. The courts have never elevated to the level of constitutional principle any set of economic principles, socialist or free market, as can be seen from the jurisprudence on the right to private property. The evolution of this goal in jurisprudence is the legal aspect of the political function of humans to search for the best means through ever-changing problems. This is done not by seeking standards thrown up by these problems themselves but by responding rationally to them having regard to the permanent values, rights and goods involved in human fulfilment. The courts, like any human institution, are fallible in this regard and may change their interpretation in the light of new rational arguments, perhaps brought to the fore by changing social circumstance. But this does not mean that the quest is different. It involves, on the one hand, nothing less than a continuing rational enquiry into the fulfilment of human persons and their communities and into the conditions of that fulfilment, and on the other hand, an appreciation of the social environment, in order to find how best persons may be protected and promoted in their environment as social actors, so that they may have the possibility of fully realising the potential they possess by virtue of human nature. The goal is to be fully human in a fully just society. (1994) 16 *DULJ* 105, at 116.

[13–50] The difficulty with mapping the commutative/distributive justice distinction onto a rigid separation of powers doctrine is highlighted by the number of enforceable constitutional obligations that have clear resource implications: the duty to provide for free primary education, the duty to provide an Irish translation of statutes, the duty to provide a residence for the President in the vicinity of Dublin, the duty not to interfere (illegitimately) with property rights, the duty not to interfere with the right to work. In these circumstances, it is difficult to see why a particular class of social rights should be singled out for special attention (or lack of attention) by the courts. Indeed, as Whyte points out, Costello J himself changed his mind on the constitutional salience of the distinction between distributive and commutative justice, accepting that the constitutional right to bodily integrity was infringed by appalling living conditions. (See *ex tempore* decision in *O'Brien v Wicklow UDC* 10 June 1994 (HC), cited in Gerry Whyte, *Social Inclusion and the Legal System: Public Interest Law in Ireland* (IPA, 2001), at 57).

[13–51] Notwithstanding these difficulties, the majority in *TD* enthusiastically endorsed the distinction between distributive and commutative justice. It may well be the ultimate rationale for the majority's conclusion that—at least in the context of socio-economic rights—the Constitution demands a rigid separation of powers. De Blacam has been critical of the Supreme Court's use of this distinction:

> [T]he question raised by the judgments in *O'Reilly* and *Sinnott* is whether there is any necessary relationship between these concepts of [distributive and commutative] justice and the separation of powers. The answer, it is submitted, is that clearly there is not. Of course it is true that in many instances the issue before a judge may be characterised as one of commutative justice and that before the legislator as one of distributive justice; but it is manifestly not the case that judges are concerned only with the former and legislators with the latter....
>
> The fallacy underlying the link between the two concepts of justice and the doctrine of the separation of powers lies in a failure to appreciate the purpose of these concepts; as John Finnis has explained: "The distinction between distributive and commutative justice is no more than an analytical convenience, an aid to orderly consideration of problems." This being so, there is no reason in principle why the resolution of questions of distributive and commutative justice must be segregated in accordance with the constitutional function of the person making the decision. Mark de Blacam, "Children, Constitutional Rights and the Separation of Powers" (2002) 37 *Ir Jur* 113, at 131.

The Separation of Powers and Competing Visions of Democracy

[13–52] The constitutional analysis engaged in by the judges in *TD* does not really seem to support their ultimate conclusions. Conclusions are presented as being axiomatic when greater argument and justification are required. What are the boundaries between the organs of government? Do the small number of review powers (Art 34.2.3° for example) justify a more general set of review powers—"checks and balances" rather than "separation of powers"? Why are socio-economic rights considered problematic? Why do the resource implications of certain rights, such as education rights, cause concern when the resource implications of other rights, such as property rights and Irish language rights, do not?

[13–53] In truth, these questions are not clearly determined by the text of the Constitution. The answers largely depend on one's own views of the practical abilities of judges for addressing these sorts of issues and the democratic propriety of such judicial activism. These views are mutually reinforcing: one's assessment of judges' abilities influences one's views on the democratic issue, and *vice versa*. The democratic issue turns not on whether one is a democrat or not but rather on what conception of democracy one is committed to. Some view democracy as largely a process concept: provided the political process is fair, its decisions should be respected. Certain process rights, such as freedom of speech, association, *etc* and a limited conception of equality, may be necessary to preserve the fairness of the process. But there the role of the courts ends. Others view democracy as a substantive concept: no matter how formally fair a process may appear, if it denies certain substantive benefits, it is not democratic. Under such an account, the courts would have a more interventionist role in ensuring that decisions reached through a democratic process are substantively democratic. The conflicting positions of Denham and Hardiman JJ can perhaps best be understood in this light. Denham J was more willing to enforce a constitutional right against the democratically expressed wishes of the people.

[13–54] Judicial enforcement of socio-economic rights, certainly at a constitutional level, requires judges to make complex, substantive decisions about the expenditure of funds in the polity, possibly reordering the allocation of funds agreed in the ordinary political process. Whyte defends this decision-making power where it is apparent that the constitutional rights of marginalised people are not adequately protected by the political process. (Gerry Whyte, *Social Inclusion and the Legal System: Public Interest Law in Ireland* (IPA, 2001), at 10). Objections to such decision-making power are generally framed in terms of the idea that the courts should limit themselves to the enforcement of formal civil and political rights, rights which ultimately protect the political process. It is in that political process that substantive choices should be made. The suggestion that the courts should enforce the substance of democracy, as against the choices made through the ordinary political process, rejects the proposition that the courts' only valid concern is with civil and political rights and the process of democracy.

At the core of the argument against judicial enforcement of socio-economic rights lie the *dicta* of Costello J in *O'Reilly v Limerick Corporation*, considered above. Although Costello J's judgment neatly captured the idea that the ordinary political process should be the arbiter of certain democratic entitlements (such as distributive justice), it offers little in support of that idea apart from reiteration of the commutative/distributive justice distinction. Arguments made by others in favour of the distinction tend to take two forms. First, it is argued that judicial enforcement of distributive justice is undemocratic. Secondly, it is argued that such enforcement is pragmatically unwise given the limited capacities of the courts. [13–55]

A majority of the Constitution Review Group rejected, on a number of grounds, a suggestion that the Constitution should provide for socioeconomic rights. Most prominently, they elaborated on a conception of the political process of democracy: [13–56]

> [T]hese are essentially political matters which, in a democracy, it should be the responsibility of the elected representatives of the people to address and determine. It would be a distortion of democracy to transfer decisions on major issues of policy and practicality from the Government and the Oireachtas, elected to represent the people and do their will, to an unelected judiciary.

Despite the observations of Costello J in *O'Reilly*, there is some basis for claiming that the Constitution commits itself to a more substantive conception of democracy. The Irish Constitution is both a basic law and a manifesto. Indeed, in his explanatory address on the 1937 Constitution, Mr de Valera indicated that he viewed the Constitution as more than a legal Charter: [13–57]

> I am aware that there are theorists who take a narrow view of the relation of the national polity to the national life and hold that a written Constitution should contain nothing more than the legal machinery for the establishment of the organs of the State. I do not share that view. In my judgment, if the constitution of a country like our own is written down at all it should not only define the character of the legislative, executive, and judicial regime, not only be a compendium of the great axioms of constitutional government, I mean *eg* that of the responsibility of the executive to Parliament or the independence of the judiciary or the principle of universal suffrage, but should contain as well a statement of some at least of the God-given rights of the individual both as a human being and as a member of society the protection of which by the State means more in the long run to the integrity and continuance of the civil society itself that the organisation of the institutions by which it is ruled. University College Dublin Archives Department, P150/2431.

[13–58] Given that the courts are the authoritative interpreters of the Constitution and that the Constitution is avowedly more than a formal charter for government, it is difficult to sustain the objection that judicial review should not deal with substantive matters. In summary, although the decision in *TD* appears to have settled that constitutional socioeconomic rights are not particularly enforceable, there remain serious concerns about how that conclusion was reached.

Judicial Impeachment

[13–59] A further example of the system of checks and balances established by the Constitution is the power of the Oireachtas—contained in Art 35.4 to remove a judge for stated misbehaviour or incapacity. In *Curtin v Clerk of Dáil Éireann* [2006] IESC 14, the Supreme Court considered the procedures being adopted in relation to Judge Curtin. Judge Curtin had been acquitted, by way of direction, of a charge of possessing child pornography. Notwithstanding his acquittal, there remained considerable public concern. Both houses of the Oireachtas by resolution adopted a new procedure to allow for investigations into judicial conduct. Following those new procedures, a motion was moved noting the concerns about the applicant's conduct and calling for his removal from office. Again following the new procedures, both houses by resolution established a joint select committee to take evidence in relation to the applicant's conduct. The Oireachtas also amended s 3 of the Committees of the Houses of the Oireachtas (Compellability, Privileges and Immunity of Witnesses) Act 1997 to allow judges be compelled to give evidence and to produce documents to Oireachtas committees, subject to the consent of the compellability committee of the Houses. Pursuant to this power, the committee ordered the applicant to produce his computer, including its hard drive, for the examination of the committee. The applicant sought judicial review of the committee's decision, challenging both the inquiry process established by the resolutions and the constitutionality of s 3 of the 1997 Act, as amended.

[13–60] On appeal, Judge Curtin made three principal contentions. First, Judge Curtin claimed that the impeachment process was inconsistent with Art 35.4.1° because it did not require the charges against him to be proved before the Houses of the Oireachtas debated the impeachment resolution. Secondly, Judge Curtin claimed that s 3 of the 1997 Act (as amended), which allowed judges to be compelled to give evidence and provide documents to the Oireachtas committee, was unconstitutional as it infringed judicial independence. Thirdly, Judge Curtin claimed that the particular direction issued by the Oireachtas committee requiring him to produce his computer was invalid, having regard to the exclusionary rule.

The Constitutionality of the Impeachment Process

[13–61] Article 35.4.1° of the Constitution, the provision on which Judge Curtin relied, provides simply:

> A judge of the Supreme Court or the High Court shall not be removed from office except for stated misbehaviour or incapacity, and then only upon resolutions passed by Dáil Éireann and by Seanad Éireann calling for his removal.

[13–62] As s 39 of the Courts of Justice Act 1924 extended to Circuit Court judges the same tenure as that afforded to judges of the High Court and Supreme Court, it was common case that the procedural protections of Art 35.4.1° applied to Judge Curtin. That said, Art 35.4.1° itself is quite vague as to the procedures to be followed. Murray CJ, who delivered the judgment of the court, reasoned:

> Some of the words in Article 35.4.1 are clear and unambiguous. A judge cannot be removed other than in accordance with Article 35.4.1: both Houses must pass the required resolution; the resolution must call for the judge's removal. This apparently refers to the resolution as proposed. A resolution of one House alone will not suffice. It is also clear, by necessary implication, that the resolution itself must specify the "misbehaviour or incapacity," as the case may be, (or indeed, though not relevant in this case, the "incapacity") which purports to justify the judge's removal.
>
> Apart from these matters, Article 35.4.1 is silent. It does not define misbehaviour or state whether misbehaviour relates to the performance of judicial duties or may be misbehaviour of a general kind. Article 35.4.1 prescribes no procedures to be followed by the Houses of the Oireachtas. Article 15.11.1, however provides that: "All questions in each House shall, save as otherwise provided by this Constitution, be determined by a majority of the votes of the members present and voting other than the Chairman or presiding member." In particular, Article 35.4.1 contains no guidance on the power of the Houses to appoint investigating committees or the powers it may delegate to any such committees.
>
> In these circumstances, it is reasonable to consider whether there is any history or background to the enactment of the Constitution capable of elucidating what was in the contemplation of the framers. More particularly, however, it will be necessary to consider the constitutional context of Article 35.4.1. [2006] 2 IR 556, at [78]–[80].

[13–63] In this regard, he considered that three elements were particularly relevant: the function and standing of the judiciary in the constitutional scheme, the express power conferred on the Oireachtas and the obligation to respects principles of fairness and justice in the exercise of that power. Murray CJ, citing a number of provisions of the Constitution, identified the role of the courts (and, by implication, judges) as follows:

> The courts are required to act as custodians of the Constitution and as such, to act as a check on the actions of the other two arms of government and to ensure that they act in accordance with the rule of law, respect individual constitutionally protected rights and observe the provisions of the Constitution.

[13–64] An essential prerequisite to the performance of this function was, he reasoned, that the independence and integrity of the courts be guaranteed and respected. This independence was effected by a number of provisions, including Art 35.4.1°. Importantly, this independence did not exist for the benefit of the judges themselves, as individuals, even though it might have that effect. Rather, it existed for the benefit of the people as it was only an independent judiciary that could ensure that the organs of the State conducted themselves in accordance with the rule of law.

[13–65] Referring to many of the seminal cases on the separation of powers, Murray CJ emphasised that each organ of the State must be allowed to exercise its own powers and that the presumption of constitutionality applies to resolutions of the Houses of the Oireachtas, including those adopted in relation to Judge Curtin. Moreover, the Oireachtas had an exclusive power—under Article 15.10—to pass the resolutions contemplated by Art 35.4.1°.

[13–66] The nub of Judge Curtin's complaint was that fair procedures could not be followed within the method adopted by the Houses of the Oireachtas. It would have been preferable, he argued, for the committee to make decisions in relation to the evidence and present a non-binding report to both Houses. Moreover, he argued that he would not be able to present evidence to the Houses even if he thought it necessary. The court was not convinced by this latter point, noting that there was nothing in the Standing Orders to prevent the Houses hearing evidence, however unprecedented that might be. That said, the court accepted that Judge Curtin's suggested approach "might well have been more satisfactory". However, based on the earlier separation of powers case law, the court reasoned that the appropriate constitutional test was whether the approach adopted by the Houses of the Oireachtas was "in clear disregard" of the Constitution. The Court concluded that it was not *clearly in disregard* of the Constitution for the Oireachtas to decline to adopt a procedure that was not, on the face of Art 35.4.1°, constitutionally required. In any event, the Court considered that Judge Curtin had taken an unduly narrow view of the powers of the committee. Although the committee was precluded from making findings of fact, recommendations concerning the facts or expressing any opinions about the facts, it was not precluded from organising the material and evidence into manageable form.

[13–67] A separate but related argument was made by Judge Curtin during the Supreme Court appeal. It was argued that there was a risk that the Houses of the Oireachtas might conflate two issues into one, by deciding on the issue of misbehaviour and the possible consequence of removal from office in one resolution. The Court considered that this issue was premature as the procedures had not yet reached that stage and as neither the standing orders nor the Resolution prescribed any method for debating the resolution. However, given the exceptional character of the case, the court felt it appropriate to provide some guidance to the Oireachtas:

> It is the opinion of the Court that, as a matter of basic fairness, the Appellant should be entitled to a distinct hearing and decision on the issues of fact before he must confront the ultimate and drastic decision to remove him from office. Some support is to be found in the words of Article 35.4.1. The first part of the sentence declares that a judge may not be removed "except for stated misbehaviour or incapacity." The second part goes on to provide that this may happen: "and then only upon resolutions passed......" These remarks are not intended to impose onerous legal requirements on the Houses. They retain a large area of discretion as to how the resolutions are put. They are not necessarily obliged to break the allegations against the Appellant into several components. They may decide that the factual issues may fairly be expressed in the form of a single proposition. [2006] 2 IR 556, at [152].

The Constitutionality of the Power to Compel Judges

[13–68] The Court held that s 3A of the Committees of the Houses of the Oireachtas (Compellability, Privileges and Immunity of Witnesses) Act 1997 was constitutional, for much the same reasons as underlay its decision in relation to the impeachment process under Art 35.4.1°. Judicial independence existed for the benefit of the people, not the benefit of the individual judge. A particular responsibility had been conferred on the Oireachtas by Art 35.4.1°. In order to consider whether to remove a judge from office, it was necessary for the Oireachtas to have a power of the type granted by s 3A of the Act.

The Direction to Produce the Computer

Judge Curtin sought to rely on the exclusionary rule to maintain that the committee could not direct him to produce his computer. The Supreme Court rejected this argument. Section 3A was a lawful basis for ordering production of the computer. This lawful basis was not undermined by the fact that the computer had been unlawfully seized in the past. Moreover, the Oireachtas had also amended the Child Trafficking and Pornography Act 1998 in order to exempt any proceedings of the Oireachtas from criminality by reason of the possession or distribution of child pornography. There was therefore no reason why it would be unlawful to provide the computer to the committee.

[13–69]

CONTENTS – CHAPTER 14

The European Union

Introduction..[14–01]
The Principal Constitutional Amendments ....[14–03]
Amendment of the Treaties ....[14–08]
Methods of Incorporating Community Law ....[14–18]

Overview

Ireland's decision to join the European Economic Community has been the most significant amendment to the constitutional structure originally established in 1937. Art 29.4 of the Constitution provides an authorisation for Ireland to join the EEC and to ratify several subsequent Treaties. It also immunises from constitutional challenge in Ireland acts of the institutions of the EC and EU as well as Irish acts that are necessitated by Ireland's membership of those organisations. In the *Crotty case*, the Supreme Court held that Ireland could sign up to developments of the EEC that did not alter the essential scope or objectives of the EEC. However, Title III of the Single European Act, which required Member States to endeavour to formulate and implement a single European foreign policy, did not come within the essential scope and objectives of the EEC and, as it amounted to a fettering of the Government's power to conduct foreign affairs, could not be ratified in Ireland without a referendum. The courts have upheld the constitutionality of section 2 of the European Communities Act 1972, which allows primary legislation to be amended by secondary legislation in order to give effect to European Community law. However, this power under section 2 can only be validly exercised where the Community law being implemented deals with all matters of principle and policy and leaves only matters of detail to be addressed by the Member State.

CHAPTER 14

The European Union

Introduction

Ireland's decision in 1972 to join the then European Economic Community remains, without doubt, the most significant amendment to the Constitution. Indeed, the changes wrought to Ireland's constitutional structure as a result of our membership of the European Union are probably more far-reaching than the changes wrought by the 1937 Constitution itself. The interaction between two legal orders, such as the Irish constitutional order and the European Union legal order, creates difficulties. A principal cause of such difficulties is that the same legal issue can be perceived differently from different perspectives. Thus the European Court of Justice will perceive the interaction of EU law and Irish law from a European perspective, principally derived from the foundational texts of the EC and the EU. In contrast, the Irish courts are likely to perceive the interaction from an Irish constitutional perspective. [14–01]

The Constitution has been amended on a number of occasions to reduce or remove the possibility of conflict between the European perspective and the Irish perspective. As Community law maintains that it is supreme (takes precedence over national law) and is in many instances directly effective within Member States, these amendments have principally been directed towards securing two outcomes, as a matter of Irish constitutional law. First, that full force and effect can be given to Community law within the Irish legal order. Secondly, that in the event of conflict, Community law takes precedence. The narrow purpose of this chapter is to trace how the Irish Constitution, as interpreted by the courts, has secured these outcomes. [14–02]

The Principal Constitutional Amendments

Article 29.4 of the Constitution has been amended on a number of occasions to allow Ireland's membership of the evolving European Economic Community. Relevant to this issue, Art 29.4 contains a discrete authorisation for Ireland to join the EEC and to sign the subsequent treaties. Thus Art 29.4.3° allows Ireland to join the EEC, Art 29.4.4° allows Ireland to sign the Treaty of Maastricht, Art 29.4.5° allows Ireland to sign the Treaty of Amsterdam, and so on. As a result of the Supreme Court decision in *Crotty v An Taoiseach* (considered below), the Government has considered it necessary to hold a referendum on each of these Treaties. The Amsterdam Treaty and the Nice Treaty raised a number of subsidiary issues, which are also constitutionally addressed in sub-articles of Art 29.4. [14–03]

Article 29.4.10° essentially immunises Community law measures from constitutional challenge: [14–04]

> No provision of this Constitution invalidates laws enacted, acts done or measures adopted by the State which are necessitated by the obligations of membership of the

European Union or of the Communities, or prevents laws enacted, acts done or measures adopted by the European Union or by the Communities or by institutions thereof, or by bodies competent under the Treaties establishing the Communities, from having the force of law in the State.

[14–05] Although this provision does not explicitly grant the force of law (within Ireland) to Community law measures, it provides two things. First, it provides that the Constitution cannot be used to invalidate laws, acts or measures of the Irish State that are "necessitated by the obligations of membership." Secondly, it provides that the Constitution does not prevent laws, acts or measures of the European Institutions from having the force of law in the State. Accordingly, if such measures can gain that force of law from elsewhere, they cannot lose their legal force and effect by reason of the Constitution.

[14–06] In *Crotty v An Taoiseach* [1987] IR 713, Barrington J identified the reason why (as a matter of Irish law) the laws of the EEC had the force of law within Ireland:

> A referendum was held on the 10th May, 1972, at which the people voted by an overwhelming majority in favour of the Third Amendment of the Constitution, and the Third Amendment of the Constitution Act, 1972, was enacted into law on the 8th June, 1972. Ireland deposited its instrument of ratification on the 16th December, 1972.
>
> These acts may have been sufficient to make Ireland a member of the European Community in international law as from the 1st January, 1973....
>
> But these acts were not sufficient in themselves to make Ireland an effective member of the Community. To make Ireland an effective member as of the 1st January, 1973, it was necessary to make the Treaty part of the domestic law of Ireland. To achieve this it was necessary to pass an Act of the Oireachtas pursuant to the provisions of Article 29.6, making the Treaty of Rome part of the domestic law of Ireland and giving the institutions of the Community a status in Irish domestic law. Had the Oireachtas not passed the European Communities Act, 1972, Ireland might still have been a member of the Community in international law but it would have been in breach of its obligations in international law under the Treaty of Rome and under the Treaty of Accession. This however would not have been a matter in relation to which the domestic courts of this country would have had any competence because the Treaty would not have been part of the domestic law. The immunity from constitutional challenge conferred by the second sentence of the Third Amendment on laws enacted, acts done, or measures adopted by the Community or its institutions would therefore have been meaningless as these laws, acts or measures would not have been part of the domestic law of this country.
>
> To make them part of the domestic law of this country the European Communities Act, 1972, was necessary. This Act cannot therefore have been passed by virtue of the second sentence of the Third Amendment but by virtue of the licence to join the European Community contained in the first sentence of the Third Amendment. It accordingly in section 1 lists the Treaties governing the European Communities and, in section 2, provides that from the 1st January, 1973, the Treaties governing the European Communities and the existing and future acts adopted by the institutions of those Communities, shall be binding on the State and shall be part of the domestic law thereof under the conditions laid down in those Treaties.
>
> The European Communities Act, 1972, was clearly authorised by the people when they authorised the State to join the European Economic Community. It must be presumed to be constitutional and would appear to be safe from constitutional challenge. But had it gone outside the terms of the licence granted by the first sentence of the Third

Amendment it would not have been immune from constitutional challenge. [1987] IR 713, at 757–758.

As a matter of Irish law, therefore, it was the European Communities Act 1972 that gave force of law within Ireland to the measures of the European Communities. Without such an Act, Ireland would have become a member of the Communities in international law but would have failed to give effect in domestic law to the obligations of membership. Without a constitutional amendment, however, the European Communities Act 1972 would unquestionably have been unconstitutional. If nothing else, it would have contravened the exclusive legislative power of the Oireachtas by giving the force of law to measures never considered by the Oireachtas. The question that has arisen in the case law in a number of different ways is the extent of the constitutional authorisation provided by Art 29.4.10°. [14–07]

Amendment of the Treaties

In *Crotty v An Taoiseach* [1987] IR 713, Mr Crotty objected to Ireland's proposed ratification of the Single European Act (the SEA). The SEA, a Treaty entered into by the then 12 members of the European Economic Community, was the first significant amendment to the Treaty of Rome. As well as adopting the name "European Community", it made a number of changes to the way in which the Communities established in 1957 operated: [14–08]

- The decision-making process of the Council of Ministers was changed in six instances from unanimity to qualified majority vote – this raised the possibility that Ireland could be outvoted on an issue;
- A power was given to the Council to attach a court of first instance to the European Court of Justice, if the latter so requested;
- The SEA gave the Community explicit competence for the first time in a number of areas, including economic and social cohesion, research and technological development and the environment;
- Title III of the SEA committed each Member State (including Ireland) to formulate and implement a European foreign policy.

The issue before the Supreme Court was whether any of these alterations was unconstitutional. As the first three changes noted above had been implemented in Ireland by the European Communities (Amendment) Act 1986, Mr Crotty's challenge in that respect was a challenge to the constitutionality of legislation. Article 34.4.5° of the Constitution therefore required that there could only be one judgment, in this case delivered by Finlay CJ. The final aspect of the case (Title III) was a matter for implementation by the Government in the sphere of foreign affairs. Accordingly, the constitutionality of legislation was not impugned, allowing each Member of the five judge Court to deliver his own judgment. [14–09]

The first issue was the extent of the authorisation provided by the phrase "necessitated by the obligations of membership". Finlay CJ noted that it was clear and accepted by the State that the ratification of the SEA was not an act "necessitated by the obligations of membership of the Communities." That is, Ireland's membership of the EEC could not oblige it to sign up to any further expansion of the Community's scope or powers. Therefore, the SEA did not benefit from the constitutional immunity conferred by Art [14–10]

29.4.10°. The State and Mr Crotty, however, offered conflicting views of the authorisation conferred by the first sentence of Art 29.4.3° which read at the time:

> The State may become a member of the European Coal and Steel Community (established by Treaty signed at Paris on the 18th day of April, 1951), the European Economic Community (established by Treaty signed at Rome on the 25th day of March, 1957) and the European Atomic Energy Community (established by Treaty signed at Rome on the 25th day of March, 1957).

[14–11] Mr Crotty contended that this provision meant that any amendment of the Treaties would require a further amendment of the Constitution. The State contended that the provision allowed Ireland to join dynamic and developing Communities, thus authorising the State to participate in and agree to amendments of the Treaties which were within the original scope and objectives of the Treaties. The Supreme Court adopted an approach that was somewhere between these two positions, albeit closer to that advocated by the State:

> It is the opinion of the Court that the first sentence in Article 29.4.3 of the Constitution must be construed as an authorisation given to the State not only to join the Communities as they stood in 1973, but also to join in amendments of the Treaties so long as such amendments do not alter the essential scope or objectives of the Communities. To hold that the first sentence of Article 29.4.3 does not authorise any form of amendment to the Treaties after 1973 without a further amendment of the Constitution would be too narrow a construction; to construe it as an open-ended authority to agree, without further amendment of the Constitution, to any amendment of the Treaties would be too broad. The issue then arises as to whether the effect of the amendments to the Treaties proposed by the SEA is such as would bring the introduction of them into the domestic law by the Act of 1986 outside the authorisation of Article 29.4.3 as above construed. [1987] IR 713, at 767.

[14–12] The Supreme Court then held that none of the SEA amendments (with the exception of Title III) altered the essential scope and objectives of the original Treaties:

> In discharging its duty to interpret and uphold the Constitution the Court must consider the essential nature of the scope and objectives of the Communities as they must be deemed to have been envisaged by the people in enacting Article 29.4.3. It is in the light of that scope and those objectives that the amendments proposed by the SEA fall to be considered.
>
> Article 2 of the Treaty of Rome provided as follows:—
>
> "The Community shall have as its task, by establishing a common market and progressively approximating the economic policies of Member States, to promote throughout the Community a harmonious development of economic activities, a continuous and balanced expansion, an increase in stability, an accelerated raising of the standard of living and closer relations between the States belonging to it."
>
> Article 3 of that Treaty set out what the activities of the Community should include for the purposes stated in Article 2, and amongst these activities are:—
>
> > "(c) the abolition, as between Member States, of obstacles to freedom of movement for persons, services and capital;
> >
> > (f) the institution of a system ensuring that competition in the common market is not distorted;
> >
> > (g) the application of procedures by which the economic policies of Member States can be coordinated and disequilibria in their balances of payments remedied;
> >
> > (h) the approximation of laws of Member States to the extent required for the proper functioning of the common market;

> (i) the creation of a European Social Fund in order to improve employment opportunities for workers and to contribute to the raising of their standard of living;
> (j) the establishment of a European Investment Bank to facilitate the economic expansion of the Community by opening up fresh resources;
> (k) the association of the overseas countries and territories in order to increase trade and to promote jointly economic and social development."
>
> For the purpose of attaining its objectives and implementing its provisions the Treaty of Rome established certain institutions. Amongst these is the Court of Justice of the European Communities which was established to ensure that in the interpretation and the application of the Treaty the law is observed. The decisions of that Court on the interpretation of the Treaty and on questions covering its implementation take precedence, in case of conflict, over the domestic law and the decisions of national courts of Member States.
>
> Another institution of the EEC is the Council, whose decisions have primacy over domestic law and which for the purpose of ensuring that the objectives of the Treaty are attained is charged with ensuring the co-ordination of the general economic policies of the Member States. Some of its decisions must be unanimous, others may be taken by qualified majority, and still others by simple majority. The capacity of the Council to take decisions with legislative effect is a diminution of the sovereignty of Member States, including Ireland, and this was one of the reasons why the Third Amendment to the Constitution was necessary. Sovereignty in this context is the unfettered right to decide: to say yes or no. In regard to proposals coming before the Council which the State might oppose, unanimity is a valuable shield. On the other hand, in proposals which the State might support, qualified or simple majority is of significant assistance. In many instances the Treaty of Rome provided a requirement that a decision on a particular topic should be unanimous, but would after the expiry of a particular stage or of the transitional period require only a qualified majority. The Community was thus a developing organism with diverse and changing methods for making decisions and an inbuilt and clearly expressed objective of expansion and progress, both in terms of the number of its Member States and in terms of the mechanics to be used in the achievement of its agreed objectives.
>
> Having regard to these considerations, it is the opinion of the Court that neither the proposed changes from unanimity to qualified majority, nor the identification of topics which while now separately stated, are within the original aims and objectives of the EEC, bring these proposed amendments outside the scope of the authorisation contained in Article 29.4.3 of the Constitution. As far as Ireland is concerned, it does not follow that all other decisions of the Council which now require unanimity could, without a further amendment of the Constitution, be changed to decisions requiring less than unanimity.
>
> The power of the Council to attach to the European Court a court of first instance with limited jurisdiction which would be subject to appeal on questions of law to the European Court, does not affect in any material way the extent to which the judicial power has already been ceded to the European Court. This Court is therefore of the opinion that the establishment of an additional court, if it occurs, has not been shown to exceed the constitutional authorisation. [1987] IR 713, at 768–770.

On Title III, however, the Court reached the opposite conclusion. Three members of the Court concluded that Title III went too far. Two dissented. Walsh J noted the effect of Title III and explained its problems in the following terms: [14–13]

> It commits the State, and therefore all future Governments and the Oireachtas, to the other Member States to do the following things:—
> 1. To endeavour to formulate and to implement a European foreign policy.
> 2. To undertake to inform or consult the other Member States on any foreign policy matters of general interest (not just of common interest) so as to ensure that the combined influence of the States is exercised as effectively as possible through

co-ordination, the convergence of their positions and the implementation of joint action.
3. In adopting its position and in its national measures the State shall take full account of the position of the other Member States and shall give due consideration to the desirability of adopting and implementing common European positions.
4. The State will ensure that with its fellow Member States common principles and objectives are gradually developed and defined.
5. The State shall endeavour to avoid any action or position which impairs the effectiveness of the Community States as a cohesive force in international relations or within international organisations.
6. The State shall so far as possible refrain from impeding the formation of a consensus and the joint action which this could produce.
7. The State shall be ready to co-ordinate its position with the position of the other Member States more closely on the political and economic aspects of security.
8. The State shall maintain the technological and industrial conditions necessary for security of the Member States and it shall work to that end at national level and, where appropriate, within the framework of the competent institutions and bodies.
9. In international institutions and at international conferences which the State attends it shall endeavour to adopt a common position with the other Member States on subjects covered by Title III.
10. In international institutions and at international conferences in which not all of the Member States participate the State, if it is one of those participating, shall take full account of the positions agreed in European Political Cooperation.

One other matter expressed in somewhat ambiguous terms at Article 6 (c) in Title II is as follows:—

"Nothing in this Title shall impede closer cooperation in the field of security between certain of the High Contracting Parties within the framework of the Western European Union or the Atlantic Alliance."

One interpretation of that is that the Member States who are members of the Western European Union or the Atlantic Alliance (Ireland is not a member of either) can develop their own co-operation in those fields without being impeded by anything in Title III of this Treaty. However, it can also amount to an undertaking on the part of this State that in the exercise of whatever powers it may have under Title III it shall do nothing to impede such co-operation in the field of security in the framework of the Western European Union or the Atlantic Alliance on the part of those Member States which belong to those institutions.

All of these matters impinge upon the freedom of action of the State not only in certain areas of foreign policy but even within international organisations such as the United Nations or the Council of Europe. That latter effect of the Treaty could amount to the establishment of combinations within these organisations. In touching upon the maintenance of the technological and industrial conditions necessary for security the Treaty impinges upon the State's economic, industrial and defence policies. The obligation on the High Contracting Parties after five years to examine whether any revision of Title III is required does not give the Treaty a temporary character.

I mentioned earlier in this judgment that the Government is the sole organ of the State in the field of international relations. This power is conferred upon it by the Constitution which provides in Article 29.4 that this power shall be exercised by or on the authority of the Government. In this area the Government must act as a collective authority and shall be collectively responsible to Dáil Éireann and ultimately to the people. In my view it would be quite incompatible with the freedom of action conferred on the Government by the Constitution for the Government to qualify that freedom or to inhibit it in any manner by formal agreement with other States as to qualify it....

In enacting the Constitution the people conferred full freedom of action upon the Government to decide matters of foreign policy and to act as it thinks fit on any particular issue so far as policy is concerned and as, in the opinion of the Government, the occasion requires. In my view, this freedom does not carry with it the power to abdicate that freedom or to enter into binding agreements with other States to exercise that power in a particular way or to refrain from exercising it save by particular procedures, and so to bind the State in its freedom of action in its foreign policy. The freedom to formulate foreign policy is just as much a mark of sovereignty as the freedom to form economic policy and the freedom to legislate. The latter two have now been curtailed by the consent of the people to the amendment of the Constitution which is contained in Article 29.4.3 of the Constitution. If it is now desired to qualify, curtail or inhibit the existing sovereign power to formulate and to pursue such foreign policies as from time to time to the Government may seem proper, it is not within the power of the Government itself to do so. The foreign policy organ of the State cannot, within the terms of the Constitution, agree to impose upon itself, the State or upon the people the contemplated restrictions upon freedom of action. To acquire the power to do so would, in my opinion, require a recourse to the people "whose right it is" in the words of Article 6 "... in final appeal, to decide all questions of national policy, according to the requirements of the common good." In the last analysis it is the people themselves who are the guardians of the Constitution. In my view, the assent of the people is a necessary prerequisite to the ratification of so much of the Single European Act as consists of title III thereof. [1987] IR 713, at 781–784.

Henchy J agreed: [14–14]

It is urged on behalf of the Government that the changes in existing inter-state relations effected by Title III are slight, that it does little more than formalise existing practices and procedures by converting them into binding obligations. This, I fear, is to underestimate the true nature in international law of a treaty as distinct from a mere practice or procedure, and to misinterpret the commitments for the future involved in Title III. As a treaty, Title III is not designed in static terms. It not alone envisages changes in inter-state relations, but also postulates and requires those changes. And the purpose of those changes is to erode national independence in the conduct of external relations in the interests of European political cohesion in foreign relations. As I have pointed out, the treaty marks the transformation of the European Communities from an organisation which has so far been essentially economic to one that is to be political also. It goes beyond existing arrangements and practices, in that it establishes within the framework of the Communities new institutions and offices (such as European Political Cooperation, the Political Director and the Political Committee) and charts a route of co-ordination, by means such as working parties, a secretariat and regular meetings, so as to give impetus to the drive for European unity. [1987] IR 713, at 788–789.

Finlay CJ and Griffin J dissented, on the basis that Title III did not amount to the sort of "clear disregard" of the Constitution that would be necessary to justify court intervention. Finlay CJ reasoned: [14–15]

I do not consider that it has been established that adherence by the State to the terms of Article 30 of the SEA amounts, in the words of FitzGerald CJ, "to a clear disregard by the Government of the powers and duties conferred on it by the Constitution." Furthermore, I interpret the decision of Griffin J in *Boland v An Taoiseach* [1974] IR 338 as being consistent with the view already expressed by me that where an individual person comes before the Courts and establishes that action on the part of the Executive has breached or threatens to breach one or other of his constitutional rights that the

Courts must intervene to protect those rights but that otherwise they can not and should not....

It was submitted that, whereas the plaintiff acknowledged that the Courts had no function to intervene with the Executive in the formation or statement of policy, either in external relations or in any other part of Government activity, a difference arose where the declaration of policy involved, as it is stated Article 30 of the SEA involves, a commitment to other states for consultation, discussion and an endeavour to coincide policies. I cannot accept this distinction. It appears probable that under modern conditions a state seeking cooperation with other states in the sphere of foreign policy must be prepared to enter into not merely vague promises but actual arrangements for consultation and discussion. I can find no warrant in the Constitution for suggesting that this activity would be inconsistent with the Constitution and would, as is suggested, presumably in each individual instance, require a specific amendment of the Constitution. [1987] IR 713, at 774–775.

[14–16] The precise implications of *Crotty* are difficult to assess. In many ways, the implications of Title III were considerably less significant than the implications of those parts of the SEA that the Court held did not require a referendum. Do the essentially procedural requirements and aspirational statements of Title III restrict Ireland's sovereignty in any real way? The minority may well have been correct in their view that the ratification of Title III was not a "clear disregard" of the Constitution. At any rate, the concrete diminution of sovereignty represented by QMV is surely greater than the efforts at consultation required by Title III. On the other hand, the apparent discrepancy between these two rulings may be explained by the Court's focus on whether a particular amendment was beyond the essential scope and objectives of the Treaty. While many of the changes represented (considerably) more of the same, Title III was a little bit of something quite new: the first formal foray into foreign affairs. In this regard, Henchy J's comment that Title III marked the transformation of the EEC from an essentially economic organisation to a political organisation may be the best explanation of the Court's greater wariness of Title III.

[14–17] Since *Crotty*, the State has taken a cautious approach to the amendment of the EC Treaties. All of the judges agreed that a Treaty requiring Ireland to enter a European Union would require a referendum, so it is not surprising that the Treaty on European Union in 1992 was put to a popular vote. Since then, the Amsterdam Treaty and the Nice Treaty have been put to a popular vote (twice in the case of the Nice Treaty), and the amendments required to ratify the Lisbon Treaty were rejected by the people in 2008. On the other hand, the relatively minor amendments made to the Treaties formally to accommodate new members of the EU and the EC have never been put to popular vote in Ireland.

Methods of Incorporating Community Law

[14–18] Section 2 of the European Communities Act 1972 provides:

From the 1st day of January, 1973, the treaties governing the European Communities and the existing and future acts adopted by the institutions of those Communities shall be binding on the State and shall be part of the domestic law thereof under the conditions laid down in those treaties.

As noted above, this provision grants legal status, within Ireland, to Community law and would clearly be unconstitutional were it not for Art 29.4.10°.

Section 3 of the 1972 Act provides: [14–19]

(1) A Minister of State may make regulations for enabling section 2 of this Act to have full effect.
(2) Regulations under this section may contain such incidental, supplementary and consequential provisions as appear to the Minister making the regulations to be necessary for the purposes of the regulations (including provisions repealing, amending or applying, with or without modification, other law, exclusive of this Act).

Within a normal Act, s 3(2) would clearly be unconstitutional as it is a Henry VIII clause. It gives to a Minister of State a power to amend by regulation primary legislation, where that is necessary to make Community laws part of the law of the State (see Chapter 11). In *Meagher v Minister for Agriculture* [1994] 1 IR 329, the applicant had been prosecuted under regulations that amended primary legislation. He challenged the constitutionality of s 3(2). The Supreme Court upheld the constitutionality of the section, Finlay CJ delivering the judgment of the Court: [14–20]

> The power to make regulations contained in section 3(1) of the Act of 1972 is exclusively confined to the making of regulations for one purpose, and one purpose only, that of enabling section 2 of the Act to have full effect. Section 2 of the Act which provides for the application of the Community law and acts as binding on the State and as part of the domestic law subject to conditions laid down in the Treaty which, of course, include its primacy, is the major or fundamental obligation necessitated by membership of the Community. The power of regulation-making, therefore, contained in section 3 is *prima facie* a power which is part of the necessary machinery which became a duty of the State upon its joining the Community and therefore necessitated by that membership.
>
> The Court is satisfied that, having regard to the number of Community laws, acts done and measures adopted which either have to be facilitated in their direct application to the law of the State or have to be implemented by appropriate action into the law of the State, the obligation of membership would necessitate facilitating of these activities, in some instances, at least, and possibly in a great majority of instances, by the making of ministerial regulation rather than legislation of the Oireachtas.
>
> The Court is accordingly satisfied that the power to make regulations in the form in which it is contained in section 3(2) of the Act of 1972 is necessitated by the obligations of membership by the State of the Communities and now of the Union and is therefore by virtue of Article 29.4, subsections 3, 4 and 5 immune from constitutional challenge. [1994] 1 IR 329, at 351–352.

Although this ruling upheld the constitutionality of s 3 of the 1972 Act, it did not establish whether, in a particular case, it was appropriate for Community legislation to be implemented into Irish law by way of secondary legislation. In essence, the Court had decided that membership of the Community necessitated a power of this type but did not of itself necessitate use of that power in any particular case. Any Ministerial exercise of the power would be presumed constitutional unless otherwise established. [14–21]

The Court then considered whether the use by the Minister for Agriculture to make the regulations at issue was legitimate. At issue was Council Directive 85/358/EEC which provided for a system of controls on certain prohibited substances in cattle. The Minister implemented this Directive by way of the European Communities (Control of [14–22]

Oestrogenic, Androgenic, Gestagenic and Thyrostatic Substances) Regulations 1988 and the European Communities (Control of Veterinary Medicinal Products and their Residues) Regulations 1990. These regulations made it an offence to be in possession of a prescribed substance and allowed search warrants to be granted and summonses in respect of an alleged offence to be issued within two years of the offence. This was an amendment of the Petty Sessions (Ireland) Act 1851, which imposes a general time limit of six months. Blayney and Denham JJ delivered judgments with which the other members of the Court agreed. Blayney J focused on whether the powers in the regulations were necessary for the purposes of giving effect to the provisions of the Directive. He concluded that they were and, by extension, that the Minister had power to make regulations to that effect under s 3 of the 1972 Act.

[14–23] Denham J agreed with Blayney J's conclusion but formulated her approach in a manner similar to the *Cityview* test employed in respect of delegated legislation (see chapter 11):

> Article 189 leaves to the national authorities the choice of form and methods. In choosing the form and method the Minister has to act in accordance with the law and the Constitution. Thus the Minister must balance the relevant Articles of the Constitution, which in this case are Article 15.2 and Article 29.4.5. His choice, under Article 189, must be in accordance with national law, the Constitution and community law. His decision is judicially reviewable.
>
> The fact that the substance of the directive is binding as to the result to be achieved, and that a Minister must initiate an enabling national process, does not determine the issue of choice of method. Whereas the State is required to implement the substance of the directive into law, the State is not required by community law to choose any particular form or method.
>
> *Form or method*
>
> In determining the form or method the State, Minister, must have due regard to the Constitution, both Article 15.2 and Article 29.4.3.
>
> Under Bunreacht na hÉireann as enacted in 1937 the sole and exclusive power of making law for the State was vested in the Oireachtas. This is a fundamental aspect of democratic government, based on the separation of powers.
>
> That basic tenet has been qualified by membership of the European Community which has established other law making authorities. *Inter alia* it has established law making in the form of directives, which are binding on the State, as to the result to be achieved, leaving to the national authorities the choice of form and methods.
>
> Were the Constitution still in its 1937 form the State, Minister, would have no choice- he would have to initiate a process of legislation through the Oireachtas.
>
> However, the Constitution has been amended, and Community law has been introduced to the domestic law, and the situation is not now governed by Article 15.2 alone. Article 15.2 cannot be read in isolation.
>
> The term "necessitated" in Article 29.4.5 together with Article 189 of the Treaty make it clear that in balancing the two the mere fact that the substance in laws enacted, acts done or measures adopted, is necessary to be incorporated into domestic Irish law, is not the end of the matter.
>
> The term "necessitated" is relevant to the choice of method, however membership has not itself obligated a special form and method of implementation. Article 15.2 and the choice of form and methods of Article 189 must then be read together with Article 29.4.5.
>
> Article 29.4.5 refers to "laws enacted, acts done or measures adopted." Clearly this refers to legislation through the Oireachtas and other methods of implementation, including the two sets of regulations herein.

The Minister made the regulations under section 3 of the Act of 1972. The directive is "binding" on the State as to the result to be achieved. The principles and policies are set out in the directive. Under section 3(2) the Minister's regulations may contain such incidental, supplementary and consequential provisions as appear to the Minister to be necessary for the purposes of the regulations, including amending an Act (exclusive of the Act of 1972). Clearly incidental, supplementary and consequential provisions are not foundation principles and policies.

If the directive left to the national authority matters of principle or policy to be determined then the "choice" of the Minister would require legislation by the Oireachtas. But where there is no case made that principles or policies have to be determined by the national authority, where the situation is that the principles and policies were determined in the directive, then legislation by a delegated form, by regulation, is a valid choice. The fact that an Act of the Oireachtas has been affected by the policy in a directive, is a "result to be achieved" wherein there is now no choice between the policy and the national act. The policy of the directive must succeed. Thus where there is in fact no choice on a policy or a principle it is a matter appropriate for delegated legislation. If the directive or the Minister envisaged any choice of principle or policy then it would require legislation by the Oireachtas....

Applying the test to this situation the test is whether the ministerial regulations under section 3 of the Act of 1972 are more than the mere giving effect to principles and policies of the said Act and the directives which are part of domestic law as to the result to be achieved.

If the regulations contained material exceeding the policies and principles of the directives then they are not authorised by the directives and would not be valid under section 3 unless the material was incidental, supplementary or consequential. In those circumstances if they were not incidental, supplementary or consequential the regulations would be an exercise of legislative power by an authority not so permitted under the Constitution. If it be within the permitted limits, if the policy is laid down in the directive and details only are filled in or completed by the regulations, there is no unauthorised delegation of legislative power.

Democracy

The separation of powers is a fundamental principle of Bunreacht na hÉireann. The power to legislate for the State is solely within the Oireachtas-save where that authority has been assigned under the Constitution to Community authorities and organs of the State to act in accordance with Community law as integrated into national law. There was no question in this case that the principles and policies of the directives were not within the Treaties.

In the directives herein the policies and principles have been determined. Thus there is no role of determining policies or principles for the Oireachtas. While the directive must be implemented there is no policy or principle which can be altered by the Oireachtas, it is already binding as to the result to be achieved.

That being the case the role of the Oireachtas in such a situation would be sterile. To require the Oireachtas to legislate would be artificial. It would be able solely to have a debate as to what has already been decided, which debate would act as a source of information. Such a sterile debate would take up Dáil and Seanad time and act only as a window on Community directives for the members of the Oireachtas and the Nation. That is not a role envisaged for the Oireachtas in the Constitution.

Consequently, solely because the Minister is making a regulation which repeals a statute, does not of itself invalidate the regulation which as a vehicle, as a choice, can be *intra vires* the Constitution under Article 29.4. To say that the regulations breach Article 15.2.1 simply because it repeals or amends a statute is to hold the false premise that the Minister is determining principles or policy.

The regulations in this case being within the policies and principles of the directives the substance of the regulation is within the directives. There are no policies and principles enunciated in the regulations that are not within the directives. There are no policies and principles in the regulations additional to the directive.

Consequently, to state that such an action-effectively an administrative implementation of policies and principles of a directive-is superior legislation as envisaged in Article 15.2.1-is a misnomer. Superior legislation involves a decision on policies and principles by the legislature and an implementation thereof in the form of a statute. Here what is at issue in essence is subordinate legislation as delegated under Community law.

No constitutional right, other than the process under Article 15.2 of Bunreacht na hÉireann, was submitted as part of the argument, or as being in issue. Nor was any issue raised as to the validity of the directives and their principles and policies under the Treaties.

I am satisfied that the regulations in issue in this case were not *ultra vires* the power of the Minister for Agriculture and Food under section 3 of the European Communities Act, 1972, insofar as they authorised the time thereby amending section 10(4) of the Petty Sessions (Ireland) Act, 1851, being as they were implementations of policies and principles in the relevant directives. [1994] 1 IR 329, at 364–368.

[14–24] The constitutional requirements for the implementation of Community law were again considered in *Maher v Minister for Agriculture* [2001] 2 IR 139. Notwithstanding that the European Communities (Milk Quota) Regulations 2000 SI 49/2000 were adopted to implement a Community law Regulation – as distinct from a Directive – it was submitted that the Regulation had left matters of principle and policy for the Member States and that therefore, as a matter of Irish constitutional law, the Minister had acted *ultra vires* in implementing them by secondary legislation. Keane CJ took the opportunity to reconsider and refine slightly the reasoning in *Meagher*:

> It is accepted in this case that, if the making by the first respondent of the Regulations of 2000 was "necessitated" by the obligations of membership of the European Union or the European Economic Community, it could not be successfully challenged by the applicants. It would seem to follow that this should be the first issue to be addressed by this court.
>
> As a result of the passage of the Eleventh Amendment of the Constitution, Article 29.4.3 empowered the State to become a member of, *inter alia*, the European Economic Community established by the Treaty of Rome. Article 29.4.5 ensured that laws enacted, acts done or measures adopted by the State which were necessitated by the obligations of membership of, *inter alia*, the European Economic Community were not invalidated by any other provision of the Constitution. Section 2 of the Act of 1972, which provided that the treaties governing the European Communities and the existing and future acts adopted by the institutions of the communities were to be binding on the State and be part of its domestic law under the conditions laid down in the treaties, was clearly necessitated by the obligations of membership of those communities.
>
> The result was a historic transfer of legislative, executive and judicial sovereignty to the European Communities and, as a result of further referenda, the European Union. In particular, the exclusive roles hitherto enjoyed by the Oireachtas in the legislative field and the courts in the administration of justice were significantly abridged. The developing jurisprudence of the European Court of Justice also made it clear that there existed effectively an autonomous European legal order and that the member states were obliged to acknowledge the primacy of Community law over national law in areas where it was applicable. It was also, moreover, clear that the member states envisaged that the communities established by treaties were to be dynamic in their nature and that the obligations of membership referred to in Article 29.4.5 would not be static.
>
> In the result, a significant new volume of legislation became applicable in Ireland and binding on all the citizens either in the form of directives which the State, as a result of its

membership, was obliged to implement in domestic legislation, or regulations which were directly applicable in Ireland and did not require such legislation for their implementation. Since, under the communities' legal order, the method by which a directive was implemented, as distinct from its substance, was to be determined by the member state, the directive itself would contain no indication as to which of the two normal methods employed in Ireland, an Act of the Oireachtas or a ministerial regulation, was to be employed. The directives in short, did not contain the enabling provision, commonplace in domestic Irish legislation, under which a minister or some other body so authorised by the Oireachtas can give detailed effect in the form of regulations to policies determined by the Oireachtas. That was not necessarily the case with regulations which, of their nature, did not require implementation by either legislation or regulation. As the present case demonstrates, however, it was also possible for the Council of Ministers to issue regulations having direct effect in a member state such as Ireland which, in defined areas, required or authorised the member state to adopt its own rules whether by way of legislation or regulation. It is also, of course, obvious that in some instances, in the case of both directives and regulations, their detailed implementation can be effected by administrative acts rather than by legislation or regulation.

Accordingly, had section 3 of the Act of 1972, not been enacted by the Oireachtas, it would have been necessary for directives to be implemented by an Act of the Oireachtas, since there would have been no parent legislation in this country enabling it to be done by way of regulations made by the appropriate minister. The same would apply to those regulations in which the member states were required or authorised to adopt rules themselves for the purpose of implementing the regulations. Thus, although a directive did no more than require the member states to reduce or increase a tariff or duty by a specified sum, leaving no policy choice to be made by the Oireachtas, it would have been necessary for an Act to be passed if Ireland was to fulfil its obligation as a member of the community....

It follows that, in the present case, the first inquiry must be as to whether the implementation of the European Communities Regulation by legislation, whether in primary or secondary form, was necessitated by the obligations of membership within the meaning of Article 29.4.5 of the Constitution. It is clear that it was. Article 7.1 expressly required the making of detailed rules by the member states as to the transfer of quotas with a holding in the case of its sale, lease or transfer by inheritance to purchasers. To that extent at least, Ireland was under an obligation to adopt such detailed rules and it was not contended on behalf of the applicants that this could have been achieved by administrative decisions, rather than legislation, either primary or secondary in form, which was binding in law on all those affected whether as persons entitled to quotas, producers of milk or purchasers of milk or milk quotas.

The second inquiry in the present case is as to whether, given that the making of detailed rules in legislative form, to at least that extent, was necessitated by the obligations of membership, their being made in the form of the Regulations of 2000 other than by an Act, was in conflict with the exclusive legislative role of the Oireachtas under Article 15.1 and was not necessitated by the obligations of membership....

[I]t is almost beyond argument that the choice of a statutory instrument as a vehicle for the detailed rules rather than an Act was not in any sense necessitated by the obligations of Community membership. There would appear to be no difference in principle between the obligation on a member state to implement a directive and the corresponding obligation under a regulation, such as the European Communities Regulation in the present case, to adopt detailed rules for the implementation of specified parts of the regulation. In each case, while the member state is obliged to implement the directive or the specified part of the regulation, the choice of form and method for implementation is clearly a matter for the member state....

[I]n the present case, it could not be said that the making of the rules in the form of the Regulations of 2000 rather than an Act were necessitated by the obligations of membership and the essential inquiry must be as to whether the first respondent in making the Regulations of 2000 was in breach of Article 15.1 of the Constitution.

In determining that issue, it is accepted that the appropriate test is as set out by O'Higgins CJ in *City View Press Limited v An Comhairle Oiliúna* [1980] IR 381...

However, in applying that test to a case in which the regulation is made in purported exercise of the powers of the first respondent under section 3 of the Act of 1972, it must be borne in mind that while the parent statute is the Act of 1972, the relevant principles and policies cannot be derived from that Act, having regard to the very general terms in which it is couched. In each case, it is necessary to look to the directive or regulation and, it may be, the treaties in order to reach a conclusion as to whether the statutory instrument does no more than fill in the details of principles and policies contained in the European Community or European Union legislation.

Thus, there are no doubt many cases, of which *Meagher v Minister for Agriculture* [1994] 1 IR 329 was one, where no choice has to be made by the member state as to the appropriate policy to be implemented. The policy in that case was unmistakably the outlawing of the hormonal substances in question and the giving of the necessary powers of search and prosecution to the competent authorities in the member states. Nor had the State any discretion as to whether any particular part of the impugned regulation was to be omitted....

In the present case, the European Community Regulations as already noted, required the member states to adopt detailed rules as to the transfer of quotas with land and it also required the authorisation of temporary transfers of quotas which producers who were entitled thereto did not intend to use. However, in three areas, it was left to the member states to decide whether they elected to pursue specified courses of action. First, they could effectively derogate from the provisions of article 7(1) by providing that quotas were not to be automatically transferred with a holding. They could only do so, however, in order to ensure that quotas were solely attributed to active milk producers. The first respondent decided to make use of this option by providing in the Regulations of 2000 that, subject to certain exceptions, quotas were not to be automatically transferred with the land. Since one of the exceptions was in favour of active milk producers, there can be no doubt that the first respondent, in making the regulation in that form, could not be accused of having effected an impermissible derogation from the general provisions of article 7(1). The Regulations of 2000 also allowed for exceptions in the case of sales or transfers to specified members of the family of the person entitled to the quota.

The member states were also entitled under article 6 to determine to what extent transfer operations might be renewed. This was availed of by the first respondent so as to restrict persons entitled to quotas who had leased their quotas for three successive years from making more than one further lease of the land and quota. Finally, article 8 enabled the member states to take one or more of five courses of action with a view to completing restructuring of milk production or environmental improvement. One of these was availed of by the first respondent to introduce the milk quota restructuring scheme....

As I have already indicated, a directive, or in this case a regulation, can be equated to the parent statute in which, in the case of domestic legislation, one would expect to find principles and policies laid down which were then to be implemented in detail by a form of delegated legislation. There is, however, manifestly a significant difference between a directive or regulation, which is applicable throughout the fifteen member states of the European Union, and an Act of the Oireachtas the effect of which is confined to a relatively small and homogeneous area within the European Union. In the case of a regulation which is intended to apply in a number of different regions throughout the European Union in which the conditions of the dairying industry may vary widely, it is not surprising to find that the regulation, in specified areas, leaves choices as to the nature of the implementing measures to be introduced by the member state. The issue in this case is as to whether the choice of the appropriate measures can be regarded as involving no determination of policy or principle, as that expression has been used in previous decisions of this court.

I have experienced some difficulty in arriving at a conclusion as to how this issue is to be resolved. Applying the reasoning which found favour in *Meagher v Minister for Agriculture* [1994] 1 IR 329, it seems self-evident that there are choices to be made by Ireland, as a member state, in determining how it will implement the regulation in those areas where it has been afforded a discretion. Once it is acknowledged that rules of this nature may be implemented in a manner requiring parliamentary scrutiny and that implementation by ministerial regulation is not necessitated by our membership of the European Union, it gives rise to natural misgivings to find that there is no role for the democratically elected institutions of the State, other than the limited one under section 4 of the Act of 1972. I am, however, persuaded by the analysis carried out by Fennelly J in the judgment that he will deliver that, in the case of the operation of the super-levy scheme, the choices as to policy available to the member states have in truth, been reduced almost to vanishing point. As he points out, the scheme which has given rise to these proceedings was essentially the creation of the European Union and, if one seeks to determine the principles and policies which underlie it, one must look, not to any parent legislation in Ireland, but to the treaties of the European Union and the regulations and directives which have established the complex machinery of the Common Agricultural Policy and the common market in milk. It follows that the making of the regulation was not an impermissible exercise of the legislative role of the Oireachtas and that the applicants' contentions to the contrary are not well founded. [2001] 2 IR 139, at 175–177; 181–186.

[14–25] In this particular case, the Supreme Court concluded that the level of choice permitted to Ireland by the Community Regulation was not such that required the intervention of the Oireachtas: implementation by way of statutory instrument did not breach the *City View* test. It is difficult to assess precisely how the courts will apply the *Meagher/Maher* test. Given the generally non-rigorous application of the *Cityview* test itself, it seems unlikely that a particularly onerous approach will be taken in relation to European legislation.

[14–26] In the more recent case of *Browne v Attorney General* [2003] 3 IR 205, the Supreme Court held that s 3 of the European Communities Act 1972 could not be used to make regulations creating an indictable offence: this followed from s 3(3) which provided that regulations under that section could not create an indictable offence. The contentious issue in the case was whether the State could rely on a principle/policy contained in a European Community law measure and a secondary law-making power contained in an Act of the Oireachtas. The Supreme Court held that this was impermissible:

> It is accepted in this case that the Council Regulation of 1998, which prohibits the use by vessels of any of the member states, either within their exclusive fishery limits or on the high seas, of drift nets exceeding 2.5 kilometres in length for the purpose of catching albacore tuna is directly applicable in the State to the same extent as if it were an Act of the Oireachtas. As is normally the case with European Community measures, it is left to the member states to provide for the effective policing of the measure in question in whatever is the appropriate manner having regard to the laws of the member state concerned. It is not in dispute in this case that, in these circumstances, the second respondent was empowered by section 3 of the Act of 1972 to make regulations for that purpose, even though the principles and policies which were being given effect to were not prescribed by the Oireachtas in primary legislation. It is clear from the decisions of this court in *Meagher v Minister for Agriculture* [1994] 1 IR 329 and *Maher v Minister for*

Agriculture [2001] 2 IR 139 that the fact that, in such cases, the principles and policies to which the regulation gives effect are not to be found in any Act of the Oireachtas, but rather in the Community measure concerned, does not affect its constitutional validity. It is beyond argument at this stage that the law as laid down by this court in *Cityview Press v An Chomhairle Oiliúna* [1980] IR 381, that secondary legislation will trespass on the exclusive law making role of the Oireachtas unless it does no more than give effect to principles and policies laid down in an Act of the Oireachtas, is not applicable to regulations intended to give effect, by virtue of section 3 of the Act of 1972, to European Community measures such as the Council Regulation of 1998. There is, however, one crucial qualification to that general statement of the law, namely, that any such regulation cannot create an indictable offence.

It is clear, in this case, that the Order of 1998 was intended to give effect to the principles and policies as to the conservation of fishery resources adopted by the Council in Council Regulation 1998. There is not any Act of the Oireachtas in existence setting out principles and policies applicable to the conservation of fishery resources both within the exclusive fishery limits of the State and on the high seas. As is clear from the judgment of the Court of Justice in *Commission of the European Communities v United Kingdom of Great Britain and Northern Ireland* (Case 804/79) [1981] 2 ECR 1045, since the 1st January, 1979, the power to adopt, as part of the common fisheries policy, measures relating to the conservation of the resources of the sea has been vested exclusively in the European Communities.

I am satisfied that it follows inevitably that the Order of 1998 was not intended to give effect to principles and policies set out by the Oireachtas in parent legislation. It was intended simply to give effect to the principles and policies adopted by the Communities in Council Regulation 1998, as, indeed, the terms of the order itself make unambiguously clear: the second respondent while purportedly invoking powers conferred on him by section 223A of the Act of 1998 says in express terms that this is being done:-

"for the purpose of giving effect to Council Regulation (E.C.) No. 1239/98."

As I have already indicated, there is not the slightest doubt as to the power of the second respondent to give effect by statutory instrument to the principles and policies contained in that measure, even though they have not been embodied in any Act of the Oireachtas: that is the clear object of section 3 of the Act of 1972. What no minister can do, in availing of the powers conferred by that section, is to provide for the creation of an indictable offence: that power was expressly reserved to the Oireachtas by subsection (3). There is no indication whatever in the language of section 223A that it was envisaged by the Oireachtas that the second respondent could give effect to principles and policies which had never been considered or adopted by the Oireachtas by means of a statutory instrument under that section which effectively circumvented the prohibition on the creation of indictable offences in section 3(3) of the Act of 1972.... [2003] 3 IR 205, at 219–220.

[14–27] This imposed a procedural restriction on the State. If a Minister sought to defend the validity of secondary legislation on the basis that it was consistent with principles and policies contained in a European Community measure, that Minister could not evade the requirement in s 3(3) of the 1972 Act to the effect that indictable offences could not be created by way of regulation under that provision.

[14–28] The European Communities (Amendment) Act 2007 seeks to reverse both the specific conclusion and the rationale of *Browne*. Section 2 of the 2007 Act amends s 3 of the 1972 Act to allow for the prosecution on indictment of offences created by regulations made pursuant to s 3. Section 4 of the 2007 Act provides that a power conferred on a Government Minister to make a statutory instrument may be exercised by that Minister for the purpose of giving effect to a European Act "if the obligations imposed on the State under the European act concerned relate, in whole, to matters to which" the statutory power relates. Section 5 of the Act provides that any statutory instrument purporting to give effect to a European Act, but that was made under a statutory provision that was not for the purpose of giving effect to a European Act, shall have statutory effect as if it were an Act of the Oireachtas. This approach takes advantage of the decision in *Leontjava v DPP and Chang v DPP* [2004] 1 IR 591 to confer statutory authority on secondary legislation that would otherwise be invalid.

Contents – Chapter 15

Referendums and the Political Process

Introduction	[15–01]
Referendums: the Constitutional Provisions and Early Cases	[15–02]
The Referendum Cases: a More Interventionist Role	[15–12]
The Substance of Referendum Proposals	[15–23]
The Electoral Process	[15–30]
Drawing of Constituency Boundaries	[15–30]
Secret Ballot	[15–41]
Rules Governing Candidates at Elections	[15–42]

Overview

Referendums and the political process have both been regulated by reference to the Constitution. Initially, the courts were wary of intervention in the conduct of referendums. However, in 1995 the courts held that it breached constitutional guarantees of fair procedures and equality for the Government to spend money on one side of a campaign in a referendum. However, the courts continue to be unwilling to intervene in relation to the content of a referendum proposal. Moreover, the courts have never overturned the result of a referendum once it has been held. In relation to the electoral process, the courts have intervened to ensure the secrecy of the ballot and to ensure that the ratio of population to representatives is reasonably uniform throughout the country. More recently, the courts have adopted the norm of fair procedures developed in the referendum context to provide some protections for election candidates from overly burdensome procedures.

CHAPTER 15

Referendums and the Political Process

Introduction

The people interact with the organs of government in two ways. Through referendums, the people can amend the Constitution. In this way popular sovereignty is realised: the people have the ultimate say on matters of national importance. However, the people more regularly have their say indirectly, through their elected representatives. Both referendums and the political process are primarily regulated by statutory law. However, litigants have occasionally called in aid the Constitution to govern the referendum process and the political process. The courts were generally quite slow to impose constitutional requirements on how referendums and the political process must be conducted. However, in the past 15 years the courts have developed a basic norm of fairness that applies to these processes. This was developed originally in the context of referendums but has also been applied to the political process. However, it is procedural rather than substantive in character. [15–01]

Referendums: the Constitutional Provisions and Early Cases

Article 6.1 of the Constitution provides that it is the right of the people to designate the rulers of the State and, in final appeal, to decide all matters of national policy. Article 46.1 provides: [15–02]

> Any provision of this Constitution may be amended, whether by way of variation, addition, or repeal, in the manner provided by this Article.

The rest of Art 46 outlines the procedure by which a referendum proposal may be put to the people. It must first be passed by the Oireachtas in much the same way as ordinary legislation, save with the obvious difference that it can only be enacted if it is approved by the people as well. Article 47.1 of the Constitution provides that a proposal to amend the Constitution will be passed if a simple majority of those voting on the day approve it. This is a lower threshold than applied under the Irish Free State Constitution whereby a referendum could only be approved by a majority of two thirds of those voting or an absolute majority of those registered to vote.

There were not many referendums in the early years of the State, although the rate of constitutional amendment has increased significantly since the 1980s. It was in the 1980s that litigants first sought to have the referendum process regulated by the courts by reference to constitutional principles. In *Roche v Ireland* 17 June 1983 (HC), Mr Roche sought to prevent the Eighth Amendment of the Constitution being put to the people on the basis that the wording was unclear. As a consequence, he argued, he [15–03] could not rationally decide how to vote and was therefore deprived of his constitutional right. Carroll J rejected this contention, noting that the Court had no jurisdiction to interfere in the legislative process and commenting that if Mr Roche was uncertain of the meaning of the Amendment, he could vote against it, thereby preserving the *status quo*.

[15–04] In *Finn v Minister for the Environment* [1983] IR 154, Mr Finn sought to restrain the holding of the same referendum to insert Art 40.3.3° into the Constitution. Article 40.3.3° proposed to grant explicit protection to the right to life of the unborn. Mr Finn argued that the Supreme Court had recognised the right to life of the unborn as an unenumerated constitutional right in cases such as *G v An Bord Uchtála* [1980] IR 32 and *Norris v Attorney General* [1984] IR 36. On this basis, Mr Finn challenged the constitutionality of the Bill passed by the Oireachtas to amend the Constitution and sought to restrain the holding of the referendum.

[15–05] In the High Court, Barrington J accepted that the right to life of the unborn was constitutionally protected. He reasoned:

> [Counsel for Mr Finn submits] that the Courts ... have a duty to uphold the Constitution and that, upon a complaint being properly made that the Houses of the Oireachtas had acted in contravention of Article 46, section 4, of the Constitution by incorporating other proposals in a Bill to amend the Constitution, the Courts would be justified in examining the Bill and taking appropriate action. Subject to this possible exception, I accept [Counsel for the Minister's] submission that the High Court has no function in relation to the content of a proposal to amend the Constitution. Certainly it is not concerned with the propriety or wisdom of any such proposal, nor has it any power to restrain the two Houses of the Oireachtas from putting any such proposal before the people....
>
> [Counsel for Mr Finn's] submission requires the restrictive interpretation which he seeks to place on the people's power to amend the Constitution. [He] contends that the Constitution can be amended by way of variation, addition, or repeal—but not otherwise. If, he contends, the rights of the unborn child are already implicitly protected by the Constitution, it is not open to the people to amend the Constitution by making that protection explicit. When the people provided that the Constitution could be amended "whether by way of variation, addition, or repeal," I very much doubt if they intended to restrict their powers in this manner....
>
> Finally, to succeed in his submission, [Counsel for Mr Finn] would have to show that the proposed amendment, if accepted by the people, would not vary or affect the protection which I believe the Constitution presently gives to the unborn child. In deference to [Counsel for the Minister's] submission, which I accept, that it is generally no function of the Court to attempt to construe a Bill containing a proposal to amend the Constitution, I feel obliged to decline to attempt to construe the present proposal. I will say only that [Counsel for Mr Finn] has failed to convince me that the present proposed amendment, if accepted by the people, will not change or vary the constitutional position of the unborn child as I have attempted to describe it earlier in this judgment. [1983] IR 154, at 160–164.

[15–06] On appeal, the Supreme Court dealt with the issue more tersely, simply holding that the courts had no power to review the constitutionality of a Bill, except under the Art 26 procedure. Accordingly, the Court could not enter into the analysis that Mr Finn urged. The Supreme Court's approach on this point creates something of a lacuna. As Barrington J had noted, it is a constitutional requirement that a Bill containing a proposal to amend the Constitution contain no other proposal. Although Barrington J accepted that the courts could review such a flawed procedure, the dicta of the Supreme Court suggested that judicial intervention in such circumstances would not be permissible.

In *Slattery v An Taoiseach* [1993] 1 IR 286, the plaintiffs sought to restrain the Government from holding a referendum to ratify the Treaty on European Union on the basis that the Government had not met its obligation to provide factual information or evidence of the benefits, disadvantages and onerous provisions of the Treaty on European Union and had not provided clarification as to the legal effects of ratification of the Treaty on European Union having regard in particular to Art 40.3.3°. The issues in this case were clouded somewhat by the failure of the plaintiffs to go to court in a timely manner. Nevertheless, the Supreme Court gave some substantial consideration to the issues, effectively affirming the position stated in *Finn*. Hederman J reasoned: [15–07]

> What is now before this Court is in effect a challenge to the Oireachtas and to the defendants in their decision to hold a referendum. That challenge is contained in the passages that I have referred to in the affidavit of the first plaintiff, which, though not before the High Court, was before this Court. The real point in this case is to ask this Court to prevent the operation of legislative and constitutional procedures which are in train. This is something the Court has no jurisdiction to do. What the defendants are doing is implementing the decision of the Dáil and the Seanad. They are not controlling the referendum. There is no constitutional or legal obligation on the defendants to provide funds for those seeking to oppose the referendum....
>
> I am satisfied that the plaintiffs have failed to satisfy this Court there is anything unconstitutional in what is being done by the defendants. The Treaty on European Union is still fully in existence. What cannot yet be decided is the issue of whether the Treaty is ultimately going to be ratified by all the Member States. It should be noted that the present date for ratification may not necessarily be the final date for such ratification. A proposal to amend the Constitution cannot *per se* be unconstitutional and the procedure adopted for so doing cannot be unconstitutional if it complies with the requirements of the Constitution. Nothing in this case has demonstrated any failure to comply. [1993] 1 IR 286, at 299–300.

McCarthy J agreed, although he addressed more directly the question of whether there was an obligation on the Government to provide information about the referendum proposal: [15–08]

> Article 6 proclaims that all powers of government legislative, executive and judicial, are derived under God from the People. In having a referendum, the People are taking a direct role in government either by amending the Constitution or by refusing to amend it. Such an amendment can only be initiated by the legislature where the relevant legislation may be promoted by any member of the legislature. When the relevant legislation has been passed by both houses the constitutional process must continue. The relevant legislation concerning the holding of a referendum makes no reference to the provision of information. It may be that an argument can be advanced that there is an obligation on the defendants to provide information concerning what may be involved in the referendum. In my view, an argument for such a requirement does not warrant interference by the judicial organ of government in this constitutional process. [1993] 1 IR 286, at 303.

McKenna v An Taoiseach (No 1) [1995] 2 IR 1 concerned the same referendum on the Maastricht Treaty in 1992. (The case was decided in 1992 but not reported until 1995). [15–09]

Ms McKenna argued that it was unconstitutional for the Government to spend money on an advertising campaign advocating a "yes" vote on the Maastricht Treaty. Costello J rejected her argument:

> Here no claim is made that a *legal* wrong has been committed or is contemplated — the allegation is that a *constitutional* wrong has been committed by the Government by the acts complained of and that the wrong will be repeated unless restrained by order of this court. As I understand the submission that the Government actions have infringed the Constitution, it is this: the Constitution requires that the People decide on whether the Constitution should be amended or not. This constitutional responsibility can only be fulfilled by the People if it is properly informed on the issues. Such a requirement calls for a public debate in which both sides of the argument can be put fairly and adequately. If a publicly funded advertising campaign undertaken by the Government is partisan and only presents one point of view, this will distort the debate because the proponents of the opposite view would not have the resources to match it. It follows, it is suggested, that unless a publicly funded advertising campaign for a "Yes" vote is accompanied by public funding for those campaigning for a "No" vote, the People will be unable to give the informed and responsible decision which is required by the Constitution. The Government, it is claimed, will act constitutionally if it campaigns for its point of view in a non-partisan way. But if it decides to campaign in a partisan way, that is by a campaign which only puts one point of view, then the Government will act constitutionally if, but only if, it makes public funds available to enable those opposing it to express their point of view in media advertisements and by means of information leaflets.
>
> I can, of course, appreciate that the plaintiff as a member of a small party opposed to the Government's point of view may feel aggrieved that her party's campaign is deprived of the benefits which the Government has conferred on itself from public funds. But not every grievance can be remedied by the courts. And judges must not allow themselves to be led, or indeed voluntarily wander, into areas calling for adjudication on political and non-justiciable issues. They are charged by the Constitution with exercising the judicial power of government and it would both weaken their important constitutional role as well as amount to an unconstitutional act for judges to adjudicate on such issues. It seems to me that this is what the plaintiff in this action is requiring the court to do. The merits of ratification or non-ratification of the Maastricht Treaty are, of course, not matters on which this court should express a view. The extent of the role the Government feels called upon to play to ensure ratification is a matter of concern for the executive arm of government, not the judicial. The Dáil decides what monies are to be voted for expenditure by the Government on information services (which would include an advertising campaign in support of an affirmative vote in a referendum). Should the Government decide that the national interest required that an advertising campaign be mounted which was confined to extolling forcibly the benefits of an affirmative vote, it would be improper for the courts to express any view on such a decision. The object of such a campaign would, of course, be to influence voters' attitudes. But to adjudicate on a claim that the use of public funds to finance such a campaign was unfair because it distorted public attitudes would involve an assessment of the effect of such a campaign on public attitudes, the strength of the opposing campaign of those propounding a "No" vote, and the forces influencing the voters' ultimate decision. Such an assessment is not just one of establishing facts but calls for a careful analysis and a balancing of complex political and social factors. It is one for political analysts to make, not for judges.
>
> I must conclude, therefore, that the plaintiff's complaint of misconduct by the Government is a complaint of *political* misconduct on which this court can express no view and that she has failed to establish any *constitutional* impropriety in the exercise by the Government of the executive power of government in the conduct of the referendum campaign.... [1995] 2 IR 10, at 5–6.

Costello J also rejected Ms McKenna's claims that her right to communicate was [15–10] infringed, as she was not precluded from communicating. He also rejected the contention that her right to equality in the exercise of the franchise had been infringed:

> [T]he plaintiff has failed to show how it has been infringed in this case. The submission would appear to be a development of the distortion argument to which I have already referred. It is claimed, as I understand the submission, that by a partisan publicly-funded publicity campaign for a "Yes" vote the electorate will be unfairly influenced so that more affirmative votes will be cast than would otherwise be the case. But even if this could be established on an issue on which the court could adjudicate, such conduct would not amount to an infringement of the right now being considered. Each vote cast in the referendum by each member of the electorate would still be of the same value — and this is not altered by the fact that some might be cast in a way which was influenced by the methods of advocacy employed by the Government. [1995] 2 IR 10, at 8.

In 1995, the Supreme Court initially reaffirmed its strong reluctance to get involved in [15–11] the supervision of referendums. In *Re Article 26 and the Regulation of Information (Services Outside the State for Termination of Pregnancies) Bill 1995* [1995] 1 IR 1, the Supreme Court was invited to rule that the Fourteenth Amendment to the Constitution, permitting the distribution in Ireland of information about abortion services abroad, was itself unconstitutional. That is, the Court was called to overturn a referendum decision on the basis that it was substantively defective, because it conflicted with the natural law. The Court refused to do so, holding that the people were entitled to amend the Constitution in accordance with Art 46 of the Constitution. Once amended, the Constitution was the supreme law of the land and not open to judicial review. (This case is discussed in greater detail in chapter 4).

The Referendum Cases: a More Interventionist Role

Later in 1995, however, Ms McKenna returned to the courts making the same [15–12] argument that it was unconstitutional for the Government to spend money supporting one side of a referendum campaign. On this occasion, she objected to the campaign being run by the Government in support of the proposal to amend the Constitution to allow for divorce. Dáil Éireann had voted that £500,000 be allocated to the Minister for Equality and Law Reform, to be used for a publicity campaign to encourage a "Yes" vote in a forthcoming referendum on the removal of the constitutional prohibition on divorce. In the High Court, Keane J followed the judgment of Costello J in *McKenna (No 1)*. However, the Supreme Court allowed her appeal, albeit on grounds that are not entirely clear. Hamilton CJ reasoned as follows:

> For the purposes of this case I am prepared to accept that the Government was acting in accordance with its rights in the giving of factual information with regard to the proposal which is the subject of the referendum, in expressing its views thereon and in urging the acceptance of such views.
>
> The fundamental issue raised by the plaintiff in this case is whether the Government was entitled to expend public funds for the purpose of promoting a campaign for a "Yes" vote in the proposed referendum to amend the terms of the Constitution.
>
> As illustrated earlier in the course of this judgment, neither the Constitution nor the Referendum Act, 1994, envisaged any role for the Government in the submission of the Bill by referendum to the decision of the People.

The action of the Government in expending public funds on the promotion of such a campaign was not an action in pursuance of the executive power of the State.

Even if it were, it would still be subject to examination and review by the Court in accordance with the *dicta* quoted in the course of this judgment.

It is admitted by and on behalf of the Government that it has expended and proposes to expend certain monies in a publicity campaign designed to influence public opinion in relation to the proposed referendum.

The question for consideration is whether such activity constitutes an interference with the constitutional process of amending the Constitution and the constitutional rights of the plaintiff.

The constitutional process for the amendment of the Constitution has been set forth in detail earlier in this judgment as being governed by the provisions of Articles 46 and 47 of the Constitution and the terms of the Referendum Act, 1994.

As stated by McCarthy J in *Crotty v An Taoiseach* [1987] IR 713, the People in having a referendum "are taking a direct role in government either by amending the Constitution or refusing to amend it".

The role of the People in amending the Constitution cannot be overemphasized. It is solely their prerogative to amend any provision thereof by way of variation, addition or repeal or to refuse to amend. The decision is theirs and theirs alone.

Having regard to the importance of the Constitution as the fundamental law of the State and the crucial role of the People in the adoption and enactment thereof, any amendment thereof must be in accordance with the constitutional process and no interference with that process can be permitted because, as stated by Walsh J in *Crotty v An Taoiseach* [1987] IR 713, "it is the people themselves who are the guardians of the Constitution".

As the guardians of the Constitution and in taking a direct role in government either by amending the Constitution or by refusing to amend, the People, by virtue of the democratic nature of the State enshrined in the Constitution, are entitled to be permitted to reach their decision free from unauthorised interference by any of the organs of State that they, the People, have created by the enactment of the Constitution.

The constitutional process to be followed in the amendment of the Constitution involves not only compliance with the provisions of Articles 46 and 47 of the Constitution and the terms of the Referendum Act, 1994, but also that regard be had for the constitutional rights of the citizens and the adoption of fair procedures.

The Bill containing the proposal to amend the Constitution was initiated in Dáil Éireann, passed by both Houses of the Oireachtas and then submitted for the decision of the People.

Once the Bill has been submitted for the decision of the People, the People were and are entitled to reach their decision in a free and democratic manner.

The use by the Government of public funds to fund a campaign designed to influence the voters in favour of a "Yes" vote is an interference with the democratic process and the constitutional process for the amendment of the Constitution and infringes the concept of equality which is fundamental to the democratic nature of the State. [1995] 2 IR 10, at 40–42.

[15–13] O'Flaherty J agreed that the funding of one side of the referendum campaign was unconstitutional, although he did not cite any constitutional provision in support of this conclusion, instead stating a number of general propositions:

> [T]he Government must stop short of spending public money in favour of one side which has the consequence of being to the detriment of those opposed to the constitutional amendment.
>
> To spend money in this way breaches the equality rights of the citizen enshrined in the Constitution as well as having the effect of putting the voting rights of one class of citizen (those in favour of the change) above those of another class of citizen (those against).

> The public purse must not be expended to espouse a point of view which may be anathema to certain citizens who, of necessity, have contributed to it. No one would suggest that a Government is entitled to devote money from the exchequer in a direct manner in the course of a general election to secure its re-election. (I leave aside legislative enactments which it may have helped to bring about with the outcome of an election in mind.) The position of a referendum is not any different.
>
> I should think it bordering on the self-evident that in a democracy such as is enshrined in our Constitution (which is not exclusively a parliamentary democracy; it has elements of a plebiscitary democracy) it is impermissible for the Government to spend public money in the course of a referendum campaign to benefit one side rather that the other. [1995] 2 IR 10, at 43.

Denham J made a similar point:

> The spirit and concept of equality applies to the process of a referendum. There is a right to equal treatment in the political process. It is a breach of the concept and spirit of the constitutional right to equality for the Government to spend public monies in funding a campaign to advocate a specific result in a referendum. [1995] 2 IR 10, at 53.

But it is hard to see how the spending of money on one side of a referendum campaign breaches the equality rights of citizens or puts the voting rights of one class of citizen above those of another. Furthermore, citizens can surely have no right to prevent the expenditure of public monies in support of views of which they disapprove. Blayney J focused more on fair procedures, albeit a conception of fair procedures that draws heavily on ideas about equality: [15–14]

> [N]either the provisions of the Constitution nor the provisions of the Act of 1994 envisage that the executive would have any role other than to submit the amendment to the decision of the People. No guidance is given as to how this role is to be carried out, but since it is a role imposed on the executive by the Constitution in connection with the very important constitutional right of the People, that is voting at a referendum, I am satisfied that constitutional justice requires that the executive should act fairly in discharging it, not favouring any section of the People at the expense of any other section. This would seem to be a minimum requirement for the discharge of any constitutional obligation. The people are entitled to be treated equally....
>
> Has the executive observed fair procedures in submitting the amendment to the decision of the People? In my view it has not. The Government has not held the scales equally between those who support and those who oppose the amendment. It has thrown its weight behind those who support it. The Government's intention, as indicated very clearly in a letter dated the 20th October, 1995, written on the direction of the Minister for Equality and Law Reform to a public relations firm engaged by the Department, is to spend a sum of over £400,000 in inserting advertisements in the national press and having leaflets printed, the object of which is to advocate a "Yes" vote. If this plan were implemented it would give a very considerable advantage to those who support the amendment as against those who oppose it. The Government would be acting unfairly in the manner in which it was submitting the amendment to the decision of the People. [1995] 2 IR 10, at 49–50.

Blayney J's conception of fair procedures seems more appealing than the equality-based rationale more favoured by Denham and O'Flaherty JJ. Although it is difficult to pinpoint the precise problem, there just seems to be something manifestly unfair about the Government using public monies to influence the outcome of a referendum. [15–15]

[15–16] The various members of the Court did provide some guidance as to the limits of their judgments. It was emphasised that members of the Government were not expected to remain neutral on a referendum proposal. The Government could spend money to inform people about the referendum proposal, provided that the information campaign was non-partisan. O'Flaherty J suggested that the judgment did not preclude Ministers from using their state transport in relation to the referendum campaign or from going on the public airwaves.

[15–17] The judgment in *McKenna* was delivered about one week before the end of the referendum campaign. Ultimately, the referendum was carried by a margin of 818,842 for and 809,728 against. This result was then challenged by an aggrieved anti-divorce campaigner in *Hanafin v Minister for the Environment* [1996] 2 IR 321. Mr Hanafin brought a petition to the High Court challenging the provisional referendum certificate to the effect that the proposal had been carried. Both the High Court and the Supreme Court rejected the petition. The Supreme Court accepted that Mr Hanafin was entitled to challenge the provisional referendum certificate on the basis that the conduct of the referendum (which included the publicly funded information campaign) was unconstitutional. The Court also accepted that Mr Hanafin only had to satisfy the Court on the balance of probabilities that the unconstitutionality had materially affected the outcome of the referendum. Hamilton CJ then addressed this issue:

> No organ of State is entitled to review or interfere with the will of the people as expressed in their votes cast in a referendum to consider a proposal for the amendment of the Constitution because the will of the people as so expressed is binding on all the organs of the State, as it is the fundamental right of the people to decide all questions of national policy *via* the referendum process.
>
> While the judicial arm of government is not entitled to interfere with the right of the people to cast their votes at a referendum or with the results of the referendum, it is entitled to intervene in order to protect the rights of the citizens to exercise freely their constitutional right to vote if the constitutional rights of the citizens in regard thereto are violated by any body or individual.
>
> The will of the people as expressed in a referendum providing for the amendment of the Constitution is sacrosanct and if freely given, cannot be interfered with. The decision is their's and their's alone.
>
> This position is undoubtedly recognised by the Oireachtas in the Act because it provides that the validity of the provisional referendum certificate, which is the document containing the result of the referendum, can only be questioned if it is established that the wrongdoing or irregularity complained of and set forth in section 43 of the Act materially affected the result of the referendum as a whole. In effect, this means that no matter what the nature and extent of the wrongdoing may be, the result of the referendum cannot be impugned or interfered with if the result of the referendum as a whole was not materially affected by such wrongdoing....
>
> [I]t is clear that the Act provided and intended that the result of the referendum as a whole could only be questioned if it was established to the satisfaction of the court that the result was materially affected by the alleged wrongdoing. The onus of so establishing rests on the petitioner who questions the result of the referendum.
>
> This is not only required by the [Referendum Act 1994] but is in accord with the constitutional right of the citizens to vote in a constitutional referendum and to have the result thereof accepted, respected and not interfered with unless it is established that such result was materially affected by alleged wrongdoing of such a nature and effect as to vitiate the referendum....

In this case, however, the petitioner claims to be entitled to:—
"an order of this Honourable Court declaring that the referendum held on the 24th November, 1995, pursuant to the 15th Amendment to the Constitution (No. 2) Bill, 1995, was null and void."

The remedy sought therein is not a remedy against the Government, who committed the breach of the Constitution, but a remedy which seeks to override and reverse the sovereign will of the people as expressed in the provisional referendum certificate containing the record of votes cast at the referendum.

It is a remedy sought by the petitioner in a referendum petition presented to the Court pursuant to the provisions of section 42 of the Act and the relief to which he is entitled is subject to the provisions of the Act, and in particular section 43(1) thereof, which provides that a provisional referendum certificate may be questioned on the grounds that the result of the referendum as a whole was affected materially by the constitutional wrongdoing....

The people are presumed to know what they want, to have understood the proposed amendment submitted to them and all of its implications.

The petitioner sought to rebut this presumption by producing evidence of the opinions of various experts with regard to opinion polls and the factors which affected the voting pattern and intentions of the electorate.

The question of the assessment of such evidence and its probative effect was a matter for consideration of the members of the divisional court. As pointed out in the earlier portion of this judgment, the members of the divisional court, for the reasons set forth in their judgments, rejected such evidence and were not satisfied that the petitioner had discharged the onus of proof of establishing that the constitutional wrongdoing had materially affected the result of the referendum as a whole.

It is not sufficient to establish an interference with the conduct of the referendum by way of a constitutional wrongdoing: it must be further established that the result of the referendum as a whole was affected materially by the said constitutional wrongdoing....

The petitioner has failed to establish that the constitutional wrongdoing on the part of the Government materially affected the result of the referendum as a whole and his appeal against the decision of the divisional court on the referendum petition must be dismissed.
[1996] 2 IR 321, at 425–431.

Barrington J noted the difficulties with meeting the standard of proof: **[15–18]**

[E]ven assuming that the petitioner's experts could have accurately assessed the movement of public opinion in the course of the election campaign, the vital question is what happened on the 24th November, 1995, the day of the referendum poll. Even assuming one could measure the effect of the Government's advertising campaign in the weeks before the 17th November, a totally new factor entered into the situation on the 17th November, when the Supreme Court ruled that the Government's advertising campaign was unconstitutional. It seems to me to be impossible to assess on any scientific basis what effect the Supreme Court ruling, and the reaction of the Government and the various parties to it, had upon public opinion. The most important week of the campaign was undoubtedly the last week but whether the Government's advertising campaign, viewed in the light of the Supreme Court ruling, had a positive or negative impact on the voters appears to me to be impossible to estimate.

It is worth emphasising that there is no suggestion in this case that the will of the people was overborne by any form of coercion nor is there any suggestion that the material placed before the people by the Government in the course of its advertising campaign was untrue. No-one has come forward to say that he was misled or that he would have voted in a different way but for the Government's advertising campaign. The Government was guilty of a constitutional wrong, but this wrong was discovered before the date of the referendum and the people voted with full knowledge of what the Government had done. We know how they voted. We don't know why they voted the way they did. We are not competent to interrogate them as to do so would amount to breaking the secrecy of the ballot. Primary evidence being thus excluded it seems to me that we cannot accept secondary evidence from experts who seek to second guess why the people voted the way they did. [1996] 2 IR 321, at 457–458.

[15–19] Mr Hanafin was thus in an extraordinary bind. He was required to prove that the government spending materially affected the referendum. However, he could not inquire how any particular person voted nor why she voted in that way. Nor was the court satisfied with expert evidence that attempted to track the effect of the Government's campaign. O'Flaherty J went so far as to comment that the standard set by the Court for Mr Hanafin was "incapable of proof". This raises the question of why the Court should require a petitioner to prove the unprovable. It is unclear from *Hanafin* how the courts might deal with more egregious breaches of fair procedures, such as bribery, fraud or voter intimidation. Would it be possible to establish that any such breach materially affected the result of a referendum without inquiring how particular persons voted?

[15–20] The difference in judicial attitude between *McKenna* and *Hanafin* may be explained (if not necessarily justified) by reference to different conceptions of referendums. On the one hand, a referendum can be perceived as an ordinary legal event, just as subject to legal norms and regulation as any other event. On the other hand, a referendum can be perceived as the foundational event that gives authority to the entire legal system. If viewed in this way, it becomes difficult for the courts to regulate referendums because, in so doing, they would be regulating the foundational event that gives them their authority to regulate in the first instance. This is awkward territory for the courts, raising difficult jurisprudential questions. If this explanation is correct, it raises the question of why the courts perceive the referendum sometimes as an ordinary legal event and sometimes as a foundational event. *Hanafin* suggests that this change occurs once the referendum occurs. That is, it is easier for the courts to view referendums as ordinary events (subject to legal regulation) before the people have actually spoken. Once the people have actually spoken, the result of the referendum becomes something that is virtually unquestionable.

[15–21] The rationale of *McKenna* has been applied in another referendum context. In *Coughlan v Broadcasting Complaints Commission* [2000] 3 IR 1, Dr Coughlan complained about the allocation of party political broadcasts at the time of the 1995 divorce referendum. Section 18 of the Broadcasting Act 1960 required RTÉ to present news and current affairs in an impartial manner, but allowed for the broadcast of party political broadcasts. By definition, these would not be impartial. In the 1995 referendum campaign, RTÉ allowed political parties, each of which was committed to a "Yes" vote, to have one party political broadcast each. In addition, it allowed a non-party group opposed to divorce and a non-party group in favour of divorce each to broadcast a programme in similar form to a party political broadcast. In total, 42.5 minutes of broadcasting time was afforded to the "Yes" side and only 10 minutes to the "No" side. Dr Coughlan challenged this discrepancy by making a complaint to the Broadcasting Complaints Commission. The Commission rejected the complaint, so Dr Coughlan sought judicial review of that decision on the basis of *McKenna*. A majority of the Supreme Court concluded that RTÉ had acted unconstitutionally, Keane J reasoning as follows:

I have no doubt that the Constitution envisaged that political parties would play a role of fundamental importance in the process of amending the Constitution by means of a referendum. The fact that political parties are not expressly mentioned in the Constitution is not of the slightest significance in this context....

An important feature of the judgments in *McKenna v An Taoiseach (No 2)* [1995] 2 IR 10, and *Hanafin v Minister for the Environment* [1996] 2 IR 321, must next be considered. It was solely the expenditure by the government of public funds with a view to influencing the outcome of the referendum which was found to be unlawful. It was made clear in the judgments in both cases that there was nothing to prevent the government from campaigning, both collectively and as individual ministers, with the utmost vigour to secure a particular result and that this would inevitably involve the use of government resources at the expense of the taxpayer. (See in particular the observations of Barrington J in *Hanafin v Minister for the Environment* [1996] 2 IR 321, at 455.) That follows inevitably, in my view, from the central role allotted by the Constitution to the Oireachtas, and by necessary implication the government, in the referendum process.

The contrast with the position of the second respondent scarcely requires emphasis. Unlike the Oireachtas and the government, it is not an organ of the Constitution given a specific and crucial role in the referendum process: it is purely the creature of a statute enacted by the Oireachtas. As the second respondent, of course, fully accepts, it is precluded from forming any corporate view as to how the people should vote in a referendum. It is enjoined by the terms of the statutes which created the second respondent to maintain objectivity and impartiality in all matters of public controversy. It would be remarkable if such a body differed from the Oireachtas and the government in enjoying a freedom to interfere with the result of a referendum by allowing political parties and other bodies which supported a particular outcome a considerable advantage in the broadcasting of partisan material over which they had unfettered control, subject only to any relevant laws such as that of defamation. I am satisfied that the High Court Judge was correct in holding that the allocation of uncontested broadcasting time in the present case in those circumstances was legally impermissible.

I do not overlook the difficulties created for the second respondent by this state of the law. As was emphasised on its behalf, it has no control over the editorial content of party political broadcasts. Even in circumstances where the opposition parties were advocating a "No" vote and, in the result, any significant imbalance would not normally arise, the second respondent would be powerless to prevent the transmission of uncontested broadcasts which were, in the event, unfairly weighted in favour of a "Yes" vote if, for example, one of the parties concerned was to change its collective mind on the relevant issue after the passage of the Bill through the Oireachtas. It may be that, having regard to those circumstances, the present state of the law leaves the second respondent in the position that it cannot safely transmit party political broadcasts during the course of referendum campaigns as distinct from other campaigns. Whether the difficulties confronting the second respondent in this area can or should be dealt with by legislation and, if so, how, are not matters for this Court. [2000] 3 IR 1, at 54–58.

In *Sherwin v Minister for Environment* [2004] 4 IR 279 (1997), however, Costello P upheld the constitutionality of s 26 of the Referendum Act 1994 which allows only members of the Oireachtas to appoint personation agents and agents to monitor the counting of votes. He rejected the plaintiff's arguments on the grounds that such agents were appointed not to advance the cause of one side or the other but rather to assist in the administration of the referendum. That said, he ordered that the Minister had acted *ultra vires* in not exercising his power under s 26 of the Referendum Act 1994 to consider whether to make an order where there was a "special difficulty". [15–22]

The Substance of Referendum Proposals

[15–23] As noted above and discussed in more detail in chapter 4, in *Re Article 26 and the Regulation of Information (Services Outside the State for Termination of Pregnancies) Bill 1995* [1995] 1 IR 1, the Supreme Court refused to strike down the Fourteenth Amendment to the Constitution on the grounds that it was unconstitutional. As well as illustrating a strong reluctance to interfere with a vote of the people after is made, this decision reflects the general approach of the courts not to supervise the substantive content of referendum proposals. Several cases have stated this position.

[15–24] In *Riordan v An Taoiseach (No 1)* [1999] 4 IR 321, Mr Riordan challenged the constitutionality of the Fifteenth Amendment to the Constitution Act 1995 passed by the Oireachtas for the purpose of putting the divorce amendment proposal to the people. Mr Riordan argued that as divorce was unconstitutional, a Bill passed by the Oireachtas allowing for divorce must be unconstitutional. The Supreme Court rejected this argument, noting that the obligation on the Oireachtas not to enact unconstitutional laws plainly did not apply to Bills to amend the Constitution itself. This must be correct insofar as it relates to the substance of the law, but there remains a question as to whether the courts can review the constitutionality of a referendum proposal on the basis that it does not comply with the procedural requirements of Art 46 itself.

[15–25] In *Riordan v An Taoiseach (No 2)* [1999] 4 IR 343, Mr Riordan sought to restrain the holding of a referendum to amend the Constitution on the basis that the manner in which the Constitution was proposed to be amended was unconstitutional. The referendum proposal consisted of a number of amendments to the Constitution for the purposes of giving effect to the Good Friday Agreement. One aspect of this proposal involved amendments to Arts 2 and 3 of the Constitution. However, it was provided that these amendments would only come into effect if the Government declared that the State had become obliged, pursuant to the Agreement, to give effect to those amendments. Thus the amendment being put to the people was essentially a conditional one that would only come into effect if the Government made a declaration that it was required. The Supreme Court rejected Mr Riordan's contention that this was unconstitutional:

> The applicant has failed to understand the problem which confronted the Government in relation to the Belfast Agreement. That agreement imposed reciprocal obligations on the various parties to it and each party wished to be reassured that the other parties would carry out their respective obligations. For instance the Irish Government undertook to have Articles 2 and 3 of the Constitution amended but only on the basis that the British Government and the unionist parties to the Agreement would establish the power sharing executive and the cross-border bodies contemplated in the Agreement. On the other hand the British Government and the Unionist parties did not wish to establish the power sharing executive and the cross-border bodies only to find that the proposal to amend Articles 2 and 3 was defeated in a constitutional referendum.
>
> The text of the new section 7 is a clever drafting device designed to resolve this problem. By means of it the people have given a conditional assent to the amendment of Articles 2 and 3 of the Constitution.
>
> The people have a sovereign right to grant or withhold approval to an amendment to the Constitution. There is no reason therefore why they should not, provided the matter is properly placed before them, give their approval subject to a condition.
>
> It is quite wrong to suggest that the people have delegated to the Government the right to amend the Constitution. This is not so. The people have consented to

an amendment to the Constitution subject to the happening of a particular future event. That future event is that the Government should have made the declaration referred to in section 7(3). Section 7(3) provides that if the Government makes that declaration "then, notwithstanding Article 46 hereof, this Constitution shall be amended as follows ...". But it is the people, not the Government who are speaking in the passage quoted. The reference to "notwithstanding Article 46 hereof", is merely an indication that the people have consented to the making of the amendment on the happening of the event referred to and that they do not wish to be consulted again.

Finally it is true that the amendment effected by the Nineteenth Amendment of the Constitution Act, 1998, is, in form, an amendment to Article 29 of the Constitution and not an amendment to Articles 2 and 3. But it is important to remember that the Nineteenth Amendment to the Constitution, having been approved by the people, and promulgated by the President as law now forms part of the Constitution. The amendment is now Article 29.7 of the Constitution. The proposed new texts of Articles 2 and 3 are now lying-as it were in the form of an escrow-in Article 29 of the Constitution. But they are there for all to see and on the happening of the anticipated future event-that is to say the Government making the declaration contemplated by Article 29.7.3°-the draft Articles 2 and 3 will, by virtue of the internal workings of the Constitution itself, move to replace the existing Articles 2 and 3.

Under these circumstances there is no substance in the applicant's objections to the Nineteenth Amendment of the Constitution Act, 1998, and for this reason, as well as the other reasons previously stated, the court will refuse leave to amend the grounds of appeal and the motion will be dismissed. [1999] 4 IR 343, at 354-355.

At a later point in the case, Barrington J put the matter as follows:

> Provided the appropriate procedures are complied with there are no circumstances in which this Court could purport to sit in judgment on an authentic expression of the people's will or an amendment of the Constitution made in accordance with the provisions of Article 46. [1999] 4 IR 343, at 358-359.

This *dictum* concisely states the attitude of the courts: they will ensure procedural fairness in the conduct of the referendum, but will not scrutinise the content of referendum proposals. [15–26]

In *Morris v Minister for the Environment* [2002] 1 IR 326, Ms Morris challenged the manner in which the Government was putting an abortion amendment before the people. The proposal was to insert a new Article 46.6 into the Constitution in the following terms: [15–27]

> 1. Notwithstanding the foregoing provisions of this Article, Article 40 of this Constitution shall be amended as follows:
> The following subsections shall be added to section 3 of the English text:
>> "4 In particular, the life of the unborn in the womb shall be protected in accordance with the provisions of the Protection of Human Life in Pregnancy Act, 2002.
>>
>> 5 The provisions of section 2 of Article 46 and sections 1, 3 and 4 of Article 47 of this Constitution shall apply to any Bill passed or deemed to have been passed by both Houses of the Oireachtas containing a proposal to amend the Protection of Human Life in Pregnancy Act, 2002, as they apply to a Bill containing a proposal or proposals for the amendment of this Constitution and any such Bill shall be signed by the President forthwith upon his being satisfied that the Bill has been duly approved by the people in accordance with the

provisions of section 1 of Article 47 of this Constitution and shall be duly promulgated by the President as a law."

2. If a law, containing only the provisions set out in *An Dara Sceideal-The Second Schedule* to the *Twenty-fifth Amendment of the Constitution (Protection of Human Life in Pregnancy) Act, 2001*, is enacted by the Oireachtas, this section, other than the amendment of Article 40 of this Constitution effected thereby, shall be omitted from every official text of this Constitution published thereafter, but notwithstanding such omission this section shall continue to have the force of law.

3. If such a law is not so enacted within 180 days of this section being added to this Constitution, this section shall cease to have effect and shall be omitted from every official text of this Constitution published thereafter.

4. The provisions of Articles 26 and 27 of this Constitution shall not apply to the Bill for such a law.

[15–28] This rather convoluted amendment provided that the life of the unborn would be protected in accordance with an Act that was envisaged by the Constitution. If that Act were passed by the Oireachtas within 180 days of the amendment, it could not then be amended save by way of referendum. Ms Morris objected to this method of amendment contending that, except in cases of proposed repeals, Art 46.1 of the Constitution requires that the proposed variation or addition to the Constitution be contained in the body of the Constitution itself and not have a separate existence in the form of an entrenched Act of the Oireachtas purporting to possess constitutionally entrenched status, and that the provisions of the second schedule constituted another proposal which Art 46.4 prohibited. The High Court rejected this argument. Kelly J reasoned:

> The applicants contend that in order to permit the Constitution to be altered so as to allow for a particular measure to stand outside the text of the Constitution and have constitutional status, Article 46 would itself have to be amended first in order to enable such a proposal to be put to the people.
> I do not agree with these propositions urged by the applicants.
> First, it is to be noted that Article 46.1 does not contain any express prohibition on an amendment in the form in which it is proposed here. Neither does it contain any mandatory obligation to the effect that an amendment must be contained in its entirety in the body or text of the Constitution itself.
> Secondly, this form of amendment by reference to a document or documents which will not be incorporated into the text of the Constitution is one which has already been utilised on quite a number of occasions.
> Whilst it is true that this is the first time on which this particular procedure to effect an amendment to the Constitution has been utilised, earlier amendments going back as far as the Third Amendment to the Constitution in 1972 have been brought about by reference to documents which were not themselves incorporated into the text of the Constitution. Some of these were challenged. The most notable in recent times was the Belfast Agreement which was at the heart of *Riordan v An Taoiseach (No 2)* [1999] 4 IR 343....
> No more than in *Riordan v An Taoiseach (No 2)* [1999] 4 IR 343, the proposal here is a clever drafting device which does not in my view offend against Article 46.1 of the Constitution. Ultimately the people have a sovereign right to grant or withhold approval to the amendment as proposed. In my opinion, insofar as this argument is concerned, the proposal is properly being placed before the people and they ought now to be given the opportunity to express their approval or otherwise without interference by this court.
> The people are being asked to approve an amendment to the Constitution which makes provision for a law relating to abortion as may be set out in a subsequent Act. They are being asked to give their approval to this amendment, subject to a specific condition that the amendment will lapse unless the subsequent Act is enacted containing a specific text

within a prescribed time. The specific text is set out in the second schedule to the Bill and is therefore being made known to the people prior to the referendum. If the people determine in the referendum to approve of the proposal they will be consenting to an amendment to the Constitution which will then become permanent, subject to the occurrence of a condition subsequent namely the passing into law of the Act in the second schedule.

I take the view that since it is competent for the people to give a conditional consent to the amendment to the Constitution then *pace* Barrington J in *Riordan v An Taoiseach (No 2)* [1999] 4 IR 343, at 363, there must be a mechanism or drafting procedure whereby the matter can properly be placed before the people. I am of opinion that the form of this Bill is such a drafting procedure and does not offend either expressly or impliedly the provisions of Article 46.1 of the Constitution. [2002] 1 IR 326, at 339.

Kelly J appears to have accepted that the courts could review a Bill containing a referendum proposal that also contained another proposal (in breach of Art 46.3). This approach, which is surely correct, prefers the reasoning of Barrington J in *Finn* to that of the Supreme Court in that case. However, Kelly J reasoned that the Protection of Human Life in Pregnancy Act (contained in the Schedule to the Referendum Bill) was not an impermissible "other proposal": [15–29]

> The term "any other proposal" in Article 46.4 of the Constitution refers to a legislative proposal, *ie* a proposal which, if the Bill to amend the Constitution is passed, will take effect as substantive law in the State. The text of the second schedule to the Bill, which sets forth the terms of an envisaged Act of the Oireachtas, is not a proposal which falls within the ambit of the prohibition contained in Article 46.4 of the Constitution.
>
> The text contained in the second schedule to the Bill has *no* legislative effect as a result of its being included in the second schedule. The Bill does not propose that the text of the second schedule should have legal effect. If the referendum proposal is carried and the Bill is signed into law by the President it will only give effect to the constitutional amendment set out in the first schedule to the Bill. It does not in any way give constitutional or legal effect to matter contained in the second schedule. That will occur if, and only if, the national parliament passes such a measure into law. There is no guarantee that that will happen. Regardless of the size of the majority achieved in the referendum (if such occurs) there is no legal obligation on parliament to pass the legislation contained in the second schedule to the Bill.
>
> The second schedule merely puts before the people the text of an Act which it is envisaged may, if the referendum is carried, be subsequently passed into law.
>
> The terms of the second schedule to the Bill require an entirely separate and distinct decision by the national parliament to enact a law in accordance with those terms before it can have legal effect. The second schedule to the Bill, is not in my view, a "proposal", in the sense in which that term is to be understood where it is contained in Article 46.4. [2002] 1 IR 326, at 341–342.

In *Riordan v Government of Ireland*, 14 February 2002 (HC), the Supreme Court upheld this approach of Kelly J in considering a similar challenge to the terms of the amendment proposal.

The Electoral Process

Drawing of Constituency Boundaries

The electoral process has also been the subject of constitutional regulation by the courts. There were several early cases in which the courts took a reasonably interventionist role. This interventionist approach waned in the 1970s and 1980s. [15–30]

However, since the 1990s the norm of fair procedures developed in the referendum context has come to be applied in relation to the ordinary political process

[15–31] A number of cases concern the drawing of constituency boundaries. Article 16.2 provides as follows

> 1° Dáil Éireann shall be composed of members who represent constituencies determined by law.
> 2° The number of members shall from time to time be fixed by law, but the total number of members of Dáil Éireann shall not be fixed at less than one member for each thirty thousand of the population, or at more than one member for each twenty thousand of the population.
> 3° The ratio between the number of members to be elected at any time for each constituency and the population of each constituency, as ascertained at the last preceding census, shall, so far as it is practicable, be the same throughout the country.
> 4° The Oireachtas shall revise the constituencies at least once in every twelve years, with due regard to changes in distribution of the population, but any alterations in the constituencies shall not take effect during the life of Dáil Éireann sitting when such revision is made.
> 5° The members shall be elected on the system of proportional representation by means of the single transferable vote.
> 6° No law shall be enacted whereby the number of members to be returned for any constituency shall be less than three.

[15–32] In *O'Donovan v Attorney General* [1961] IR 114, the plaintiff challenged the distribution of elected representatives throughout the country. At that time, the ratio of constituents per elected representatives varied considerably throughout the country. The highest ratio was in the constituency of Galway South where the ratio of members to population was of the order of one member to 16,575.3 of the population. The lowest ratio of one member to 23,128.2 of the population was in the constituency of Dublin South (West). That is, there was a disparity in ratio between members and population in these two constituencies of 6,553. Budd J considered whether this arrangement was adequate compliance with the requirement in Article 16.2.3° that the ratio of TDs to population be the same throughout the country, "as far as practicable". He first addressed the meaning of the phrase "as far as practicable":

> This sub-clause 2 has to be given effect and put into operation by legislation. The Oireachtas has the task of dividing the country into appropriate entities to form constituencies. To each must be allotted a number of members, and in doing this, regard must be had to the matter of ratio. All this must involve the formation of some plan. Considerable calculation of figures and much adjustment of areas and boundaries and numbers of members must be called for in order to obtain a result in accordance with the Constitution. The sub-clause is thus not one concerned with merely philosophical concepts but deals with highly practical matters of practical politics. That, then, is the context in which the phrase, "sa mhéid gur féidir é," is used and the clause itself is part of our fundamental law intended to work in a practical fashion. That context therefore calls for giving the phrase a liberal, commonsense construction, and, in my view, that involves construing the phrase as limiting the principle of near equality of ratio between members and population in the constituencies by what is "feasible" or "practicable," as distinct from any notion of mathematical accuracy. [1961] 1 IR 114, at 131.

The parties had different conceptions of the sorts of issues that could be considered relevant in assessing what was practicable. Mr O'Donovan argued that the only difficulties that might legitimately be considered in arriving at a conclusion as to what was practicable were those involved in the administrative machinery of elections. In contrast, the Attorney General argued that a wide range of considerations were relevant. The following extract gives some sense of the breadth of considerations which the State wished to take into account: [15–33]

> It was suggested that it was part of the duties of deputies to keep continuous touch with their constituents in order to hear their views and thus be able to reflect those views and represent them properly in the Legislature and also to assist them in their everyday problems. The latter function, it was said, would involve helping them in connection with securing their legitimate rights in such matters as loans and grants to which they might be entitled and seeing that they secured the full benefit from Government schemes with regard to such matters as health, housing and agriculture. For this purpose it was often necessary, it was said, for deputies to visit Government departments in their constituents' legitimate interests. Deputies were also expected to forward the interests of their constituents with local authorities in connection with matters of interest to them administered by such authorities. It was pointed out that on the western seaboard particularly the indented coastline, large sparsely-populated areas, mountains and other geographical considerations gave rise to difficulties of communication and thus made it hard for constituents to see their deputies and for deputies to serve their constituents properly. Furthermore, deputies for these areas had to spend much time in travelling to and from Dublin where the Dáil sits. These difficulties, it was suggested, did not affect the deputies and their constituents in the Dublin area in the same way because of the ease of communication and high density of population. Moreover, it was suggested that the population in Dublin did not have occasion to make such great demands on their deputies as people in the west of the country and the loss of time in travelling did not occur. It was submitted that in order to make the parliamentary system operate properly and effectively, it was necessary to have a higher ratio of members to population on the western seaboard in order to achieve a fair equality. That is to say, it was necessary to have more deputies in these areas in relation to the population than elsewhere so that they could adequately perform their functions having regard to the difficulties that faced them.
> [1961] 1 IR 114, at 134–135.

Budd J rejected this submission. Noting that the constitutionally envisaged duties of TDs were to enact laws and elect the Taoiseach and referring to the text of Art 16.2 as a whole, he reasoned that equality of representation was the central concept: [15–34]

> The clause must, however, in the circumstances be read in the context of the Constitution as a whole, and other Articles of the Constitution may have a bearing on the construction of this sub-clause affecting its construction. There are several Articles which I believe it is relevant to consider in this respect which entirely support the view I have expressed. Article 5 provides, *inter alia*, that Ireland is a democratic State. Article 16.1.4° provides that no voter may exercise more than one vote at an election for Dáil Éireann. Article 40.1 provides that all citizens shall, as human persons, be held equal before the law. There is an explanatory addition to this Article, not relevant to what I am dealing with here. A "democratic state" is one where government by the people prevails. In modern usage of the words I believe it to be correct to say a "democratic state" denotes one in which all citizens have equal political rights. That the words should be given such a meaning in our Constitution seems to be supported by the other two Articles I have referred to as to the restriction of voting power to one vote per person and the equality of all before the law.

That equality is not maintained if the vote of a person in one part of the country has a greater effect in securing parliamentary representation than the vote of a person in another part of the country. To illustrate this simply, if 80,000 people in one part of the country can return five deputies, while 80,000 people in another part of the country can only return two deputies, the spirit of equality is not maintained. There are thus contained in the Constitution other Articles the spirit of which demands equality of voting power and representation. The Articles I have just referred to admittedly have reference to equality of voting power, but are relevant in construing [Article 16.2.3°] to this extent, that if it be established, as I believe it is, that the spirit and intendment of these other Articles is that the notion of equality in political matters is to be maintained, it would be illogical to find a different and inconsistent principle adumbrated elsewhere in the Constitution. If a departure from the principles to be implied from those Articles was intended, one would at least expect to find such form of words used as would clearly indicate a different principle. On examining [Article 16.2.3°] nothing of the kind is apparent. On the contrary, the whole object of the clause would seem to be designed to achieve the spirit of equality to be found in these other Articles. Thus, all of the relevant clauses harmonise. This all leads to the conclusion that any construction of [Article 16.2.3°] which would have the effect of destroying the dominant principle of equality should be rejected.

On due deliberation as to the proper inferences to be drawn from all these considerations as to the proper construction of Article 16, 2, 3, I have arrived at the following conclusions. First, that the dominant principle of that sub-clause is the achievement of as near an equality of the parliamentary representation of the population as can be attained, paying due regard to practical difficulties. Secondly, that there are difficulties of an administrative and statistical nature so plain to be seen that it may be safely assumed they, at any rate, must have been in the minds of those enacting the Constitution. Thirdly, that these difficulties are of them-selves alone sufficient to explain and justify the qualification of the principle of equality. Fourthly, that there is no indication to be found in the Constitution that it was intended that any of the difficulties as to the working of the parliamentary system should be taken into consideration on the question of practicability. Fifthly, that if matters of the kind mentioned as to the working of the parliamentary system were to be taken into consideration, the result would be that the dominant principle of equality would be departed from so far as to be destroyed and the intention of the people in enacting the relevant sub-clause would be entirely frustrated. Finally, that this fifth conclusion involves rejecting, with one qualification, the contention that the difficulties of the operation of the parliamentary system should be considered in determining what is practicable. In the result, it would seem to me that the difficulties to which the Legislature should have regard are those of an administrative and statistical nature, and the principal question to decide will be as to whether equality of ratio of members to population has been achieved in so far as practicable having regard to such difficulties. There is, it seems to me, only one possible qualification of this: that if it be shown that the result would involve the collapse of the parliamentary system that factor would have to be most seriously considered, having regard to the view that I have expressed that our fundamental law must be deemed to have been intended to be workable. I proceed to consider these administrative difficulties and the others so far as relevant.

Taking this approach, he held that the Electoral (Amendment) Act 1959 authorised substantial departures from the principle of equal voting rights, for which there was no justification. Accordingly, it was unconstitutional.

[15–35] The Oireachtas quickly passed the Electoral (Amendment) Bill 1961, which was referred by the President to the Supreme Court. The Court upheld the validity of the

Bill in a manner that was far less interventionist in its assessment of whether the Oireachtas had complied with Art 16.2.3°:

> The sub-clause recognises that exact parity in the ratio between members and the population of each constituency is unlikely to be obtained and is not required. The decision as to what is practicable is within the jurisdiction of the Oireachtas. It may reasonably take into consideration a variety of factors, such as the desirability so far as possible to adhere to well-known boundaries such as those of counties, townlands and electoral divisions. The existence of divisions created by such physical features as rivers, lakes and mountains may also have to be reckoned with. The problem of what is practicable is primarily one for the Oireachtas, whose members have a knowledge of the problems and difficulties to be solved which this Court cannot have. Its decision should not be reviewed by this Court unless there is a manifest infringement of the Article. This Court cannot, as is suggested, lay down a figure above or below which a variation from what is called the national average is not permitted. This, of course, is not to say that a Court cannot be informed of the difficulties and may not pronounce on whether there has been such a serious divergence from uniformity as to violate the requirements of the Constitution.
>
> To justify the Court in holding that the sub-section has been infringed it must, however, be shown that the failure to maintain the ratio between the number of members for each constituency and the population of each constituency involves such a divergence as to make it clear that the Oireachtas has not carried out the intention of the sub-clause.
>
> In the opinion of the Court the divergencies shown in the Bill are within reasonable limits.
>
> Accordingly, the Court is of opinion that this ground of objection has not been established. *Re Article 26 and the Electoral (Amendment) Bill 1961* [1961] IR 169, at 183.

The Court also confirmed that the Oireachtas is entitled to work on the basis of the last completed census.

Another issue that arises from Art 16.3 is the relevance of census changes to the drawing of constituency boundaries. As just noted, in *Re Article 26 and the Electoral (Amendment) Bill 1961*, the Supreme Court confirmed that the Oireachtas was entitled to rely on the last completed census. In *O'Malley v An Taoiseach* [1990] ILRM 461, the plaintiff sought an interim injunction restraining the Taoiseach from advising the President to dissolve the Dáil on the grounds that constituencies had not been properly revised in light of census changes. Hamilton P refused this injunction largely on separation of powers grounds: the Constitution clearly gave the right to the Taoiseach to advise the President with regard to the dissolution of Dáil Éireann. However, Hamilton P made a number of comments as to the import of Art 16.2.4°. As the injunction application was heard *ex parte*, these comments were strictly *obiter*: [15–36]

> It is clear from these figures that the ratio between the numbers of members to be elected at any time for each of these constituencies and the population of these constituencies as ascertained at the last preceding census are not the same, so far as is practicable.
>
> The responsibility for revising the constituencies with due regard to changes in the distribution of the population rests on the Oireachtas. Article 16.2.4° provides that:
>
> The Oireachtas shall revise the constituencies at least once in every 12 years with due regard to changes in distribution of the population.
>
> The constitutional obligation placed on the Oireachtas is not discharged by revising the constituencies once in every 12 years. They are obliged to revise the constituencies with due regard to changes in distribution of the population and when a census return

discloses major changes in the distribution of the population there is a constitutional obligation on the Oireachtas to revise the constituencies.

No revision has taken place since the last census in 1986 and I am satisfied that the Oireachtas is in breach of its constitutional obligation to revise the constituencies particularly when the census discloses a major change in the distribution of population and the fact that the ratio between the number of members to be elected at any time for each constituency and the population of each constituency as ascertained at the last preceding census is not so far as is practicable to be same throughout the country. [1990] ILRM 461, at 463–464.

[15–37] More recently, in *Murphy v Minister for Environment* [2007] IEHC 185, the plaintiffs challenged the constitutionality of the Electoral (Amendment) Act 2005 on the basis that the census conducted in April 2006 showed that the ratio of TDs to population varied considerably throughout the country. The average ratio throughout the country was one TD to 25,000 people. However, five constituencies deviated from this figure by 10 percent or more. It was accepted that this breached the principle laid down in *O'Donovan*. Although proceedings were initiated shortly prior to the 2007 general election, the plaintiffs did not seek to prevent the election or overturn its results.

[15–38] Clarke J approved Hamilton P's judgment in *O'Malley* to the effect that there was an obligation to review boundary constituencies in the light of the latest statistics, not just every 12 years. However, this did not mean that the Electoral (Amendment) Act 2005 automatically became unconstitutional.

While the comments of Hamilton P in *O'Malley*, in relation to the obligation on the Oireachtas to revise constituencies, are obiter, it was not suggested by counsel for either side that they do not represent a correct statement of the law. I agree. I am, therefore, satisfied that the Oireachtas has an obligation, as soon as significant and unjustifiable disproportionality is revealed by census figures, to act to remedy that difficulty.

One final consideration that needs to be taken into account under this heading stems from the fact that the constituencies which currently exist under the 2005 Act were, at the date of their enactment, entirely consistent with the last census then available (that is the census taken in 2002 whose results became available throughout 2002 and 2003). There can be no suggestion, therefore, that the 2005 Act was unconstitutional as of the time of its enactment.

In all those circumstances I am satisfied that a more harmonious construction of the various sub clauses of Article 16, favours the view that the immediate consequence of the publication of census figures which show that the constituencies then currently provided for by law are no longer proportional "so far as it is practicable", leads to a situation where the Oireachtas has an immediate and pressing obligation to put in place measures designed to remedy that problem by enacting appropriate amending legislation. Unless, therefore, the alternative construction argued for by the plaintiffs was mandated by the clear text of the Constitution, I would not favour the view that an existing Electoral Act is, in those circumstances, immediately unconstitutional. I would leave to a case where it specifically arises, the question of what the proper approach of a court should be to circumstances where, in purported reliance on that obligation, the Oireachtas enacts constituencies which, themselves, fail to meet the proportionality test.

However, I am satisfied that, in fact, the approach which I have indicated, is in conformity with a proper construction of the wording of the Article itself. While it is true to state that the Article requires that the "ratio" be proportionate "insofar as it is practicable", it seems to me that the ratio can only be provided for by law as the ratio is determined by the constituencies which must themselves be determined by law. Therefore, the ratio can only be changed by the enactment of a new law. Thus it is not practicable to change the ratio until such time as a reasonable opportunity has been given to the Oireachtas to bring about that change. Even though the ratio itself might be disproportionate it is not a breach of the obligation that it be proportionate "insofar as it is practicable", if it can be shown that there was no reasonable opportunity, after the results of a relevant census had become available, to change the ratio. In all the circumstances I am satisfied that an existing Electoral Act does not, as a matter of principle, become unconstitutional immediately upon the publication of census figures showing a disproportion between the level of representation from one constituency to another. Such a situation gives rise simply to an obligation on the Oireachtas to take appropriate remedial action. [2007] IEHC 185, at [4.21–4.24].

A particular issue arose in this case as to what was meant by "last preceding census" in Art 16.2.4°. This arose because in 2006, the Central Statistics Office has published a preliminary report showing figures from the 2006 census. Although these figures were largely accurate, the definitive report was only published in 2007. Clarke J reasoned that Art 16.2.4° aimed to provide a clear standard by which the legitimacy of constituency boundaries could be assessed. Accordingly, he concluded that the obligation of the Oireachtas to revise constituency boundaries only arose on publication of the definitive report, not the preliminary report. [15–39]

The next issue was the length of time that could elapse between the publication of the definitive census figures and the revision of constituencies. Clarke J accepted the reasonableness of the procedure for the review of constituency boundaries under the Electoral Act 1997. As that procedure was statutorily envisaged to take up to six months, such a delay in the revision of boundaries was reasonable. On that basis, Clarke J concluded that it would not have been possible for the Oireachtas to revise the constituency boundaries between 29 March 2007, when the figures became available, and the time of his judgment (7 June 2007). [15–40]

Secret Ballot

In *McMahon v Attorney General* [1972] IR 69, the plaintiff challenged the constitutionality of the Electoral Acts 1923 and 1963. Rule 22 in Part I of the Fifth Schedule to the Act of 1923 required that an elector's number on the register of electors would be marked on the counterfoil of his ballot paper immediately before that paper was delivered to him. The directions mentioned in s 16(2) of the Electoral Act 1963 required that a particular serial number should be printed on the counterfoil of a ballot paper and also on the ballot paper. The Fifth Schedule of the 1923 Act also allowed for counted ballots to be inspected and for sealed packets of counterfoils to be opened. The combined effect of these provisions was that it was possible to identify how a particular person had voted. The State sought to defend these arrangements on the basis of protection against fraud. If it transpired that a person had voted illegitimately, it would be possible to identify the vote cast by that person and remove it. The Supreme Court rejected this argument, Ó Dálaigh CJ reasoning: [15–41]

> Article 16.1.4 of the Constitution speaks of voting by secret ballot. The fundamental question is: *secret to whom?* In my opinion there can be only one plain and logical answer to that question. The answer is: *secret to the voter.* It is the voter's secret. It is an unshared secret. It ceases to be a secret if it is disclosed. The Constitution guarantees the voter that his vote will be secret. In my opinion the Constitution therefore requires that nothing shall be done which would make it possible to violate that secrecy. The acknowledged

purpose of marking the voter's counterfoil is to disclose how he voted if that should be necessary in order to avoid the inconvenience of a re-poll. But this is what the Constitution says shall not be done; of course, the Constitution is speaking of the *bona fide* voter. Where votes cast at a particular polling station are destroyed, the Oireachtas has authorised a re-poll limited to that station: see section 17 of the Act of 1963. This device could be made available wherever personation, to a significant degree, was proved to have occurred. In any event, inconvenience cannot prevail against the clear mandate of the Constitution. [1972] IR 69, at 106–107.

Rules Governing Candidates at Elections

[15–42] In *Loftus v Attorney General* [1979] IR 221, the Supreme Court considered the constitutionality of s 13(2) of the Electoral Act 1963 which establishes that the registrar of political parties shall register as a political party any political party that in his opinion is a genuine political party and is organised to contest a general or local election. Parties already represented in the Dáil at the time of the Act were automatically registered. The main benefit of registration was that it allowed the name of the party to appear beside the candidate's name on the ballot paper. The registrar refused to register the plaintiff's political party, "the Christian Democratic Party of Ireland." The plaintiff challenged the validity of this decision and the constitutionality of s 13(2) on several grounds. The Supreme Court, *per* O'Higgins CJ, rejected the challenge to s 13(2) based on Art 40.6.1°(iii) on the following grounds:

> It seems proper and in the public interest to regulate such statutory rights and facilities as are given by this legislation. If some control and regulation were not provided, genuine political action might be destroyed by a proliferation of bogus front organisations calling themselves political parties but with aims and objects far removed from the political sphere. [1979] IR 221, at 242.

[15–43] In *O'Reilly v Minister for the Environment* [1986] IR 143, the plaintiff, who intended to present himself as a candidate in the local elections and afterwards for Dáil Éireann, sought a declaration that the procedure provided by s 16 of the Electoral Act, 1963, whereby candidates' names on ballot papers were listed in alphabetical order, offended Art 40 of the Constitution in failing to provide fairness of procedures or to hold the plaintiff equal before the law, and was therefore repugnant to the Constitution and invalid. Although Murphy J accepted that there was a bias in favour of candidates listed towards the start of the ballot paper, he rejected the constitutional claim on the basis that the problem lay not with the electoral scheme—although a more closely tuned one could be devised—but with inattentive voters.

[15–44] In a number of more recent cases, the courts have applied the principles of equality and fair procedures developed in *McKenna* to the electoral process. In *Kelly v Minister for the Environment* [2002] 4 IR 191, the High Court held that it was unconstitutional, in assessing the election expenses of Dáil candidates, to exclude the office expenses of sitting TDs, Senators and MEPs. McKechnie J reasoned:

> Having reviewed the evidence, I am satisfied beyond doubt that the facilities which are available to outgoing members of the Dáil are of particular relevance and value to those members who seek re-election. No tools could be more helpful or appropriate than postage, access to communications equipment, and all of the other services which is theirs as of right. Even if there was no cap on the expenditure which a candidate could incur,

the availability itself, of such facilities and services out of public funds, could be said to be unfair and discriminatory, but when one adds to that a newcomer's inability to match the value of such services by increased spending, the resulting situation is unjust, unreasonable and arbitrary. [2002] 4 IR 191, at [38].

In the Supreme Court, it was accepted by the State that the legislation would be unconstitutional if it did mean that publicly funded facilities did not count towards a candidates permitted expenses. The State sought (but failed) to persuade the Court that the double construction rule would allow the Court to read the statute in a different way. (This is discussed further in chapter 16). [15–45]

In *Redmond v Minister for the Environment* [2001] 4 IR 61, Herbert J held unconstitutional the requirement that election candidates pay a deposit that would not be refunded if they received less than a certain number of votes: [15–46]

> In my judgment a law which has the effect, even if totally unintended, of discriminating between human persons on the basis of money is an attack upon the dignity of those persons as human beings who do not have money. This is far removed for instance from issues such as alleged rights to wage parity or increases or issues of the uneven impact of taxation upon citizens in various marital or non-marital relationships or on farmers or householders or occupiers. The history of poverty and of social deprivation in Ireland, but by no means exclusively in Ireland, demonstrates overwhelmingly the extent to which the essential dignity of persons as human beings is involved. In my judgment this is exactly the type of discrimination for which the framers of the first sentence of Article 40.1 of the Constitution were providing. [2001] 4 IR 61, at 80.

This decision was not appealed. The Electoral (Amendment) Act 2002 introduced a new regime for the nomination of candidates which distinguishes between candidates approved by political parties and candidates not so approved. Whereas the former are entitled to stand for election upon proof that their nomination is approved, the latter must gain the assent of thirty persons registered as Dáil electors in the particular constituency. In *King v Minister for Environment* [2006] IESC 61, a number of plaintiffs challenged the constitutionality of this provision with regard to both Art 16 and Art 40.1 of the Constitution. The High Court upheld this provision but the Supreme Court declared it unconstitutional on appeal. The Court noted the difficulties for such non-party candidates in meeting such a requirement, observing at 30–31: [15–47]

> The Court considers that such an imposition is *prima facie* disproportionate to the particular objective to be achieved, namely the due authentication of the nomination papers.... Considering that this aspect of the measures in question is *prima facie* disproportionate to the objects sought to be achieved, that provision must be considered incompatible with the Constitution in imposing an undue impediment on the otherwise lawful right of the candidate to be nominated unless the State can establish there are objective reasons why this is necessary. Notwithstanding the evidence given on behalf of the State, the Court is not satisfied by that evidence that there are no other administrative arrangements which are significantly less onerous regarding the verification of a signature on a nomination paper. It is not for the Court to designate what other form of administrative arrangements might be provided for in legislation.

In *Ring v Minister for the Environment* [2004] 1 IR 185, Mr Ring challenged the constitutionality of s 13A of the Local Government Act 2001, as inserted by s 2 of the Local Government (No 2) Act 2003. The effect of this section was to remove the dual [15–48] mandate and prevent a person from being simultaneously a TD and a county councillor. Mr Ring objected on constitutional grounds. Laffoy J first rejected Mr Ring's argument that he had a constitutional right to stand for election to local government. Article 28A—inserted by referendum in 2001—did not provide such a right. Comparing Article 28A with Art 16, it was reasonable to conclude that the Constitution envisaged that eligibility for election to local government was a matter for regulation by the Oireachtas.

[15–49] Laffoy J also rejected Mr Ring's argument that the new law interfered with his right to stand for election to the Dáil:

> [T]here being no constitutionally protected right to stand for election to a local authority, section 13A imposes no constraint on the plaintiff's eligibility for membership of the Dáil. It is not an impediment to him remaining in the Dáil until the next general election nor to him standing at the next general election. He does, however, have to choose between his desire to be a member of the Dáil and his desire to be a member of Mayo County Council. However, in that regard he is not in any different position from a member of, say, the Competition Authority or indeed a member of any of the other statutory authorities or boards to whom membership of the Houses of the Oireachtas is not open while remaining a member of the authority or board. If such a person is eligible under Article 16.1.1 to stand for the Dáil, stands and is elected to the Dáil, he or she must resign membership of the authority or board before taking his or her seat. [2004] 1 IR 185, at 206.

Finally, Laffoy J rejected Mr Ring's argument that his rights to equality in the democratic process had been breached.

Contents – Chapter 16

Principles Governing Constitutional Litigation

Introduction.	[16–01]
Standing	[16–02]
The Presumption of Constitutionality.	[16–12]
Judicial Restraint	[16–16]
The Double Construction Rule	[16–20]
Severance.	[16–23]
Effects of a Finding of a Declaration of Unconstitutionality	[16–26]
Introduction	[16–26]
When Do Declarations of Unconstitutionality Date To?	[16–29]
What is the Effect of a Declaration of Unconstitutionality?	[16–33]
The Continuing Effect of Official Decisions Taken Before the Declaration of Unconstitutionality	[16–43]

Overview

The courts have elaborated a number of rules and principles governing constitutional litigation. The rules of standing require that, in general, only a person particularly aggrieved (actually or potentially) by a government action can challenge the constitutionality of that action. However, any person with a *bona fide* concern can challenge the constitutionality of an action that affects everyone in general but no-one in particular, such as the conduct of a referendum campaign. In seeking to challenge a government action, a person cannot rely on an argument that the action is unfair vis-à-vis someone else if it is not unfair vis-à-vis the litigant herself. The courts have identified the presumption of constitutionality as a fundamental principle of constitutional law. It follows from this that the courts will exercise judicial restraint, assessing the constitutionality of government action only if absolutely necessary. Where a statutory provision is open to two interpretations, one constitutional and the other not, the courts will adopt the constitutional interpretation. Moreover, it is presumed that statutory powers will be exercised constitutionally by the recipients of those powers. The courts have had difficulty in ascertaining what retrospective effects a declaration of unconstitutionality should have. Following the *A case*, the position seems to be that declarations of unconstitutionality normally have no retrospective effects apart from for those immediately involved in the litigation itself.

Chapter 16

Principles Governing Constitutional Litigation

Introduction

So far this book has focused largely on constitutional cases, identifying the decisions that have been taken and the principles that have emerged. At many points, allusion was made to the principles that govern the process of constitutional litigation: who is entitled to bring cases (standing); who bears the onus of proof (presumption of constitutionality); how should a statutory provision be interpreted (the double construction rule). It is now appropriate to focus specifically on these issues. Although these questions may appear technical, they actually strike to the core of the constitutional dispensation in the country. The ideas that not everyone may challenge the constitutionality of a statute, that the courts should show deference to the Oireachtas when interpreting legislation, that the effects of a declaration of unconstitutionality should be limited, all raise fundamental issues about our structure of government.

[16–01]

Standing

A legislative provision cannot be constitutionally challenged by just anyone. Generally speaking, a litigant must be able to point to some way in which she is personally affected by the provision in question. She must demonstrate that she has standing (often referred to as *locus standi*). This requirement was first stated in *Cahill v Sutton* [1980] IR 269. Section 11(2)(b) of the Statute of Limitations 1957 provided that an action in contract for damages arising out of personal injuries must be instituted within three years of the injury. Mrs Cahill instituted proceedings for injuries allegedly caused to her by Mr Sutton, a medical practitioner, outside the three-year limit. Mr Sutton pleaded the Statute of Limitations in his defence and Mrs Sutton challenged the constitutionality of the absolute time limit of three years. She argued that the provision was unconstitutional because it did not contain any exception in favour of an injured person who did not become aware of the relevant facts, on which her claim was based, until after the expiration of the period of limitation or until a short time before its expiration. The Supreme Court did not accept that she had standing to raise this point. Henchy J identified the issue in the following way:

[16–02]

> The first thing to be noted about this submission is that even if section 11(2)(b), were qualified by such a saver, it would avail the plaintiff nothing. At all material times she was aware of all the facts necessary for the making of a claim against Dr. Sutton. Her present claim is founded on breach of contract. Within weeks of the commencement of her treatment in 1968 she knew of the facts which, according to her, constituted a breach of contract, and of their prejudicial effects on her. Yet she did not bring her action within

the three-year period. It is clear—indeed, it is admitted—that the plaintiff would still be shut out from suing after the three-year period of limitation even if the suggested saving provision had been included in the Act of 1957.

That being the legal predicament in which the plaintiff finds herself, the argument formulated on her behalf is not that she is unjustly debarred from suing because of the alleged statutory defect but that a person to whom the suggested saving provision would apply if it had been enacted could claim successfully in the High Court a declaration that section 11(2)(*b*), is unconstitutional because the suggested saving provision is not attached to it. Therefore, the plaintiff is seeking to be allowed to conjure up, invoke and champion the putative constitutional rights of a hypothetical third party, so that the provisions of section 11(2)(*b*), may be declared unconstitutional on the basis of that constitutional *jus tertii*—thus allowing the plaintiff to march through the resulting gap in the statute. The question which the Court has to consider is whether such an indirect and hypothetical assertion of constitutional rights gives the plaintiff the standing necessary for the successful invocation of the judicial power to strike down a statutory provision on the ground of unconstitutionality. [1980] IR 269, at 280.

He then identified several reasons why it would be undesirable to allow any person to challenge a constitutional provision:

> There is also the hazard that, if the Courts were to accord citizens unrestricted access, regardless of qualification, for the purpose of getting legislative provisions invalidated on constitutional grounds, this important jurisdiction would be subject to abuse. For the litigious person, the crank, the obstructionist, the meddlesome, the perverse, the officious man of straw and many others, the temptation to litigate the constitutionality of a law, rather than to observe it, would prove irresistible on occasion.
>
> In particular, the working interrelation that must be presumed to exist between Parliament and the Judiciary in the democratic scheme of things postulated by the Constitution would not be served if no threshold qualification were ever required for an attack in the Courts on the manner in which the Legislature has exercised its law-making powers. Without such a qualification, the Courts might be thought to encourage those who have opposed a particular Bill on its way through Parliament to ignore or devalue its elevation into an Act of Parliament by continuing their opposition to it by means of an action to have it invalidated on constitutional grounds. It would be contrary to the spirit of the Constitution if the Courts were to allow those who were opposed to a proposed legislative measure, inside or outside Parliament, to have an unrestricted and unqualified right to move from the political arena to the High Court once a Bill had become an Act. It would not accord with the smooth working of the organs of State established by the Constitution if the enactments of the National Parliament were liable to be thwarted or delayed in their operation by litigation which could be brought at the whim of every or any citizen, whether or not he had a personal interest in the outcome. [1980] IR 269, at 283–284.

[16–03] Henchy J identified the primary rule on standing as being that "the person challenging the constitutionality of the statute, or some other person for whom he is deemed by the court to be entitled to speak, must be able to assert that, because of the alleged unconstitutionality, his or that other person's interests have been adversely affected, or stand in real or imminent danger of being adversely affected, by the operation of the statute." He accepted that Mrs Cahill was obliquely affected by the alleged unconstitutionality as, if the statutory provision were struck down, her personal injuries action would not be statute-barred. However, this oblique benefit was not sufficient to confer standing on her. Henchy J emphasised, however, that the standing requirement was a constitutional rule of practice that would need to be applied flexibly. If there were good countervailing reasons as to why the standing rule should be

Principles Governing Constitutional Litigation

relaxed, then that should be done. There were no such reasons in Mrs Cahill's case, but several relaxations of the rule have been developed in subsequent cases.

At first glance, the conclusion that Mrs Cahill did not have standing may seem slightly odd. She was clearly prejudiced by the operation of the statutory provision (as it prevented her from suing) yet she was found to lack *locus standi*. However, this oddness disappears if one explores the distinction between *locus standi* and *ius tertii* (right of a third party) to which Henchy J alluded. Essentially, Mrs Cahill sought to make an argument that was not hers to make. Although she was prejudiced by the operation of the statutory provision, the *reason* advanced as to why the statute was unconstitutional did not relate to her personal circumstances. She knew full well the fact that she had suffered an injury well within the three year time limit; accordingly, while the statutory provision may have been hypothetically unfair, it was not unfair vis-à-vis her. She essentially sought to conjure up a hypothetical third party by reference to whose situation the statutory provision would appear unfair and might be struck down. She would then be able to waltz through the gap in the law (the absence of any time bar), notwithstanding the fact that, even if the statute allowed for an extension of time where an injury was discovered late, Mrs Cahill would equally fall foul of such a provision. Thus although the Supreme Court in *Cahill v Sutton* made many general statements about standing, its ultimate conclusion turns on the concept of *ius tertii*. [16–04]

This distinction between standing and *ius tertii* is further borne out by the decision in *Norris v Attorney General* [1984] IR 36. Mr Norris challenged the constitutionality of constitutionality of s 61 of the Offences against the Person Act 1861 (criminalising anal sex) and s 11 of the Criminal Law Amendment Act 1885 (criminalising "gross indecency" between men). As a preliminary objection, the State argued that Mr Norris had no standing to challenge the legislation as he had never been prosecuted for any offence nor intimidated in any way. The State also argued that Mr Norris was not entitled to rely on the right to marital privacy, established in *McGee v Attorney General* [1974] IR 284, as he himself was not married. The first objection was a general standing objection; the second was an objection based on *ius tertii*. The Supreme Court unanimously held that the standing objection was not well founded; a majority (McCarthy J dissenting) held that the *ius tertii* objection to the marital privacy argument was well founded. O'Higgins CJ put the matter as follows: [16–05]

> In my view, the defendant's objection, in so far as it applies to that part of the plaintiff's case which is based on marital privacy, is well founded and should be upheld. The basis of the plaintiff's case is that there exists in our society a significant number of male homosexual citizens, of whom he is one, for whom, sexually, the female offers no attraction, and who, desiring a stable relationship, must seek such amongst male companions of a similar outlook and disposition. For these, as the plaintiff clearly implied in his evidence (see transcript, Book 1, Q. 153), marriage is not open as an alternative either to promiscuity or a more permanent sexual relationship with a male person. This being so, it is *nihil ad rem* for the plaintiff to suggest, as a reason for alleviating his own predicament, a possible impact of the impugned legislation on a situation which is not his, and to point to a possible injury or prejudice which he has neither suffered nor is in imminent danger of suffering within the principles laid down by this Court in *Cahill v Sutton*.
> However, I do not agree with the defendant's submission that the plaintiff lacks standing to complain merely because he has not been prosecuted nor has had his way of life

disturbed as a result of the legislation which he challenges. In my view, as long as the legislation stands and continues to proclaim as criminal the conduct which the plaintiff asserts he has a right to engage in, such right, if it exists, is threatened and the plaintiff has standing to seek the protection of the Court. [1980] IR 36, at 58–59.

[16–06] This decision was fully consistent with *Cahill v Sutton* on the *ius tertii* point. In relation to the general standing issue, it demonstrated that a reasonably flexible approach would be adopted. On a very strict interpretation, it could be argued that Mr Norris was not directly prejudiced by a law that was not enforced. Nevertheless, the Court was prepared to accept that an apprehended prejudice or chilling effect was sufficient to give standing.

[16–07] In *Society for the Protection of Unborn Children v Coogan* [1989] IR 734, the Supreme Court again relaxed the rule on standing. In this case, the plaintiff (SPUC) sought injunctions restraining the publication by UCD Students Union of material giving information on abortion and pertinent addresses. SPUC contended that this giving of information was in breach of Art 40.3.3° of the Constitution. In the High Court, Carroll J held that SPUC did not have standing, but this was appealed to the Supreme Court. A majority of the Supreme Court held that it was open to SPUC to seek the injunctions, Finlay CJ reasoning:

> [T]he test is that of a bona fide concern and interest, interest being used in the sense of proximity or an objective interest. To ascertain whether such *bona fide* concern and interest exists in a particular case it is of special importance to consider the nature of the constitutional right sought to be protected. In this case that right is the right to life of an unborn child in its mother's womb. The threat to that constitutional right which it is sought to avoid is the death of the child. In respect of such a threat there can never be a victim or potential victim who can sue. If it were to be accepted, as is contended on behalf of the defendants, that only the Attorney General could sue to protect such a constitutional right as that involved in this case, that would, I am satisfied, be a major curtailment of the duty and the power of the courts to defend and uphold the Constitution. On the evidence adduced in the High Court, there can be no question of the plaintiff being an officious or meddlesome intervenient in this matter. I would accept the contention that it could not acquire a *locus standi* to seek this injunction merely by reason of the terms of its articles and memorandum of association. The part, however, that the plaintiff has taken in the proceedings to which I have referred, which were successfully brought to conclusion by the Attorney General at its relation, and the particular right which it seeks to protect with its importance to the whole nature of our society, constitute sufficient grounds for holding that it is a person with a *bona fide* concern and interest and accordingly has the necessary legal standing to bring the action. [1989] IR 734, at 741.

A litigant may therefore have standing even where it is not directly prejudiced and where the right asserted very definitely belongs to a third party, if that third party is not in a position to institute proceedings itself. Not any person can litigate such a point: there must be genuine concern and interest.

[16–08] A more general exception was articulated in *Crotty v An Taoiseach* [1987] IR 713, in which Mr Crotty sought to restrain the State from ratifying the Single European Act. The State challenged his standing to seek these reliefs, but both the High Court and the Supreme Court held that he had standing. In the High Court, Barrington J reasoned:

> There is no doubt that the present issue raised in these proceedings is a controversial political issue but it appears to me also that, right from the start, it has been an issue dealing with the powers of the Government and with constitutional rights which are matters of law and in which a responsible citizen — be his attitude to them right or wrong — could take a legitimate interest and that, in so much as it is a matter which affects the whole constitutional and political structure of the society in which he lives, it is a matter in which the individual citizen might have a legitimate interest which might be accepted in a court of law....
>
> It does appear to me, assuming the plaintiff were otherwise devoid of constitutional standing, that he has raised matters which are common to him and to other citizens and which are weighty countervailing considerations which would justify, on their own, a departure from the rule in relation to *locus standi*. But it does appear to me that in relation to one matter — and it is a basic matter — the plaintiff clearly has a *locus standi* because his contention is that what is being done involves an amendment to the Constitution which should be submitted to a referendum, and that he, as a citizen, has the right to be consulted in such a referendum and that his right is being infringed. He may be correct in making that submission or he may not but it appears to me that it is a serious and important issue and that he has the *locus standi* to raise that particular issue. [1987] IR 713, at 732–734.

The Supreme Court upheld this conclusion on appeal, Finlay CJ commenting:

> The Court is satisfied, in accordance with the principles laid down by the Court in *Cahill v Sutton* [1980] IR 269, that in the particular circumstances of this case where the impugned legislation, namely the Act of 1986, will if made operative affect every citizen, the plaintiff has a *locus standi* to challenge the Act notwithstanding his failure to prove the threat of any special injury or prejudice to him, as distinct from any other citizen, arising from the Act. [1987] IR 713, at 766.

It thus appears that where a particular governmental action affects everyone in general, but no-one in particular, a concerned member of the public will have standing to challenge the constitutionality of that governmental action. This approach has been followed in a number of cases. For instance, in *McKenna v An Taoiseach (No 2)* [1995] 2 IR 10, Ms McKenna challenged the Government's spending of public monies on one side of a referendum campaign. Both the High Court and the Supreme Court accepted, with little discussion, that Ms McKenna had standing to challenge the Government's spending, even though it did not affect her in particular. [16–09]

A different issue arose in *TD v Minister for Education* [2001] 2 IR 259. This case principally concerned whether, and in what circumstances, the courts could grant mandatory orders requiring the State to take certain actions in order to comply with constitutional rights. An issue arose as to whether the applicants had standing to seek the orders given that it was unlikely the facilities would be built before the applicants reached the age of 18 (at which point they would no longer have a constitutional right to the facilities). Two members of the Supreme Court addressed this issue. Keane CJ held that the applicants did have standing, largely because of the effect on their asserted rights to date: [16–10]

> The law in general requires that a person who seeks to challenge the validity of laws passed by the Oireachtas or actions or omissions of the executive and demonstrates that a particular right which he/she enjoys is threatened or endangered by the alleged invalidity, cannot rely on the fact, if it be the fact, that the invalidity will have that effect on the

rights of others, although not on his/hers: see the decisions of this court in *Cahill v Sutton* [1980] IR 269, *King v Attorney General* [1981] IR 233, *Madigan v Attorney General* [1986] ILRM 136 and *Mac Mathúna v Attorney General* [1989] IR 505. That general principle, however, must on occasions yield to the overriding necessity that laws passed by the Oireachtas or acts and omissions of the executive should not go unchallenged, simply because it is difficult, if not impossible, for individual citizens or groups to establish that their individual rights are affected. Thus, in cases where legislation affected all the citizens in the same manner, as in the case of the electoral laws challenged in *O'Donovan v Attorney General* [1961] IR 114, the State's becoming a party to the Single European Act in *Crotty v An Taoiseach* [1987] IR 713 or the expenditure of money for an allegedly unlawful purpose by the Oireachtas and Executive during a referendum campaign (*McKenna v An Taoiseach* (*No 2*) [1995] 2 IR 10), the courts have afforded *locus standi* to persons whose *bona fide* concerns were not in doubt but who could not demonstrate that their individual rights or interests were particularly affected.

In the present case, it is clear that, having regard to their respective ages, some of the applicants will derive no conceivable benefit from the order granted by the High Court. Indeed, since all of them are in the catchment area of the Eastern Health Board and the units to be provided on foot of the order are, without exception, situated outside that area, it is difficult to see what benefit will accrue to any of them from the provision of these units. While it may be that a general improvement in the provision of facilities on a national basis would ensure that the facilities available in the Eastern Health Board area were not being used to meet any deficiencies in other areas and that, in that indirect manner, children in need of facilities, including the applicants, might derive some benefit from their provision, the fact remains that, as the evidence clearly demonstrated, the damage was already done in the case of the applicants by the undoubted failure of the State to deal adequately with this problem in the past.

However, I am satisfied that the submission advanced on behalf of the applicants that these considerations are relevant to the form of relief to which the applicants might be entitled rather than to their *locus standi* or lack of it is well founded. They have undoubtedly been affected by the failure on the part of the State agencies to meet their particular needs and that, of itself, would appear to me to afford them *locus standi* in these proceedings. [2001] 4 IR 259, at 282–283.

Hardiman J, with whom Murray J agreed, held that the applicants—while having *locus standi* in general—did not have *locus standi* to seek the specific mandatory orders.

[16–11] In more recent years, there have been very few constitutional cases in which *locus standi* has been an issue, suggesting that the principles governing this area have now been settled. The principles seem to be that ordinarily a person should be personally affected by legislation in order to have standing to challenge it. However, the courts take a relatively broad view of what affects a person, including anticipated effect and chilling effects. The major exception to this rule of personal effect is that macro political and constitutional developments, which affect everyone in general but no-one in particular, can be challenged by any concerned citizen. In addition to the rule of *locus standi*, there is also a rule that a litigant cannot invoke the right of a third party (*ius tertii*) in order to strike down legislation. That is, even if personally affected by the legislation, one cannot rely on the fact that the legislation is (or might be) unfair vis-à-vis a third party if it is not unfair vis-à-vis oneself. As an exception to this rule, however, where the person affected by the legislation is not in a position to assert her own constitutional rights, those rights may be asserted by another citizen or organisation that has a *bona fide* concern.

Principles Governing Constitutional Litigation

The Presumption of Constitutionality

In *Pigs Marketing Board v Donnelly* [1939] IR 413, the defendant challenged the constitutionality of the Pigs and Bacon Acts 1935 and 1937 which allowed the Board to authorise a hypothetical price. This provision was challenged on the grounds that amounted to an unconstituitonal delegation of legislative power. Hanna J made the following observations:

[16–12]

> When the Court has to consider the constitutionality of a law it must, in the first place, be accepted as an axiom that a law passed by the Oireachtas, the elected representatives of the people, is presumed to be constitutional unless and until the contrary is clearly established. In Éire we have a written Constitution which enacts that the Oireachtas is the only body to pass laws for the peace, order and good government of the State, and it is submitted that their power of legislation is to be limited to these purposes and that any law passed by them must conform to this test. It seems to me difficult, if not impossible, for any Court of law to give all analytical definition of these words—"peace, order, and good government of the State," based upon any known principle of law, or upon which any principle of law could operate. I am certainly unable to do so. The question of peace, order and good government of the State in reference to legislation is primarily a matter for the Oireachtas, and the application of the phrase would seem to be more a guide than a positive law. The reason for this opinion is that upon this question there is no rule of law to guide the Court. It is a question entirely of practical political science and of the theory of government, a question which, if it were to be decided by the Court, would be determined, not by any principle of law, but would depend on the individual view of each particular Judge, or body of Judges, on the theory of government and their knowledge of political science. It seems to me to be a vague phrase, a kind of political shibboleth, the meaning and application of which has changed and will continue to change from one generation to another.
>
> These remarks apply with more force to the submission that the laws passed must be consistent with social justice, assuming that the use of that phrase in Article 43 is to apply to legislation. I cannot define that phrase as a matter of law. It cannot be the old standard of the greatest good of the greatest number, for, at the present day, it may be considered proper that the claim of a minority be made paramount on some topic. As to the meaning of social justice, opinions will differ even more acutely than on the question of "good government." I cannot conceive social justice as being a constant quality, either with individuals or in different States. What is social justice in one State may be the negation of what is considered social justice in another State. In a Court of law it seems to me to be a nebulous phrase, involving no question of law for the Courts, but questions of ethics, morals, economics, and sociology, which are, in my opinion, beyond the determination of a Court of law, but which may be, in their various aspects, within the consideration of the Oireachtas, as representing the people, when framing the law. [1939] IR 413, at 417-418.

This was one of the first cases in which a challenge was brought under the 1937 Constitution. Hanna J's reluctance to assess the common good and social justice has clearly been overtaken by later developments. Nevertheless, his views on the presumption of constitutionality are now firmly established. Apparently because the Oireachtas is democratically elected, its legislation is presumed to be constitutional. In other cases, the presumption has been rationalised as following from the "respect which one great organ of the State owes to another"—*Buckley v Attorney General* [1950] IR 67.

[16–13]

Foley has argued that the presumption of constitutionality finds its justification in two different conceptions of the national Parliament: the Oireachtas as democratic body and the Oireachtas as constitutional interpreter:

[16–14]

> [T]he presumption of constitutionality can be understood to premise its foundational deference on an idealised image of legislative process.....
>
> Suppose that a younger brother defers to the views of his oldest brother about how best to play a particular computer game. Insofar as little brothers actually think about these kinds of things, there are two general types of reason for such deference. First are reasons which relate to his brother's *identity* as the eldest. He may defer simply because the fact-of-being-the-eldest warrants some degree of "respect". Alternatively, he may defer because he equates the fact-of-being-the-eldest with assumptions about how good his brother *qua* the eldest actually is at playing the game. The latter deference is not justified simply by reason of the older brother's identity-as-the-eldest, what he *is*, but by reason of assumptions made about how the eldest actually does a particular thing, *ie* what he *does*.
>
> A similar distinction can be drawn in the constitutional sphere. For example, deference in the United Kingdom has been justified, in the words of *R(S) v Chief Constable of South Yorkshire*, on the basis of the "unimpeachable democratic credentials" of Parliament. It is the fact-of-being-elected which counts here-a fact about the legislature's *democratic identity*. On the other hand, one may defer not simply because of the democratic identity of the legislature-a factor relevant to what the legislature "is"-but because of assumptions made about how a democratic legislature actually conducts constitutional scrutiny-assumptions about what parliament "does". That, for example, seems to be the guiding principle behind one form of the "due deference" approach whereby some British courts have held that deference must be based on a preliminary assessment as to whether the legislature has actually reached an opinion on the matter now before the court. The presumption of constitutionality, it is submitted, appeals *both* to images of what the legislature "is" and what it "does." Brian Foley, "Presuming the Legislature Acts Constitutionally: Legislative Process and Constitutional Decision-Making" (2007) 29 *DULJ* 141, at 147.

[16–15] In Foley's view, however, even the image of what the legislature is appeals to some sense of how the Oireachtas goes about its job of legislating. The difficulty, for Foley, is that the manner in which the Oireachtas does its legislative job in fact does not warrant any deference (such as the presumption of constitutionality). The Oireachtas takes too much direction from the Government to be considered a democratic, deliberative assembly; the Oireachtas does not seriously consider whether its legislation is consistent with the Constitution, too often just accepting the conclusion of the Government (based on the advice of the Attorney General) that the legislation is constitutional. Foley considers what might take the place of the presumption of constitutionality:

> The suggestion in *Wilson* is that *some* parliamentary reasoning over the choice of alternatives would make deference appropriate. The difficulty, however, is with defining precisely what degree of reasoning is required. We can illustrate this problem as follows. We may hypothesise that a legislative measure may be proposed and passed in at least the three following different situations:
>
> A. Legislation is proposed by the Minister who baldy states his, and the government's belief in its constitutionality without elaboration. The legislation is passed without comment on issues of constitutionality.
> B. Legislation is proposed by the Minister who states his, and the government's belief in its constitutionality but also goes into careful detail in respect of this belief, setting out the potential problems and reasons why he believes the Bill is sound. The minority raises issues over the legislation, which the Minister rejects out of hand saying they will not be considered.
> C. Legislation is proposed by the Minister who states his, and the government's belief in its constitutionality but also goes into careful detail in respect of this belief,

setting out the potential problems and reasons why he believes the Bill is sound. The minority raises issues over the legislation, in respect of which the Minister seeks further advice. At committee stage, and upon the return to open house, the Minister outlines his reasons for rejecting minority amendments.

If we believe that scenario *A* represents a good way of deciding constitutional matters, then it is likely that legislative process, as it is, should be afforded a presumption of constitutionality. On the other hand, if one believes that *A* is not good enough, then one is less likely to believe that the legislative process, as it is, should be worthy of deference when it decides constitutional issues. Indeed, the more one thinks about how legislation may earn its "democratic credentials," the more complicated the relevant factors become....

The point here is really a very simple one. Once we move beyond the internal critique, we come face to face with the question of how "good" legislative process has to be in order to attract deference. Any answer to this question, however, will *necessarily* depend on what it is we are asking the legislature to do. If, for example, we believe that constitutional interpretation must *necessarily* be deliberative in the technical sense of deliberative democracy, then it is unlikely we will believe that the legislature will perform it as much because, as noted above, our legislative assembly is simply *not* a deliberative body in that sense....

The primary aim here has simply been to suggest that there are serious problems with presuming that the legislature actually makes constitutional decisions in any sense which can reasonably be described as "legislative." The presumption, in other words, cannot be justified as a general proposition about legislative behaviour. This, of course, may prompt one to ask what may take its place. In this respect, the model of due deference whereby deference must be *earned* seems intriguing. It seems to base deference on the basic notion that legislative constitutional deliberation must actually be *seen to be done* and may dovetail with a growing culture of justification. Nevertheless, accepting this model in any form would require one to work out just what degree of legislative reasoning suffices for deference to be "due" which leads one inexorably to the need to provide a theory of what constitutional interpretation "is" around which comparative institutional abilities and competences may be compared. *ibid*, at 173–177.

Judicial Restraint

A number of principles follow from the presumption of constitutionality and from the great respect which the courts consider that they owe to the Oireachtas. The first of these is the principle of judicial restraint: the courts will not undertake an assessment of a constitutional issue if the case can be resolved on another basis. In *M v An Bord Uchtála* [1977] IR 287, an unmarried mother placed her son for adoption. In an effort to regain custody of her child, she alleged both that certain sections of the Adoption Act 1952 were unconstitutional and that certain statutory procedures had not been followed by the Adoption Board. O'Higgins CJ explained the order in which the courts had to address the issues:

[16–16]

> Where the relief which a plaintiff seeks rests on two such distinct grounds, as a general rule the court should consider first whether the relief sought can be granted on the ground which does not raise a question of constitutional validity. If it can, then the court ought not to rule on the larger question of the constitutional validity of the law in question. Normally, such a law as a statute of the Oireachtas will enjoy a presumption of constitutionality which ought not to be put to the test unnecessarily. However, there may be circumstances of an exceptional nature where the requirement of justice and the protection of constitutional rights make the larger enquiry necessary. Such, in my view, do not exist in this case. [1977] IR 287, at 293.

[16–17] This approach was restated in *Murphy v Roche* [1987] IR 106. Mr Murphy was a member of an unincorporated members club. While dancing at a club function, he fell. He sued the club in negligence. The club claimed that, as a member, he was estopped from suing the club. He sought to argue that any such estoppel would be unconstitutional. Both Mr Murphy and the club were happy to have the estoppel and constitutional issues determined as preliminary issues, but the Attorney General contended that this would be inappropriate. The Supreme Court agreed, Finlay CJ reasoning:

> There can be no doubt that this Court has decided on a number of occasions that it must decline, either in constitutional issues or in other issues of law, to decide any question which is in the form of a moot and the decision of which is not necessary for the determination of the rights of the parties before it. Secondly, it has also clearly been established that where the issues between parties can be determined and finally disposed of by the resolution of an issue of law other than constitutional law, the Court should proceed to consider that issue first and, if it determines the case, should refrain from expressing any view on the constitutional issue that may have been raised.
>
> These principles, however, must, of course, be subject in any individual case to the overriding consideration of doing justice between the parties. [1987] IR 106, at 110.

This judgment indicates that the rule is merely one of practice that ought to be applied in a practical way. In this case, having regard to the undesirability of the plaintiff having to mount a full negligence action that might then be barred by estoppel, the Supreme Court directed that the estoppel issue (but not the constitutional issue) be tried as a preliminary issue.

[16–18] *White v Dublin City Council* [2004] 1 IR 545 is a case that well illustrates the lengths to which the courts will go, however, to ensure that constitutional issues are reached last. Fennelly J outlined the correct approach in the following way:

> The applicants' claim is, of course, *prima facie* statute-barred. It is not contested that, in order to succeed, they have to show that section 82(3B)(a) of the Act of 1963, as amended, is unconstitutional. The first respondent suggests, in its written submissions, that it may be appropriate to consider the constitutional issue in advance of the other issues. If the section is not unconstitutional, there is no need to reach a conclusion on the planning issue. That approach is not permissible.
>
> It is well-established in the case law of this court that a challenge to the constitutionality of a statute will not normally be addressed until the person mounting the challenge shows that he is affected by the provision....
>
> In my view, the logic of those decisions is that it would not suffice for the applicants to show that they wish to impugn the validity of the planning permission. It is, no doubt, possible to say that it would be simpler and more convenient for the court to address the constitutional issue first. However, there is no overriding consideration, in the interests of justice, for departing from the normal rule. I am satisfied that it must be shown that their claim is well-founded, in short that it would succeed. If, on the other hand they fail on the planning issue, it will be unnecessary to consider the constitutional issue. [2004] 1 IR 545, at 556–557.

[16–19] Thus, the applicants had to demonstrate that their judicial review application, which was statute barred, would succeed. Only if the application would hypothetically succeed could the Court consider whether the statute barring the application was unconstitutional. The Supreme Court held both that the judicial review application would succeed and that the statutory bar (an aboslute two-month limit) was unconstitutional. However, if the Court had held that the statutory bar was constitutional, it would—in the interests of judicial restraint—have engaged in a full consideration of a judicial review application that transpired to be statute-barred.

The Double Construction Rule

In *McDonald v Bord na gCon* [1965] IR 217, the Supreme Court considered a challenge to the constitutionality of certain provisions of the Greyhound Industry Act 1958. The provisions empowered an Bord na gCon to exclude a person from (a) being on any greyhound race track, (b) being at any authorised coursing meeting, (c) being at any public sale of greyhounds. Mr McDonald argued that this provision allowed the Board to exercise a judicial power. Walsh J identified a rule of statutory interpretation that was required by the presumption of constitutionality:

[16–20]

> The Greyhound Industry Act of 1958, being an Act of the Oireachtas, is presumed to be constitutional until the contrary is clearly established. One practical effect of this presumption is that if in respect of any provision or provisions of the Act two or more constructions are reasonably open, one of which is constitutional and the other or others are unconstitutional, it must be presumed that the Oireachtas intended only the constitutional construction and a Court called upon to adjudicate upon the constitutionality of the statutory provision should uphold the constitutional construction. It is only when there is no construction reasonably open which is not repugnant to the Constitution that the provision should be held to be repugnant. [1965] IR 217, at 239.

In order to ensure that the legislation could be held constitutional, Walsh J read in provisions to the effect that a proper investigation with natural justice would be carried out before an exclusion order was made:

> The wording of the provisions of sections 43 and 44 does not exclude the application of the principles of natural justice to these investigations. While the Board may determine the manner in which the investigation shall be carried out the clear words or necessary implication which would be required to exclude the principles of natural justice from such investigation are not present in the sections. [1965] IR 217, at 243.

The double construction thus mandates the courts to write in any saving provisions provided they are not clearly excluded by the wording of the Act.

In *East Donegal Co-operative Livestock Market Ltd v Attorney General* [1970] IR 317, Walsh J emphasised the force of the double construction rule and also articulated a further rule to the effect that it was presumed that the Oireachtas intended that powers granted under an Act would be exercised constitutionally. Accordingly, a statutory provision that assigned a power to a public body could not be declared unconstitutional simply because—on one construction—the power might be exercised unconstitutionally:

[16–21]

> [A]n Act of the Oireachtas, or any provision thereof, will not be declared to be invalid where it is possible to construe it in accordance with the Constitution; and it is not only a question of preferring a constitutional construction to one which would be unconstitutional where they both may appear to be open but it also means that an interpretation favouring the validity of an Act should be given in cases of doubt. It must be added, of course, that interpretation or construction of an Act or any provision thereof in conformity with the Constitution cannot be pushed to the point where the interpretation

would result in the substitution of the legislative provision by another provision with a different context, as that would be to usurp the functions of the Oireachtas. In seeking to reach an interpretation or construction in accordance with the Constitution, a statutory provision which is clear and unambiguous cannot be given an opposite meaning. At the same time, however, the presumption of constitutionality carries with it not only the presumption that the constitutional interpretation or construction is the one intended by the Oireachtas but also that the Oireachtas intended that proceedings, procedures, discretions and adjudications which are permitted, provided for, or prescribed by an Act of the Oireachtas are to be conducted in accordance with the principles of constitutional justice. In such a case any departure from those principles would be restrained and corrected by the Courts.[1970] IR 317, at 341.

[16–22] Although many statutory provisions have been saved from a declaration of unconstitutionality by means of the double construction rule, there are limits to what can be achieved: statutory language is not infinitely malleable to ensure constitutionality. In *Kelly v Minister for the Environment* [2002] 4 IR 191, the applicant challenged the rules for the computation of election expenses. Section 31 of the Electoral Act 1997 (as amended) set out what were and were not electoral expenses by reference to the Act's Schedule. Paragraph 1 of the Schedule listed items that constituted electoral expenses. Paragraph 2 provided that the following were not electoral expenses: any expenses in respect of any property, services or facilities so far as those expenses fall to be met out of public funds. Mr Kelly argued that this breached the principle of fairness in the political process (see chapter 15) as it allowed public representatives not to count as an electoral expense the use of their support services for electoral purposes. As there was a cap on electoral expenses, this would put elected representatives at an advantage compared to unelected persons. In the Supreme Court, the focus was not on whether such an arrangement was constitutional but rather on whether the Act could be read in such a way as to ensure that the apparently excluded expenses were actually included. The Court concluded that, notwithstanding the double construction rule, such an interpretation was impossible:

> The wording of paragraphs 2(a) and (c) of the schedule to the Act of 1997 is, in the opinion of the court, plain and unambiguous. It provides that the expenses therein mentioned, including matters such as the provision of office accommodation, secretarial facilities and telephone and postal facilities to members of the Oireachtas and of the European Parliament, are not to be treated as "election expenses" for the purposes of Part V of the Act of 1997. No other construction of the provisions in question is, in the view of the court, reasonably open.
>
> It may well be the case, as urged by counsel for the respondents, that the Oireachtas did not contemplate that expenditure of this nature would be availed of by outgoing members of the Oireachtas or members of the European Parliament for the purposes of their election campaigns. It may be that they were intended to be availed of only for the performance of their duties as legislators or public representatives. The fact remains that the Oireachtas, in plain and unambiguous language, said that such expenditure was not to be treated as "election expenses". The fact, if it be the fact, that the Oireachtas did not contemplate the utilisation of these expenses for the purpose of election campaigns and may even be deemed to have regarded it as, in some sense, improper cannot conceivably justify a construction of the provision which, far from being reasonably open, is directly at variance with what the legislature actually said. [2002] 4 IR 191, at 231.

Severance

Article 15.4 of the Constitution provides that every law enacted by the Oireachtas which is in any respect repugnant to the Constitution or to any provision thereof shall, but to the extent only of such repugnancy, be invalid. Accordingly, an element of unconstitutionality in an Act does not contaminate a whole Act. Most obviously, this means that a whole statute will not be struck down simply because one provision is unconstitutional. More difficult questions arise, however, when it is suggested that the constitutionality of a provision could be saved by deleting certain words from it. Although such an approach is consistent with the idea of judicial restraint (statutory provisions should not be unnecessarily declared unconstitutional), it runs the risk of the courts performing a legislative function. For by deleting only some words in a constitutional provision the courts might in effect be enacting a statutory provision that was never legislatively intended. The courts have addressed these issues in a number of cases. [16–23]

In *Maher v Attorney General* [1973] IR 140, the Supreme Court held that s 44(2)(a) of the Road Traffic Act 1968 was unconstitutional. This section provided that a certificate prepared by a designated, registered medical practitioner to the effect that a certain level of alcohol was present in a person's blood would be "conclusive evidence that, at the time the specimen was taken or provided, the concentration of alcohol in the blood of the person from whom the specimen was taken or by whom the specimen was provided was the specified concentration of alcohol". The Court held that this was an impermissible intrusion on the judicial power. However, the Court then considered whether the word "conclusive" could be severed from the statute to render it constitutional, Fitzgerald CJ delivering the judgment of the Court: [16–24]

> The submission means that it is within the jurisdiction of the Court to sever or separate the word "conclusive" so as to give the paragraph, with that word removed, constitutional validity. The application of the doctrine of severability or separability in the judicial review of legislation has the effect that if a particular provision is held to be unconstitutional, and that provision is independent of and severable from the rest, only the offending provision will be declared invalid. The question is one of interpretation of the legislative intent. Article 15.4.2 of the Constitution lays down that every law enacted by the Oireachtas which is in any respect repugnant to the Constitution or to any provision thereof shall, but to the extent only of such repugnancy, be invalid; therefore there is a presumption that a statute or a statutory provision is not intended to be constitutionally operative only as an entirety. This presumption, however, may be rebutted if it can be shown that, after a part has been held unconstitutional, the remainder may be held to stand independently and legally operable as representing the will of the legislature. But if what remains is so inextricably bound up with the part held invalid that the remainder cannot survive independently, or if the remainder would not represent the legislative intent, the remaining part will not be severed and given constitutional validity. It is essentially a matter of interpreting the intention of the legislature in the light of the relevant constitutional provisions, and it must be borne in mind in all cases that Article 15.2.1 of the Constitution provides that "the sole and exclusive power of making laws for the State is hereby vested in the Oireachtas: no other legislative authority has power to make laws for the State." If, therefore, the Court were to sever part of a statutory provision as unconstitutional and seek to give validity to what is left so as to produce an effect at variance with legislative policy, the Court would be invading a domain exclusive to the legislature and thus exceeding the Court's competency. In other words, it would be seeking to correct one form of unconstitutionality by

engaging in another. The usurpation by the judiciary of an exclusively legislative function is no less unconstitutional than the usurpation by the legislature of an exclusively judicial function. The right to choose and formulate legislative policy is vested exclusively by the Constitution in the national parliament.... [The Chief Justice reviewed the background to the enactment of the statutory provision in question and continued.]

The proposition that section 44(2)(*a*), should be saved by severing from it the word "conclusive" necessarily involves setting aside the legislative decision arrived at after mature consideration that the certificate should prove conclusively that the blood-alcohol level determined in the certificate was that of the person from whom the specimen was taken at the time it was taken. In its place, legislative effect would be given to the certificate as merely "evidence" of that fact—thus giving legislative force to the rejected recommendation, or something akin to it. Apart from doing violence to the verbal integrity of the provision as enacted by the legislature, a judicial preservation of section 44(2)(*a*), with the word "conclusive" omitted, would amount to an impermissible usurpation of the legislative function by setting up as law something that the legislature had deliberately and unambiguously rejected. The unlikelihood that section 44(2)(*a*), with the word "conclusive" omitted would represent the will of the legislature is borne out when one considers how it would operate in that form. The certificate of the result of the analysis would then be merely "evidence" that the blood-alcohol level of the person from whom the specimen was got was the specified amount. But what sort of evidence? The immediately preceding and succeeding parts of the same section state meticulously that the certificate in question shall, as to the matters specified, be "sufficient evidence... until the contrary is shown." Would section 44(2)(*a*), with the word "conclusive" omitted, have the same probative effect, or more, or less? It is scarcely conceivable that, if the word "conclusive" were to be dropped, the legislature would have been content to use the word "evidence" without the precision of qualifying words which is to be found elsewhere in the same section.

All the indications lead to the conclusion that the legislature, in opting to make the certificate conclusive evidence of the analysis, had not directed its attention to what would happen if the certificate were not conclusive and that, if it had, it would not have allowed section 44(2)(*a*), to go forth merely with the word "conclusive" omitted. The decision of the Court is that section 44(2)(*a*), of the Act of 1968 in its entirety must be declared invalid as being repugnant to the Constitution. Because of the crucial part played by the paragraph in the scheme of this important legislation, the Court reaches this conclusion reluctantly and with regret; but to hold that the paragraph could survive with the word "conclusive" omitted would amount to an amendment rather than an interpretation, thus requiring the Court to act in a legislative rather than a judicial role. The Court accepts as correct the argument on behalf of the Attorney General that if the paragraph is invalid it is totally invalid. The plaintiff's appeal will be allowed and his conviction will be declared invalid. [1973] IR 140, at 147–150.

[16–25] *Desmond v Glackin* (*No 2*) [1993] 3 IR 67 provides a good illustration of a situation in which the courts considered that severence was possible. The Companies Act 1990 allowed for the appointment of inspectors with power to inquire into the affairs of companies. Section 10(5) of the Act allowed an inspector to certify a person for non-co-operation and present the certificate to the High Court. The High Court could then inquire into the matter and, having heard witnesses who might be produced against or on behalf of the alleged offender, "punish the offender in like manner as if he had been guilty of contempt of court". Section 10(6) also allowed the High Court, after an inquiry under s 10(5) to make orders or directions requiring the person (in effect) to co-operate with the inquiry. Both the High Court and the Supreme Court held that the clause "punish the offender in like manner as if he had been guilty of contempt of court" was a breach of Art 38.1. However, it was held that that clause could validly be severed from s 10(5). Finlay CJ delivered the judgment of the Court:

> The Court, having considered the original provisions of section 10(5) and (6) of the Act of 1990, and having considered the deletion therefrom contained in the order of the High Court removing from section 10(5) only the words: "punish the offender in like manner as if he had been guilty of contempt of court", has come to the following conclusions concerning the severance so created.
>
> The provisions of the two subsections as contained in the Act provide two quite separate methods of procedure....
>
> It is the provision for punishment "in like manner as if he had been guilty of contempt of court" which this decision holds to be inconsistent with the Constitution. A procedure as is contained in section 10(6) whereby the Court may, upon certification by the inspector of a refusal to answer questions or produce documents, inquire into the matter in a proper manner and either absolve the person from the obligation so to do, or direct by court order the answering of particular questions or, possibly, of all questions of a particular category, and the production of particular documents or of all documents of a particular category, does not contain any constitutional flaw.
>
> The Court is satisfied that the proper interpretation of these two subsections leads to a conclusion that the legislature intended not only the provision for punishment which is held to be inconsistent with the Constitution, but also, as a separate discretionary jurisdiction in the court, the powers contained in section 10(6). If, in addition to the words deleted from section 10(5) by the order of the High Court, there is added a consequential deletion of the words contained in section 10(6):— "Without prejudice to its power under subsection (5), the court may, after a hearing under that subsection", then there remains in the combined provisions of the two sub-sections one of the two original intentions of the legislature, and such a severance in the view of the Court would be permissible, having regard to the applicable principles which have been set out.
>
> The Court therefore holds that section 10(5) of the Companies Act, 1990, is invalid having regard to the provisions of the Constitution to the extent only that it contains the words: "punish in like manner as if he had been guilty of contempt of court", and declares that consequent upon such finding there must be deleted from the provisions of section 10(6) of the Companies Act, 1990, the words: "Without prejudice to its power under subsection (5) the court may, after a hearing under that subsection". [1993] 3 IR 67, at 118–120.

Effects of a Finding of a Declaration of Unconstitutionality

Introduction

[16–26] The effect of declaring legislation unconstitutional is an exceptionally difficult issue. In terms of strict theory, the meaning of the Constitution does not change. Accordingly, a law declared unconstitutional must either have been unconstitutional since it was enacted or, if it is a pre-1937 law, since the date of the enactment of the Constitution. However, if laws are treated as void from either of those dates, questions arise as to how we treat persons (public and private) who acted on the assumption that the law was invalid. Can we (or should we) unravel all actions taken on foot of laws subsequently declared invalid?

[16–27] The courts have wrestled with these questions in a number of cases. Most recently, considerable public controversy was caused by *A v Governor of Arbour Hill Prison* [2006] IESC 45. On 15 June 2004, A had pleaded guilty to the offence of unlawful carnal knowledge of a girl under the age of 15 years, contrary to s 1(1) of the Criminal Law (Amendment) Act 1935. The girl in question was the 12-year-old friend of A's daughter. When sleeping over at A's house, she was plied with alcohol by A who then raped her. For this crime, A was sentenced to a term of imprisonment of three years. Subsequently, the DPP initiated a prosecution of C also for an offence contrary to s 1(1). C initiated judicial review proceedings, seeking a declaration either that s 1(1) allowed him to plead a defence of reasonable or honest mistake as to age or, in the alternative, that s 1(1) was unconstitutional. The Court held on 23 May 2006 that s 1(1) was inconsistent with the Constitution. (See chapter 2 for discussion of *C v Ireland* [2006] IESC 33). On 26 May 2006, A instituted habeas corpus proceedings. Article 40.4.1° of the Constitution provides that no citizen shall be deprived of his personal liberty save in accordance with law. Article 40.4.2° prescribes a procedure whereby detained persons can seek an order from the High Court declaring their detention illegal and ordering their release. On 29 May 2006, the High Court ordered the release of A, Laffoy J principally reasoning that A's continued detention in custody had been rendered unlawful by the declaration that s 1(1) of the 1935 Act was unconstitutional. The State appealed and on 2 June 2006, the Supreme Court allowed the appeal, ordering the re-arrest of A. The Court provided its reasons on 10 July 2006.

[16–28] The judgments of the Supreme Court in *A* significantly developed the jurisprudence on declarations of unconstitutionality. In order to assess the current position, the best approach is to consider what the answer to three questions would be, both before and after *A*:

(a) When do declarations of unconstitutionality date to?
(b) What is the effect of a declaration of unconstitutionality?
(c) If declarations of unconstitutionality do not have fully retrospective effect, can official acts taken before the declaration of unconstitutionality continue to have legal effect after the declaration of unconstitutionality?

When Do Declarations of Unconstitutionality Date To?

[16–29] The answer to this question depends on whether the statutory provision declared unconstitutional was enacted before or after the Constitution came into force. In *Murphy v Attorney General* [1982] IR 241, the Supreme Court considered the question in relation to post 1937 statutes, a majority concluding that post 1937 statutes were void *ab initio*. Henchy J rested this conclusion primarily on a characterisation of the Oireachtas as a delegated legislative body. Article 15 of the Constitution grants to the Oireachtas the power to legislate, but Art 15.4 provides that the Oireachtas shall not enact any law that is in breach of the Constitution:

> The Constitution, therefore, as part of its inbuilt checks and balances, has made it abundantly clear that the delegated power of legislation given to the Oireachtas (a power which may in turn be sub-delegated by the Oireachtas pursuant to Article 15.2.2) is a power which, regardless of any interim presumption of constitutionality that may attach to its enactments, cannot be exercised save within the constitutionally designated limitations of that power; and once it has lost the presumption of constitutionality as a result of a judicial condemnation on the ground of unconstitutionality, it must, in accordance with Article 15.4.2, be held to "be invalid"—not, be it observed, to have "become invalid." It is to be deemed null and void from the moment of its purported enactment, no less than if it had emanated from a person or body with no power of legislation. In my judgment, the constitutional disposition of the powers of the State in this respect falls into line with the general principle that, when a constitution or

Principles Governing Constitutional Litigation

a constitutional statute gives a specifically confined power of legislation to a legislature, laws found to have been enacted in excess of that delegation are *ultra vires* and therefore void *ab initio*. [1982] IR 241, at 309.

Although the point did not arise for decision in the case, Henchy J also reasoned that pre-1937 statutory provisions that were found unconstitutional were void from the date of the enactment of the Constitution: [16–30]

> If it is a pre-Constitution enactment, Article 50.1, provides in effect that the statutory provision in question shall, subject to the Constitution and to the extent that it is not inconsistent therewith, continue in full force and effect until it is repealed or amended by enactment of the Oireachtas, *ie*, the Parliament established by the Constitution. The issue to be determined in such a case is whether, when the impugned provision is set beside the Constitution, or some particular part of it, there is disclosed an inconsistency.
>
> If the impugned provision is shown to suffer from such inconsistency, it may still be deemed to have survived in part the coming into operation of the Constitution, provided the part found not inconsistent can be said to have had, at the time of that event, a separate and self-contained existence as a legislative enactment. Otherwise, the impugned provision in its entirety will be declared to have ceased to have a legislative existence upon the coming into operation of the Constitution in 1937.
>
> Such a declaration under Article 50.1, amounts to a judicial death certificate, with the date of death stated as the date when the Constitution came into operation. *ibid*, at 306–307.

All other members of the Court agreed with this proposition in relation to pre-1937 statutes. However, as the point was conceded by the Attorney General in argument and did not arise for decision in the case, it cannot be stated that it has been definitively decided. [16–31]

Although certain members of the Supreme Court in *A* mentioned arguments that had been advanced for the overruling of *Murphy*, none was prepared to take this step, particularly in the context of habeas corpus proceedings, which are designed primarily for speed. The position, therefore, continues to be that pre-1937 statutes are deemed void from the date on which the Constitution was enacted and that post-1937 statutes are deemed void *ab intitio*. [16–32]

What is the Effect of a Declaration of Unconstitutionality?

Although the word "void" seems to suggest that a measure is ineffectual or of no legal effect, the courts have consistently held that not everything done on foot of a void statute will itself be declared void. Put another way, void statutes have been held to have given legal effect to other measures. These issues were first directly considered in *State (Byrne) v Frawley* [1978] IR 326. On 12 December 1975 in *de Búrca v Attorney General*, the Supreme Court had declared unconstitutional the method of preparing jury lists under the Juries Act 1927. Five days later, the prosecutor was convicted of larceny by a jury empanelled on 10 December 1975 under the provisions that had been declared unconstitutional. Some five months later, the prosecutor sought an order of habeas corpus on the ground that he had been convicted by an improperly constituted jury. A majority of the Supreme Court held that the jury that had convicted the prisoner suffered from the same constitutional defect as the Juries Act 1927 in that it was not sufficiently representative of the community. However, the same majority held that the prosecutor was now debarred from seeking release: [16–33]

As to the prisoner in this case, his position is uniquely different from that of other persons convicted by a jury selected under the provisions of the Act of 1927. He was the first person entitled to plead successfully in the Circuit Court the unconstitutionality of such a jury. As a result of the decision in the *de Burca Case*, he was presented with that opportunity in the middle of his trial. An informed and deliberate decision was made to turn down that opportunity. His then counsel, instead of applying to have the jury discharged, elected—and I make no criticism of that choice—to allow the trial to proceed without any objection to the jury as constituted. It was obviously thought to be in the best interests of the prisoner that he should take his chances before that jury, notwithstanding its constitutional imperfection. Had he been acquitted by that jury, doubtless we would have heard no complaint that the jury was selected unconstitutionally.

Because the prisoner freely and knowingly elected at his trial to accept the empanelled jury as competent to try him, I consider that he is now precluded by that election from claiming that the jury lacked constitutionality.... The prisoner's approbation of the jury was affirmed by his failure to question its validity when he formulated grounds of appeal against his conviction and sentence, and when his application for leave to appeal was argued in the Court of Criminal Appeal. It was not until some five months after his trial that he first put forward the complaint that the jury had been formed unconstitutionally. Such a *volte face* is impermissible. Having by his conduct led the Courts, the prosecution (who were acting for the public at large) and the prison authorities to proceed on the footing that he accepted without question the validity of the jury, the prisoner is not now entitled to assert the contrary. The constitutional right to a jury drawn from a representative pool existed for his benefit. Having knowingly elected not to claim that right, it would be contrary to the due administration of justice under the Constitution if he were to be allowed to raise that claim in the present proceedings when, by deliberate choice, it was left unasserted at the trial and subsequently in the Court of Criminal Appeal. What has been lost in the process of events is not the right guaranteed by the Constitution but the prisoner's competence to lay claim to it in the circumstances of this case. [1978] IR 328, at 349–350

[16–34] In *Murphy v Attorney General*, as noted above, the Supreme Court held that certain provisions of the Income Tax Acts were void *ab initio* on the ground that they treated married persons living together less well than unmarried persons living together, thereby breaching Art 41 of the Constitution. Nevertheless, the Court held that there were significant limits on the effects of that declaration of voidness and the extent to which the plaintiffs—or others—were entitled to claim back the taxes that had been unconstitutionally levied. Henchy J considered the sort of factors that might lead the courts to recognise the effect of measures taken on foot of void statutes:

But it is not a universal rule that what has been done in pursuance of a law which has been held to have been invalid for constitutional or other reasons will necessarily give a good cause of action: see, for example, the decision of this Court in *The State* (*Byrne*) v *Frawley*. While it is central to the due administration of justice in an ordered society that one of the primary concerns of the Courts should be to see that prejudice suffered at the hands of those who act without legal justification, where legal justification is required, shall not stand beyond the reach of corrective legal proceedings, the law has to recognize that there may be transcendent considerations which make such a course undesirable, impractical, or impossible.

Over the centuries the law has come to recognize, in one degree or another that factors such as prescription (negative or positive), waiver, estoppel, laches, a statute of limitation, *res judicata*, or other matters (most of which may be grouped under the heading of public policy) may debar a person from obtaining redress in the courts for injury, pecuniary or otherwise, which would be justiciable and redressable if such considerations had not intervened....

For a variety of reasons, the law recognizes that in certain circumstances, no matter how unfounded in law certain conduct may have been, no matter how unwarranted its operation in a particular case, what has happened has happened and cannot, or should not, be undone. The irreversible progressions and bye-products of time, the compulsion of public order and of the common good, the aversion of the law from giving a hearing to those who have slept on their rights, the quality of legality—even irreversibility—that tends to attach to what has become inveterate or has been widely accepted or acted upon, the recognition that even in the short term the accomplished fact may sometimes acquire an inviolable sacredness, these and other factors may convert what has been done under an unconstitutional, or otherwise void, law into an acceptable part of the *corpus juris*. This trend represents an inexorable process that is not peculiar to the law, for in a wide variety of other contexts it is either foolish or impossible to attempt to turn back the hands of the clock. [1982] IR 241, at 314–315.

Following the decision in *Murphy*, the Oireachtas enacted s 21 of the Finance Act 1980, which provided for a system under which the tax collected from married persons, in respect of the tax years prior to 1979/1980, would not be any less than would have been collected under the provisions impugned in *Murphy*. This gave rise to the situation in *Muckley v Ireland* [1985] IR 472. The plaintiffs had overpaid their tax in 1979/1980. However, they had underpaid their taxes in the years 1975/1976–1978/1979. The inspector of taxes sought to offset the previous underpayments against the more recent overpayment, with the result that the Revenue Commissioners would not have to repay the amount of the overpayment. This would have been the correct position if s 21 of the 1980 Act were constitutionally valid; however, both the High Court and the Supreme Court held that s 21 was unconstitutional on the grounds that it penalised the married state. On that basis, Barrington J summarised the situation as follows, casting considerable light on the extent to which the declaration of voidness in *Murphy* had retrospective effects: [16–35]

It appears to me that the logic of the Supreme Court judgment in the *Murphy Case* [1982] IR 241 indicates that there was no power to compute and to levy taxes under the impugned provisions of the Act of 1967. If these taxes have not been paid there is no power to collect them. Taxes which have been paid under the impugned provisions cannot, generally, be recovered but this is not because the impugned provisions ever had any validity but because of the unfortunate fact that it is not possible to rectify all the injustices of life.

This line of reasoning has however the unpalatable result that conscientious citizens who paid their taxes on time cannot recover them but people who delayed or defaulted may escape liability altogether. Mr. O'Neill, on behalf of the Attorney General, referred to this as a "monstrous" result.

It is however only fair to point out that there is no question of Mr. and Mrs Muckley being defaulters. They met all their tax liabilities in accordance with the PAYE system and, in retrospect, we now know that they in fact paid more tax than they were constitutionally obliged to pay. The logic of this would appear to be that, on the basis of the Murphy decision, they are not obliged to pay any further taxes in respect of the financial years 1975/76 to 1978/79 (inclusive), and that they are entitled to a refund of the full amount of tax over-paid in the year 1979/1980 free of any set off in respect of the earlier years. [1985] IR 472, at 477.

This clarifies a number of points. First, the decision in *Murphy* was characterised as an exception justified by the practical difficulties of paying back taxes that had already [16–36] flowed into the central fund. It was an exception to the general principle that voidness means having no legal effect. Secondly, the Muckleys were in effect able to avail themselves of the declaration of unconstitutionality granted in *Murphy* to affect transactions entered into prior to *Murphy*. Although these points were not argued before the court, they certainly reflect the understanding of *Murphy* at the time.

[16–37]   The next relevant case concerned s 34 of the Offences against the State Act 1939, which provided that where a person holding an office in the civil service was convicted by a Special Criminal Court of a scheduled offence, such as membership of an unlawful organisation, that person would immediately on conviction forfeit her position. In July 1991, in the case of *Cox v Ireland* [1992] 2 IR 53, the Supreme Court held that this provision was unconstitutional. In *McDonnell v Ireland* [1998] 1 IR 134, the plaintiff sought to avail himself of this ruling. In May 1974, he had been deemed automatically to have forfeited his position in the civil service upon his conviction of a scheduled offence. After his release from prison, he applied for reinstatement in 1975 and again in 1984 but was refused on each occasion on the basis of his forfeiture. Following the decision in *Cox*, Mr McDonnell instituted proceedings claiming that his purported dismissal was unconstitutional and had no legal effect, as s 34 of the 1939 Act was void *ab initio*. The Supreme Court affirmed the orthodoxy that a post-1937 statute is void *ab initio*. Barrington, Keane and Barron JJ all held against the plaintiff on the basis that he was statute-bound and/or defeated by laches. Barrington J expressly approved of the Supreme Court majority decision in *Murphy*, noting that Art 15.4 can only be read as meaning that an unconstitutional provision can never become valid law. O'Flaherty J, however, made some *obiter* comments:

> [S]ince the provision was in place when the plaintiff was prosecuted on the 30th May, 1974, he cannot now avail of its extirpation as giving him a cause of action. This is established in both the majority judgments, as well as in the minority judgment, of the Court in [*Murphy*]....
>
> The approach of the majority in [*Murphy*], while holding that declarations of invalidity of legislation worked to make the impugned legislation void *ab initio*, produced more or less the same results [as the minority judgment of O'Higgins CJ that such legislation was void only from the date of the declaration]. It was held that the plaintiffs were not entitled to recover tax paid by them for any period prior to the tax year 1978/79, which was the tax year in respect of which the constitutionality of those sections was first effectively impugned....
>
> The correct rule must be that laws should be observed until they are struck down as unconstitutional. Article 25.4.1 of the Constitution provides that:
>
> "Every Bill shall become and be law as on and from the day on which it is signed by the President..." and that, unless the contrary is expressed, that law is effective from that day forth....
>
> From that date, all citizens are required to tailor their conduct in such a way as to conform with the obligations of the particular statute. Members of society are given no discretion to disobey such law on the ground that it might later transpire that the law is invalid having regard to the provisions of the Constitution. Every judge on taking office promises to uphold "the Constitution and the laws"; the judge cannot have a mental reservation that he or she will uphold only those laws that will not someday be struck down as unconstitutional. We speak of something as having "the *force* of law". As such, the law forms a cornerstone of rights and obligations which define how we live in an ordered society under the rule of law. A rule of constitutional interpretation, which preserves the distinct status of statute law which, as such, is necessitated by the

requirements of an ordered society and by "the reality of the situation" ... should have the effect that laws must be observed until struck down as unconstitutional. The consequence of striking down legislation can only crystallise in respect of the immediate litigation which gave rise to the declaration of invalidity. This is what occurred in *Murphy v The Attorney General* ... as well as in *Cox v Ireland*.... [1998] 1 IR 134.

Although this approach is consistent with the result in *Murphy*, it is not consistent with the reasoning of the majority. The majority clearly viewed the limitation in *Murphy* as an exception to a general principle of retroactive effect for declarations of voidness. For O'Flaherty J, however, there is a general principle against retroactive effect for declarations of voidness, with perhaps a limited exception for those engaged in the litigation in which the declaration of constitutionality is granted. Moreover, the approach suggested by O'Flaherty J is inconsistent with the result in *Muckley*. For if laws must be observed until struck down and the consequences of striking down legislation only crystallise in respect of the immediate litigation, the Muckleys should not have been able to avoid the effects of their underpayment of taxes prior to the declaration that such legislation was unconstitutional as they themselves had not challenged the constitutionality of that legislation. However, the minority position of O'Flaherty J appears to have become the Court's position in *A*. [16–38]

Murray CJ, for instance, put the matter as follows:

> [O'Flaherty J's] statement of the law I am quite satisfied is correct. It is the logical and ineluctable application of the principles and considerations set out in the judgment of this Court in *Murphy* and indeed other judicial dicta which I have cited.... Save in exceptional circumstances, any other approach would render the Constitution dysfunctional and ignore that it contains a complete set of rules and principles designed to ensure "an ordered society under the rule of law" in the words of O'Flaherty J.

Although Murray CJ was correct to note that the courts have not enforced a rigidly retroactive effect for declarations of unconstitutionality, it is arguable that he reversed the principle and the exception. O'Flaherty J's statement of the law does not logically and ineluctably follow from the principles and considerations laid down in *Murphy*. Indeed, as O'Flaherty J himself had implicitly conceded, his proposition was consistent with the result of *Murphy* but not with the reasoning employed. Moreover, it was inconsistent with the result of *Muckley*. That said, as no member of the Supreme Court in *A* referred to *Muckley*, this point did not need to be addressed. [16–39]

The judgment of Denham J neatly captured the way in which the implications of *Muckley* was overlooked by the Supreme Court: [16–40]

> The plaintiffs [in *Murphy*] were the only tax payers entitled to maintain a claim for restitution of tax in pursuance of the Court's decision, unless proceedings had already been instituted by any other taxpayer challenging the validity of the sections impugned in the proceedings. Thus, this decision on unconstitutionality did not render the State liable to repay all excess monies gathered, *bona fide*, by the State, since 1967, to the plaintiffs, or to the many affected married couples. There was no retrospective application of unconstitutionality.

This is not correct, however, There was retrospective application of the declaration in *Murphy*; otherwise, the plaintiffs in *Muckley* could not have maintained their claim

[16-41] In addressing *Murphy*, Hardiman J focused on Henchy J's assertion that a condemned provision would *normally* provide no legal justification for any acts done or left undone or for transactions undertaken in pursuance of it. He relied on the word "normally" to support Murray CJ's restatement of the principle:

> In a criminal prosecution where the State relies in good faith on a statute in force at the time and the accused does not seek to impugn the bringing or conduct of the prosecution, on any grounds that may in law be open to him or her, including the constitutionality of the statute, before the case reaches finality, on appeal or otherwise, then the final decision in the case must be deemed to be and to remain lawful notwithstanding any subsequent ruling that the statute, or a provision of it, is unconstitutional. That is the general principle.
>
> I do not exclude, by way of exception to the foregoing general principle, that the grounds upon which a court declares a statute to be unconstitutional, or some extreme feature of an individual case, might require, for wholly exceptional reasons related to some fundamental unfairness amounting to a denial of justice, that verdicts in particular cases or a particular class of cases be not allowed to stand.

[16-42] Although Henchy J's use of the word "normally" clearly envisaged exceptions to retroactive application of declarations of unconstitutionality—a point supported by the decision in both *Murphy* itself and *McDonnell*—it is questionable whether it is consistent with a general principle that criminal convictions will stand notwithstanding a subsequent declaration of unconstitutionality. Such a general principle seems to substitute the rule for the exception.

The Continuing Effect of Official Decisions Taken Before the Declaration of Unconstitutionality

[16-43] This was a crucial issue in the *A* case. If the effects of a declaration of unconstitutionality crystallise only in the immediate litigation and thereafter have prospective effect, what happens to a situation brought about by an official decision prior to the declaration but that continues after the declaration? In A's case, what happens to a detention begun on foot of an official decision prior to the statute being struck down but that continues after the statute is struck down. The courts had never directly addressed this issue prior to *A*. In *A* itself, in the High Court, Laffoy J ordered the release of Mr A largely on the basis that his continuing detention could not be justified on the basis of the statute declared to be void *ab initio*. She put the matter as follows:

> As I have said, the only consequence of the declaration of the inconsistency of section 1(1) with the Constitution with which I am concerned on this application is whether it has rendered the detention of the applicant unlawful as of now. If is undoubtedly the case that the consequences of a declaration under Article 50.1 may be determined by a variety of factors, for example, the conduct of the person relying on the declaration or the fact that an irreversible course of events has taken place, so that what was done on foot of the condemned statutory provision may not necessarily be relied on as a ground for a claim for mollification or other legal redress, as Henchy J noted in *Murphy v The Attorney General*, citing the decision of the Supreme Court in *The State (Byrne) v Frawley*.

However, on this application I am not concerned with whether the applicant may be in a position to maintain a civil action for wrongful imprisonment in the future.... In the light of the declaration by the Supreme Court of the inconsistency of section 1(1), the only offence of which the applicant was convicted, the conviction is a nullity, and the warrant is bad on its face.... [H]is detention was rendered unlawful by the declaration and cannot continue.

However, the Supreme Court's view was implicitly to the contrary. Not only would the courts give effect to actions taken on foot of legislation subsequently declared unconstitutional, but the courts would continue to give effect to those actions even after the legislation was declared unconstitutional. Rossa Fanning has been critical of the Supreme Court's decision on the basis that it did not directly deal with this issue: [16–44]

> This is an important aspect of the case that appears at many stages lost in an abstract discussion about the principles surrounding retrospective application of judicial decision-making in the main. Lengthy passages were cited to demonstrate that, in short, the past cannot easily be undone. But the judgments contained very little analysis of the question of whether A was seeking to undo the past at all.
> The proceedings were brought pursuant to an Article 40.4.2 inquiry whereby A alleged, at the time the proceedings came before Laffoy J in the High Court, that he was at that time being "unlawfully detained." Unique amongst personal rights protected by the Constitution, the personal liberty of the individual is expressly protected by the in-built mechanism of an Article 40.4.2 inquiry into the legality of his detention.
> The proceedings can accordingly be seen as present-tense proceedings based on a live and continuing complaint. They were far removed from the notion of an historic claim for damages that might have been brought by a person convicted under the section decades previously and long since released. Such a hypothetical person could certainly have been met by the *ratio* of the decision in *McDonnell* and *Murphy*.
> But that was not the position here. A did not seek to retrospectively impugn his trial or re-open the question of an appeal in respect of his conviction, the time-limit for which having long since expired. Instead, he brought what the judgments repeatedly characterised as a "collateral challenge" to his conviction and sentence based on the decision in *CC*. A slightly different way of looking at matters is that the challenge he brought was not a collateral challenge to the legality of his conviction and sentence at all, but rather was solely a challenge to the legality of his continued detention, having regard to the *prospective* effect of the Supreme Court decision on May 23, 2006.
> Despite the repetition of something approaching a mantra in the judgments of the Supreme Court that A's application was barred by the absence of a general principle of retroactive application of constitutional decision-making, no relief sought on behalf of A in fact required any retroactive application of the decision in CC.
> The narrow Article 40.4.2° proceedings brought on his behalf did not seek an Order of *certiorari* quashing his conviction. Nor could they of course, as such an Order would have been beyond the remit of the court in determining the narrow inquiry into the legality of the detention of A. Nor were damages sought by A, which following similar logic, would have required the initiation of appropriate plenary proceedings on his behalf. The only relief that was sought was relief against his *continued* imprisonment after the date the Supreme Court had announced that section 1(1) of the 1935 Act was inconsistent with the Constitution and of no legal effect. Thus, the only issue in the case was the legal basis for the *prospective* detention of A and not his historical or *retrospective* detention. To borrow the metaphor used by Griffin J in *Murphy*, A was not asking that the court attempt to unscramble any eggs. Rossa Fanning, "Hard Case; Bad Law? The Supreme Court Decision in *A v Governor of Arbour Hill Prison*" (2005) 40 Ir Jur 188, at 207–208.

[16–45] Perhaps the courts should overrule *Murphy* and provide that statutes will be void only from the time they are declared unconstitutional. Estelle Feldman and I have elsewhere criticised the reasoning, but not necessarily the result, in *A*:

> The *A case* demonstrates a legitimate concern for the proper ordering of society. However, all the dicta (perhaps not surprisingly, given the context of the case) focus on situations where public officials have acted. But the law also plays a role in guiding the activities of private individuals. It seems likely that cases will emerge in the next few years in which a person is accused of committing acts that breached section 1(1) prior to it being struck down as unconstitutional. The rights of victims and the proper ordering of society would seem to be prejudiced just as much by not prosecuting such persons as they would have been by releasing Mr A. Yet nothing in the judgments of the Supreme Court would allow any action to be taken on foot of the statute in those cases.
>
> The Supreme Court's decision in *A* thus creates and/or entrenches three contentious distinctions. First, there is the distinction between a legal measure being void on the one hand and providing near absolute legal authority for official action on the other. Secondly, there is the distinction between those for whom release would be an unjustified windfall and those for whom release would not be an unjustified windfall. Finally, there is the distinction between giving continuing effect to official actions taken in reliance on the law but not giving any recognition to the extent to which private citizens have ordered their lives in reliance on the law. All these distinctions could be avoided if the Supreme Court were to reverse *Murphy* and simply hold that statutes declared unconstitutional are void only from the date of the declaration forwards, perhaps with a limited exception for those who had instituted the litigation. Although such a re-interpretation might not be the best interpretation of Article 15.4 and Article 50.1, it would produce a more consistent and defensible set of propositions than exists in the current case law. Raymond Byrne and William Binchy, *Annual Review of Irish Law 2006* (Thomson Round Hall, 2007), at 184–185.

CONTENTS – CHAPTER 17

Constitutional Interpretation

Introduction. . . . . [17–01]
The Constitution: Interpreting Words. . . . . [17–04]
The Constitution: Interpreting Values. . . . . [17–14]
Conclusions. . . . . [17–31]

Overview

Constitutional law requires that current decisions about what the organs of government can and cannot do must be made on the basis of the past decision represented in the text of the Constitution. Constitutional interpretation is the manner in which sense is made of the past decision for the present circumstances. Where this is unclear, problems arise for three reasons: the method of interpretation may determine the result in the case; the Constitution itself does not determine the method of interpretation; judges do not have an electoral mandate to make important decisions for society. In some constitutional cases, the focus is on the interpretation of words. In these cases, the courts tend to view the words of the Constitution in a broad or harmonious way, attempting to make sense of the whole context. In other cases, the focus is on the interpretation of values. In these cases, the courts have oscillated between giving a living interpretation to the values and assuming that the values must be interpreted in line with prevailing beliefs in 1937. The general lack of consistency in methods of judicial interpretation leads to concerns about coherence in constitutional law.

Chapter 17

Constitutional Interpretation

Introduction

At its most basic, law functions as a method of decision-making. Often when making a decision, one makes an unfettered decision about what one *should* do—by reference to morality, consequences, needs, wants, desires, *etc*. For instance, which political party will I vote for? Will I support a referendum to outlaw the death penalty? Which chocolate will I eat? Society also makes many collective decisions in this way: how should we run the health system? What would be an appropriate tax rate to stimulate economic activity? What incentives should we provide for the production of chocolate? [17–01]

Law is a different method of decision-making. When a decision is governed by law, we decide what to do *now* by reference to a decision made *then*. When a driver decides to drive on the left hand side of the road (in Ireland, at any rate), this decision is not based on a full assessment of what would, all things considered, be best but rather on the fact that in the past it was stipulated that it was mandatory to drive on the left hand side of the road. In this way, the law brings a number of desirable elements into human affairs. It ensures efficiency by removing the need for all decisions all the time to be made by people undertaking a full assessment of what would, all things considered, be best. It ensures predictability by allowing people to plan their affairs because—when a matter is legally regulated—people can have an expectation of how other people will act and what the consequences of their own actions will be. It also facilitates democracy: it would be impossible for all decisions to be the subject of democratic debate. However, general laws can be agreed democratically and then applied (initially by private persons but ultimately by legal officials in the case of disagreement or default). This is not to argue that all decisions should be governed by law. Clearly it is possible to over-regulate society by making decisions for people which should really be left to the individuals themselves. The correct balance between regulation and freedom is the stuff of political debate. Nevertheless, in order to understand the law properly—and to approach legal problems intelligently—it is important to understand the unique ways in which law contributes to the common good. [17–02]

The correct legal answer to a question will not always be clear. Sometimes, legal provisions are deliberately left vague so that a sensible decision can be taken after the fact (a reasonableness standard, for example). More controversially, sometimes legal provisions will appear to conflict and sometimes it will be unclear whether a particular factual situation is covered by a particular legal rule. In these cases, resolution is called for. In our legal system officials—ultimately judges—have the role of resolving these disputes. This raises the question that is the focus of this chapter: in what way (if at all) does the *past* decision (for the purposes of this book, the decision at issue is the Constitution as amended) affect how we must *now* determine this dispute? Put another way, how should we interpret the Constitution? These questions arise in all areas of the [17–03] law but are particularly acute in the context of a constitution that allows for judicial review of legislative and executive decisions. For the courts' interpretation of a constitutional decision (the text of Art 40.1, for example) can lead to the overturning of a democratic choice (a rule that women be presumptively excluded from jury service, for example). By subjecting legislation to the power of judicial review, the Constitution clearly envisages counter-majoritarian decision-making of this type; however, where the constitutional text is unclear, the process of rendering it clear assumes crucial importance. The chosen method of interpretation often determines the interpretation reached which determines the result in the case. To complicate matters further, no method of interpretation is constitutionally stipulated. The Constitution does not provide guidance as to the method which should be used for its own interpretation. So judges' choice of interpretative method, which is likely to be determinative of many constitutional cases, is itself based on something other than the Constitution. It is therefore important that judges' choice of interpretative method be clearly articulated, cogently defended and consistently applied.

A considerable amount of judicial attention and a huge amount of academic attention has been paid to the questions of how a constitution ought to be interpreted. The purpose of this chapter, however, is primarily to focus on judicial attitudes in Ireland.

The Constitution: Interpreting Words

[17–04] In *Sinnott v Minister for Education,* Murray J made the following basic statement:

> It is axiomatic that the point of departure in the interpretation of a legal instrument, be it a constitution or otherwise, is the text of that instrument, albeit having regard to the nature of the instrument and in the context of the instrument as a whole. [2001] 2 IR 545, at 671.

This is undoubtedly correct. As the purpose of legal interpretation is to work out what the past decision (the text) means for the current dispute, that process must start with the text. This does not overlook the fact that interpreters bring their experiences to the text. Nevertheless, although a psychological examination of how such experiences bear on interpretation is a worthwhile area of study, it is not directly relevant to the normative question being addressed here: how ought the Constitution to be interpreted?

[17–05] Stating that interpretation must start with the text does not tell us very much about what to do with the text. It is generally accepted in Irish constitutional law that a narrowly literal approach, parsing carefully each provision, should not be taken to the Constitution.

[17–06] There is more support for a broadly literal approach. This approach is still based on the text but does not rely on a narrow parsing of textual provisions. It is more likely to harmonise two provisions than to apply the *expressio unius est exclusio alterius* (the expression of one thing is the exclusion of the other) rule to emphasise the differences between constitutional provisions. Costello J stated this approach in *Attorney General v Paperlink* [1984] ILRM 373, at 385:

> The Constitution is a political instrument as well as a legal document and in its interpretation the courts should not place the same significance on differences of language used in two succeeding sub-paragraphs as would, for example be placed on

differently drafted sub-sections of a Finance Act. A purposive, rather than a strictly literal, approach to the interpretation of the sub-paragraphs is appropriate. I do not, therefore, think that any significance should be attached to the fact that the State's duty towards the citizens' unspecified personal rights in Article 40.3.1° is phrased in somewhat different language to its duty towards the citizens' specific personal rights set out in Article 40.3.2°. Accordingly, I am prepared to hold that the State has a duty by its laws to protect as best it may from unjust attack the personal right of each of the defendants to earn a livelihood.

Once one begins to broaden the interpretative context in this way, it is difficult to stop. That is, once one seeks to interpret two provisions in a coherent manner, there is a natural tendency to try and interpret more and more provisions coherently. This tendency manifest itself in Henchy J's harmonious approach, first stated in *Dillane v Attorney General* [1980] ILRM 167, at 170: [17–07]

> Under the doctrine of harmonious interpretation, which requires, where possible, the relevant constitutional provisions to be construed and applied so that each will be given due weight in the circumstances of the case, it would not be a valid form of constitutional interpretation to rule that the immunity given to a Garda by Rule 67 is necessarily permitted by Article 40.1 and in the same breath to hold that it is proscribed by [Article 40.3.2°]. This subsection guarantees protection of property rights only in the case of unjust attack, and vindication of them only in the case of injustice done. For the reasons I have given for holding that the second paragraph of Article 40.1 warranted the denial under Rule 67 of an application by the plaintiff for costs against the prosecuting Garda, even if it could be held that a right to apply successfully for costs is a property under the subsection, I would have to decide that there was no breach of the subsection; for there was no "unjust attack" which was required to be protected, and no "injustice done" which was required to be vindicated. What happened when the plaintiff was denied his costs under the rule was categorically permitted by Article 40.1, so it cannot be part of the injustice which Article 40.3.2° was designed to prevent. In my judgment, this ground of constitutional attack also fails.

This approach appears sensible. In particular, it is difficult to see how the common good would be sufficient to override one constitutional right but not another. However, the process of harmonising constitutional provisions is not without its problems. An approach that minimises the differences between different constitutional provisions may overlook the fact that different provisions might quite legitimately be trying to achieve different things. In *Quinn's Supermarket v Attorney General* [1972] IR 1, at 24–25, Walsh J considered the interaction between the freedom of religious conscience in Art 44.2.1° and the prohibition on religious discrimination in Art 44.2.3°: [17–08]

> [Article 44.2.1] of the Constitution guarantees freedom of conscience and the free profession and practice of religion in terms which do not confine these to Christianity and Judaism. It appears to me, therefore, that the primary object and aim of Article 44, and in particular the provisions of section 2 of that Article, was to secure and guarantee freedom of conscience and the free profession and practice of religion subject to public order and morality; and to ensure that the practice of religion and the holding of particular religious beliefs shall not subject the person so practising religion or holding those beliefs to any disabilities on that account, or permit distinctions on the ground of religious profession, belief or status between persons in the State who are free to profess and practise their religion. If, however, the implementation of the guarantee of free profession and practice of religion requires that a distinction should be made to make possible for the persons

professing or practising a particular religion their guaranteed right to do so, then such a distinction is not invalid having regard to the provisions of the Constitution. It would be completely contrary to the spirit and intendment of the provisions of Article 44.2 to permit the guarantee against discrimination on the ground of religious profession or belief to be made the very means of restricting or preventing the free profession or practice of religion. The primary purpose of the guarantee against discrimination is to ensure the freedom of practice of religion. Any law which by virtue of the generality of its application would by its effect restrict or prevent the free profession and practice of religion by any person or persons would be invalid having regard to the provisions of the Constitution, unless it contained provisions which saved from such restriction or prevention the practice of religion of the person or persons who would otherwise be so restricted or prevented.

[17–09] It is arguable that the purpose of a guarantee against religious discrimination is to prohibit religious discrimination, not to facilitate free practice of religion. By rendering the prohibition on discrimination subordinate to the guarantee of free practice, the courts have—in the interests of harmony—turned Art 44.2.3° into a virtual dead-letter. A better approach might be to attempt a more sophisticated harmonious interpretation that gave due weight to both constitutional provisions. Under this approach, however, it can be difficult to work out which provision should—in a particular case—be given more weight.

[17–10] Somewhat similarly, a particular textual provision may come into conflict with a perceived constitutional ethos. This problem is well illustrated by the case of *People (DPP) v O'Shea* [1982] IR 384. The issue in this case was whether a clear constitutional provision could be modified by reference to a more amorphous constitutional ideal. Article 34.4.3° provides:

> The Supreme Court shall, with such exceptions and subject to such regulations as may be prescribed by law, have appellate jurisdiction from all decisions of the High Court, and shall also have appellate jurisdiction from such decisions of other courts as may be prescribed by law.

[17–11] The DPP sought to appeal an acquittal in the High Court (the Central Criminal Court) to the Supreme Court. It had been the accepted common law practice that acquittals could not be appealed. Henchy J argued that the provision could not be looked at in isolation:

> I agree that if the relevant sub-section of the Constitution is looked at in isolation and is given a literal reading, it would lend itself to that interpretation [of permitting the DPP to appeal against an acquittal]. But I do not agree that such an approach is a correct method of constitutional interpretation. Any single constitutional right or power is but a component in an ensemble of interconnected and interacting provisions which must be brought into play as part of a larger composition, and which must be given such an integrated interpretation as will fit it harmoniously into the general constitutional order and modulation. It may be said of a constitution, more than of any other legal instrument, that "the letter killeth, but the spirit giveth life." ... The letter [gives] way to the spirit, the spirit being the paramount principle of autrefois acquit. [1982] IR 384, at 426.

[17–12] This analysis is seriously open to question. If Henchy J was contending that all provisions of the Constitution should be read harmoniously so as to provide a "larger composition", it is difficult to see how the court could ignore Art 34.4.3° in coming to that larger composition. It is the Constitution itself, *ie* the words contained in it, that provides us with our only sense of what the Constitution's spirit is. It is permissible to resolve a conflict between two provisions in favour of a spirit evidenced by other provisions. But it is not permissible to over-write one clear provision in favour of an amorphous spirit that has no particular textual foundation. On the other hand, if Henchy J was contending that the express provisions of the Constitution can legitimately be overridden by reference to a sense of the spirit that need not be grounded in any text, it is difficult to reconcile that proposition with any democratic account of judicial review.

A majority of the Supreme Court disagreed with Henchy J, O'Higgins CJ putting the matter as follows:

> The Constitution, as the fundamental law of the State, must be accepted, interpreted and construed according to the words which are used; and these words, where the meaning is plain and unambiguous, must be given their literal meaning. Of course, the Constitution must be looked at as a whole and not merely in parts and, where doubt or ambiguity exists, regard may be had to other provisions of the Constitution and to the situation which obtained and the laws which were in force when it was enacted. Plain words must, however, be given their plain meaning unless qualified or restricted by the Constitution itself. The Constitution brought into existence a new State, subject to its own particular and unique basic law, but absorbing into its jurisprudence such laws as were then in force to the extent to which these conformed with that basic law. It follows that existing laws, or formerly accepted legal principles or practices, cannot be invoked to alter, restrict or qualify the plain words used in the Constitution unless the authority for so doing derives from the Constitution itself. Indeed, the very existence of an inconsistency between what was formerly the law and what the words of the Constitution declare, according to their literal meaning, repeals and abrogates what had been the law. [1982] IR 384, at 397–398.

This reasoning perhaps goes to the opposite extreme of Henchy J. Although O'Higgins CJ left open the possibility of looking to other provisions of the Constitution, that could only be done where there was doubt or ambiguity. The best approach perhaps lies somewhere between the two. A narrowly literal approach ought never be the end-point in constitutional interpretation. However, in seeking to read the provisions of the Constitution harmoniously, determinative weight must be attached to what (all) the provisions actually say. It is not permissible to overlook a clearly worded provision in favour of an unstated "spirit". Other cases may be less clear-cut. A clearly worded provision should take interpretative precedence over an unclear provision. An absolute obligation should take interpretative precedence over a conditional obligation. But how should the courts harmonise two values that appear to be in irreconcilable conflict? [17–13]

The Constitution: Interpreting Values

Some constitutional provisions do not lend themselves easily to a semantic interpretation. For instance, if one were to look up the words "equality", "before" and "law" in a dictionary, one would not be particularly confident of having identified the correct interpretation of Art 40.1. Equality before the law is a moral value to which the State is committed by virtue of Art 40.1. Other values to which the State is committed include the protection of property, family, freedom of expression, marriage and religious freedom. Difficult questions arise in relation to how these values should [17–14] be interpreted. Any form of literal approach, even a harmonious one, seems unfit for purpose: the question is not what the words "equality" or "protection of property", *etc* mean but rather what the values connoted by those words require. Such values can be treated as concepts, the task of the courts being to adopt a more concrete, albeit contested, conception of the concept. That conception can then be applied to the particular facts of the case.

[17–15] Ronald Dworkin has argued in favour of this approach to constitutional interpretation:

> [There is] a particular way of reading and enforcing a political constitution, which I call the *moral* reading. Most contemporary constitutions declare individual rights against the government in very broad and abstract language, like the First Amendment of the United States Constitution, which provides that Congress shall make no law abridging "the freedom of speech." The moral reading proposes that we all – judges, lawyers, citizens – interpret and apply these abstract clauses on the understanding that they invoke moral principles about political decency and justice. The First Amendment, for example, recognizes a moral principle – that it is wrong for government to censor or control what individual citizens say or publish – and incorporates it into American law. So when some novel or controversial constitutional issue arises – about whether, for instance, the First Amendment permits laws against pornography – people who form an opinion must decide how an abstract moral principle is best understood. They must decide whether the true ground of the moral principle that condemns censorship, in the form in which this principle has been incorporated into American law, extends to the case of pornography.
>
> The moral reading therefore brings political morality into the heart of constitutional law. But political morality is inherently uncertain and controversial, so any system of government that makes such principles part of its law must decide whose interpretation and understanding will be authoritative... Ronald Dworkin, *Freedom's Law* (Oxford, 1996), at 2, Reproduced with the kind permission of Oxford University Press.

[17–16] On occasion, the Irish courts have articulated an approach that is close to this method of constitutional interpretation. For instance, in *McGee v Attorney General* [1974] IR 284, at 318–319, Walsh J described constitutional interpretation in the following terms:

> In this country it falls finally upon the judges to interpret the Constitution and in doing so to determine, where necessary, the rights which are superior or antecedent to positive law or which are imprescriptible or inalienable. In the performance of this difficult duty there are certain guidelines laid down in the Constitution for the judge. The very structure and content of the Articles dealing with fundamental rights clearly indicate that justice is not subordinate to the law. In particular, the terms of Article 40.3 expressly subordinate the law to justice. Both Aristotle and the Christian philosophers have regarded justice as the highest human virtue. The virtue of prudence was also esteemed by Aristotle as by the philosophers of the Christian world. But the great additional virtue introduced by Christianity was that of charity—not the charity which consists of giving to the deserving, for that is justice, but the charity which is also called mercy. According to the preamble, the people gave themselves the Constitution to promote the common good with due observance of prudence, justice and charity so that the dignity and freedom of the individual might be assured. The judges must, therefore, as best they can from their training and their experience interpret these rights in accordance with their ideas of prudence, justice and charity. It is but natural that from time to time the prevailing ideas of these virtues may be conditioned by the passage of time; no interpretation of the Constitution is intended to be final for all time. It is given in the light of prevailing ideas and concepts.

These comments were admittedly expressed in the rather peculiar context of the unenumerated rights doctrine. Nevertheless, they evidence a view that the Constitution is committed to certain moral values, that guidance as to the import of these moral values is to be found in the text, but that judges should interpret the provisions in light of present-day understandings of them.

[17–17]

Many decisions of the courts interpreting constitutional values appear to fit this method of interpretation. Thus in *Re Article 26 and the Health (Amendment) (No 2) Bill 2004* [2005] IESC 7, at [120], the Supreme Court characterised constitutional property rights in the following way:

[17–18]

> The right to the ownership of property has a moral quality which is intimately related to the humanity of each individual. It is also one of the pillars of the free and democratic society established under the Constitution.

In *State (Nicoloau) v An Bord Uchtála* [1965] IR 567, at 643–644, Walsh J identified the sort of family that the Constitution protected:

[17–19]

> It is quite clear from the provisions of Article 41, and in particular section 3 thereof, that the family referred to in this Article is the family which is founded on the institution of marriage and, in the context of the Article, marriage means valid marriage under the law for the time being in force in the State. While it is quite true that unmarried persons cohabiting together and the children of their union may often be referred to as a family and have many, if not all, of the outward appearances of a family, and may indeed for the purposes of a particular law be regarded as such, nevertheless so far as Article 41 is concerned the guarantees therein contained are confined to families based upon marriage.

Again, this is a method of constitutional interpretation that begins with the text, but in both cases the courts were not simply reading the text to work out what the words literally meant. Instead, they were reading the Constitution to find out what values were protected.

[17–20]

An issue arises as to whether an approach that emphasises the present-day understanding of values is appropriate to all provisions of the Constitution. Kelly has proposed a useful distinction in this regard:

[17–21]

> Are the rules in the Constitution to be understood in 1987 to mean what we can suppose the Dáil and people in 1937 intended them to mean? Or is the text, despite having been debated and approved only once, fifty years ago, to be interpreted in the light of today's contemporary understanding, one by one, of the terms it contains? The former method, what Gerard Hogan calls the historical approach, certainly contains difficulties, chief among them the difficulty (which will increase with the years) of deciding what opinions, standards, etc we ought to impute to our parents and grandparents. As McCarthy J said in the Norris case, it is not easy to be sure what even today's public opinion on this or that point may be. And in fact the Supreme Court, in several cases, has taken the line that the Constitution is a living, developing organism, and that its elements – for instance, the standard of what is an inherent "personal right" – change over the years. This indeed was an unavoidable line for the court to take if, for instance, it was to give Mrs McGee a favourable decision in her case about what she said was her personal right to import contraceptives for her own marital use, because nothing is more certain than that the Supreme Court of 1950, let alone that of 1940, although looking at the very same constitutional Article, would have thrown her case out. This approach, then, is not

"historical", in Gerard Hogan's sense; it does not consider a case from what it thinks would have been the standpoint of Dáil and people in 1937; to use Walsh J's neat expression, it takes the Constitution to be "speaking always in the present tense".

But there are serious difficulties with the present-tense approach too; and they get worse if you move away from the bare words of the Constitution, and consider whether some constitutional term, or value, or element, is to be presumed to carry with it some well-understood corollary....

How is one to achieve a balance between the competing claims of the historical approach and the "present-tense" approach? I think the answer is this. They both have a role to play in constitutional interpretation, but in different areas. I would propose the following rough rules.

1. The "present-tense" approach is appropriate to *standards* and *values*. Thus elements like "personal rights", "common good", "social justice", "equality", and so on, can (indeed can only) be interpreted according to the lights of today as the judges perceive and share them. The same would go, as Walsh J says in the context of the private property guarantees of Articles 40.3 and 43, for concepts like "injustice".
2. The historical approach, on the other hand, is appropriate where some law-based *system* is in issue, like jury trial, county councils, the census. These the Dáil and the people built into the case of the state; if their removal or transformation is needed, it must be authorised by the people in a referendum; they cannot be whittled away by ordinary legislation subject only to "present-tense" constitutional scrutiny.
3. This need not mean that the shape of such systems is in every respect fixed in the permafrost of 1937. The courts ought to have some leeway for considering which dimensions of a system are secondary, and which are so material to traditional constitutional values that a willingness to see them diluted or substantially abolished without a referendum could not be imputed to the enacting electorate. John Kelly, "The Constitution: Law and Manifesto" 208, at 212, 215 in Frank Litton ed, *The Constitution of Ireland 1937–1987* (Institute of Public Administration, 1988).

[17–22] A good example of a historical approach being applied to technical issues is *Conroy v Attorney General* [1965] IR 411, in which the Supreme Court considered what constituted a "minor offence", triable summarily under Art 38.1:

Article 71 of the Constitution of Saorstát Éireann was similar in essentials to the provisions of Article 38 of the Constitution. In the year 1922 the existing law for the trial of offences authorised the summary trial of a wide range of offences which were not trivial either by their nature or by the punishments they attracted. After the enactment of that Constitution the Courts of Justice Act, 1924, recognised that many of such offences should be tried summarily and the Act also recognised the obvious fact that a particular offence might be considered to be minor or non-minor according to the circumstances of the particular case. After the enactment of the present Constitution the same fact was recognised by the Criminal Justice Act, 1951. The Constitution of Saorstát Éireann may be considered to have accepted the existing pattern of distinction between offences to be tried in a Court of summary jurisdiction and offences to be tried on indictment by a jury.

In 1937 the people with full knowledge of the existing structure of the Courts and the modes of trial gave themselves the present Constitution.... [T]he procedure for prosecuting offences of drunken driving prescribed by that Act was part of the procedural pattern in existence and was widely known in 1937. Its creation by Act of the Oireachtas sufficiently indicates that it reflected public opinion. The procedure prescribed by section 49 of the Act of 1961 in form corresponds to the pattern in existence in 1937 and the offence thereby created does not, by reason of the punishment prescribed, differ in character from the corresponding offence in the Act of 1933. [1965] IR 411, at 433.

However, it can sometimes be difficult to identify what is a technical issue and what is not. In *Sinnott v Minister for Education* [2001] 2 IR 545, the issue was whether a person's right to free primary education extended beyond the age of 18. Murray J reasoned that the question of what constituted "primary education" was a question of standards or values to be determined by reference to current understandings of the term while the duration of primary education was a technical issue to be determined by reference to the historical understanding of the Constitution: [17–23]

> What is understood by "primary education" in Article 42.4? It was not in contention in this appeal that historically primary education has always been understood as the basic education given to children in primary schools by primary teachers up to the age of 12 or 14 years. For immediate purposes I don't think it is necessary to review the definition given to primary education by reference to its content in a number of judicial authorities. However education as a concept is defined, primary education has always been understood to be a form of basic education given to children in the primary school cycle. It stands in contrast with secondary education and third level education as well as, nowadays, pre-school attendance of infants. The precise age at which the primary cycle begins and ends may be a variant of history, culture and policy in any given country but in the end it has been traditionally understood as referring to that primary cycle in which children, as opposed to adults, are taught.
>
> Primary education has been part of the education system in this country since the nineteenth century. As Murnaghan J observed in *McEneaney v Minister for Education* [1941] IR 430, at 438: "For now more than a century it has been recognised that the provision of primary education is a national obligation; and for very many years this duty was entrusted to a corporate body created by Royal Charter called to the Commissioners of National Education in Ireland". The Constitution of 1922 made express provision for the availability of primary education.
>
> In short, primary education in the pre-1922 and post-1922 education system was understood as ordinarily and naturally referring to the education of children. This was the system in place when the Constitution of 1937 was adopted. Counsel for the first plaintiff argued that in adopting the Constitution of 1937, Article 42.4 represented a dramatic decision of the people to ensure that there was a financial commitment of constitutional status to the provision of free primary education. It certainly was a fundamentally important statement in the Constitution of the State's obligation to provide free primary education but there is nothing to indicate that it had any dramatic or any material effect on the existing structure. In fact the Constitution was not a catalyst for change in that regard. Primary education as naturally and generally understood, continues to be afforded to children to the present day.
>
> In my view even today the generally understood meaning of primary education, (and primary school and primary teacher) is the teaching of children and contemporary English dictionaries define it in such a way....
>
> [Murray J quoted from Professor Kelly's work as extracted above and continued.] There is undoubted value in such an approach which Professor Kelly clearly had in mind as a *guide* to, rather than formal canons of, interpretation.
>
> As correctly emphasised by counsel for the first plaintiff, the obligation to provide for free primary education in Article 42.4 is unique in the extent to which it circumscribes the discretion which the organs of State, government and Oireachtas, normally enjoy under the Constitution as to the allocation of national resources. That particular obligation is limited to primary education. It excludes other forms of education. If Article 42.4 was intended to extend that constitutional obligation to the provision of free primary

education to all adults, irrespective of their age, according to their need, I think it can fairly be said that one would have expected that such a far reaching limitation on the powers of the Oireachtas to have been expressly stated in the provision.

That is not to say that the content or nature of the education to be provided for cannot be interpreted in the light of present day circumstances. The nature and quality of the primary education to be provided is a more abstract concept with connotations of standards and values. Historically there is no doubt that many persons who suffered from mental or physical handicap were not capable of benefiting from the kind of education that was traditionally available. However, with greater insight into the nature of people's handicaps, the evolution of teaching methods, new *curricula* as well as new tools of education there is no doubt that the nature and content of primary education must be defined in contemporary circumstances. That means where children are capable of benefiting from primary education (however its content is defined) the State have an obligation to ensure that it is provided free to children who can benefit from it including those who suffer from severe mental or physical handicap.

In my view, primary education taken in its ordinary and natural meaning is at once both inclusive and exclusive. It relates to the teaching of children only. It includes children but excludes adults. I do not find in the Constitution authority for interpreting it otherwise. [2001] 2 IR 545, at 680–682.

[17–24] This is a difficult distinction to maintain. If one is prepared to expand what is understood to be the content of primary education by reference to present-day understandings, why should one shut off the possibility that the duration of primary education could be interpreted in a manner different from that prevalent in 1937? This is not to argue that the right to free primary education necessarily extends beyond the age of 18. Rather, it simply suggests that the duration question is just as much a values issue as the content question.

[17–25] More recently, the courts have adopted a further method of working out whether a present tense approach is appropriate. In *Gilligan v Revenue Commissioners* [2006] IEHC 404, at 126, Dunne J considered whether a lesbian couple had a right to marry under the Constitution. In order to address this point, she considered whether she could adopt a present-day understanding of the term "marriage":

> I accept that the Constitution is a living instrument as referred to in the passage from the judgment of Walsh J [in *McGee v Attorney General*] relied on by counsel for the plaintiffs but I also accept the arguments of Mr O'Donnell to the effect that there is a difference between an examination of the Constitution in the context of ascertaining unenumerated rights and redefining a right which is implicit in the Constitution and which is clearly understood. In this case the court is being asked to redefine marriage to mean something which it has never done to date.

[17–26] This approach requires the court to make a distinction between an implicit right and a judicially enumerated right. That is, in order to work out what method of interpretation is appropriate, a court must decide whether the right is one that was textually implicit in the Constitution or one that was enumerated on the basis of the unenumerated rights doctrine. Given that most judges involved in the unenumerated rights doctrine understood themselves (rightly or wrongly) to be enumerating rights that were implicit in the Constitution, this will be a very difficult distinction to draw. Indeed, in *Ryan v Attorney General* [1965] IR 294 itself, Kenny J identified the right to marry as a right stemming from the unenumerated rights doctrine. There is nothing particularly wrong with difficult distinctions, but a considerable amount will turn on this distinction to no particular purpose. It is difficult to see what is achieved by making rights with a textual basis less capable of evolution than rights with no textual basis. Depending on whether a right is "implicit" or "judicially enumerated", it will attract a historical or present-day interpretation. However, the benefit of employing such a distinction—particularly when it conflicts with the standards/technicalities distinction suggested by Professor Kelly—is impossible to discern. All told, this development in constitutional law is regrettable. Professor Kelly's approach—for all its difficulties in application to borderline cases—is preferable. It at least articulates some rational basis as to why different constitutional provisions should be accorded different interpretative treatment.

In recent years, the courts seem to be undertaking greater recourse to the historical method of interpretation. As noted above, it was used by Dunne J in *Gilligan*. In *Leontjava and Chang v DPP* [2004] 1 IR 591, at [87], Keane CJ rejected the proposition that the Oireachtas was precluded from legislating by way of incorporating another instrument. Among several grounds for his conclusion, he reasoned: [17–27]

> This court cannot accept the proposition that the framers of the Constitution in 1937, while conferring on the Oireachtas the exclusive role of making laws for the State, intended to limit their powers to legislate by prohibiting them from incorporating other instruments, such as secondary legislation and treaties, in an Act and giving them the force of law without setting out their provisions *in extenso*. As the decision of the House of Lords in *Institute of Patent Agents v Lockwood* [1894] AC 347 demonstrates, that precise form of statutory incorporation by reference was already established towards the end of the nineteenth century and there is nothing in the Constitution to indicate that the choice of the Oireachtas to legislate in that rather than another form was in any way inhibited.

What is interesting about this quotation is that there is little reference to what the framers, ratifiers or enacters of the Constitution actually thought. This is most probably for two reasons: (a) documents evidencing the views of these people are not easily accessible, and (b) many of the issues that now arise were not even considered in 1937. However, the lack of any attempt empirically to ascertain the views of the framers renders it questionable whether the historical method—as practised by the Irish courts—can properly be characterised as a method of interpretation. It does not aim at an understanding of how words were used and understood in 1937. Rather it rests on an assumption that nothing that was permitted prior to 1937 was intended to be upset by the Constitution, and therefore cannot be held unconstitutional, unless there is a clear textual basis for so doing. As this assumption does not relate to the interpretation of the text (and indeed seeks to stymie interpretation), it is best characterised as a political assumption. [17–28]

Whether or not this assumption is warranted, it is worrying that the courts adopt it only intermittently. *McGee v Attorney General* is probably the most famous example of the courts holding unconstitutional a criminal prohibition that had been enacted by the same legislature as ratified the Constitution. More recently, in *C v Ireland* [2006] IESC 33, the Supreme Court held unconstitutional section 1(1) of the Criminal Law (Amendment) Act 1935 on the basis that no element of *mens rea* was required in respect of the offence of unlawful carnal knowledge of a girl under the age of 15. Hardiman J reasoned: [17–29]

> It appears to us that to criminalise in a serious way a person who is mentally innocent is indeed "to inflict a grave injury on that person's dignity and sense of worth" and to treat him as "little more than a means to an end." [2006] IESC 33, at [44].

[17–30] No consideration was given as to whether the state of affairs in 1937 should lead the court to the conclusion that s 1(1) could not be constitutional. If Professor Kelly's distinction between values issues and technical issues were consistently applied by the courts, this would not be such a problem. However, in the absence of such consistency, one is at a loss to understand how the courts in some cases decide to assume that the Constitution was intended not to change the law while in other cases conclude that the Constitution did change the law.

Conclusions

[17–31] As noted at the start of this chapter, methods of interpretation play a crucial role in constitutional law. Most constitutional cases arise precisely because the constitutional text is unclear. Therefore, the method chosen to reach a clear result from an unclear text will likely be determinative of the result of the case. As this method cannot be determined by the Constitution itself and is instead a matter of judicial choice, it is especially important that the method chosen be justified and consistently applied. However, that consistency of method is lacking in the case law. Indeed, in *Sinnott* Hardiman J implied that inconsistency of interpretative approaches is a constitutional virtue:

> There has been considerable academic debate, some reflected in the arguments in the hearing of this appeal, as to the correct approach to the construction of a constitutional provision. Tensions are said to exist between the methods of construction summarised in the use of adjectives such as "historical", "harmonious" and "purposive". In my view, much of this debate is otiose, because each of these words connotes an aspect of interpretation which legitimately forms part, but only part, of every exercise in constitutional construction. [2001] 2 IR 545, at 687–688.

[17–32] In these circumstances, it is difficult to avoid the conclusion that—in Irish constitutional law—methods of interpretation function as *ex post facto* justifications for intuitively reached conclusions rather than as fetters on judicial power. Until some consistency of interpretative method is achieved, it is unlikely that there will be much coherence in constitutional law.

INDEX

A
Administrative state
    emergence of [11–30]
All Party Oireachtas Committee
    regarding Cabinet confidentiality [12–33]
    regarding carers within the home [9–69]
    regarding interests of the child citizen [9–57], [9–100]
    regarding State's deferring to parents [9–98]
Anglo-Irish Agreement [12–23]
    definition of [12–24]
    objections to [12–23]
Aristotle
    regarded justice as [4–18], [17–16]
    regarded prudence as [4–18]
Aristotelian equality
    see Equality
Attorney General
    representative of public [13–10]

B
Belfast Agreement [1–03], [15–25]

C
Children's rights [9–109]
    "child" as term regards education [9–119], [9–121]
        does it include? [9–122]
    description of [9–74]
        childhood [9–121]
            "young persons" [9–121]
        "functional child" approach [9–122]
    infant child [9–95]
    of paramount consideration [9–100], [9–101]
    regarding the State [9–74]
    unless explicitly age-related [9–73]
    who asserts on behalf of child? [9–75], [9–93], [9–95]
        judicial attitude to parents [9–96], [9–99]
Citizenship
    constitutional amendments [1–05], [1–06]
    ius sanguinis [1–05]
    ius soli [1–05]
Cityview Test
    see Legislative power
Clarke, Desmond
    describes a State [1–11]
    integration of religion in education [10–24]
    analysis [10–25], [10–26]
    on 'natural law' problems [4–28], [4–29]
    what constitutes a nation [1–01]
Commutative/distributive justice [13–48]
Constitution
    basic law/manifesto [13–57]
    committed to certain moral values [17–17]
    must be upheld [13–47]
    separation of powers as "overlapping" [12–12]
    "silence" regarding Oireachtas powers [11–50]
    "silent as to form of legislation" [11–46]
    "silent as to how government should function" [12–32]
Constitution Review Group
    regarding non-marital families [9–07]
    rejected providing for socio economic rights [13–56]
Constitutional interpretation [17–01]
    description of [17–16]
    judicial attitudes in Ireland [17–04]
        broad literal approach required [17–06]
        difficult to stop [17–07]
        harmonizing provisions [17–07], [17–08]
        problems with [17–08], [17–09]
            due weight must be allotted [17–09], [17–13]
            versus ethos [17–10], [17–11]
        to provide "larger composition" [17–12]
        start with text [17–04], [17–05]
    method of, is crucial [17–31]
        ex post facto justifications [17–32]
    "plain words must be given plain meaning" [17–12]
    "*the* constitutional family" [17–19]
    vague legal provisions [17–03]
    values [17–14]
        equality before the law [17–14]
        historical approach [17–22]
            favoured by courts [17–27]
            intermittently [17–29]
            method of interpretation? [17–28]
            assumes nothing permitted pre-1937 [17–28]
            does not relate to interpretation [17–28]
        what was "minor offence" [17–22]
            identifying technical issues [17–23], [17–30]

primary education [17–23], [17–24]
present-day understanding of [17–21], [17–25]
   implicit/judicially enumerated right [17–26]
should be treated as concepts [17–14], [17–15]
   popular approach [17–17], [17–18]
when decision is governed by law [17–02]

Constitutional litigation [16–01]
challenging provisions [16–02]
   undesirable to allow anyone to [16–02]
declaration of unconstitutionality [16–26]
   exceptionally difficult issue [16–26]
     for the courts [16–27]
     three questions [16–28]
   when do they date to? [16–29], [16–30]
     pre-1937 statutes void from [16–31], [16–32]
declaration of voidness [16–33]
   decisions taken before [16–43]
     Supreme Court's view [16–43], [16–44]
       statutes void from point of declaration? [16–45]
   effects of [16–33]
     certain limits on [16–34]
     retrospective [16–35]
       application [16–40]
       general principle [16–38]
         courts not rigid [16–39]
   means no legal effect [16–36]
   unconstitutional provision can never be law [16–37]
     condemned provisions [16–41]
     criminal convictions [16–42]
double construction rule [16–20]
   force of [16–21]
   limits to achievement [16–22]
   mandates the courts to [16–20]
locus standi [16–11]
   principles [16–11]
     cannot invoke right of third party [16–11]
presumption of constitutionality [16–12]
   Oireachtas as democratic body/interpreter [16–13], [16–14]
     how it legislates affects perception [16–15]
       direction from Government [16–15]
   principle of judicial restraint [16–16]
     protecting rights/requiring justice [16–16], [16–17]

reaching constitutional issues [16–18], [16–19]
severance [16–23]
   positive example [16–25]
   words from State [16–24]
standing, primary rule [16–03]
   affect on asserted rights to date [16–10]
   apprehended prejudice sufficient to give [16–06]
   concept of ius tertii [16–04]
     differs from standing [16–05]
     object to marital privacy argument [16–05]
   general exception [16–08]
   must be genuine concern/interest [16–07], [16–09]

Criminal charges
definition of [2–05], [2–07]
legal provisions [2–08]
vary in seriousness [2–25]

Criminal law [2–01]
see also Evidence; Right to be provided with lawyer; Unconstitutionally obtained evidence
"due course of law" [2–02]
legitimacy of courts actions [2–04]
"principles of fairness" [2–03], [2–25]

Criminal offences [2–86]
blameworthiness [2–88]
character of [2–90]
constitutional defects [2–86]
self-evident rule against vague [2–87]
without *mens rea* elements [2–89], [2–90], [2–91]

Curtin, Brian Judge
see Judicial impeachment

D

Defence of coercion [3–16]
Democracy [14–23]
   as a substantive concept [13–53]
Derrynaflan Chalice [1–16]
District Court Rules [1–24]
Doctrine of popular sovereignty [1–08]
"Due course of law"
   possible meanings [2–02]
Dwelling place
see Liberty/Dwelling place

E

Electoral process [15–30]
candidates [15–42]
   being TD/county councilor [15–48]
   can choose only one position [15–49]

Index

benefits of registration [15–42]
names on ballot paper [15–43]
not/approved by political parties
  [15–47]
permitted expenses [15–45]
principles of equality/fair procedure
  [15–44]
  non-refundable deposit [15–46]
  office expenses [15–44]
constituency boundaries [15–31]
disparity in ratios [15–32]
"last proceeding census" [15–39]
obligation on Oireachtas [15–38]
State's considerations [15–33]
  TD's duties [15–34]
secret ballot [15–41]
Equality [3–01], [3–02]
"as human persons" [3–33]
"basis of discrimination" [3–36], [3–37],
  [3–42]
  age, regarding employment [3–44],
    [3–45]
    easier to classify than race/sex
      [3–46]
  context of [3–35]
    to guarantee equality [3–35]
    irrelevance of [3–40]
    versus "basis" [3–38], [3–39]
  interpretation of human personality
    [3–47]
  property ownership [3–41]
onus of justification [3–43]
  falls on State [3–46]
  hypothetical [3–46]
suspect classifications [3–49]
"before the law" [3–03]
  Aristotelian [3–07]
  equals should be treated equally
    [3–08]
    no obligation to treat unequals
      unequally [3–24]
    identifying ir/relevant differences
      [3–09]
      justifying discrimination [3–13]
        courts' general principle
          [3–23]
        onus on State [3–20], [3–46]
        legitimate reasons [3–21]
          which serve other values
            [3–22]
        persistent [3–13]
      property qualifications [3–09]
      relevant, touchstone of
        inequality [3–14]
      sex discrimination [3–10],
        [3–15], [3–17]

adoption orders [3–19]
in choosing jury [3–18]
obligations towards women
  [3–10], [3–11]
  distinctions between
    [3–12]
social welfare code [3–20]
testing legislative
  classifications [3–27]
indirect discrimination [3–31]
  classic example [3–32]
objectionable distinctions [3–04]
protection of formal [3–05]
  obligation of consistency [3–06]
standards of review [3–26], [3–43]
  four aspects [3–28]
    developing rules [3–30]
    leveling up/down [3–29]
summary of development [3–50]
  invalid legislation [3–54]
  possible changes [3–51], [3–52]
European Union [14–01]
amendments of Treaties [14–08]
  Constitutional consequences? [14–11]
    according to Supreme Court
      [14–12], [14–13]
    changes are "slight" [14–14]
    is Irish sovereignty restricted?
      [14–16]
    not "clear disregard" [14–15]
  "necessitated by obligations" [14–10]
  State's cautious approach [14–17]
  un/constitutional? [14–09]
communities legal order [14–24]
Constitution amended to maintain
  relations [14–02]
  cannot validate laws of Irish State that
    are [14–05]
  does not prevent "European" laws from
    [14–05]
    have force within Ireland [14–06]
  principle Amendments [14–03],
    [14–04]
incorporating Community Law [14–18]
  breach City View test? [14–25]
  constitutional requirements [14–24]
  contentious issue [14–26]
  creating indictable offence [14–26]
  defending secondary legislation [14–27],
    [14–28]
  primacy over national law [14–24]
  via Minister of State [14–19], [14–20]
    deemed constitutional [14–21]
    Minister for Agriculture [14–22]
      delegated legislation approach
        [14–23]

milk quota regulations [14–24]
    how will Ireland implement
    [14–24]

Evidence
  see also Unconstitutionally obtained
    evidence
  duty to seek and preserve [2–50], [2–51]
    Braddish principles reconsidered [2–54]
    court interference [2–53]
    on the gardaí [2–52]
    "real risk of unfair trial" [2–54]

Executive powers [12–01]
  see also Government; Immigration
  conduct of foreign affairs [12–02]
  delegated legislative power [12–16]
    power to deport, two justifications
    [12–17]
  description of [12–06]
    with historical approach [12–07]
      control of aliens [12–12]
        characterised by Supreme Court
        [12–13]
        courts' case law [12–14]
  do not depend on legislative grant of power
    [12–04]
  explicit, over external relations [12–19]
    courts exercise power of judicial review
    [12–20]
      disagreement [12–21], [12–22]
      Shannon airport as stopover
      [12–26], [12–27]
      Supreme Court's activist approach
      [12–23]
        request to strike Anglo-Irish
        Agreement [12–23]
        defence [12–24]
  if assertion made by Oireachtas [12–18]
  immigration law [12–09]
    jurisprudence of [12–09]
    State's power to deport [12–10]
  implicit [12–03]
    existence of, recognised by Supreme
    Court [12–05]
    presumptively assigned to government
    [12–15]
  separation of powers [12–12]

F

Family and Education [9–01], [9–02]
  see also Children's rights; Primary
    Education
  autonomy [9–90]
    correct constitutional position [9–91]
  definition of [9–05], [9–29], [17–19]
    non-marital, excluded [9–06]
      alternative protection [9–35], [9–36]

      amendments to extend [9–07]
    discrimination regards children
    [9–33], [9–34]
      fathers [9–38], [9–39]
        amendment [9–41]
        "rights of interest/concern"
        [9–40]
    legislative recognition of [9–11]
    position of [9–33]
  non-nationals [9–42]
    being adopted by Irish couples
    [9–44]
    bringing their children to Ireland
    [9–43]
    right to reside in Ireland [9–46],
    [9–47]
      for child citizen [9–51]
      not if right cannot be
        asserted [9–52], [9–53]
      procedural right [9–55]
      right to his/her parents
      [9–54], [9–59]
    how to restrict? [9–48]
      deportation [9–49]
        affects child [9–60],
        [9–61]
        justifying [9–56]
          factors considered
          [9–57]
      non-Irish parents [9–58]
      strong derivative, when [9–50]
  same-sex couples [9–29]
  turns on marriage [9–09]
    definition of [9–09]
    more complex than family [9–10]
  existed before/established by Constitution?
    [9–03]
  marital autonomy [9–70]
    children's rights [9–73]
    decisions jointly made [9–72]
    strongly protected [9–71]
  parent primacy in education [9–04]
  parental autonomy [9–76], [9–77]
    in custody cases [9–76]
      marital/natural [9–85]
      natural/adoptive [9–79], [9–80],
      [9–82]
        primary rule [9–81], [9–83]
        "compelling reasons" test
        [9–84]
    versus rights/welfare of child [9–78]
    in education context [9–102]
      State's interest in compulsory
      [9–112], [9–113]
      teaching children at home [9–103]
        less/bright children [9–111]

Index

"minimum" required by State [9–104]
  "actual conditions" determine [9–107]
  examinations [9–110]
  "suitable elementary" [9–108], [9–109]
    Supreme Court's stance [9–108]
  must be certified by minister [9–107]
  reluctance to raise standard [9–123]
primary/fundamental group of society [9–118]
  in health context [9–86], [9–87]
    State intervention [9–88], [9–89]
      compulsory vaccination programme [9–94]
      exceptional circumstances [9–92]
    State overly deferential to [9–98]
right to marry [9–25], [9–26]
  same-sex couple [9–27]
    discrimination against [9–28]
rights [9–30]
  for members against other family members [9–31]
  "inalienable and imprescriptible" [9–30], [9–36]
  of married couples [9–32]
taxation [9–12]
  constitutionality of [9–15]
  courts should be deferential [9–17]
  prohibit inducements not to marry [9–13], [9–16]
  prohibit penalisation of marriage [9–14], [9–16]
    penalisation/inducement test [9–18], [9–19]
      partnership recognition [9–20], [9–22]
        enhanced rights for cohabitation [9–22]
          unconstitutional [9–23]
          for legislature? [9–24]
        qualitative/quantitative approach [9–21]
women/mothers in home [9–04], [9–62]
  breach of children's education rights affects [9–66]
  certain discrimination [9–63]
    socio-economic context [9–64], [9–65]
  justice of care arrangements [9–68]
    proposals for change [9–69]

Finlay, CJ
  reviews treasure trove [1–17]
Freedom of assembly [8–27], [8–50]
Freedom of association [8–28]
  coercion, question of [8–54]
  compared to freedom of expression [8–50]
  extent of [8–49]
  includes right to "run and manage" [8–51]
  political parties [8–38]
  restrictions [8–42]
    exercise of the right concept [8–48]
    trade unions [8–43]
      Supreme Court's approach [8–44], [8–45], [8–46]
  sports clubs [8–39]
    unconstitutional coercion [8–40]
    "discriminating clubs" [8–41]
  trade unions [8–29], [8–30], [8–43]
    employees under pressure to join [8–32]
      does not imply no choice [8–33]
      particular type of association [8–52]
    right to fair procedure [8–35], [8–36]
  meaning/purpose of association guarantee [8–31]
Freedom of expression [8–01]
  see also Religion
  blasphemy [8–24]
    although clearly a crime [8–25]
    courts' attitude [8–26]
  includes freedom of association [8–32]
  of whom [7–10]
    media speech [8–11]
      entitled to greater protection [8–11]
  methods of communication [8–21]
  personal dignity/autonomy [8–03]
  public order/morality [8–02]
  to express what? [8–04]
    divisions [8–05], [8–06]
      express/communicate [8–07]
      political speech [8–08], [8–09], [8–22]
        ban [8–23]
        "criticism of government policy" [8–08]
      religious [8–22], [8–23]
    restrictions [8–13]
      by State on religious speech [8–23]
      Defamation law [8–20]
      for newspapers [8–14]
      prior restraint orders [8–16]
        confidential interests [8–18], [8–19]
        defamatory article [8–17]
  value of [8–19]
"Fundamental rights" [4–18]
  "man in virtue of his rational being" [4–38]

G

Gardaí
    see also Liberty/Dwelling place
    common law duty of [7–28]

Government [12–01]
    cabinet confidentiality [12–32]
        accepted by narrow majority of Supreme Court [12–32]
        judicially enumerated principle [12–32]
            amendments to [12–33]
    composition of [12–30]
        Tánaiste [12–30]
        Taoiseach [12–30]
            duties of [12–31]
            when "absent" [12–31]

H

Hogan, Gerard
    on difficulties of unenumerated Rights Doctrine [4–30]

Human Personality Doctrine [3–33]
    regarding guarantee of equality [3–35]

I

Immigration
    see also Executive powers
    controlled by state [1–12]
        as characterised by Supreme Court [12–10]
        executive/government power [12–11]
    is an inherent state power [1–21], [12–10]

Ireland
    "is a sovereign, independent, democratic state" [1–20], [12–27]
    language of [1–22], [1–23]
        for state business [1–24]
            with translations [1–24], [1–25]

Irish Free State
    see also Royal prerogatives
    as recognised by British crown [1–13]
    not "sovereign" [1–19]

Irish language [1–22]
    see also Ireland
    inclusion in home education [9–107]
    required by State for funding primary education [9–125]

Irish legal system
    character of [4–44]

Irish unity
    by peaceful means [1–04]

Ius sanguinis
    see Citizenship

***Ius* soli**
    see Citizenship

J

Judicial impeachment [13–59]
    constitutionality of process [13–61]
        Circuit/High/Supreme Court judges [13–61], [13–62]
    exclusive power of Oireachtas [13–65]
    Judge Curtain [13–59]
        made three principal contentions [13–60]
        Supreme Court appeal [13–67]
        tried to use exclusionary rule [13–69]
    "misbehaviour" not defined [13–62]
    power to compel judges [13–68]
    role of courts/judges [13–63]
        essential prerequisite [13–64]

Judicial independence
    exists for benefit of people [13–68]

Judicial power [13–01]
    can courts intervene in government duties? [13–18]
        enforce constitutional rights? [13–19]
            socio-economic rights [13–54]
                argument against [13–55]
    character of [13–02]
    commutative/distributive justice [13–48]
        distinction between [13–48]
            finding positive support for [13–49], [13–51]
            onto rigid separation of powers doctrine [13–49]
                difficulties with [13–50]
            as ultimate rationale [13–51]
    considering constitutionality of provision [13–07]
        lack of judicial oversight [13–08]
        no entitlement to intervention [13–09]
    could/not be delegated? [13–03]
    courts making mandatory order [13–25], [13–34]
        duty to vindicate constitutional rights [13–37]
        majority view [13–25]
        difficulties [13–39]
        formula to test legitimacy [13–27]
            "clear disregard" [13–29]
                causing tension [13–41]
                interpretations [13–42], [13–43]
                "conscious and deliberate" [13–30]
            "exceptional circumstances" [13–28]
        minority view [13–32], [13–35]
            difficulties [13–39]
        supervising actions of Executive [13–40]

Index

when declaratory order not feasible [13–36]
is/not investigative/determinative [13–04], [13–05]
oversight of other government powers [13–17]
no law is unconstitutional [13–18]
reservation of, to the courts [13–10]
   constitutional separation of powers [13–10]
      as a concept [13–23], [13–24]
      majority's view [13–21], [13–31]
      minority view [13–32]
      must be balanced with [13–33], [13–45]
         difficulties with [13–46]
      no organ should have "paramountcy" [13–24]
      rigid/non-porous [13–22]
      status of [13–20]
      strange concoction [13–44]
      versus visions of democracy [13–52]
         attitude to Constitution [13–57]
         authoritative interpreters [13–58]
         judges' abilities [13–53], [13–54]
   impermissible intrusion [13–12], [13–13]
   imposing sentences subject to review [13–15], [13–16]
      remit/commute to Minister of Justice [13–16]
   interference by Oireachtas is repugnant [13–11]
      can stipulate a penalty [13–14]

Jury service
   method of [2–79]
   sex discrimination [3–18]
   unconstitutional limitations [2–78]
      exclusion of women [2–80]

Jury system
   majority verdicts [2–81]
   Oireachtas entitled to adapt [2–81]

K

Keane, J
   calls for restraint when enumerating new rights [4–51], [4–52], [4–53]
      socio-economical rights [4–54]

Kingsmill Moore, J
   ingredients of a criminal offence [2–07]

L

Legal aid
   constitutional right [2–27]
   no one compelled to accept [2–25]

Legislative power [11–01], [11–02]
   see also Constitution; Oireachtas; President
   character of [11–03]
      not absolute [11–04]
   distinguished from administrative [11–08], [11–30]
      liberal democratic demand [11–30]
   exclusive, to Oireachtas [11–06]
      poses problems [11–06], [11–07]
         delegation is necessary [11–07]
         but is it permissible? [11–09], [11–14]
      principals/policies versus details [11–10]
         Cityview test [11–23], [11–25]
            restrictions on Minister [11–25]
            should be reformulated? [11–28]
            socio-economic rights [11–26], [11–27]
         in Supreme Court [11–16], [11–18]
            deportation [11–16], [11–17]
         "particular provisions" [11–21]
         relaxed application [11–19], [11–24]
      test results [11–11], [11–12]
   Henry VIII clauses [11–36], [11–37]
      impermissible unless [11–38]
   non-delegation doctrine [11–29]
      with *Ultra Vires* Doctrine [11–31], [11–32], [11–39]
         example [11–35]
            High Court directs Attorney General [11–35]
            narrow interpretation adopted [11–36]
      illustrative diagram [11–34]
   primary, as deliberate process [11–41]
   primary/secondary [11–23], [11–43]
      exceeding power [11–40]
      regarding delegation to Minister [11–37]
   reservation of, of government [11–05]
   statutory power cannot exceeds statute [11–05]

Liberty/Dwelling place [7–01]
   see also Prisoners' rights
   illegal/unconstitutional deprivation of [7–13]
      courts' tardiness [7–14]
      Gardaí arrest power [7–15], [7–31]
         treatment of prisoner [7–16]
         extreme situation [7–17]

"in accordance with law" [7–05]
   detention warrants [7–08]
   different interpretations [7–06]
     "ordinary legislation"/"higher law view" [7–07]
     procedural/substantive [7–10], [7–11]
       State's reliance on [7–12]
inviolability of dwelling [7–39], [7–41]
   search warrant error [7–40]
of person is inviolable [7–04]
procedural guarantee? [7–02]
   Executive Council [7–03]
un/constitutional provisions [7–09]
versus legal detention powers [7–27]
   common law duty of GardaÚ [7–28]
     can arrest on suspicion [7–31]
     conflicts with constitutional guarantee? [7–29], [7–30]
   continued detentions [7–35]
   non-criminal contexts [7–32]
     mentally ill [7–33], [7–34]
       paternalistic attitude to [7–35]
   preventive detention [7–36], [7–38]
     according to Supreme Court [7–37]
   provisions on arrest [7–31]
     not convincing [7–32]

M

Marriage
   see also Family and Education
   definition of [9–05], [9–09]
McQuaid, John Charles
   regarding property rights [6–05]
McGovern, J
   distinction between law/morality [5–27]
     questionable [5–28]

N

Nation
   broad term [1–02]
   can choose own government [1–03]
   rights of, regards national policy [1–07]
Natural law
   see also Unenumerated Rights Doctrine
   death of [4–45]
   defending judicial reliance on [4–31]
   definition of [4–19]
   source of constitutional rights [4–18]
   superior to positive law? [4–43], [4–44]
   ultimate governor of laws of man [4–35]
Non-delegation doctrine
   see Legislative power
Non-nationals
   see Family and Education
Northern Ireland Parliament [11–02]

O

Oireachtas
   see also Judicial power; Legislative power
   cannot legislate inconsistently with Constitution [11–04]
   constrained by Constitution? [11–43], [11–44]
   every Act passed by, in Supreme Court office [11–47]
   incorporating by reference [11–46]
   interpreting Constitutional rights [4–50]
   is not sovereign [11–04]
   investigative powers of [11–49]
     according to Supreme Court majority [11–50]
     impugning good names of citizens [11–50], [11–51]
       unconstitutional [11–51]
     no explicit power [11–50]
   time limits for bringing of actions [5–43]
   to determine legal status of embryos *in vitro* [5–28]

P

Penal sanctions
   no retroactive [2–83], [2–84]
   imposition of death penalty [2–85]
People, the
   are the sovereign authority [4–40]
   gave themselves the Constitution to [4–18]
   power to amend Constitution [1–10], [4–39], [4–42], [4–45]
Personal Rights [5–01]
   right of access to courts/right to litigate [5–41]
     balancing constitutional rights/duties [5–43]
     to challenge one's detention [5–42]
     to civil legal aid [5–45]
   right to a good name [5–29]
   right to bodily integrity [5–31]
     carries positive obligations [5–32]
     courts' reluctance to become involved [5–33]
     includes freedom from torture/degrading treatment [5–32]
   right to life [5–02]
     and to die a natural death [5–03]
     dubious reasoning regards quality of life [5–04], [5–05], [5–06]
     of the unborn [5–09], [5–10]
       distinction between law/morality [5–27]
         questionable [5–28]

Index

enforced by court [5–14], [5–15]
  harmonious interpretation of
    Constitution [5–14]
  explicit protection [5–11]
  permissibility of abortion [5–13]
  right to travel [5–23]
  risk of self destruction [5–15], [5–21]
  socio-economic entitlement [5–08]
right to marital privacy and autonomy [5–35]
  bugging telephones [5–36]
  contraceptives/sex [5–35]
  rape victims [5–37]
  to refuse medical treatment [5–38]
  ward/sentient person [5–39], [5–40]
right to work and earn a livelihood [5–34]
  breached by compulsive retirement age? [5–34]
  not absolute [5–34]

Pope Pius XI
regarding property rights [6–05]

President
referring Bills to Supreme Court [11–48]

Presumption of innocence [2–63]
constitutionally protected [2–64]
  "burden of proof" [2–65]
    infringed by impugned provisions? [2–65]
      by the Oireachtas [2–66], [2–69]

Primary education
"child" as term regards [9–119], [9–121]
  "young person" [9–120]
envisages higher than "certain minimum standards" [9–125], [9–126]
for children
  at risk [9–127], [9–128]
    frustration with State's response [9–129]
  with mental/intellectual disabilities [9–117], [9–118], [9–119]
Irish language a pre-requisite for funding [9–125]
meaning of [9–114], [9–121]
  High Court's expansive interpretation [9–116]
  historical approach [17–23], [17–24]
parental choice in [9–124]
  subverting through higher standard [9–126]
reluctant to raise standard [9–123]
State's obligation to provide free [9–115]
  fundamental/important right [9–118]
    for all children [9–118], [9–119]
      whether or not within family units [9–121]

"Primary punishment"
definition of [2–73]
distinguishing from "secondary" [2–74]

Prisoners' rights [7–19]
to communicate, with media [7–24]
  proportionality analysis [7–25]
    constitutional principles [7–26]
to vote [7–21], [7–22]
  suspended/incompatible? [7–23]
which cannot be denied [7–20]

Property rights [6–01], [6–02]
anomalous legislation
  difficult to justify [6–62]
    courts unwilling to uphold restrictions [6–63]
compensation [6–64]
  courts' approach [6–66], [6–67]
  for near/expropriation [6–65]
    distinguish from restriction [6–66]
  payment of, defeats whole purpose of [6–68], [6–69], [6–70]
  role of [6–71]
economic value created by law [6–19]
  impact of regulatory schemes [6–20]
    courts' attitude [6–21], [6–22]
  milk quotas [6–26]
    constitutionally protected? [6–28]
    regulated markets [6–29]
    naturalise ownership? [6–30]
      reference to the common good [6–31]
  taxi licenses [6–32]
  planning permission [6–23], [6–24]
    and development [6–25]
imposing cost of achieving a public good [6–57]
  on employers [6–58]
  opposing [6–59], [6–60]
  vulnerability of targets [6–61]
intellectual [6–16]
invoking constitutional [6–33]
  arguments [6–34]
land use [6–49]
  must obtain planning permission [6–50]
  places restrictions [6–51]
ownership rights [6–44]
  courts' concerns [6–45], [6–46]
    inequity in the system [6–47]
    "unjust attack" [6–48]
postscript [6–72]
protection of [6–03]
  constitutional [6–04]
  dual [6–12]
retrospective restrictions on [6–55]
  stringent test [6–56]
Roman Catholic Church on [6–05]

problems for the courts [6–06]
shareholders [6–18]
Supreme Court's judicial activism [6–08]
   defence of judicial role [6–09]
      problems for Oireachtas [6–10]
         restricting exercise of property rights [6–14]
         reviewing judgment of [6–11]
taxation [6–52]
   legislation unconstitutional [6–54]
   special deference [6–53]
testing legitimacy of restrictions on [6–35]
   inquiry into justice of legislation [6–38]
   proportionality [6–36], [6–40]
      advantage of [6–42]
      approved by Supreme Court [6–42], [6–43]
      between means /object [6–41]
      should assess interference [6–37]
what is property? [6–15]

R

Referendums [15–01]
   attitude of courts [15–26], [15–35], [15–36]
   constitutional provisions/early cases [15–02]
      by variation, addition, repeal [15–05]
      courts' power to review constitutionality of Bill [15–06]
         "authentic expression of people's will" [15–25]
      Government funding/advocating way to vote [15–09], [15–12]
         affects balance of probabilities [15–17]
            difficult to present proof [15–18]
            "incapable of" [15–19]
         concept of fair procedures [15–14]
            more appealing than equality [15–15]
         equality concept applies to referendum [15–13]
         neutrality not expected [15–16]
         unconstitutional [15–13]
      Government's obligation for factual information [15–07]
         is there an obligation? [15–08]
      monitoring counting of votes [15–22]
      ratio of TDs to population [15–37]
      right to life of unborn [15–04], [15–28]
         granting explicit protection [15–04]
      RTÉ' airtime for party political broadcasts [15–21]
      Supreme Court's reluctance to get involved [15–11]
      unclear wording affects voting right [15–03]
   different conceptions of [15–20]
   substance of proposals [15–23]
      Good Friday Agreement [15–25]
      method of [15–28]
         "any other proposal" [15–29]
      reviewing constitutionality of [15–24]
Religion [10–01]
   see also Freedom of expression
   as school subject [10–20], [10–21], [10–24]
      context particular to Ireland [10–25]
   endowment [10–15]
      guarantee against [10–15]
      involves [10–17]
      payment of school chaplains [10–15], [10–17]
         remains constitutional [10–18]
            harmonious interpretation [10–19]
      State funding [10–16]
         is not an [10–17]
   "education" or "instruction?" [10–15]
   freedom of conscience/practice/profession [10–02]
      State's guarantee [10–07], [10–22]
      subject to "public order/morality" [10–06]
      to manage own affairs [10–10]
   non-discrimination [10–07], [10–22]
      distinguish between teachers/ministers [10–12]
      guarantee invoked [10–12]
         successfully [10–13], [10–14]
      preferential treatment [10–07]
         necessary discrimination [10–09], [10–10]
         purpose of [10–11]
   non/secular education [10–26]
   overview [10–22]
   religious/political advertisements [10–04]
      "minimalist" restriction? [10–05]
   State's commitment to [10–08], [10–23]
      should fund only secular? [10–26], [10–27]
   State funding for religious institutions that provide education [10–16], [10–17]
   "we are religious people" [10–07]
   what is a? [10–03]
Right of access to courts/right to litigate
   see Personal rights
Right of natural child
   to know natural parents [4–47]
Right to a good name
   see Personal rights

Index

Right to be provided with lawyer [2–25]
  see also Right to silence
  constitutional versus legal [2–28]
  reasonable access [2–28]
    criticisms regarding [2–32]
    precise parameters [2–29]
Right to bodily integrity
  see Personal rights
Right to civil legal aid
  see Personal rights
Right to confrontational cross-examination [2–70]
  no such constitutional right [2–70]
Right to early trial [2–55]
  Courts' view [2–57]
    "real/serious risk of unfair trial" [2–57]
      question of prejudice [2–62]
      sexual abuse cases [2–58]
      other than [2–59], [2–60]
        death of alibi witness [2–61]
Right to freedom of expression
  not absolute [2–36]
Right to jury trial [2–71]
  must be representative [2–81]
  precise role of [2–82]
  three exceptions [2–71]
    non-minor offences [2–72], [2–73]
      emphasis on severity of punishment [2–74], [2–75]
  value of [2–76], [2–77]
Right to life
  see Personal rights
Right to marital privacy and autonomy
  see Personal rights
Right to marry
  see Family and Education
Right to privacy
  see Unenumerated Rights Doctrine
Right to reside in Ireland
  see Family and Education
Right to silence [2–32]
  constitutional [2–43]
  non/voluntary confessions [2–42], [2–44]
  privilege against self-incrimination [2–33]
  freedom of expression [2–34]
  justified limit [2–35]
    penalty for maintaining silence [2–36]
    weak protection [2–37]
      courts conclusion [2–38]
        European Court of Human Rights [2–39]
          adverse inferences [2–40]
Right to work and earn a livelihood
  see Personal rights

Rights of mother and child [4–22]
Royal prerogatives
  attached to British crown [1–13]
    immunity from suit [1–16]
    not carried over to Irish Free State [1–14], [1–15]
    strong attitude against [1–18], [1–19]
Rule of absolute protection [2–16]
Rule of Law [2–84]

S

Separation of powers doctrine [2–23]
  see also Judicial power
  as a concept [13–23], [13–24]
  is fundament/constitutional [13–31], [13–38], [14–23]
  majority's view [13–21], [13–31]
  minority view [13–32]
  must be balanced with [13–33]
  status of [13–20]
  strange concoction [13–44]
Shannon Airport
  see State
State
  see also Clarke, Desmond; Religion
  can dictate manner/method of education [9–108]
  cautious approach to amending treaties [14–17]
  "Christian and democratic" character [4–04]
  defending legislative restrictions on liberty [7–12]
  interest in compulsory education [9–112]
  intervention regarding parental autonomy [9–88]
    general needs of society [9–113]
    in education context [9–105], [9–106]
    too deferential? [9–98]
  "is the guardian of common good..." [4–18], [9–106]
  must justify appropriate discrimination [3–20]
  must outlaw termination of pregnancy [5–16]
  no authority over natural rights? [4–43]
  powers of [1–12]
    to deport aliens [12–10]
  providing Shannon airport as a stopover [12–25], [12–27]
  provides free primary education [9–115], [10–18]
    and facilitate matters of religious/moral formation [10–18]
  restricting freedom of expression [7–23]
  subject to the People [1–09]

Sunningdale Agreement
    challenge to [12–19]
    inconsistency with Constitution [12–19]
Supreme Court
    disagrees with investigative powers of Oireachtas [11–50]

T

Tánaiste
    see Government
Taoiseach
    see also Government
    right to advise President [15–36]
        on dissolution of Dáil [15–36]
Treasure Trove
    history of this prerogative [1–17]
    Supreme Court's alternative [1–20]
    is an inherent state power [1–21]

U

***Ultra Vires* Doctrine**
    see Legislative power
"Unborn"
    lack of definition [5–25]
        does it include embryos *in vitro*? [5–26]
            status to be decided by Oireachtas [5–28]
Unconstitutionally obtained evidence [2–09]
    forced entries [2–12]
    search warrant errors [2–11]
        lack/defects [2–18]
    treatment by courts [2–10]
        "conscious and deliberate" [2–14], [2–15], [2–16]
            searches of dwellings [2–17]
        "extraordinary excusing circumstances" [2–13], [2–20], [2–21]
            phrase considered [2–19]
        should take strict view [2–12]
Unenumerated Rights Doctrine [4–01]
    by virtue of personality [4–11], [4–12]
    current status of [4–46]
    difficulties with [4–28]
        judges lack "sophistication" [4–29]
        restraint advocated regards new rights [4–51], [4–53]
            not to conflict with privacy [4–52]
        summary of [4–30]
    identifying [4–08]
    implied from other constitutional provisions [4–26], [4–27]
    judicial reliance [4–31]
        ambiguities [4–32]
    natural law/rights [4–17]
        death of [4–45]
            right to know parents' identity [4–46], [4–47]
        interaction with Constitution [4–34], [4–35], [4–41]
            Executive Council [4–37]
            to strike down legislation [4–36]
        of child [4–24]
        of mother and child [4–22], [4–24]
        problems [4–20], [4–21], [4–25]
        reliance on [4–18]
        structure of constitution provides guidance [4–19]
        superior to Constitution/State? [4–43]
    right to bodily integrity [4–02], [5–31]
        three very different arguments [4–03], [4–04]
            "Christian and democratic" nature of State [4–04], [4–08]
            distinguish between law/ morality [4–05]
            opposing Catholic teaching [4–14]
                judges to interpret individually? [4–15]
        right to privacy [4–10]
            dignity and freedom of individual [4–11]
                homosexuality? [4–16]
            intrusion by legislation [4–12], [4–13]
            traveling to another State [4–09]
    skeptical attitudes to [4–49]
    withering doctrine [4–55]
    time to abandon? [4–56]
Unfair pre-trial publicity [2–45]
    consequences for fair trial [2–46]
    fade factor [2–48]
    newspaper photographs [2–47]

W

Westminster Parliament [11–02], [11–04]
Women
    see also Equality
    distinctions between [3–12]
    previously excluded from jury service [2–80], [3–11]
    within the family [9–04]